Blake's
Visionary Forms Dramatic

BLAKE'S
VISIONARY FORMS
DRAMATIC

EDITED BY
DAVID V. ERDMAN
AND
JOHN E. GRANT

PRINCETON UNIVERSITY PRESS

PRINCETON, NEW JERSEY

1970

The inclusion of color plates was made
possible by a gift from J. Lionberger Davis
Illustrations printed by
The Meriden Gravure Company, Meriden, Connecticut

This book has been composed in Linotype Baskerville
Printed in the United States of America
by Princeton University Press

Oft would he stand & question a fierce scorpion

glowing with gold
—*The Four Zoas* VI 71

Preface

THE twenty new essays presented here show, even in their differences and variety, I believe, that we are learning at last to read Blake's pictorial language: to read its hieroglyphics, to see, to hear, to follow its choreography, its music, its mental drama. In recent years literary scholars have tended less to panic at the idea of taking Blake's pictures seriously, art scholars less to shy at talk of the "Poetical Personifications & Acts, without which" (Blake said) his works "never could have been Executed." Both have made increasingly serious overtures of collaboration. Recent advances in the filming and facsimulating of Blake's songs and prophecies have brought the range and the minute particulars of his Illuminated Works into our libraries and classrooms. But it is the earlier and now more fully advanced learning of his poetical language that prepared us. We have still to put fully into practice the dawning realization that all Blake's languages are one.

In the reading of Blake's poetry there has been a steep if not revolutionary increase in comprehension and appreciation, marked specifically by a great explicative conquest of the moderately difficult and even of many of the incredibly difficult poems, chapters, passages. Intellectual warfare rages, but today proponents of differing readings of, say, *The Mental Traveller* or *Visions of the Daughter of Albion* share a wide tract of common ground. In the reading of Blake's illuminations the advance has been slower and less steady; common ground has been gained, plate by plate, but some has been lost. At times we seem to be deeper in the woods but further from the light that shone in 1951 from the wonderfully luminous and also compendious eight-page essay on "Poetry and Design in William Blake" by Northrop Frye.

Frye spoke of Blake's inventing "a form in which text and design are simultaneously present and contrapuntally related"; of the "union of musical and poetic ideas in a Wagner opera" as but "a remote analogy" to the unity of "independent" poetry and painting in Blake; and of Blake's having perfected, while he "hardly seem[ed] to notice" it, "a difficult and radical form of mixed art, for which there is hardly a parallel in the history of modern culture."

Some four years later my first slide lecture on *America* was called "The Cinerama of William Blake" in an effort to suggest that appeals to the tradition of *ut pictura poesis* were wide of the mark, or short of it, as well as to signal Blake's contemporaneity. During the following years John E. Grant, in critical reviews and rigorously particularizing essays, has taught us to look and look again at Blake's visionary details—and at our efforts to describe them (a role in which he has given indefatigable service as coeditor of this volume). Gradually the superb Blake Trust facsimiles and the Fitzwilliam and British Museum transparencies have made available almost "the whole impact of Blake" which Frye had wished for; the excitement is reverberating; and we all turn to the 98th plate of *Jerusalem* for words to describe the consequent "regenerations terrific [and] complacent." Here Blake supplies a climactic definition of what we are talking about and how we should try to talk about it, as he describes the discourse of those who awake in and awake (rejoicing) *to* "Unity In the Four Senses in the Outline the Circumference & Form, for ever":

> And they conversed together in Visionary forms dramatic
>   which bright
> Redounded from their Tongues in thunderous majesty,
>   in Visions
> In new Expanses, creating exemplars of Memory and
>   of Intellect. . . .

Our topic inevitably widens. We began speaking of a mixed form of graphically illuminated poetry or poetically embroidered painting, then glanced at the analogy of opera, where the mixture includes music, sung and played, and spectacle. Plate 98 emphasizes the dramatic, the exemplary (or emblematic), and the apocalyptic ("Visionary," "new Expanses") within a unity of senses and form. Toward such unity we are still perhaps only groping, but its possibility we have begun to accept, and it is this that provides the excitement running through the contemporary discovery of Blake.

Our thanks are due to the English Institute, whose 1968 program at Columbia University elicited the nuclear papers of this volume, three as invited contributions and many of the others as entries in the related essay contest; and to Princeton University Press, for encouragement when the idea of a collected volume first arose and for a liberal realization of it. With exceptions due to accidents of timing or of topic, these essays have all more or less been shaped in the give and take of critical discussion which began at the formal and informal sessions of the Institute and was continued until press time by correspondence, long telephone calls, and the exchange of xeroxed copies with accumulated marginalia. The papers of the collaborating editors have been forged in these furnaces, and we in turn have fastened link upon link of query or comment on all the others. It will be seen that some of the papers take cognizance of some of the others; some could not, and some were not available in time for circulation. In this respect the volume falls short of being a single book by twenty authors, as also it does in respect of full and systematic coverage of the works of Blake.

The coverage nevertheless is widely representative—of the works and of ways of viewing them—and the arrangement though it escapes being chronological or categorical has its logical progressions. The first two essays concern early and unillustrated writings: *An Island in the Moon*, Blake's medley of satiric prose and stageworthy lyrics recognized as fun in itself and as a mine of theatrical-musical-literary sources constituting Blake's London apprentice environment; and his dramatization of the first days of *The French Revolution* as an inversion of Revelation and its celestial machinery. The next papers explore and debate the nature of Blake's mixed art and the current critical approaches to it. Three essays of explication follow, concerned with the verbal, visual, and musical structures of the prophecies *America* and *Europe* and *The Book of Urizen*.

A systematizing essay follows, devoted to the classification and interpretation of Blake's repetitions of attitude and gesture as consistent elements of symbolic language. The next essay, on the *Songs of Innocence and of Experience*, focuses on the aesthetics of visual design in the illuminated plates. It is followed by an iconological study of the presence, in the Songs and elsewhere, of graphic as well as literary variants of the traditional motif of Cupid and Psyche. Blake's deeply ambivalent feelings about the mental power he called Urizen are next followed throughout his work to the psychic serenity and creativity and clarity of his sixties. The ensuing essay on Orc, Blake's creative *enfant*, as a paradigm and personification of his poetic method attempts to penetrate to still more elemental formal processes.

Blake's way with the texts of other geniuses, as original and ironic as his way with texts of his own, is examined closely in the three essays on his illustrations, respectively, of Thomas Gray's *Ode on the Death of a Favourite Cat*, of the first of Edward Young's *Night Thoughts*, and of the Book of Job. His absorption and transformation of epic traditions afford at least a *point d'appuis* for the next three papers, on Blake's *Milton, The Four Zoas*, and *Jerusalem*—three not at all parallel treatments of various formal-visionary considerations. Moral and Judgmental considerations, however, properly determine the climactic positioning of the respectively urban and agrarian sermons that conclude the volume.

D.V.E.

From Fable to Human Vision
A Note on the First Illustration

"The Youthful Poet sleeping on a bank by the Haunted Stream by Sun Set sees in his dream the more bright Sun of Imagination. under the auspices of Shakespeare & Jonson. in which is Hymen at a Marriage & the Antique Pageantry attending it" (E665/K618). Thus Blake captioned the water color reproduced as our first illustration {1}, the last of six designs for *L'Allegro* that are complemented by a more somber six for *Il Penseroso*. These contrary illuminations of Milton's double poem, which is a prototype of Blake's "Two Contrary States of the Human Soul," depict an integrated progression from innocent poetic visions, through visions of experience, to the culmination in a "peaceful Hermitage" where, wide awake, the Poet "bursts forth into a rapturous Prophetic Strain" (see illustration {106}). "The Haunted Stream by Sun Set" challenges us to advance from enjoyment in the picture to something like prophetic comprehension of it and of the poem that prompted it.

This last scene of *L'Allegro* is to the last scene of *Il Penseroso* as the first plate of Blake's *Illustrations of the Book of Job* is to the twenty-first. And if we are to be instructed as well as delighted by Blake's art, it is to such progressions and such conjoinings of the poetic and the prophetic imaginations that we must attend. "Inspiration" so obviously occurs in the *L'Allegro* picture that at first we discern only the evident pleasures of the sleeping poet. But Blake insists that true Art is a product of and for awakened minds. The diminished consciousness of sleep can betray the artist by permitting absorption in fantasies deriving from his personal weaknesses: the gray river and gray figures in the foreground warn us of this. And when the faculties are not fully roused to act, they can drift into subservience to some "Great Tradition" in art—such as is implied by the warbling Shakespeare and the ceremonial Jonson depicted here.

Time after time Blake admonishes us to consider the sun; here the abstraction of the "more bright Sun" from the temporal sun signifies, after all, that the sun is setting. Now the youthful poet, at the end of his innocence, is preoccupied with antique pageantry in the "more bright Sun" and is willing to accept the dictations of Shakespeare, who appears as a piper of innocence but also gestures toward the Druid oaks which overarch the scene. These "woodnotes" can only be the ratio of what is already known (E2/K97) and the poet who responds to them cannot be just and true to his own Imaginations (E94/K480). In the end he must dis-illusion his vision in order to achieve the wisdom of the hermitage from which the ancient bard can see the mental fight of Orion enacted among the stars.

When we compare the scenes revealed within "the more bright Sun" with the uncritical words of the poem, we recognize how the sleeping poet has failed to perceive the depicted discordant elements for what they are, signs of experience. In the upper section of the Sun the proposed union between Mirth and Milton is shown as a marriage that recalls not only Jonson's *Masque of Hymen* but also the fateful marriage of Orpheus and Eurydice alluded to in Milton's lines. The fact that the woman is carrying Hymen's tall lighted candle—a departure from decorum not mentioned in the poem—portends the uncreative dominance of the Female Will; the stairs, as in many of Blake's scenes, lead down to the realm of death. In the lower section we are shown that more takes place under Shakespeare's auspices than his "fancy" at first indicates. The music and graceful dancing of the women flanking the central figure are revealed to be art in the service of tyranny; their bodies emit flames while above them six infants remain tethered by chains in spite of aspirations upward to achieve sweet liberty. Freed, these "Infant Joys" could rise no higher than the pale fire of the wedding guests at the top. On second thought this Sun is no more promising than "This World" as diagramed in *Jerusalem* 54. The central figure amidst the passionate fire and dance holds a censer in its left hand (ritual incense is "a cloudy pestilence"—*J* 79) while evidently keeping an apocalyptic trumpet unblown in its right.

Milton's poem has it that the amorous ditties produced by these Shakespearean Daughters of Memory are able not only to ease the "eating Cares" of the would-be cheerful man, but perhaps to disencumber the soul and even resurrect Orpheus or persuade the king of death finally to surrender the poet's emanation. Such pining for liberation is too paradoxical for Blake, who knows that the "Lydian" erotic mode is inadequate to deal with the world of experience. In this world, represented in the poem by the "cities" and epitomized by the theatres, ostensible pleasures ought to be exposed as scenes of bondage by a true poet with his eyes open. Our Youthful Poet is as yet not ready to become one with the unshod seer, guided from above and within, who is depicted in the frontispiece of *Songs of Experience* {15}. Instead he appears as a supine dandy who wears a pretty suit and tries with one hand to write like "learned" Jonson while gesturing ambiguously with the other toward the Shakespearean oak. The art that issues from such divided states of imagination, Blake is saying, may entertain or distract the world but cannot change it. At the poet's feet the tiny figure who runs to the brink with uplifted arms is undeceived and raises the alarm.

What he wishes to expose and denounce cannot be the licentiousness of the stage or even the illusory nature of theatricality, for Blake would not have endorsed those venerable charges, made by the "Platonic" enemies of vision in every age. In the cell of the true visionary, shown in the final design of the series {106}, there is better dancing and warmer embracing than anything displayed on these stages. Blake demands a strenuous encounter with the Exuberance that is Beauty, for his "Spectator" to attain Wisdom and Happiness too (see E37/K152 and E550/K611). Art accepted as entertainment is truly pernicious; the spectator who allows himself to be lulled into a "Rapturous delusive trance" (E318/K290) is not a happy man but a victim.

That tiny alarmist represents the prophet or "true poet" appealing to the spectator. From *Songs of Innocence* to the designs for Dante, he alone escapes to tell us that the sleep of death is contagious. The river of death he must cross is named Lethe in one context and Jordan in another. At the front left Orpheus and Eurydice, the poet and his wife, embrace in the reunion that cannot occur on the dreamer's side of the river, where twilight will soon fall. On the surface of the stream, evidently not making headway against the adverse current and the wind, Milton's three Daughters of Inspiration, his threefold artistic emanation, are borne back in their distress to Death's other kingdom. They direct us to three objects of concern. The first girl points up to the derelict dreamer, the second looks woefully at *us*, and the third gazes fearfully back at Pluto's seat of power, all too visible to her.

It can seem quite wonderful that a youthful poet should enjoy

"the more bright Sun of Imagination" while the presumably insignificant mundane sun is setting. But when he sleeps in these
Beams of Light he is unable to recognize the human cost of exclusively "spiritual" vision. What Blake referred to as "the more
sublime" does not shine with enough clarity to reveal the Human
Forms Divine hidden by the round disk of fire at Sun Set. The
presence of two suns marks a declination from the "Great Sun"
displayed in the third design for *L'Allegro* (not shown here); that
vision began to provide sufficient illumination because it engaged
temporal as well as eternal resources for a Last Judgment. The
disjunction begun there, and widening as the "innocent" poet
sleeps, cannot be rectified until Milton finds a dream which contains all his emanations and the strength to confront the wrath
of the temporal sun, as he does in the penultimate design for *Il
Penseroso* (not shown). Recognizing his mundane bondage, he
can reject it, internalize the reunified Sun as inner light, and
"open a center" even in the depths of midnight. With the strength
of this illumination he is able to take delight in the true marriages
that fill his mossy cell and to understand the human dramas implicit in the stars {106}.

J.E.G.

Contents

Preface, by David V. Erdman   vii

A Note on the First Illustration, by John E. Grant   xi

List of Illustrations   xvii

List of Figures   xxii

Key to References   xxiii

1. Apprenticeship at the Haymarket? by Martha W. England, Queens College   3

2. *The French Revolution*: Revelation's New Form, by William F. Halloran, University of Wisconsin–Milwaukee   30

3. Blake's Composite Art, by W.J.T. Mitchell, University of Ohio   57

4. Blake and the Sister-Arts Tradition, by Jean H. Hagstrum, Northwestern University   82

5. *America*: New Expanses, by David V. Erdman, State University of New York at Stony Brook   92

6. *Europe*: "to those ychain'd in sleep," by Michael J. Tolley, University of Adelaide   115

7. *Urizen*: The Symmetry of Fear, by Robert E. Simmons, York University   146

8. Blake's Use of Gesture, by Janet A. Warner, York University   174

9. *Songs of Innocence and of Experience*: The Thrust of Design, by Eben Bass, Slippery Rock State College   196

10. The Presence of Cupid and Psyche, by Irene H. Chayes, Silver Spring, Maryland   214

11. Blake and Urizen, by John Sutherland, Colby College   244

12. Orc as a Fiery Paradigm of Poetic Torsion, by George Quasha, State University of New York at Stony Brook   263

13. Metamorphoses of a Favorite Cat, by Irene Tayler, Columbia University   285

CONTENTS

14. Envisioning the First *Night Thoughts,* by John E.
Grant, University of Iowa   304

15. Text and Design in *Illustrations of the Book of Job,*
by Ben F. Nelms, University of Missouri–Columbia   336

16. Epic Irony in *Milton,* by Brian Wilkie, University of
Illinois   359

17. The Formal Art of *The Four Zoas,* by Helen T.
McNeil, Hunter College, City University of New York 373

18. Narrative Structure and the Antithetical Vision of
Jerusalem, by Henry Lesnick, Queens College   391

19. Blake's Cities: Romantic Forms of Urban Renewal,
by Kenneth R. Johnston, University of Indiana   413

20. "Forms Eternal Exist For-ever": The Covenant of
the Harvest in Blake's Prophetic Poems, by Edward
J. Rose, University of Alberta   443

Index   465

Plates   477

List of Illustrations

For permission to reproduce the pictures listed here we are grateful to their respective owners. For clarity of reference, these illustrations will be cited by number within ornamental brackets: {1}.

1. For Milton's *L'Allegro*, water color, no. 6. Pierpont Morgan Library

2. *Infant Joy, Songs of Innocence*. From *Songs of Innocence and of Experience*, copy Z. Library of Congress, Rosenwald Coll.

3. *The Marriage of Heaven and Hell*, title page, copy E. Coll. Sir Geoffrey Keynes

4. *The Sick Rose, Songs of Experience*. From *Songs of Innocence and of Experience*, copy Z. Library of Congress, Rosenwald Coll.

5. *Jerusalem*, title page, copy E. Coll. Paul Mellon

6. *Jerusalem*, pl. 25, colored proof, detail. Coll. Kerrison Preston

7. *Jerusalem*, pl. 46[32], colored proof, detail. Coll. Kerrison Preston

8. *The Ancient of Days*, color print, variant of *Europe* frontispiece. Library of Congress, Rosenwald Coll.

9. *Songs of Innocence and of Experience*, general title page, copy I. Harvard College Library, Widener Coll.

10. *Songs of Innocence*, frontispiece. From *Songs of Innocence and of Experience*, copy I

11. *Songs of Innocence*, title page. From *Songs*, copy I

12. *Introduction, Songs of Innocence*. From *Songs*, copy I

13. *The Blossom, Songs of Innocence*. From *Songs*, copy I

14. *The Divine Image, Songs of Innocence*. From *Songs*, copy I

15. *Songs of Experience*, frontispiece. From *Songs*, copy I

16. *Songs of Experience*, title page. From *Songs*, copy I

17. *Infant Sorrow, Songs of Experience*. From *Songs*, copy I

18. *London, Songs of Experience*. From *Songs*, copy I

19. *The Marriage of Heaven and Hell*, pl. 11, copy E. Coll. Sir Geoffrey Keynes

20. *Visions of the Daughters of Albion,* title page, copy L. Princeton University Library

21. *Visions of the Daughters of Albion,* Argument, copy L. Princeton University Library

22. *Visions of the Daughters of Albion,* pl. 4, copy L

23. *A Breach in a City the Morning after the Battle,* water color, earliest version. Coll. Charles E. Rosenbloom

24. *America, frontispiece,* copy K. Yale University Library

25. *America,* title page, copy K

26. *America,* Preludium, pl. 1, copy K

27. *America,* Preludium, pl. 2, copy K

28. *America,* pl. *a* (canceled). Library of Congress, Rosenwald Coll.

29. *America,* pl. 3, copy K. Yale University Library

30. *America,* pl. *b* (canceled). Library of Congress, Rosenwald Coll.

31. *America,* pl. 4, copy K. Yale University Library

32. *America,* pl. *c* (canceled). Library of Congress, Rosenwald Coll.

33. *America,* pl. 5, copy K. Yale University Library

34. *America,* pl. 6, copy K

35. *America,* pl. 7, copy K

36. *America,* pl. 8, copy K

37. *America,* pl. 9, copy K

38. *America,* pl. 10, copy K

39. *America,* pl. 11, copy K

40. *America,* pl. 12, copy K

41. *America,* pl. 13, copy K

42. *America,* pl. 14, copy K

43. *America,* pl. 15, copy K

44. *America,* pl. 16, copy K

45. *Europe,* Preludium, pl. 1, copy I. Auckland Public Libraries, Sir George Grey Coll.

46. *Europe,* pl. 3, copy I

47. *Europe,* pl. 4, copy I

48. *Europe,* pl. 5, copy I

49. *Europe,* pl. 8, color print. National Gallery of Victoria, Melbourne

50. *Europe,* pl. 12, copy I. Auckland Public Libraries, Sir George Grey Coll.

51. *Book of Urizen,* pl. 1, copy F. Harvard College Library

52. *Book of Urizen,* pl. 28, copy F

53. *Book of Urizen,* pl. 13, copy F

54. *Book of Urizen,* pl. 18, copy F

55. *Book of Urizen,* pl. 17, copy F

56. *Book of Urizen,* pl. 15, copy F

57. *Book of Urizen,* pl. 6, copy F

58. *Book of Urizen,* pl. 23, copy F

59. *Book of Urizen,* pl. 7, copy F

60. *Book of Urizen,* pl. 8, copy F

61. *Book of Urizen,* pl. 16, copy B. Coll. Mrs. L. K. Thorne

62. *Book of Urizen,* pl. 22, copy F

63. *The Great Red Dragon and the Woman Clothed with the Sun,* water color, for Revelation 12:4. National Gallery of Art, Rosenwald Coll.

64. For Gray's *Ode on the Death of a Favourite Cat,* water color, no. 1. Coll. Paul Mellon

65. For Gray's *Ode,* no. 2

66. For Gray's *Ode,* no. 3

67. For Gray's *Ode,* no. 4

68. For Gray's *Ode,* no. 5

69. For Gray's *Ode,* no. 6

70. Richard Bentley, for Gray's *Ode.* From *Designs by Richard Bentley, for Six Poems by Mr. Thomas Gray* (London, 1753)

71. For *Il Penseroso,* water color no. 3, detail. Pierpont Morgan Library

72. For *L'Allegro,* no. 1, engraving, detail.

73. For Young's *Night Thoughts,* water color no. 5. British Museum

74. *Night Thoughts,* no. 6, title page for Night the First

75. *Night Thoughts,* no. 7

76. *Night Thoughts,* no. 8

77. *Night Thoughts,* no. 9

78. *Night Thoughts,* no. 10

79. *Night Thoughts,* no. 11

80. *Night Thoughts,* no. 12

81. *Night Thoughts,* no. 13

82. *Night Thoughts*, no. 14
83. *Night Thoughts*, no. 16
84. *Night Thoughts*, no. 17
85. *Night Thoughts*, no. 18
86. *Night Thoughts*, no. 20
87. *Night Thoughts*, no. 34
88. *Night Thoughts*, no. 272
89. *The Four Zoas*, p. 26 (infra-red photograph). British Museum
90. *The Four Zoas*, p. 86 (infra-red photograph). British Museum
91. *Albion rose*, engraving. National Gallery of Art, Rosenwald Coll.
92. *Milton*, pl. 29, copy C. Rare Book Division, The New York Public Library
93. *The House of Death*, color print. Tate Gallery
94. *Elohim Creating Adam*, color print. Tate Gallery
95. *Jerusalem*, pl. 28, proof copy, detail. Pierpont Morgan Library
96. *Jerusalem*, pl. 53, detail, copy D. Harvard College Library
97. *Jerusalem*, pl. 33[37], copy D
98. *Jerusalem*, pl. 76, copy D
99. *Jerusalem*, pl. 78, detail, copy D
100. *Jerusalem*, pl. 84, detail, copy D
101. *Jerusalem*, pl. 95, detail, copy D
102. *Jerusalem*, pl. 97, detail, copy D
103. *Jerusalem*, pl. 99, copy E. Coll. Paul Mellon
104. *Jerusalem*, pl. 100, copy E
105. *Satan's and Raphael's Entries into Paradise*, water color. Henry E. Huntington Library
106. For *Il Penseroso*, water color no. 6. Pierpont Morgan Library
107. For Dante's *Inferno*, no. 10, engraving. Harvard College Library
108. *Satan Exulting Over Eve*, color print. Coll. Gregory Bateson, Honolulu, Hawaii
109. *Illustrations for the Book of Job*, pl. 9. Harvard College Library
110. *Job*, pl. 11. Harvard College Library

111. *Job*, pl. 12. Harvard College Library
112. Michelangelo, Sistine Chapel ceiling, detail
113. *Job*, drawing for pl. 14. Pierpont Morgan Library.
114. *Job*, pl. 14. Harvard College Library
115. *Job*, pl. 15. Harvard College Library
116. *Job*, pl. 17. Harvard College Library
117. Cumberland, *Psyche Disobeys*, engraved by Blake (*Thoughts on Outline*, pl. 12)
118. Cumberland, *Conjugal Union of Cupid and Psyche*, engraved by Blake (*Thoughts on Outline*, pl. 15)
119. Van Coxie, *Discovery of Cupid*, engraved by Agostino Veneziano. Prints Division, The New York Public Library
120. Van Coxie, *Punishment of Psyche*, engraved by the Master of the Die. Prints Division, The New York Public Library
121. Montfaucon, *Antiquity Explained* (1721-1722), vol. I, pl. 61, nos. 4, 5, 6; 9, 10; 14, 15

LIST OF FIGURES

1. Levels of Action in *The French Revolution*   51
2. Thrust of Implied Movement in the Title Page of
   The Marriage of Heaven and Hell   65
3. The Symmetry and Orientation of *Urizen*   164
4. The Four Elements in *Urizen*   170
5. *There is No Natural Religion* (b), pl. 7. Pierpont
   Morgan Library   180
6. *All Religions Are One*, pl. 4. Henry E. Huntington
   Library   180
7. The wedding of Cupid and Psyche. Montfaucon,
   Antiquity Explained (1721-1722), vol. I, pl. 61, no. 3   222
8. Spence, *Polymetis* (1747), pl. 6, no. 4   224
9. Spence, *Polymetis*, pl. 6, no. 6   224
10. Chrysalis. Bryant, *Mythology* (1775-1776), vol. II, pl. 10   227
11. Aurelia. Bryant, *Mythology*, vol. II, pl. 10   227
12. Musca. Bryant, *Mythology*, vol. II, pl. 10   227
13. *The Gates of Paradise*, pl. 7   229
14. Spence, *Polymetis*, pl. 6, no. 3.   233
15. Spence, *Polymetis*, pl. 6, no. 5   233
16. *Jerusalem*, pl. 50, detail, copy D. Harvard College
    Library   396
17. *Jerusalem*, pl. 19, detail, copy D.   402
18. *Jerusalem*, pl. 57, details, copy D.   434
19. *Jerusalem*, pl. 92, detail, copy D.   435
20. *Jerusalem*, pl. 14, detail, copy D.   461

Key to References

1. The following abbreviations are employed for Blake's works:

A	*America*
DC	*A Descriptive Catalogue*
E	*Europe*
FR	*The French Revolution*
FZ	*The Four Zoas* (earlier title, *Vala*)
J	*Jerusalem* (variant plate numbers for chapter II in copies D and E are given in brackets [ ])
Job	*Illustrations for the Book of Job*
M	*Milton*
MHH	*The Marriage of Heaven and Hell*
N	*Notebook* (the Rossetti MS)
NT	Designs for Young's *Night Thoughts*
PA	*Public Address* (in *N*)
PS	*Poetical Sketches*
T	*Tiriel*
U	*Book of Urizen*
VDA	*Visions of the Daughters of Albion*
VLJ	*A Vision of the Last Judgment* (in *N*)

2. Roman numerals indicate chapter or scene or "night" divisions marked or implied by Blake.

3. Arabic numerals indicate plate or page and line numbers, thus: *A* 5:2 means *America*, plate 5, line 2. But numerals with *FR* refer simply to lines.

4. When useful, reference is given to pages in *The Poetry and Prose of William Blake*, ed. David V. Erdman, commentary by Harold Bloom, Garden City, 1966; fourth printing, 1970, indicated by the letter "E"—followed by reference to pages in *The Complete Writings of William Blake*, ed. Geoffrey Keynes, London, 1966; fourth printing, 1968, indicated by "K" (pagination identical to the Nonesuch edition first set in 1957); but the text quoted is, in accidentals, E.

5. Abbreviations for other frequently cited references:

B&N	Books or articles, by number as listed in G. E. Bentley, Jr. and Martin K. Nurmi, *A Blake Bibliography*, Minneapolis, 1964
Bentley, *Vala*	G. E. Bentley, Jr., ed., *Vala, or The Four Zoas*, Oxford, 1963
Bloom, *Apocalypse*	Harold Bloom, *Blake's Apocalypse: A Study in Poetic Argument*, Garden City, 1963, 1965

Blunt	Anthony Blunt, *The Art of William Blake*, New York, 1959
BNYPL	*Bulletin of The New York Public Library*
Census	Geoffrey Keynes and Edwin Wolf 2nd, *William Blake's Illuminated Books: A Census*, New York, 1953
Damon, *Dictionary*	S. Foster Damon, *A Blake Dictionary: The Ideas and Symbols of William Blake*, Providence, 1965
Damon, *Philosophy*	S. Foster Damon, *William Blake: His Philosophy and Symbols*, New York, 1924, 1947
Digby	George Wingfield Digby, *Symbol and Image in William Blake*, Oxford, 1957
Erdman, *Prophet*	David V. Erdman, Blake: *Prophet Against Empire; A Poet's Interpretation of the History of His Own Times*, Princeton, 1954; revised, Princeton and Garden City, 1969 (page nos. of revised edition in brackets)
Frye, *Essays*	Northrop Frye, ed., *Blake: A Collection of Critical Essays*, Englewood Cliffs, 1966
Frye, *Symmetry*	Northrop Frye, *Fearful Symmetry: A Study of William Blake*, Princeton, 1947
Hagstrum	Jean H. Hagstrum, *William Blake: Poet and Painter; An Introduction to the Illuminated Verse*, Chicago, 1964
JWCI	*Journal of the Warburg and Courtauld Institutes*
Keynes, *Bible*	Geoffrey Keynes, comp., *William Blake's Illustrations to the Bible: A Catalogue*, London and New York, 1957
Raine	Kathleen Raine, *Blake and Tradition*, Princeton, 1969, 2 vols.
Rosenblum, *Transformations*	Robert Rosenblum, *Transformations in Late Eighteenth Century Art*, Princeton, 1967
Rosenfeld, *Essays for Damon*	Alvin H. Rosenfeld, ed., *William Blake: Essays for S. Foster Damon*, Providence, 1969

Blake's
Visionary Forms Dramatic

1

Apprenticeship at the Haymarket?

MARTHA W. ENGLAND

MY PURPOSE is to compare William Blake's *jeu d'esprit* which we call *An Island in the Moon* with *Tea in the Haymarket*, a generic name for a variable product of the satiric personality and dramatic genius of the actor Samuel Foote.

The actual evidence that Blake ever heard of Samuel Foote can be quickly stated. *An Island in the Moon* was written in 1784. Many years later, in his letter "To the Deists" which opens chapter III of *Jerusalem*, he wrote: "Foote in calling Whitefield, Hypocrite: was himself one: for Whitefield pretended not to be holier than others: but confessed his Sins before all the World." By the time he wrote this subtle and complicated discussion of hypocrisy, Blake must have seen, read, or at least heard about Foote's most famous character, Squintum, in *The Minor*.

From this statement on, all is conjecture, and all is qualified by varying degrees of probability. My hypothesis is that Blake knew of Haymarket procedures and wrote a Haymarket piece of his own modeled on *Tea*. The evidence, such as it is, is in the piece itself.

The comic dramatic topicality of this early work suggests that Blake was aware of many Londons: the world of high fashion, the competitive world of painters and engravers, the world of passionate preachers and flamboyant pseudo-scientists, the public and private entertainment worlds of trained monkeys and meditating philosophers and performing bluestockings, the world of antiquarian absurdities and solemnities, the world of the streets in his neighborhood with its street song and burlesque and hawked sideshows. On the stage of the Little Theater in the Haymarket, all these impinging worlds met their distorted image in the theatrical artifice of Samuel Foote, the master parodist of the illegitimate theater. *Tea in the Haymarket* was never published, and was indeed unpublishable in its wild improvisation, but there are sober records of its mood and method in Foote's published plays, in various books, literary and theatrical reviews, and periodicals.[1] Foote died in 1777. It is possible that Blake saw not Foote himself but stage offerings of the seasons immediately preceding his writing of *An Island in the Moon*, when Foote's plays were on stage, his roles played by Bannister and other long-time associates. Also on stage were plays by Foote's imitators and dramatic sketches using as characters Foote and actors trained by him. If Blake saw none of this, he may have read the theatrical reviews. He may have listened to gossip about Foote and his exploits. Dead or alive, on stage or off, Foote was much talked about.

But Blake may have seen Foote himself. He was twenty years old when Foote was buried in Westminster Abbey—a signal honor for a "mere clown." Blake always had unusual freedom. His father was as indulgent as his means allowed, and *Tea* was not expensive. Young Blake need not even have been out at night to see *Tea*, for it was usually performed at noon, and thus Samuel Foote is credited with having instituted the first theatrical matinees in English stage history.

Samuel Foote's stage career was approximately contemporaneous with that of David Garrick, his rival and friend. At his first attempt, Foote discovered that he was unable to sustain a role on stage, either in tragedy or comedy. With the intrepidity that was always his, he made a virtue of necessity, success of failure, a career of his faults, and advantages of all his handicaps. Thenceforth he refused to "act." He was a mimic, and he was eternally himself. Whatever role he was playing, whatever costume he wore, he would turn to the audience (as Blake does in *An Island in the Moon*) and address it in his own person and voice. He made a life and made a living by deriding those who took language seriously—actors, singers, orators, preachers, and teachers of rhetoric.

After the Licensing Act of 1737 (recently revoked with appropriate celebration on the London stage) there were two Theaters Royal in London, Drury Lane and Covent Garden. In the Hay-

[1] This essay, in expanded form with extensive footnotes and nine appendices, has been published as "The Satiric Blake: Apprenticeship at the Haymarket?" *BNYPL*, LXXII (Sept., Oct. 1969), 440-464, 531-550. The final appendix is a survey of London theatrical seasons of 1782-1784, preceding Blake's writing. Others concern sources of information about Foote; William Hayley's theatrical writings; Blake's and Foote's language; Handel, Milton, and Blake; *Daphnis and Amaryllis*; Blake's street cries; "good English Hospitality"; and Blake and Handel.

market there were two houses, one called the King's Theater, where opera was performed, the other called the Little Theater. From 1747 on, Foote was often in occupancy in the Little Theater with a company of about twelve actors, plus singers, dancers, and instrumentalists. When he was abroad or otherwise engaged, Christopher Smart took over. During the 1750's Smart drew large crowds with a vaudeville, *Mrs. Midnight's Entertainments*, which was performed at taverns when Foote had the Little Theater, just as Foote might at times perform in taverns or fair booths. Foote, unlike Smart, had close associations with the major houses. He acted his own plays and many other roles at Drury Lane and Covent Garden. His plays were popular there, with or without him in the cast.

In 1767 he had an accident while riding and one leg had to be amputated. The Duke of York was present at the hunting party and felt himself to be in part responsible. He made such restitution as he could. Through his influence Foote was given a patent to perform during the summer months when the two major houses were closed, and the Little Theater, rebuilt and refurbished, became a Theater Royal, where Foote had a company of about fifty.

This new dignity did not cause his work to lose its raffish flavor. He had borne with jesting courage the pain of amputation without anesthesia, and thereafter he wrote his roles so as to emphasize what Doctor Johnson called his depeditation. His lusty old characters were all the funnier because of puns on his name. The young heroines whom he pursued queried, "Why should I marry a man with one foot in the grave?" Coarse—but a coarse courage which extended his license, as it were, to comment on the defects of others. Although he was fully licensed during the last ten years of his career for the summer months, and although during his entire career he performed often at the major houses, for twenty years it had been illegal to stage plays in the Haymarket, and he had consistently made that legal handicap into a peculiar strength. Those subterfuges by which he was enabled to perform there remained always his best jokes.

The contrast between his own unlicensed stage and the "license to perform" granted to various others was the foundation of his standing jokes. One result was that his work seemed to be a direct reflection of life going on around the theater door. In the Hay-

5

market were held auctions of pictures and antiquities. Foote would announce such auctions, sometimes with elaborate catalogues and parodies of ancient and modern art. One name for him was "the Auctioneer." When he was translated to the higher world of Drury Lane, far from relinquishing his low ways, he emphasized them. *Taste* was his first success as a playwright. Garrick wrote and spoke the prologue in the guise of one of those Haymarket auctioneers. Thirty years later, Foote acted *Taste* by royal command for the King and Queen, who greatly enjoyed seeing him play Lady Pentweazle.

Opera could be performed. Members of the company came and went around his theater door, and his operatic neighbors were the butt of his constant ridicule. One part of *Tea at the Haymarket* often was *The Cat's Opera*. Foote advertised that he desired the yowling to be authentic, so he had imported a brace of cats from Italy (just as many of the favorite singers were Italian). One of his "Italian cats" came to be known as "Cat" Harris. The other was Edward Shuter, who had been marker in a billiard room when Foote took him under his tutelage. Shuter was in the very first performance of *Tea*, and became a very popular comedian. At mid-century, the most popular comic turn was Shuter's *Cries of London*, sometimes billed as a "roratorio."

In Panton Street near by, the puppets were licensed to perform. Foote carried on sparring matches with these neighbors also. His puppets at times were ordinary little wooden figures, at times life-sized; at times like his cats, they were human. At times they were merely metaphors of man's ageless silliness, man's eternal playing with toys, man's illusion that he is free, when he is actually pulled by the strings of his own fads and fancies and vanities. Or they might be any combination of these things. His puppets partook of his other standing jokes, such as his twitting of Garrick about his small stature. "Will your puppets in this play be life-sized?" "Oh no, madam; only about as large as Garrick."

Philanthropical organizations enjoyed certain privileges in the performing arts. Foote persistently pilloried all philanthropies, especially the Foundling Hospital and Magdalen Hospital. He would announce his performances as being "For the Relief of the Sufferers by a Late Calamity." These tricks were not meant to deceive; he collected no money under such false pretenses. It was his premise that those who promoted such charities were hypocritically imposing upon the public.

The hypocrisy of the Methodists was his constant target, and this subject found its way into many of his published plays. Here again, part of the satire was based on their "license to perform." It was charged against him that the Establishment in some obscure way subsidized and encouraged his attacks, so that he derided the Methodists "upon authority." He answered:

> Under authority! What! Do you suppose I play, as you preach, upon my own authority? No, sir. Religion turned farce is by the constitution of this country the only species of drama that may be exhibited for money without permission.

"I am within the law," was the Haymarket stance. The first matinee in English stage history opened in 1747 under the title *The Diversions of the Morning*; legal authorities objected, and Foote quickly advertised that his friends should come and have *A Dish of Chocolate* with him at noon. The generic title became *Tea at the Haymarket*, which properly should be served at half past six (and sometimes was), but whether auction, lecture, concert, opera, cat's opera, chocolate, it was *Tea*. Modified forms took place at the major houses, but *Tea at the Haymarket* was its general name. He mimicked other actors without mercy (it has been said the whole idea grew out of *The Rehearsal*), they were eager to retaliate, and the public loved this battle of mimes. How the composite titles were used can be seen from an advertisement published by Harry Woodward, a Harlequin second only to John Rich. "As the Auctioneer gives *Tea* tomorrow at Covent Garden, Mr. Woodward (by particular desire) on Saturday next will present him with a dish of his own chocolate, with an addition of one Mew at his Cats." Of all evasions of the Licensing Act, *Tea* was the most famous. The public paid for tea; whether or not it ever got any tea was immaterial. The performance was gratis. Since by law the performance could not be a play, *Tea* was Foote's free form at its freest.

His oldest jokes were new every day. Major disasters and minor foibles were his provender. Often he pretended to read his lines from a newspaper, but he had sources of information other than the daily press. He was familiar with levels of society lower than might seem prudent for a man in public life, and higher than might seem possible for a mere clown.

7

He was no mere clown. He was called "the British Aristophanes." Not his writing, but his miming deserved the title. His pen could never carry his full power. Great satire occurs when its contrary is present in the world. Aristophanes wrote in the presence of great tragic playwrights. *The Rehearsal* was evoked by John Dryden. *The Beggar's Opera* came when Handel's pastoral music drew forth a "Newgate pastoral" to match it. The greatest acting the world has ever seen evoked Foote's mimicry of acting. David Garrick made Foote possible, confronted and challenged him at every turn; and Foote in his own way was great also. He was wildly, irresistibly funny.

An Island in the Moon: The Libretto

The first general similarity between *An Island in the Moon* and *Tea at the Haymarket*, then, is that they are not plays but antiplays. Foote's plays have plots. Blake set up *King Edward the Third* in the form of a play. In contrast, *An Island* and *Tea* do not have plots as frameworks, but both are framed on social occasions. The whole point is: We are only drinking tea or rum & water. Despite the fact that *An Island* contains virtually nothing but lines, acting directions, descriptions of sets and placement of properties; despite the fact that it is more stageworthy than *King Edward the Third*, one can tell at a glance that it is "not a play."

The second general similarity is that Blake's characters are accepted as grotesque portraits of himself, his brother, and people known to him—or possibly combinations of their traits which have been distorted for the purposes of comedy. Blake's fifteen characters, ten male and five female, meet upon seven occasions, drifting in with no stated pretext. They are inhabitants of the moon, who fortunately speak English. They meet at four homes, which may be satiric reproductions of houses known to Blake's social circle, giving opportunity for amusing changes of sets chosen to represent philosophy, law, mathematics, and science. The first, third, and fifth meetings are in the home of the three Philosophers, where, in happy lunacy, dwell Quid the Cynic (Blake), Suction the Epicurean (Robert, his brother), and Sipsop the Pythagorean (a young medical student who has a cat). The fourth and seventh meetings are with Steelyard the Lawgiver (John Flaxman). The second meeting is in the home of Obtuse Angle

8

the Mathematician, and the sixth is an explosive episode in the house of Inflammable Gass the Windfinder. Obtuse and Inflammable have been variously identified as members of Blake's circle of friends.

The third similarity is the variety and importance of Blake's offstage characters, those figures which never appear on stage in their own persons but are described and mimed by one or another of the fifteen members of the cast.

The fourth similarity is that Blake's offstage characters as well as his cast are modeled on real people. His "Jack Tearguts" is identified in his manuscript as Dr. John Hunter. His text makes almost as clear the identity of Richard and Maria Cosway among these offstage characters, and others have been conjecturally identified.

In presenting offstage characters, it was Foote's technique to layer role on top of role. He quoted himself in contrasting mood. He told about eccentrics who in recounting their own experiences would subdivide into several characters or traits. He represented real people on stage, sometimes with no effort at disguising their identity.[2] These might be in the *dramatis personae*; but some of his most celebrated representations were offstage characters only. This is true of Sir Penurious Trifle, and as a rule it was true of his most famous role, Squintum. I have checked cast lists, and find in the 1770's some few instances when Squintum was an actual member of the cast, played by Bannister or Weston or Wilkinson, while Foote played Mrs. Cole.[3] But almost always Foote kept this "double role" for himself alone; he played Mother Cole, and, as Mother Cole, told about Squintum. Foote slid from character to character before one's eyes with startling speed and clarity. Those actors whom he trained, such as Shuter and Weston, could almost equal his dexterity. Blake demands this ability of most of his cast of fifteen.

Fifth: Blake mirrors the Man in the Street. His folk allude to Jerome, Goethe, Voltaire, Plutarch, and Pliny in a great show

[2] Foote staged several portraits of Thomas Sheridan, one being Doctor Gruel; he alluded to Clive's wealth gained in India and parodied his Commons speech; he ridiculed openly and in their own names the medical impostors West, Cleland, Rock, and Stevens.

[3] See George Winchester Stone, Jr., ed., *The London Stage*, IV (Carbondale, Ill., 1962), 1341, 1485, 1504.

of erudition, but *An Island in the Moon* is geared to the urgencies of daily life. This is an especially good framework within which to stage moments of nostalgia and sentiment later in the program.

Sixth: Foote attempted on stage to join two irreconcilable elements: the maximum of "identification" and the maximum of grotesquerie. London afterpieces impressed foreign visitors because of the close relationship between the stage and the daily lives of the audience. This quality was general, but Foote was preeminent for establishing such relations. No one (certainly not Blake) had quite Foote's finesse, but Blake used the same methods and made a fair success.

Seventh: Blake used Foote's own formulaic jokes, and used them as Foote used them on stage. They were dropped quickly, like nods and winks for the delectation of the cognoscenti. As Mozart in *Don Giovanni* quoted *The Marriage of Figaro* with feigned boredom at his own popularity, so Foote in one role alluded to his other roles. Mozart's joke is not very funny if you do not know "Non più andrai," but everyone knows "Non più andrai," and in 1784 everyone knew Foote. When he was on stage, he made all his roles build on one another. It was part of his basic premise that he was always himself. The method kept his jokes alive for decades. Any audience Blake may have had in mind in 1784 would have recognized unerringly those jests of reverend ancestry. It was not necessary to play them out, just as it is not necessary for Jack Benny to play *The Bee* complete on his violin. A hint is enough, and in both cases part of your pleasure arises from recalling how your grandfather laughed at that joke.

For example: Blake gives us right away a character named Etruscan Column the Antiquarian. His name suggests those modern and native "imported antiquities" staged for many years by Foote and auctioned off by Garrick. The name suggests about as awkward and obvious a fake as one can imagine. Phoebus Apollo, when he is "brought on stage" in a song by Quid, talks like an auctioneer. The old jokes are established in their familiar ambience.

The Antiquarian "seems to be talking of virtuous cats." Why should an antiquarian ponder this particular subject? Any London theatergoer would answer, "Don't they always?" For, according to Foote, the chief preoccupation of antiquarians was precisely

10

that creature known for feline virtue, Whittington's cat. For years *The Nabob* had been showing the public a meeting of the Society of Antiquarians with this cat as the chief item on the agenda. So deeply was the British mind impressed with the staging that even today the article on Whittington in the *Dictionary of National Biography* prudently assures the reader that Foote's interpretation of the cat was only Foote's joke. It may have been known to Blake, however, as it was known to many, that Foote's joke was based on fact.

At times there appeared in the newspapers, not an invitation to tea, but this announcement: "The Members of the Robin Hood are summoned to the Jury." Complete audience participation was solicited. The Robin Hood was a debating society, famous in its own right, and over the years made more so by Foote's stage parodies. At meetings of the Robin Hood, difficult questions were assigned for impromptu discussion so that the debaters might develop quick wit in controversy and familiarity with correct procedures. When Foote put the Robin Hood on stage, either the subject would be carried to ridiculous lengths, or the question would be left pending in mid-air. Blake demonstrates both tricks. He turns his lunatics loose on subjects which were to be his own lifelong concerns. One is the relation of classic myth to the Bible.

After Quid has sung of Apollo's physical degeneration and mercantile preoccupations, the company goes into a disquisition on "Phebus," raising the following "material points" in good Robin Hood style:

1. Who was he?
2. Did he understand engraving?
3. Was he as great as Chatterton?
4. Is he in the Bible?
5. Is he identical with Pharaoh?
6. (The moral issue properly comes last.) Is it profane to speak lightly of him and/or Pharaoh in general conversation?

The discussion is an extended one, in the course of which Phebus becomes inextricably mixed up with Chatterton.

The second topic raised is one always near the surface of Blake's mind: How is poetry related to the visual arts? A profound problem in this area is broached: "Is Pindar a better poet than Ghiotto was a painter?" The Jury gives no definitive answer, but this time leaves the question hanging.

One technique of relating a text to the visual arts had been brought to a high degree of excellence in the London theaters: the use of the stage set to reinforce drama. Loutherbourgh was at Drury Lane. Published stage pieces acknowledged the contribution of Richards and Dahl to the success of the total production. George Lambert, in whose workrooms the Beefsteak Club was organized, was another set designer and scene painter of note. Actual houses and gardens were parodied or portrayed in stage scenes. Blake's four sets—the Philosophers' House, the Mathematician's Study, the Lawgiver's Library, the Scientist's Laboratory—represent merely as settings much of the farcical nature of the piece, and the most satirical parts of the show take place against the most satirical of the settings, the Philosophers' House.

We are, of course, on the moon. The room opens out on an Oriental garden, some lunar-lit monstrosity, with the inappropriate cynosure of a statue of a fat-bellied Apollo. The two contrasting elements represent visually the clash between the neo-Palladian landscaping of "Capability" Brown and Sir William Chambers' taste for Oriental gardening. Blake may have had an immediate inspiration direct from the Haymarket of 1784 in *The Mogul Tale: or, the Descent of the Balloon*, by Mrs. Elizabeth Inchbald.[4]

Certain of the plays on stage in 1784 may have suggested to Blake such details as names of characters, but in language, characterization, and structure *An Island in the Moon* is closer to Foote's own work than to that of Foote's imitators. Foote's imitators used his linguistic tricks but simplified them. Blake's language has greater density than Pilon's or Sheridan's or Murphy's.

Blake's characters, at the opening of his piece, are dramatizing an alienation that is deeper than that of Mrs. Inchbald's folk, or Sheridan's, or Murphy's.[5]

---

[4] Moon-pieces had a stage history dating from Elkanah Settle's *The World in the Moon* (1697). When Blake wrote, *Harlequin Emperor of the Moon* was a popular puppet show. Mrs. Inchbald's play (which is in her collected works) combined the old seraglio stories with the new science, having the balloon come down by accident in an Oriental garden.

[5] Notice that the deepest division of Blake's lunatics is created by the figure of Chatterton. See my appendix on "Foote's Language and Blake's Tone" in *BNYPL*.

Even more strongly, one is reminded of the violent and reason-less fluctuation of mood which characterizes Foote's stage work. Chaos and order alternate. Bitter words give way to fraternity and sorority. Quarrels as well as restorations of amity seem cause-less. The cause, indeed, is not primarily logical or psychological, but is based in dramaturgy. The actors are thus given pretext for dazzling displays of quick-change artistry. This trait gives the structure and the dramatic nature to Foote's work and Blake's.

Offstage characters are chosen to give gross, not subtle, con-trast with the person who tells about them. Sipsop, a timid soul whose name suggests milksop, mimes Jack Tearguts, the domi-neering surgeon. Tilly Lally, the la-de-da of assumed elegance, mimes low characters, one-eyed Joe in the sugar house and some rough-and-ready brats whose conduct of a cricket game is deplora-ble. Etruscan Column, towering in perpendicular antiquity, de-scribes "a little outre fellow" who obtrudes himself rudely into his valuable meditations on Pliny and the migration of birds. Even animals are offstage characters. "Do you think I have a goat's face?" a character asks, and presumably distorts himself into a goat—or a tyger. Some of these secondary characters have direct ancestry in Foote. He often mimed the one-eyed actor Delane.

When Blake's scientist gives a slide lecture, he has the example of Foote's Doctor Hellebore, who represented to the very garments and eyeglasses Sir William Browne, President of the Royal Col-lege of Surgeons. As Blake's Inflammable Gass shows us a flea, a louse, and other unsavory exhibits, so Doctor Hellebore magni-fied for his auditors slides showing those yellow insects that hatch out in the blood and cause jaundice, and the standard cure: spiders must be introduced into the blood stream. The spiders eat all the flies, thus curing the jaundice, then obligingly starve to death.[6]

One popular candidate for the original of Blake's Inflammable Gass is Joseph Priestley. In case you have been assuming that Priestley would have been inconsolably offended, I suggest, on the contrary, that Blake probably meant him to play the role himself. Sir William Browne was so delighted with his prototype that he sent Foote his own muff after the opening night of *The Devil upon Two Sticks*, so that Doctor Hellebore might gesticu-

[6] D.V.E.: See the "Memorable Fancy" in *MHH* 17-20, where Blake is shown his eternal lot as "between the black & white spiders."

late with it as Sir William did when he lectured, and might be even more unmistakably Sir William instructing the Royal College in the cause and cure of jaundice. If Blake had asked Priestley to play Gass and lecture on flogiston, I have no doubt all would have been Gass and gaiters. Certainly there is no bigger fool on stage than Quid. And all who feel affection for Blake like to think that Robert Blake laughed with him when he penned the lines of Suction, while time was given for that noble Epicurean to laugh and sing and enjoy his rum.

Not all Foote's victims were as amused as Sir William. The stage representation of George Whitefield drew many protests, one from John Wesley and one, as we have seen, from Blake himself years later. Charles Churchill, in *The Rosciad*, took this play as exemplary of all Foote's stage work.

> By turns transformed into all kinds of shapes,
> Constant to none, Foote laughs, cries, struts, and scrapes:
> Now in the centre, now in van or rear,
> The Proteus shifts, bawd, parson, auctioneer.
> His strokes of humour, and his bursts of sport
> Are all contained in this one word: *Distort.*

In *The Minor*, Shift is a professional mimic. The auctioneer is on stage only because Shift is paid to pretend to be an auctioneer. The bawd, Mother Cole, is an actual member of the cast. The parson is Squintum, George Whitefield, who had a defective eye, hence the name. In some stagings (as Churchill indicates) Foote played all four roles. The audience felt no difference in the "levels of reality" of the four characters. Assuredly Squintum was "real" to the audiences, although Foote, dressed in women's clothes, described and mimed him as seen through the eyes of Mother Cole.

In like manner Blake shows us Mr. Huffcap, his enthusiastic preacher, through the eyes of one of his female admirers, Mrs. Sigtagatist. Like Mother Cole, she plays for us a series of roles in rapid succession: her defense of religion, her helpless state without it, her younger and more enthusiastic self, and a brisk quarrel in which she champions the clergy. It seems that Blake may have considered giving her yet another role, a hypocritical confession, for at times in his manuscript the name is written "Mrs. Sinagain." Foote's Mother Cole (whose original, Mother Douglas, was drawn

14

three times by Hogarth)[7] is a procuress who has joined the Methodists for business reasons and for the consolation of Squintum's doctrine, which (whatever Whitefield's was) is gross antinomianism. Mrs. Cole, under Squintum's tutelage, has no difficulty in reconciling her old calling with the New Call. "Salvation is not the work of a day," he has taught her, and so she will have another drink, thank you, and take the bottle when she leaves. Parson Squintum has said, "A woman is not worth saving that won't be guilty of a swinging sin; for they have no matter to repent upon." A Mrs. Sinagain would not thus be graveled for lack of matter. But Blake rejected the name. His representation of enthusiasm, while it is very like Foote's in dramatic method, differs from it in essence.

The close of this incident demonstrates another similarity between Foote's work and Blake's. Foote, even in the more formal structure of his published plays, was notorious for the casual way in which he extricated his characters from difficulties. Blake at this point sets up an impossible situation. Mrs. Sigtagatist has described Mr. Huffcap in the pulpit, setting his wig afire and throwing it at his congregation for the good of their souls. Blake now has Inflammable set his hair afire and run about the room—a fine effect, with stage fire and utter confusion. How is Inflammable to be extricated? Easily enough. Draw the curtain, and tell the audience it never happened. Our master of ceremonies, Blake, speaks in his own person. "No No he did not. I was only making a fool of you."

This is an example of Blake's means of establishing those close relations to his audience for which London afterpieces (and Foote's supremely) were remarkable. The direct address by the one man who is completely in charge of the whole show—the totally unrealistic intervention which was Foote's policy. Blake intervenes, as shown above, in the action, and intervenes between cast and audience, as when he says directly to his house: "If I have not presented you with every character in the piece call me ass."

The use of current events in the afterpieces deeply impressed foreign visitors, and Foote was past master of blending the new-

[7] Hogarth's pictures of the notorious Mother Douglas are *Enthusiasm Delineated, Industry and Idleness* plate 11, and *The March to Finchley*.

est news with his oldest jokes. Three events of 1784 which had extensive coverage in the newspapers served Blake particularly well. Two of these will be discussed later (the Handel Festival and the death of Samuel Johnson), but the Great Balloon Ascension seems to have been his point of departure for lunar regions, and will be briefly outlined here.

Englishmen, after more than a year of reading about the triumphs in France of the aerostatic machines, saw their first balloon ascension on September 15, 1784. Filled with the dreadful inflammable gas, the balloon rose from Moorfields in the sight of 150,000 Londoners. The *Gentleman's Magazine* jocularly compared this space travel to Foote's *Devil upon Two Sticks*, the Bottle Imp borrowed from Le Sage, who had power to transport people through space. This periodical reviewed at length a novel, *The Man in the Moon*, mentioning the use made there of the Bottle Imp and Swift's Laputa. By fortuitous circumstance, the pilot was named Lunardi. Many were gripped with an impulse to rhyme moon with balloon and make puns about Lunardi and lunatics. On the Continent, and in England, stage farces made use of ballooning. Mrs. Inchbald's play *The Mogul Tale: or the Descent of the Balloon* opened in July at the Haymarket, set in an Oriental garden; and Frederick Pilon's *Aerostation: or the Templar's Stratagem* opened at Covent Garden in October, with a bookseller named Quarto in the cast who possibly prompted Blake to use a bookseller called "the Dean of Morocco," hinting at the mysterious East as well as the leather of fine bindings.

But these were not musical pieces. Blake's is. Albert Friedman has shown its relation to the ballad revival,[8] and it has relations with the ballad opera, as can be seen from the history of that form.[9] And it also has relation to the songs set within Foote's more formal plays. But Blake's use of music is in every way closer to Foote's use of music in *Tea at the Haymarket* than to ballad opera or a play with incidental music. We turn now to a consideration of his songs, a more important matter than his libretto.

[8] *The Ballad Revival: Studies in the Influence of Popular on Sophisticated Poetry*, Chicago, 1961, 264-267.

[9] Edmund Gagey, *Ballad Opera*, New York, 1937. Earlier "moon" pieces are described, their staging, their association with Harlequin.

An Island in the Moon:

The Songs, Suggested Divisions

ACT I

The Philosophers' House (chapters 1-4)
1. Trumpet Voluntary—Suction and Sipsop (tenor and bass)
2. To Phebus—Quid (baritone)
3. Honour & Genius—Quid, with Suction and Sipsop

The Mathematician's Study (chapter 5)

The Philosophers' House (chapters 6-7)
4. Old Corruption—Quid

The Lawgiver's Library (chapter 8)
5. Phebe and Jellicoe—Miss Gittipin (soprano)

ACT II

The Philosophers' House (chapter 9)

6. Lo the Bat—Quid and Suction
7. Want Matches?—Quid and Suction with entire company
8. I cry my matches—Mrs. Nannicantipot (contralto)
9. As I walked forth—Steelyard (baritone)
10. This frog he would a wooing ride—Miss Gittipin
11. Solfeggio—Sipsop
12. Hail Matrimony—Quid
13. The Ballad of Sutton—Obtuse Angle (tenor)
14. Good English Hospitality—Steelyard and entire company

INTERLUDE

The Scientist's Laboratory (chapter 10)

ACT III

The Lawgiver's Library (chapter 11)

15. Holy Thursday—Obtuse Angle
16. When the tongues of the children are heard—Mrs. Nan.
17. O father father—Quid (baritone)
18. Joe and Bill—Tilly Lally (buffo)
19. Leave o leave me—Miss Gittipin
20. Doctor Clash—Little Scopprell (countertenor or falsetto)
21. William of Orange—Sipsop and entire company

At the Haymarket, business was better if room were made within satire for sentiment. In Foote's plays, he usually treated the young lovers quite without satire, and some parent-child relationships were also thus treated. In *Tea at the Haymarket*, music and dance took the place of sentiment in plot. Foote wrote no songs, but used whatever was most popular. At his theatrical discretion, he would use the material straight or satirically. His chief source was the pastoral as it came down from Milton and Handel by a sharp and devious descent through the theaters, public gardens, and fair booths of the eighteenth century.[10] He hired the best singers, dancers, and instrumentalists he could afford, and he had great skill in presenting his performers on stage. The show was under his control at every moment. He knew when to give a performer the stage, and knew as well when to interrupt "Consider, Fond Shepherd," or "The Amorous Swain." He would stop his performers, parody, deride, criticize—thus giving them opportunity to play a role within a role: comic subservience, rage, chagrin, pique. Then when he asked for another song, perhaps a favorite of his, no one was better equipped to lead the applause. For if the British Aristophanes found a song touching, what red-blooded Englishman but should dissolve in tears? Foote prided himself on the sweep of emotions he could inflict on an audience. From the depths of laughing at something so low they ought not to be amused (but were), he jerked them to higher planes of patriotism and sentiment.

Blake thus deploys the twenty-one songs in his musical score, all but one of which he wrote. The songs are wept over, interrupted, criticized, so as to control audience reaction and shape a unified whole.

The singing begins as soon as the entire company is on stage, and it begins under the auspices of Phebus, though we well may

[10] Milton and Handel existed separately on the eighteenth-century stage, of course; from about 1739 on, they were linked on stage, not only by the actual works which joined them, but also by derivative works which, at the level of the minor stages especially, were almost infinite in number and almost completely predictable in their sameness. Milton-and-Handel formed a sort of universally acceptable vocabulary in pastoral writings for the stage. It is this vocabulary of cliché that Blake derides. Any comprehensive history of the stage supplies information. Perhaps best of all is Paul Henry Lang's brilliant evocation of an era, *George Frideric Handel*, New York, 1966.

For Blake's immediate situation in 1784, much information is given by Charles Burney's book, published in 1785: *An Account of the Musical Performances in Westminster-Abbey, and the Pantheon, May 26, 27, 29, June 3, 5, 1784*. Of the newspapers, *Lloyd's Evening Post* gives the best feeling for the Handel Festival, both in detail and in enthusiasm (see LVI, 507, 508, 511, 519, 534, 543).

ask what the sun god is doing on the moon and why he presides over an Oriental garden. "In the Moon as Phebus stood over his oriental Gardening O ay come Ill sing you a song said the Cynic." Quid the Cynic is Blake. He does more singing than anyone else. The other two hosts halt him long enough to give him the correct formal introduction of a trumpet fanfare, scatological in words, but rendered with straight faces. Suction's tenor voice moves up the trumpet's tonic chord, Sipsop's bass moves downward on the same notes.

"Ill begin again said the Cynic," and he sings of Phebus, launching the wandering minds of the moon-dwellers on a discussion of Phebus, Chatterton, and Pharaoh.

The three Philosophers led by Quid sing:

> Honour & Genius is all I ask
> And I ask the Gods no more.

This is a parody of a song from *Daphnis and Amaryllis* by James Harris, staged at Drury Lane during Garrick's regime. Harris, along with his many attainments, was an excellent amateur musician, trained in the music of Handel, who was his friend. Most of the music in this pastiche is from Handel, most of the words are adapted from Milton, but the words of this song are Harris' own.[11] Later in Blake's piece the song is repeated when spirits are high and music has induced a mood of utter contentment: "I ask the gods no more."

The fourth song is "Old Corruption," sung by Quid. The stage background of the song is the satire of the medical profession and especially of the conduct of hospitals in *The Devil upon Two Sticks*, which play was then on stage, and was part of the jesting about the balloon ascensions. The literary background is Book II *Paradise Lost*, the genealogy of Sin, Death, and the hell hounds. Its future lay ahead; it is a Blakean fable of the ancestry of disease, and the first of many grotesque births Blake would contribute to literature.

The fifth and last song of Act I has its background in James Harris' pastoral—or, to be more precise, it pokes fun at the many, many stage songs derived from *L'Allegro*. It was almost required that someone sing about the light fantastic toe, and Miss Gittipin

[11] On Harris' stage pastiche and the tradition Blake is satirizing, see Appendix H of my *BNYPL* article.

does so. The company is gratified. The song is jocund in mood, mildly satirizing the *L'Allegro* tradition, but not much sillier than some of the genuine songs in the tradition. It provides a minor musical climax needed at this point.

Act II opens with the sociable suggestion, "Let's all get drunk." The Blake brothers sing first: an anthem to Doctor Johnson. The text was inspired by Collins' *Ode to Evening*: "Now air is hushed, save where the weak-eyed bat,/With short shrill shriek, flits by on leathern wing." The anthem opens:

> Lo the Bat with Leathern Wing
> Winking & blinking
> Winking & blinking
> Winking & blinking
> Like Doctor Johnson

The music might be an "animal imitation" such as Purcell's "Lo, hear the gentle lark," or Handel's nightingales in *Solomon*, or Haydn's snakes in *The Creation*.[12] The "short shrill shrieks" could be voiced *ad libitum*.

Blake is never more like Foote than at this point. One would need to cite all references to Foote in Boswell's *Life of Johnson* to present an argument that the anthem, with its duetto miming Johnson and Scipio Africanus greeting one another among the shades, was an appropriate tribute at the time of Johnson's death. In an age of wits, the acknowledged wits were Johnson, Quin, Garrick, and Foote. In the long battle of wits between Johnson and Foote, jests were rough on both sides. Johnson said of him, "For loud obstreperous broad-faced mirth, I know not his equal."

[12] I am not forgetting that *The Creation* was not written until 1798; I am only citing the most familiar examples of animal imitations. Haydn had long desired to write an oratorio in the manner of Handel, and his triumphant visits to England in 1791 and 1794 were in part his inspiration for writing *The Creation* and *The Seasons*. It probably was the impresario Salomon who brought to Haydn's attention the libretto for *The Creation*. Part of its attraction lay in the fact that it had been prepared by Linnell for Handel, but had not been set. It is a "pastiche" of Genesis and *Paradise Lost*. Such work went on at all levels, from the sublime down to the farragoes that Blake is satirizing. Odes and anthems were very popular on stage. I know of no staging of Collins' *Ode to Evening*, which stands (at considerable distance) behind Blake's lyric, but his *Ode to the Passions* was staged at Drury Lane on April 18, 1774.

In precisely these terms Blake pays his tribute—and we remember that it was entirely a private and unpublished tribute.

So far I have said nothing about a member of the cast called Little Scopprell. I think he was a countertenor, or had a high and effective falsetto at his command. Any actor who can laugh on stage as he does will earn his pay in a company of comedians. The loud obstreperous broad-faced mirth of the anthem leaves Little Scopprell quite undone. For some time the whole company can only echo it.

Then, led by Quid and Suction, they sing a part-song "Want matches?" in "Great confusion & disorder." This song brings us into a stage tradition for which Foote's pupil Shuter was famous. The most popular specialty act of the mid-century was Edward Shuter's *Cries of London*. Blake wanted a song of this type. No good stage director lets confusion reign on stage very long, and the next three songs are calming.

Mrs. Nannicantipot sings another street cry, a contrasting song of the children who sell matches on the street. It is Blake's own; so far as I can discover, there is nothing like it in the records of street cries of the period. If Mrs. Nan's original is Mrs. Anna Barbauld, then Blake gave her music to an expert in children's songs, but the words are pure Blake, not "Anna Barbauld." I think "I cry my matches" is the first really lovely musical effect of the program. Certainly I myself would stage it for such an effect. I know what Adelaide Van Wey could do on stage with New Orleans street cries. One of these, "Tant sirop est doux," speaks to me as this one does, of the pathos of a child's uncomprehending acceptance of the human condition. Blake's little match vendor moves from us toward the distant Guild Hall, and this first Song of Innocence fades as the child blesses those who sit in authority therein.[13]

In the hush that follows, Steelyard sings a pastoral about a young maid among the violets. Critics have spoken slightingly of the words, but I have heard Leonard Warren accomplish wonders in recital with a very similar song, "Early one morning just as the sun was rising." Steelyard's baritone as it followed and contrasted with the contralto may be supposed to have made it very sweet to the ears. In fact, Tilly Lally's reaction indicates this. The key word is *sweet*; he times his lines so as to allow the song to

[13] See Appendix J, of my *BNYPL* article, on street cries and street children.

have its full effect before he breaks the mood, but when he does, he uses the suggestion of "too much sweetness" for a transition to low comedy. He mimes one-eyed Joe Bradley licking up much too much sweetness in the sugar-house.

Miss Gittipin then sings the only song not tampered with at all by Blake. This version of "Frog went a-wooing" was active in London then, and is still active in America.[14]

Little Scopprell praises her voice by saying it is like a harpsichord. At this date, the harpsichord represented the good old days of Handel et al., in contrast with that shocking innovation, the pianoforte, which Johann Christian Bach had made popular in London to the dismay of all conservative souls.

Sipsop is getting restive. He has been silenced in his solo work since his trumpet voluntary at the opening. Perhaps mindful of the florid bass tricks of "And the trumpet shall sound," he begins singing a bass solfeggio. Quid stops him. He wants no Italian nonsense. (The Haymarket was one of the headquarters for this battle throughout the century.) He prefers "English Genius," and anyway he himself wants to sing a solo. He sings a satiric tribute to matrimony and the combined English genius of Milton, Handel, and the "English Blake." Scopprell interrupts "Hail Matrimony" just as Blake is alluding to his own publication of the year before, "How sweet I roam'd," having taken a swipe at "Hail wedded love," *L'Allegro*, and Handelian pastiches. Scopprell is the self-appointed music critic for the evening, and seems to have his eye on Miss Gittipin; so he professes to be outraged at Quid's cynical view of wedlock. But the rest of the company is as amused as the audience is supposed to be. Obtuse Angle has to wipe away his tears of laughter before he can sing the next song, a ballad of Old England. Blake knew well the real ballads and the imitation ones, and wrote a good imitation of the casual rhyming of folk ballad. One of the hits of the century had been *Shakespeare's Garland*, Garrick's imitations of Percy's collection of old ballads, written for the Shakespeare Jubilee. Blake's ballad

---

[14] Cecil J. Sharp, ed., *Nursery Songs from the Appalachian Mountains*, 2nd series, London, 1923. The refrain there is "Collum a carey"; Blake's is "cock I cary."

Friedman, *The Ballad Revival* (p. 265), says Blake's is "the broadside version of the traditional 'Marriage of the Frog and the Mouse.'" An active version, then, in Blake's London when he wrote.

uses a Shakespearean tag as Garrick used them. Obtuse Angle's song is a tribute to Thomas Sutton, who by building a hospital did more for humanity than Locke, Newton, South, Sherlock, and other Hamletlike souls who sat around wondering whether to be or not to be.

Blake, since he is making an *omnium gatherum* of all the most popular turns, could hardly neglect "The Roast Beef of Old England," from *The Grub Street Opera* by Henry Fielding, that great Haymarket emeritus. The closing song of Act II is, like that beloved song, addressed to the inward parts of Common Man, and, like it, attributes national virtue to England's careful concern for eating and drinking. Steelyard's baritone leads, and the whole company joins in the fine, noisy closing.

Between Act II and Act III is an interlude without song, a scientific demonstration given at the home of Inflammable Gass, when the deadly gas flogiston is accidentally released all over the house to kill us all with a plague.

The seven songs of Act III are placed with care. Since no such program can end with sentimental songs, the beginning of the last act is the place for them. Blake opens with three marvelous songs of childhood. The tenor first sings *Holy Thursday*. This song and the next were used in *Songs of Innocence*. Critics use *Holy Thursday* to demonstrate the degree of irony in that book. Critical opinion covers a wide spectrum, from equating Blake with Foote's own derision of the Foundling Hospital, Magdalen, and all philanthropic endeavors, to the other end of the spectrum, Handel's attitude. Handel, in a gesture which has a place in the history of public charity as well as in the history of music, gave *Messiah* to the foundlings. It has been estimated that minimum royalties would have put the foundlings in a position to buy out some respectable segment of the city. Their chapel was the only consecrated place where Handel's oratorios could be performed during his lifetime, and the chapel was associated with "He shall feed his flock like a shepherd and gather the lambs in his bosom." Thus the foundlings came to be linked with song, and singing was an important part of the children's lives. From here the singing spread to Magdalen Hospital and other institutions for orphaned and abandoned children, until it became a custom to unite them annually at St. Paul's. The singing of the children came to be a feature of London life, drawing the general public to the hospital chapels as well as to the annual service at St. Paul's. There is fairly good evidence that Blake heard the children sing,[15] and the poem itself evinces his knowledge of the custom. When he speaks of the children, the "multitude of lambs" who "raise to heaven the voice of song," what his attitude is seems to be anybody's guess.

Mrs. Nannicantipot then sings "When the tongues of children are heard on the green." Once again, the critics are widely divided as to how Blake meant us to hear her song.

The third song is "O father father," rather like Goethe's *Der Erlkönig*. At this point the manuscript shows Blake's hesitation. First he assigned the song to Miss Gittipin; that is wrong, for the song needs a deep voice. Then he considered the buffo Tilly Lally. But that is wrong. So he gave it to himself, trusting it to Quid's baritone. That is the right choice. A child's lone voice calls in the dark for his father, but we hear it through the father's consciousness. Schubert set *Der Erlkönig* for the baritone Johann Vogel, who sang it into his first big success in 1821, and the song is Opus 1 in Schubert's published works.

In Blake's three songs, the three voices, tenor, contralto, baritone, should move as the songs move, step by step from full morning light to twilight to dark. They move from public ceremony to social play to secret fear of some Erlking who may steal a child away from his father. In each song, the threat to innocence is more explicit. They stop the show, as well they might.

Now we can see the rationale of the ponderings of Maestro Blake. He knew the audience ought to hear the soprano and the buffo, and now we do. Tilly Lally moves us out of this mood with

---

[15] Benjamin Heath Malkin, who had interviewed Blake for his report in *A Father's Memoirs of His Child*, 1806, says of *Holy Thursday* (p. 319): "It expresses with majesty and pathos the feelings of a benevolent mind, on being present at a sublime display of national munificence and charity." Louis Benson, *The English Hymn*, New York, 1915, 344, gives some history of the singing of the London Charities. Special books were prepared from 1762 on, and from 1774 on there was a series of hymnbooks for the Foundling Hospital. The children sang not only the metrical psalms (the only congregational song permitted as a rule), but also hymns by Addison, Ken, Doddridge, and others, and as they visited taking their hymns with them, made free-composed hymns familiar and popular. One fine hymn to come from this source is Psalm 148, "Praise the Lord! Ye heavens adore Him." The author is quite unknown, but the children from the very first sang it to Haydn's tune, as we sing it today.

another song of childhood, sung with verve and good humor, his ditty of the two urchins (lost souls by English standards) who fail to observe the niceties in the game of cricket.

Then the soprano with the harpsichord voice gives us a pre-Romantic song about one of those girls who is determined to die of thwarted love and haunt her faithless lover in the breeze. (Betty in *The Cozeners* by Foote sings such a song, but there were many others floating around to serve as models.) It is not a bad song, and gives a needed contrast between two broadly comic numbers.

Little Scopprell has served the other performers well all evening by his applause and laughter. It is only fair that he be given the last and best of the comedy turns. He has his day in the sun. His song is based on the best of all stage jokes, *The Rehearsal*. Long ago it had been made into a musical rehearsal on stage. Such a skit as *Bayes in Chromatics*, done while Garrick was at Drury Lane, was even at that date a joke with decades of stage history behind it. Blake's character Doctor Clash has a progenitor in Foote's character Doctor Catgut in *The Commissary*, one of Foote's plays that was on stage. The original of Foote's Catgut was Dr. Thomas Arne. Blake's Doctor Clash, played by Scopprell, is having a hard time rehearsing his orchestra and an Italian castrato. He yells, pounds on the podium, and (as all conductors will do) sings for his singer.[16]

Steelyard complains about the song. He says he wants something better than Doctor Clash, and asks for the best—the most popular single piece of stage music of the era, Handel's "Water Music." The line would get a laugh, for the "Water Music" is not written for singing.

[16] At Covent Garden in the season of 1782-1783, *The Commissary* was a main attraction, not an afterpiece, and was considerably expanded. Doctor Catgut (but certainly not the original of the character, Dr. Arne) was an elderly flirt, contemptible as man, poet, and composer. He offers his new duet as a model for pastoral writing:

> There to see the sluggish ass
> Through the meadows as we pass,
> Eating up the farmer's grass, etc.

Blake's Doctor Clash uses as his model for instruction the child's rhyme, "Great A, little A, bouncing B." Foote's Catgut does not use this in the printed version, but he does promise to rhyme "from Z quite to great A." Both musicians are being well paid for instructing in the merest elements of the solfeggio.

Something Handelian is needed for the closing number, and something in Handel's "big bow-wow tone." So the bass leads the company in singing a masterpiece of utter irrelevancy, "Victory! twas William the Prince of Orange." Well, hooray for him, whoever he may be and whatever he may have to do with anything! The chorus is indiscriminately patriotic. Trumpets sound. Banners wave. The hero on a white horse fights his way through the smoke of some undesignated battle while thousands cheer. I think it is one of the funniest things Blake wrote. Certainly it is very loud, and at this point in the proceedings, this is the necessary quality. What more could any Haymarket audience desire? At the finale, we are an inner circle, loyal Englishmen, castigators of folly, but rather chivalric in a vague way, and not ashamed of a bit of honest sentiment.[17]

How aware of stage work Blake was is an unanswerable question, but there is value in asking unanswerable questions.

Was he ever present when the greatest of all Lady Macbeths chilled the air of London with her sleepwalking? Mrs. Siddons was at her most powerful as Lady Macbeth and as Queen Katherine, and accounts by those who saw the two roles border on the incredible. So does W. Moelwyn Merchant's assessment of Blake's *Queen Katherine's Dream* border on the incredible; yet both judgments do persuade the reader: "the richest, most penetrating

[17] The Handelian atmosphere of Blake's close can be accounted for by the fact that in the spring and early summer of 1784 Westminster Abbey was filled with carpenters, and London periodicals were filled with Handeliana, in preparation for the Festival. Blake's character Clash was be-doctored, but Handel was not. He went to Oxford to take the degree, his doctoral offering being *Athalia*, which Winton Deen has called the first great English oratorio. For some unguessed reason the degree was not given. Later Handel used much of the music from *Athalia* in *Il Parnasso in Feste*, splendidly staged at the opera house in the Haymarket on March 13, 1734 to celebrate the marriage of his loyal friend and pupil, Ann, Princess Royal, to William, Prince of Orange. Blake's curtain song suggests the chorus from Part II of that work, "O quanto bella gloria è quella del cacciator." *The London Stage* gives the story of the great expense and confusion that the staging of the nuptial pageants and masques entailed for the theaters. Blake is making fun of musicians in general and Handelism in particular; he may also be taking Handel's side as an artist who served an Establishment whose judgments really did seem erratic: church doors closed to his biblical oratorios, no scholastic honors for his great name, and so on.

comment by any artist on the work of Shakespeare."[18] If any actress influenced Blake's *Jane Shore*, it was Mrs. Yates, not Mrs. Siddons, for that tidal wave had not struck the London stage when his picture was made. Before he illustrated Stedman's *Narrative*, had his nerves ever been harassed by Garrick's or Kemble's overwhelming portrayals of slavery in Surinam in *Oroonoko*? Did his *Mad Song* owe anything to any Ophelia or Belvidera of the boards? Did he see Tom King's Touchstone? Is there anything in Blake's *Samson* that he owed to Handel's *Samson*? When Blake's metrics moved from simple song forms to the rolling baroque rhythms of prophecy, did he owe to Handel some sense of a vast yet symmetrical shape of sound waiting to be filled up with syllables?

David Erdman, reading again Blake's letters to Hayley, dropped me a note quoting Blake on the child actor Master Betty, and commented, "Sounds like an old theatergoer. Yes?" Yes. And at the very least, it is evident that Blake wrote all his life as if the theater were a part of life to be taken into consideration.

Such knowledge as he needed to write *An Island in the Moon* could have been had elsewhere; it is simpler to conclude that he saw Foote himself in the Haymarket. The text as it stands is essentially complete, a unified whole, the parts arranged with tact, the style appropriate to the intention. The sense of a show under the complete control of one man is present. The stock jokes are there, and are handled so as to come through with novelty and freshness. We could wish for more: more stage directions to tell how the Blake brothers planned to bring down the house with their weak-eyed bat, any sketches for stage sets, and, most of all, any sketches for those lecture slides. Think what the man who drew *The Ghost of a Flea* could have done with those slides! Still, the shape and substance of a Haymarket show is there.[19]

[18] W. Moelwyn Merchant, "Blake's Shakespeare," *Apollo* (April 1964), 318-325, referring (p. 325) to Blake's six drawings in an extra-illustrated Second Folio, among them one of Blake's four depictions of *Queen Katherine's Dream from Henry VIII*. Another, *Richard III and the Ghosts*, is considered by Merchant "almost alone in Blake's work on Shakespeare in being directly influenced by recollections of the stage." See also Merchant's *Shakespeare and the Artist*, London and New York, 1959.

[19] D.V.E.: There *are* some sketches on the MS, all on the back of the final page reproduced in *BNYPL*, LXXIII, facing p. 454. They relate to the text, slightly, but not to its stage possibilities. I think "English Genius" is the theme: a center profile of Robert Blake (?), laurel-crowned; above it a

For all that, it is imitation Foote. Blake dramatizes at the beginning the breakdown of communication between the characters. This alienation does not resolve itself on any basis of reason. It yields to song, and finally all the characters are one in their singing. This is a Blakean belief set in a Haymarket formula.

Blake did not have the "single vision" necessary for Foote's type of allegory. He was unable to deal with characters or even with institutions as Foote did. It is always possible to make the College of Surgeons the object of satire. But all Foote's doctors are quacks, idle, aimlessly cruel. Jack Tearguts is no quack. He works hard, and the pain he gives is not aimless. Almost any medical student, given enough rum & water, may refer to Old So-and-So in derision and fear. But Sipsop, when he did so, was aware that a surgeon whose duty it was to operate on cancer patients nerved himself for his day's work as best he could. Even today, with anesthetics at command, it is not an easy life. And Sipsop, lunatic though he is, cannot forget the pain he has seen. Even on the moon, Blake could not dismiss compassion. To call anything human "Sir Penurious Trifle" or "Mrs. Sinagain" and really follow through in his characterization was not William Blake's dish of tea.

We are lucky to have this "failure" left unpublished in a notebook. We can watch a great metrist and a born parodist searching for his tunes, trying out dramatic systems and metrical systems, none of which were to enslave him. Here he cheerfully takes under his examining eye song and satire, operas and plagues, surgery and pastoral song, Chatterton and science, enthusiasm and myth, philanthropy and Handelian anthem, the Man in the Street and those children whose nursery is the street—while he

---

tiger's face; above that "William Blake" (twice); opposite the face, about to eat the laurel (?), the head of a goat. Then there is a lot of smudging out, while the ink was wet—especially of Blake's name; also of another profile, below the crowned one, more certainly William's face. One suspects some brotherly horseplay; indeed, the page fills up with profiles of horses' heads, and backs; of lion and lamb (twice); and some practice strokes and letters of graver's script, the only full words being "Numeration" and "Lamb" and (on top of Lamb) "n no." Yet no "Robert Blake." Applying Quid's question on the recto page, however, the face (or faces) cannot be said to look like the tiger or the lamb or the goat, but—the drawings seem to insist—that noble beast the horse. According to Palmer Brown, who first called my attention to the page and its details, these sketches were made in the original ink of the text and not in the second ink of the textual emendations.

is making up his mind what William Blake shall take seriously. Our chief interest in the work is and properly will always be in those songs of childhood and what grew out of them. The work may also raise the question: Are those "visionary forms dramatic" more *dramatic* than we had thought? At any rate, here a master ironist flexes his vocal cords with a wide range of tone. It is good to know that this ironist (unlike some others) enjoyed a joke.

2

The French Revolution
Revelation's New Form

WILLIAM F. HALLORAN

FEW would now accept Swinburne's 1868 assertion that *The French Revolution* consists "mainly of mere wind and sputter."[1] Yet praise of selected passages is still tempered by doubts about the integrity of the poem's form and the clarity of its images.[2] It is generally regarded as an experiment that failed, an apprentice work that helped pave the way for Blake's later achievements in narrative poetry.[3] Objections center upon the attempt to elevate real people and events into a cosmic drama. Blake's apparent loss of interest in the poem and his turn to mythic figures of his own invention in the prophetic works that followed might indicate that he became impatient with the poem's realistic frame.[4] Whether or not that was the case, *The French Revolution* as it

---

[1] B&N no. 2032C (reissue, New York, 1967), 15. The title page of the only surviving copy of *FR* (a set of proofs in the Huntington Library) is dated 1791.

[2] Damon, *Philosophy*, 82; Frye, *Symmetry*, 204-205; and David Halliburton, "Blake's *French Revolution*: The *Figura* and Yesterday's News," *Studies in Romanticism*, v (1966), 158-168. Bloom, *Apocalypse*, 60-67, suggests that the confusion of symbolic values is deliberate, a function of the apocalyptic nature of the poem.

[3] Contrary views have been expressed by Pierre Berger (B&N no. 887B), 329-337; Jacob Bronowski (B&N no. 954A), 50; and Erdman, *Prophet*, 138 [152].

[4] Halliburton, "Blake's *French Revolution*," 168; John Beer, *Blake's Humanism*, New York, 1968, 106; and Frye, *Symmetry*, 204: "The form of *The French Revolution* is dictated by the sequence of historical events, and as a result the comprehensive view of the states of liberty and tyranny which Blake affords us in other poems, in which their political, educational, economic, religious and psychological aspects are all presented as a unit, is lacking; and the cause of liberty at least has not a definite enough protagonist to represent all its various aspects at once. This is a defect which Blake attempted to remedy in *America* by creating Orc."

stands may be an incomplete realization of Blake's initial plan;[5] and the surviving text may be in part inaccurate or unfinished.[6] Claims of perfection are not in order, but it is equally unwise to settle quickly into negative judgments. When the work is set against its principal source and approached not as a truncated epic but as a visual and dramatic prophecy, its structure becomes clearer and its place in the Blake canon more central than most critics have recognized or allowed.

Similarities have been noted between the first two books of *Paradise Lost* and the debate that forms the heart of *The French Revolution*.[7] There are other ties between the two works. Indeed, Blake may have set out to construct a mirror image of *Paradise Lost*, an epic account of man's return to the earthly paradise from which he had been unjustly excluded.[8] Yet the poem he produced is not an epic, but a prophecy; and its main source is not *Paradise Lost*, but the Book of Revelation. Rather than looking back to chronicle a cycle of history, it brings narrative and dramatic features of the epic to bear upon contemporary events and presents those events as prophetic of a regenerate world. Like Revelation, Blake's *Revolution* is an intensely visual account of the death of

[5] On the other hand, Bloom, *Apocalypse*, 66, makes the following provocative comment: "The poem ends on a token of fulfillment, with the revolutionaries, who 'in peace sat beneath morning's beam.' Blake had nothing to add, and the course of events had little to add to Blake's desired consummation." The only evidence that seven books were intended appears in the front matter of the proof copy in the Huntington Library. The present analysis of the structure of the first book seems to bear out Bloom's suggestion that, whatever Blake may have intended at first, the poem as we have it is essentially complete. (See note 17, below.)

[6] In "William Blake's *The French Revolution*: A Note on the Text and a Possible Emendation," *BNYPL*, xxii (1968), 3-18, I have discussed the state of the text and suggested the reordering of one passage. Other difficulties remain. For example, lines 62-63 strike me as irrelevant and intrusive in their present position, but I see no satisfactory rearrangement.

[7] See Mark Schorer, *William Blake, The Politics of Vision*, New York, 1959, 258 and John Beer, *Blake's Humanism*, 106.

[8] Against Milton's emphasis upon salvation by obedience and grace, Blake glorifies the free play of human energy, and he conceives the apocalypse not as a gift from above but an expression of man's determination to overthrow unjust limitations. The poem thus carries forward the debate with Milton that underlies *The Marriage of Heaven and Hell*.

an old order and the birth of a new, but he responded to his source argumentatively and creatively. Retaining the apocalyptic thrust and prophetic fervor of Revelation, he rejected its violence and focused on the present rather than the future. A peaceful interlude in France enabled him to portray the revolution as he envisioned the apocalypse, as a bloodless removal of the social and religious hierarchies that enslave men's minds and cause them to inflict pain upon each other. An imaginative recasting of Revelation thus forms the core of *The French Revolution*, and it will be useful to review the main features of the biblical prophecy before proceeding to examine the structure and imagery of Blake's poem.

The visual emphasis of Revelation is established at the start when John tells us that Christ appeared to him on the island of Patmos and commanded him to write down what he was about to see. After reproducing Christ's messages to the seven churches, John reports that he saw an open door in heaven, obeyed a command to rise in the spirit, and saw the throne of God surrounded by twenty-four elders and four living creatures.[9] John's ascent initiates vertical movement among three spatial levels. Linear movement at the upper level begins in the sixth chapter, when Christ steps forward as the lamb to open the first of seven seals on the scroll in the right hand of God. Interaction between the two kinds of motion—vertical and linear—determines the work's structure.

Continuity is maintained by a series of events in heaven: the opening of the seals, the sounding of the seven trumpets, and the emptying of the seven bowls of God's wrath by the seven angels with the seven plagues. This linear sequence moves the reader forward in time to the final victory over Satan and the descent of the New Jerusalem from heaven to earth. Yet the twenty-one events are arranged arbitrarily or ritualistically.[10] Emphasis falls

[9] For Blake's illustration of this scene, see Keynes, *Bible*, pl. 160.

[10] For an informed and perceptive analysis of Revelation, see Austin Farrer's *The Revelation of St. John the Divine*, Oxford, 1964. Recognizing that apocalyptic events on earth do not follow "a single or continuous time-scheme," Farrer remarks: "In following such an order of composition St. John gives no just cause of complaint. There is not a line in the book which promises (for example) a continuous exposition of predicted events in his-

not upon their interdependence but upon their results at the two lower levels of the work—earth and hell. While events at these levels create the impression of mounting catastrophe, they are largely independent of each other and have no influence upon their heavenly causes. At several points John breaks the sequence of events to describe an apparently unrelated vision. In this episodic scheme, the reader's sense of time becomes increasingly confused.[11] Just as the frequent leaps among the three spatial levels prepare us for the coalescence of space with the descent of the heavenly city, so the deliberate distortions of time prepare us for the timelessness of eternity. It is only in the last chapter, which forms with the first a frame or envelope, that we regain our normal spatial and temporal orientations. The complex interaction of vertical movement in space and linear movement in time highlights the separate visions and thus reinforces the narrator's effort to show the reader what he saw.

To compensate for the absence of a strong narrative line, the work relies for unity upon devices of recurrence: displacement, juxtaposition, and repetition. The final displacement of Babylon by Jerusalem, for example, provides the sense of fulfillment that normally comes with the resolution of plot. The visionary interludes, in turn, reinforce the significance of this event. The portraits of the woman clothed with the sun and attacked by the dragon in chapter 12 and that of the whore of Babylon astride the scarlet beast in chapter 17 are digressions from the main chain of events. Yet the juxtaposition of the two women—one representing God's chosen people and the other the profligacy of pagan Rome— enriches the texture of the final displacement when the New Jerusalem comes down "prepared as a bride adorned for her hus-

---

torical order. Our difficulties are of our own making; we are victims of our own unjustified expectations. The secret of reading St. John is simply that of discovering what he is doing, and of being content to let him do it" (pp. 22-23). The last two sentences apply equally to Blake and might serve as an epigraph to the present essay. My comments on Revelation predate my reading of Farrer's book, but they conform for the most part with the more detailed discussion and should suffice to establish the relationships between Revelation and *The French Revolution*.

[11] In chapter 20, for example, an angel throws Satan into the bottomless pit for a thousand years. The narrator shifts immediately to the past tense to describe his release and permanent immersion in the burning lake.

band" (21:2).[12] Finally, repetition links events on all three levels and provides a sense of order. The numerical groupings—with seven recalling the first creation and implying completeness—is the most obvious repetitive device. Each group of seven events builds to a crescendo in which the seventh produces an earthshaking storm with thunder, lightning, hail, and the relocation of mountains and islands. With its emotional effect, this recurrent image group functions as a chorus. Others bind the work on a wider scale: The opening of the first seal, for example, reveals Christ on a white horse with crown and bow (6:2). The last heavenly event—the emptying of the seventh bowl—produces, after the whore of Babylon interlude (17 and 18), Faithful and True riding out of heaven on a white horse to subdue the seven-headed beast that supports Babylon-Rome (19:11-16). After defeating the beast, Christ as warrior-hero takes the New Jerusalem for his bride. The entire chain of events between the first seal and the seventh bowl thus becomes an extension of the single quest. With the discovery of such patterns, the work gradually acquires the order and unity it seems at first to lack.

In writing *The French Revolution*, Blake proceeded, like John, by creating a series of verbal pictures.[13] He also borrowed the central images of Revelation—those of war, storm, and harvest. Less apparent, and more important, he incorporated the basic structure of Revelation: the episodic organization, devices of recurrence, movement within a tri-part division of space, and manipulation of time to imply timelessness. A difference in narrative point of view may obscure these structural similarities. John rose in spirit to heaven and thereby gained the ability to see throughout the universe. Blake as narrator stayed on earth and accepted the limitations of his own and his readers' sense of space and time. So limited, he could not move his characters into heaven and hell without sacrificing plausibility; neither could he ignore chronology and causality in arranging his scenes. The poem's action thus proceeds along a narrative line that is firmer than Revelation's.[14]

---

[12] I have used the Oxford Revised Standard Version of Revelation and noted chapter and verse references, as here, within the text.

[13] He later illustrated at least eleven scenes from Revelation (see Keynes, *Bible*, pls. 159-170), and his masterpiece, *The Last Judgment*, incorporates many details from these illustrations and from other passages in Revelation.

[14] For an account of the relationship between events in the poem and events in France, see Erdman, *Prophet*, 135-137 and 148-150 [149-151 and 162-165].

To gain the flexibility necessary for his apocalyptic theme, Blake assumed the stance of a visionary who could see in historical events their supernatural overtones.[15] Thus while focusing on the poem's middle level and without violating it, he gained a broader scope by means of figurative language and a symbolic landscape. Like the author of Revelation, he used images, metaphors, and symbols to deepen the poem's texture and bind it together, but he also used them to gain the expanded temporal and spatial framework that John attained through heavenly omniscience. Therein lies a difficulty. Those who have complained that certain images appear too frequently and with confused symbolic values have not come to terms with their dual function of expansion and limitation.[16] The comparison with Revelation clears the way for a better understanding of *The French Revolution*'s structure and the operation of its imagery. By examining the poem not as the first book of a traditional epic but as a visual and dramatic prophecy,[17] an imaginative recasting of Revelation from a different perspective, we can hope to form a sounder judgment of its relative success or failure.

The French Revolution proceeds by a sequence of scenes defined by place. Except for the second and third, these scenes, un-

[15] For Blake, who claimed to have seen the heavenly hosts in the rising sun, the amount of contrivance in this choice should perhaps be deemphasized.

[16] See Damon, *Philosophy*, 82, and Halliburton, "Blake's *French Revolution*," 162.

[17] This approach invites a tentative extension of an earlier suggestion that the poem as it stands may be essentially complete. (See note 5.) Is it possible that the front matter ("A Poem in Seven Books" and "Advertisement. The remaining Books of this Poem are finished, and will be published in their Order.") was added by Joseph Johnson or someone in his employ without Blake's approval, in an effort to dignify the poem and set it in a more familiar and acceptable context? As an epic rather than a prophecy it would have been less likely to raise the ire of Royalists who were apprehensive that the revolution would spread across the channel. The failure of the poem to appear might have been due to a difference of opinion between Blake and the publisher-printers about the form in which it would appear. That Blake did not himself take it up and engrave it is easily explained by the fact that the revolution began to take on qualities of violence that undercut the poem's central theme. In retrospect, of course, history's failure to follow the course set for it has no bearing on the poem's aesthetic value. For Blake, who refused to make a distinction between the roles of poet and prophet, the failure of the prophecy would have been sufficient cause for discarding the poem or, more precisely, for not spending time and effort engraving it.

like those in Revelation, are joined chronologically by cause and effect. Not formally marked in the text, they are as follows: In the first (lines 1-15), the King and Necker, his Minister of Finance, rise at dawn in an upper room of the Louvre and descend to meet forty troubled nobles in the council chamber. The next two scenes (16-58) form an interlude. The first of these (16-53) presents a view of Paris which includes the Hall of the Nation where the Commons meets. It then moves to the Bastille (18) and describes the Governor-Jailor stalking "like a lion" and a "wolf gorg'd" through its seven towers (19-26). Then, in a sequence of tableaux, we view seven prisoners in seven dens beneath the seven towers (26-51). The third scene (54-58) offers another overview of Paris and centers this time on the Hall of the Nation that has shaken the King and offered hope to the prisoners in the Bastille and the people of Paris.

The fourth scene (59-254), the main body of the poem, returns to the King's chamber and the action that began in scene one. The lengthy debate among nobles and clergy produces the King's banishment of Necker and, later, his rejection of the Commons' request that he move his army ten miles out of Paris. In scene five (255-269), the Abbé de Sieyès, who argued the Commons' cause before the King, returns to report the King's refusal, whereupon the Commons votes to defy the King and asks Fayette to order the removal of the army. The sixth scene (270-292) offers another broad landscape and focuses this time upon the army, which accepts Fayette's command and leaves the city. Finally, in scene seven (293-306) we return again to the palace for a view of the King and nobles in defeat.

Even this brief résumé demonstrates Blake's forming power. The scenes are arranged symmetrically: Louvre, Bastille, Commons—Louvre—Commons, Army, Louvre. The correspondence of scenes two and six—Bastille and Army—implies ironically that the King's forces are really his prisoners. The link is overtly established by Burgundy's cynical response to Sieyès (248-254): The King will remove his army only if the Bastille will depart ten miles into the country. When the army later obeys Fayette, it frees itself and leaves the people of Paris free to release the prisoners in the Bastille. The arrangement of scenes highlights the fourth with its crucial decisions by presenting three background studies and then three views of the result of those decisions. The seven-part division, a borrowing from Revelation, is complemented by the seven towers and dens of the Bastille. The scenic pattern also establishes a double motion: events move forward in time while settings provide two harmonious returns to the inner space of the palace. Consideration of movement forces us beyond the externals of setting and actions. Figurative language implies a positioning of each scene at one of three spatial levels and a vertical movement among those levels that interacts with the pattern of settings and the chronological progress of events. To come to terms with Blake's use of image and symbol to expand his canvas and control his ideas, each scene must be carefully examined.

As the poem opens, the King, sick on his couch and wreathed in a mist, can no longer lift his scepter to bruise in cruelty "the mild flourishing mountains" of France (5).[18] After the harsh light of Sun-Kings, those mountains—the people of France—are now flourishing because the "Prince"—the Prince of Light—is "wreath'd in dim / And appalling mist" (2-3). To the King, who equates France with his noblemen, the mountains seem sick and pale like himself (6-7). The dimming of Lucifer—the star of the old morning—signals the approaching apocalypse, the birth of a new light and a new world. *The French Revolution* does not follow Revelation in recording the displacement of satanic rule by another sun-court descending from heaven. The scepter, we are told, is "no more / To be swayed by visible hand" (4-5). Whether it will be taken up by an invisible hand or by no hand at all remains uncertain, but we are alerted to the egalitarianism underlying Blake's version of the apocalypse. The King's loss of power will put an end to authoritarianism in France.

Despite its satanic allusions, the first scene treats the King as a well-meaning victim of his ancestry and events. Under the influence of Necker, he has begun to accept his loss of power as inevitable and resistance as futile: "Rise, Necker: the ancient dawn calls us / To awake from slumbers of five thousand years" (7-8). While common sense thus pushes him toward the new dawn, habit and memory pull him back into the false light of the five-thousand-year dream of history (8-9). The inevitability of his fall

[18] The hand of the fallen Saturn is "unsceptered" in Keats's *Hyperion* and *Fall of Hyperion* (lines 19 and 324, respectively). I suspect a common source.

from power, signaled by the imagery of the first scene, is dramatized as he descends—"troubled, leaning on Necker" (10)—to his council chamber. With the King's fate sealed at the start, interest centers upon the division within him. Whether he decides to accept or resist events will determine not the result of the revolution but the course it will take, its quality.

After the King's figurative descent from sky to earth, his nobles —"shady mountains, . . . each conversing with woes in the infinite shadows of his soul" (10-13)—gather round like clouds and further obscure his light. Their fearful thunder is softened ("embosomed") by the "woods of France" (11) and echoed by the higher "clouds of wisdom prophetic" that "roll over the palace roof" (12). The stage is set for a battle between lower clouds (nobles) and upper clouds (people). The God of Revelation uses war to destroy his enemies. Blake shifts the imagery to imply that if the nobles decide to imitate God and use war as their instrument they will destroy not their enemies but themselves. The morning clouds of prophetic wisdom (15) in the sky are dominant.

Downward motion continues in the second scene (16-53). From an overview of Paris, we pass to the dens of the Bastille that form the lower level of the poem. Just as the Hades of Revelation holds men and women who have defied God, this hell holds men and women who have defied the King. Blake uses the scene to move back in time and present visually the injustices that led to the revolution. With each tableau our indignation increases until finally, when the prisoners look up and laugh at the jailor's light, we feel a power rising from below to consume the King in the hell he has created. The transvaluation—with dynamic energy, creativity, and virtue attributed to the inhabitants of hell—corresponds to Blake's more extensive refutation of Milton and orthodox Christianity in *The Marriage of Heaven and Hell*. The shaking of the seven dens (52) ironically echoes the breaking of the seven seals in Revelation. In both cases destructive forces are released upon a group of usurpers, but Blake shows the power originating within human beings and directed against an earthly court that has set itself up in imitation of the heavenly court in Revelation. The object of his attack is the Judaic-Christian tradition that created and perpetuated an authoritarian God and allowed certain men to decree themselves his representatives on earth.

From the Bastille's hell, we rise in the third scene (54-58) for a closer view of the Commons which reinforces the poem's scheme of displacement and clarifies Blake's apocalyptic vision. The Hall of the Nation is fixed by an extended simile: "For the Commons convene in the Hall of the Nation; like spirits of fire in the beautiful / Porches of the Sun, to plant beauty in the desert craving abyss, they gleam / On the anxious city" (54-56). The people "look up to the morning Senate" (58). Having figuratively occupied the sun, the Commons displaces the King at the upper level of the poem. In the name of order and justice, the Sun-Kings made a desert of human life by serving themselves and the abyss or chaos that craves a desert. With an optimism soon to be tempered by the course of events, Blake portrays revolutionary government as a gleaming, creative sun that dispels clouds of despair ("visions of sorrow," 58), nourishes life, and fosters beauty.

The opening of the fourth scene (59-254) implies another descent, this time from the Hall of the Nation: "But heavy brow'd jealousies lower o'er the Louvre" and "terrors of ancient Kings / Descend from the gloom and wander thro' the palace" (59-60). While the scene takes place at the middle or earthly level of the poem, images repeatedly associate characters and events with the upper and lower levels. The nobles persist in thinking themselves in the sky, but Blake implies that they are slipping toward hell. Like Satan's band of fallen angels in *Paradise Lost*, they "fold round the King" in "thick shades of discontent" on "soul-skirting mountains of sorrow" (64-67). Bound down with iron and marble, they burn "in flames of red wrath" that represent the hell within them and their desire for revenge. Concurrently, they dim the King's light and infect him with their fire. The confluence of light and dark, heat and cold, echoes Milton's treatment of hell in *Paradise Lost*.

Quickened to speech by the nobles' fire, the King describes his perception, through the clouds rolling round him, of "the spirits of ancient Kings" who come out of the sky as though out of their graves (72-73). Frightened by the escaped prisoners who shout in the fields, these spirits counsel the King to hide with his nobles in "the nether earth . . . in stones, among roots of trees" (75-77). Strategic retreat may halt the apocalyptic "plague and wrath and tempest" (78) and enable the rulers to regain their authority. The advice of the ancient kings is that of Belial: "If we can sustain and bear, / Our Supreme Foe in time may much remit / His anger" (*Paradise Lost* II,209-211). As he prepares to sit down, the King sees out his window the fire-breathing army, and his bosom expands like the "starry heaven" (82). Having moved away from the wiser counsel of Necker, he is tempted now to reject the advice of the ancient kings and submit to his nobles' desire for war.

The spokesman for the stronger course is the Duke of Burgundy, whose role is that of Milton's Moloch. He urges the King to "stretch the hand that beckons the eagles of heaven" (103), to order the army against the rebels "with clarions of cloud breathing war."[19] Blake summons the imagery of Revelation to Burgundy and turns it against him. In lines echoing the description of the harvest and winepress of war in Revelation 14:17-20, Burgundy appears "red as wines / From his mountains," and from his garments rises "an odor of war, like a ripe vineyard" (83-84). The chamber becomes "as a clouded sky" as he stretches "his red limbs, / Cloth'd in flames of crimson" over the council (85-86). Infant souls, victims of his past tyranny and potential victims of the war he urges, weep in his burning robe (87-88). He proceeds to describe with vigor and clarity the pastoral life of primitive simplicity that threatens to put an end to the "great starry harvest" (90), the "eternal reason and science" (95) of Western civilization that he wants preserved at all costs. Blake thus sets before the reader indirectly his own vision of postapocalyptic life, an ideal that forms the positive pole of the poem.

Under the spell of the Duke's fire, the King looks again at his armies that tinge the morning with "beams of blood" (105-106).[20] Weak and confused, surrounded by "dark mists" that "blot the writing of God" in his bosom (108-109), he is torn between distress for his nobles (107-108) and pity for the women and children who will suffer from the war he hears coming (111-113). Honestly trying to do what will be just and merciful for his people, he quietly sides with the nobles and banishes Necker from the kingdom. Despite his good intentions, the choice aligns him with the Old rather than the New Testament God, and he concludes

[19] Line 101. With "cloud" rather than "loud," I follow the proof copy in the Huntington Library. See E737, and my note: *BNYPL*, LXXII, 4-5.

[20] Line numbers here depart from all editions except the third (1968) and subsequent printings of E.

his speech as the stern lawgiver: "The tempest must fall, as in years that are passed away" (115). Despite his sympathy for the women and children, it is the writing of God as pastoral shepherd that is blotted from his bosom (108-109). That role now passes to Necker. Having slipped back into the old rather than firmly grasping the new order, the King now fades to the background and becomes a passive observer.[21] Blake thus implies that the rulers who formed the keystone of the old political, religious, and social structure were bound to fall by their weakness of character and lack of vision.

That the King's act of banishment will bring about his displacement by Necker at the upper level of the poem becomes explicit in the passage following his speech. The extended simile marking Necker's pause portrays a pastoral world wherein he will be honored by the tears of husbandmen and women and bright children before they turn to their "pensive fields" (118-120). His face covered with clouds that suggest his sadness and the burden he has assumed, Necker drops a tear and leaves his "place" (121). As he passes out of the chamber, women and children kneel round, kiss his garments, and weep. The actions recall the honor paid Christ as he moved to his crucifixion and subsequent ascension.[22] Embodying principles of liberty and fraternity, Necker becomes the exemplary spiritual leader of the new age. Indeed, his might be the invisible hand that takes up the scepter now too heavy for the King, though he would use that symbol to protect rather than

[21] He speaks only one more line: 197.

[22] Necker's flight to Geneva introduces yet another kind of motion into the poem. Burgundy had asked if the nobles would allow the "mowers / From the Atlantic mountains" to mow down the "harvest of six thousand years" and permit "Necker, the hind of Geneva" to "stretch his crook'd sickle o'er fertile France" (89-91). Later allusions to Voltaire and Rousseau (276 and 282), both associated with Geneva, clarify the pattern. Originating in the Swiss mountains, revolutionary ideas passed westward to join forces with the exiled Titans in Atlantis and then moved on to infect the Americans with the desire for independence. Now those ideas are returning across France in a southeasterly direction that retraces the course of the old sun and moves toward the new. Necker thus becomes the vehicle of their transmission to Switzerland, where, tempering justice with mercy, he will preside from those high mountains over the European harvest and then tend his flocks as the true shepherd. This pattern of global movement receives more extensive treatment in Blake's *America* and *Europe*. For a succinct account of Blake's use of this myth, see Frye, *Symmetry*, esp. 174-175 and 206.

punish the people. The imagery portrays Necker as the New Testament God who will nourish rather than bruise the mild flourishing mountains (see line 5) and oversee a bountiful harvest for all human beings.

After Necker's departure, the Archbishop of Paris rises as a scaly serpent amid hissing flames and "sulphurous smoke" (126-127). Just as Blake used Burgundy's speech to establish indirectly his ideal political and social order, he uses the Archbishop's to castigate orthodox religion and suggest an alternative moral order. By carefully framing the Archbishop's description of a vision he saw during the night, Blake guides our opinion of it. At midnight in his "golden tower," the Archbishop tells us, "the repose of the labours of men / Wav'd its solemn cloud" over his head (129-130. Then he awoke, felt a cold hand passing over his limbs, and saw a vision. After describing it, he says: "I slept, for the cloud of repose returned, / But the morning dawn'd heavy upon me" (151-152). The sleep which returned like a dark cloud represents absence of true vision; it is a rest from labor, a state of unimaginative repose. The dreamlike interval, which seemed a nightmare to the Archbishop, was in fact an awakening to truth.

As the Archbishop describes his vision, Blake moves for the first and only time directly into the heaven of Revelation. Near the end of that prophecy, the heavenly court descends to earth in glory; here the court petrifies at its center and falls apart at its edges. God on the throne is the sad Urizenic figure who appears frequently and in various contexts in Blake's later poems and drawings:

> An aged form, white as snow, hov'ring in mist, weeping
>   in the uncertain light,
> Dim the form almost faded, tears fell down the shady
>   cheeks; at his feet many cloth'd
> In white robes, strewn in air censers and harps, silent
>   they lay prostrated;
> Beneath, in the awful void, myriads descending and
>   weeping thro' dismal winds,
> Endless the shady train shiv'ring descended, from the
>   gloom where the aged form wept.   (131-135).

These lines depict the heavenly counterpart of the collapse of the French court. It is significant that Necker's displacement of the King at the upper level of the poem intervenes between the victory of the wrathful nobles over the King's mind and this description of the disintegration of the heavenly monarchy from which the King had derived his temporal authority.

Having set the ruinous scene, the Archbishop reproduces the words whispered to him by the "aged form" in a voice like that of a grasshopper (136). Although not specifically identified by the Archbishop, this "form" is the God of orthodox religion who sees himself, after having been so long worshiped, going out like a lamp without oil (137-138). From his vantage point, men seem to be "descending to beasts" as they look downward, labor, and forget his "holy law" (139). In the spreading chaos, nobles who served him are failing and dying (143); all that has been sacred is profaned. Even the "holy choir / Is turn'd into songs of the harlot in day, and cries of the virgin in night" (146-147). For Blake, of course, the dissolution of the heavenly court of the fourth chapter of Revelation is cause for rejoicing; the apocalyptic tremors running through the speech as reported by the Archbishop signal a healthy release from restraints, the shedding of a gigantic illusion, the birth of a new moral order.

As the hoary God reflects morbidly upon death, with the possibility of his own no doubt in mind, his sense of hierarchy lashes back upon him. If everyone drops "unredeem'd, unconfess'd, unpardon'd" (148), priests will have to rot next to lawless lovers. What is worse, the "King, frowning in purple," will be buried "beside the grey plowman, and their worms embrace together" (150). Blake's ironic laughter breaks through in a telling blow for egalitarianism. But the Archbishop, frightened out of his Christian charity by the oracle, calls upon the King to follow "the command of Heaven" and "shut up this Assembly in their final home" (153-154). Fearing the safety of his own head and heart, he addresses the King as "O Annointed" and urges him to assume the role of the antichrist by turning the Hall of the Nation and the Bastille into living tombs. Since the rebels "threaten to bathe their feet / In the blood of Nobility" (155-156), the King, in the name of his ancient God, should cause the buildings to devour the rebels.

At this point, midway in scene four, as Blake's irony reaches its peak, he shifts out of that mode to prepare for the speeches of a nobleman and a clergyman who, in contrast to Burgundy and the

Archbishop of Paris, support the revolution. With the two earlier characters, he worked indirectly to undercut the old order and describe the new. He now moves to a direct portrayal of the new order through characters who share his vision. In a transitional passage, a man named Aumont, whose soul is an "eternally wan-d'ring" comet, enters the chamber "like a man that returns from hollow graves" (160-161). He announces that the Abbé de Sieyès, who has come with a message from the Commons, was preceded through the ranks of the King's army by "a dark shadowy man in the form / Of King Henry the Fourth" (164-165), who walks in fires and has struck the soldiers dumb with fear. A king who accepted democratic principles and thus betrayed his heritage, Henry poses a special threat to the council.[23] Several nobles rise in anger and stalk the chamber like thunder clouds. The Duke of Bourbon madly draws his sword, challenges the "spectre of Henry," and offers to lead the army against the people (171-174).

In this tense situation, Orleans, "generous as mountains," rises and lifts a "benevolent hand" to calm his fellow nobles (175-176). Like Henry, he is an aristocrat who values human liberty. In a speech that ranks among Blake's most brilliant, Orleans attempts to convince the councilmen that they would profit as human beings by accepting the revolution. Addressing his fellows as "princes of fire," he urges them to use their human flames to create rather than destroy and assures them that the fire of true nobility is unquenchable (179-181). Then, changing the meta-phor, he asserts that the body whose members are healthful can-not be diseased (182). Referring first to the body politic, he then enters the metaphor to dwell upon the bodies of individual men and women. The Archbishop had warned that the collapse of orthodox religion would turn men into beasts. In words that re-call the Archbishop's concern with heart and head, Orleans asks: "Can the soul whose brain and heart / Cast their rivers in equal tides thro' the great Paradise, languish because the feet / Hands, head, bosom, and parts of love, follow their high breathing joy?" (183-185). The political theme is thus grounded in the bedrock of human nature. Remove restraints, Orleans asserts in the mood of Blake's "Proverbs of Hell," and men will quicken into creative and responsible human beings. The flaming forth of the people

[23] See Erdman, *Prophet*, 154-155 [169-170].

will not, Orleans assures the nobles, dim the luster of their own crimson, "for fire delights in its form" (189). Finally, Orleans issues a challenge to the Archbishop that expresses a central principle of Blake's prophetic writings:

> But go, merciless man! enter into the infinite labyrinth
>   of another's brain
> Ere thou measure the circle that he shall run. Go, thou
>   cold recluse, into the fires
> Of another's high flaming rich bosom, and return un-
>   consum'd, and write laws.
> If thou canst not do this, doubt thy theories, learn to con-
>   sider all men as thy equals,
> Thy brethren, and not as thy foot or thy hand, unless
>   thou first fearest to hurt them.   (190-194)

The appeal for personal freedom against the cold bonds of the established church quiets the councilmen into reflectiveness. Bourbon replaces his sword, and the nobles sit "like clouds on the mountains, when the storm is passing away" (195-196). There is a ray of hope that earlier presages will prove wrong, that the nobles will acquiesce to a peaceful revolution.

At this point the King rises and speaks his last line in the poem: "Let the Nation's Ambassador come among Nobles, like incense of the valley" (197). The source is Revelation 8:3-5 where, in the silence following the opening of the seventh seal, incense mingles with the prayers of saints rising before the throne of God. The silence in Revelation is followed by the casting down of the censer and an earth-shattering storm. With this pattern in mind, we can guess that the peaceful mood in France is only an interlude. And the King's speech, though low-keyed and conciliatory, shows him clinging to his position. He will *allow* the prayers of his people to come up before him and sends Aumont to summon Sieyès. When Aumont emerges from the palace as a "cold orb of disdain" (199), the sight of him causes King Henry's soul to shudder, whereupon Henry departs indignantly on "horses of heav'n" (201) to prepare for apocalyptic battle.

Addressing the nobles as "Heavens of France," the Abbé begs them to hear the voices of the oppressed people rising from "valley and hill / O'erclouded with power" (206-207). His deferential manner is emphasized by the simile preceding his speech: "As a father that bows to his son; / Whose rich fields inheriting spread their old glory, so the voice of the people bowed / Before the ancient of the kingdom and mountains to be renewed" (203-205). The contrast with Orleans' bold assertiveness is sharp and purposeful. Sieyès' humility signifies weakness and reminds the nobles of the power they retain over men's minds. The possibility of losing that power stirs them again, reawakening the mood of battle. Blake's psychological insight strikes deep. Habits of subservience among lower members of the religious and social orders are deeply ingrained. Like the banishment of Necker, rejection of the Abbé's message is a necessary prelude to the abolition of slavish deference among men. Although change does not in the end come about through war, the conclusion of the fourth scene makes the point that it will not come as a gift of the nobles.

While the Abbé's manner reminds the nobles of their power, what he says reminds them of the material comforts they may lose. His speech dramatizes Burgundy's earlier warning that the "marble built heaven" would become a clay cottage (89). Since ancient kings joined with priests to systematize the universe ("blights of the fife" and "blasting of trumpets," 209), men have been locked into that system, enslaved by a "sulphur heaven" (213) that is hell. Through Sieyès, Blake asserts that the chaos the Archbishop's God feared for the future has been a feature of common life for centuries. Human suffering gains intensity, the Abbé asserts, until "the dawn of our peaceful morning" (214-216), whereupon man raises "his darken'd limbs out of the caves of night, his eyes and his heart / Expand" (218-219). The Abbé then shifts to the future tense (220) to describe the results of this expansion. In response to the valleys of France, soldiers will lay down their arms (220-221), nobles will put off their symbols of rank and authority (221-223), and a priest will weep in his thunderous cloud, bend down to embrace the valleys, and put his hand to the plow (223-224). Orleans assured the nobles that the relaxing of restraints upon individual freedom would not produce the chaotic orgy imagined by the Archbishop. Sieyès reproduces the sermon of a regenerate priest who sees the new age not as the end of European civilization, as Burgundy had forecast, but as its flowering into a truly civilized and creative society.

After proclaiming the end of oppressive terrors, this priest will instruct his people in the new patterns: song, guiltless love, universal education, and productivity at all levels of society (227-236). Suffering and deprivation removed, "the happy earth" will "sing in its course, / The mild peaceable nations be opened to heav'n, and men walk with their fathers in bliss" (236-237).[24] In the guise of a priest of the future which is imagined by a redeemed religious man of the present, Blake presents his first extensive description of the ideal life that formed the core of his apocalyptic vision.

Finally, Sieyès adjures the nobles: "Hear the first voice of the morning: Depart, O clouds of night, and no more / Return; be withdrawn cloudy war, troops of warriors depart, nor around our peaceable city / Breathe fires, but ten miles from Paris, let all be peace, nor a soldier be seen" (238-240). Rather than dispersing, the noble clouds stir and "cast their shadows" in anger until the palace appears "like a cloud driven abroad" with blood running down its "ancient pillars" (241-246). Between the sounding of the sixth and seventh trumpets in Revelation, a mighty angel, a messenger from God, descends to describe the remaining events of the apocalypse in a voice that becomes the seven thunders.[25] Blake may have had this passage in mind as he described Burgundy stepping forth to cast the King's doom upon Sieyès and the people: "Thro' the cloud a deep thunder, the Duke of Burgundy, delivers the King's command" (247). Whereas the angel of the Revelation prohibited John from reproducing what the thunder said, there is no reticence on the part of Burgundy. With heavy cynicism he announces that the "bands of the murmuring kingdom" (254) will be retained and thus sets the stage for an apocalyptic battle.

The long fourth scene contains only two crucial decisions—the banishment of Necker and the rejection of the Commons' message—and one follows from the other. The measure of suspense following Orleans' speech is short-lived. Considering the scene's length and the inevitability of its actions, it contributes minimally to plot. Its purpose is rhetorical: to dramatize in a mental war the poem's substructure of ideas. Three men blinded by tradition and self-interest are set against three men of vision in a battle of words that is the poem's only realization of the

[24] The image picks up that of the Learlike father paying suit to his son in the simile preceding the Abbé's speech.

[25] Blake's illustration of this passage in the tenth chapter of Revelation, *The Angel of the Revelation*, is reproduced as pl. 162 in Keynes, *Bible*.

apocalyptic storm. Through the dialectical interplay of speeches and through images implying position and motion, the scene imprints upon the reader's mind a victory for the new order. The weak and ineffectual King is displaced by the Christlike Necker. While the bloody Burgundy strives to maintain his place in the sky, Orleans rises above him by the force of his majestic bearing and the depth of his perceptions. Sieyès easily overcomes the Archbishop of Paris with the verbal weapons of true religion delivered by an imagined priest who bends down from the sky to work among the people. With its intricate pattern, its visual imagery, its subtle characterizations, the force of its ironies, and the beauty of its visions, the scene carries the weight of the poem's prophetic mission.

In the fifth scene (255-269) Sieyès returns to the Commons "like the morning star arising above the black waves, when a shipwreck'd soul sighs for morning" (255). The Assembly hears his provocative message in silence, whereupon "a thunder roll'd round loud and louder" (257). The thunder subsides as Mirabeau rises to the sound of rushing wings and calls Fayette, who responds "sudden as the bullet wrapp'd in his fire" (262). "Bowing like clouds, man towards man" (263) and "like a council of ardors seated in clouds, bending over the cities of men" (264), the Assembly votes "the removal of War" (267). Beneath them, at the poem's middle level, "their children are marshall'd together to battle" (265), but rather than allowing the battle to begin the Assemblymen ask Fayette to lead the King's army out of the city. During the vote, "pestilence weighs his red wings in the sky" (267). The image fuses the horse of war of the second seal in Revelation with the pale horse of famine and pestilence which emerges from the fourth seal carrying Death (6:3-7). The democratic leaders of the new age reject those violent horsemen and move toward the apocalypse as Blake envisioned it, as the nonviolent removal of the social and political hierarchies of eighteenth-century Europe.[26]

[26] Kathleen Raine (I, 348) has recently characterized *The French Revolution* as "a celebration of war." The people are ready for war if it must come, and the imagery implies an impending battle; but that imagery is realized only in the verbal contest of scene four. Among the liberals, Necker, Orleans, the Abbé de Sieyès, and Mirabeau prevail over the fiery spirit of King Henry the Fourth and the horses of war. The two significant actions of the Commons

The sixth scene (270-292) presents the enactment of the Commons' decision. "The aged sun rises apall'd" and for the last time "from dark mountains."[27] It is obscured by a cloud on the eastern hill that casts a shadow on the city, the army, and the Louvre; but it "gleams a dusky beam / On Fayette" (270), who becomes a "flame of fire" (273) before the dark ranks of the army. Around him "flow frequent spectres of religious men weeping" (274), an ironic reversal of the bright cloud of infant souls in Burgundy's burning robe (87-88). These spectres have been driven out of the abbeys by the "fiery cloud of Voltaire, and the thund'rous rocks of Rousseau" (276), the verbal warriors of the new age. While the imagery continues to imply the possibility of violence, Fayette, increasingly an independent source of light, lifts his hand to quiet the army (278) in a gesture that recalls Orleans raising his hand to calm the nobles (175-176). As he stands silently, with the fiery soul of Voltaire and the white cloud of Rousseau[28] over his head (282-283), the officers rush round him to hear his words: "The Nation's Assembly command, that the Army remove ten miles from Paris; / Nor a soldier be seen in road or in field, till the Nation command return" (285-286).

Obedient now to the "Nation," the officers rush back to their stations and await "the sound of trumpet": "Then the drum beats, and the steely ranks move, and trumpets rejoice in the sky. / Dark cavalry like clouds frought with thunder ascend on the hills, and bright infantry, rank / Behind rank, to the soul shaking drum and shrill fife along the roads glitter like fire" (290-292). Revelation's trumpet and storm imagery is neatly turned.[29] The trumpets signal

---

are the deployment of a message of peace and a defiant ploy that strips the nobles of their power to make war. "The first voice of the morning," as delivered by Sieyès, is "let all be peace" (238-240).

[27] Line 270. Like the author of Revelation, Blake distorts clock time. Since there has been no break in the action to allow for the passage of a night, we may assume that we have simply moved further into the dawn that began in the poem's opening lines. Blake wished simply to set the poem in the apocalyptic morning and draw a contrast between the old and new dawns.

[28] The image recalls "one like a son of man" on a "white cloud" in Revelation 14:14.

[29] The first four trumpets in Revelation produce a rapid succession of cataclysmic events on earth and in the sky (8:6-12). The next three produce the "woes" that inflict those inhabitants of earth who have not been sealed

renewal without destruction; while the dark clouds that dimmed cheerful France at the start of the poem ascend on the hills as the cavalry responds to Fayette, the representative of the Commons, the new sun. The texture of this climactic passage is deepened by its ironic echoes of the ninth chapter of Revelation, where a fallen star releases the locusts that become the war horses whose king is the angel of the bottomless pit. Fayette descends as a new Lucifer to take the army away from the satanic King and thus avert a battle that would have destroyed the King's insectile minions as well as the saintly rebels. Rather than spreading the plague of war upon all the inhabitants of France, the dark hosts consent to rise out of their hell into the morning sun. By shifting allegiance, they save themselves, break the bands that enslave the country, and clear the sky of dark clouds so that the apocalyptic radiance can embrace all the "mild flourishing mountains" (5) of France.

In the last scene, the noise of the departing army and the wind of trumpets smite "the palace walls with a blast" (293). The removal of war strikes the nobles like a storm. Growing "pale and cold" (294), the King falls deeper into the sickness described in the poem's opening lines. His heart sinks, his pulses fade in faint death (294-296). His nobles, the sick mountains of line 6, become "pale like mountains of the dead, / Cover'd with dews of night, groaning, shaking forests and floods" (296-297). In the darkness of the palace they fall among slimy snakes and toads (297-300); yet they do not enter the earth or descend to the lower level of the poem. Their fate is not that of the Satan of Revelation, who is finally thrown into the burning lake to suffer eternal torment (20:10). Rather, in actions that fuse vision and reality, the "bottoms of the world" open, the graves of the archangels are unsealed, and the "enormous dead" come to life as "pale fires" (301-302). Blake stays with the twentieth chapter of Revelation where the sea, Death, and Hell give up their dead to be judged by their deeds, but his emphasis is upon reconciliation rather than retribution:

---

by God: at the fifth a star falls from heaven to earth and releases the army of locusts which rises amid the darkening smoke from the bottomless pit (9:1-11); at the sixth a host of cavalry, the horses breathing fire and smoke and sulphur, destroy a third of mankind (9:13-21); and at the seventh there is rejoicing in heaven, God's temple opens (11:15-19), and finally Christ appears on a white cloud (cf. FR 282) to begin the harvest (14:14-20).

"A faint heat from their fires [the pale fires of the dead] reviv'd the cold Louvre; the frozen blood reflow'd. / Awful up rose the king, him the peers follow'd, they saw the courts of the Palace / Forsaken, and Paris without a soldier, silent, for the noise was gone up / And follow'd the army, and the Senate in peace, sat beneath the morning's beam" (303-306). The upward movement includes the king (now uncapitalized) and his nobles. Along with the "enormous dead," they are figuratively reborn into a new age where suppressors and suppressed will live together in liberty and fraternity.

The French Revolution does not take the simple form of a transfer of place and power between King and Commons. The last scene projects a general rising as king and peers pick themselves up off the ground to see the palace forsaken and the city of Paris silent and soldierless. Noise and army have "gone up," and finally, in a subtle reversal of that upward motion, the Senate sits *beneath* the morning sun. The poem's vertical movement can be diagramed as follows:

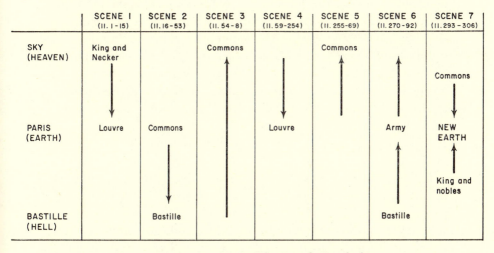

	SCENE 1 (ll. 1-15)	SCENE 2 (ll. 16-53)	SCENE 3 (ll. 54-8)	SCENE 4 (ll. 59-254)	SCENE 5 (ll. 255-69)	SCENE 6 (ll. 270-92)	SCENE 7 (ll. 293-306)
SKY (HEAVEN)	King and Necker ↓		Commons ↑	↑	Commons ↑	↑	Commons ↓
PARIS (EARTH)	Louvre	Commons ↓		Louvre		Army ↑	NEW EARTH ↑ King and nobles
BASTILLE (HELL)		Bastille				Bastille	

Fig. 1. Levels of action in *The French Revolution*

Although the heavenly city does not descend as it does in Revelation (21:2), the new heaven and new earth coalesce at the center of the poem. Vertical motion becomes irrelevant, Blake implies, in a regenerate world where mankind lives peacefully and productively, without hierarchies of power and privilege, beneath a beneficent sun. Man, if he chooses, may create a true heaven on earth. The possibility of his doing precisely that through the medium of the revolution in France is the final point toward which all the disparate elements of the poem move.

The spatial structure of *The French Revolution* and the pattern of its development depend heavily upon figurative language. It may be useful in conclusion to look more closely at Blake's management of the single image and the extended simile. Among the poem's images, the cloud is most prominent. Some have objected that there are too many clouds and that their symbolic values are too numerous and contradictory.[30] Opinions differ on their meaning and purpose.[31] Again, the best starting place is the Book of Revelation. Whatever else they may do, the clouds signal the apocalyptic storm with its dual function of destruction and renewal. In Revelation the storm functions as an independent phenomenon; throughout *The French Revolution* the clouds are closely associated with war. Dark clouds and clouds of fire are linked with nobles and King; while higher, lighter clouds represent the revolutionaries. At this level of perception, the clouds mark a distinction between the conservative and liberal forces that clash in the rhetoric of scene four and threaten to meet in the thunder and lightning of a real battle. At a deeper level, all the cloud images are positive because the apocalyptic war, verbal or otherwise, is a vehicle of renewal. "Clouds of wisdom" in line 12 may refer only to the upper clouds, but "O cloud well appointed" refers specifically to the dark cloud that descends on "chearful France" in line 1. Men of true vision will see beyond the darkening effect of the "well appointed" cloud to the new order it will bring.

Blake also uses clouds to make a qualitative distinction between possible forms of the apocalypse. In a moment of anger Necker pauses "like a dark cloud" (117); and when Orleans momentarily subdues the nobles they sit around "like clouds on the mountains, when the storm is passing away" (196). Yet Necker as dark cloud

[30] "No less than thirty-six of them in three hundred and six lines of the poem" (Damon, *Philosophy*, 82). "The [cloud] image is employed so often and in so many ways that we become unduly conscious of its presence, and when it occurs in an unexpected context, we are confounded" (Halliburton, "Blake's *French Revolution*," 162).

[31] "Blake attached no important and occult meaning to the word; it means, quite simply, a focus of power—but not always even that" (Damon, *Philosophy*, 82). "In its elevation, its immateriality, it is a convenient emblem of transcendence" (Halliburton, 162).

releases only a tear (121); and immediately after Sieyès' speech the noble "clouds cast their shadows" (241) and return to their stormy mood. By marking temporary shifts of emotion with reversals of the image pattern, Blake reinforces the dominant association of lighter clouds with the Commons and emphasizes the people's and his own preference for a peaceful resolution.

Finally, the clouds mark the relative abilities of characters to see clearly.[32] An obvious example occurs in the poem's first line, where the fusion of cloud and vision—"The dead brood over Europe, the cloud and vision descends over chearful France"—may be confusing in isolation. The phrase occurs later in the Archbishop's lamentation: "my cloud and vision [will] be no more" (143). For the Archbishop, "cloud" may signify the transcendence of his vision. Blake, a step behind him, implies that his vision is a cloud that prevents true seeing. It is this cloud-vision that descends in line 1 and establishes an ambiguity central to the poem: In coming down to earth it increases the darkness and subdues the cheer of France, but in becoming less transcendent it will begin to disintegrate and to clear the way for true vision and permanent cheerfulness. Its descent, represented by the King's movement down to his council chamber (10), initiates the verbal storm that results finally in the ascent of the "dark cavalry like clouds frought with thunder" (291). In this way the clouds reinforce the essential distinction between two kinds of seeing, two views of human life, and move through the poem's landscape as agents of visual renewal.

Along with their symbolic functions, the clouds of *The French Revolution* also serve to block off, deepen, and enrich the poem's scenes.[33] When Rousseau unfolds his white cloud over

[32] Harold Bloom has recognized this point: "The dominant image of *The French Revolution* is the cloud, which represents at once the failure of vision to achieve clear form, and the failure of less imaginative perception to form a clear image" (*Apocalypse*, 62).

[33] Blake often used clouds to separate groups of figures and give shape to his paintings and designs, sometimes to divide spiritual and material events within a single scene. They are used extensively in the Job illustrations. In *The Last Judgment* the spiritual forms rising toward heaven at the left resemble clouds, and they are separated from the material bodies falling into hell at the right by a cloud-flame form in the center. These clouds are most prominent in the 1806 water color formerly in the Butts Collection and reproduced as pl. 131b in Keynes, *Bible*. In this version the heavenly throne is also framed by clouds. In the Petworth water color (E, pl. 2), these clouds assume human forms.

the army (282-283), for example, we see that event in the sky and mix with it our perception of the material events below. The dark clouds and red clouds that fold round the King when he descends to his chamber (59-69) are visual counters implying his descent toward hell. Light clouds tend to enable the reader to see more clearly—because Blake follows them with more detailed descriptions—while dark clouds tend to obscure or shut off vision. Besides marking levels and implying vertical placement, the clouds add depth, motion inward, and thus a third dimension to the poem.

A more complex visual motive underlies Blake's management of similes. The following lines exemplify his use of this figure to expand the poem's space:

> For the Commons convene in the Hall of the Nation;
>   like spirits of fire in the beautiful
> Porches of the Sun, to plant beauty in the desart craving
>   abyss, they gleam
> On the anxious city; all children new-born first behold
>   them; tears are fled,
> And they nestle in earth-breathing bosoms. So the city
>   of Paris, their wives and children,
> Look up to the morning Senate, and visions of sorrow
>   leave pensive streets.   (54-58)

The two basic analogies are set in the first three lines: The Hall of the Nation is like the porches of the sun, and the members of Commons gleam on the city of Paris like the spirits of fire that surround the sun and plant beauty in the abyss. The return to "city" followed by the semicolon in the third line seems to bring the simile to a close; but "them" in the next phrase could refer either to the Commons in Paris or to the spirits of fire within the simile. The word "So" in the fourth line, a conventional mark for the close of an extended simile, joins "them" in line 3 to push "new-born" children back into the "spirits of fire" simile. The initial analogies are thus extended: the people of Paris who look up to the "morning Senate" and lose "visions of sorrow"[34] are *like* "new-born" children who first behold a new world fashioned by a creative sun from the "desart craving abyss." In other words, the "new-born" children seem at first to be the real children of

[34] These are the "cloud and vision" of the old order (1 and 143) which caused sorrow among the common people.

Paris looking at the sunlike Commons. Then we move to the suggestion that the men, wives, and children of Paris *are* the first-born of a newly created world. Besides extending and enriching the analogies, the syntactical ambiguities obscure the distinction between what is happening in Paris and what is happening in the mind of the poet, between reality and vision. Movement in and out of the simile leads the reader from a recognition of analogy (two separate pictures) to the impression of identity (one picture doubly conceived). The poem's space is not only expanded, but transformed.

We should recall, at this point, the distortions of space and time in the Book of Revelation and my earlier suggestion that Blake, to compensate for his lack of heavenly omniscience and to make the most of his limited point of view, used images and symbols to establish three spatial levels and movement among them. The porches of the sun simile suggests that the limitation of narrative focus may have been a deliberate effort to demonstrate that men need not be taken in the spirit to heaven like St. John, or even imagine themselves so transported, to gain a more inclusive and penetrating vision. The syntactical structure of the simile is purposefully manipulated to break down the barrier between inner and outer space, to encourage readers to see the supernatural within the natural, the visionary within the real. Moreover, the kind of seeing it fosters is an essential ingredient of the rebirth experienced by the people of Paris, who see the "morning Senate" as the rising sun, and by the reader, who sees the Parisians as new-born children looking up to the Senate-sun. By fostering imaginative vision, the complex verbal figure contributes directly to the poem's prophetic mission.

The simile marking Necker's pause illustrates a disruption of the reader's time sense for a similar purpose:

> Like a dark cloud Necker paus'd, and like thunder on
>   the just man's burial day he paus'd;
> Silent sit the winds, silent the meadows, while the hus-
>   bandman and woman of weakness
> And bright children look after him into the grave, and
>   water his clay with love,
> Then turn towards pensive fields; so Necker paus'd, and
>   his visage was cover'd with clouds.   (117-120)

Again the analogy is firmly set: Reacting stormily at first to the King's decision, Necker becomes *like* a dark cloud. Then, *like* the thunder that sounds or pauses to honor the just man on his burial day, Necker pauses. The clouds covering his visage in the last line move the initial simile ("like a dark cloud") into metaphor; analogy again gives way to identity. Necker seems to move up among the clouds which carry the thunder of the second simile. Within that simile, Blake presents a cinematic forward-flash into the postapocalyptic world where Necker, no longer pausing like the thunder in honor of the just man, *becomes* the just man who is honored by the elements and by the people shedding tears at his graveside. Functioning dramatically to extend the pause, this simile shows the reader, at the low point of Necker's fortune and of the poem, the ideal toward which events are moving. Confirmation of the jump into the future occurs after the simile when, as Necker leaves the palace, we see the future beginning: "the women and children of the city / Kneel'd round him and kissed his garments and wept" (122-123).

At its deepest level, *The French Revolution* attempts to work a change upon the reader by expanding his spatial and temporal vision, by moving his "imaginative eye" inward as well as up and down in space and back and forward in time. Images and similes are carefully structured to prepare the reader for the coalescence of vision and reality at the end of the poem, where Blake abandons analogy and invites the reader to *see* gleams of fire shooting from the sun that is Fayette (278), Rousseau unfolding his white cloud (282-283), and the pale fires of the enormous dead—those dead who brood over Europe in the poem's first line—reviving the cold Louvre (302-303). Along with other formal elements such as juxtaposition, displacement, and repetition, figurative language encourages the reader to see the revolution as revelation, as the apocalypse, and thus to make a new life for himself and for all men. Convinced that the potential for imaginative sight lies within every human being, Blake brought all his artistic resources to bear within the verbal medium in an effort to show how the advancing present can become the eternal "now." Later, as other essays in this volume demonstrate, he buttressed the words of his narratives with pictures in order to approach more nearly his prophetic goal and thereby created complex interrelationships between verbal and graphic images whose subtleties we are only beginning to appreciate.

3

Blake's Composite Art

W. J. T. MITCHELL

THE illuminated poetry of William Blake presents a unique problem in the interpretation of the arts, for although there have been many artists who have worked in several different media, rarely do we find one equally renowned in more than one field, and even more rarely do we encounter an artist who can successfully combine several art forms. Michelangelo's sonnets would not be read if he had not carved in marble, and Wagner's libretti survive, not for their inherent value, but because of their musical settings. Blake's "sister arts" of poetry and painting, on the other hand, have survived at least a century of misunderstanding without the mutual support of one another. In the twentieth century his paintings and etchings have risen in market value to equal and surpass those of his formerly better known contemporaries, and the bare words of his poetry have appeared in edition after edition. Until recently, Blake's two arts have gone their separate ways in criticism as well, with only occasional bursts of cross fire between the art historians and the literary critics. Today, however, the question is no longer *whether* Blake's poetry and painting have anything to do with one another, but *how* their relationship may best be understood.

Since the two sides of Blake's genius have made their ways in the world without the help of one another, it is proper to ask what is gained by yoking them together. Suzanne Langer's observation that there are no marriages of the arts, only successful rapes, must serve as a warning to anyone who would deflower either of Blake's arts for the sake of elucidating the other. It is one thing to say that one form helps to explain or amplify the other; quite another to claim (as this essay does) that the illuminated poems constitute a composite art, a single, unified aesthetic phenomenon in which neither form dominates the other and yet in which each is incomplete without the other.

There may be a kind of ironic virtue, then, in the long period of division that Blake's composite art has undergone. If, as seems apparent from the tendencies of the present volume,[1] the next major step in Blake studies is to be a critical reunification of text and design, it will be important to remind ourselves of how well the two art forms have done on their own, and to account for this fact even as we bring them together. The word "illustration," for instance, will have to be redefined when applied to Blake. It will simply not do to say that his designs illustrate the text if we mean only that they throw light upon, explicate, or provide a visual rendition of matters which have been sufficiently expounded in the text. If this were an adequate definition, it would be very difficult to explain the fact that Anthony Blunt has been able to write a very fine study of the paintings on the assumption that they are completely superior to the poems (especially the later prophecies), and that the text is in reality only a kind of pre-text for the real art in the designs.[2] The poetry, thanks to the endless vocabularies of literary critics, will take care of itself; but the art is in danger of being infected by the concept of illustration. As a kind of verbal prophylactic, therefore, it might be appropriate at the outset to remind ourselves that when Blake "illustrates" a text, he expands and transforms it, and often provides a vision which can operate in complete separation from it.

Blake's reluctance to permit this separation has often been remarked. In referring to a friend's request for separate plates from *The Marriage of Heaven and Hell, The Book of Urizen*, and several other minor prophecies, he objected strongly: "Those I Printed . . . are a selection from the different Books of such as could be Printed without the Writing, tho' to the Loss of some of the best things. For they, when Printed perfect, accompany Poetical Personifications & Acts, without which Poems they never could have been Executed."[3] It is interesting to note, however, that a substantial number of the designs he sent to his friend do

---

[1] See also Blunt's full-length study, and his series of more specialized articles in *JWCI*, II (1938) and VI (1943). Other studies of interest include Geoffrey Keynes's *Blake Studies*, London, 1949, and the works cited in the present volume as Digby and Hagstrum. E. J. Rose has been issuing a series of articles based upon his "Mental Forms Creating: A Study of Blake's Thought and Symbols," Ph.D. diss., Univ. of Toronto, 1963-1964. The most recent specialized essay is Thomas Connolly and George Levine, "Pictorial and Poetic Design in Two Songs of Innocence," *PMLA*, LXXXII (1967), 257-264.

[2] Blunt, 2.

[3] Letter to Dawson Turner, 9 June 1818 (K867).

not illustrate specifically any of the "Poetical Personifications & Acts" in the poems to which they were attached.[4] It is no accident that amid all the meticulous Blake scholarship that has appeared in recent years, there is still no authoritative index or commentary identifying the subjects of his illustrations.[5] In *The Songs of Innocence and of Experience*, of course, the problem of specification of content is greatly simplified by the direct juxtaposition of the design with a limited text, but even in the case of these poems (especially *Experience*) there are problems. In the longer prophetic works, however, the relationship becomes very attenuated: illustrations often seem purposely placed as far as possible from their textual reference—when there is a reference to be found at all. As Blake increased his mastery of both poetic and pictorial techniques, it seems that he tended to minimize the literal, denotative correspondences between the two forms.

There is no difficulty in locating a context for composite art forms in Blake's intellectual milieu. The eighteenth century was, after all, the age which discovered that art could be spelled with a capital A, and Abbé Batteaux could title his 1746 treatise *Les Beaux Arts reduits à un même principe.*[6] Book illustration was expanding into a minor industry, and individual poems such as Thomson's *Seasons* were illustrated so often that it has been possible for one modern critic to construct a history of late-eighteenth-century criticism largely on the basis of the illustrations of this one poem.[7] Since the Renaissance an elaborate apologetics had developed around the illustrated book, especially

---

[4] An examination of the poetical contexts of the plates in *The Small Book of Designs* (conjectured by Keynes in his *Census* of Blake's illuminated books to be the plates which Blake sent to his friend) convinces me that at least 9 out of the 23 designs in this series have no apparent textual referent (pls. 1, 2, 5, 8, 9, 11-13, 18), and several others are quite ambiguous. One need only compare the specifications of content of these designs by Damon (*Philosophy*) and Keynes to see how unsure and contradictory the identifications are likely to be. Furthermore, the captions which Blake wrote at the bottoms of the plates in this series are in no instance taken from the poem that they illustrate.

[5] In lieu of such a work, it is often useful to consult the Keynes-Wolf *Census* or Damon's *Philosophy*, exercising considerable caution.

[6] For this general subject see Paul O. Kristeller, "The Modern System of the Arts, A Study in the History of Aesthetics," *Journal of the History of Ideas*, III (1951), 496-527.

[7] Ralph Cohen, *The Art of Discrimination*, Berkeley, 1964.

the emblem book, taking the Horatian maxim *ut pictura poesis* for its central principle.[8] The critical dogmas which calcified around Horace's innocent phrase had already provoked an adverse reaction from Lessing,[9] however, and we should be surprised to find an independent mind like Blake's receiving them passively.

The two basic premises of the doctrine of *ut pictura poesis* were, first, that all art is to be understood as a species of imitation, and second, that the reality which is to be imitated is essentially dualistic. The personification of poetry and painting as the "sister arts" was no accident; it expressed concisely the eighteenth century's conviction that the two arts were daughters of the Nature which they imitated, and that they provided complementary representations of a dualistic world of space and time,[10] body and soul, *dulce et utile*,[11] sense and intellect.[12] The emblem book enjoyed a particularly privileged position because it not only fulfilled the classical ideal of uniting the arts, but also could be seen as a means of providing the most comprehensive possible imitation of a bifurcated reality. "The emblem," as Jean Hagstrum points out, "seemed to be the completest and most satisfying form of expression imaginable, since body (the picture) and soul (the verse) were vitally connected."[13] Painting was supposed to appeal to the senses, poetry to the intellect, and the union of the two arts, it was presumed, would counteract that "dissociated sensibility" which T. S. Eliot had not yet invented. Cesare Ripa, per-

---

[8] Some of the more important studies of these ideas are Arthur Kenkel and Albrecht Shöne, eds., *Emblemata: Handbuch zur Sinnbildkunst des XVI und XVII Jahrhunderts*, Stuttgart, 1968; Robert J. Clements, *Picta Poesis: Literary and Humanistic Theory in Renaissance Emblem Books*, Rome, 1960; Jean Hagstrum, *The Sister Arts*, Chicago, 1958; and Rensselaer Lee, "'Ut Pictura Poesis': The Humanistic Theory of Painting," *Art Bulletin*, XXII (1940), 197-269.

[9] *Laocoön: An Essay on the Limits of Painting and Poetry*, 1766.

[10] See, for example, the anonymous essay in *The Free Thinker*, no. 63 (22 October 1718; repr. London, 1722), II, 34-36, which argues that poetry is chiefly effective in time because mass publication permits it to endure. Painting, on the other hand, is ineffective in time because it is perishable, but conquers space because it leaps the language barrier.

[11] See Mario Praz, *Studies in Seventeenth Century Imagery*, London, 1939, I, 155ff.

[12] Giabattista Marino, *Dicerie sacre*, Vicenza, 1662, Essay I, Part ii, 52f. Quoted in Hagstrum, *The Sister Arts*, 94.

[13] *The Sister Arts*, 96. I owe several of the following examples to Hagstrum and Lee.

haps the most important of the emblematists, plagiarized Marino to affirm that the union of the arts "causes us almost to understand with the senses, . . . to feel with the intellect."[14] An even more extravagant claim was made by the anonymous essayist of *The Plain Dealer* in 1724: "*Two Sister Arts,* uniting their different Powers, the one transmitting *Souls,* the other *Bodies* (or the outward Form of Bodies) their combining Influence would be of Force to frustrate *Death itself*: And all the ages of the World would seem to be Cotemporaries."[15]

Blake's critique of the implications of *ut pictura poesis* can be understood most clearly in terms of his reception of the idea of Nature assumed by this doctrine. For Blake, the dualistic world of mind and body, time and space, is an illusion which must not be imitated, but which must be dispelled by the processes of his art: "But first the notion that a man has a body distinct from his soul, is to be expunged; this I shall do by printing in the infernal method, by corrosives, melting apparent surfaces away, and displaying the infinite which was hid" (*MHH* 14). The methods of relief etching here become a metaphor for the destruction of the appearance of dualism. Blake would agree with the attempt of the emblematists to unite the two arts, not, however, as a means of representing the full range of reality, but as a means of exposing as a fiction the bifurcated organization of that reality. The separation of body and soul, space and time, Blake sees as various manifestations of the fall of man, "His fall into Division" (*FZ* 1 4:4). The function of his composite art is therefore twofold: it must "melt apparent surfaces away" by exposing the errors and contradictions of dualism; and it must display "the infinite which was hid," and overcome the "fall into division" with a "Resurrection to Unity" (*FZ* 1 4:4).

Blake never refers to his painting and poetry as "the sister arts," a curious omission for a man who lived at the end of the age which had systematized this relationship so carefully. The reason lies in his conception of the nature of the dualities that his art was designed to overcome. Blake's most pervasive metaphor for the "fall into Division" is the separation of the sexes. In particular, the apparent division of the world into space and time is described as a sexual antinomy: "Time & Space are Real Beings, a Male & a Female. Time is a Man, Space is a Woman" (*VLJ*:

[14] *Iconologia,* Padua, 1618, 416; translated in Hagstrum, 94.
[15] *The Plain Dealer,* II, no. 60 (London, 1730).

E553/K614). In Blake's myth, the sexes do not exist as part of the ultimate reality, but are the product of pride and egotism: "When the Individual appropriates Universality / He divides into Male & Female" (*J* 90:51-52). The danger is, according to Blake, that this sexual polarity will be mistaken for the final nature of things: "when the Male & Female / Appropriate Individuality, they become an Eternal Death" (*J* 90:52-53). That is, in terms of space and time, when space becomes an individual, an end in itself, it becomes a prison-house, the "Mundane Shell" of matter which is mistakenly supposed to be independent of consciousness. In like manner, time becomes a nonhuman phenomenon, an endless Heraclitean flux or the "dull round" of a fatal, mechanistic determinism. Blake's poetry and painting must begin by invalidating these incontingent views of time and space, and end by replacing them with visions of eternity and infinity. His primary disagreement with eighteenth-century conceptions of composite art, then, is that they presuppose an incontingent Nature which is to be copied and represented in a complementary, additive manner. For Blake, the coupling of poetry and painting is desirable not because it will produce a fuller range of imitation, but because it can dramatize the interaction of the apparent dualities in experience, and because it can embody the strivings of those dualities for unification.

If we conceive of text and design as Blake did, as organized expressions of the polarized phenomena of space and time, their relationship becomes intelligible in terms of his theory of contrariety. If a purpose of his art is to dramatize the struggle of the antinomies of our experience into a unified vision, the vehicles of spatial and temporal form must embody this dialectic as well. Regarded in this way, the separation of text and design can be seen as having two functions. First, it has a hermeneutic function, in that the disparity between poem and illustration entices the mind of the reader to supply the missing connections. In this light, the illuminated book serves as an "Allegory address'd to the Intellectual Powers" which is "fittest for Instruction because it rouzes the faculties to act."[16] Second, the separation has a mimetic function, in that the contrariety of poem and picture reflects the world of the reader as a place of apparent separation of temporal and spatial, mental and physical phenomena.

[16] Letters to Thomas Butts, 6 July 1803, and Dr. Trusler, 23 August 1799 (K825, 793).

It is important to remember the adjective "apparent" when talking about the discrepancies between Blake's designs and text, however, for if we are correct, the most disparate pictorial and verbal structures must conceal a subtle identity of significance. The title page of *The Marriage of Heaven and Hell* {3} exemplifies the way in which the apparent unrelatedness of content in design and text belies the close affinities of formal arrangement. A pair of nudes embrace in a subterranean scene at the bottom of the page, the one on the left emerging from flames, the one on the right from clouds. The top of the page is framed by a pair of trees, between which are two sets of human figures. No scene in the poem corresponds to this picture,[17] and yet it is a perfect representation of the poem's theme, the marriage of contraries:

[17] It has been suggested by John E. Grant that the title page "illustrates" the text of *MHH* 24, which describes the dialogue of an angel and devil, and the conversion of the former into the latter. A considerable number of qualifications would have to accompany this view of the relationship: 1) the textual devil and angel are males, while the pictured figures are female; 2) the text describes a conversation followed by a self-immolation, while the design depicts a sexual encounter; 3) the other details of the design do not seem to refer to the text of plate 24. An accurate understanding of the relationship between the design and any textual echoes of its details must take into account, it seems to me, the complex transformations involved in transposing the elements of one to the other. One could argue, for instance, that self-immolation and sexuality are a kind of natural metaphor, and certainly a very Blakean one; yet this would still only scratch the surface of the complex metaphorical layers that would be involved in any equation of *MHH* 1 with *MHH* 24.

J.E.G.: I agree that some of these reservations need to be borne in mind lest one assume, as Damon does, that the episode depicted is intended as an "illustration" in the sense of a literal depiction of the last Memorable Fancy. The hazards of descriptive generalizations based on a single copy, however, need also to be guarded against: the round buttocks and long hair on the figure at the left in copy F (Blake Trust facsimile) make the figure seem female, the more svelte buttocks in copy H (Dent facsimile) could easily be those of a male; hair length is not a safe guide; and Blake often chose not to depict the genitalia of indubitably male figures. One could argue that the pictured "Devil" and "Angel" are both androgynes, but it seems simplest to treat them as male and female respectively, as I have done in my discussion of the page in "Two Flowers in the Garden of Experience," in Rosenfeld, *Essays for Damon*, 363-364. For one thing, the word "Marriage" in the title and these embracing figures on the same page (though the page contains other details, since it is designed for viewers, not just readers) require readers to concern themselves with implications that make sense of the conversion of the Angel at the end of the poem. This conversion is described as his encountering "a Devil in a flame of fire" (cf. the left-hand figure in flames in

> Without Contraries is no progression. Attraction and Repulsion, Reason and Energy, Love and Hate, are necessary to Human Existence.
>
> From these contraries spring what the religious call Good & Evil. Good is the passive that obeys Reason. Evil is the active springing from Energy.
>
> Good is Heaven. Evil is Hell. (*MHH* 3)

---

the title page) and, from where he sits "on a cloud" (cf. the right-hand figure), stretching "out his arms embracing the flame of fire"—upon which "he was consumed and arose as Elijah," who, we are reminded later, "comprehends all the Prophetic Characters" (*VLJ* 83). To summarize this as "self-immolation" is to ignore the transparent and traditional sexual symbolism and to forget there was a Devil in this flame. Were not Blake's title and title page designed to make the human presence of a long-haired Devil in the flame embarrassingly obvious to angelic readers? One must, so to speak, take a Black Panther to lunch before he is fit to enter the kingdom of prophecy.

Those who find anything but the expression of this principle anachronistic are invited to observe several facts. The first is that in copy F, the Blake Trust facsimile, the figure at the right is colored dark brown, quite dark enough to be counted as "black" either in the eighteenth century or now, especially when it is contrasted with the very pinkish "white" figure at the left. It would be more convenient for the reader if this color symbolism were reversed so that the infernal character were black, but the viewer will find the further ironies of the actual coloration both intelligible and satisfying. He will also observe that Blake did not employ this color symbolism in most versions of the book, but understand that this does not negate the significance in copies where he did so.

If a contemporary racist, such as Gillray, had seen the title page of copy F, he might have concluded that Blake was advocating miscegenation. But two other considerations will assist the appreciation of Blake's point in all versions of this design. Although the relationships indicated in the background are more intimate, the central consummation depicted is clearly no more than a kiss. In the text of *MHH* 24 Blake neglects to mention the human form in the flame embraced by the Angel—and thus prevents the conversion of angelic character from seeming easy. In the introduction to this section, in plate 22, Blake declares that the writings of Dante are infinitely more informative than those of the angelic Swedenborg; perhaps Blake had already read that episode in the *Purgatorio* where Dante, like all pilgrims to eternity, must pass through the circumambient fire of love to return, like Adam into paradise, to where Beatrice is.

There have been many accounts of what *The Marriage of Heaven and Hell* is about. I say it is about the education of the Prophetic Character. Blake is committed to showing how much pain and dislocation such an education demands. Though he was honest about the magnitude of the task, he was glad to join with Moses and Milton in praying that all the Lord's people become prophets.

Every aspect of the composition is deployed to present this vision of contraries: flames versus clouds, red versus blue, the aggressive inward thrust of the female flying up from the left versus the receptive outward pose of the figure on the right. At the top, the trees on the left reach their branches across to the right, while the trees on the right recoil into themselves. The couple beneath the trees on the left walk hand in hand toward the right. The couple on the right face away, and are separated, one kneeling, the other lying on the ground. This last detail suggests that the composition is not simply a visual blending of contraries, but also a statement about their relative value. The active side presents a harmonious vision of the sexes; the passive, an inharmonious division, in which the male seems to be trying to woo the female from her indifference by playing on a musical instrument.[18] This tipping of the balance in favor of the "Devil's Party" is accentuated by the direction of movement that pervades the whole design. If we were simply to have a balanced presentation of contraries such as the text suggests, we would expect a simple symmetrical arrangement, with a vertical axis down the center (see fig. 2a). But, in fact, the whole kinesis of the composition,

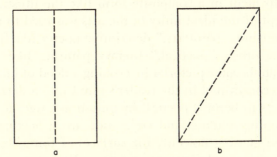

Fig. 2. Thrust of implied movement in the title page of *The Marriage of Heaven and Hell*

accentuated by the flying nudes in the center, produces an axis which goes from the lower left corner to the upper right. If one were to draw vectors indicating the probable course of the figures in the center of the design, the result would be the diagonal axis of figure 2b.

[18] The reclining figure is clearly a woman in copy C (Morgan Library) and in copy D and the Trianon Press facsimile of this copy; the instrument held by the kneeling figure is only suggestively etched—probably a flute or shepherd's pipe, or it could be a lyre.

This tilting of the symmetry of the contraries, is, of course, exactly what happens to the theme of the *Marriage* as Blake treats it. Although the contraries are theoretically equal, Blake has all his fun by identifying himself with the side of the devils. The poem is not simply a self-contained dialectic; it is a dialogue with Blake's own time, and he felt that the "Angels" already had plenty of spokesmen, such as Swedenborg and the apologists for traditional religion and morality. At his particular historical moment, Blake felt that the axis needed to be tilted in favor of energy. Hence, all the good lines in the work and the advantageous pictorial treatments are reserved for the representatives of Hell. But the style of lettering in the title page returns us to the theoretical equality which Blake sees between the contraries. Both "Heaven" and "Hell" are printed in rather stark block letters; the flamboyant, energetic style of free-flowing lines and swirls is reserved for the key term in the poem, "Marriage."

Blake's departure from the literalist implications of *ut pictura poesis* was not, however, simply confined to the avoidance, in his own work, of mere illustration. The doctrine also had implications for the nature of poetry and painting in general, apart from their employment in a composite form like the illustrated book. The concept of the ideal unity of the arts was used to encourage, on the one hand, "painterly," descriptive poetry like Thomson's, and on the other, "poetical," literary painting like Hogarth's. Poetry was to become pictorial by evoking a flood of images which could be reconstituted in the reader's mind into a detailed scene. Painting was to become poetical by imitating a significant action, with beginning, middle, and end,[19] not just a fleeting moment, and by representing not only the surfaces of things but also the interior passions and characters of men. Each art was expected to transcend its temporal or spatial limitation by moving toward the condition of its sister.

This conception of the unification of the arts can only be applied very meagerly to Blake's practice. His poetry, like Milton's, avoids "painterly" descriptions in favor of visual paradoxes like "darkness visible" and "the hapless Soldiers sigh" which "Runs in blood down Palace walls." When he does have an opportunity for "iconic" passages describing a fixed object, such as the build-

[19] See ch. 9, "The Unity of Action," in Lee's " 'Ut Pictura Poesis.' "

ing of the art-city of Golgonooza in *Jerusalem,* the result is anything but a set of visualizable images:

> The great City of Golgonooza: fourfold toward the north
> And toward the south fourfold & fourfold toward the east
>   & west
> Each within other toward the four points: that toward
> Eden, and that toward the World of Generation,
> And that toward Beulah, and that toward Ulro:
> Ulro is the space of the terrible starry wheels of Albions sons:
> But that toward Eden is walled up, till time of renovation:
> Yet it is perfect in its building, ornaments & perfection.
>
> <div align="right">(<i>J</i> 12:46-53)</div>

It is no accident that Blake, for all his ability to visualize the unseen, never illustrated this passage. In fact his prophetic illustrations generally do not provide visual equivalents for specific passages, but often expand upon some point of only minor importance in the text, or even convey an opposed or ironic vision.

Blake's refusal to illustrate an "iconic" passage such as the description of Golgonooza is a clue, moreover, to the extent of his departure from the tradition of "literary" painting. Architectural backgrounds, the standard setting of the history painting, naturally generated a more or less "objective" and mathematically constructed spatial container for the human form. But Blake, who considered himself a history painter (see the subtitle of his *Descriptive Catalogue*) could hardly be more perfunctory in his treatment of this kind of subject matter. He is interested not in the mechanically determined form of the material city but in its spiritual (i.e., human) form, as in *Jerusalem* 57, where he specifies the cities of York, London, and Jerusalem with tiny geographical emblems (fig. 18), but defines them pictorially as gigantic women. Jerusalem, particularly, while both a city and a woman in the text, is primarily a woman in the illustrations.

Blake's rejection of the architectural background is only one symptom of his general refusal to employ very extensively the techniques of three-dimensional illusionism which had been increasingly perfected since the Renaissance.[20] This kind of illusion-

---

[20] See Rosenblum, *Transformations,* 158, for an account of Blake's "regression" from the illusionistic style and an intriguing explanation of its relation to other primitivistic experiments in the arts.

ism was particularly popular with "literary" painters, since it provided an easy metaphor for the temporal structure of the scene being depicted. The earliest event in the narrative could be placed in the foreground, and the later events could be placed in increasingly distant perspective planes.[21] Blake avoids this kind of illusionism in his designs for his own works. As a rule, he concentrates on a few foreground images, often arranged symmetrically, to encourage an instantaneous grasp of the whole design rather than an impression of dramatic sequence. Sometimes, to be sure, he does present metamorphic sequences across the foreground plane, usually in his marginal designs, where (for obvious reasons) radial and bilateral symmetry must give way to some kind of linear presentation. These mural-like tableaux, however, embody the passage of time not as a progression from the near to the distant, or the clear to the obscure, but as a movement from the near to the near. All moments in the sequence are immediate and "immanent"; just as in the poetry, the prophet-narrator "present, past, & future *sees*" as an eternal *now*.

The other desideratum of "poetical" painting, the representation of the interior life of its human subjects, not just their outward features, likewise seems inapplicable to Blake's practice. His human figures have a kind of allegorical anonymity, and are clearly designed as types, not as subtly differentiated portraits. We see very little subjectivity in the faces of Blake's figures for the same reason we do not find "motivation" or novelistic personalities in his poetical personifications. Urizen cannot have his own interior life like the character of a novel; he is only an aspect of the interior life of the single human mind which constitutes the world of his poem. Blake certainly expresses the passions in his painting: but he does not present them as residing *within* particular human figures; he presents them *as* human figures. His portraits are not of men with minds, but of the mind itself.

The methods of pictorialist poetry and literary painting, then, shed only a negative light on the specific manner in which Blake

[21] Hogarth's interiors provide a striking example of conscious use of this technique. See particularly Ronald Paulson's "*The Harlot's Progress* and the Tradition of History Painting," *Eighteenth Century Studies*, I (1967-1968), 73. For an explanation of the use of a similar device in landscape painting, see Jeffrey Eicholz, "William Kent's Career as a Literary Illustrator," *BNYPL*, LXX (1966), 620-646.

approaches the problem of unifying the arts. He rejects the practice of mutual transference of techniques in favor of a methodology which seems rather to emphasize the peculiar strengths and limitations of each medium: the shadowy, allusive metamorphoses of language, and the glowing fixity of almost abstract pictorial forms.

In Blake's view, the attempt to make poetry visual and to make pictures "speak" and tell a story was bound to fail because it presumed the independent reality of space and time and treated them as the irreducible foundations of existence. As we have seen, Blake considers space and time, like the sexes, to be contraries whose reconciliation occurs not when one becomes like the other, but when they approach a condition in which these categories cease to function. In the simplest possible terms, his poetry exists to invalidate the idea of objective time, his painting to invalidate the idea of objective space. To state this positively, his poetry affirms the power of the human imagination to create and organize time in its own image, and his painting affirms the centrality of the human body as the structural principle of space. The essential unity of his arts, then, is to be seen in the parallel engagements of imagination and body with their respective media, and in their convergence in the more comprehensive idea of the "Human Form Divine." For Blake, in the final analysis the body and the imagination are separable principles only in a fallen world of limited perception; the business of art is to dramatize their unification: "The Eternal Body of Man is The Imagination. . . . It manifests itself in his Works of Art" (*Laocoön*: E271).

Blake's specific techniques for constructing his art forms as critiques of their own media are quite clear. In the poetry he creates a world of process and metamorphosis in which the only stable, fixed term is the imagining and perceiving mind. Cause and effect, linear temporality, and other "objective" temporal structures for narrative are replaced by an imaginative conflation of all time in the pregnant moment. The prophetic narrator-actor perceives "Present, Past & Future" simultaneously, and is able to see in any given moment the structure of all history: "Every Time less than a pulsation of the artery / Is equal in its period & value to Six Thousand Years" (*M* 28:62-63). Consequently, the narrative order of the poem need not refer to any incontingent, non-human temporal continuum. Most narrative structures employ

69

what Blake would call "twofold vision": that is, the imaginative arrangement of episodes is always done with reference to an "objective" time scheme. The narrative selects its moments and their order in terms of some imaginative order: *in medias res, ab ovum,* or *recherche du temps perdu.* All of these selective principles assume, however, that there is an order of nonhuman, "objective," or "real" time which flows onward independent of any human, "subjective," or "imaginary" reorganization of its sequence. For Blake, this objective temporal understructure is an illusion which is to be dispelled by the form of his poetry. The beginning, middle, and end of any action are all contained in the present; so the order of presentation is completely subject to the imagination of the narrator. Hostile critics have always recognized this quality in Blake's major prophecies when they indicted them for being "impossible to follow." That is precisely the point. Blake's prophecies go nowhere in time because time, as a linear, homogeneous phenomenon, has no place in their structure. *Jerusalem* is essentially a nonconsecutive series of poetic "happenings," not a linear ordering of events. The one continuous and stable element in the course of the narrative is the idea of consciousness as a transformer of itself and its world. That is why Los, the vehicle of the imagination, is also cast as the personification of time. In this way, Blake could depict the poet's management of time and the prophet's quarrel with history as the struggle of the individual with himself.

An analogous technique can be observed in the whole range of Blake's paintings. Historical parallels have tended to confuse attempts at defining Blake's style because the historical concept always carries with it a freight of alien associations which have no relevance to the work at hand. His art has recognizable affinities with Michelangelo, Raphael, and the Mannerists in his treatment of the human figure, with Gothic painting in his primitivism and anti-illusionism, and with contemporaries such as Flaxman in his stress on outline, Fuseli in his use of the terrific and exotic. It is also clear, however, that these elements are transmuted into something unified and unique in Blake's hands. His art is a curious compound of the representational and the abstract, the picture that imitates natural forms and the design that delights in form for its own sake. The "flame-flowers" which are so ubiquitous in his margins, and which later provided inspiration for art nouveau, serve as a prime example of the interplay between representation and abstraction that informs all his work. The abstract vorticular composition may assume specific representational form as a whirl-pool, a dance of lovers, or a spiral ascent to the heavens. The circle may serve as the structural skeleton of the mathematical enclosures of Urizen, or of the glowing sun created by the hammer of Los. Plate 39 [44] of *Jerusalem* makes this technique explicit by showing a serpent metamorphosing into a flame, then a leaf, and finally the tendrils of a vine. The effect of this pictorial strategy is to under-cut the representational appearance of particular forms and to endow them with an abstract, stylized existence independent of the natural images that they evoke. Pictorial form is freed from the labor of accurately representing any idea of nature, and in-stead serves to show that the appearances of natural objects are arbitrary and subject to transformation by the imagination. All art, of course, even that which claims only to provide a mirror image of external reality, transforms its subject matter in some way. But the subject of Blake's art is precisely this power to trans-form, this ability of the artist to reshape and control his visual images, and, by implication, the ability of man to create his vision in general. That is why at the center of Blake's visual world of process and metamorphosis the form of the human body tends to retain its uniqueness and stability. The backgrounds of Blake's designs, his landscapes and prospects, all serve as a kind of evanes-cent setting for the human form. There are no mathematically determined perspectives, and very few landscapes which would make any sense without the human figures they contain. Pictorial space does not exist independently as a uniform, objective con-tainer of forms; it exists to provide contrast and reinforcement to the human figures it contains. The image of evil in Blake's designs, consequently, is not an arbitrary emblem, or simply a devil with horns, but the sight of the human body surrendering its unique form and dissolving into a nonhuman landscape, as in many designs in the Lambeth books and the later prophecies where bodies take root in the ground or sprout bestial appendages.

The essential unity of Blake's composite art, then, lies in the convergence of each art form upon the single goal of affirming the centrality of the human form (as both imagination and body) in the structure of reality. Blake's art imitates neither an external world of objective "Nature" nor a purely internal world of sub-

71

jective, arbitrary abstractions. Neither representationalism nor allegory satisfactorily defines the nature of his art. This latter point perhaps needs to be stressed most forcefully, since no one is about to mistake Blake for a Dutch painter, and since the allegorists generally have more to say about Blake than anyone else. Interpretation would indeed be easier if certain colors and certain abstract linear patterns had fixed, iconic meanings, but Blake would certainly be less interesting. The whole vitality of his art arises from his refusal to settle for the fixed, the emblematic, and the abstract, and from his decision to concentrate instead upon dramatizing the activity of the imagination in its encounter with reality. "Men think they can Copy Nature as I copy Imagination This they will find Impossible" (*PA*:E563). Blake's use of the word "imagination" as an object here has misled many critics into supposing that he has in mind the archetypal forms of some Platonic system as the objects of his copying. But imagination is not simply a product for Blake, a fixed body of well-defined forms; it is the *process* by which any symbolic form comes into being. When Blake says he "copies imagination," then, he means that he renders faithfully the activity of the mind as it alters the objects of perception: both the finished product and the process by which it comes into being are "imagination."

The consequences of this definition of Blake's art are perhaps more apparent in his poetry than in his art. Since Northrop Frye's *Fearful Symmetry* the nonallegorical nature of Blake's poetry has regularly been acknowledged, if not fully grasped. Nevertheless, the question of form in the major prophecies is still open. *Jerusalem* is still treated primarily as a quarry for Blakean "philosophy," not as a poetic structure with its own nondiscursive logic. When attempts are made to understand its form, they usually concentrate on one of the structural topoi to which Blake often alludes—the prophecy, the epic journey, the dream vision— rather than on Blake's own peculiar ideas about the principles of narrative form.[22] When these traditional ideas of form are recast

[22] Two exemplary studies of *Jerusalem* are E. J. Rose, "The Structure of Blake's Jerusalem," *Bucknell Review*, XI (1963), 35-54, and Karl Kiralis, "The Theme and Structure of Blake's Jerusalem," *ELH*, XXIII (1956), 127-143. Both critics try to construct a linear, sequential model for *Jerusalem*, and both fall short. It is interesting to note, however, that the two studies are about equally accurate in what they do say about the progressions in the

in terms of Blake's own understanding of poetry as a critique of temporality and as a means of transcending it, we will see, I suspect, that *Milton* and *Jerusalem* have as much in common with *Tristram Shandy* as with *Paradise Lost*.

The basic groundwork for understanding Blake's pictorial symbolism remains to be done. Critics still tend either to content themselves with identification of subject matter (which assumes that the designs are mere illustrations) or to search for a fixed set of pictorial conventions. The attempts to formulate a color glossary, a left-right convention, or a set of denotative linear forms persist in spite of their continued failure to account for more than a very few pictures.[23] Blake makes clear, however, that no system of abstractions is to be found beyond or behind his art, and gives us instead a fairly straightforward set of general principles for understanding the generation of symbols by the dialectics in his compositions. His emphasis on the superiority of form and outline to light and color is well known yet misleading:

> The great and golden rule of art, as well as of life, is this: That the more distinct, sharp, and wiry the bounding line, the more perfect the work of art: and the less keen and sharp, the greater is the evidence of weak imitation.   (DC:E540)

> The Beauty proper for sublime art is lineaments, or forms and features that are capable of being the receptacles of intellect;   (DC:E535)

Blake's preference for linearity was probably in large measure a product of his early apprenticeship to James Basire, a master of the old-fashioned school of austerity in line engraving. The change

---

poem, and yet they say diametrically opposite things. Kiralis sees the structure as analogous to the stages in human growth; Rose sees it as precisely the reverse, a journey backward in time. (See Lesnick's essay, pp. 391ff.)

[23] Attempts to impose a lateral convention are quite persistent in spite of their inadequacies. E. J. Rose ("Visionary Forms Dramatic: Grammatical and Iconographical Movement in Blake's Designs and Verse," *Criticism*, VIII [1966], 111-125), and Claudette Kemper ("The Interlinear Drawings in Blake's Jerusalem," *BNYPL*, LXIV [1960], 588-594) propose with equal assurance diametrically opposed interpretations of the meanings of right and left in *Jerusalem*. The point is, of course, that neither right nor left has any fixed meaning but that pictorial reversals and inversions, in particular and local contexts, may produce meaning.

in taste in late-eighteenth-century reproductive engraving to the softer lines and tonal emphasis of Woollett, Strange, and Bartolozzi[24] left Blake in possession of an increasingly unfashionable style, and probably accounts for some of his bitterness at the "painterly" schools. He was not isolated, however, in his preference for linearity. The neoclassical primitivism which Winckelmann had introduced was having its effect both in England and on the Continent. Diderot's hope for a reincarnation of Poussin was being fulfilled by David's meticulous historicism and sculpturely purity;[25] Flaxman and Cumberland, to name two of Blake's friends, were insisting on an even more radical purity and simplicity of outline.[26] The seeds of this preference for linearity had always been present in idealist conceptions of art,[27] and the theorists of the seventeenth and eighteenth centuries had consequently felt it necessary to defend the equal importance of color and light in painting long after it had been established in practice. Du Fresnoy, for instance, calls outline and color sisters, and defends the latter against the charge of prostituting outline: "And as this part, which we may call the utmost perfection of Painting, is a deceiving Beauty, but withall soothing and pleasing: So she has been accus'd of procuring Lovers for her Sister, and artfully engaging us to admire her. But so little have this Prostitution, these false Colours, and this Deceit, dishonour'd Painting, that on the contrary, they have only serv'd to set forth her praise."[28] The writers on *ut pictura poesis* likewise justified the use of color by comparing it to the expressive qualities of poetry: the relationship of color to outline is regularly equated with the relationship of verse to fable.[29] Color is seen by the Platonists as "art," a kind of

[24] Arthur M. Hind, *A History of Engraving and Etching*, London, 1923; rev. 1963, 204-206, 209.

[25] See Jean Seznec, "Diderot and Historical Painting," in *Aspects of the Eighteenth Century*, ed. E. R. Wasserman, Baltimore, 1965, 139.

[26] Blake did all the engravings from Flaxman's drawings for *Compositions from the Works Days and Theogony of Hesiod*, London, 1817, and a few for *The Iliad of Homer*, London, 1805. He also taught Cumberland how to engrave, and executed his designs for *Thoughts on Outline*, London, 1796.

[27] See Dora and Irwin Panofsky, *Pandora's Box*, New York, 1956, 91.

[28] *The Art of Painting*, tr. John Dryden, 2nd edn. London, 1716; excerpts in *A Documentary History of Art*, ed. Elizabeth Holt, New York, 1958, 170.

[29] See Dryden's preface, "A Parallel of Poetry and Painting," to Du Fresnoy's *De Arte Graphica*, in *The Essays of John Dryden*, ed. W. P. Ker (Lon-

cosmetic allurement to the "real meaning" which is contained in outline. To the Aristotelians, color permits a faithful imitation of nature's variety, and provides a verisimilitudinous setting for the general forms revealed by outline.

It is easy to say that Blake rejects these justifications of color, just as he rejects the Venetian "painterly" schools, and virtually makes a demonic trinity out of Rembrandt, Rubens, and Titian (see *DC*:E537-538). But it is not so clear what we should make of his actual use of color. We cannot say of Blake's designs, as we can of Flaxman's illustrations to Hesiod, Homer, and Dante, that they would gain nothing by the inclusion of color. Blake rarely produced an illustration to his own work without color, and black-and-white reproductions of his work are notoriously unsatisfying. Furthermore, to take at face value his claim that coloring is sub-servient to and determined by outline simply falsifies a good deal of his practice. In spite of his theoretical preference for clear out-line and form, Blake often obscures his outlines with opaque pigments and heavy drapery.

The resolution of this apparent contradiction between theory and practice lies in a fuller understanding of the theory. The subservience of light to form is, for Blake, a visual equivalent of an ideal condition:[30]

> In Great Eternity, every particular Form gives forth or
>   Emanates
> Its own peculiar Light, & the Form is the Divine Vision
> And the Light is his Garment.   (*J* 54:1-3)

The relation of form to light is defined as that of the Individual and his Emanation, or of consciousness and the external world which it projects. With the fall, however, consciousness becomes egotism (male will) and the external world becomes an inde-pendent Nature (female will). Form and light become, in this world, sexual principles working in opposition. The resolution

---

don, 1900), II, 147f. See also Abbé Batteaux, *Les Beaux Arts reduits à un même principe*, Paris, 1746, 247 for the equation of "desseing" with "fable" and "coloris" with "versification."

[30] In the discussion which follows I will not distinguish rigorously between the terms "color" and "light," and "outline" and "form." Blake uses the terms almost interchangeably, and sees them as completely interdependent in theory.

of this opposition is attained by a procedure rather similar to the one we observed in the relation of text and design, a dialectic of contraries. When female nature, for instance, assumes an independent existence, it becomes "An outside shadowy surface superadded to the real Surface; / Which is unchangeable" (*J* 83:47-48); that is, color freed from outline and obscuring it is the visual equivalent of nature's obfuscating the imagination. The veil or garment is often used as a metaphor for this idea of color, and the disposition of drapery in Blake's pictures can be seen to follow the same principles as his treatment of color. Even though "Art & Science cannot exist but by Naked Beauty displayd" (*J* 32:49), Blake clothes many of his figures to exhibit their immersion into the fallen world of space and time. The frontispiece of *Jerusalem*, for instance, presents the clothed figure of Los-Blake entering the fallen world, the "Void outside of Existence, which if enterd into Englobes itself & becomes a Womb." The return of Los (*J* 97 {102}) from this world of Ulro or "Eternal Death" into the world of imagination (or true existence) displays his naked beauty. In the "Death's Door" illustration to Blair's *Grave* Blake similarly contrasts the entry into death (i.e., the fallen world) with the "awaking to Eternal life" by setting the clothed figure who enters the grave against the naked figure atop the grave. "The Drapery is formed alone by the Shape of the Naked" (Annotations to Reynolds: E639/K462) in theory, but in practice Blake often covers his figures (especially Urizen) with heavy, oppressive garments which obscure rather than reveal their lineaments.

It would be a mistake, however, to conclude that Blake's art is constructed simply on the principle that outline is "good" and the color or drapery which obscures it is "bad." The two compositional elements, like the two aspects of his composite art, engage in a dialectic that ranges from antagonism (when color becomes "An outside shadowy Surface" obscuring outline) to unity (when light serves as an aureole or halo around form), and all the stages of this dialectic are integral to the total vision. Blake provides us with a vocabulary for describing the range of his possible uses of form and light in the terms which he probably drew from his own experience as a painter. When man falls from his state of visionary perfection in Blake's myth, a universe or space must be created to set a limit to his fall: "The Divine Hand found two Limits: first of Opacity, then of Contraction" (*M* 13:20).

These two limits are personified as Satan and Adam, and represent the lower boundaries of man's fall into spiritual darkness and the shrinking of his soul into an egotistic, self-enclosed organism. "But there is no Limit of Expansion! there is no Limit of Translucence" (*J* 42:35), except in the limitations of the painter's ability to create glowing images of bodily freedom. The applicability of these two terms to Blake's art is strongly suggested by his making them the basic structural principles of his art-city, Golgonooza, like Yeats's Byzantium, a regular metaphor for the total form of his artifices of eternity. (See *FZ* viia 87:E354.)

Two of Blake's most famous designs, the frontispiece to *Europe* and *Albion rose*, exemplify the contrast between contraction / opacity and expansion / translucence. The figure captioned "Albion rose from where he labourd at the Mill with Slaves . . ." {91} expands in a veritable sunburst of radiance. Blake wisely avoids trying to convey this radiance by direct means, such as mere whiteness, and instead depicts Albion as the light-source of all the colors of the spectrum; he serves as both the hub and spokes of a color-wheel. Just below Albion's knees the outer boundary of his radiance seems to expand into and dispel the darkness around his feet. The ground, which corresponds to the spiritual darkness and deformity from which he has risen, is presented as a riot of disorganized, opaque pigments, such as Blake used in depicting the seat of "that most outrageous demon," Newton.[31] Anthony Blunt has shown that this figure may have been derived from a diagram of the perfect human proportions in Scamozzi's *Idea dell'architettura universale*, in which the limbs of the figure are measured against a wheel with the center located at the navel.[32] Blake has moved the center of his figure down to the loins to enforce his idea that "The improvement of Sensual Enjoyment" (which corresponds, among other things, to the use of the erotic image, "Naked Beauty Display'd") is the proper means for reawakening the infinite in man. More important, Blake has freed his figure from the enclosing wheel, except perhaps for the token reminder of enclosure just below Albion's knees. If the design is indeed to be taken as employing a quotation from Scamozzi's treatise, it is certainly an ironic allusion, expressing Blake's conviction that his

[31] Reproduced in Blunt, pl. 30c.
[32] "Blake's Glad Day," *JWCI*, vi (1943), 225-227.

art is to be seen as a triumph over the tyranny of "mathematic form."

The contrasts with the frontispiece to *Europe* {8} need hardly be elaborated. Urizen is shown with his body bent and contracted into itself, enclosed in a circle. His one outward gesture is a thrust downward into the darkness to inscribe another circle on the abyss. Unlike Albion, who is the center of all the dynamism in his design, Urizen is the subject of the elements, as is revealed by the wind blowing his hair and the clouds closing in to obscure his radiance. If Albion is to be seen as bursting the circle of mathematical restriction, Urizen is the creator of that circle, and Blake's treatment of him must remind us of one of his most audacious epigrams:

To God

If you have formd a Circle to go into
Go into it yourself & see how you would do

(E508/K557)

The concepts of expansion and translucence, contraction and opacity are not to be placed in a simple equation with "good" and "evil," any more than outline and color can convey value in themselves. Blake always had a "contrary vision" in mind, in which any given symbolic organization could reverse its meaning. The act of creation, for instance, is a demonic act in that it encloses man in the "Mundane Shell," but it is, from another point of view, an act of mercy in that it prevents man from falling endlessly into the "Indefinite." In like manner, there is a sense in which contraction is a good, as in the state of Innocence when the mother creates a womblike space to protect the child. In *The Songs of Innocence* this aspect of contraction is given visual expression by "embracing" compositions. The space of the design is generally encircled in vines, or framed by an overarching arbor. Opacity also has its beneficial aspect, as can be seen in both text and design of *The Little Black Boy*, where it serves as a temporary protection from the overpowering translucence of God:

And we are put on earth a little space,
That we may learn to bear the beams of love,
And these black bodies and this sun-burnt face
Is but a cloud, and like a shady grove.

The protective functions of opacity and contraction in Innocence are transformed, of course, in *The Songs of Experience*. The tranquil, angel-guarded darkness of *Night* gives way to the threatening opacity of the "forests of the night" in Experience. The protective contraction of the arbor becomes the stark frame of a dead tree, the encircling vines become choking briars.

On the other hand, expansion and translucence are not unequivocally good. Blake often presents the figures of warfare or revolution as bright, expansive nudes. The figure of Orc, for instance, the personification of energy and rebellion against the circumscribed order of Urizen, is often depicted as a bright, youthful nude in an expansive pose. A good example of this kind of composition is plate 10 of *America* {38}, which shows Orc surrounded by flames, his arms extended in a kind of parody of the exultant expansion of *Abion rose*. Just two plates before this appears the well-known "Urizen on the Stone of Night," a design which has a completely different affective value from plate 10. But a close comparison of the two figures and the positions of their limbs reveals a point-for-point similarity. (See {36} and {38}.) The two pictures have, of course, completely opposite effects. Orc seems to rise and burst outward, the downward movement of his hands only providing thrust to his expansive movement, which is accentuated by his flaming hair and the exploding surroundings. The old man in his white robes, on the other hand, anatomically identical to Orc, produces the effect of contraction. His arms seem to merge into the stony background, pressed down by a great weight and weariness. The horizontal curves of the rocks reinforce the gravity which seems to push against and bend down the space of the picture. The juxtaposition of these two designs provides us with a visual equivalent of what Northrop Frye calls "the Orc cycle," the cyclical repetition of tyrannic repression and rebellious reaction. This essential identity of the rebel and his oppressor becomes the basis of Blake's critique of his own historical time, and in the later prophetic books a structural metaphor for time in the fallen world.

This identity of Orc and Urizen is also a further example of the interplay between abstraction and representation which is the basic mode of Blake's symbolism. The linear skeleton which permits us to identify these two figures has no particular meaning in itself: it does not "equal" Urizen or Orc, or the sum of their qualities. On the other hand, the particular representation of each of these mythical figures does not achieve its full symbolic status until we recognize that each is potentially the other, each is a metaphor for the other. Orc *is* Urizen, because the spirit of violent rebellion always degenerates into oppression when it has gained power. Urizen *is* Orc, because the tyrant inevitably begets the revolutionary reaction against his rule.[33] Neither abstraction nor representation, however, is permitted to become in itself the locus of this meaning. Significance is located in the dialectic between the permanence of outline and the mutability and momentary reality of color, just as in the poetry the continuity of consciousness is affirmed and realized in its ability persistently to give form to the changing manifestations of itself and the world it perceives.

The total design of the illuminated page affirms the identity of poem and picture by actualizing the continuity and interrelatedness of the most abstract linear patterns with the most representational forms. At the one extreme, visual form is constructed in accord with what is, from the point of view of the visual arts, a completely abstract, nonvisual system (language); at the other extreme, the picture exists to imitate the peculiarly visual aspects of experience. The word "Marriage" on the title page of *The Marriage of Heaven and Hell* affirms, appropriately enough, the actual marriage of these two concepts of form by serving as a bridge between the abstraction of typography and the mimesis of naturalistic representation. This may sound like an unnecessarily involved way of pointing out that Blake decorates his letters with foliage, as the medieval illuminators did. But the keystone of a complicated structure is always in the obvious, the inevitable place. The continuity which Blake manages to establish between the

[33] David Erdman has shown in this volume ("*America*: New Expanses") that Blake does not express this vision of the Orc cycle in the text of *America*, and suggests that he did not develop this concept of the cycle until the 1800's. My interpretation, therefore, may be subject to considerable qualification, although, as we have seen elsewhere, Blake was certainly capable of saying things in his designs which he never expressed in the accompanying text. The significant point, nevertheless, is the method by which meaningful interplay between outline and color is established in related designs. It may be an overstatement to say that "Orc is Urizen" in the context of these two plates, but it is certainly accurate to note that some kind of metaphorical relationship has been created by the similarities of the two designs.

worlds of ideality and reality, subject and object in the dynamics of his two art forms is an integral part of the process of uniting these two forms into a single entity. And it is also the means by which the strange and wonderfully consistent world of his imagination manages to retain its own uncompromising otherness while establishing a continuity with and relevance to our own worlds.

4

Blake and the Sister-Arts Tradition

JEAN H. HAGSTRUM

IT HAS SEEMED obvious to some students of Blake that a painter-poet whose "canonical" works united those two arts that for centuries had been called sisters belonged to the venerable tradition of literary pictorialism, which had in his own period of artistic development reached one of its many recurring climaxes.[1] That view has recently been challenged. In this volume, for example, David Erdman says that "traditional appeals to the tradition of *ut pictura poesis,* pro or contra, were wide of the mark," and W.J.T. Mitchell denies that Blake stands in the pictorialist tradition, finding him much closer to the "non-pictorial Milton than to verbal scene-painters like Thomson or conventional personifiers like Collins and the Wartons."[2]

In a later section of this essay I shall attempt to argue that Blake, however often he may have stretched out of easily recognizable shape the forms he inherited, did in fact remain profoundly indebted to the pictorialist masters of his youth. But in viewing the largest relevant context for Blake's union of the arts, we must understand that literary pictorialism is by no means confined to scene-painting of the kind that Lessing attacked or to the visual personifications of the anti-Pope school. The tradition we are concerned with in defining the verbal-visual in Blake goes far beyond Collins, Thomson, or the Wartons in time and quality. It includes the sacramental icon as well as the natural image, prophetic vision as well as empirical imitation. It is a complex and ageless tradition that has been variously embodied at different moments of cultural history.[3] Blake, as he always did with the

---

[1] Mark Schorer calls Blake's pictures "restatements" of his poems: "This is *ut pictura poesis* with a vengeance, the sister arts are joined at birth" (*William Blake: The Politics of Vision,* New York, 1946, 11). Northrop Frye (*Essays,* 125) sees *ut pictura* in Spenser and Blake as a means of achieving integrity of meaning. See also Hagstrum, 8-20.

[2] For Erdman's remark, see above, p. viii. Mitchell, in revision, has dropped this formulation but not his argument (see p. 67). See also Mario Praz's review of Hagstrum in *Il Tempo* (Rome), 16 April 1965.

[3] See Jean H. Hagstrum, *The Sister Arts,* Chicago, 1958, *passim.*

influences that played upon him, adapted this broad and diverse tradition to his own special purposes. But reject it or ignore it or treat it as irrelevant—that he seems not to have done. To Blake and his picture-poem inheritance may be applied what Christ said of Jewish law and prophecy: that he came not to "destroy but to fulfill" it (Matthew 5:17).

The three sections of this essay are designed to divide the problem into its essential components. In "Blake and the Sister Arts" we shall discuss his and his predecessors' union of the two arts. "Blake and *Ut Pictura Poesis*" will narrow the focus and concentrate on Blake's words alone, as embodiments of persistent pictorialist conventions. "Word and Vision" will attempt to relate the verbal and visual of Blake's form to the spoken and the seen that have together characterized prophecy and apocalypse.

Blake and the Sister Arts

There is abundant precedent for Blake's union of the arts in illumination, the emblem, the *impresa*, the book of icons, and book illustration. These forms have been insufficiently studied. It may be stated, categorically, that Blake's practice will not be fully understood in all its nuances and his originality not fully appreciated until these antecedent forms and the conventions peculiar to each are known. For Blake was not merely a frequent borrower and adapter of motifs from preceding practitioners of the sister arts. He was himself an emblematist, an illuminator, and an illustrator. These were his genres, whose techniques he had consciously mastered and of whose problems, old and new, he was fully aware.

Thus Blake used most of the conventions of the illustrated book, which was reaching a kind of apogee in Blake's early life—the frontispiece, the title page, head and tail illustrations, borders, and interpolated pages of design alone. Sometimes—and this should not be forgotten by the new generation of Blake commentators who are discovering subtle relations between word and design—the poet-painter is highly conventional and duplicates in line and color the literal scene of his verbal description. Blake often "literally" renders his allegorical landscapes. Then again he illustrates a metaphor or trope, even when it is fleeting or submerged. Often he follows a complex scheme of complementarity and antithesis. For most of these habits there is precedent in con-

temporary book illustration, particularly as that art was being sub-
tilized and refined by Fuseli and others.

The interests of Blake's circle of friends—and enemies—and
the pressures of his artistic milieu must have kept alive in Blake's
conscious mind the issues raised by the sister-arts tradition and
its adaptation to contemporary culture.[4] Blake's age, to a degree
hard to exaggerate, loved to pair poet with painter, selecting
"characters in these Sister Sciences, that would exactly match &
tally with each other."[5] The poetical lights of Blake's youth were
arch-pictorialists. Fuseli begins as a pictorialist and struggles with
Lessing's challenge.[6] Hayley and Romney, like Goethe and Tischbein, dream of collaborating in order to produce something
superior to what each art could do alone.[7] Blake's own pictorial
pantheon—Raphael and Michelangelo, Florence and Rome, with
Germany added—was that of the typical *ut pictura poesis* critic and
poet. When Blake exalts the art of painting, he does so in terms
precisely reminiscent of the Leonardesque *paragone*, which sought
to make the visual intellectually respectable by associating it with
the verbal. Blake was as sympathethic to those immemorial pictorialist values (clarity, outline) as he was hostile to the newer
and antipictorialist ideals (chiaroscuro, chromatic richness).[8] In
fact, on one occasion Blake seems, without mentioning his name,
to strike at the most potent foe of *ut pictura*, Edmund Burke,
exactly at the point at which Burke tried to weaken the pictorial:
"Obscurity," Blake exclaimed, "is Neither the Source of the Sublime nor of any Thing Else."[9]

[4] Mitchell, who in the preceding essay argues a point of view different
from the one in this paragraph, finds Blake's failure to use the term sister
arts "a curious omission." We should, however, beware of assuming too much
from Blake's silences, since so much, particularly of his conversation, has
been lost.

[5] Quoted by Charles Ryskamp in "Wordsworth's *Lyrical Ballads* in their
Time," *From Sensibility to Romanticism*, ed. Frederick W. Hilles and Harold
Bloom, New York, 1965, 364.

[6] See Eudo C. Mason, *The Mind of Henry Fuseli*, London, 1951, 203-207.

[7] William Hayley, *The Life of George Romney, Esq.*, Chichester, 1809, 78.

[8] See Hagstrum, *The Sister Arts*, 66-70, on the *paragone*; Hagstrum, *Blake*,
9 (on Blake's elevation of painting), 15 (on Blake's pantheon), 59-60 (on
Blake's reaction to "tonality").

[9] Annotation to Reynolds' Discourse VII (E647/K473). Here Reynolds' expression of Burke's philosophy has aroused Blake. In annotating Discourse
VIII Blake attacks Burke's treatise by name (E650/K476).

No one detail is persuasive alone. But cumulatively the evidence suggests that Blake was incontrovertibly a practicer of the sister arts and also that his practice was supported by a theoretical commitment to the values of pictorialism, broadly conceived.

Blake and *Ut Pictura Poesis*

If we narrow our consideration from the larger sister-arts tradition to *ut pictura poesis*, which usually bade the poet use words in a painterly fashion, we arrive at the conviction that Blake was not only a uniter of painting and poetry but that in language alone he was a verbal pictorialist. For Blake's words, taken alone, reveal, not everywhere but prominently, the most characteristic features of pictorialist poetry. (1) His verse is filled with verbal icons—that is, his imagery suggests or is organized into pictures or other works of graphic art. (2) His manner of proceeding can be called a version of picture-gallery form, in which the reader moves like a spectator from tableau to tableau. (3) Blake uses, almost obsessively, one of the most conspicuous devices of pictorialist poetry, the visualizable personification.

1. The Verbal Icon

From Homer's description of the shield of Achilles to Keats's Grecian urn, the poet has attempted to describe real or imaginary works of visual art.[10] Sometimes, as in Keats's poem, the icon lends its shape, as it were, to the whole poem. Sometimes, as in Homer and occasionally in Milton, an interpolated visual stasis causes time to come to a stop. The eye is arrested as the epic or narrative movement slows down or halts. Western poetry of all kinds is thickly sown with iconic passages or entire iconic poems. Poets have described or suggested temples, palaces, portraits, stained-glass windows, frescoes, tapestries, teapots, carvings, dishes, landscapes, gardens, statues, carved animals, altars, and pavement. Blake's pages are perhaps denser with such icons than almost any other poet's. We encounter verbal allusions to or renditions of cities, architectural drawings, pillars, canopies, arches, cromlechs, curtains, beds, statues, tents, gates, bridges. Blake's personae are frequently makers of icons, workers in one or another of the visual arts. Urizen is an architect, Jesus a goldsmith and jeweler, Los a forger of metal, Milton a sculptor. Men and gods win victories—

[10] *The Sister Arts*, index under "iconic poetry."

over time, the fall, nonentity—by making icons that occupy space. Highly unvisual concepts are represented iconically. Language is a structure with a basement. Spiritual conditions are places or monuments that can be entered and left, often physical objects that are made by an artist or an artisan. Blake, like Keats, proves that the Romantic poets were by no means all iconoclastic singers of songs, verbal artists aspiring to the condition of music (*ut musica poesis*).[11] Some of them were conscious contrivers of verbal icons. None was more so than Blake.

2. *The Manner of Proceeding*

Persistent in the Western tradition is an un-Aristotelian or anti-Aristotelian literary form.[12] This form does not unfold an action in time or move logically from one premise to another toward a conclusion. The author moves, instead, from picture to picture, transforming his reader into a spectator who also moves, as it were, through a gallery or from detail to graphic detail as though analyzing a single tableau. Pindar's progress is from image cluster to image cluster. A typical Greek romance is made to grow out of a pictorial frontispiece. An ancient allegory advances by interpreting the successive details of a picture. Some medieval narratives, much of Spenser, and Shakespeare in *Venus* and the *Rape* proceed from wall hanging to wall hanging. Marino presents an anthology of poems as a gallery. And Marvell obviously and Pope more subtly organize single poems as galleries. Thomson and Gray move from one picturable scene to another, virtually creating a program for the almost inevitable illustrator. Collins groups characters around a central personification.

Such forms as these are not always exclusively visual. More precisely, they are often a kind of literary "see and tell": pictorial scenes or objects produce exclamatory, epideictic, interpretative responses as visual words and conceptual words alternate in larger or smaller masses.

Such a manner of proceeding, so prominent among pictorialist poets, Blake appears to have adopted. In fact, the addition of literal pictures to his books of verse reinforces the form already

[11] For a discussion of Keats's and other Romantic poets' relation to the pictorialist tradition, see Hagstrum, "The Sister Arts: From Neoclassic to Romantic," in *Comparatists at Work*, ed. Stephen G. Nichols, Jr. and Richard B. Vowles, Waltham, Mass., 1968, 169-194.

[12] *The Sister Arts*, index under "picture-gallery form."

present in the words alone. The unilluminated *French Revolution* proceeds in the picture-gallery manner from tableau to tableau. So would *America* and *Jerusalem* even without the designs. The proper movement in Blake is, both literally and metaphorically, from plate to plate. There is no onward rush of temporal movement. Some devices tie the plates together, to be sure—a phrase at the bottom of one page may be illustrated on the next, visual analogues and repetitions send the mind forward and backward, occasionally a verbal image is not rendered visually until much later, and earlier poems are recalled in later designs and vice versa. But all these tyings-together are within the basic pictorialist form.

Erdman properly stresses the movement and music that accompany Blake's "Visionary Forms Dramatic,"[13] for both are present and the poet's words and pictures both suggest orchestration and action. Even so, Blake's form is essentially painterly, not linear or temporal—visual in the agitated manner of Bernini and the Baroque, but still basically visual. One is constantly amazed at how much action the visibilia alone can suggest.

Blake's form must, in the end, be authenticated by the sensitive and trained reader of his pages. But every now and then the artist drops a hint of how his imagination moves. The redeemed Job, his arms extended in a position of benediction, displays to his daughters the walls of his house. On them are some of the crucial scenes of his experience. "Reading" Blake's *Job*, we proceed as in a gallery, and Job himself, contemplating his past, *sees* it in frescoes on a wall. Eno opens the center of an atom of space and expands it "into Infinitude." Immediately Blake has Eno make of the expanded space a decorated gallery: she "ornamented it with wondrous art." Sometimes Blake views all human history and life as though in a gallery: "All things acted on Earth are seen in the bright Sculptures of Los's Halls." Every possible human story, says the poet, is engraved. Each sorrow and distress is carved here. The relations of man and man, man and woman, the family, marriage, and friendship are all "wrought with wondrous Art." Human history, emotions, institutions—all these are seen as bright art on bright walls.[14]

[13] In the following essay.
[14] For the Blake references in this paragraph, see *Job* 20; *FZ* I 9:12-13 (E300/K270); *J* 16:61-69.

3. Personification

Perhaps the most striking characteristic of pre-Romantic pictorialism is the painterly personification.[15] Blake's personifications are also visualizable—and of course more substantial and real than those of his early masters. He actually *saw* his, while Thomson, Collins, and Gray only imagined theirs, building them up from their detailed recollections of Grecian marbles and Renaissance paintings.

But even though Blake's persons are flesh and blood and not the "shadowy tribe" of Collins, they do not leap up *ex nihilo*. In *Poetical Sketches* the personifications that riot are clearly of the anti-Pope school. And even the latest Blake creates verbal personifications that always betray their filiation.

Genetics aside, Blake's personifications are absolutely central to his verbal art, which is a *display* of human forms, giant and otherwise. Beneath his landscapes are human forms. The faculties of man are personified. The story of art and society is beheld "as men walking." Nature as a whole is Vala, but its individual parts are also animated:

> The grey hoar frost was there
> And his pale wife the aged Snow they watch over the fires
> They build the Ovens of Urthona.
> *(FZ* IX 138:9-11:E391/K378)

The universal family is one man. God is man, and Christ is man, for in Blake theology is always "anthropology." Like Milton, Blake had an "all-personifying fancy."

Many of Blake's prophetic persons ultimately go back, in style though not always in name and meaning, to the Scriptures. But their line descends through the pictorialist tradition, including the eighteenth-century branch. That lineage explains why Blake's persons often resemble those of the Bible but at the same time reveal important differences. Blake read the Bible, but he also *saw* it. The white page came stained with color and scored with line, for Blake's Bible was also the Bible of Raphael, Michelangelo, and the great masters of Western religious art, engraved by such masters as Raimondi. Blake's personifications are, as one would expect, more graphic, more emblematic, and more human than those of the Bible. The Oriental, mystical, diagrammatic

---

[15] *The Sister Arts*, index under "personification."

grotesques of apocalypse and prophecy (consider the shapes in *Ezekiel,* for example) Blake has usually transformed into the Human Form Divine. And that Form is the creation of Western thought and art, refined and humanized by ideals of naturalness and humanity that animated much of the pictorialism of the eighteenth century. In spite of their occasional emblematic awkwardness, Blake's persons are the real men and women that a critic like Shaftesbury called for; they are not often the shapes the philosopher deplored, designed only to bear meanings.[16]

Compare St. John's Jerusalem with Blake's (Revelation 22 and *J* 86). The Evangelist beheld her in the spirit on a mountain as a bride and as a city, but as more city than bride. She descends in general glory, in the dazzling light of precious stones. She is highly symmetrical, with a wall, twelve gates, and as many angles and as many foundations. Her splendor is that of bejeweled geometry, and her light is not that of the natural sun but of a universal and unexplained radiance.

If John's icon is a city with only a hint of a woman, Blake's is a woman with only a hint of a city. Blake's more human and pictorial vision is of course not entirely free of emblematic grotesqueness. Jerusalem has six wings, there are gates of pearl on her forehead, and her wings are a chromatic spectrum of gold, azure, and purple. But the human figure dominates. The wings grow from white shoulders, and the pectoral gems do not conceal the snowy bosom. The sandals of gold and pearl engird real feet, and the bells of silver surround feminine knees.

Thus Blake's Jerusalem is a city with gates and walls. But mostly she is "the soft reflected Image of the Sleeping Man," and the "sublime ornament" on her breasts does not obscure the outline of beauty.

Word and Vision

In the previous section we confined our discussion mostly to Blake's words, in order to show that even the verbal Blake was saturated with influences from the traditional and contemporary *ut pictura poesis* and that his language embodied visual icons, the picture-gallery method of proceeding, and pictorial personifications. We now return to Blake's full form, the union of word and design.

[16] *The Sister Arts,* 123, 159.

Both Erdman and Mitchell rightly argue that Blake's form requires the reader to transcend its composite parts and leap beyond them into meaning and vision. The sister arts must be transcended; they must lead the disciple, as Mary and Martha did, to the Master, who stands at the heart of Blake's apocalypse and fuses with man and his mind. Although he differed with many of his pictorialist predecessors about where ultimate value lay, his aim of transcending the allied arts he shared with most of them.

Goethe hoped to achieve with Tischbein a "perfect unity," one that "neither poetry nor painting alone could ever adequately describe."[17] Pictorialists of different persuasions differed as to what that unity was or where it lay. But in general they agreed that their arts should combine forces in order to lead the beholder beyond themselves to nature, or nature's God, or the mind of man. Giarda in 1626 saw colored forms not as conventional signs for abstract concepts but as ideas that actually dwelt in the intelligible world.[18] Daniel Webb ("le plus littéral des interprètes anglais du *ut pictura*")[19] wanted the sister arts to achieve two ends: mechanical imitation (real objects in nature) and ideal representation (images existing in the mind).[20] Bielfeld outlined three kinds of sensuous imagery: the historical, the allegoric, the mystical.[21] Hurd explained the picturesque qualities of language as arising from religion and the religious impersonations of natural details.[22]

With respect to the three traditional aims of composite art (the religious, the natural, or the subjective), Blake can be precisely located. His verbal-visual forms do not point to the mystical, the otherworldly, the conventionally religious. Nor does one leap from his media to external nature. His forms are displayed in order to bring us to what his predecessors called "ideal" reality and what he himself called the "Intellectual" or "Mental." Blake is more radically subjective than his idealist predecessors, only because his commitment to the mind is more uncompromising and

[17] *Goethe's Travels in Italy* (Bohn's Standard Library), London, 1885, 121.

[18] E. H. Gombrich, "*Icones Symbolicae*: The Visual Image in Neo-Platonic Thought," *JWCI*, XI (1948), 164.

[19] A. Lombard, *L'Abbé du Bos*, Paris, 1913, 347.

[20] *An Inquiry into the Beauties of Painting*, London, 1760, 4-6.

[21] *The Elements of Universal Erudition . . . by Baron Bielfeld*, tr. W. Hooper, II, London, 1770, 358.

[22] Richard Hurd, *Moral and Political Dialogues*, London, 1759, 124.

because from the mind he expected the total conversion of man and society. For him, as for few others, the *mens creatrix* is, if an uncongenial voice may be heard,

At once the source, and end, and test of Art.

Blake's radical and individual idealism, then, is not religious in any orthodox sense of the term. He does not seem to believe in the objective "otherness" of God. But Blake's inwardness does not prevent him from using the language of the external apocalypse. That prophetic language, like *ut pictura poesis* and the sister arts, unites the verbal and the visual in ways strikingly parallel. The God of Israel *speaks* in *visions* (Genesis 46:1, Psalms 89:19), and the prophet Nathan (2 Samuel 7:17) addresses David "according to . . . vision" and "according to . . . words." Milton alternates between vision and word. In *Paradise Lost,* when Adam's outer vision has been purged by euphrasia and rue and his "inmost seat of mental sight" has also been cleansed, he is bidden by Michael to open his eyes and *behold* the great prophetic-historical tableaux of Book XI. These visions are replaced by speech in Book XII, where Adam *hears* verbal "relations" of Christian events and truths.

So the prophetic tradition, and so Blake, who also united word and vision, believing it impossible to "*think* without *images* of somewhat on earth."[23] In Blake's apocalyptic climax language also reaches its climax: human forms redound from the tongue and "every Word & Every Character / Was Human" (*J* 98). Vision similarly reaches its climax. The new man, now one man, is an object of sight—"clearly seen / And seeing." In the great consummation word and vision become, as it were, the sister arts. *Ut pictura poesis. Ut poesis pictura.* "And I *heard* Jehovah speak, . . . & *saw* the Words."

Surely Blake's great power as artist and prophet springs from a remarkable union of the aesthetic (painting and poetry) and the prophetic (vision and word).

[23] Annotations to Lavater 225 (E590/K88).

5

America
New Expanses

DAVID V. ERDMAN

TODAY the inquiry into the art of Blake's Illuminated Printing is moving far beyond the simple but long prevailing question whether the design on a given page illustrates or illuminates or counterpoints the text: whether poem is like picture or picture like poem. We are now, at a minimum, concerned with what the two arts are doing in harness, pictura *atque* poesis. At maximum we are concerned with much more. But allow me at this level to make a point about the interchange or sharing of pictorial imagery between picture and text. On the seventh plate of *Jerusalem* the words describe the "opake blackening" Spectre of Los as one who "panting like a frighted wolf and howling . . . stood over the Immortal . . . among the Furnaces." The etched picture (*Jerusalem* 6) shows us the blacksmith with tongs, fire, hammer, anvil, bellows, and a chain that operates the bellows; but the Spectre is not standing; it has no visible feet but hovers over the smith on wings, like a bat not a wolf. A moment later, in the text, the Spectre "groaning" kneels before Los at the furnace—presumably more like a man than a wolf or a bat. The effect may be called metaphorical density, but it is more than that and not quite that. Whether the Spectre is bat, wolf, or man (we are to realize) depends on how the mind sees it or him. These are alternative or simultaneous visionary forms of one form that hint at metamorphoses to tease us *into* thought, for their one form is in turn a shadow form of the human blacksmith, who is the metaphorical heroic form of the poet-artist, William Blake of South Molton Street (as he tells us within the poem). *Because* he faints at the anvil he is haunted by his spectral self-shadows: *or* because they are in his mind, he faints at the forge. The action of the poem-picture is larger and more complex than would be indicated by the pictures or the words taken separately, for these point not at each other (as in the usual picture book) but beyond themselves. The artifact only opens the sensory doors to the mental theater.

In other words, the text is not there to help us follow the pictures, nor the pictures to help us visualize the text; both lead us to an imaginative leap in the dark, a leap *beyond* the dark and the fire—from perception to Intellectual Vision, a last judgment in which fools perish.

We must attend to Blake's definition (*Jerusalem* 98) of true communication as practised by humans in paradise:

> And they conversed together in Visionary forms dramatic
>   which bright
> Redounded from their Tongues in thunderous majesty,
>   in Visions
> In new Expanses, creating exemplars. . . .

Their converse involves mastery of all the arts of discourse, ornamentation, dramaturgy, exploration, and moral suasion (exemplars). Using only the arts of poetry and painting (and engraving) Blake must suggest all the others. And all must serve Intellectual Vision, seen through the window of the artifact. His illuminated pages become a prompt book of suggestions for Visions, Expanses, New Songs, and Thunderous Dramatic Forms, in which he wishes us to converse. "I give you the end of a golden string," he says. "It will lead you. . . ." His text is a clue-thread. On the thread of text the emblematic etchings are mere sketches for cosmic motion-pictures, or rather color-motion-music pictures, on a four-dimensional mental screen—the cinerama of William Blake.

The man who tried "all experiments" in art and mixed art might have been delighted at the potentialities of the cinemonsters of our day—if horrified at their Satanic intellectual focus. The man who, when the sun rose, did not fixate on a "round disk of fire" but saw (and heard) "an Innumerable company of the Heavenly host crying Holy Holy . . ." abhorred the kind of realism which does not open the interior and exterior worlds.[1]

[1] *DC* 9 (E539/K583), *VLJ* (E555/K617). For a more thoughtful consideration of the "problem in visualization that presents itself everywhere in Blake's poetry" see Harold Bloom, "The Visionary Cinema of Romantic Poetry," *Essays for Damon*, 18-35. "Blake, I think, like his master Milton (as Eisenstein hinted) wants his reader to be more of a film-script reader or even a director than a film-viewer."

It was a sense of Blake's objective that led Northrop Frye to go on, after suggesting the (remote) analogy of "the union of musical and poetic ideas in a Wagner opera," to the proposition that Blake's work involves the building up of a unified structure of meaning as "a total image, a single visualizable picture."[2] This view is valid, at a distance from the work, but dissolves as we approach; for the visualizable picture is in motion—and is not really single. It is usually at least twofold, with a polar or antiphonal or dialectical tension between two contrary images (or image systems), each striving to be determinate—as, for example, the rival cities of Jerusalem and Babylon in *Jerusalem*. Beyond that, it can be apocalyptically threefold or fourfold, as I hope to reveal in the present close look at *America, A Prophecy*, 1793.

Physically *America* is an eighteen-page folio booklet "in Illuminated Printing" consisting of a frontispiece, an illustrated title page continuing the picture of the frontispiece, a Preludium of two and a Prophecy of fourteen illuminated pages (see {24-44}). The work concerns a cycle of history that begins with the birth and rising of an Orc or human serpent of Independence, during the American War and Revolution, and concludes with the end of the war (in 1781) and that spirit's repression for "twelve years." The cycle is viewed prophetically from 1793, a time of auguries of a new cycle. That year, on January 21, the King of France was guillotined. In February, France and England went to war. In June, Blake issued an engraved print of a king hysterical, flanked by two chief warriors gripping sword and spear, above the caption *Our End is Come*. In October he offered *America* for sale, with the specific prophecy in its concluding lines that "their end should come"—the end of "Angels & weak men" who "govern o'er the strong"—"when France reciev'd the Demons light."[3]

---

[2] Frye, "Poetry and Design in William Blake," *Journal of Aesthetics and Art Criticism*, x (1951), 35-42; reprinted in John E. Grant, *Discussions of William Blake*, Boston, 1961, 44-49.

[3] *A* 16 (E56/K302); Prospectus of 10 October 1793 (E670/K207); *Our End is Come / Published June 5 1793 by W Blake Lambeth* (E660): behind the alarmed trio is an oaken door frame; in later versions flames are added beside or behind them; in the color print the door frame has been burnt up. See G. Keynes, *Engravings by William Blake: The Separate Plates*, Dublin, 1956, 19-22, pls. 12-14. But first and second states are confused by Keynes: the physical evidence is that the third state shows traces of the second-state inscription, and that proves to be "When the senses . . ." not "Our End. . . ." E660 is also mistaken, before the fourth printing.

Joel Barlow in his *Vision of Columbus*, Book Five, had re-arranged the chronological and geographical materials of the historical American War into an epic pageant viewed prophetically by Christopher Columbus from a Mount of Vision in Spain.[4] Barlow's stage was the American coast, which Columbus could see from his Spanish mountain; his machinery consisted of one angel; his main stage device was a cloud that hid the scene during intermissions. Blake extended the stage to include the British coast, swelled the machinery to a large cast of angels and demons, replaced the Mount of Vision with the "vast shady hills" of an archetypal Atlantis "between America & Albions shore," and replaced Columbus as European spectator with the King of England, who, "looking westward" from Albion, trembles at a "vision" which is, largely, the relevant part of Barlow's *Vision*. But of course Blake's symbolic fusion of military and political and psychic history, heightened by apocalyptic imagery from descriptions of the Black Death, soars beyond the troubled fountains of Barlow's couplets. Blake's choreography is utterly new; action as well as communication crisscrosses the Atlantic and leaps from its depths to the zenith; and he departs further from the narrative form of history, epic or chronicle, in the direction of musical form and mural allegory as in paintings of the Last Judgment by the Italians or by Blake himself. *America* we might look upon as an acting version of a mural Apocalypse.

Drawing upon both text and pictures, let us examine first the music of it and then the visualizable drama—an order which will stress Blake's departure from narrative but not from progression.

Blake, working as a musician, first gives us silence, then the early emergence of articulate sound, and finally a conflagration of apocalyptic thunders and war-clarions. Silent are all the figures in the illustrations of the frontispiece and title page: slain warriors, anguished maiden[5] (and, above, the preoccupied—yet also the alert—reading public);[6] the mother and children who seem

---

[4] See my "William Blake's Debt to Joel Barlow," *American Literature*, XXVI (1954), 94-98; also *Prophet*, 22-26, 54 [23-27, 57], and, for the addition of Black Death imagery, 55-56 [58-59].

[5] J.E.G.: Breathing, not lamenting.

[6] Clouds separate these two readers, and four attendant spirits, from the work itself. The alert female is reading properly; her position echoes that of Michelangelo's Delphic sibyl, as Janet Warner notes, and her feet and her attendant's fingers point to "PROPHECY." The male's reading requires redirecting.

95

to have been, but are not now, weeping; the chained angel in the broken wall, his *face* buried; the dismounted cannon and broken sword in the foreground, the brokenness suggesting an irreversible silence (though later we shall see the sword reforged). Utterance begins in the Preludium, but first (in the text) in the silence of dark air stands "dumb" the dark virgin of nature; "for never from her iron tongue could voice or sound arise." (In the illustration the first implied sound is the wailing of Eve over the chained Orc: see identifications later on.) Then, as "an eagle *screaming,*" a lion *raging,* or whale or serpent, the hairy youth *howls* his joy. "Silent as despairing love" (*A* 2), he *rends his chains,* seizes the womb. Then *bursts* the virgin *cry*—the birth of articulate desire, a "first-born smile." Fire and frost mingle in the "*howling* pains" of a Behmenesque Genesis.[7]

Then in the center of the first page of "A Prophecy" is pictured a trumpet from which are blown flames undoubtedly ear-piercing as well as, according to the text, soul-piercing—indicative of the music to come, which is chiefly of flames and terrible blasts of wind and strong speeches. Here are the opening lines (with emphasis added):

J.A.W.: The flying figure in the right-hand corner, one of the spirits or energies that Damon and Keynes call "joys," is escaping right out of the picture, while no one pays the slightest attention; the eye of the reader is invited by the line of the figure's arm to turn the page and become involved in the prophecy, where this escaping energy is transformed into Orc.

J.E.G.: But this leader is a woman; she is seen from the front still stirring things up at the end of the engraved *Night Thoughts* designs, where the reader who has used his head is with her (*NT* no. 153). See her also beside "Vala / Night the First" in *FZ* 3; she is related to Ahania in *Ahania* and in *Urizen* 13 {53}. For a similar pair of readers see *MHH* 10. The motif of a woman and children with a book also occurs in *Songs of Innocence* title page {11} and in *NT* no. 6 {74}.

[7] This reference some find obscure. I am thinking of such embracings as the following from ch. 3, "Concerning the Birth of Love," Jacob Behmen, *Works,* London, 1763, vol. II: "And so when the first desire . . . is *filled* with Glance of the Light, then all the Essences (which have *laid hold* on the Light) stand in the first desiring will, and the will thereby becometh *triumphant,* and full of joy, that the child of Light is generated in it . . . and the Joy (*viz.* the source of the Fire) flieth upward, and the Center retaineth it. . . . one form embraceth the other. . . . the sourness retaineth its fierce might . . . in the sharpness of the Love; but . . . is very soft; and . . . maketh voices, tunes and sounds . . . and with the breaking through of the source, they *feel* one another" and so on. (Italics in original.)

96

The Guardian Prince of Albion *burns* in his nightly tent.
Sullen fires across the Atlantic *glow* to America's shore:
Piercing the souls of warlike men, who rise in *silent*
 night.
Washington, Franklin Paine & Warren, Gates, Hancock
 & Green:
Meet on the coast *glowing with blood* from Albions *fiery*
 Prince.

Out of this pierced silence Washington speaks. When his "strong voice" ceases, a terrible blast sweeps over the heaving sea, and the eastern cloud curtains part, to reveal the Prince (over England) in his dragon form "clashing his scales." Whereupon arises in demon form the giant Orc of independence with a voice whose "thunders" shake the temple. Heard by a sympathetic ear, however, these thunders are a sweet and lusty hymn of resurrection: "The morning comes, the night decays, the . . . bones of death . . . breathing! awakening! / Spring like redeemed captives . . ." (plate 6 {34}).

Note that our imagination must have two ears as well as two eyes. To the Prince of Albion, rebellion is a horrid spectre with voice of thunder. To "coarse-clad honesty" it is "the soul of sweet delight" singing of "a fresher morning." The page is Blake's rendition of the Declaration of Independence; after "darkness and . . . sighing" the "inchained soul" and "his wife and children" (remember the frontispiece) burst into laughter and song, and their song is that the Sun "has left his blackness" and the "fair Moon rejoices" and those roarers "the Lion & Wolf shall cease." It is this sort of "duality in union" in Blake which Mrs. Bodkin approves of as "harmonized clash."[8]

An interchange of loud challenges between Orc and Albion's Prince—or Angel, for George III has modulated to a higher spiritual form—ends in a climactic chant of escalation delivered by the Angel (plate 9 {37}). Structurally this twenty-seven-line chant opens and closes with a two-line refrain:

Sound! sound! my loud war-trumpets & alarm my
 Thirteen Angels!
Loud howls the eternal Wolf! the eternal Lion lashes
 his tail!

[8] Maude Bodkin, *Archetypal Patterns in Poetry*, London, 1934, 317.

The first of these lines is also repeated internally twice, making cadences at the thirteenth and twenty-first lines of this trumpet voluntary; musically as well as pictorially the page is organized as a unit.

Uttering these lines, the Angel-Prince is acting as the magician or conductor of an orchestral whirlwind of war. "Thus wept the Angel voice," we are told in a kind of stage direction, "& as he wept the terrible blasts / Of trumpets blew a loud alarm." Even the answering silence is described in orchestral terms:

> No trumpets answer; no reply of clarions or of fifes,
> Silent the Colonies remain. . . .

In the remaining pages of text, trumpeting and challenging give way to action. The fires "roaring fierce" are so often given as sound effects (and remember the flaming trumpet of the first page of "A Prophecy") that even where sound is not specified it is connoted. The fires and deep rolling thunder become less and less musical, however, and more and more evidently the fire and thunder of incendiary cannonades. In the final page (plate 16) the fire is said to rage so high it melts the heavens, rousing the old man Urizen (the Prince's highest spiritual form) who damps the flames and noise with "icy magazines" of "stored snows"; and for "twelve years" the only sound is of his "Weeping in dismal howlings" (the phrase repeated as a refrain).[9] Barlow's focus on the December hailstorm which prevented the revolutionists' capture of Quebec evidently prompted these "snows poured forth, and . . . icy magazines"; perhaps we may see Niagara Falls at the right edge of the plate—see, not hear, because the bottom of the falls is not represented. Yet the reversion to silence is incomplete and temporary. In the final eight lines "shudderings" are shaking thrones and there is a crackling (though so sharp a word is not used) of "fierce flames . . . round the heavens, & round the abodes of men."

[9] *A* 16:2. J.E.G.: The flames' going up rather than over is a kind of allusive parody of the Phaëton myth. Unable to manage the sun chariot he had borrowed, Phaëton burned up the Sahara before Jove knocked him down with a thunderbolt. Orc's melting the heavens is like Phaëton's devastation below; Urizen tries to extinguish with snow while Jove used Nelsonian fire. One of Michelangelo's three drawings of the fall of Phaëton lies just behind *MHH* 5. And compare the Satan-Palamabron foul-up in *Milton*. The old cold man first appears in *To Winter*.

Let us now consider what we are shown and what we are told to visualize. Working as a painter, Blake begins not on a fresh canvas but on one filled with a vision he does *not* want. The scene pictured in the frontispiece and on the title page is taken, we discover, from his early painting, exhibited at the end of the American War: *A Breach in a City the Morning after the Battle* {23}. We shall find out later whose shell the wall is; Orc placed in the broken wall is stopping a gap or has made a breach, but is manacled; he represents the strong governed by the weak.[10] We must understand that in Blake's view the Revolutionary War was sad not only because of the bloodshed and possibly some continuing impairment of liberty in America[11] but also because it ended with tyranny still enthroned in Britain and the rest of Europe; at the end of the Prophecy it is Orc's chains that melt as thrones totter.[12]

But just as, musically, Blake starts with a long silence; so pictorially he starts with a static tableau before moving into the dynamic vision. In this sad scene of the frontispiece and title page, motion is still, life is at its low ebb; the warriors are horizontal, the women exhausted with weeping, the sword broken, the cannon dismounted; the Titan is chained by his wrists to the horizontal stone. Below the heavens, where hope springs, there is no

[10] See *Prophet,* 71 [75]. On the three extant versions of *A Breach* see *Romantic Art in Britain*, ed. Frederick Cummings and Allen Staley, Philadelphia, 1968, 159-160. In the version called *War* and inscribed "Inv WB 1805" the Orc figure, wingless but the same naked, curly-headed youth with face buried, is added on top of the heap of bodies in the breach; the wings of the *America* title page remain on the eagle. Reproduced in Mark Schorer, *William Blake: The Politics of Vision*, New York, 1946, opp. 254. For different interpretations of this figure, see below, p. 194.

[11] J.E.G.: I think it was the Constitution, ratified in 1791, that wrought those manacles. D.V.E.: I don't like guessing (when *I'm* not doing it); wasn't America still a symbol of freedom to Blake in *Jerusalem*? J.E.G.: The soul of America is a female; the male, *born* free, is in chains.

[12] J.E.G.: This is not literally the imagery Blake uses, however, but the melting of the "bolts and hinges" of the gates of the "law-built heaven." When the book swings back again to the start, we see (in the frontispiece) that the manacles are on Orc while the *gate* has been melted or blown up. The recent doings at London School of Economics remind us how controversial it can seem to Establishmentarians if insurgents decide to remove the gates just set up to maintain law and order. Getting rid of the gates is one way of cleansing the doors of perception: remember how Samson was always carrying off the gates of the Philistines.

motion except (in the title page) the slanting rain or sleet; no vegetation, except that imitated in the stone. There is silence also in the absence of text. This is not the "single visualizable picture" Blake wants us to *see* but one that is to be erased or seen through or burnt away by the dynamic vision of the Prophecy itself, announced by the flaming trumpet on its first page. Yet he does not step at once from death to life, from stone to flame, from horizontal to spiral. He supplies first the two transitional pages of the Preludium, in which silence is broken by the very fact of the introduction of text (beneath the design at first, then above it) and by various *rehearsals* of the moment of revolutionary birth. In the text a "silent" youth suddenly, as "an eagle screaming," seizes a "dumb" (and "shadowy") female, who utters the virgin cry of articulate desire, a "first-born smile," and so on. In the pictures we are shown first that the chained Promethean lies in a middle state between the cave dweller and the man standing free.

This first page of the Preludium {26} is a progressive cartoon, to be read clockwise; and then counterclockwise. Forgetting the headless worm (of six coils: sixty winters?), which is there at the start and finish of the journey only if you are committed to corporeality and intellectual death, man is, at his lowest *living* stage, the self-clutching cave dweller in the dark, though he can sit up and look about even there, and next a metamorphosing root-shoot rising to air and light. Reaching the surface, he is (1) horizontal with his eyes shut, as the title-page warrior, i.e., dead or mentally asleep, or (2) able to sit up (the Titan in the wall) but still self-clutching, eyes buried despite demonic-angelic wings, or (3) chained flat, cruciform, but with open eyes looking straight up, as in Preludium 1.[13] The picture leaps ahead to upstanding man, and woman, already Adam and Eve, *turning about*, looking backward.[14] They are compelled to, hearing the youth's cry, seeing him crucified; yet this dangerous retrospection is apt to reverse the progression. This plate traps hope, risen from the worm,

[13] In a pen and water color variant at the Tate there is horror in Orc's face: the vultures are descending just above the picture. (In Martin Butlin's Tate Gallery *William Blake*, London, 1966, pl. 5.)

[14] J.E.G.: As at the end of the (earlier Huntington) *Paradise Lost* series of illustrations, and prototype of the Cain and Abel pictures. D.V.E.: In Blake's subsequent myth, of course, they are Los and Enitharmon.

and sends it back to the worm. Even the almost leafless tree droops.[15]

On the second Preludium page {27}, however, we are shown dynamic growing things reaching up from the earth though rooted in it—a vine shooting up taller than Adam, a sprout of wheat, hopeful metamorphoses upward in the dynamic scale, and between them chainless man crouching in a furrow, ready to spring up— a stage skipped in the first page, the good news rehearsed and announced by the youthful female on the title page. Blake has reversed the direction again, forward, and turned the angle of our vision. Seeing this burgeoning phase to be *where we are now*, we know we are out of the trap, are looking and springing up free of death—even while, in the words above our eye as we crouch to spring, the virgin pathetically fearful, in joy and pain of giving birth, imagines with Sophoclean irony: "This is eternal death: and this the torment long foretold." Consider the interaction: while the text rehearses struggle and outcry and change, the pictures subdue these to the potential mode yet prepare the *release* of potentials.

A grace note of yellow light behind the crouching Orc (in copy M at least)[15a] calls attention to the rising-sun position of his head against the curve of the earth, and on the next page (plate 3 {29}) we see him aloft, soaring free of the trap—yet dangling chains.[16] How reassuring this token: he did not bypass that stage but broke through it. In this figure the manacled Orc of the frontispiece is freed, the earth-chained crucified slave of plate 1 is risen. We have the central prophecy of the poem—that tyranny is not eternal, that freedom is worth a second try—even as we reach

---

[15] J.A.W.: The Eve figure is recognizable as Oothoon, "the soft soul of America" in this same distraught pose in *VDA* 6, an ironic contrast to the vision of love and freedom her words there suggest. In the Preludium she can thus be identified as America itself, distraught before its rebellious energies are unbound, soon to be parent of its own revolution in the same way that in the text of the next plate the shadowy daughter of Urthona finds her own voice after Orc is released. There too we *see* Orc released.

[15a] In copy K (shown here, {27}) the sunrise is beginning to the right of Orc's head.

[16] J.E.G.: Compare *FZ* 2, and on the chains see *MHH* 16. For a regrouping of the whole sequence, in comparable relation to a prophetic title, look at *J* 4.

"A Prophecy," the very lettering of which is vibrant with flight and exuberance and fruition.

Everything Blake's mind touches grows to his purpose. Even his title lettering heralds the progression from geometry to vitality. "AMERICA" on the title page is square, static, carved in stone; *"PROPHECY"* below it begins a forward tilt and takes color. Then *"Preludium"* introduces the more curved, vital lines of italic lower case with a swash capital.[17] Finally, *"A PROPHECY"* is all swash, flowing, swirling, fruitful, flowering, with leaves and lilies and ripe heads of wheat.[18]

And only now, in the Prophecy itself, we begin to focus on the central dynamic and apocalyptic picture of the drama. The stage areas of it are indicated in the opening lines: on the right side, Albion's cliffs, where the Prince burns in his nightly tent; on the left side, the coast of America, where Washington, Franklin, Paine, and others rise and meet and stand. The two coasts are linked by fire *or* blood "glowing" across the Atlantic. The Atlantic itself fills the center of the area; Orc is born there; and we can see from its deeps to the zenith—and beyond, for we are told that "above all heavens" resides Urizen, old Nobodaddy aloft.

Notice the link of the coasts by blood *or* fire: we need twofold vision to see that the same relationship can be vital or destructive. Words can give the twofold vision in one image: the Americans "Meet on the coast glowing with blood from Albions fiery Prince." And in one picture (plate 15 {43}) we can see flames as tendrils— or tendrils as flames.

In the fourteen pages of the Prophecy, the main body of the work, the actions and persons of the American War and Revolution, interpreted as Armageddon and Apocalypse, are arranged choreographically on this world stage into a single Judgment Day picture—with God at the top above several cloud layers of angel-filled heavens, and the Atlantic deeps at the bottom, whence God's

[17] Copy M (used for the Blake Trust facsimile) is not representative; by the time of its printing the separate slip of copper with the word "Preludium" was lost; adding the word by brush, Blake reverted to the simpler italic capitals of the title page.

[18] Grant warns that the vine entwining the "P" is "a lookout type, which can scourge." I too used to identify these triangle-leaved and/or flowered vines as scourge vines but cannot recall the source or basis of the idea. The flowers here are lilies, as Grant agrees; nowhere in Blake's *text* do lilies combine with cruel leaves.

mocking adversary arises, mocking his stance, defying repression with naked energy. On the eastern side are Tory angels ascending and circling above Albion's cliffs, led by George the Third in his dragon form; on the western are rebel angels, led by the Angel of Boston, descending to assist the warlike patriots standing on the American shore.

For twelve of the fourteen pages the jealous wrath from Albion hurtles upon America fires, chains, insults, and a bacteriological attack of forty millions of Albion's angels armed with disease. The stern Americans *stand* unconsumed, the standing representing the unity of their rushing together. In the last two pages the whirlwind recoils upon Albion and inflames Bristol and London and unhinges the gates of the senses throughout Europe.[19]

This is Blake's dynamic "single" visualizable picture—of shifting multiple perspectives. Reaction makes more noise, smoke, and mileage, but freedom in two hours makes more progress. On the last page (plate 16 {44}) the silent, static image of the "Morning after the Battle" threatens to reassert itself as the tyrant god Urizen pours down ice and snow to reduce the rebel Orc to his Atlantic deeps, and the picture subdues to quiet: Niagara Falls as hair. We think again of the rain or sleet of the title page. Yet the work concludes with a reassertion of the main image of the conflagration of the old heaven and earth.

In the illumination of the Preludium we saw a progressive movement (in plate 1) reversing upon itself, then (in 2) springing forward again. In the concluding pages a progressive movement is resumed, beginning (in the text) with "the fierce rushing of th' inhabitants together" (14:12) described as a sort of general strike and transposed, in the illumination of plate 15, to a gentle ascent from clusters of flaming grapes at the bottom, up the left margin but halted near the top, to be frozen on the ultimate plate. The figure in these designs is female, an Eve for our Amer-

---

[19] Here, as in *A Song of Liberty*, the poet conflates the whole revolutionary era of the tottering of thrones in "France Spain & Italy" because people defeated redcoats in America. To quote *A* 14, *MHH* 12, *PA* 18, and *A* 14-15: the "wrath" of their unity is "the voice of God," i.e., of honest men, the "Public Indignation of Men of Sense in all Professions"—"citizens . . . mariners . . . scribe . . . builder"—against war and obedience to tyranny; its infectious civic fire inspires the citizens of Albion to *stand* also, naked of "their hammerd mail." Compare the vision of alternative communities in *Jerusalem* discussed in Kenneth Johnston's essay in this volume.

ican Adam (we saw them together in Preludium 1), the inspiring "soft soul of America" who must light the fierce youth's rising.

Toward the end of his life Blake would combine the male and female lovers' cycles, in the circle of lovers illustrating Dante's Inferno, where, in a clockwise whirlwind reversing the Dantean hopelessness of hell, figures at first self-sufficient develop mutual awareness, embrace with increasing ardor, and arrive at the full union of Paolo and Francesca, which constitutes so bright a luminary as to make the poet swoon.

In *America* the embrace of youth and virgin as of fire and frost is portentously narrated in the Preludium text; the sexes are out of phase; their progressions are separately pictured. The male's progress we observed in the Preludium and first Prophecy plates. The female's we see in plate 15: first self-entwined, then in a group embrace (female), then alone, free and upward moving in a rising wave-flame. But the metamorphosis of the next phase appears to stultify; free underground, as she enters the surface this Daphne becomes rootbound, and the next phase is a non-human tree on the surface of the earth, with a small, clothed woman bent over in blind servility ("pining in bonds of religion," we gather from the text) or discouragement (compare Orc in the broken wall). A sort of bird-flower does get up into the tree, but that indicates a possibility rather than the actuality. It is the superstitious, face-burying female, enlarged in size perhaps to match the bent Orc of the frontispiece, who dominates the "finis" page, her hair a waterfall. Despite the text's announcement of Orc's fires' renewal and the end of tyranny, the design suggests barren virginity (the almost leafless tree-women at the top left) and a failure of the Muse's nerve; only in nonhuman or very small images, some of them almost invisible, is life maintained and a fire-glow suggested.

A moment of perceptive lingering can draw sustenance from these minute intimations of life, nevertheless. Though the four flower buds, two of them large, almost open roses, glow with color only in the painted copies of *America* (such as copy M, used for the Blake Trust facsimile) and only in these copies is the square-lettered FINIS across the snake's belly painted out, the snake even in outline is the irrepressible American rattlesnake, there are no "mildews of despair" on these flowers—and there are among them, and at the top of the page, several fairy-sized human forms worth watching. In Blake's illustration (*NT* no. 190) of line 560 of Young's Fifth Night, "From *Sorrow*'s Pang, the Birth of Endless Joy," Sorrow is represented by a large huddling woman somewhat like the large one here, and Joy by a slender dancer tiptoe on Sorrow's head and about to soar straight up. Several potential soarers gathering about the sorrowful Niagara figure include, at her feet, an embracing couple (the woman clad in rose, in copies K and M); on the hill of her back a couple finished with a book and looking up; and on her head an absorbed reader, perhaps a composite of the two readers on the title page. No Joy is about to spring up. Yet John Grant calls attention to the fact that the lines which seem to sketch a girdle at the woman's waist are actually drawn as a living tree, sheltering a piping piper, our man of Innocence for all seasons![20]

And notice that the serpent's head among the rosebuds and of similar shape is opening as they shall; we have not returned to the headless worm of the beginning. Night it may be; nature and man, female and male, have not arisen together. Yet if both man and woman slept at the same time, no one would watch and no waking would ever occur. In those first pages, when the warrior is dead asleep, it is the woman who with her embrace is to restore him; when the giant in the breach hides his head, the woman faces the world and upholds the children. (The Blakean analogues are Theotormon-Oothoon and Albion-Jerusalem.) Viewing the work as a whole, then, the reader can nowhere rest discouraged if nowhere rest content. At least this is true for the whole picture we have been examining. But there is more to see. The tale of this multiple simultaneous drama is slavery-freedom-slavery-freedom, with a gently but firmly planted hope that slavery's periods are shortening or can be escaped. The open graveyard picture of the beginning is surely erased by this active scene, of disobedience from Boston to Bristol, of fierce flames burning "round the heavens, & round the abodes of men," to quote the concluding

[20] There are sheep in front of the piper, as Michael Tolley points out, and another figure, with sheep, on the ledge formed by the rock-woman's calf. We see the same man, with a somewhat longer pipe, leaning against the letter "I" of the *Songs of Innocence* title page, and again, much later, at the top of *J* 9. Compare the man kneeling in the *MHH* title page, with lyre or very badly drawn short pipe (see above, p. 63 and n, and {3}).

words. Yet this also is to be transcended, as we must finally discover.

Consider the nature of Blake's presentation of what I have been calling his central prophetic image, the revolutionary Armageddon or battle of "that great day of God Almighty." We are given only a fragmentary sketch. The poet does not attempt to present it in one vast painting. On the Prophecy's first page we see a portion of the American stage area, with citizens fleeing from burning homes presumably, but we never see the stern Americans who are named, the central visualizable group. On the second page (plate 4 {31} or the variant canceled plate b {30}) we see a bit of the coast of Albion and indeed its king but not as a fiery prince in a royal tent. In a progressive cartoon we see the King successively in dragon, angel, and human form (as the text explains), a series of metamorphoses that Blake rather loses interest in when revising the text, though he keeps the pictures.

Again the particulars are worth an excursus. In the original text the "wrathful Prince" arises as "A dragon form clashing his scales," with voice, glowing eyes, and other features that "Reveal the dragon thro' the human." He then courses "swift as fire" down to a meeting of "his Lords & Commons" in the valley of the Thames, "where his Angel form renews." The latter form looks more human but is only an "aged apparition." Pictured at the top of the page is a slightly absurd dragon—intentionally so, for its limp human hands replace more clawlike fingers (in b) to reveal the human through the dragon (an effect contrapuntal to the original text).[21] Plummeting down the left margin, identified by scepter and book of rules, is the King's angel form with "snowy beard" and "white garments" that cast "a wintry light" (heavily emphasized in colored copies). The bolt of lightning in front of the dragon is repeated in front of the angel like a trademark. At the bottom of the page we are not shown the "hall of counsel" (collapsing anyway, according to the original text) but a stout naked man clutching his head—the pathetic reality beneath these

---

[21] Compare the human hands of the Urizenic lamb in *The Number of the Beast is 666* (Keynes, *Bible*, pl. 167, or *Romantic Art in Britain*, pl. 96). Canceled plate *A* (*a*) was replaced by the almost identical plate 3; *b* by 5, very different in text; *c*, continuing *b*, disappears from the poem—except for its influence on the conception of the Preludium, discussed below. See {28, 30, 32}. For the texts see E57-58, 724-725/K203-205.

disguises; we will recognize him again on the next plate, where he meets a revolutionary tribunal. Here what he views in anticipatory terror is an "orc" or killer whale beside him on the shore, a sea monster or spectre of his imagination. This happens to rulers who start crusades against nations seeking freedom. Revision of the plate moved the monster to the left, keeping the King's eyes toward it, and placed just above his head the line, "The King of England looking westward trembles at the vision" (the account of the downfall of George and his Lords and Commons being replaced by an account of the birth of Orc). Possibly the image originated in the illumination (the Preludium text was written latest of all); the first orc looks like a tree trunk with exposed roots; in redrawing it is much more like a whale or at least a manatee. A large, rooted tree takes its original place.[22]

We could see from the start that the Dragon-Angel-King was only human: those hands, a device used later in the Epilogue to *The Gates of Paradise* to help us see a bat-winged Urizenic Satan as truly "but a Dunce."[23] The King sees only monsters. On the next page a similar contrast in perception is pictured in more purely symbolic terms: we see three soaring naked men with (Christ's) fiery sword and scales of justice; the King sees a coiled serpent awaiting him amid hellfire. (The serpent is mentioned in the text, but the revolutionary tribunal is not.) This cartoon reads only counterclockwise; it could hardly be reversed. At the top the King, bound and presumably gagged, is tried by the three

[22] The redrawn plate (*A* 4 {31}) has two, possibly three, new figures to the right of the head-clutching man and against the tree. One is a bearded man looking up behind him; his arms clasp a gowned child; to the right of these lies a woman's face, white like the child, tilted back as if in a faint; her body presumably is out of sight, behind the man's. The face is fairly clear in copy M but not visible in copy K. The man might be one of the councillors from *Our End is Come*. Perhaps we are being shown consternation in the Royal Family. (Grant cites the half-buried heads in *Gates of Paradise* 16 and *J* 92, but this head is neither buried nor on the ground.)

[23] In the drawing on *FZ* 70 mere human hands and bare human feet betray the human form within a crocodilelike "fierce scorpion glowing with gold"; the scorpion is a son of Urizen, like King George, but in the *FZ* text Urizen himself is the only male who has a "Dragon Form" (see *Concordance*). Echoes of *A* 4 appear on the facing page (*FZ* 71, one of the *NT* proofs selected, one feels, as appropriate): snowy-bearded elder with bow and arrow (cf. the scepter); book; alarmed, curly-headed, stout man at bottom. (This is *NT* no. 18).

youths, found wanting, and sent hurtling and clutching his head to the bottom, where his possibly decapitated body is encircled by a blood-red serpent. January 1793, if you will:[24] this is at the center of the prophecy, and Blake was less afraid to picture it than to describe it.[25] (The central figure carrying the bound King was repeated years later when Blake depicted, for "Hell, Canto 21," a devil casting a corrupt official into boiling pitch.) More literal violence is described and depicted in canceled plate c {32}. King George, uttering "hollow" grief over America as he dons his "armour of terrible gold," is "like an aged King in arms of gold / Who wept over a den, in which his only son outstretch'd / By rebels hands was slain." Pictured in the margin is a young man outstretched in a cloud cave—not very dead looking; George is mistaken to think that rebellion has destroyed America. Pictured, but not described, is a violent scene in which a "terrible boy" (to borrow text from the Preludium) is forcing a dark-haired female to writhe and cry out.[26] This rejected plate may be out of our bounds, but it shows the Preludium being generated by an attempt

[24] The time of the guillotine for the King of France, to be succeeded shortly (theme of *Europe A Prophecy*) by the outbreak of war between England and France. For the apocalyptic sword and scales, see Revelation 6:4-5.

[25] The visible effect in most copies of *America* is that the head is gone— or wrenched back into opaque shadow. Grant reports that in a late copy, O, the drawing has been fiddled with to make a sort of face, looking down into the coils (and this can be seen in the Micro Methods transparency of this Fitzwilliam copy). Simmons notes the symbolic economy:
R.E.S.: The "King" is judged, cast through the snake vortex, and then— if you carry the same man through the succeeding plates—emerges as the "renovated" man on top of the ground (*A* 6). Ideally, this is what should happen —change the tyrant, don't replace him. However, this figure is still a "vegetative" fellow, an Adam, not an eternal.
John Grant calls my attention to further evidence of Blake's fascination with the decapitation of a king (and of its dangerous relevance in the 1790's) in a striking change made between the water color and the engraving of *NT* no. 20. The text refers to Death's power "To tread out Empire"; in the drawing (see {86}) Death stands on two royal bodies, one crowned, the other headless but with crown beside severed neck. From his own or his publisher's caution, Blake carefully restored head and crown when he engraved these two kings. People would think of Louis—and George.

[26] It may be these two who appear in pl. 16, the woman in rose. Descending to them is the trumpeter of the first Prophecy page; in this plummeting position he will appear again in *NT* II, 5 (no. 38) and as the title-page angel of *The Grave*.

to illustrate an epic simile. The "son outstretch'd," by turning his head awake, becomes Orc chained to the rock in Preludium 1; the rude assault becomes the symbolic painful-joyous embrace of dumb virgin and fiery youth. And once the Preludium had been designed and written, the first "Prophecy" plate had to be re-designed to change the angle of ascent of the soaring, freed Orc: originally rising from the page, he now can be seen to have sprung from the furrow of Preludium 2.

To return to the central picture, in three further illustrations we are given glimpses of the Atlantic. Urizen in his clouds (plate 8 {36}), but with ocean waves beneath, confronts Orc on the waves, which appear as flames (plate 10 {38}). In plate 13 {41} we see on the watery shore the female in Promethean state and the male sunk to sea bottom. Blake is here using his stage center for the physical-mental horror of war.[27] All the other pictured "visionary forms" are either metaphors of textual detail not in the idiom of the main picture, not located on its stage, or constitute emblems of persons and events quite outside the poem we have been per-ceiving.

By the text, too, we are supplied only a few graphic elements of the single picture, plus a wealth of metaphorical and contrary or ambivalent visionary forms to fill the canvas: so that we are able to see this single dynamic vision in motion and inside out or upside down. For example, in the view that accepts Urizen as a God above all heavens in thunders wrapped, the place of Orc is that of Satan in the abyss. But in the eyes of democrats Urizen is a god of snow and ice and is really just an arbitrary shell harden-ing on the outer surface of mundane life; Orc is not Satan but Christ in the fearful symmetry of his Second Coming (for this was Armageddon); and the Atlantic where he appears is not an abyss but a mountain rising above the abyss of nonentity. In this view Albion and America are not separated by a great gulf but are parts of the base of the Atlantic Mountains. There are many indications that the apparently central image of continents *divided* by an Atlantic deep is a false or temporary image. A more "eter-nal" image is of Atlantean hills, seen as the One Earth of true human geography: a picture of "vast shady hills between America

[27] J.E.G.: For the effect of subsequent horror on female and male bodies, see *J* 58. But in *M* 38 they are shown reunited on a mountainous shore, being awakened rather than tormented by an eagle.

& Albions shore . . . from [whose] bright summits you may pass to the Golden world" (plate 10). It is "Here on their magic seats" that "the thirteen Angels" sit by right, before the divisive behavior of Albion's Prince forces them to come down and side with "warlike men." The Promethean female in plate 13 is the "soul of America," as we know because the picture is a "quotation" from *Visions of the Daughters of Albion*, and her rock must be the mountaintop now sunk to the water's edge.[28]

But finally the central vision is dynamic because *it is going to change*, to *hatch* into a vision of Eternity beyond the flames which are referred to as giving "heat but not light." Observe that the stage is global, not in the usual sense but as the inside of a mundane egg framed by the orbed concave sky and the concave deeps of the sea. Blake's single (but twofold) visualizable picture has a third "fold"—that it can be seen as the seed or egg or embryo of a change beyond the change. Orc is born in fire "o'er the Atlantic sea" (plate 4), but observe that this world of bloody fire is embryonic: "enrag'd the Zenith grew, / As human blood shooting its veins all round the orbed heaven." What look like clouds rising from burning towns, Barlow's Falmouth, Charlestown, Bristol, Groton, Fairfield, Kingston, [New] York, and Norfolk, are really "vast wheels of blood," the veins of a vast embryo.

As the Preludium hinted, this process cannot stop short of a further and more complete metamorphosis. A further or fourfold vision must follow the breaking of the Urizenic shell or, in a cognate image, the throwing down of the spears of the old cold heavens. A new humanity, a new human form of society, is the vision Blake wants us to see *beyond* the revolutionary drama presented on this split stage of the American and British shores of the Atlantic.

Some of the pictured and verbal images of the Prophecy are there to suggest the third or generative view of the central picture, while some are glimpses of the picture beyond the Revolution. The children sleeping with a sheep (plate 7 {35}) are under a tree of paradise (an identification confirmed by specific *Night Thoughts* illustrations, e.g., VI, 23—no. 244) in which sit recognizable birds of paradise.[29]

[28] Suggested by Shelley Goldenberg.

[29] In copy K two of these birds are colored bright red, and that color is repeated in pl. 11 {39} in two similar birds in flight beside the swan and

In other words, when we wind up the thread of the illuminated poem into the golden ball of a single, dynamic, visualizable orb, we are ready to enter into new expanses, through heaven's gate, built in Jerusalem's wall—or, in this instance, through the "breach in the city . . . after the battle." It may be, as Frye says, that Blake "hardly seems to have noticed that he had perfected a radically new form of mixed art." He hardly seems to have cared, any more than he cared to question a window concerning his sight. It mattered little to him whether picture penetrated poem or poem penetrated picture, if only their human, apocalyptic meaning would penetrate our hearts and minds.

A Note on the Mundane Shell

That breach in the city wall is nicely ambiguous, for while Tyranny or Urizen made the breach, attempting to overwhelm the inhabitants and let in the chaotic ocean to devastate a "portion of the infinite," the breach is also a rift in the rock-shell of his tyrannous universe. Note that Urizen dwells outside the human world, above all heavens; and from where he sits the shell or skull of intellectual Life looks like a millstone or a grain of sand.

Once at least when Blake speaks of seeing "a world in a grain of sand" he means a world *inside a translucent grain*. To eyes focusing on its surface, a grain of sand may seem rough and round, the millstone world of Newton's complicated but mechanical universe. But the world inside a grain of sand is what we see when we peer into its interior as if it were one of those Easter eggs with an interior peepshow. It was *America* and other illuminated prophecies that Blake referred to collectively as a grain of sand. "There is a Grain of Sand in Lambeth" (where he wrote these Prophecies) that is "translucent & has many Angles." He "who finds it will find . . . within" the hidden Jerusalem and indeed within each angle "a lovely heaven." But if an

---

above the snake. Their direction of flight is a spiral reverse of the direction in which the swan and the snake are moving, and it suggests a return to paradise that will be made possible by peace. Because of the fires hurled from Albion, the snake is bearing the children inland to safety, and the swan (whose adult rider looks back into the flames) suggests (a) Paul Revere's ride to spread the alarm, (b) the quill of Tom Paine (see *A* 14:15) put to earth-saving use, and, as an illustration of the text of pl. 11, (c) the speech of Boston's Angel (Samuel Adams) carrying the message of disobedience.

informer should see it, i.e., were it seen from Urizen's point of view, such a Watch Fiend would accuse its inhabitants of Sin and Sedition and have them destroyed "in blood of punishment"—again the ambiguity (*J* 37[41]).

For details of the "Concave Earth" and "Mundane Shell" see *Jerusalem* 13; for the hatching human, see illustrations to *Night Thoughts* (nos. 13 and 16 {81, 83}): in no. 13 a winged boy rises like the dawn from a sphere which is at once the earth and an egg.

A Note on the "Orc Cycle"

As history moved on, the Orc that appeared "in the vineyards of red France" (*Europe* 15:2) became Napoleon; by 1804 Blake, instead of humming "ça ira," was arguing that "Resistance & war is the Tyrants gain," that the "iron hand" which "crushed the Tyrants head . . . became a Tyrant in his stead" (*The Grey Monk*). Orc *became* (not the specious Urizenic dragon but) the serpent that Urizen believed him to be. This suggests a very different kind of progression: slave-rebel-tyrant, not to be equated with the cycle in *America* and the *Marriage* of restraint-freedom-restraint-freedom, i.e., slave-rebel-slave-rebel. Northrop Frye wrote a brilliant mythopoeic chapter on the "Orc cycle," and the term is now so current that some people father it upon Blake (Frye, *Symmetry*, ch. 7, esp. pp. 206ff.). Frye ranges through the Lambeth works but with his focus on the *America* pattern. Recent criticism often focuses on the Napoleonic cycle, implying the corruption of revolutionary energy (equated with "power") into tyrannic cruelty. To call this the "Orc cycle" and then read that kind of corruption into *America* is to wander far astray.

The *prophetic* importance of the distinction makes it worth laboring. The cycle of history prophetically examined in *America* and *Europe* is not that of rebellion-vengeance-tyranny; it is of enslavement-liberation-reenslavement, the prophet's concern being how to escape the reenslavement. After the American Revolution the strong let themselves be governed by the weak:

> They are obedient, they resist not, they obey the scourge:
> Their daughters worship terrors and obey the violent:

—to quote Bromion only slightly out of context (*VDA* 1:22-23). The failure of free man to remain free is blamed on his weakness of desire, not vengefulness; politically the people lack vision and sufficient rushing-together; they permit their senses to be shut and their minds manacled. No form of the words revenge or vengeance appears in the Lambeth prophecies, nor does the concept of what we might define as escalation generated by resistance seem to be present. Things do get bloodier at the end of *Europe,* the bard does fling down his harp (but then pick it up again by canceling the lines) in that "sick & drear" quatrain at the end of the *America* Preludium. But Blake sees these as symptoms of a struggle he does not redefine: Nobodaddy is fighting hard to perpetuate hanging and slaughtering, sheep-people put out horns and grow bloodthirsty, the poet grows silent, "asham'd of his own song." But the need is not to draw back but to meet the occasion. Blake *never* advocates violence and terror, but that was not the English problem in the 1790's. He does not use the parable of the French Terror or anything like it. Only much later does the "second Napoleon" (see *Prophet,* 455 [493]) exemplify Jacobin Tyranny—and this is so much against Blake's expectations that he cannot fit it in. "Orc in his triumphant fury" in the *Four Zoas* (vɪɪb 91:21:E395) must have the word "triumphant" erased, but with no replacement.

The subsequent *Grey Monk* formula, developed at or after Felpham and applying to the years after Amiens (after 1801), does focus on, i.e., against, vengeance; yet it, too, cannot accurately be equated to Damon's "formula for all revolutions" (*Dictionary,* s.v. "Orc"). In these later decades what Blake sees and opposes, for Englishmen, is the vengeful attempt to destroy France by war. The way to resist that "iron hand" is not to imitate its career nor to escalate violence but to be seditiously pacifistic: the tear is the "Intellectual Thing" that "can free the World. . . ." In short, Albion's foolish going off to war against Luvah is no consequence of his having danced the dance of throwing-down-muskets in 1780 (see *America,* plate 15 {43} and the captioned engraving *Albion rose* {91}). It is more accurately speaking a nonconsequence of that; Albion has forgotten about casting "swords & spears to earth" and "Giving himself for the Nations."

A recent article by Gerald E. Enscoe, "The Content of Vision: Blake's 'Mental Traveller," *Papers on Language & Literature,* ɪv (1968), 400-413, points out the "danger of missing what the poem is about"—in this case *The Mental Traveller*—inherent in its schematic reading as a mere "instrument through which certain mythic phenomena [predefined as the "Orc-Urizen cycle"] are recorded." Let me quote Enscoe's concluding paragraphs:

> The vision the poem presents is a terrifying one: one recognizes in it the "state" in which many men and women are now living. If the reader is so inclined, he can call it "the fallen world," implying that such a world has a kind of objective existence.

113

He may see it as a representation of reality, and the Orc cycle as a built-in aspect of all human experience in a finite, time-limited world.

To say this is to miss the main point of the poem. Blake has presented an alternative to this world of the male-female struggle for domination. The poem contains in the persona of the mental traveller himself, as well as in the momentary interludes involving the introduction of new life into the cycle, what Herbert Marcuse has called the basic content of most genuine aesthetic activity: the "tabooed images of freedom" which all men retain unconsciously and which the artist is constantly in the process of trying to liberate. Surely this is the alternative to the present reality, this voice speaking from a state that allows men to see beyond present reality that forms the essential content of Blake's vision.

Further discussion of the Orc cycle will be found in notes in the essays by Mitchell, Simmons, and Grant in this volume; see also E. J. Rose, "Blake's Human Insect," *Texas Studies in Literature and Language*, x (1968), 215-232, esp. 217-218.

And see Rose's "Harvest" essay, below, on the visionary use of the seasonal cycle.

6

Europe
"to those ychain'd in sleep"

MICHAEL J. TOLLEY

BLAKE in *Europe,* more overwhelmingly than in *America,* is a prophet of doom. While the Prophecy in each poem ends like a revenge tragedy, with the purging "strife of blood," in *America* we hear Orc's hopeful celebration of the coming liberty. In *Europe* Orc is silent; the whole spirit of the earlier poem is lighter, even joyous. The beings in *Europe,* with the equivocal exception of the nameless shadowy female, seem ignorant of futurity: they are chained by the past, or act blindly in the present. The revolutionary action in the poem is as secret as a time fuse, and works on the same principle.

There are some joyful forms in both the text and the designs of *Europe,* but we find more that are horrific or depressing. Caterpillars and snails feed on the pages; spiders festoon them with their webs; more than forty flies decorate one page; serpents dominate two more. Other illustrations confront us with a lurking assassin and with sufferers from plague, cannibalism, imprisonment, and fiery war. There are angels, but they minister to a scaly warrior-king and a bat-winged pope; there are two fine young nudes, but they blast pestilential hail over their page; another angelic figure clutches the back of her head in terror or despair. Rintrah's clouds swag heavy, and there are several night scenes: oily nudes wrestle in a dark cloudy sky; at the edge of a cliff (perhaps) an old man balefully wards off an unseen threat beyond the blackness. Even a relatively lighthearted scene (*E* 4 {47}) shows, we suspect, a mother meditating incest (Enitharmon with Orc). True lightheartedness is seen only in a few smaller decorative figures. Yet many birds, in unexpected places, aspire upwards, like the one above the appealing small girl on the final page: there is aspiration always, as in *Ah! Sun-Flower,* but little comfort. Perhaps most typical of all *Europe*'s denizens is the

115

pathetic girl on page 12, meshed by spider-threads, who, out of her despair, prays, her face turned upward. (See {50}.)

Constituting an anatomy of the corruption of Blake's Europe, a dreamworld in which one finds "every man bound," the designs begin in mathematical creation and end in flames of Armageddon —with no visible line of progress from one to the other. Perhaps we are to see what Blake shows us in the *America* text: that plagues recoil upon the tyrants who hurl them; that the serpents and spiders poison and the caterpillars eventually fret away "the paind heavens."[1]

Rich in allusion, simple in outline, grand in the sublime tradition of painting, the frontispiece, envisioning the creator as a windswept old man who kneels in a sun that breaks through clouds to set his compasses on the void beneath, expresses a fundamental protest against the theodicy of Blake's time. While the design stands independent of *Europe* in conception, it is fittingly placed to introduce this poem, and may even have germinated its basic idea. To the right of the pencil sketch on page 96 of the *Notebook* are the words "who shall bind / the Infinite," a crucial phrase in the *Europe* Preludium. This *Notebook* sketch is in close association with others used for *Europe*; it is dated by Keynes as pre-1793. Whether or not Blake had *Europe* already in mind when he drew the sketch, his application to it of a key question from the poem shows how ironically he viewed the creator's attempted circumscription of the unbounded abyss.

The design is a crystallization of many images. Several eighteenth-century Bibles include an illustration of the compasses when outlining the seven days of creation. These compasses derive

[1] Most of the really good work on *Europe* has been done in Erdman, *Prophet*, esp. chs. 9 and 12. I take for granted the reader's awareness of Erdman's discussion, also knowledge of Damon's commentary, *Philosophy*, 342-351. Damon gives most of the Cumberland inscriptions in the British Museum copy of *E* (copy D in *Census*); I am grateful for new readings supplied by J. E. Grant and sorry there is no space here to present them fully. Damon was convinced that Blake was "directly responsible for their insertion," but I prefer to treat each motto according to its merits.

As we go to press it is good to hear that the Blake Trust facsimile of *Europe* has been published by Trianon Press; Grant reports that an exhibition in Manchester showing original and facsimile pages side by side proved the latter amazingly accurate. (Most of the *Europe* plates in the present volume are from the copy I have worked with, copy I in the Auckland Public Library.)

from Proverbs 8:27 (Blake's image may also have been shaped partly by the words of the following verse, with its reference to "the clouds above" and "the deep"), but the major source for Blake must be Milton's account of the creation in *Paradise Lost*, Book VII.[2] It seems that Blake's systematically diabolic method of reading sacred works came into play here: Milton's creator is the Son, but we are carefully informed that he was "Girt with Omnipotence" and other attributes, "and all his Father in him shone" (VII, 194-196). Thus, ironically enough, Milton warrants the Jehovahlike appearance of Blake's creator. Blake, under the shadow of Newton's mathematical pantocrator, could see the creator only as an old Urizen, not as a vigorous young man. In the *Marriage*, Blake had defined the Miltonic creation as an account of the rational power's exhibition of God as a circle of destiny ("in Milton, the Father is Destiny, the Son, a Ratio of the five senses"). The compasses of this ratio form the circular horizon which limits man, spatially and mentally, hence Blake's name for the creator, Urizen, who in *The Book of Urizen*, chapter VII, characteristically "formed golden compasses / And began to explore the Abyss" before planting the garden of Eden. Blake's way of showing men that the Miltonic-Newtonic creator their reason accepts as God is only a projection of their guilty fears was to labor with loving care a definitive image of this creator as Urizen. Once clearly seen, he believed, this image must be rejected as blasphemous error.

Europe 2:14-16

In the Preludium to *Europe*, the nameless shadowy female ends her complaint with the words:

> And who shall bind the infinite with an eternal band?
> To compass it with swaddling bands? and who shall cherish it
> With milk and honey?
> I see it smile & I roll inward & my voice is past.

Blake's phrasing suggests that he had in mind here three accounts of the creation, which we must add to the two already discussed. One of these comes in *Paradise Lost*, Book III. Explaining the creation to Satan, Uriel says (710-711):

[2] See also Martin K. Nurmi, "Blake's 'Ancient of Days' and Motte's Frontispiece to Newton's *Principia*," in *The Divine Vision*, ed. V. de S. Pinto, London, 1957, 207-216. The Cumberland inscription quotes *PL* II, 226-231.

Confusion heard his voice, and wild uproar
Stood rul'd, stood vast infinitude confin'd. . . .

Blake's phrase uses the same paradox. Further, in his previous stanza Blake seems to have reshaped, in terms of the relationship between the nameless shadowy female and Enitharmon, another idea from the same passage in Milton, echoing the captive stars of lines 716 through 721 in his "myriads of flames" that are stamped with Enitharmon's signet. Milton's idea in line 721 of the stars "in circuit" walling the universe is one worthy of Urizen, though the idea is more closely related to the Covering Cherub or the mundane shell in Blake's later mythic weaving.

Another account of the creation that obviously lies behind Blake's words is that of Job 38. Verse 31 has a phrase similar rhetorically to Blake's "who shall bind the infinite," viz. "Canst thou bind the sweet influences of Pleiades, or loose the bands of Orion?"[3] Job 38:9 has Blake's image of swaddling bands: "When I made . . . thick darkness a swaddlingband for [the sea]." The image of the compass in Blake's "To compass it with swaddling bands" may well come from Proverbs 8:27. The third creation account is one that may have suggested the Job references to Blake, stanza XII in Milton's Hymn from *On the Morning of Christ's Nativity*: in that stanza Milton takes most of his imagery from Job 38, and Blake was closely engaged with Milton's poem, as I shall show later.

However this may be, the conclusion of Blake's questions makes it clear that he is talking about more than compassing the depth. The words "and who shall cherish it / With milk and honey?" seem to recall the food to be given to Immanuel in Isaiah 7:15: "Butter and honey shall he eat, that he may know to refuse the evil and choose the good." Perhaps Blake specified milk rather than butter to emphasize his theme of maternal domination. The "swaddling bands" are of course the "swaddling clothes" of Luke 2. Milton also, in the Nativity Hymn, mentions Christ's "swadling bands," presenting the paradox of Christ's physical weakness and spiritual power:

[3] Dennis Douglas originally gave me the reference to Job 38:31, in correspondence. Cf., besides Blake's *Job* 14 {114}, *FZ* II 24:6, 9; VIII 103:8; *J* 60:60; *Then she bore* . . . ; and *Paradise Lost* VII, 374f.

Our Babe to show his Godhead true,
Can in his swadling bands controul the damned crew.

(227-228)

Further, the nameless shadowy female sees the Infinite "smile," taking up Milton's presentation of the Babe as lying in "smiling Infancy" (151). But Blake's Babe smiles in conscious triumph.

Milton's Hymn helps us to see that the questions of the nameless shadowy female here are oracular; indeed, the first two are rhetorical. She knows that it is impossible to "bind the infinite with an eternal band": this is a contradiction in terms. The birth of Christ represented the crucial challenge to Urizen's compasses: by circling Him tight round with swaddling bands, by the very milk of His mother's breast, Urizen and Enitharmon, forces of mortality, attempted to control the Infinite.

Annotating Swedenborg's *Divine Love*, Blake wrote, "When the fallacies of darkness are in the circumference they cast a bound about the infinite." In *The Marriage of Heaven and Hell* he asserted that "Energy is the only life . . . and Reason is the bound or outward circumference of Energy." The infinite will find its own form, which can never be imposed successfully from without; energy must find its own reasonable bound. *Europe* is, structurally, an analysis of what happens when an attempt is made, on a global scale, to marshal energy under reason. The final result is the explosion of Armageddon: as Blake saw it in political terms, the war between the allied forces of established government and priestcraft and the revolutionary armies of self-liberating people. The birth of Jesus was the turning point in the struggle. Milton celebrated this in terms of Christ's victory over the various pagan gods; Blake restated the nature of Christ's achievement and redefined the demons with whom Christ contended. But throughout *Europe* we find Blake looking very closely at Milton's Hymn, and it is not going too far to say that *Europe* is primarily a reworking of Milton's poem to fit Blake's understanding of the significance of the events Milton celebrated.

The Secret Child

Several commentators have remarked upon the similarity between the first words of the Prophecy proper and the first words of Milton's Hymn proper. Formally, Blake's Preludium echoes Milton's first four stanzas, which act as an introduction to the Hymn. It is unthinkable that Blake could have designated his work a "Hymn," and his choice of the term "Prophecy" in itself demonstrates the deep difference between Milton's approach, celebrating the holy birth, and Blake's, using the birth as the foundation for a threatening prophecy.

In his opening to "A Prophecy," besides making use of obvious verbal parallels, Blake echoes the meter of the opening three lines of Milton's stanza form, though he makes the third line an alexandrine, as if to assert (having once for all indicated his source to the reader) his own emancipation. He also carefully avoids the rhyme, rephrasing Milton's first line in his own version. Blake begins:

> The deep of winter came:
> What time the secret child,
> Descended thro' the orient gates of the eternal day:
> War ceas'd, & all the troops like shadows fled to their abodes.

Compare the first lines of Milton's Hymn proper:

> It was the Winter wilde,
> While the Heav'n-born-childe,
> All meanly wrapt in the rude manger lies. . . .
>
> (29-31)

(Oddly enough, Blake mollifies his departure from Milton by substituting the more Miltonic locution, "What time," for Milton's own "While.") Earlier in Milton's poem is the phrase "Forsook the Courts of everlasting Day" (13), which suggested Blake's "eternal day," while Blake's gates may come from a later passage where, speaking of Truth, Justice, and Mercy descending, Milton suggests that "Heav'n . . . / Will open wide the Gates of her high Palace Hall" (147f.). The fact that Blake's gates are "orient," and the detail of the troops fleeing like shadows to their abodes, are suggested by Milton's lines where the sun

> Pillows his chin upon an Orient wave,
> The flocking shadows pale,
> Troop to th' infernall jail. . . .
>
> (231-233)

120

Both Blake and Milton, though Blake more closely, draw here also upon Song of Solomon 2:17 and 4:6, verses which both begin: "Until the day break, and the shadows flee away." Blake again follows Milton (and a more general tradition) when he notes that "War ceas'd" (see 52-54). Finally, it has even been thought that Blake's word "secret" comes from the last line of Milton's prelude to the Hymn: "From out his secret Altar toucht with hallow'd fire." Be this as it may, Blake's phrase "secret child" suggests most particularly the secret circumstances of Christ's birth. In Matthew 2 we read how Jesus was hidden from Herod by angelic intervention. But it is surely no coincidence that the last line of Blake's Preludium also, with Milton, refers to a "secret" place:

> She ceast & rolld her shady clouds
> Into the secret place.

The nameless shadowy female is a kind of personified womb in the Preludium to *Europe* (her words "My roots are brandish'd in the heavens" may describe the placenta). On her appearance in the *America* Preludium, she is described as "Invulnerable tho' naked, save where clouds roll round her loins" (1:7), and Orc's rape of her is described in these terms:

> Round the terrific loins he siez'd the panting struggling
>   womb;
> It joy'd: she put aside her clouds & smiled her first-born
>   smile. . . .   (2:3-4)[4]

Her "secret place" is thus the place of generation. The secrecy of Jesus does not however seem to refer to his birth from the womb, an interpretation which would clash with the poetical symbolism of the third line. Rather, it seems to me that Blake drew attention to the secrecy with which the infant Jesus was surrounded, in

---

[4] Superficially, the nameless shadowy female in *Europe* and the shadowy daughter of Urthona in *America* are not identical. Bloom, *Apocalypse*, 146, considers that in *Europe* "she is one stage further onwards in the sorrow of the natural cycle." Blake's view of the female's function shifted later, probably in accordance with his more sinister reading of the generative process. When he recapitulates the *America* Preludium in *FZ* viib 91, the "nameless shadowy Vortex" becomes Orc's seducer and is identified as Vala. She even tends to supplant Enitharmon as propagator of false religions (*FZ* viii 103:22). She has an important speech in *M* 18.

order to account for the lies Enitharmon was able to spread about his birth and his mission. The secrecy, like the swaddling bands, becomes another weapon in the hands of the restrainers. Thus, seeing her opportunity, Enitharmon rejoices (E 5):

> Now comes the night of Enitharmons joy!
> Who shall I call? Who shall I send?
> That Woman, lovely Woman! may have dominion?
> Arise O Rintrah thee I call! & Palamabron thee!
> Go: tell the human race that Womans love is Sin:
> That an Eternal life awaits the worms of sixty
>   winters
> In an allegorical abode where existence hath never
>   come:
> Forbid all Joy, & from her childhood shall the little
>   female
> Spread nets in every secret path.

Blake had earlier (1789) objected to those who "suppose that Womans love is Sin. in consequence all the Loves & Graces with them are Sin," when annotating Lavater's *Aphorisms* (E 590). Enitharmon's injunction, "Go: tell the human race that Womans love is Sin," an attempt to restrict men and women by making them fear moral condemnation unless their union is legitimized by priest and king (Palamabron and Rintrah), perhaps draws fuel from the notion of the virgin birth. If the normal process of generation be considered insufficiently holy for God's son, who had to be, according to Milton, "Of wedded Maid, and Virgin Mother born" (3), then logically "Womans love is Sin." Blake's own careful avoidance of a reference to the fleshly processes of birth in *Europe* 3:3 does not contradict Enitharmon's reading. Enitharmon seems also to be deliberately perverting Christ's offer of a more abundant life (as in John 10:10) to one of "pie in the sky when you die," aiming here to make men feel that what happens in this life can be endured, to postpone fatally all thoughts of revolutionizing the present system.[5]

[5] Blake was a devout believer in the possibility of a heavenly life after death: his communion with Robert is a token of this. His attack in *Europe* (as in *Ah! Sun-Flower*) is against the false doctrinal emphasis on future rewards and punishments which tends to keep man timid and a tame prisoner of the shadowy life on earth. Enitharmon has a gift for twisting Blake's most

Oothoon

Europe 3 {46} is dominated by a large winged female figure who floats from left to right across the page. Her hands are clasped behind her head, her face hidden by her hair, which hangs down below her head in four wavy locks. Her arms and left leg are bare; her waist is girdled. Perhaps from the girdle extends a curiously long thick tail of fabric, passing between her knees and calves, and out below her ankles, ending in a truncated *s* curve, like a reversed question mark. This tail of cloth has a marked resemblance to the trailing intestines on the bat-winged foetus at the bottom of *Europe* 1. (Also see below, p. 208 n.)

Following Cumberland's mottoes, from passages in Rowe, Milton, Homer, and Shakespeare, this figure has been traditionally identified as an ominous comet, in Damon's words "shaking the evils, which she presages, from her hair." Blake's comets in the *Night Thoughts* series (nos. 149 and 313) are very different from the *Europe* figure, and the mottoes given by Cumberland do not adequately describe her, yet I am inclined to grant that they help define her role and so, perhaps, her identity. Although the nameless shadowy female is, in the immediate context of the poem, the obvious candidate for the role (her appearance apart), typologically the figure looks more likely to be Oothoon, as depicted in *Visions of the Daughters of Albion* and particularly in *Milton* 42.[6] Oothoon's appearance over the shores of Albion at the end

---

valuable insights. Thus in *FZ* II 34 she has a "delusive" speech in which she perverts the meaning both of a favorite dictum of Blake's and, shifting her ground, of the Nativity again:

> Arise you little glancing wings & sing your infant joy
> Arise & drink your bliss
> For every thing that lives is holy for the source of life
> Descends to be a weeping babe
> For the Earthworm renews the moisture of the sandy plain
>
> (34:78-82)

In Enitharmon's book, Christ's coming sanctified life (sc. mortal life) and so all life (sc. all mortal life) is holy. She conveniently ignores Christ's desire to awaken man to life (eternal). In *Jerusalem*, the doctrinal value of the incarnation for Blake is as a sign of God's forgiveness of man, as in *J* 7:65-67, 27:57-64, for instance.

[6] In *VDA* Oothoon's general appearance as a youthful woman with flowing hair is similar to that of the winged *Europe* figure. Though not so pictured, Oothoon is described as "wing'd" in *VDA* 1:14. I am aware that the

of *Visions* could more plausibly be described as cometlike than it is here, which is probably a sign of Blake's growing conviction that European soil is less favorable than American to the growth of liberty. Oothoon, "the soft soul of America" (*VDA* 1:3), emblem of independence, is a fearful portent to the European powers, and her future depends on the struggle in Europe between re-actionaries and revolutionaries. The winged figure seems to be protecting her neck with her hands, a sign that she fears decapita-tion.[7] In *Europe* itself Oothoon is, apart from Orc, the only re-bellious child of Enitharmon, directly opposed as she is to Enithar-mon's key principle of secrecy (*E* 14:21-25).

The hunched child inside a flaming circle that floats below the tresses of the flying woman is even more intriguing. Possible identities abound. Damon apparently sees here one of Homer's "sparkles" shot from the comet's hair, which may have been Cum-berland's fancy. Blake's text on this page refers to Enitharmon's sons and daughters, who "rise around / Like pearly clouds." Again, Blake could have been influenced by the stars in Milton's Hymn that "in their glimmering Orbs did glow" (75). It is very likely that the child is an illustration of the nameless shadowy female's "vig'rous progeny of fires." But from its position in the design, Blake must surely have intended us to relate this child to "the secret child" in the first lines of the poem, which "Descended thro' the orient gates of the eternal day." Because of the child's sullen

---

typological problem is complicated by Oothoon's resemblance to Enitharmon, to Earth, to Eve, and to other Blakean women. Posture can be misleading, as it is in *A* 1, where a figure who must be Enitharmon according to the line of Blake's myth looks very like the Oothoon of *VDA* 6. However, the help given us by *VDA* and *M* 42 in identifying the *Europe* figure as an Oothoon-type is not likely to be misleading. The whole problem will be more fully discussed elsewhere.

Another curious question is the relationship of Blake's winged figure to a similar one by Fuseli, the subject of a water color now in the British Museum Print Room (1885-3-14-200). The Fuseli work is untitled and, as far as I know, undated, though Paul Ganz dates it 1808 (*The Drawings of Henry Fuseli*, London, 1949, pl. 106). Ganz describes the design as "The spirit of Night; grasping her hair, the spirit flies across a dark, cloudy sky." Fuseli's figure flies from right to left, and her head is drawn up and back, but the wings are similar to those of Blake's figure. Perhaps this is a case of Fuseli's finding Blake "damned good to steal from"; perhaps they share a common ancestry.

[7] See Erdman, *Prophet*, 188-189 [205], and above, p. 108.

(and so sinister) appearance, one is inclined to fend off the suggestion that it is the infant Jesus, but the proposal must be faced. The child covers the lower half of its face, and this could be read as a sign of secrecy. It appears, however, not through the gates of dawn, but through a dark vaginalike opening in the clouds (cf. that in *A* 14 {42} particularly). The opening lines of Blake's Prophecy and this "burning babe" seem equally to be in ironic counterpoint to the Nativity celebrated by Milton. With the birth of Jesus, the spirit of desire (to recall the terms of Blake's *Marriage*) was reborn, incarnated in the fiery form of Orc (with whom we must identify the encircled child), to provide no cause for angelic rejoicing. Blake must surely also intend us to see Orc as emerging from a vortex at the opposite pole from that in which Urizen appears on the frontispiece. Orc's small circle, though formed by Urizen's compasses, is fittingly in flames; the child within waits to leap out.

The Peaceful Night

The opening lines of the Prophecy proper suggest that the secret child comes with the dawn. It is surprising, therefore, that we should move immediately into evening: "Now comes the night of Enitharmons joy!" The time of approaching night is stressed by Blake. Los, we are told, "joy'd in the peaceful night," and this echoes Milton's words in the Hymn:

> But peacefull was the night
> Wherein the Prince of light
> His raign of peace upon the earth began. . . .
>
> (61-63)

Blake, while wishing to preserve some essential features of Milton's time scheme, extends and alters it. Milton, though he refers both to Creation and Last Judgment, confines his immediate narrative to the night of Christ's birth and the dawn that follows. In the course of this peaceful night, the pagan gods feel the power of "The dredded Infants hand" and are all ready to flee at sunrise. But Blake's night lasts "Eighteen hundred years." Thereby he suggests that the first and second coming are essentially one, that the Nativity is not effectually completed till eighteen hundred years are past, but that an important change did begin to take effect even from the first coming. The birth was like the sowing of a seed, which will grow underground in secret, will even "die," in the words of St. John, but continues to grow whatever evil appears openly above ground.[8]

This change, however, is marked by such odd signs that it is not surprising that Blake's commentators as well as Enitharmon have been misled by them. The fact that night comes immediately after dawn has been announced looks ominous. Enitharmon and her crew rejoice, thinking they are in command of the situation. There are pointed contrasts with the situation in Milton's Hymn. Milton's Nature, the obvious counterpart of Enitharmon, hid "her guilty front with innocent Snow" and "doff't her gawdy trim." Milton says

> It was no season then for her
> To wanton with the Sun her lusty Paramour.
>
> (35-36)

Blake, no doubt, approved the sentiment, but he himself asserts that Enitharmon did wanton with the Sun, that is to say, with Los, "possessor of the moon" (*E* 3:7), an obvious antonomasia. Enitharmon, or possibly Los (the syntax is ambiguous),[9] misreads another ominous sign:

---

[8] John 12:24. Mark 4:26-29 practically gives the program for the action of *Europe*, with even a suggestion of Enitharmon's sleep. Blake was so steeped in biblical patterns of thought and action that his own patterns were often, naturally, emanations of the biblical ones. It was not for nothing that he described the Bible as the Great Code of Art.

[9] *E* 3:9-4:14 is treated by Keynes as a single speech. Erdman (E725) distinguishes three speakers: "Los (3:9-14), the envious sons of Urizen (4:3-9), and Enitharmon (4:10-14)." Erdman takes 4:1f. as narrative, but the evidence I cite from Milton's Hymn makes it more natural for these lines to be part of the speech begun in 3:9. The possibility that all the lines should be given to Enitharmon has not been considered previously, but it is syntactically possible and an easier reading. The reference to "his num'rous sons" in 3:8 makes Los the more natural speaker, but the attribution to Los makes the prior mention of Enitharmon somewhat purposeless and the whole speech sounds awkward in his mouth. One can ignore the full stop at the end of line 5 (it could possibly be meant as a comma). Giving the speech to Enitharmon clarifies the reference to "strong Urthona" in 3:10, which would come oddly from Los (who *is* Urthona, essentially). The words at the end of the poem, on Los's reappearance, "Then Los arose" (15:9), may mean that he awoke after sleeping, giving point to 3:7, 10.

D.V.E.: Well, there *is* a syntactical difficulty, although this is an attractive suggestion. The first words spoken are introduced, in 3:7-8, thus: "Los . . .

And Urizen unloos'd from chains
Glows like a meteor in the distant north
Stretch forth your hands and strike the elemental strings!
Awake the thunders of the deep,
The shrill winds wake!

The intention is obviously to contradict stanza v of Milton's
Hymn, where

> The Windes with wonder whist
> Smoothly the waters kist,
> Whispering new joyes to the milde Ocean,
> Who now hath quite forgot to rave. . . .
>
> (64-67)[10]

Urizen's appearance in the role of Lucifer should have warned
Enitharmon off, as the stars are warned in the Nativity Hymn,
but Enitharmon apparently sees Urizen only as a competitor in
the task of binding the joys of life. However, that Urizen is "unloos'd from chains" I take as a reference to Revelation 20:7f.,
where we are told that "Satan shall be loosed out of his prison,
And shall go out to deceive the nations which are in the four
quarters of the earth, Gog and Magog, to gather them together
to battle." Certainly this is effectively Urizen's role in *Europe*; he
is loosed only that he may gather the nations together for Armageddon.

As Urizen, spirit of repression, is unloosed, it follows that Orc,
Urizen's opposite, must be bound, and we find Enitharmon immediately calling up the bound Orc to rejoice over him "in the

---

joy'd . . . / Thus speaking while his . . . sons shook their bright fiery wings."
Don't "speaking" and "his" refer back to Los? And if we are to suppose
Enitharmon speaking, the normal Blakean meaning of the image of the
sons' fiery wings disappears: the poet's works displayed their bright pages,
i.e., Los uttered the following Illuminated Prophecy. Or do you take it that
Enitharmon speaks while Los's sons illuminate?

[10] The same stanza has referred to "the Prince of Light" beginning his
reign of peace upon earth. This title of Christ is also Urizen's in *FZ*, and
most naturally belongs to Lucifer. Thus there is irony in Urizen's arrival
as a meteor, usurping Christ's role here just as he blasphemously usurps his
title elsewhere. Urizen's place is in the north to parallel Satan's in *Paradise
Lost*, Book v, where his royal seat is described as "far blazing" (755ff.), while
in Book ii Satan "like a Comet burn'd"—in the passage (708ff.) suggested
by Cumberland as related to the design on this page of *Europe*.

127

hour of bliss" (E 4:10-14). This page, *Europe* 4 {47}, shows Enitharmon playfully lifting the coverlet from the bed on which Orc, with radiant head, lies sleeping. She wishes to play with the captive Orc as the Philistines played with Samson: the analogy indicates the nature of her error.[11] Simultaneously, Blake is probably mocking lines in Milton's poem, in a spirit similar to that of the *Marriage*. In lines 167 through 170 Milton rejoices that

> . . . from this happy day
> Th' old Dragon under ground
> In straiter limits bound,
> Not half so far casts his usurped sway. . . .

—Orc or *orcus*, the old dragon, being feared by timid or perverted minds. (Blake presents Orc as a young Cupid in order to correct this reactionary notion. He warns us instead to look out for old Urizen-Lucifer, who is quietly exercising his starry influences over us, unchallenged.)

Enitharmon goes on to call up her other children, who represent, basically, different attitudes of mind, the forces which help to keep men self-bound or (in Oothoon's case) cause them to rebel. Rintrah and Palamabron are enrolled as Enitharmon's chief assistants. They represent the limiting authority of king and priest. Rintrah is portrayed in *Europe* 6 as a scaly warrior-king, Palamabron in *Europe* 11 as a bat-winged pope. Both are described in terms that partly echo biblical phrases. Rintrah is asked to "Bring Palamabron horned priest, skipping upon the mountains." The latter phrase, no doubt intentionally ludicrous, is a contraction

[11] The Cupid-Psyche suggestion of this design has a similar moral: it is not safe for a Female Will to take a young Eros for granted, as if he were her toy. The Cumberland motto for this design seems to have reference only to the various figures in the background. As Damon notes (p. 349), the first of these lines is from Dryden's *Aeneis* VI, 409. The following couplet, however, is from Dryden's *Metamorphoses* 8 ("Meleager and Atalanta"), lines 316f. Cumberland's immediate source is Bysshe, whose attribution is incomplete. As John E. Grant has pointed out to me in correspondence, some of the forms below the text resemble others in *VDA*. We can identify two at the left as Bromion and Oothoon, from their positions at the bottom of *VDA* 1, after the rape. To the left of these, the pensive figure resembles one (reversed) above and to the left of the rainbow on the *VDA* title page. The two embracing figures at right are in the spirit of the dancers in the rainbow, or the embracing couples on the *MHH* title page. They are all, evidently, younger sons and daughters of Enitharmon.

of part of Song of Solomon 2:8, "The voice of my beloved! behold, he cometh leaping upon the mountains, skipping upon the hills." One remembers that the Song of Solomon was read as an allegory of Christ and his church and that the priest should be Christ's representative. But his horns suggest that he is more closely allied to the devil. Blake alludes to the two horns of the mitre, which were symbolic of the horns of Moses.[12] Enitharmon sees Rintrah as "Prince of the sun," accompanied by his "innumerable race" of warriors, "Thick as the summer stars," each ramping and shaking "his golden mane," while Rintrah's own eyes "rejoice because of strength" (8:8-12). Though Rintrah is "lion Rintrah" (8:2), her words recall the description of a war-horse in Job 39:21, who "rejoiceth in his strength," as well as the description of the sun in Psalms 19:4f., which "rejoiceth as a strong man to run a race." Palamabron, who generally represents Pity, thus seems effeminate on his first appearance, in contrast to Rintrah (Wrath), and Blake uses biblical allusion to point the contrast.

After calling up Rintrah and Palamabron, Enitharmon, giving us very little warning ("My weary eyelids draw towards the evening"), falls asleep for eighteen hundred years (*E* 9:1-5). The course of history becomes a "female dream" as Enitharmon's plans are enforced. For Enitharmon, "Man was a Dream!" But as Blake puts it we are made to feel that this was not only her illusion: after eighteen hundred years have passed, Enitharmon still "laugh'd in her sleep to see (O womans triumph) / Every house a den, every man bound" by commandments such as "Thou shalt not commit adultery" and "thou shalt not covet thy neighbour's wife" (Exodus 20:14,17). Such commandments acted as mental chains, restricting the fulfillment of desire except in secret. Men became, in effect, sleepwalkers, never allowing themselves to be fully awake and alive.[13] However, Enitharmon could not see beyond her own dream; had not reckoned with the secret process of revolt initiated by Jesus the law-breaker, which continues to feed the spirit of

[12] In Exodus 34:29f. and 35 the Vulgate gave Moses horns, an error avoided by the Authorized Version, but springing from an ambiguity in the Hebrew, as Blake doubtless was aware.

[13] Blake at this time considered that wisdom might come through satiety but not through abstinence. Besides the Proverbs of Hell, his provocative view of the golden age in *The Book of Los* 3:7-26 offers a contrast to Enitharmon's scheme of deprivation that should help to explain Blake's objection to the commandments.

Orc. Blake does not stop to explain the process, but takes us immediately to the time just before the dawn, when Enitharmon will awake, aroused by Newton, who blows the last trump (13:5-10). It takes time for Newton's influence to be felt, and there are other signs of awakening in the American War of Independence, the French Revolution, and the succeeding events in London as Pitt fights for power, deposing Thurlow (who receives special treatment by Blake in *E* 12:14-20), and prepares, as an extreme reactionary, to engage in the war of Armageddon.

Blake seems to have taken the hint for his broad sequence of events from stanza XVI of Milton's Hymn. Milton says that before Christ can come "himself and us to glorifie":

> Yet first to those ychain'd in sleep,
> The wakefull trump of doom must thunder through the
> deep. . . .   (155-156)

By "those ychain'd in sleep" Milton means the dead, but Blake saw that the phrase could apply just as well (in fact more properly, as we have seen) to the living. It can also apply just as well to Enitharmon as to the "Shadows of men in fleeting bands" who "Divide the heavens of Europe" (9:6f.) or to the citizens, suburban dwellers, and villagers more obviously bound (12:29-31). That Enitharmon should have been put to sleep at the birth of Christ represents a most subtle triumph: her power is suspended in the midst of her schemes: she is allowed only to project them. Before Christ's birth Enitharmon had open control: though she cannot be so narrowly identified, she was worshiped principally as Venus (as Los is the blacksmith Vulcan, and Orc their son is Cupid). Although she has succeeded in delegating some powers to Rintrah and Palamabron (who combat Orc in 12:22-24), she has effectually lost control. Orc's revolt takes her completely by surprise.[14]

Famine, Pestilence, War, Imprisonment, Fire

Though the night was peaceful for Enitharmon, the shadows in her dream of eighteen hundred years suffered the range of miseries possible to mortal men. The function of many of the illustrations is to give visible form to those miseries. *Europe* 6, a full-page design labeled "Famine" by Cumberland, shows two

---

[14] Blake views Christ's essential triumph in similar terms in *To Tirzah*, probably written after *Europe* (E722).

women preparing to feed on a dead child. A cauldron boiling over a fire dominates the design. Neither woman is noticeably lean, and the one at right looks positively plump and conspicuously wears a pearl necklace.[15]

Two designs show the effects of plague. *Europe* 7, another full-page design, is labeled "Plague" by Cumberland; his motto refers to the bellman who walks grimly past the door of a plague-stricken house (Damon, *Philosophy*, 350). Before the door, one woman appeals to heaven for the mercy the door demands (it is inscribed "LORD [H]AVE MERC[Y] / ON US"); another, seated on the ground, seems already stricken. She is supported by a man, who shares her anguish. *Europe* 9 is a surprisingly attractive page, considering the subject of the illustration: two nude spirits literally blasting a harvest. Inside stems that curve in a large *S* around the text, young male and female spirits blow serpentine trumpets from which dark pestilential flakes fall over the page and particularly over the dying ears of what I take to be barley. Other commentators identify the plant as wheat, but the long whiskers on the ears suggest barley rather, except perhaps in copy K. Blake could have had in mind specifically one of the plagues of Egypt (Exodus 9:31): "And the flax and the barley was smitten: for the barley was in the ear, and the flax was bolled." Since on other pages Blake includes flies and other insects reminiscent of the Egyptian plagues (perhaps even a locust on a grain stem, in *Europe* 4), such a reference would be germane to his purpose. The pestilence on the present page suggests the "hail" of Exodus 9:18ff., and, indeed, a text on this same page shows that Blake had Egypt in mind here. We read that "Albions Angel smitten with his own plagues fled with his bands" (9:8), which recalls the climax of *America*, where Albion's Angel gives "the thunderous command," whereupon

> His plagues obedient to his voice flew forth out of their
> clouds

---

[15] Written above the design in copy D is the pencil heading "Famine," and at right is another pencil inscription, "Preparing to dress the Child." Similar children are in *A* 11, *Holy Thursday* (*Experience*), and above the text in *NT* I, 8 (no. 13). John E. Grant points out that the sorrowing woman at left resembles the praying statue at the end of *America*. Janet Warner mentions the pearls in *Blake Newsletter*, II (1969), 60. See Erdman, *Prophet*, ch. 12, n. 15 of rev. edn. See also note 21, below.

Falling upon America, as a storm to cut them off
As a blight cuts the tender corn when it begins to
  appear. . . .
Then had America been lost, o'erwhelm'd by the
  Atlantic,
And Earth had lost another portion of the infinite,
But all rush together in the night in wrath and raging
  fire
The red fires rag'd! the plagues recoil'd! then rolld they
  back with fury
On Albions Angels; then the Pestilence began in streaks
  of red
Across the limbs of Albions Guardian, the spotted plague
  smote Bristols
And the Leprosy Londons Spirit, sickening all their
  bands. . . .   (*A* 14:4-6, 17-20; 15:1-3)

Though the parallel with Egypt is not exact, the Egyptian pattern, of a despotic Pharaoh imposing slavery on his people and then himself suffering all the effects of plague before the people could be liberated, is close to that in *Europe, America*, and chapter III of *The Book of Urizen*.[16] This kind of imagery goes back to *Tiriel* 5 (E279), a reference essential to our understanding of the *Europe* 8 design. Tiriel leaves home with Hela after cursing his sons and daughters. In Blake's account of the effects of the curse there is a patent suggestion of Egypt. One of the *Tiriel* illustrations shows an Egyptian pyramid in the background ("Tiriel Supporting Myratana," plate 1 in Bentley's edition). *Europe* 8 {49} is a variant of another *Tiriel* illustration, "Tiriel Denouncing his Four Sons and Five Daughters" (Bentley's plate 6). In *Europe* 8, Blake uses only two of the ten figures, the old denunciator and one of his daughters, who kneels in front of him clasping his

[16] Note also *FR* 209f. In *U* 4:41-49 the name given by the children of Urizen to the "pendulous earth" is Egypt. Blake would have been alive to the irony in Deuteronomy 28, where Moses-Jehovah threatens law-breakers with the same curses as were suffered by the Egyptians under Pharaoh. Note esp. verse 22, to which Blake refers in *A* 16:20f. This passage at the end of *America* is an anticipation of the main narrative in *Europe*; *A* 16:15 forecasts *E* 15:2. Blake frequently illustrated the subject of plague or pestilence; see the four designs listed in Keynes, *Bible*, under no. 38 and especially the horrific *Pestilence—the Death of the First-Born*, no. 39.

thighs, head bowed. (Elsewhere, he uses the group of four sons separately, in the design best known as *Our End is Come.*) The old man in *Europe* is given a longer beard than Tiriel's, and the figures are reversed: the old man now appears not so much to denounce as to ward off an invisible evil and the girl appears to cling to her father for protection, not to plead with him. But with *Tiriel* as a check, these appearances do not convincingly alter the original nature of the design. We can interpret the girl as a type of Oothoon or Hela, or simply a daughter of Albion pleading with the father-figure. He himself must be Albion's guardian angel, simultaneously denouncing the Americans and warding off the clouds of pestilence he himself has provoked with his curses. He is described as "ancient" in *Europe* 10:24, and in the canceled plate *c* of *America* we find the Angels of Albion, once armed, described collectively as "a frowning shadow, like an aged King in arms of gold," whose "white beard wav'd in the wild wind" (24-27). Another relevant passage is *America* 15:6-8. The suggestion in the design that the man is looking to the left or westward, standing on an eastern shore, strengthens the identification.[17]

Europe 13 shows us the horror of imprisonment, grotesquely exaggerated by the pockmarked jailor, who retreats up the stone stairway at the right, taking a giant stride and holding two huge keys on a ring in his right hand. In the Fitzwilliam copy K,

[17] Though one cannot be sure whether left is west in Blake (as Grant has pointed out, this depends on whether one is looking from north or south), the deduction seems safe here, especially as the left-to-right movement of the Oothoonesque figure in *E* 3 suggests movement from America to Europe (the direction in which the infectious idea of liberty was spreading, a plague to priest and king). Cf. the final *VDA* design. The Cumberland motto for *E* 8, from Dryden's *Aeneis* II, 409f., describes the burning Troy as it appears to *young* Aeneas looking out from his terrace: "Thus Deluges descending on the plains / Sweep o'er the yellow year &c." Though not obviously relevant to Blake's design, by association this is curiously close, like a half-buried idea. Priam, as his son expires at his feet, curses his Greek murderer. Aeneas' account of his escape from Troy, with his father on his back and his son hanging on his arm, presents a vivid image more than half like that of *E* 15, and the brilliant accounts of fire in the passage must have influenced Blake deeply.

D.V.E.: More directly, the aged king of *E* 8 represents the yellow year threatened by the revolutionary deluge; in *E* 13 his hosts fall, "Yellow as leaves of Autumn," when the trump is blown. George Cumberland's inscriptions seem guided by an understanding of the poem—and its sources—that was, perhaps, Blake's own.

this jailor is given green and blue flesh. The prisoner, looking with startled eye back at the retreating figure, hands up, palms open and fingers distended in horror, sits cross-legged on a stone step at the left, with heavy chains round his ankles, seeming more terrified of the jailor than of his situation. A spider weaves its web on the wall above him. In this way, Blake makes the Godwin-esque comment that the one who imprisons is more inhuman than the "criminal" who is his victim. The keys, ironically enough, suggest a reference to Revelation 20:1-3, where an angel locks up Satan. Recall Urizen's unchaining in *Europe* 3:11. Again the question is asked: who is to be feared—Orc or Urizen?[18]

The final *Europe* design (*E* 15) shows something of the terror and distress generated by fire. A strong young nude carries his fainting wife over his right shoulder and extends a hand behind him, looking back to his daughter whose head is turned to the flames in the background, her right arm up in a vain attempt to ward them off. The man's left foot is on the first step of a ruined edifice at the left: we see only a broken classic pillar, which Damon interprets as a symbol of the Reason which the revolutionary flames will overwhelm. Although the design befits Orc's appearance in France at the end of the poem, associated as he is with the rising sun glowing "fiery red," it also continues the catalogue of earthly woes. The design is a recapitulation and enlargement of a motif in *America* 3, where husband, wife, and child hold hands as they flee from flames. It can also be considered as a preliminary essay for the great Job illustration (pl. 3), which shows Satan overwhelming Job's children. One of Blake's marginal texts there is from Job 1:16, "The Fire of God is fallen from Heaven," and the central figure, a strong young man advancing up a stone stairway, carrying his frightened child on his left shoulder and extending an arm to rescue his wife, is remodeled from the *Europe* figure. Lightnings and tremendous flames fill the background.[18a]

[18] In *Blake's Humanism*, Manchester, 1968 (129, 155, 157 and pls. 48, 49) John Beer suggests that *E* 15 shows Newton horrified by the plague-spotted victim of his own analysis. There seems no basis for the suggestion other than the superficial resemblance between the prisoner and Blake's Newton in the 1795 color print. Newton is mentioned in this page of *Europe*, but a Newton without compasses or last trump is no Newton, in this context, and Beer's suggestion seems irresponsible, though no more so than Digby's (p. 45), according to which the jailor is Newton and the prisoner Orc.

[18a] For the latent image of Aeneas in burning Troy, see n. 17, above; see also Irene H. Chayes's essay below, p. 214.

Fall

I regard *Europe* 10 as an interpolated page. The narrative passes naturally from pages 9 to 11, and page 10 is the only *Europe* print that was not etched on the back of a copper plate.[19] Blake decided for the sake of completeness to hold up his contemporary narrative of events following the American War to recapitulate his version of the creation and fall. Milton too had glanced at the creation in his Hymn, as we have seen, but Blake's version differs widely from the Miltonic and biblical accounts.

The account of the fall in *Europe* is a revision of those in *The French Revolution* and a canceled plate of *America* (*b*). The latter tells us that the Prince of Albion's counsel hall was built at the same time our present universe was formed. By this poetic license Blake suggests that the tyranny of George III was ultimately born with the tyranny of the fallen world and is thus bound up with its fate. In *Europe* the hall of counsel becomes the "ancient temple serpent-form'd" of Avebury, as Damon pointed out (*Philosophy*, 344). This Blake identified with Verulam, the seat of Bacon, one of those thinkers who "chang'd the infinite to a serpent." Blake describes the temple partly in biblical terms. In talking of "massy stones, uncut / With tool," Blake, Paul Miner suggests, is "Most probably . . . extending the imagery of Deuteronomy xxvii." Miner notes that "When the Israelites passed over Jordan they set up on Mt. Ebal an altar of 'great stones' upon which the laws of Israel were written. This altar was untouched with 'iron tool.' "[20] Blake's purpose in suggesting this reference is, I suppose, partly to reinforce the antiquity of the temple, partly to bring to mind the law and cursing associated with the altar on Mt. Ebal. These are, however, precious stones and derive ultimately from Ezekiel 28:13 and from Aaron's breast-

[19] I set out the evidence in "The Auckland Blakes," *Biblionews and Australian Notes & Queries*, II (1967), 6-16. Gerald E. Bentley, Jr. has measured the plate sizes of most copies of *A* and *E*, and this evidence suggests the possibility that sixteen plates had *A* on one side and *E* on the other. Two of the eighteen *A* prints, 2 and 6, were printed from the reverse side of the copper plate. I am grateful to Professor Bentley for sharing with me much bibliographical information. (This account excludes prefatory plate iii.)

[20] Paul Miner, "William Blake's 'Divine Analogy,' " *Criticism*, III (1961), 58n. Exodus 20:25 is the closer reference, in view of "unhewn," for *J* 66:1; cf. also Joshua 8:31.

plate (Exodus 28:17-21). The latter connection is more obviously significant, but in Blake's total thought the Ezekiel reference looms larger. Blake saw Ezekiel's Covering Cherub as the Serpent of Eden: in the words of *Jerusalem*, 96:12, "like a Serpent of precious stones & gold." And, given the association with Aaron, the jewels make the Serpent more specifically the "Prester Serpent," according to Blake's popular etymology. The jewels have a specious quality, giving the Serpent, and the "ancient temple serpent-form'd" of Verulam, connotations similar to those of Leutha, the "Sweet smiling pestilence" (*E* 14:12). Blake's punctuation suggests that the stones themselves do, however, have an eternal function, giving light in the Opake. In this connection, we note that their number, twelve, may also be suggested by the number of precious stones that comprise the foundations of the wall of Jerusalem in Revelation 21:19f. "Twelve" is also the zodiacal number, and the stones are "Plac'd in the order of the stars" to suggest this. Frye's comment (*Symmetry*, 140f.) is relevant: "This zodiacal pattern, which is frequent in Blake, always has the sinister significance of the unending cyclic repetition of time."

Blake's account of the fall presents it in terms of the shrinking and inversion of the five senses (*E* 10:10-15). He relates how "the five senses whelm'd / In deluge o'er the earth-born man," synchronizing fall and flood, since the latter marks off the days when there were giants in the earth, that is to say, beings with expanded senses. His next paragraph is a recapitulation with variations. Blake significantly rejects, in charging that "Thought chang'd the infinite to a serpent," the obvious emblem of infinity as a serpent with its tail in its mouth, the circular uroboros. The serpent he actually draws on this page stands on its tail and rears its body up the whole length of the left margin, projecting its flaming, crested head over the top of the text. Its body is in seven coils: this is presumably what Blake intends by his "image of infinite shut up in finite revolutions."[21] The seven coils project his-

[21] The temple at Verulam was not in the uroboros form and was quite dissimilar to Blake's serpent in *E* 10. Blake portrays it in *J* 100. *NT* no. 163 (*V*, 8) is very close to *E* 10, showing a man beneath a dead tree worshiping a serpent that rears in coils (there are seven loops) up the left margin. See Hagstrum, pl. 66b. Interestingly, this worshiper is very similar to the stone figure in *A* 16: his state is that of hypnotized petrifaction. Beer,

tory as the spiral repetition of cycles, as Blake suggests in his later "Seven Eyes" symbolism (*FZ* I 115:41ff.; *M* 13:12ff.). The Seven Churches of Beulah (or, perhaps, as this is *Europe,* more specifically those of Leutha) are also suggested. In this system, revolution is only a turning round of the wheel: those who subscribe to the system thus entirely miss the millennial potential in each struggle of the people toward liberty.[22] To Blake the prophet the words "French Revolution" must have been a libel: by accepting the implications of the words, the French cheated themselves. Blake wanted continual uprising that would be limited in the end only when desire was satiated: his message is, however, primarily addressed to the English, in order that they may join in the vision, beyond politics or national boundaries, to see their enemies as the governing, reasoning, and religious powers only. Blake's Milton contrasts forcibly the "Laws of Eternity" with what he calls, addressing Satan, "the Laws of thy false Heav'ns" (*M* 38:28ff.). The coils of the serpent are not expansive: in *Europe* itself they can be contrasted with the "ever-varying spiral ascents to the heavens of heavens" (10:13), that is, man's aural power in eternity; so reminiscent, as Damon (*Philosophy,* 345) has noted, of Blake's beautiful illustration of Jacob's Ladder.

Blake insisted that the fall is man's own error, that he wasn't turned out of paradise, but fled from it, under a mistaken notion of God. God, "that which pitieth," was seen as "the flaming sword" of Genesis 3:24, "which turned every way to keep the way of the tree of life" and was described as a "devouring fire" in Exodus 24:17 and Isaiah 29:6 and 30:30. Blake synchronizes the idea with that in Genesis 3:8, of Adam and his wife hiding from "the presence of the LORD God amongst the trees of the garden." The image of the flood is used again to describe the limiting effect of Space— later Blake will identify Enitharmon herself as Space (*M* 24:68). All except "this finite wall of flesh" is overwhelmed, because Adam is the limit of contraction (*M* 13:20f.). The phrase "man became

---

Blake's Humanism, 127f., sees the snake of *E* 10 as a representation of the "raging whirlpool" of 10:21; his description accordingly is in reverse of mine: "The page . . . is illustrated, economically and tellingly, by the figure of a serpent, spiralling down from top to bottom of the page." This "snakes and ladders" reading is attractive but secondary.

[22] See the notes on Orc in the essays in this volume by Mitchell, Erdman, Grant, and Simmons.

an Angel" looks out of line with the other degrading imagery, unless we are familiar with Blake's inversion of angel and devil in *The Marriage of Heaven and Hell.* The biblical basis for Blake's ironic statement is found in Genesis 3:22: "And the LORD God said, Behold, the man is become as one of us, to know good and evil."

This evocation of the fall was not to Blake a recapitulation of history but an account of beliefs that condition the lives of each of us at this moment, preventing us from breaking out of our den. However, he is less successful in *Europe* than in *Visions* in giving his concept immediacy: here the account is in terms of man in general, there it is Oothoon's own story (2:30-36).

In the succeeding paragraph there are two main difficulties, the significance of the "Stone of Night" and the symbolism of north and south. Frye (*Symmetry*, 224) saw a reference here to Jacob's stone, a suggestion we can endorse for several reasons. The phrase "Once open to the heavens" is suggestive, and Jacob's was a stone of night. As Blake very likely had Jacob's Ladder in mind earlier in *Europe*, the link is more convincing here. We should note, though, that Blake is referring not so much to Jacob's stone as to Jacob's skull. The Stone of Night is the human brainpan. This idea was already present when Blake mentioned the Stone of Night in *America*, for Orc prophesies that he will "renew the fiery joy, and burst the stony roof" (*A* 8:9).

The dominance, on English maps, of north over south, was to Blake another expression of the universal inversion accompanying the fall. The furthest point north in the present scheme is the Pole Star.[23] But, as the *Introduction* to *Songs of Experience* suggests, we should really be standing on top of the stars, controlling (that is, overmastering) the "starry pole." While we are under the

---

[23] Beer, *Blake's Humanism*, 78f., 98f., 127, has some interesting notes on the Pole Star's domination of the universe, but he is surely mistaken on p. 127 when he says that "The 'attractive north' has an ideal polar magnetism without the polar coldness and hardness." This is to read "attractive" as connoting "charming, glamorous," but the term is primarily Newtonic in this context, in keeping with Blake's account of a fall that is the product of "Thought." Urizenic thought began things by projecting the fallen universe; Newtonic thought exposed the universe as mechanical, thus making the stars fall, as inferior productions of the Infinite Mind of man. Newton, if drawn by Blake in *Europe*, would be in a small globe reaching *upwards* with his compasses.

Pole Star, we are creatures of night (the main stress in *Introduction*) and of northern winter (the main stress in *Holy Thursday* of *Experience*). Such is the world of Experience, in which we are controlled by what Earth in *Earth's Answer* comes to see as "Starry Jealousy," an abstract, cold, distant, arbitrary law that restricts love instead of liberating it. Earth invokes the spring as an emblem of free fruition openly displayed. This is quite the opposite vision from that of the little black boy, who was born "in the southern wild" and was taught by his mother to see God as a sun, who benevolently provides clouds to protect the fallen mortals from his excessive heat. So in *Europe* the fall is described as a movement of the south, once on top of the north, down through the whirlpool of the magnetic north to its sunken position in the present world.

Toward Armageddon

Blake's continuation of his historical narrative is a restatement, in somewhat different terms, of reactionary measures described in *America*. There (13:10-12) Albion's Angel

> . . . enrag'd his secret clouds open'd
> From north to south, and burnt outstretched on wings
>   of wrath cov'ring
> The eastern sky, spreading his awful wings across the
>   heavens. . . .

Later (16:2), "The Heavens melted from north to south," as a result of the revolutionary flames, and Urizen's reaction was to pour snow and ice on the Atlantic to hide the revolution from European eyes in a thick fog (no doubt literally of rationalization and false propaganda). In *Europe* 11 it is Urizen's Book that "Expanded from North to South," i.e., along the line of the Atlantic, apparently with the same effect (12:3f.):

> Rolling volumes of grey mist involve Churches, Palaces,
>   Towers:
> For Urizen unclaspd his Book! feeding his soul with
>   pity. . . .

Perhaps Urizen's pity was reserved for the dethroned tyrants: a good weapon at least in the mouths of such as Burke. However,

> Between the clouds of Urizen the flames of Orc roll heavy
> Around the limbs of Albions Guardian, his flesh
>   consuming   (12:32f.)

and he prepares for war, in desperation.

"The youth of England" are compelled "Into the deadly night" to see the form of Albion's Angel. "They saw his boney feet on the rock, the flesh consum'd in flames" and "They heard the voice of Albions Angel howling in flames of Orc. / Seeking the trump of the last doom" (12:5-12). This vision contrasts with Orc's triumphant statement in *America* (8:15f.):

> Fires inwrap the earthly globe, yet man is not consumd;
> Amidst the lustful fires he walks: his feet become like
>   brass. . . .

His words involve not only a reference to the three in Daniel who walked in the fiery furnace but also, apparently, one to Revelation 1:15, for the detail of the brazen feet: "And his feet like unto fine brass, as if they burned in a furnace; and his voice as the sound of many waters." Albion's Angel, not representing humanity, cannot make his feet become like brass, and so is painfully consumed by the fires of Orc. Blake here may be suggesting an ironical reading of Revelation 10:1-6, where we have an angel "clothed with a cloud," as Albion's Angel seems to be, with "feet as pillars of fire," who "cried with a loud voice, as when a lion roareth" and who swore "that there should be time no longer."

If Blake did have in mind the phrase "cried with a loud voice," from Revelation 10:3, he may have been reminded by it of Exodus 19:19, which is echoed in the next line of *Europe*: "Above the rest the howl was heard from Westminster louder and louder:" (12:14). Exodus 19:19 reads, "And when the voice of the trumpet sounded long, and waxed louder and louder, Moses spake, and God answered him by a voice." This could, however, be only an indirect reference, though Blake has Exodus 20 in mind a few lines later. David Erdman (*Prophet*, 200 [217]) compares a passage in the sixteenth "Probationary Ode" of the *Rolliad* (1784, 1791), in which Chancellor Thurlow (whose fate Blake's next lines announce) warns "every rebel soul" to tremble as he grows "profane" with a "louder yet, and yet a louder strain." The *Rolliad* itself, of course, echoes Exodus 19:19, and while the *Rolliad* seems the primary reference, Blake would have been inevitably reminded of the passage in Exodus because Milton refers to it in stanza XVII of the Nativity Hymn, describing the noise of the "Wakeful trump of doom":

> With such a horrid clang
> As on mount *Sinai* rang
> While the red fire, and smouldring clouds out brake. . . .

In fact, the howl from Westminster and Europe, the "Howlings & hissings, shrieks & groans, & voices of despair" (12:34) were probably suggested by the "voice of weeping heard and loud lament" of the departing spirits in stanzas XIXf. of the Hymn. Although Orc's flames are consuming the flesh of Albion's Angel, a paragraph interrupts this account to remind us that, meanwhile, all appears to Enitharmon to be under rigid control:

> Enitharmon laugh'd in her sleep to see (O womans
>   triumph)
> Every house a den, every man bound: the shadows are
>   filld
> With spectres, and the windows wove over with curses
>   of iron:
> Over the doors Thou shalt not; & over the chimneys Fear
>   is written:
> With bands of iron round their necks, fasten'd into the
>   walls
> The citizens: in leaden gyves the inhabitants of suburbs
> Walk heavy: soft and bent are the bones of villagers.
>   (12:25-31)

In this way Blake elaborates on Milton's image of "those ychain'd in sleep." Exodus 20:3-17 gives the ten commandments, most of which begin "Thou shalt not." Exodus 20:20 may have suggested "Over the chimneys Fear is written." It reads, "And Moses said unto the people, Fear not: for God is come to prove you, and that his fear may be before your faces, that ye sin not." Blake's placing of this paragraph lends dramatic irony to Enitharmon's hubris, which he continues to build up when she awakes with the sound of the last trump.

The appropriateness of Newton's blowing the last trump has

141

been well explained by other commentators.[24] To describe the effects of the blast, Blake conflates two Milton passages and a biblical sign of apocalypse.

> Yellow as leaves of Autumn the myriads of Angelic hosts,
> Fell thro' the wintry skies seeking their graves;
> Rattling their hollow bones in howling and lamentation.
>
> (13:6-8)

This recalls the effect of the rising sun at the end of the Nativity Hymn (232-236):

> The flocking shadows pale,
> Troop to th' infernall jail,
> Each fetter'd Ghost slips to his severall grave,
> And the yellow-skirted *Fayes*,
> Fly after the Night-steeds, leaving their Moon-lov'd maze.

The suggestion of autumn leaves recalls Milton's fallen angels in *Paradise Lost*, Book I, 301-303:

> His Legions, Angel Forms, who lay intranst
> Thick as Autumnal Leaves that strow the Brooks
> In *Vallombrosa*. . . .

The basic image is, however, biblical, drawn from passages associated with the Last Judgment (and from one, in Matthew, with the last trump): "And all the host of heaven shall be dissolved, and the heavens shall be rolled together as a scroll: and all their host shall fall down, as the leaf falleth off from the vine, and as a falling fig from the fig tree" (Isaiah 34:4, cf. Matthew 24:29ff.; Revelation 6:13).

Although Enitharmon is roused by the "wakeful trump of doom," she does not realize she has slept, and says scornfully, "Arise Ethinthus! tho' the earth-worm call: / Let him call in

---

[24] Before Newton blows the last trump, "The red limb'd Angel" makes three unsuccessful attempts to "awake the dead to Judgment." Erdman's explanation of this seems satisfactory. He finds here "the three crises contrived by Pitt in the half decade before the war with France finally came" (*Prophet*, 195 [212]). In this reading, the "red limb'd Angel" is Albion's Angel (red because of Orc's flames). Sloss and Wallis identified the Angel as Orc; Bloom refines this by calling him one "stimulated by Orc's fires." The Angel seems goaded rather than stimulated, and the narrative sequence makes an identification of the Angel with "Albions Guardian" of 12:33 more natural.

vain." Newton is to her merely a worm "of sixty winters," not "A mighty spirit." Yet she is herself only a creature of man's imagination! She continues to call up her sons and daughters (who are clearly of a different order from the fallen angelic hosts, the stars supported by Newton's laws of attraction) to the "sports of night."[25]

Morning

After Enitharmon has completed her roll call, she appeals once again to Orc to "give our mountains joy of thy red light" (14:31). Her appeal is answered, but not in the way she intended:

> She ceas'd, for All were forth at sport beneath the solemn
>   moon
> Waking the stars of Urizen with their immortal songs,
> That nature felt thro' all her pores the enormous revelry.
> Till morning ope'd the eastern gate.
> Then every one fled to his station, & Enitharmon wept.
>
> But terrible Orc, when he beheld the morning in the
>   east,
> Shot from the heights of Enitharmon;
> And in the vineyards of red France appear'd the light of
>   his fury.   (14:32-15:2)

Thus abruptly, Blake returns us to the situation of the opening lines of his Prophecy, pointing the return by using similar language, reminiscent of the end of Milton's Hymn (stanza xxvi) and of Song of Solomon 2:17 and 4:6. So the long night at last wakens to the day of judgment. Blake's apocalyptic imagery continues to echo the Nativity Hymn and the Bible.

Erdman's interpretation (*Prophet,* 249 [269]) identifies Orc with Christ: "During the long night he has grown and now has burst his chains. The 'secret child' of Innocence is, on his second coming, the 'just man' of Experience, ready to tread the vintage

[25] For these sports of night, Blake may well have had in mind, as Frye suggests, the "Midnight shout and revelry" in *Comus*. Attempts to find sources and analogues for the sons and daughters of Enitharmon have not hitherto been very rewarding: though the catalogue parallels that of the deities in the Hymn, Blake's persons are deliberately original. Two verbal reminiscences can be noted. *E* 14:4 is a reminiscence of Psalms 94:17-19; 14:5 was suggested by *Paradise Lost* III, 30f.

of wrath. He is the avenging Christ of Saint John's prediction: his eyes are as a flame of fire and his clothes bloody, 'and out of his mouth goeth a sharp sword . . . and he treadeth the wine-press of the fierceness and wrath of Almighty God.' " Erdman's quotation here is from Revelation 19, a chapter Blake undoubtedly had in mind, as it deals with the war of Armageddon. However, on comparing the passages, I am not happy with the identification, and on other grounds it seems an oversimplification to identify Orc with Christ. The two are clearly differentiated at the beginning of the Prophecy. It is less confusing to see Orc in terms of the representative of Edom in Isaiah 63:1-6, a passage related to Revelation 19. There the avenger's red garments are stressed, as well as his fury and independence: "I have trodden the winepress alone."[26] The second coming remains implicit; Blake wished to prophesy liberation and independent war, not the reimposed law of an external power.

Europe ends with the twisting of an image from Revelation 19:

> Then Los arose his head he reard in snaky thunders clad:
> And with a cry that shook all nature to the utmost pole,
> Call'd all his sons to the strife of blood.

In Revelation 19:17-18 we have this equally macabre preparation: "And I saw an angel standing in the sun; and he cried with a loud voice, saying to all the fowls that fly in the midst of heaven, come and gather yourselves together unto the supper of the great God; That ye may eat the flesh of kings, and the flesh of captains, and the flesh of mighty men, and the flesh of horses, and of them that sit on them, and the flesh of all men, both free and bond, both small and great." I have already pointed out the connection of Los with the sun; he stands in the sun in *Milton* 21 as well as in the vision at Felpham recorded in Blake's letter of 22 November 1802 to Butts. A later passage in *The Four Zoas* clinches the link with Revelation 19:17f., for there Los is seen with flaming head "like the bright sun seen thro a mist," with Eagles and

---

[26] There is a possible link here with "the vineyards of red France" which Orc will be treading. In *MHH* 3, Blake's eschatology involves "the dominion of Edom, & the return of Adam into Paradise." Some commentators prefer to read "dominion of" as meaning "dominion over" rather than "dominion by," though in context the second is more natural. The weight of evidence is swaying toward this second reading, though there is much to be said on the other side.

Vultures crying and laughing round his loins.[27] Los's cry "shook all nature to the utmost pole," a detail reminiscent of the glance at the Last Judgment in Milton's Hymn, where, hearing the trumpet,

> The aged Earth agast
> With terrour of that blast,
> Shall from the surface to the center shake;
> When at the worlds last session,
> The dreadful Judge in middle Air shall spread his
>   throne.

Thus Blake, in 1793 or 1794, viewed the contemporary situation and related it to the great biblical pattern of history. Milton's poem on the Nativity provided him with a framework and a stimulus: the beautiful meditation of Milton became Blake's terrible prophecy.

[27] *FZ* viib 96:19ff. It is in the course of this battle, an extensive recasting of that initiated in *Europe*, that Orc turns into a "Serpent round the tree of Mystery" (93:24). The morphology of Orc here and elsewhere does not support the proposal to identify him with Christ in *Europe*. But one must remember that Blake, when writing *Europe*, had not yet projected Orc's perversion: his Prophecy was written in the hope that Orc would continue to expand. This is why, writing to "Christian" England, Blake wished to assimilate the Orc movement to Christ's teaching, to gain credit for the movement toward liberation and, at the same time, to strip the Christian gospel of its Mosaic or Enitharmonesque accretions.

7

Urizen

The Symmetry of Fear

ROBERT E. SIMMONS

In *The Book of Urizen* a number of complex but symmetrical forms, in both text and design, are used to present an account of the origin and nature of the fallen world. The work is divided into symmetrical parts, and the meanings and juxtapositions of these parts amount to a rigorous and scathing satiric critique of the whole basis of eighteenth-century rationalism and its offspring: natural religion. Blake called the Tyger a work of "fearful symmetry," and so is the world defined by the structure of *Urizen*, becoming ultimately a four-sided house of mirrors, finitely limited, but infinitely reflecting fallen man within it.

This essay will try to show, first, the symmetry of *Urizen*, and second, why that symmetry is fearful. The conclusion is that symmetry not only is, but must be, a central conception behind all Blake's symbolic descriptions of the fallen world. Put simply, symmetry is fixity and therefore finite, though repeatable; whereas for Blake the eternal world is the infinite flux of energy, where all forms appear.

The Symmetry of *Urizen*

Symmetry is defined as similarity of form or arrangement on either side of a dividing line. Three modifications of this concept must be made in applying it to *Urizen*. First, the similarity of arrangement, because of the "book" nature of *Urizen*, takes a sequential form, matching the first and last, second and penultimate, and so on, textual divisions or designs. In this sense the structure of *Urizen* is cyclical as well as symmetrical, since the first and last events will have similarities.

Second, the similarities themselves may be conceptual as well as visual in both text and design. That is, a strong correspondence in meaning may occur between two parts of the text or two designs, although the particular images used to present the meaning may differ. Frequently enough, however, the symmetry is also visual or physical; actual similarities in words, images, or compositional details do occur.

Third, and this is a difficult point, the correspondences between parts of the text, or between designs, are based on the conception of opposites as well as similars. For example, a separation may be paralleled by a union, a birth by a death, a cause by its effect. The general justification for this lies in the fact that at a certain scale of abstraction birth and death, for example, are both subsumed by the larger concept of mortality; hence, both births and deaths may be images of mortality. Similarly, both causes and effects may signify causality; both unions and separations signify division. The particular reason, however, derives from the mirror nature of symmetry—the fact that an object and its identical, but reversed, image in a mirror together form a perfect symmetrical structure. Thus, a death is conceptually the identical but reversed image of a birth. The reversal of lefts and rights involved in mirror symmetry, as well as mirror imagery generally, and, most importantly, the archetypal mirror event—from the myth of Narcissus—all contribute as well to *Urizen*'s symmetrical symbolism.

Subject and Object

The first indication of the symmetry of *Urizen*'s structure is the similarity of the designs on the first and last plates (1, 28 {51, 52}).[1] The two designs operate like "before" and "after"

[1] This essay is based primarily on copy A (Dimsdale, now Mellon Collection; Dent facsimile 1929), while the illustrations are reproduced from copy B (collection of Mrs. Thorne) and copy F (Harvard College Library). The Blake Trust facsimile represents copy G (Rosenwald Collection). Because no two copies of *Urizen* are arranged in the same way, the plate numbers cited are those of the model established by Keynes in the *Census*.

Urizen is a complex work bibliographically. The seven known copies all have different plate sequence and coloring and vary in minor details and in number of plates. Thus the shape of the work is more fluid than would seem to be indicated by my emphasis on symmetry and fixed form. To attempt here to detail all the variations on that form would make an already complex argument more complicated. I am preparing a bibliographical treatment which will examine the possibly accretive nature of the work's development as well as the varying symmetries of the different copies. For help on

pictures in Blake's story of the fall, and in their combination of similarities and opposites illustrate very well the form symmetry will take in the rest of *Urizen*. Both plates have text at the top of the page, the illustration at the bottom. Both illustrations show Urizen with a long, white beard, in a crouched or sitting position, looking downwards, his hands symmetrically away from his body on each side, with one foot showing beneath his robe.

However, the designs also show some striking contrasts. In plate 1 Urizen is very old and feeble, crouched in an almost fetal position, writing simultaneously with both hands in books on either side of him. His right foot only is shown, but it is placed on his left side (his right leg apparently crossing his body under his robe) and rests on a third book in front of him. He appears to be in a low valley or cave, eyes peering down at his book, and behind him stand the two stone tablets of the law. He appears kindly, or foolish, rather than menacing. His long robe is blue.

In plate 28 Urizen is old but very strong, sitting on something like a throne, his hands resting on two objects, possibly stones, on either side. He holds, in both hands, strands of a net that reaches below him and on which his left foot (the only one shown) rests. He seems to sit high up, on a mountain range, and looks down as though from a commanding height. IIe appears strong and cold, perhaps stupidly so, but his strength and the net make him menacing. His robe is white, like snow on the mountain.

These first and last plates define the end points of *Urizen*'s symmetrical structure. The first seems to show a primarily mental Urizen: the book and writing implements, the physical weakness, the tablets of moral law. The last shows a physical Urizen: the net, the insensitive physical strength, the stones of the mountains— perhaps representing the "tablets" of natural law. The largely symmetrical composition, vertically, of both designs, particularly the fact that the Urizen of the title page is writing with both hands, directs us to further symmetries.

---

all these bibliographical problems I am indebted to G. E. Bentley, Jr., who first introduced me to Blake's texts and supplied special information about *Urizen*.

Readers interested in *Urizen* and further relationships between its pictures and text should also see the fine article by W.J.T. Mitchell: "Poetic and Pictorial Imagination in Blake's *The Book of Urizen*," *Eighteenth-Century Studies*, III (1969), 83-107.

The central dividing line of the work also draws attention to itself by its design. It occurs on plate 13 {53},[2] where the illustration is placed midway on the plate, with text both above and below, the only plate so designed. *Urizen* has nine chapters,[3] and chapter v begins on this plate. It has twelve numbered verses. Verse 6 ends:

> He [Los] saw Urizen deadly black,
> In his chains bound, & Pity began. . . .

Verse 7 begins:

> In anguish dividing & dividing
> For pity divides the soul

and goes on to tell of the separation of Los and the globe of blood that soon becomes Enitharmon. At the exact center of *Urizen*, then, begins the story of a division, thus separating the work into two halves.

That the two halves are intended to be symmetrical is indicated by the mirror imagery of the designs illustrating this event. The design on plate 13 shows a wispy, floating Enitharmon,[4] in a night sky among clouds. In the A and B copies, and possibly in the G, she appears to be touching the moon with one hand. In the floating form of the design there is a suggestion of a reflection in water. The moon, of course, is a mirror, becoming visible only by reflecting light from the sun. Los is strongly associated with the sun in the first half of *Urizen*. Enitharmon in her night sky and Los, the creating sun, or day, show the reflected "opposite" aspect of symmetry.

[2] Plate 13 is near the center of all copies, though the varying placement of the full-page designs tends to obscure this fact.

[3] The highest numbered chapter is IX, although there seem to be two versions (two different plates) of the first six verses of chapter IV. Both versions are retained in all but copy C. Only one is counted in my textual calculations.

[4] A similar design is used on the title page of *Ahania*, dated by Blake a year after *Urizen*. If unilateral identification were called for, this should indicate that the *Ahania* design shows Enitharmon, rather than the *Urizen* design Ahania. But there is ample evidence of Blake's tendency to use certain compositions and gestures in more than one work for more than one purpose. See the essay in this volume by Janet Warner, to whom I owe thanks for introducing me to the concept of repeated gesture in Blake's designs.

149

The full-page design on Plate 17 {55} illustrates this same central event, and adds another aspect to the mirror symmetry of *Urizen*. The design itself is symmetrical vertically as are those on plates 1 and 28. It shows Los leaning over, apparently squeezing the round globe of blood out of the top of his head with his hands over his ears. The globe of blood hangs beneath him, suggesting the shape of a pool, with Los leaning over it, both looking in it and creating it. This design of a figure bending over a round form beneath him is a repeated one in Blake. The most famous example is that on the frontispiece of *Europe*: the "Ancient of Days" {8} leaning out of a round globe with a compass, about to describe a similar round world beneath him. Plate 15 of *Urizen* {56} shows an "Eternal" in the same position as the "Ancient of Days." Both figures reach down with their left or "mirror" hands. In plate 15 the curving mortal world appears below. I would argue that all these designs are variations on the central form of Narcissus creating the divided image of himself in a pool, as in plate 17 Los creates the divided image of himself as a round globe, which then becomes a woman.

The designs on plates 13 and 18, considered together, confirm both the Narcissus interpretation and the mirror symmetry of the two halves of *Urizen* represented by Los and Enitharmon. Verse 8, on plate 18, reads in part:

> At length in tears & cries imbodied
> A female form trembling and pale
> Waves before his [Los's] deathy face

Verse 9, also on plate 18, reads:

> All Eternity shudderd at sight
> Of the first female now separate
> Pale as a cloud of snow
> Waving before the face of Los

The design on plate 18 {54} shows Los in flames, arms outstretched in a crucifix position, gazing upwards. The design on plate 13, referred to earlier, fits the female portion of the description given in the verses above. The arms of the floating amorphous female figure in the sky are outstretched like those of Los in plate 18. The heads of both figures are tilted to one side. In addition, in plate 18 Los's left foot is more clearly defined and in advance of his right—a proper position for creating the mirror form of woman. Together, the two designs fit the single description of the text, and form a picture of a man transfixed by his floating mirror image.

If the myth of Narcissus is seen as being at the center of *Urizen*, both physically and conceptually, the meaning of the two symmetrical halves symbolized by Los and Enitharmon becomes clearer. The Los or Narcissus half begins with plate 1, the thinking, reading, writing Urizen, his subjectivity symbolized by the cave or valley in which he works. The Enitharmon or reflected-image half ends with the powerful, physical Urizen, his objectivity symbolized by the mountains or stones on which he rests. Thus Blake is using the story of Narcissus' perception of his own image in the water as a parable for the origin of the philosophical problem of the split between subject and object. It is the perception of this distinction between "self" and "other" that creates the divided physical world—a world everywhere in Blake associated with water.

But there is a second part to the Narcissus story, the examination of which establishes the meaning of the last, or Enitharmon, half of *Urizen*. Narcissus not only created his own divided image, he compounded the disaster by falling in love with it, and wound up as one of the "flowers" of the vegetative world. This "love" aspect of the myth is reflected in the fact that the globe Los creates turns into a woman. This acknowledges also the traditional Western form of the myth—the eyes in the pool in the garden that begin the quest of courtly love. The use Blake makes of this part of the myth becomes clearer in chapter VI, where Los and Enitharmon appear as Adam and Eve, living, like Narcissus, in the fallen vegetative garden of the natural world. Courtly love, as well as Adam and Eve's behavior after the fall, is summarized succinctly in the first verse:

> But Los saw the Female & pitied
> He embrac'd her, she wept, she refus'd
> In perverse and cruel delight
> She fled from his arms, yet he followd

The creation of Enitharmon, then, represents not only a division of subject and object, but also the beginning of Los's fallen attempt to reunite the two by pursuing the objective world and making himself (sexually) a part of it.

If the last half[5] of *Urizen* represents man "embracing" the objective world, the symmetrically identical but reversed first half should show man rejecting the subjective world. And so it does in the first half of chapter v, where Los turns in despair from the subjective, sleeping Urizen, "Cut off from life & light frozen" (v, 5), and begins the creation of Enitharmon. But also, if the last half of *Urizen,* as seems likely, shows the working out of the consequences of electing to live in the objective world, the first half should show those consequences of upholding subjectivism which lead to its rejection in chapter v. With this overall scheme in mind, we can begin to explore these two symmetrical halves in more detail, beginning with the first one.

Reason and The Senses

The first point of interest is the discovery of a second dividing line, again indicated by a division of Los, this time from Urizen. Chapter III is intermediate between chapters I and v. It has fourteen verses. Verse 7 ends:

> Like a human heart strugling & beating
> The vast world of Urizen appear'd.

Verse 8 begins:

> And Los round the dark globe of Urizen,
> Kept watch for Eternals to confine,
> The obscure separation alone. . . .

This completes the creation of Urizen's world, as well as his division from Los, and is the first mention of Los in the poem.

Again the symmetry, this time of Los and Urizen, on either side of this dividing line is confirmed by the illustrations. The confirmation is made by pairing similar designs, however, rather than by using the mirror imagery of the Narcissus myth. Shortly beyond the dividing line we are shown a symmetrical matching of Los and Urizen in the illustrations on plates 7 and 8{59, 60}. The designs on both these plates appear at the bottom of the page, with text above, and they are of similar size. They show Los and Urizen, respectively, in similar circular, huddled, embryonic positions.

---

[5] "Half" here refers primarily to the text.

Los has the ruddiness of a newborn baby; Urizen is shown as a skeleton. Los is enveloped in flames, mouth howling in pain; Urizen floats in dark space, silent and dead.

The text confirms the identification of Los with the sun and Urizen with the earth that is suggested by the circular form of the designs. Verse 9 of chapter III reads:

> Los wept howling around the dark Demon:
> And cursing his lot for in anguish,
> Urizen was rent from his side;
> And a fathomless void for his feet;
> And intense fires for his dwelling.

Verse 11 reads:

> The Eternals said: What is this? Death
> Urizen is a clod of clay.

The rending of Urizen from Los's side suggests in turn a geophysical theory of the origin of the earth as a chunk of matter thrown off by the sun, just as Enitharmon, the moon, is born in chapter V after "Los's bosom earthquak'd with sighs."

The full-page designs of plates 16 and 22 {61, 62} form a second, highly similar pair, again supporting the symmetry of the Los-Urizen division. The first shows Los as the sun;[6] the other Urizen as the earth. These designs, however, illustrate the sun and earth at a later stage, after the geophysical evolution of the earth described in the first verse of chapter IV has taken place:

> Ages on ages roll'd over him!
> In stony sleep ages roll'd over him!
> Like a dark waste stretching chang'able
> By earthquakes riv'n, belching sullen fires

Los here is in despair rather than in anguish, and Urizen is shown in a solid, fully-fleshed, mountainlike form rather than as a skeleton.

In this division, then, the emphasis in the imagery is on the

---

[6] The figure, clean-shaven in copies B and G, is bearded in A. The beard, however, is not incompatible with Los, as the later plate 21 shows a bearded Los with Enitharmon and Orc. The beard in A can be read as a sign of Los's beginning mortality, which the later plate 21 (in all three copies) confirms. Copy F lacks pl. 16.

153

splitting into two of what was once one organic body, rather than on the creation of a mirror image. If we keep in mind that this division happens in the first, subjective half of *Urizen* and look at the events that precede and follow it, we can see more clearly what this separation means.

First, from the beginning of the poem up to chapter III the growth of Urizen's world has been presented as a process of thought. This process is a literal "abstraction" that results in Urizen's subjective withdrawal from the sensible world of the Eternals into a space of pure mind. The Eternals can perceive him only as a "void" or "vacuum":

> Lo. a shadow of horror is risen
> In Eternity! Unknown, unprolific!
> Self-closd, all-repelling: what Demon
> Hath form'd this abominable void
> This soul-shudd'ring vacuum?—Some said
> "It is Urizen," But unknown, abstracted
> Brooding secret, the dark power hid.
>
> (I, 1)

Second, following the division in chapter III, Urizen becomes the fallen human body and forms the fallen senses, as well as beginning the solar system as the planet earth. The changes of Urizen, beginning in verse 6 of chapter IV, depict Urizen successively forming a skeleton, a heart, eyes, ears, nose, tongue, and hands and feet.

The first half of *Urizen*, therefore, shows the cause-and-effect sequence set in motion by attempting to take a completely subjective view of reality. First, the attempt is made to organize all experience rationally. Urizen's battle with the four elements, recounted in verse 5 of chapter II, shows him mentally organizing the physical world. The writing of the "Book of eternal brass" in the same chapter shows his corresponding attempt to fix the mental or moral world.

But with the announcement of this new, codified world, eternity is split, since the infinite eternal world has been made finite:

> For Eternity stood wide apart,
> As the stars are apart from the earth
>
> (III, 8)

Urizen is cast out and simultaneously Los appears. Los is the original eternal man, now made mortal by the division of Urizen from his side. Hence he appears as a howling newborn babe as well as the sun of the newly created solar system. Urizen appears as the earth, and in the skeletal form of death, because the defining and categorizing powers of Reason can work only with fixed, finite material, in the "abstract," separated from the complex sensory data and imaginative organizations of it that create the infinite, changing flux of experience:

> The Eternals said: What is this? Death
> Urizen is a clod of clay.   (III, 11)

Together, the birth of Los and the death of Urizen signify man's new mortality—the result of his new rational, subjective view of reality which sees stasis as the good. Los is now in agony in the flames, since Reason sees intense sense experience as only the painful prelude to the quiescence of satisfaction. Los is now a believer in the kind of reality outlined by Urizen in his rebellious speech of chapter II:

> Why will you die O Eternals?
> Why live in unquenchable burnings?

Urizen and Los now exist in an isolated, finite, subjective world. Moreover, Reason is dead, having nothing to work with, while the rest of man is miserable, unable to cope, without Reason, with his apparently chaotic sense experiences. Subjective man must therefore organize his sense experience in order to reactivate Reason by supplying it with the limited, quantifiable, isolated data it requires. Reason has thus become the first of the Los-created mirrors for reality.

Los therefore, following the view of the world supplied by Reason, hammers out the new body of Urizen: the fallen body with all the fallen senses—the progressively bound body of chapter IV. This process ends, appropriately enough, with a crucifixion:

> Enraged & stifled with torment
> He threw his right Arm to the north
> His left Arm to the south
> Shooting out in anguish deep,
> And his Feet stampd the nether Abyss.
> (IV, 12)

The design on plate 6 also shows Urizen's revolt and its consequences in the form of a crucifixion. The three upside-down, falling figures of the design are wrapped in snakes, indicating the
new mortality and sexuality of their bodies.[7]

The completed Urizen is again identified with Los by the
parallel full-page designs on plates 16 and 22 {61, 62}. Urizen in
his new form has become Los's second, divided mirror for reality:
the fallen, isolated Senses. Or rather, Los himself has become this
second mirror, having constructed it according to Urizen's definition. Los only binds the changes of Urizen. He does not create
them.

But then, in chapter v, comes the unexpected but logical next
event in the cause-and-effect sequence initiated by Urizen's revolt.
He who decides to live by Reason must progressively die by Reason. Los, having constructed the restricted portholes of the fallen
senses in order to give "life" to the subjective view of reality,
finds that his new senses, being still contained in an entirely subjective world, can apprehend only nonexistence:

> But the space undivided by existence
> Struck horror into his soul.   (v, 5)

In order to bring Urizen and himself back to complete life,
Los must now create an objective world after all. He sees himself
in Urizen's "death image" (v, 7, plate 10), and in horrified (self)
pity begins the creation of Enitharmon. This objective world,
however, since it takes shape in the finite space created by Urizen's
and Los's separation from eternity, is really contained in the subjective world as well. Los is still within his globe of selfhood, within the world of Urizen. The true, original fall occurs with the
first embracement of subjectivity, which means in itself the conceptual splitting of once-whole, infinite experience into subjective
and objective parts. This has already been done, and so the
creation now of the Enitharmic, objective world is really a repetition or reflection of the act that begins *The Book of Urizen*:
Urizen's rebellion by withdrawal into himself.

The sequence thus far has been all too logical. Urizen (or
eighteenth-century man) has affirmed the primacy of Reason, thus

---

[7] Compare the worm-enwrapped body of Adam in *Elohim Creating Adam*
{94}.

dissociating himself from his Senses. Sensory data, however, is necessary to give Reason something to work with. This data, therefore, though normally infinite and various, must now be defined, limited, and categorized; and so the fallen, separated senses develop. To use one's senses, however, requires something to be perceived, and so what has begun as the affirmation of the primacy of a subjective principle ends with the recognition of an objective world. This objective world, however, will in reality be merely the reflection or projection of subjective man himself—the watery image of Narcissus.

Natural Religion

We now have two symmetries to pursue instead of one. The original symmetry is formed by the division of *Urizen* into subjective and objective halves of experience, represented by the separation of Los and Enitharmon in chapter v. The subjective half itself, however, has also turned out to be symmetrically divided, by the division of Urizen and Los, representing the separation and definition of Reason and the Senses, in chapter III. The objective half has a similar secondary dividing point. Chapter VII is intermediate between v and IX. It has ten verses. (Verse 4 tells of the chaining of Orc beneath "Urizen's deathful shadow.") Verse 5 reads:

> The dead heard the voice of the child [Orc]
> And began to awake from sleep
> All things. heard the voice of the child
> And began to awake to life.

Verse 6 reads:

> And Urizen craving with hunger
> Stung with the odours of Nature
> Explor'd his dens around

The central events of chapters III and VII, being corresponding points in the opposed subjective and objective mirror halves, are symmetrically similar but opposite. In chapter III Urizen dies and Los appears, howling. In chapter VII Orc (Los's son) howls and disappears, and Urizen comes to life. In chapter III the solar system begins, which Blake sees as the quintessentially subjective

157

event because it is supposed to have happened before man—the objective perceiver—existed. In chapter VII the cycle of generative life begins—the archetypal objective event because capable of being directly experienced every spring. In chapter III the central event is a splitting of one original whole into two parts by an act of rebellion. In chapter VII the central event seems to be the simultaneous vivifying of two dead "parts" by an act of repression.

In chapter III the two parts of the secondary symmetrical division were seen to represent Reason and the Senses. The first point to establish in chapter VII is the meaning of these two dead "parts." The part described in verse 5 is called variously "the dead" and "All things" and seems to refer to the natural world, which, having slept through the winter, now stirs and awakens in the spring. Orc, whose sacrifice in the preceding verse 4 starts the process, is the product of Enitharmon and Los in the first sexual union, and Enitharmon soon after (verse 10) bears "an enormous race," indicating her place as the generative mother of the world. This first part could then be called Nature and be associated with Enitharmon. It represents the third of the mirrors for reality created or "lost" by Los.

Urizen is the other part and he goes immediately to work in a manner suggesting both the quantitative scientist and the Biblical and Miltonic creator:

> He formed scales to weigh;
> He formed massy weights;
> He formed a brazen quadrant:
> He formed golden compasses
> And began to explore the Abyss
> And he planted a garden of fruits
>
> (VII, 8)

His subsequent actions in witnessing the birth of the four elements (science), and cursing his race and weaving the Net of Religion, confirm his simultaneous scientific and religious function. Urizen's rebirth is the beginning of rational religion, not "given" but deduced. The net Urizen creates is "twisted like to the human brain" (VIII, 9). The sacrifice of Orc is the sign of this religion, which rests on the repression of man's being by cultural mores, the control of the son by the father. It is Los as the father and the priest who chains his son to the rock with the chain of jealousy, thus producing the fourth mirror for reality: Religion.

Rational religion is deduced, of course, from Nature, the other product of Orc's sacrifice. Just as Religion is created or justified by calling it "natural," so Nature is created by making it moral or "law-abiding." The laws of Nature as defined by science and the laws of morality as defined by Religion become identified. Whereas chapter III recorded the divorce of Reason from the Senses, chapter VII tells of the wedding that produces the one flesh of Natural Religion.

Once again the sequence has been a logical one. Forced to recognize an objective world, but insisting on viewing it through the finite and defined fallen Senses, Reason can only find in this world evidence of finiteness and definition: evidence, that is, of rationality. This in turn is taken to mean that some other "rational" being has created the objective world, and so an abstract God is born, identified with, and derived from, the "laws" of Nature.

Reason has now come full circle, like Narcissus: first projecting its conception of the world as an "other," and then using the resulting projected world as evidence of the "truth" of its conception. *The Book of Urizen*, as its name implies ("the book of your reason"), is an extremely logical critique-satire of eighteenth-century rationalism, making the circularity of the deist argument manifest in its own symmetrically enclosed structure.

Finite and Infinite

There remains to discuss the closing point of that structure, the fourth and final symmetrical dividing line, where first and last come together. This union was indicated at the very beginning by the similarity of the designs of the first and last plates (1, 28). It is further indicated now by the similarity of Fuzon's and Urizen's revolts. The fact that both chapters I and IX have one-digit verse totals (I, 6; IX, 9), whereas the chapters within which the other points of division occur have two-digit totals (III, 14; V, 12; VII, 10),[8] suggests that these first and last chapters come together

[8] This coincidence in verse numbers may seem trifling, but see the table in figure 3 for further "coincidences."

to form a single symmetrical whole just as the halves of the divided chapters do. The last verse of Chapter IX reads:

> And the salt ocean rolled englob'd

The first verse of chapter 1 begins:

> Lo, a shadow of horror is risen
> In Eternity! Unknown, unprolific!
> Self closd, all-repelling: what Demon
> Hath form'd this abominable void
> This soul-shudd'ring vacuum?

Chapter IX ends with the completion of the fourth mirror-for-reality of the Urizenic world: Religion. Urizen's world is now complete and finite, self-closed and circular, as the last verse indicates. Everything in it is contained and reflected inward by the four surrounding mirrors or symmetries of its structure: Reason, the Senses, Nature, and Religion. Consequently, Urizen's world can appear to Eternals, outside it, only as a "void" or a "vacuum," as indicated in the first verse of the work.

In a sense, the vacuum-solid contrast of the beginning-end of *Urizen* corresponds to the contrasts of its symmetrically opposite point in the "circular" structure: the shadowy image of Enitharmon created by the dying-sun Los in chapter V. The "vacuum" of Urizen complements "the space undivided by existence" (V, 5) that horrifies Los, and the "tears & cries imbodied" that make up Enitharmon appear to become the "salt ocean" of Urizen's world.

But while this interpretation confirms the basic shape of *Urizen*'s structure, it seems secondary to the entirely new aspect of symmetry which the correspondence of beginning and ending introduces: the contrast between outer and inner,[9] incomplete and complete, infinite and finite. At the beginning the Eternals, with their outer, infinite vision, literally cannot see a finite, self-bounded world; to them, it does not exist. Fuzon, on the other hand, sees Urizen's world as all too real, too solid, too objectionable. The very fact that he revolts against it proves the finiteness of his point of view, proves that he is merely the symmetrical other half of the Orc

[9] For the contrast between the finite and eternal sides of death's door, see Henry Lesnick, "The Function of Perspective in Blake's *Jerusalem*," *BNYPL*, LXXIII (1969), 49-55.

(Fuzon)-Urizen cycle now initiated.[10] He can only imitate Urizen's revolt (and later, in *The Book of Ahania*, his tyranny); not create. He lives now within a finite space.

The identity of beginning and end in *Urizen* also makes a point

[10] D.V.E.: I am not sure that this logical trap is Blake's. When he promised a Bible of Hell he did not intend a place where all who enter must abandon hope. Just as in *America* Orc is seen capable of soaring free, so in *MHH* a new future is prophesied, and here the calling "together" of the "remaining children" to leave Egypt marks one more chance to find the promised land. (See Orc note, p. 112.)

R.E.S.: Isn't the Fuzon exodus a sort of fallen analogy (mirror image) of the eternal reality? It's bad in itself, but its resemblance to eternity suggests that hope remains. I would agree that in Blake hope always remains, simply because man began there and can conceive of it. But I think one should distinguish between telling the story of the fall and telling the story of redemption. I think Blake's works up to the end of *The Four Zoas* tell the story of the fall—after that, the struggle is upward again: fall *and* redemption.

I see *Urizen* as Blake's intellectual, symmetrical, Urizenic version of the fall; and *America* as his emotional, vegetative, Orc version of the same event. The two characters are inextricably linked, as they are in both books. Blake may favor, personally, the Orc version, because it's most "alive," but the struggle is unresolved until both Urizen and Orc *forgive each other*—mutual suicide—the theme of the later prophecies. Thus the late, copy G version of *Urizen* plays down the symmetry and left and right imagery, and shows Los in gold, as potential, in plate 16; as a sign that hope is in the integration of both Urizen and Orc into the psyche, not in the conquering of one or the other. See Sutherland's essay, in this volume.

You may argue that Blake himself *thought* that Orc must win *over* Urizen *at that time*. Then you have the choice of believing Blake was mistaken in *America*, or that *America* is the story of a fall, not the beginnings of redemption. I prefer to believe the latter because I think that it is Blake's realization of this—that *America* is another version of the fall—that results in the despair that produced *Urizen* and left *The Four Zoas* unfinished, ending only in 1804. Moreover, to put the argument where ultimately it must be answered, look at *America*: a false dawn, a spring that must turn to winter— a world of vegetation; look at the imagery of the pictures, overwhelming anything positive in the text. Look at the beginning and ending plates— forerunners of *Urizen*. Look at the inconclusiveness of the text that drifts off into cycles of history, with a gesture toward some dim final redemption. The book, I think, crystallized Blake's conviction that he must explore the fall first, before redemption. Hence *Urizen*; hence *The Four Zoas*, an expansion of *Urizen*.

D.V.E.: I see that the flame of argument threatens to consume your picture of the *Book of Urizen* as a feast for laughter. But the piper is undaunted on the ending plate of *America*; so not to worry.

161

about finite and infinite time. At the moment of completion of Urizen's world at the end of the work, it appears as a void to the Eternals at the beginning. In my end is my beginning; in my beginning is my end. Urizen completing the logical cause-and-effect sequence of the creation of his world is identical with Urizen beginning it. This is another paradox of Reason—the fact that cause is indistinguishable from effect except through the orientation of time. Urizen enters Time at the beginning of *Urizen*, as he encloses space at the end, and so disappears from Eternity.

The enclosure of space, like the definition of time, is a matter of orientation. Orientation, or definition, produces the finite from the infinite. The story of *Urizen* is simply a succession of such orientations. Orientation, too, is the basis of any description or analysis of mirror symmetry, defining what is left or right, up or down, in successive reflections.

We can now begin to see a point to *Urizen*'s orientation symbolism. The shift in plates 1 and 28 from a single right foot to a single left suggests that a finite, oriented "material" world is being created, and also that it is a mirror world, not the "right" one. We can also remark the prominence and position (ahead of the right) of left feet in three key designs illuminating the three dividing points of the work: of the left foot of the central figure in plate 6, showing the fall occurring simultaneously with the described division of Urizen from Los; of that of Los in 18, where the text describes Enitharmon as separating from him; most prominently of Urizen, in 23, exploring his dens after Orc's sacrifice has brought him and Nature simultaneously to life. The up-down orientation is supplied by various upside-down "falling" figures in the designs of 6, 17, and 20, and these too illustrate dividing points in the text. Plate 6 {57} has been discussed; 17 {55} illustrates the beginning of Los's creation of Enitharmon; and 20 (not reproduced) shows the birth of Orc, whose sacrifice revivifies Urizen. In addition plate 14 shows an inverted Urizen battling with air, part of the struggle with the elements that initiates his revolt. Also, a front-back or inward-outward orientation is indicated in designs 3, 10, 14, and 27. Each of these depicts Urizen at some stage in creating his world: 3, battling fire; 10, erecting a roof against the Eternals' fire; 14, fighting the air; 27, weaving the Net of Religion.

With this in mind, let us look now at *Urizen*'s oriented, finite structure. The orientation is provided by two main axes. (See fig.

162

3, below.) If we visualize the structure as a four-sided diamond figure, the first axis of symmetry will run vertically from the center of chapter v at the top point to the junction of the combined chapters i and ix at the bottom. This line divides the work, as we have seen, into left, subjective, and right, objective, halves.

The second axis of symmetry will run horizontally from the center of chapter iii at the left point to the center of chapter vii at the right. If we consider for a moment the four "mirrors" which form the walls of this figure, we can see what the top and bottom halves of *Urizen* represent. The Senses occupy the upper left quarter of the figure, Nature the upper right. Together they form the "physical" upper half of Urizen. Reason and Religion form the "mental" lower half.

These two orientations, then, subject-object and physical-mental, create and define the four mirrors, represented by the four symmetrical quarters of the twice-bisected diamond. The fact that the axes of symmetry run from point to point means that the quarters are triangles, appropriate again to the fallen world Blake is creating, and reflecting the trinity of books with which Urizen works in plate 1 and the trinity of his two arms and single, central foot in 28. Subject-mental defines Reason; subject-physical defines the Senses; object-physical defines Nature; and object-mental defines rational Religion, or holy science, which to Blake are the same thing.

This completed, orientated world of Urizen, as the last verse tells us, is circular and enclosed. Therefore all the mirrors reflect the same image, although it is distorted by reversals of left and right, up and down, front and back. Therefore all the inhabitants of this world see the same world, or rather the same image of the world. Any variations they seem to perceive are only distorted products of the multi-mirrored environment.

This world, or image of a world, begins and ends with Reason, which decrees that all phenomena perceived by all men may be reduced to one common phenomenon. Therefore all experience is finite. But a finite experience, or world, can only exist in a finite time; we must know the beginning and end of it in order to apprehend it: hence the cyclical nature of our apprehension of this world. The theme of the origin and growth of the solar system supplies imagery for both the space and time orientations of *Urizen*. Los as the sun and Enitharmon as the moon both measure time as well as defining the space of the solar system.

163

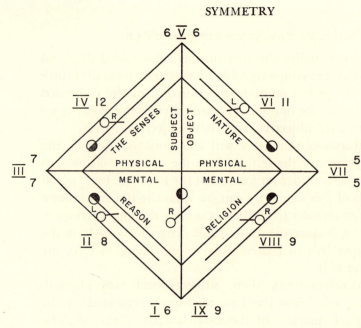

$6 \ \underline{V} \ 6$

$\underline{IV} \ 12$ $\quad$ $\underline{VI} \ 11$

THE SENSES — SUBJECT | OBJECT — NATURE

PHYSICAL $\quad$ PHYSICAL

$\dfrac{7}{\underline{III}}$ $\dfrac{}{7}$ MENTAL $\quad$ MENTAL $\quad \underline{VII} \ \dfrac{5}{5}$

REASON $\quad$ RELIGION

$\underline{II} \ 8$ $\qquad$ $\underline{VIII} \ 9$

$\underline{I} \ 6$ $\quad$ $\underline{IX} \ 9$

Verse Totals

Physical half,
two-digit figures,
total 47
Mental half,
single-digit figures,
total 44

Objective half,
odd figures,
total 45
Subjective half,
even figures,
total 46

ORIENTATION

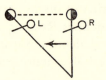

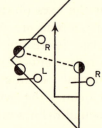

1. Left-right reversed; mental error; Urizen's right foot on left side, pl. 1.

2. Up-down reversed; physical error; upside-down falling figures, pl. 6.

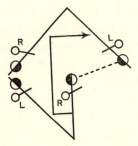

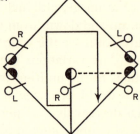

3. Up-down reversed; physical error; Orc falling upside-down, pl. 20.

Back-front reversed; objective error; Enitharmon, pl. 13.

Left-right reversed; left as sign of materialism (physical and objective); Urizen's left foot only, central, pl. 28.

4. Back-front reversed; all orientations restored, except that world is now objectively orientated, not subjectively; man sees the back side of himself as an exterior world, and exterior self; Urizen, fleeing, back to us, creating Net of Religion, pl. 27.

Fig. 3. The symmetry and orientation of *Urizen*

Los, the fallen, divided Eternal man, is the inhabitant of this world. Just as the unfallen Los was the infinite total of the myriad perceptions of all the Eternals, so the fallen Los is the finite, divided sum of the repeated and mirrored perceptions of all mortal men. Since the world, and man, has been given a beginning and ending, the sum must be finite, even if the perceptions were not repeated. It is the repetition, however, that makes finitude observable by mortal men. Urizen's is thus the ultimate symmetrical world, orientated in both space and time, and thus a world of mirrors and of repeated copies of reality, as the design on plate 1, of Urizen copying simultaneously into two books on either side of him from a third book in front, illustrates.

Thus, the infinite world of Eternal man becomes the finite world of mortal man, because of, or through, mutually agreed upon orientation or definition: the consensus of a common perception producing a fixed, unchanging, predictable, symmetrical world.

The Fearfulness of Symmetry

Essentially, the reasons for Blake's use of symmetry, as well as the extent to which he used it, have been indicated already by the foregoing analysis. In *Urizen*, as Blake insisted must everywhere be true, there is no separation of form and content. The symmetry of *Urizen*'s structure is itself a description and a cause of the fallen world that Blake set out to recount. It is symmetry itself—the generalizing and abstracting habit of reducing the world to similars and opposites, ups and downs, lefts and rights, rights and wrongs—that crystallizes the symmetrical world of the isolated, lowest common-denominator, solely quantitative, fallen senses. Being symmetrical, this world is also predictable and universal, a world of futurity and fixity. Man's birth is accompanied by the inevitable symmetry of his death. A symmetrical world links joy with pain, love with hate, master with slave, desire with dread. In the world of Urizen, symmetry is both the sign and the seal of fear.

There remain, however, some emphases to be affirmed.

The "Tragedy" of Symmetry

The first of these would stress, paradoxically as usual, the basic un-fearfulness of symmetry. The fear of symmetry is an illusion, just as symmetry itself is an illusion. This is the terror of the bogey-man at the top of the stairs—old Nobodaddy. The foolishness of this fear is illustrated everywhere in the designs of *Urizen*, which show in Los and Urizen a couple of red-faced, pseudo-tragic, comic blunderers engaged in the most incomprehensible and ridiculous activities—the archetypal Laurel and Hardy.

But although both the basis of the fear and the reaction to it are inane, the suffering still exists. The child, silly as he seems to adults, still refuses to climb the stairs. This simultaneous stupidity, but power, of the fearful world of symmetry is re-peatedly touched on by Blake. For example, *The Tyger* itself can be read as an account of the growth of an illusion of terror in what amounts to a symmetrical précis of *Urizen*. The first two lines with their strong rhythm seem to be a nursery-rhyme chant, but a chant that swells to dark poetry as the tygerish conception of the world increases its power over the questioner's mind. By the end of the poem, in "dares," the terror is complete; the end echoes the beginning, amplified, just as the powerful physical Urizen of plate 28 echoes the weak priest of plate 1. The range of treatments Blake gave the tyger design in different copies (from Cheshire cat to heroic) suggests the spectrum of such self-created bogeymen, from foolishness to power.

Other illustrations of the combined strength and stupidity of the fallen world of symmetry occur in Blake's works. The draw-ing of *The Man Who Built the Pyramids* shows a formidable, bulging-eyed, thick-necked "engineer," obviously capable of reckoning to the nearest slave the number of lives required per tier of stones. The painting of Newton working out geometrical problems on the ocean's floor emphasizes strength and an enor-mous power of intellectual concentration at the cost of complete sensory oblivion. Again, the range of combinations of strength and subtlety that projected worlds may assume and their creators possess is suggested.

Blake's illustrations in *Urizen* are thus not alone in depicting bullnecked strength combined with inner concentration and outer unawareness. In the illustration on plate 23 we even come full circle back to the tyger. The design {58} shows Urizen striding to the left, unseeing, like some sensorily oblivious, absentminded elder, toward a bulky, massiveheaded, inanely smiling catlike creature.

For an explanation of this repeated coupling of power and stupidity, one has only to remember *The Marriage of Heaven and Hell*: "One Law for the Lion & Ox is Oppression" (plate 24). In all the above-mentioned illustrations, the individual, varying, unique powers of the tyger, the man, and the ox have been reduced to one single common denominator: brute strength. With Newton, quantity, which is only one aspect of quality, has become the tyrant of experience.

Thus symmetry—the obsession with conceptual and fragmented phenomena at the expense of a unified and sensory experience— is equated with power and stupidity—quantity and mass—rather than with quality and energy. Recognition of this leads to a new appreciation of Blake's powers as an artist. One cannot criticize Blake for not being "noble" or "awesome" enough when he depicts the fallen condition, because there may well be nothing noble or awesome about it. Perhaps this is why *Urizen* is also, amongst other things, a parody of *Paradise Lost*.

It follows that when Blake depicts human suffering, in either design or verse, there is frequently something grotesque and ridiculous about it. The agony of Los's creation of Enitharmon, the original fall in the garden, is undercut by the fact that Los is shown (plate 17 {55}) squeezing her out of the top of his head, his hands over his ears, like some new kind of toothpaste from the brain of a mad chemist. Similarly, the Net of Religion that entraps mankind in chapter VIII is spun out of Urizen's bowels, as though he too had read more theology than he could stomach. Blake, in his penchant for both satire and the grotesque, is very much an eighteenth-century gentleman. Another example of the same sense of humor (and remember also Los, the born los-er) is Urizen's book of eternal brass. "Brass" as effrontery is as old as Shakespeare; it may well be complemented here by the unmitigated "gall" that the Eternals pour on Urizen in chapter III. Blake is often, like Joyce, a visionary of the comic, of change, of "eternal life sprung" (II, 1). The solemn, the painful, the tragic may ultimately be seen as only food for laughter.

The Extensiveness of Symmetry

The second point of emphasis is the usefulness of a symmetrical "model" for describing, and thus reading, Blake. Northrop Frye uses a "diabolical" and "divine" symmetry for elucidating Blake's imagery, but I would stress the symmetrical forms of his structures —and even his grammar—as well. The *Songs of Innocence and of Experience* and *The Marriage of Heaven and Hell* are obvious examples. *The Tyger, The Crystal Cabinet, The Mental Traveller* all end where they begin, with the difference of a mirror image. The last plate of *Job* reflects the first—with a significant difference. *America, Europe*, and the "Asia" and "Africa" sections of *The Song of Los* combine to form a symmetrical structure related to the four continents. *The Book of Los* (four chapters) and *The Book of Ahania* (five chapters) frame *The Book of Urizen* (nine chapters) to form another symmetrical structure.

The similarity of the structure of *The Four Zoas* (nine nights) to *Urizen* (nine chapters) might also be remarked upon, together with the fact that material from *Urizen* recurs in all the long prophecies. The orientation, or directional, symbolism of *Urizen* also recurs, suggesting that the investigation of structural symmetries in the late works may well be profitable.

But the concept of symmetry not only may be applied broadly to other Blake works, it may also be used in much greater depth, with more precision and delicacy, on individual works than has been possible in the limited space of this essay. Such an exact application and description may reveal that Blake's "system" of symbolism is even more systematic and extensive than it has been thought to be. This suggestion, if it is confirmed, would fit in well both with the basic concept of the fallen world as symmetrical and cyclical and with Blake's very extensive knowledge and use of contemporary science as revealed in his imagery.[11]

The Crystal Cabinet illustrates these points in miniature. The poem turns on the notion of a "three-fold" symmetry. The speaker

---

[11] J.H.H.: It might be well, at the same time, to take into account the tradition of *chiasmus*, a basic form of Hebrew poetry, where the climax is in the middle, and where one moves in the following fashion:

    A
       B
          C
          C'
       B'
    A'

This form explains much in Blake and is somewhat truer both to his tradition and to his own manner of proceeding than is the overworked term "cyclical."

enters a "crystal" and sees three women where once was one. He tries to seize the "inmost form," or fix the exact, mathematical shape of these images, and breaks the crystal instead, thus revealing their threefold symmetry as illusory. But symmetry, the exact, repeated life in the crystal world, now seems to him delightful, and he is filled with woe to find himself outside once more with what seems to him to be the anguished chaos of a nature impossible to organize into such pretty, repeated shapes. The final point of this analysis is that in the science of crystallography, or the analysis of the symmetries of crystals, "three-fold" symmetry (the same terminology is used) is one of the commonest forms and is illustrated by rock quartz.

For yet another example of the application of symmetry, let us look at the use of the "four elements" symbolism in *Urizen*. In chapter II, verse 5, Urizen recounts his struggle with the four elements:

> First I fought with the fire; consum'd
> Inwards, into a deep world within:
> A void immense, wild dark & deep,
> Where nothing was; Natures wide womb
> And self balanc'd stretch'd o'er the void
> I alone, even I! the winds merciless
> Bound; but condensing, in torrents
> They fall & fall; strong I repell'd
> The vast waves, & arose on the waters
> A wide world of solid obstruction.

In chapter VIII, verse 3, the four elements are born:

> Weeping! wailing! first Thiriel appear'd
> Astonish'd at his own existence
> Like a man from a cloud born, & Utha
> From the waters emerging, laments!
> Grodna rent the deep earth howling
> Amaz'd! his heavens immense cracks
> Like the ground parch'd with heat; Then Fuzon
> Flam'd out! first begotten, last born.

In both descriptions the order of appearance of the elements is emphasized. In Blake's later works the four "Zoas" are each associated with an element and a direction: Urthona (earth, north),

169

Urizen (air, south), Luvah (fire, east), and Tharmas (water, west). Blake provides a diagram showing these figures and their directions on plate 33 of *Milton*. If we diagram the elements described in *Urizen* in the same way, and use an arrow to show the sequence of their appearance, figure 4a results for the first description. This diagram seems to correspond with Urizen's movements as described in the text: "consum'd inwards" (that is, leftwards); "condensing in torrents / They fall & fall" (downwards); "arose on the waters" (upwards); "A wide world of solid obstruction" (at the top).

Fig. 4. The Four Elements in *Urizen*

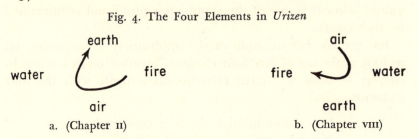

a. (Chapter II) b. (Chapter VIII)

TABLE OF SOME MAJOR CHAPTER CORRESPONDENCES
ALONG THE SUBJECT-OBJECT AXIS

Urizen loses sight of Eternity. Urizen-Los identified.	V *(first half)*	V *(last half)*	Eternals weave tent "That Eternals may no more behold them" (v, 11). Enitharmon created by Los from himself.
Urizen develops as an embryo Internal events of "birth." Los, howling, hammers out Urizen.	IV	VI	Orc goes through the stages of evolution. External events of "birth." Enitharmon, groaning, produces Orc.
Urizen-Los divide. Urizen builds his world.	III	VII	Urizen-Orc unite. Urizen measures and plants his world.
Urizen battles four elements. Urizen writes his laws.	II	VIII	Urizen sees birth of four elements. Urizen spins Net of Religion.
Urizen revolts by withdrawing from Eternity, creating a "void." Parody of Genesis description of spirit brooding on waters.	I	IX	Fuzon revolts by leaving Urizen's "englob'd" world. Parody of Genesis description of seven days of creation.

If, in keeping with mirror symmetry, we reverse all the positions of the elements, figure 4b results. This fits the sequence of the birth of the elements in chapter VIII, with fire moved from first to last. What the two diagrams represent is the world as seen from two different points of view: first, that of the revolutionary Urizen, thinking himself repressed by his "low" position (fig. 4a); and second, that of the successful, tyrannic Urizen, triumphantly at the top (fig. 4b). The first plate of *Urizen* introduces him in a valley, the last represents him on, or as, a mountain. And the Preludium tells how, though presumably he is identified with the south element, as in the *Milton* diagram, he was given "a place in the north" after his revolution.

This illustrates the depth of detail of symmetry in *Urizen*, but it also suggests interesting possibilities for other Blake works as well. The two descriptions of the elements in *Urizen* amount to a shorthand notation of the "plot" or the change of "states" that occurs in the work. Perhaps in other prophetic works a similar orientation is provided for the reader.

The Alternative to Symmetry

The third point of emphasis is the nature of Blake's alternative to symmetry—the unfallen human experience. A glimpse of this experience is provided in chapter II, verse 1, of *Urizen*:

> Earth was not: nor globes of attraction
> The will of the Immortal expanded
> Or contracted his all flexible senses.
> Death was not, but eternal life sprung

Even in this brief vision, the key components emerge: perpetual flux or change, a creatively sensual existence, the union of all men's experiences into one man's. Such an existence makes all abstract notions, including that of the shape or movement of the planets, irrelevant. Similarly irrelevant, and thus nonexistent, is the abstract notion of death.

Thus, in *The Book of Urizen*, Blake has described both of the possible worlds of men: the finite, symmetrical, and fixed; and the infinite, sensual, and changing. This leads to the question of what is the essential factor, difference, similarity—link—between them. What shift of what medium produces the two different points of view, the two different worlds? I would like to suggest that this link—this catalyst—is language. By this, I mean language in the widest sense: the exchange of all the items men create, their art objects and technologies as well as their words: all the exchanges that create one man out of many men.

Language in this sense has two aspects, the finite and the infinite. The first is mathematical; it gives men the means to create a symmetrical, repeated world, because it allows them to communicate their conceptions to others with precision. All men speaking the same language can agree on a left and right for the solar system, and can agree, or submit themselves, to the fixed predictability of such a system. In fact, it is on the exact communication of this agreement that the "existence" of the solar system depends. This is language as finite and defined, communication as the re-creation of exact copies: Urizen writing and re-writing his books. It produces a common denominator for sense experience and so a measured, "mean" world.

The second aspect of language is opposite and extreme: language as the creation and exchange of forms for reality, language as art. This is language as ambiguous, reverberating, additioning, multifoliate. *Urizen* is one of Blake's finer examples of this kind of communication—a work that compels creation, rather than conveying a copy. Simultaneous with its vision of symmetry it suggests an infinity of other meanings. The central event of chapter v, for example, alludes not only to the Narcissus myth but to the growth of an embryo from a placenta, the division of male and female as recounted in Plato's *Symposium*, the birth of Athena from Jove's forehead, the origin of the moon thrown off by the sun, the beginning of courtly love, the growth of Los's testicles, the fall in the garden, the oozing of a single drop of blood from a wound, Adam's (wet) dream of Eve, the crucifixion, Milton's view of the earth as a ball hanging beneath heaven, and a simple fainting spell, probably from vertigo. Further, Blake uses his peculiar grammar and punctuation to compound ambiguities, and adds the designs to the text to compound all the meanings once again.

This is language as art, as infinite. And all men using language in this way create a different, infinite, changing world, a world of warring contraries of meaning, and conception, and perception that forces all men to create and define and change continuously. Each man's vision becomes the material for other men's visions—

material not to be copied, but to be transformed, as poets borrow from other poets.

But whether language is used to create the finite or to permit the infinite, Blake is pointing out that language *is* man's world, the medium that enables all men to become one man, whether mortal or eternal, and to create one world, whether finite or infinite. The world of man is language, and in this sense all language is poetry.

8

Blake's Use of Gesture

JANET A. WARNER

> In these books the same attitudes and movements appear
> again and again. It is the weak side of Blake's art. . . . We
> forgive the endless repetitions of attitude and gesture
> because of the genius which has made them rush, and
> float, and fly through the air, embrace with ecstacy or
> collapse in despair.   —Laurence Binyon, 1926

> . . . Painting admits not a Grain of Sand or a Blade of
> Grass Insignificant much less an Insignificant Blur or Mark.
>   —Blake, *VLJ* (E550/K611)

QUITE early in his career as an artist, Blake developed a set of
visual forms or gestures which he came to use repeatedly. Though
both art and literary critics have regarded these repeated forms
with some embarrassment,[1] it is my contention that Blake perceived archetypes of gesture and stance in the work of painters
and sculptors, and used them in his own art, just as he perceived
and employed archetypes of literature in his poetry—in both their
apocalyptic and demonic states. Blake's repetition of visual images
must be recognized as a highly sophisticated pictorial language,

---

[1] Blake's "borrowings" from earlier art and his use of "the great traditions
to which he was heir" have, since the 1940's, been documented principally
by Sir Anthony Blunt, Collins Baker, and Jean Hagstrum. These scholars
have shown how Blake became familiar with classical art through engravings
after Raphael, Michelangelo, and Giulio Romano, and that he adapted from
Salviati, Caracci, Scamozzi, and from Flaxman, Romney, and Fuseli. Scholars
have, in fact, proved Blake familiar with a singularly wide range of artistic
works and traditions. Demonstrating that he took over these images, critics
point out that Blake learned figure drawing by such copying, and then pay
tribute to his capacity for "breathing living flame into driest bones." And
while some, like Blunt, conjecture the processes of Blake's imagination and
sensitively show Blake in relation to the artistic heritage of the eighteenth
century, few have suggested there may be other than technical reasons for
his use of the same images again and again. See Anthony Blunt, "Blake's
Pictorial Imagination," *JWCI*, VI (1943), 190-212; Collins Baker, "The Sources
of Blake's Pictorial Expression," *Huntington Library Quarterly*, IV (1940-
1941), 359-367; and Blunt (1959) and Hagstrum (1964).

a complement to the poetry yet infinitely suggestive in itself. I shall attempt to demonstrate both the consistency and the variety of this language by a survey of several of his recurrent forms, and a detailed analysis of one in particular, the gesture of outstretched arms.

Northrop Frye's observation (*Symmetry*, 15) that "form" and "image" meant the same thing to Blake, the unit of mental existence, provides a helpful approach to the study of his designs. The "Mental Things" which are alone real, the forms and images which constitute the "Living Form" that is eternal existence, can remain unchanged ("In Eternity One Thing Never Changes Into Another Thing") while constantly in creative motion, walking "To and Fro in Eternity"—which is to say that the images of art can have various contexts through the ages while still retaining their perceptible identities. To define and explore Blake's language of forms, then, does not require the assumption that their meanings are fixed or static; indeed, the most "dramatic" thing about his "visionary forms" may be that they are as ambivalent as his metaphors.

In *Anatomy of Criticism*, Frye defined archetype as "a symbol, usually an image, which recurs often enough in literature to be recognizable as an element of one's literary experience as a whole."[2] The forms I consider here may be called archetypes in an analogous sense, recurring often enough in Blake's work to be recognizable as an element of one's experience of his art. Like his poetic archetypes, Blake's visual images are indicative primarily of *states* of man, which is one reason the human figure in various gestures is so central to his designs. Symbolic meanings tend to cluster around these figures as we become aware of how consistently they are used.

Before proceeding to an extended discussion of the gesture of outstretched arms, I shall list, with representative examples, some other frequently repeated images which appear to constitute basic visual archetypes.[3] These include the flying figure, springing up-

[2] Northrop Frye, *Anatomy of Criticism*, Princeton, 1957, 365.

[3] Blunt noted "there were certain motives and certain images which were, one might almost say, the common property of the whole group to which Blake, Fuseli, Flaxman, Romney, and Stothard belonged, and that each member of the group produced his own particular interpretation of the motive" (Blunt, 41).

Sources and similarities, however, do not sufficiently explain Blake's de-ward, one leg bent, usually nude, female and wingless, viewed from the back (Argument, *VDA*); and the falling male, clutching his head (*Urizen* 6). The corpse, a supine figure with arms tight at its sides, can be adult (title page of *Songs of Experience*; *MHH* 14) or child (*America* 9; *Europe* 6).

Additional repeated motifs include: the nude male, seated, with legs apart, looking upward (*America* 6); the bent old man with staff and windblown garment (*Gates of Paradise* 15); and female figures imitating the stance of a traditional Venus: standing (the Arlington Court picture) and reclining (*America* 7).

Very frequently observed also are huddled forms, such as the kneeling, bent-over figure, apparently grieving, often a woman (*Job* 8, *America* 16); and hunched figures, facing forward with knees drawn up (*America* frontispiece, *Urizen* 22, *Gates of Paradise* 4 and 16). The worm-serpent-dragon complex makes up another group of images. (This motif is already an established symbol.)

Certain recurring details in Blake's designs also invite consideration as symbols. Among these are: mirror images (*Jerusalem* 76) and hand positions, to be considered here only in conjunction with outstretched arms—palms up (*Albion rose*) and palms down (*America* 8). There is also a hand position employing what I have called "creative fingers," a variation of pointing (*Job* 20). (I use this term because this position appears to be copied from the hand of God on Michelangelo's Sistine Chapel ceiling.) Finally, forms of birds and flowers can also be seen as repeated images in Blake's art (*America* 7 and title page of *Thel*, respectively).

That these recognizable repeated images have consistent symbolic meanings will take detailed study to establish; the following

---

signs or his reasons for repeating images, and whereas Blunt makes suggestive comments and recognizes the schematic, symbolic nature of Blake's visual forms, no one has made a systematic study of Blake's visual images and their analogues in art history in conjunction with the knowledge that Frye and other Blake literary scholars have provided.

Keynes's Notes in the *Catalogue of Blake's Separate Engravings* (Dublin, 1956) are a beginning. Digby's study, *Symbol and Image In William Blake*, also approaches the subject, within the framework of Jungian psychology, but does not go beyond Blake's own use of forms into art history. Hagstrum has all the material at his fingertips but does not discuss it in that manner. And none of these studies takes up the phenomenon of the repeated symbolic image.

discussion attempts such a study for the motif of outstretched arms. Of the various visual images in Blake's designs, this gesture is probably the most frequently observed. Figures with arms in this position (the Latin cross position—arms extended horizontally, at right angles to the body) can be seen primarily in four poses: standing; seated or kneeling with one knee raised; hovering, with only head and arms visible; and prostrate. Representative examples of these attitudes are: for the standing figure, *Albion rose* {91}; for the raised-knee figure, plate 8 of *America* {36}; for the hovering figure, *The House of Death* {93}; for the prostrate figure, Adam in *Elohim Creating Adam* {94}. These four forms are discussed in some detail in this section.

There are also other forms which incorporate this gesture: prone or supine figures, flat on the ground, viewed head on (*A Poison Tree*); and striding figures (*Urizen* 3, *Jerusalem* 26). These, together with further variations—figures with arms outstretched forward (Elohim, in *Elohim Creating Adam*) and figures with arms outstretched at an oblique angle (*Jerusalem* 99)—are considered briefly later. Even this short list indicates the consistent presence of the gesture in Blake's art, and as the discussion proceeds I hope to demonstrate that it is an important visual symbol, both eloquent in itself and useful in the interpretation of a poetic text in which the design occurs.

The traditional image suggested by outstretched arms is of course the Cross, a symbol of divinity rich with associations of self-sacrifice or death, and regeneration. The cruciform gesture also carries in Western art traditional connotations of creativity, e.g., Michelangelo's God creating Adam {112} or Raphael's God in designs for the Vatican Loggie. Thus the gesture can be seen to be complementary to the main themes of Blake's poetry and thought: man's essential divinity and capacity for regeneration— or from the aspect of fallen vision, man's own error of turning that divine creativity into mental tyranny or spiritual death. Blake appears consistently to associate the gesture with these themes. The four attitudes which repeatedly carry these connotations each have a regenerative and a demonic aspect, and also can subtly be distinguished one from the other as indicators of mental states. Yet it is always with some aspect of divinity that outstretched arms are associated.

The crucified Christ is a frequent image in Blake's art, his outstretched arms a metaphor for his voluntary self-sacrifice. In this Blake follows the iconographic tradition of Western art. His crucifixion illustrations include *Jerusalem* 76, *The Prophecy of the Crucifixion* (*Paradise Lost*, 1808), and the water color design *The Crucifixion: Christ Taking Leave of His Mother*. In these designs the sacrificial aspect of the symbol is underlined both by the sadness and passivity of Jesus and by the extended arms nailed to the bar of the Cross. In *Jerusalem* 76 the arms of Albion reflect the gesture of Christ, Albion taking upon himself the divine act of sacrifice. (See {98}.) His is the human form which most closely approximates the shape of Christ on the Cross; it is this form I have called the standing figure.

Interestingly, Blake appears to have used this figure most often for personifications of man at his spiritual extremes: Albion and Satan. Redeemed man, Albion, assumes this attitude in *Albion rose*. Albion in *Jerusalem* 76 is the back view of the same figure. The famous inscription on the *Albion rose* engraving emphasizes the sacrificial overtones of the image, while a demonic version appears in Satan's figure in *Job* 6. (A variant of the standing figure is Satan in the painting *Satan Calling Up His Legions*.)

Blake's using the same form for such dramatically opposed states as Albion and Satan makes his point emphatically that the divinity in man can be turned to malevolence and death. Supporting evidence for the association of these figures with human divinity will be found in the evident sources of the preliminary pencil drawings of front and back views of the standing Albion.[4] Anthony Blunt has suggested that these sources are Scamozzi's engraving of a proportion figure and an engraving of a bronze figure of a faun from Herculaneum (1767-1771).[5] Though an image long associated with mankind, the Scamozzi figure,[6] Blake must have thought, needed the addition of lightness and grace found in the dancer-like bronze faun, which indeed the pencil sketches more closely

[4] The pencil sketches are dated 1780 because the signature on the engraved *Albion rose* reads "W B inv 1780," though the plate was not likely engraved until the 1790's.

[5] Blunt, 34. Blunt's first discussion of Blake's sources for this picture, calling attention to the Scamozzi figure, appeared in *JWCI*, II (1938), 65-68.

[6] It is a Renaissance example of Vitruvian man, used to demonstrate that the proportions of the human body are the ideal pattern for architecture and design. Désirée Hirst (*Hidden Riches*, London, 1964, 53-54) points out that Blake was also probably familiar with Agrippa's Vitruvian figures.

resemble. Both figures associate universality and vitality with out-stretched arms, and these are important elements in Blake's later use of the penciled figures. The poet who wrote of "the human form divine" and who said "All deities reside in the human breast" made his visual divine image reflect traditional icons of the human body as an ideal measure and gave it also the quality of motion. For the dancelike movement of Albion in both *Albion rose* and *Jerusalem* 76 is the subtle but central quality which distinguishes Albion, the living human, from the passive, crucified Jesus. It expresses visually the idea of the way the divine must live in the human—that eternal life for man is a dance "of Eternal Death," continuous self-sacrifice for one's fellows. The outstretched arms of the standing form are the connecting link between Christ and Albion which contributes to the visible expression of Albion as the "spiritual body of mankind."

The same gesture on the three other forms I have mentioned is found to have similar associations with the inherent divinity in man. In the tractates of 1788, *There Is No Natural Religion* and *All Religions Are One*, Blake used each of these forms, the knee-raised, the hovering, and the prostrate, associated with texts equating the human and divine. Accompanying Proposition VII (E2/K97), which with the Application on the following plate links "God," "Man," and "the Infinite," he etched a torso of a nude male with outstretched arms, who looks somewhat Christlike (fig. 5). The Application itself stresses the divinity of this link ("He who sees the Infinite in all things sees God") and thus, as it were, authenticates the cruciform implication of the illustration. The plate illustrating the third sentence of this Proposition, "Therefore God becomes as we are, that we may be as he is," shows a prostrate figure on the ground with a halo of lines like sun rays around its head. In *All Religions Are One* the first Principle (pl. 4 [fig. 6]) is illustrated by an old man in the knee-raised position; the text identifies God with the Poetic Genius and Imagination. In that same work, Principle 7 (pl. 10) associates the hovering form, again a bearded old man, with "The True Man," the Poetic Genius.

In the last two examples, Blake represents the Poetic Genius-God-Man in the traditional artistic image of divinity in the Judeo-Christian world: both Michelangelo and Raphael show God the creator with outstretched arms, as I have mentioned, and Hagstrum (42-43) sees the Raphael as a possible source of Blake's

Jehovah-Urizen. Since Blake in *All Religions Are One* specifically mentions "The Jewish & Christian Testaments" and calls them "an original derivation from the Poetic Genius" (Principle 6), the image of the patriarchal creator conventional to Western art is a natural association for him to make. The aspect of divinity most suggested by the outstretched arms of the knee-raised and hovering forms, then, is not so much sacrifice as creativity.

Because of these associations, the second or knee-raised form can perhaps be said to suggest at best God-in-man, the Poetic Genius, and at worst, fallen man's idea of God as authority. Poetic Genius is implied in the figure of an old man with raised knee in plate 4 of *All Religions Are One* (fig. 6); the similar figure in

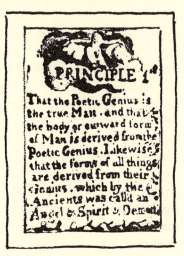

Fig. 5. *There is No Natural Religion* (b), pl. 7

Fig. 6. *All Religions Are One,* pl. 4

America 8 represents Urizen, man's perversion of his Poetic Genius into authority {36}. In the *Job* engravings this form represents one of Job's ideas of God (pl. 14, "When the morning stars sang together" {114}). In the Dante engravings the same form, with some demonic refinements, appears as "The Angry God of This World" (pl. 3). Some variations of this pose appear to have similar connotations. A figure very like *America* 8 is used in *Urizen* 5, where a bearded old man holds open with outstretched arms a book which resembles stone tablets of law (cf. *Milton* 15). And in *Gates of Paradise* 11 a bearded old man sitting with one arm outstretched holds the wings of a youth in one hand while he clips them with scissors held in the other.[7]

There is one important instance, however, where the raised-knee form is not an old man, but a young one, and since both versions occur within two plates of each other in America, the relation between them becomes worth examining. We have seen already that this is the stance of the Poetic Genius. Blake had written that the Poetic Genius was "everywhere call'd the Spirit of Prophecy" (E2), and *Marriage*, plate 24, relates outstretched arms to this faculty. At the point where Hell (i.e., the free imaginative realm) and Heaven become "married," the Angel "stretched out his arms," embraced the fire, was consumed, and arose as a prophet (Elijah).[8] Gleckner points out that in terms of the conclusion of *Marriage* it is Orc, the "newborn terror," who arises,[9] and it is consistent with this idea to note that plate 10 of *America* shows a young man usually regarded as Orc surrounded by flames with his arms outstretched {38}. When, turning the pages, we see that the young man's stance is quite like that of the old man (except that his left knee is raised rather than his right, making him a mirror image) we are invited to see a relationship between them. Also, beneath the image of Urizen on plate 8, the text demands that we hear the voice of Orc: "The terror answered: I am Orc, wreath'd round the accursed tree." The possibilities of their relationship hinge on the fact that both figures make the gesture associated with the Poetic Genius. In Urizen the Poetic Genius has become part of a repressive system, the spiritual form of Albion's guardian prince, symbol of authority and restraint. His mirror image on plate 10 reflects his other self, the imaginative

---

[7] Engraved in 1793; the later additions of 1818 include the key for this plate: "Holy & cold, I clip'd the Wings of all Sublunary Things." The association of repressive authority with a bearded old man occurred earlier in Blake's drawings for *Tiriel*, which represent the tyrannical king as a bearded patriarch. Tiriel is never shown in the specific poses I am discussing, though he is pictured raising one arm to curse. (See Bentley's edition of *Tiriel*, Oxford, 1967.)

[8] Blake's picture *Ezekiel's Vision* (Boston Museum of Fine Arts, reproduced in the magazine *Blake Studies*, 1 [1968], 59) shows the prophet with outstretched arms in a standing-figure variation.

[9] Robert E. Gleckner, *The Piper and the Bard*, Detroit, 1959, 193.

power of creative desire, the spirit of rebellion. Orc's pose mocks Urizen, for they are adversaries, but it also links them. Blake's Orc-Urizen myth underlies all the Lambeth books, and significantly, in *America*, the first of the prophecies, these designs provide a key to it.

The dynamic nature of these Blakean forms and the subtle way outstretched arms bring associations of divinity to each pose is further evident in the third design involving this gesture, the hovering figure. Because this form frequently hovers *over* someone, it develops, I believe, connotations of divinity separated in some way from the whole man or human form. The divine quality is thus in danger of being lost or becoming a spectre, as its bat-winged variations suggest. The hovering, bearded man in plate 10 of *All Religions Are One* may illustrate "The True Man" (as I have suggested), but in his next appearance, in *Marriage* 11, the text concerns the separation or abstraction of divine from human and how "men forgot that All deities reside in the human breast." Beneath "deities" is drawn the hovering figure, in a cloud; beneath "human breast" is a small human form, in darkness; they are about an arm's length from each other. (See {19}.)[10] In a more

[10] D.V.E.: Their horizontality is a nice equivoque. This is like a "God creating Man" picture, the Michelangelo for instance, but sideways. Who creates whom? The text tells us: "some" people attempt to "abstract" and then pronounce the abstraction to be more real than the human. The hovering deity looks more alive than the poor bare forked animal we see alongside him in the dark.

J.E.G.: The old man with outspread arms can be no other than the deity as a human artifact, a prefiguration of the malign divinity who presides in the color print of *The House of Death* {93}. The smaller nude to the left is usually taken to be a boy fleeing from this fearsome image of divinity. In some copies he seems to face the reader in a position like that of the leaping infant at the top of the page. But in other copies (see the Dent facsimile of copy H) he has his back to the reader, in a position like that of the infant at the bottom of *MHH* 4, a design that prefigures the later *Good and Evil Angels*. Dynamically the picture also resembles the title page of *VDA*, in which a sky-god, Urizen with characteristics of both Theotormon and Bromion, flies in pursuit of a fugitive woman, Oothoon, while his outstretched right wing disrupts a ring dance. These closely related images point to a connection with "the new born terror" and "the starry king" of *A Song of Liberty* 9-10. That the allegory of the concluding Song is primarily political while the exposition in *MHH* 11 is primarily theological will not seem discrepant to the student of Blake. The intertextual design at the end of the penultimate sentence, which deals with the growth of "Priesthood," in-

menacing aspect the hovering old man appears on the title page of *Visions of the Daughters of Albion* {20}, as Death in *The House of Death* {93}, and as a wielder of vipers in *Christ's Troubled Dream* (*Paradise Regained*).[11]

A similar but female hovering form appears in *Marriage* 14 and *Visions* 8, in each instance suggesting separation and potential but unfulfilled creativity. The first of these may be taken to show the process of change, the consuming flames of creation producing an infinite and holy state, the soul hovering over and awaiting union with the body, as the text suggests.[12] Here the hovering figure, though still separated from the human form below it, could suggest a creative state. In the final plate of *Visions*, on the other hand, the female form in this pose, Oothoon hovering in the sky above the Daughters of Albion, is a sad and ironic echo of the hovering bearded form menacing her on the title page, whose wings, rather than arms, are outstretched. What seems to be suggested is that Oothoon's failure to become one with Theotormon has made her an image of the very forces she was trying to overcome.[13]

Although I am tempted to suggest that after *Marriage* 11 no hovering figure could be completely positive in implication be-

---

deed makes the link: four devotees are bidden by a priest to worship a headless warrior with a sword. The impositions of priestcraft are necessarily as firmly based on a veneration of power as on a terror of God. Many of the same symbols are utilized in the somewhat different context of the design for *A Little Boy Lost* in *Songs of Experience*.

[11] In Darrell Figgis, *The Paintings of William Blake*, London, 1925, pl. 30; Digby, pl. 60. Blunt (p. 41) has suggested the figure of Jupiter Pluvius in a Roman relief as the source of this motif, tracing its appearance in the work of Blake, Flaxman, and Romney and finding Blake's first use in his Nile engraving of 1791 after Fuseli. The earlier *All Religions Are One* figure, however, does seem to be the same except for its lack of wings.

[12] D.V.E.: A title for the picture, "The Body of Hector," is penciled in the Cumberland-Beckford copy, perhaps by Blake's friend Cumberland; the fall of Troy is a suggestive analogue; compare the woman kissing her fallen warrior in the *America* title page {25}.

[13] D.V.E.: I incline to resist these total identities; if the hovering man in *MHH* 11 is deity abstracted, perhaps the hovering woman at the end of *VDA* is liberty abstracted, her eloquent pleas falling on deaf ears. But the reader-viewer will see that these appearances are to be consumed; Oothoon's flames are as rosy as the strongest color in the rainbow of the title page; the duller flames around Urizen beneath it are of *his* consuming.

cause of associations of separation, the potentially demonic aspect of this form is made obvious when it appears as a hovering bat-winged creature (e.g., *Jerusalem* 6 and 33[37]{97}; *Gates of Paradise* tailpiece). Blake's color print *Satan Exulting Over Eve* {108} shows Satan with outstretched arms and bat wings in a related variant of the hovering pose, over a serpent-wrapped Eve. It is important to note that bat-winged creatures hover over corpse forms (i.e., arms tight at sides), but eagles or eagle-winged figures hover over cruciform prostrate forms (*America* 13, top {41}; *VDA* 3; *Milton* 42). The eagle-winged Elohim in *Elohim Creating Adam* {94} suggests the creative force behind the act of separation, while the worm-wrapped cruciform Adam retains the image of his potential divinity. (It may be suggested that the bat is the demonic aspect of the eagle, another image for two sides of a creative impulse.)

Satan and the Elohim are *variations* of the hovering pose I have called a recurring form; they are not "head-and-arms-only" designs. Yet hovering forms like them, whole hovering bodies seen at various angles, are also familiar Blakean images: *Job* 11 {110} ("With Dreams upon my bed thou scarest me"); *Job* 13 ("Then the Lord Answered Job out of the whirlwind"); *Job* 20 (hoverers in the background); *Jerusalem* 31[35]; *David Delivered Out of Many Waters; The Good and Evil Angels Struggling For Possession of a Child*; and the same figures in *Marriage* 4. The one feature all these have in common is outstretched arms; all seem to generate associations that concern the separation of divine from human.

Discussion of the hovering forms has introduced us to some of the figures they hover over; so most examples of the fourth extended-arm form—the prostrate figure—have already been cited. (Because it is lying on the ground, this form is viewed from the side, and strictly speaking only one arm can be seen extended. It should be distinguished from the corpse image, whose arm is close to its side.) While this pose reminds us of the potential for regeneration, especially in its first use in *There Is No Natural Religion*, the connotations of mortality are usually uppermost, for Blake often draws the figure on a bierlike stone just above the water, or winds the serpent about it. Thus, at best, the form may connote Generation—or perhaps in the case of *Milton* 42, Beulah —and at worst the fall, a spiritual death (Adam in *Elohim Cre-*

ating Adam). This, I think, is what the serpent-wrapped, extended-arm figure means even when it is not, strictly speaking, prostrate. *Urizen* 6 uses the symbol of a serpent-wrapped cruciform figure, probably man falling upside down into material existence.[14] (See {57}.) Blake also drew an illustration for Young's *Night Thoughts* which uses a serpent-wrapped, semiprostrate man with outstretched arms as a symbol of spiritual death in the material world.[15]

Each of the four basic outstretched-arm forms can be seen, then, to suggest various aspects of divinity, and within each form either the benevolent or the malevolent aspects of the divine creative impulses may be connoted. As we can see, there are details, like the presence of the serpent, which help to contextualize the forms, so that the variations or additional facets of meaning become clear. In this respect, subtly differing hand positions can modify the meanings of the outstretched arms, like signals helping us to experience the designs with greater delicacy.[16]

For example, the hands of the figure in the sketched and in the engraved *Albion rose* are turned upwards, palms out; the palms of the figure in *There Is No Natural Religion* (fig. 5) are turned forward; the hands of the old man with raised knee are inclined downward—until the figure is used in its final engraved form in *Job*, when the hand position changes to the creative fingers of Michelangelo's God. (See {114}.) The hands of God in *Elohim Creating Adam* are sloping downward, while those of Adam himself, whose arms are more specifically in the Latin cross position, are turned forward. In *Songs of Innocence*, any of the figures from cherubs to children whose arms are outstretched to express delight or inspiration appear to have their hands inclined upwards; see *The Ecchoing Green* and *The Blossom*.

[14] See Robert Simmons' essay in this volume.

[15] No. 27 (I, 22). The text illustrated (*NT* I, 315-343) supports this interpretation. Words evoking the snake image—"rises," "sting," "envenom'd," "beware," "death"—are collocated with abstractions—"rises" with *misfortune*, "sting" with *distress*, "envenom'd" with *rage* and *peace*, "beware" with *happiness*, "death" with *joys*. Thus we are invited to see the serpent-wrapped dead man as representative of a mental state.

[16] E. J. Rose has described and commented on hand positions in "Blake's Hand: Symbol and Design in *Jerusalem*," *Texas Studies in Literature and Language*, VI (1964), 48-49.

This detail becomes more consistent as Blake's art develops. Hand position may not have been a deliberate symbol in its earliest use on the Poetic Genius form, but certainly, during the Lambeth period, the position of the hands in an outstretched-arm figure seems decidedly a symbol, especially when the figure is a bearded old man. In *Marriage* 11, *America* 8, and *Urizen* 28, for example, the drooping, downturned hands suggest the enfeebled or misdirected creativity of the God of this world.[17]

The use of the hand detail to modify the meaning of a form can be observed in the *Job* designs. In the water color drawing for plate 14 the hands of Jehovah droop (see {113}); yet when Blake engraved the design, he gave the right hand "creative fingers" (see {114}) and opened the left-hand fingers as well. This change more graphically suggests the awakened vision of Job. Job is himself shown in the outstretched-arm attitude with the creative-fingers position on both hands in the engraved plate 20, where he is recreating his experience for his daughters. The overall form of plate 14 is still an image of fallen man's idea of God, the authoritarian God of the state of Experience, but that form at its best. As Job realizes his idea of God in himself, his gestures become like Jehovah's.

It may be argued, of course, that if Blake had been consistently using this creative-hand position symbolically he would have used it at first in the water color for plate 14; my suggestion is that the case is rather like revisions in a poem. The right gesture, like the right word, alters or modifies a theme; the artist experiments till he is satisfied.

The pattern of using a receptive palms-up or outward position on Adam, Albion, or Christ figures was a usual practice of Blake's, as even a cursory examination of designs will reveal (e.g., *Jerusalem* 76 or the *Paradise Lost* series). In *Milton* the upturned hand is found in two important places: in the plates which represent Robert and William Blake receiving the divine spirit, the figures are shown leaning back with arms outstretched, palms turned up {92}.

In contrast, downturned hands are used to powerful effect in *The House of Death* {93}, where the "hovering" figure of death (as the bearded old man) has his palms turned down, or in the

[17] And compare the feeble hands of George III in his dragon form in *America* 4 {31}.

figure of the Evil Angel in *The Good & Evil Angels Struggling For Possession of a Child*. The downturned hands on the hovering variant of the outstretched-arms form are to be seen in plate 4 of Blake's *Paradise Lost* series, *Satan's and Raphael's Entries into Paradise* {105}, where once again the figure seems to represent the God of the fallen world, the Hebraic God of Milton's *Paradise Lost*. The association of the downturned hand with creativity turned to rationalism and abstraction can be seen vividly in Blake's color print *Newton*, where the left hand of Newton, sloping downwards, holds the triangular compasses. The detail of the downturned hand may bear, then, a message in regard to the Orc figure of plate 10 of *America*. This form has the same downturned hands as the Urizen figure of plate 8: perhaps Orc here may not be a completely regenerated figure: indeed, as a representative of the cycle of time he could hardly be the completely redeemed man. Blake himself drew attention to the importance of such details in his art when he wrote, "I intreat then that the Spectator will attend to the Hands & Feet . . . they are all descriptive of character & not a line is drawn without intention & that most discriminate and particular" (E550/K611).

Taking into consideration the four basic outstretched-arm images and the significant related details we have been discussing, it can be suggested that these four forms may approximate mental states. There appears to be a progression from the prostrate form to the standing: implied is a movement from the *separation* of human and divine suggested by hovering and prostrate forms, through *creation* (of the mortal and finite) as suggested by Jehovah-Urizen associations of the knee-raised form, to divine sacrifice or *union* of man and divine in the standing form. And because the standing figure can be either of the extreme states, Albion or Satan, this form most vividly expresses the dynamic potential of all these states in one man.

One design which uses many of the symbols I have been discussing is the water color *The Great Red Dragon and the Woman Clothed with the Sun* {63}. The hovering figure is here taken to its ultimate Satanic form, encompassing bat wings, serpent tail, and outstretched arms with downturned hands. According to Revelation the dragon is "that old serpent, called the Devil, and Satan, which deceiveth the whole world." The woman clothed with the sun and given the wings of an eagle represents the good *in nature* (she sits on a crescent moon) that the dragon is trying to vanquish; Blake indicates this also by her outstretched arms, her upturned hands, and her position on a stone in the sea, rather reminiscent of Urizen in *America* 8. The natural world of sun, moon, stone, and sea are her province, as they are his. Blake tells us how he reads the passage in Revelation, however, by the way the positions of woman and dragon reflect each other: these are two aspects of the same psyche, as powerful an image of the demonic and regenerative impulses of fallen man as he ever painted.

The symbolic gesture of outstretched arms, then, can be associated consistently with the main themes of Blake's work: the essential divinity of man, his capacity for regeneration, his error in turning the divine creativity into mental tyranny or selfhood. The importance of the four attitudes which repeatedly represent these ideas in Blake's art may remind us of his exclamation, "What kind of Intellects must he have who sees only the Colours of things & not the Forms of Things" (*PA*, E567/K577). The outstretched-arms motif, perhaps the most evident of several of Blake's repeated visual images, should not, then, be ignored or dismissed as a technical weakness; it is a symbol as powerful as any verbal symbol, and essential to that union of sight and sound, that reintegration of the senses which Blake strove to achieve in all his work.

APPENDIX

Ten Frequent Forms

Notes Toward Classification

Blake's work yields meanings on many levels: I attempt here to indicate further that some of this richness is revealed when a visual image is traced through the canon. Of course this can only be a gesture toward what could be an exciting and complicated series of studies if done on the comprehensive scale that Blake's art demands. What I hope will be clear is that Blake repeated his forms or "borrowed" them with conscious and precise intent. They are the components of a language of which "Every Word and Every Character was Human."[18]

[18] Blake even drew sketches of the Hebrew alphabet (in which letters are shown as names of things) as human figures. See G. Keynes, ed., *Pencil Drawings of William Blake*, London, 1927, pl. 27.

Form I. Other variations of the outstretched arms

1. Supine or prone figures, flat on the ground, viewed head on (*Poison Tree; Gates of Paradise* 7; title page of *America*).

This appears to mean death by violence; spiritual or physical murder. The most conclusive proof I have found of this meaning cannot be illustrated at this time: in the unpublished *Night Thoughts* designs are several uses of this image connected with texts of violence. For example, the design for Night VIII, 66 (no. 413) shows a strangled figure in this position;[19] and the design for Night IX, 16 (no. 435) shows a Urizenic figure in this position with an arrow sticking out of his chest, associated with the lines: "He falls on his own Scythe; nor falls alone; / His greatest Foe falls with him, Time, and He / Who murder'd all Time's offspring, Death, expire." However, the text for plate 7 of *Gates of Paradise* also suggests murder. There appears to be no "regenerative" use made of this form: when the opposite state is to be indicated, the upright standing figure is used. Sometimes the "flying figure," noted below, is contrasted to this form, as in the title page of *America* or *NT* VIII, 56 (no. 403).

2. Striding figures, arms outstretched (*Urizen* 3; *MHH* 3; *Jerusalem* 26).

This seems to be an image of either creative or demonic energy. It is often associated with flames. Rose has written interestingly of *Jerusalem* 26 in his article on Hand (see n. 16).

3. The outstretched arms at oblique angle (*Jerusalem* 99; Angels in *Job* 14, "When the morning stars . . ."; Satan in *Satan Calling Up His Legions*; *Gates of Paradise* 7; *Visions*, title page; *Thel*, title page).

A welcoming or worshiping gesture; a "demonic" aspect of the symbol is fear or flight (see the last three examples above).

4. The outstretched arms forward (Elohim in *Elohim Creating Adam*; the Accusers in *Job* 10; God in *Job* 17; the man in the Arlington Court picture; *Jerusalem* 93, Three Accusers).

Means casting a spell; creating an error, or a self-image. The regenerative aspect of the symbol is blessing (*Job* 17). The position of the fingers is an important detail of this gesture: they are usually "creative."

Form II. The flying figure, back view, springing upward, one
leg bent, one arm higher, usually nude, female, and wingless

(*Visions*, Argument; *America*, title page; *Europe* 9; *NT*, title page [no. 2] and *passim*; *FZ* pages 3 and 139; *Jerusalem* 46 [32].)

[19] See also no. 21 (I, 16) and Grant's essay, below.

One of Blake's favorite means of depicting forces of spiritual or physical energy, from joy or delight to its more sinister aspect as a destructive force. Though there is a basic recognizable shape to this form, the curve of hip or angle of arm or torso may vary, and figures spring from either right or left leg. The first two examples seem to represent joy or inspiration, as they often do in *Night Thoughts*; when this energy is turned to destructive channels, the visual image becomes more sinister, like *Europe* 9, where two figures in this pose are spreading mildew on corn, one of the plagues Albion's Angel has brought upon his country through tyrannous repression.

See also *Jerusalem* 46[32], where the figure is used for one of the children of Vala, or England at the crisis of her division into Jerusalem and Vala, according to Wicksteed, and called by him Erin, a symbol of the spiritual life (Energy) which springs from the Body (*Blake's Jerusalem: A Commentary* [B & N no. 2140]). The final page of the *Vala* manuscript had also used this form for a "spirit," according to Bentley (*Vala*, 183), "broken free of the earth."

Form III. The head-clutching falling male

(*America* 5; *Urizen* 6; *VLJ*.)

Seems always to be a version of the fall, connoting death or mortality. (In *America* 5 he falls into the coils of a serpent. Erdman gives a historical context for this figure in his reading of this plate elsewhere in this volume.) The head-clutching gesture is frequently used on upright and hunched-over figures also: *Gates of Paradise* 5 and 6; *Visions* 7; *America* 1, 4, and 5; *Europe* 3; and continues throughout the canon to indicate horror, despair, and doom. In his description of his *VLJ* design Blake calls them "various figures in attitudes of contention representing various States of Misery which alas every one on Earth is liable to enter into & against which we should all watch" (E547/K608).

Form IV. The corpse: a note on the "child" form

(*There Is No Natural Religion; Holy Thursday; America* 9; *Europe* 6; *NT* 1, 8 [no. 13] and 1, 14 [no. 19].)

This figure was first used in *There Is No Natural Religion* to illustrate the lines, "Reason or the ratio of all we have already known is not the same that it shall be when we know more." The little corpse may suggest dormant potential, the killing power of reason or selfhood, before we know more through imagination and can redeem ourselves. In *Holy Thursday* (*Songs of Experience*) Blake used the same figure to illustrate the dormant spiritual potential of "a land of poverty," not just the extreme result of hunger as one level of meaning might suggest. In *America* 9 the use of the form in connection with food and harvest images (wheat stalks) may be a symbol of something now dormant but redeemable when the killing power of reason is recognized and harvested. Digby (p. 36) sees this image as Jung's Puer Eternus, the symbol of creative possibility latent in life and waiting to be realized. In *Europe* 6 the same infant corpse is central to the design illustrating famine, where it appears that the body will be eaten to keep others alive. Yet David Erdman points out the social symbolism: "what we so clearly see in the picture is people who eat bodies they don't need; it is the rich, it is kings and queens (see *Fayette* and *The Song of Los*) who 'call for Famine.'" Perhaps the moral symbolism of this image associated with nourishment or the lack of it implies a mental condition.

Form v. The nude male, seated, legs apart, looking upward

(*Marriage* 21; *America* 6; Blair's *Grave* 13; *Jerusalem* 4; Dante 14.)

This image has often been called the "renovated" or "resurrected" man, but I feel these are misnomers. The redeemed man, we have seen, stands up with his arms out. Perhaps the label has been accepted for this seated form because of its occurrence over "Death's Door" in the Blair illustration, or because of the text of *America* 6: "The grave is burst."

The form itself appears to be patterned on Michelangelo's Adam, which suggests that "the created man" would be more apt. For the paradox of creation must not be overlooked; man on earth is "born but to die" even though he may achieve a spiritual rebirth. Blake depicts man's entry into Generation as a fall (*Urizen* 7; *Elohim Creating Adam*). Even Michelangelo's Adam looks quite pensive as the hand of God recedes from him. Therefore this Adam figure of Blake's suggests the birth of man (and the corresponding possibility of redemption), but the birth of man into the material world. In the *America* plate, the skull, toad, newt, and frog, leaves, and grass are all symbols of the veil of nature (cf. *Europe* 12). The exposed genitals also suggest man in Generation and the birth of sexuality, which is simultaneously the mark of his mortality and the agent of his delivery from it. Blake's first use of this figure in an illuminated book was in *Marriage* 21, where sexuality is a key to the "doors of perception." The pyramids which rise behind the figure in one version of this plate seem also to indicate associations with the tyranny of time.[20]

That this form represents man in nature is also strongly suggested

[20] The pyramids occur in copy D (see the Blake Trust facsimile); in some copies there is a sunburst behind the naked man; the title penciled in the Cumberland-Beckford copy is "Satan addressing the Sun."

by *Jerusalem* 4, where he is next to a seated female figure (very like the "Worm-mother" of *Gates of Paradise* 16) who has her arms outstretched in the Urizen manner, the whole combination intensifying the opening lines "Of the Sleep of Ulro!" Not yet regenerated, but still in the temporal world, this man is expectant, listening for redemption.

The form in Blair's *Grave* is slightly different: his knee is so placed that he seems preparing to stand, a stage closer to the upright attitude of complete regeneration.

At the opposite pole, a demonic variation of the basic image is used for Plutus in the Dante designs, where he is given the hair and beard of Urizen.

Form vi. The bent old man with staff and windblown garment

(*There Is No Natural Religion* 1; *Gates of Paradise* 15; *Death's Door*; *London*; *America* 12; *Jerusalem* 84; *NT* no. 26.)

This appears to be a symbol of the possibility of regeneration through death. Blake's first use of this old man figure was in plate 1 of *There Is No Natural Religion*, where the words, "Man cannot naturally Perceive but through his natural or bodily organs," seem to be related to King Lear, trying to become "unaccommodated man" and understand the secrets of the universe. Yet Lear had to divest himself of his old identity before he became regenerated, and as the removal of his garments was like a death for Lear, the design often shows this aspect of the symbol, in that the old man frequently enters the door of a tomb. In his use of this form in *Gates of Paradise* 15, the couplet speaks of the "worm weaving in the ground," that is, weaving a new garment, suggesting rebirth.

In the Blair's *Grave* plate, this form is combined with the "renovated man" and may have ironic overtones, or suggest the recurring cycle of time. However, the image suggests regeneration through death when we see Los entering a door with his windblown garments in the frontispiece to *Jerusalem*.

Form vii. Female figures imitating the stance of a traditional Venus

1. Standing (the Arlington Court picture; *Eve Tempted by the Serpent*, Victoria and Albert Museum).

2. Reclining (*America* 6; *Little Girl Found*; *Songs of Experience, Introduction*).

While there are many examples of Blake's adaptation of traditional iconographic poses, the two I have cited here are unusual in that they are quite clearly close copies. The female figure in the Arlington Court picture stands exactly like the Hellenistic *Venus genetrix* (see

Kenneth Clark, *The Nude*, New York, 1956, 79). (Blake adds arms, of course.) When we see the same pose also for Eve, except that her *right* arm is raised and she is naked, we see how Blake demonstrated the unfallen and fallen versions of the female nature.

The reclining pose can be seen in Velasquez' *Rokeby Venus*. Blake has used it as an image of innocence.

Form VIII. Bent-over kneeling figure, often a woman, apparently grieving, side view

(*Little Boy Lost; My Pretty Rose Tree; Job* 6 and *passim; America* 16; *NT* nos. 19, 28.)

One of Blake's most familiar images. It seems to mean a lament, with all the connotations of a despair born of mistaken worship. The form is not always female.

Form IX. Hunched figures with knees drawn up, front view

(*Visions* 4; *Urizen, passim; America*, frontispiece; *Gates of Paradise* 4, 16; *Jerusalem* 41 and 51.)

As Frye noted, Blake used this "foetus posture" through the years for mental cowardice; it is an image of the mind-forg'd manacles, and chains are often also part of the design. An interesting variation is the skeleton in Urizen—a profile shot of this form—which reminds us that this womb position is a symbol of self-involvement. An image that belongs to the fallen world, it is used for Theotormon in *VDA* 4, and in *Jerusalem* 51 for Hyle, sunk in despair. One of its earliest uses (varying only in that the head is not bowed) was in *Gates of Paradise* 16 ("I have said to the Worm: Thou art my mother and my sister"). Fallen Nature, then, is an association we should have with this image, named Tirzah in the *Songs of Experience*, who in being mother of mortal man has bound the senses and "closed my Tongue in senseless clay." The Tongue, for Blake, by the time he was writing *Vala*, was associated with Tharmas, whose region in the unfallen world is Beulah. When Tharmas fell, and turned into the Spectre of Tharmas, he became the Covering Cherub. In the *Vala* manuscript (p. 5) there is sketched a winged form, identified by Damon as the Spectre of Tharmas, which is extremely similar to the image in the frontispiece to *America*. At the time of engraving *America* Blake may not have named the state as yet, but it is very likely that the human condition itself, with its manacles of mental cowardice resulting from the closing up of the senses in the state of mortality—mental tyranny, in other words—is what this figure in the frontispiece represents. He is winged, like Eros, because he was once a symbol of love and his perversion into a spectre has resulted in war, symbolized by the cannon at his feet. In that the King of England or Albion's Angel is a symbol of tyranny in the poem, that identification is understandable, but we must also be aware that he is in addition a form of the Covering Cherub. Damon thought that the figure could be Urizen and the scene was "the eternal side of the Northern Gate."[21] But though the Covering Cherub is another form of Urizen and Blake used this form for Urizen frequently, the scene is more likely to be the Western Gate, the closed entrance to Eden seen from the side of Generation. That despair is a tyranny the mind forms for itself is implied further by the pencil drawing Blake made for plate 37 [41] of *Jerusalem*, called *Albion and the Letter That Killeth*.

Form x. The worm-serpent-dragon complex

This symbol already has been well defined by Damon, Frye, Digby, and others. The number of loops in its tail is quite often suggestive: one for Ulro (*Elohim Creating Adam*); two for Generation or Experience (*America* 13); five for the fallen senses (*Europe*, title page). John Grant points out that Blake numbered the coils of the serpent in the Epilogue to the *Gates of Paradise*.

Other details: birds, flowers

These symbols have already been explored by others, particularly in John Grant's article on *The Fly*. I should only like to call attention to the repetition of the *same* forms as constant motifs, and note that they subtly indicate a state or define a context which helps interpret the complete design.

A Note on Mirror Images

Mirror images in Blake's designs show the human form becoming what it beholds. The Elohim creates Adam in his own image; Albion mirrors Christ in plate 76 of *Jerusalem*; Job's God is as Job; David is delivered out of many waters by his own higher self. In the plates of *America*, to the reader, Orc is an aspect of Urizen, a mirror image, while Urizen beholding Orc sees only terror. Poetically, in *Milton* and *Urizen*, Los beholds Urizen and becomes like him.

A mirror image can be a vision or a spectre: essentially it belongs to the realm of the fallen, for there are no conventional mirror images

[21] D.V.E.: For an interpretation of the figure in the breach as chained Orc, see above, p. 99. In the narrative, it is Albion's Angel who causes (or begins) the war, but Orc whose spirit is in chains before and after the breach has been made.

in Eternity—there, all human forms have their own identity, even while "reflecting each in each." The mirror images of vision were conceived by Blake as Illuminated books, each one a movable feast, whose separate plates need not be read in a sequential manner. Robert Simmons has demonstrated how both the poetic and visual structure of Urizen can each be seen as a series of "reflections"—a suggestive approach to structure in Blake's other writings.

The "spectral" mirror images are depicted by Blake as representations of self-involvement: the narcissism which creates the fall; the creation of an image which becomes an object of worship. Mirror imagery is a natural field of symbolic speculation to a man involved in printing and engraving, a man both fascinated and repelled by Newton's Optics, a man who admonishes us to look through, not with the eye.[22]

[22] I should like to acknowledge my debt to Northrop Frye, who introduced me to Blake studies, and to Gerald E. Bentley, Jr., who read the first draft of this essay and whose encouragement is much appreciated. I have also benefited greatly by continuous discussion with my colleague, Robert E. Simmons, and correspondence with the editors.

9

Songs of Innocence and of Experience
The Thrust of Design

EBEN BASS

THE technology itself of William Blake's copper plates has its likeness in the "Two Contrary States" of Innocence and Experience. The design on each plate gave to Blake's eye the mirror image of what was to be printed. As a trained engraver he knew this almost by instinct, but working out his own method for printing with copper which in fact reversed the intaglio principle of steel engraving must have made him reconsider the whole matter of opposites. He even turned some of his plates over and worked other designs and poems on the reverse side. Because the designs resolve opposing thrusts, they furnish an important dimension to the meaning of the poems themselves. To examine the compositional "line" of Blake's drawings for the *Songs,* one begins with the simple diagonals, and ends with the various types of curves; all contribute to an understanding of the "Contrary States." Both diagonals and curves may appear in the same drawing, but I will consider the straight-line movement first, as a conceptual means for approaching the more complex curved movement.

The general title page for *Songs of Innocence and of Experience* (pl. 1 {9}) ornaments the letters of the word "Songs" with flying volutes, and accompanies it with the figure of a bird in flight. The lettering of "Innocence" and "Experience" is nearly without flourish, but these words are surrounded by flamelike curves of carmine, violet, yellow.[1] Mainly, however, the curves emphasize

---

[1] Blake greatly varied his coloring of different copies of the *Songs.* I refer mainly to copy Z of *Songs of Innocence and of Experience,* a very late copy made for Henry Crabb Robinson in 1825-1826, but for the first group I give some comparative descriptions of the coloring in copy B of *Songs of Innocence,* assigned by Geoffrey Keynes to a date of "about 1790." For the latter I have relied on the London 1954 Blake Trust facsimile. The former, copy Z of the combined *Songs,* was issued in facsimile by the Blake Trust in 1955, but I have had to rely on the Orion Press reissue of 1967 (New York), which

196

the leaning posture of Adam and the nearly prostrate one of Eve whereby Blake implies the "Innocence" of Eden and the "Experience" of expulsion. Adam hovers over and shields Eve, in turn protecting his own head with curved arms. The flame of the archangel's forbidding sword is suggested by the tongues of fire sweeping in a diagonal from lower right to left across the page, but not reaching up to the word "Songs." It alone is independent, as is shown by the graceful foliate curves serving for tails on the letters "S" and "N." These flourishes contrast with the more irregular sweep of the flames below, even though the two kinds of curves meet at a few points above the letters for "Innocence." Blake used the same lower right to upper left diagonal for the flame over the archangel's head in the "Expulsion from Eden" drawing in the *Paradise Lost* series, except that this flame ends in a volute over the angel's head and shoulders.[2]

The title page for *Songs of Innocence* (pl. 3 {11}, done before the general title page) elaborates the word "Songs" much more, into acanthuslike curves, almost as if the letters were an upper portion of the actual tree that embraces the word "Innocence." Although both the tree and the curved lettering for "Songs" are vegetal and therefore seem "innocent," the tree originates at the lower right of the design, sweeps up, over, and to the left in much the same movement as do the forbidding flames of the general title page. Also initiating that same curve are two loops of a vine embracing the trunk of the tree[3] whose fruit hangs above the heads of the "innocents," children learning to read from a book offered them by the seated figure of the mother. The word "Innocence" is in simple but decorative cursive letters. But above

---

has the advantage of added introduction and commentary by Keynes but was produced by an inferior process, I understand, and is considerably less faithful in tone and color.

(J.E.G.: Using hand stencils on top of collotype, the Blake Trust facsimiles do separate the colors and suggest the glitter of applied gold; yet the edges of color-wash areas are crudely managed and give no indication of how masterfully Blake was able, for example, to blend blue into pink while managing several other adjacent colors as well. The reissue by high-speed offset printing is strictly two-dimensional, with unBlakean shadows.)

[2] Blake's illustrations to *Paradise Lost*, in the Studio Publications edition, New York, 1947 (B&N no. 312).

[3] Damon, *Philosophy*, 271: "This is certainly symbolic of Christ embracing what we consider the Tree of Sin."

it is the fruit, hanging in two pairs, presumably knowledge of both good and evil. The children are boy and girl, to remind us of Adam and Eve before the fall. Although the mother wears a white cap and a broad white collar or shawl, her dress has the fullness and authority of a robe, and its color of purple is authoritative. The mother-children grouping suggests that the children's Innocence must encounter the authority of Experience too, through knowledge contained in the book and implied by the fruit of the tree. The three faces, each looking at the book, are on the same rising diagonal, from lower right to upper left, as that followed by the flames of the general title page and the tree branches of the Innocence title: the line of Experience. Thus, although the general title suggests lost Innocence (Adam and Eve after their disobedience, clad only in fig leaves), it more directly shows the First Parents' flight from the expelling flame of Experience. In similar manner the title page for *Innocence*, though literally depicting that subject, also suggests the counterpart of Experience by the first exposure of the children to knowledge. This is done not only in the pictorial sense of the mother teaching the children to read, but also in the compositional sense of the diagonal moving upward and left.

Before further defining the "meaning" of the upward-and-left line, a simple distinction should be made among the drawings and decorations with which Blake chose to couple the *Songs* themselves. Some plates have formal illustrations depicting actual scenes from the poems; these may fill a half or a third of the page. Thus *The Lamb* (pl. 8) is accompanied by a drawing of a young boy kindly reaching out to an affectionate lamb, with the flock and a cottage in the immediate background. *The Ecchoing Green* (pls. 6, 7), whose text Blake could have fitted on a single page, begins with a drawing at the top of the first page of the "old folk" seated under a spreading oak tree, young children at their knees and older ones standing or playing about them. Another illustration fills the lower half of the second page. It shows Old John admonishing the children about him, a mother behind him. The entire group is standing, Old John in the central authoritative position of the oak tree of the first drawing. Neither scene has a major diagonal. The first group of figures circle about the trunk or beneath the spread branches of the tree; the second group form a procession moving left. But the main feature in each compo-

sition is the center vertical. A grapevine fills the right margin of
the second page, its branches circling about the last two stanzas
of the poem. One figure at the top left reaches for the grapes of
joy; another at the right hands down a bunch of them to the
last child on the right. Although the vine and two figures are
decoration rather than formal illustrations, they too are verticals
and laterals, somewhat softened by minor vegetal curves. Many
of the plates for *Songs* have scene-type drawings,[4] though in fact
some scenes supplement, and others even contrast with, what the
poem "says." My purpose here is to consider the drawings not so
much as illustrations for the poems, but rather as compositions,
and to that extent congruent with the motion and arrangement
of the margin decorations. Two examples, *The Sick Rose* (pl. 39)
and *The Divine Image* (pl. 18), serve to show the point in Blake's
art where "illustration" merges into "decoration." In *The Sick
Rose* {3} the design surrounds the entire poem; in *The Divine
Image* {14} it surrounds the poem and divides it into two portions.
The Sick Rose is still basically an illustrated poem, though the
total curved embrace of the weakened stem anticipates Blake's
other device, as in *The Divine Image*, of using a suggestive rather
than a representational design to weave about the text. As I will
show later, the Rose's "embrace," that of love in one sense, is also
constricting; that of the Divine Image, an embrace which is also
partly open and free.

The most staid of the suggestive decorations, as distinguished
from the illustrative ones, is that for the *Introduction* to *Innocence*
(pl. 4 {12}), in which formally cross-looped vines make their way
up either margin and more delicately twine across the page above
the title. A dozen smaller tendrils approach from left and right
between stanzas. The symmetrical balance of this page is not
typical of Blake's designs. The center verticals of the two illustrations for *The Ecchoing Green* described above are in keeping
with the controlled balance of the decoration for this *Introduction*, just as are the less formal, more pleasantly curved saplings
and vines that twine up either margin of *The Lamb* (pl. 8) and
benevolently shade the text of the poem, which itself hovers over
the illustration. Designs such as these suggest harmony and bal-

[4] Plates 5, 9, 10, 13, 14, 15, 17, 22, 23, 24, 32, 33, 35, 36, 37, 38, 40, 41,
42, 44, 45, 46, 47, 48, 49, 50, 52, 54.

ance, but they neither suggest nor resolve tensions, and they are not Blake's chief compositional resource in the drawings for the *Songs*.

More like the dynamic movement in many of Blake's poems of Innocence and Experience are those designs, both the illustrations and the decorative motifs, with striking diagonals that move across the page. To see how Blake gets from the symmetry described above to a diagonal movement, we can contrast the balanced marginal vines of the first *Introduction* (pl. 4) with the off-balance trees, one at left, two entwined at the right, of the accompanying frontispiece (pl. 2 {10}).[5] The thrust of the frontispiece is also to the right, in a diagonal beginning at the roots of the single tree at the lower left and the noses close by of the grazing sheep. One's eye follows the curve of the sheep's necks and backs, up the length of the shepherd's pipe, to his face turned expectantly up and right toward the "child on a cloud" who inspires the shepherd to write verses rather than to sing songs. The counterpart to this full-page drawing is the frontispiece for *Experience* (pl. 28 {15}). Now the shepherd-poet is facing straight forward and advancing confidently, right foot forward (the first frontispiece shows the left foot advanced, the right tentatively arrested).[6] The shepherd's arms in the second drawing are raised. He joins hands with the child, who now has wings, and who now is seated on the poet's

[5] A full-page drawing with its text on another page may not seem a relevant comparison to a drawing with text on the same page. Still, Blake's versatile arrangement of the pages with text allows for as much or as little movement as his theme requires. When he wishes, he can even give the illusion that a full page of text is also a full-page drawing. In any case, the poem is always part of the design; it is never a printer's block superimposed upon it. Pls. 5, 17, 38, 40, 48 are virtually "full-page" drawings with the compositional line free to follow the direction Blake the artist chose. Also, Blake the poet governed the line lengths of the poems, and the number of stanzas to appear on any page, in accordance with the total compositional effect.

[6] Joseph H. Wicksteed, *Blake's Innocence and Experience: A Study of the Songs and Manuscripts*, New York, 1928, 143, remarks the left and right symbolism of these companion drawings. He contends that gestures of left body limbs mean Innocence, those of the right, Experience. This is true of the two frontispieces, but the hesitant right foot of the piper in pl. 2 is also a compositional resource. It helps lift the diagonal eye-movement of the viewer from the vicinity of the lower-left corner toward the center of the drawing, up and to the right, where the child floats on a cloud, the stance of his left and right feet matching that of the piper's feet.

head. Their arms thus joined encircle the poet's confident face, and the child's head is surmounted by a bright halo, the only portion left white in the colored Robinson version. The lower-left to upper-right diagonal of the earlier drawing is retained in the second. The scene of the second, however, is no longer the "woodlands wild," but a more open area. The sheep of the second illustration again nuzzle at the lower left, their necks and backs curving up and right, behind the shepherd, but the viewer's eye is then swept up by a stout tree also leaning right, only half its trunk visible, the protective leaves arching back to the left and over the haloed child. Purple hills in the distance of the colored version also stress the up-and-right diagonal. The tree at the reader's left (the poet's right) has receded into the distance, whereas its counterpart in the first frontispiece was located on the same plane as the one at the opposite side of that drawing. Thus the first drawing has a fairly flat perspective; a thick forest just in back of the sheep forbids distance. The second drawing has a distinct far horizon which is part of the up-and-right diagonal, but a diagonal in which the poet and cherub no longer participate. The poet's advanced right foot is at a strong center and makes him the decisive center vertical of the design. This motion takes him forward and "out" of the rest of the picture with its up-and-right diagonal. Unlike him, the piper in the first drawing was still oriented to the up-and-right movement of the whole design, the pipe itself marking the exact direction of the reader's eye-movement. There is no pipe in the second drawing. The poet's hands are now joined with those of the cherub, balancing him on the poet's head. In the two frontispieces, then, the up-and-right thrust is Innocence; just as in the two title pages the up-and-left thrust is Experience.

More complex than the diagonals are Blake's boldly curved vegetal designs for three poems of Innocence: *The Blossom* (pl. 11 {13}), *The Divine Image* (pl. 18 {14}), and *Infant Joy* (pl. 25 {2}). The first two designs feature amazing semi-acanthus curves; the third displays a great flower with petals embracing a mother, child, and fairy guardian. The flower stem in the third drawing and the adjacent stem of a bud of the same species almost entirely encircle the poem. Human figures inhabit all three of these designs, but on a small scale, and for the first two, mostly to dramatize the flying volute motion. The figures in *The Blos-*

201

som are, with the exception of the one at the right, provided with wings, each seated upon or launching from the curved ends of the acanthus device. The basic design is massive, and though flame-colored (the Robinson copy shows orange and gold shades), the form itself is stylized vegetation.[7] A similar curved-leaf design margins *The Divine Image*, but it is less bulky, and its motion and countermotion are more complex. The curved, rising foliage depicted in the right margin of *The Blossom* has a stable base of volutes flowing left across the bottom of the page. The broad trunk rises up the right margin and then flames out to the left above the poem to be populated by spirits in or close to flight.[8] The more sinuous curving leaves of *The Divine Image* begin at the lower right, follow a gentle "S" curve to the left and then up the left margin to repeat themselves in a reverse curve across the page, isolating the last two stanzas of the poem. The design moves up the right margin once more and finally sweeps in branching tongues to the left, above the title. The whole pattern is a giant "S" (though an additional tongue nearly closes off the upper opening), reminiscent of the great capitals of medieval manuscripts, but it is the mirror image of a great "S." The lower half of the reversed letter moves clockwise, which is the movement of the stem of the Sick Rose; but the more impressive upper half reverses to a counterclockwise flow and "blossoms" into figures and volutes at the top of the page. In harmonious cursive poses, the four figures at the top of this design may suggest in their order the "Mercy, Pity, Peace and Love" of the poem, all aspects of the Divine Image.[9] Wicksteed and Damon both note the figure of Christ raising up a reclining human figure in the lower right of the drawing. The initial sequence of the four virtues is slightly changed to "Mercy,

[7] It seems more "vegetal" in copy B, in a pale green; in Z, the gold shades appear. The same change has occurred in the colors of *The Divine Image*: in B the "Image" is green, in Z it is gold.

[8] Wicksteed (p. 125) sees the prone and erect foliage groups as two states of the phallus. The seven spirits at the crest of the plant device move clockwise in "passage through life-experience" (p. 127). The "clockwise" design of *The Sick Rose*, discussed below, is conceptually different, since a single *line*, not a ring of figures, is involved.

[9] Keynes (note on pl. 18) identifies the erect, robed figure at the left as representing all four virtues, which the two kneeling figures at the right pray for, and which are being given them by the attending angel. Even so, in the sense of composition, four figures are expressive of four virtues.

Pity, Love, Peace" in stanza 3. This is cut off from stanza 4 by the great reversed "S" curve. Stanzas 4 and 5, embraced by the lower half of the "S," change the sequence further, and stanza 5 reduces the four virtues to three: "Mercy, Love & Pity." The unmentioned "Peace," then, must be the harmony of the "human form" in which the three other virtues dwell, and which is also the "Divine Image," the full configuration of poem and decorations. There are but three human figures at the base of the "S" curve, in contrast to four at the top; the "fourth" is the harmonious embrace of the reversed "S."

The large cradling blossom of *Infant Joy* {2}, rather like an open parrot tulip in carmine, is the only colored drawing to use that shade so profusely after the general title page {9} with its carmine, yellow, and violet flames.[10] But the blossom protects Innocence, the mother, child, and guardian at the heart of the flower, whereas the rich-hued flames of Experience threaten the First Parents, who have lost Innocence. The stem of the great flower grows clockwise from the lower right, but it is countered by the stem of the bud that begins with the opposite movement in the opposite margin and then reverses itself in an "S" curve. The major stem plus the right outer contour of the flower itself comprise most of a great "S" curve in reverse, the same composition as that of *The Divine Image*. Where the Christ-figure stood at the right base of *The Divine Image* with a slim vine bordering it and twining upward, the secondary stem with its bud rises in *Infant Joy*. An ordinary "S" curve, it is the earlier stage of the main stem and its great blossom. Presumably when the bud matures and opens, the stem too will lengthen, and bending over to the left with the blossom's weight, will then become the reversed "S" curve: the *Divine Image* form is thus being born in *Infant Joy*.

A number of the poems in *Innocence* complete the meaning of their formal illustrations with a small design in the narrow left margin, and with a larger one in the right, varied by the interplay of line lengths which relate to the sort of design rendered there. Thus in *Spring* (pls. 22, 23), after the formal illustration of the mother with her infant leaning to the right toward the flock of sheep, the benevolent tree leaning over all as if to extend the

[10] In copy B, the flower and bud are a rose-sepia, with less startling highlight and shading than in Z.

movement, small motifs fill out the spaces to the right of the short lines of each stanza. The concluding long lines skip across the page, in the case of the first and third stanzas not even fitting into the space allotted them. The little motifs for each group of short lines are curving leaves and grains of wheat, each with a tiny attendant angel suggesting the theme—e.g., stanza 1 "Sound the Flute!" has a flute-playing angel ensconced on the main curve of the leaf volutes. The poem ends on the second page with the illustration reversed: The child is now to the right, now embracing, not just reaching for, the lamb. The child and sheep now recline, but the mother is missing. The marginal leaf volutes that flow from the headpiece to the tailpiece play at being irregular spirals and reversing curves. The one beside stanza 1, for example, is a fanciful "S" curve, an outflow of the capital "S" of the title *Spring*. These two pages well exemplify Blake's art of joining formal drawings to the poems by way of the marginal decorations. The various curve forms are particularly important, as I will show by further examples.

Other pages without formal illustration also capitalize on the broad, uneven right margin. *A Dream* (pl. 26) has marginal and interlinear grace notes of grass, ivy, and insects (the "glow-worm" and "beetle" of the poem). The dreaming speaker is suggested by the small figure reclining upon the opening curve of the capital "A," and by the nodding one leaning against the right curve of the capital "D" of the title. *On Anothers Sorrow* (pl. 27) and *Night* (pl. 20) have similar graceful saplings growing up the right margins, the trunks of both loose-coiled with vines, whose tendrils mingle happily with the tenuous branches of the trees to accommodate the flight or perch of birds. The verses of *Night* vary in length, from long to short in each stanza, and thus allow for longer branches of the tree. On the second page the poem itself "becomes" a more substantial tree, and the interplay of line length down the right margin permits room for a varied but ample fringe of pleasant leaves that moves toward the bottom right of the page, where stand two figures, one of whom gestures to another group of three standing to his left. The half-hidden lion of danger at the lower right of the first page is replaced by the strolling figures of peace more formally illustrating the end of the poem. Damon (*Philosophy*, 273) sees these figures as angels.

The two decorated pages of *A Cradle Song* (pls. 16, 17) also convey a surprise, but a more abrupt one, and in reverse of the danger-to-safety theme of *Night*. The first page of *A Cradle Song* features highly involuted curves approaching those of an acanthus, although the leaves are still slim.[11] They are, however, unlike the light, easy flourishes of the wheat leaves for the poem *Spring*. The right and even the narrower left margins of the first page of *A Cradle Song* are heavily foliated, almost bizarre, and each stanza is entirely separated from the next by frills and tendrils. The hedging in of each stanza implies protection for the cradled child, but the stanzas are also in fact nearly oppressed by the design, as indeed the ambiguous opening line, "Sweet dreams form a shade," could imply the mother's clouding, as well as protective, influence. The second page is dominated by a formal illustration that fills the lower two-thirds of the plate. The seated mother leans toward the child, who sleeps in a large wicker cradle, and a heavy draped pall forms the somber backdrop for the scene. A rhyme for "pall" occurs in the words "all" and "small," both repeated in the two stanzas on this page. The marginal leaves to the right of the first stanza of plate 17 are now more than ever like those of an acanthus, sweeping down in the direction of the infant's head, which in fact is nearly adult-size. The cradle's hood, and the draped cloth behind, are the mother's way of sheltering her child from cold and drafts, but both testify as much to danger and mortality as they do to protection. The great, oppressive cradle suggests God assuming manhood in Christ, assuming also the weakness of an infant, and thus the suffering of physical death.

Blake's only Song with no strong vertical margin design is *Holy Thursday* (pl. 19) in *Innocence*. Even the potentially ominous *Chimney Sweeper* (pl. 12), with its strong laterals, is composed basically upon the verticals of the left and right margins. *Holy Thursday* has no vertical decorations at all. The text marches from the left edge of the plate to the right, barely squeezing into the space, just as the regimented pairs of boys follow the beadles to the right all the way across the top of the page, and as the pairs of girls move almost as oppressively in the opposite direction across the bottom. Both processions tread a formidable linear path which

[11] Wicksteed (p. 99) feels that they represent the child's sleep.

Blake ruled off with a straightedge. The title, all in capitals, is in heavier and darker letters than are the titles of any other of the *Songs*. Aside from the occasionally embellished capital letters within the poem, the only space for grace notes lies between the stanzas, and here too, despite the small flourishes of tendrils, leaves, an occasional bird, is implied the regimented lateral procession of charity children to St. Paul's Church. Presumably for Blake the deadest line is the horizontal: except in the literal portrayals of death in the title page of *Experience* (pl. 29) and in the *Holy Thursday* of *Experience* (pl. 33), his compositions abjure it. Here, in the first *Holy Thursday*, the dead horizontal furnishes a deadly commentary on institutional religion.

In describing Blake's illustrations and decorations for the *Songs* thus far, I have noted three basic lines of composition: the strong vertical, suggesting stability and perhaps serenity (*Introduction*: "Piping down the valleys wild," pl. 4; and *The Ecchoing Green*, pls. 6, 7); the threatening diagonal thrust of the flames from lower right to left on the general title page (in irregular "S" curves, pl. 1); and the constructive diagonal thrust from lower left to right in the full-page illustrations to the two "Introductions." In the frontispiece for *Experience* (pl. 28 {15}), the thrust is not only a diagonal from lower left to right, but it continues in a counterclockwise sweep about the page. The reversal of that line, a clockwise motion, is most conspicuous in *The Sick Rose* (pl. 39 {4}). The composition of the Rose drawing is the opposite of nearly every other tree or vine design in *Songs*: except for those stems or tree trunks that evenly balance each other in opposite margins (*Introduction* to *Innocence*, pl. 4; *The Lamb*, pl. 8), Blake's stems and trunks rise up the right margins (*The Shepherd*, pl. 5; *Night*, pl. 20; *The Little Girl Lost*, pl. 34; general title page for *Innocence*, pl. 3). Admittedly the formal illustrations for *Spring* (pl. 22) and *The Little Black Boy* (pl. 9) have substantial trees rising at the left and arching clockwise over the top of the page, but both of these shelter a mother and child, the mother in each (implicitly in *Spring*) giving her child his first lessons in religious faith. The child in *Spring* reaches out to a lamb that raises its head; the Little Black Boy salutes the rising sun, where "God does live." Also, the trunks of these trees are not verticals for an entire left margin, as is the perverse stem of the Sick Rose, and the movement of these two left-margin trees is clearly benevolent, arching and ending over a mother and child; not malignant, and strangling life with a completed, perverse circle.[12]

Other lower-right to upper-left diagonals that also are "wrong" appear in four drawings for *Experience*: the title page itself (pl. 29 {16}), the tailpiece for *Introduction*: "Hear the voice of the Bard!" (pl. 30), *The Clod & the Pebble* (pl. 32), and *The Chimney Sweeper*: "A little black thing among the snow" (pl. 37). The drawing on the title page of *Songs of Experience* bears interesting analogies, as well as contrasts, to that on the general title page. Adam and Eve of the general title (pl. 1) respectively lean and lie to the left (Eve's face is turned to Adam's), their body contours outlined by a rising left motion of the flames. The colors of the Robinson copy are rich and passionate. The aged parents depicted on the more somber title page of *Experience* (pl. 29) lie supine and rigid, faces at the left but turned upward, their linear death-pose emphasized by the formally draped purple bier and by the square-paneled, tomblike background. Above it, the lettering of the word "Experience" has the Roman formality of a tomb inscription. The word "Songs," however, is graced by two cavorting figures, male and female, and its capital "S" has flowing tendrils and branches. Reminiscent of the general title page, nevertheless, are the leaning mourners of the parents, daughter in the foreground beside the long-bearded father, son at the far side of the bier by the mother. The thrust of the children's figures is again to the left; and their hands clasped in prayer, hidden at the far sides of their faces, carry the left thrust upward to relieve the left thrust at dead level of the parents. Though there are some pastel shades in the Robinson copy of this title page, all colors in it are either subdued or dull, contrary to the lively richness of the general title. The male and female figures of all three title pages lean and face left (the deceased parents of *Experience*, nonsentient, face upward with eyes closed). Thus all three pairs turn sadly toward Experience, the children nascent but absorbed in the mother's book (pl. 3 {11}), Adam and Eve cowering before the menacing

[12] Damon (p. 273) remarks, "The 'gesture' of Blake's pictures is very apt to be clockwise: from left to right above the text, and the reverse below the text." This is true of the following: pls. 5, 6, 8, 9, 12, 19, 21, 22, 23, 24, 34, 35, 36, 39, 42, 44, 46, 48, 50. But it is not true for pls. 10, 13, 14, 15, 17, 20, 33, 37, 38, 40, 41, 43, 45, 47, 52, 54. Damon's observation applies to about half of the drawings in *Songs*.

flame (pl. 1 {9}), the mourning son and daughter bowing in grief (pl. 29 {16}). In copy Z the color of apparel for the *Innocence* title page is reversed in the one for *Experience*; now the mourning adult male wears blue, the female a subdued green. The mother's purple robe of the *Innocence* has become the purple drape of the bier for *Experience*, though lighter in shade: Experience as learning becomes Experience as death.[13]

The colors of the other left-thrust drawings in *Songs of Experience* are also subdued, dark, or threatening. The text for *Introduction*: "Hear the voice of the Bard!" (pl. 30) is mounted on a gray-washed, white-edged cloud. The sky behind is a deep, dull indigo sprinkled with stars. The left thrust comes from the rear view of the figure of the Bard, in a naked reclining Roman pose, left elbow on the head of a cloudlike lounging divan.[13a] The thrust is left, but the figure faces right. The neat row of animals in *The Clod & the Pebble* (pl. 32) also faces right as the beasts bend their heads to drink from the same stream, but the neck and back contours are of course up and left. These sheep and their companion cattle face the opposite way from those in the two frontispieces. In no other drawing for Blake's *Songs* do the sheep so persistently face right; the flocks look left (as in *Spring*, pl. 22) or else turn both ways (*The Lamb*, pl. 8; *The Shepherd*, pl. 5). The lonely dark figure of the chimney sweeper in *Experience* (pl. 37) also walks to the right, barefoot, but he looks backward and up into the bleak threatening diagonal of the falling snow. It descends from upper left to lower right in harsh straight lines, the boy's only protection against the thrust of the elements being his ragged clothes and the pack of soot he carries on his back. Adam and Eve

[13] In copy Z, mothers wear purple in pls. 3, 6; so does the mother (or nurse) in 24. The mothers in the companion pls. 17 and 48 wear plum. In copy B, the mothers' gowns in pls. 3 and 24 are lavender; in 17, the dress is rose-sepia. The children's clothes in pl. 3 are uncolored.

[13a] D.V.E.: That this figure is indeed the Bard—and not (pace Geoffrey Keynes) Earth (who has not risen "from out the dewy grass")—becomes manifest when we examine the similar but more explicit drawing of *NT* no. 5 (see {73} and John Grant's discussion below, pp. 330-331) and of Blake's preliminary sketch in *N* 57. It is the scroll of the Bard's MS that constitutes or *curls into* his divan.

Perhaps bardic symbolism should also be inferred from such scroll-like details as the "trailing intestines" and "tail of cloth" in *Europe* 1 and 3 which Michael Tolley calls attention to above, p. 123.

of the general title page (pl. 1) also turn from and seek to escape the diagonal but curving, upward thrust of flames, whose direction opposes that of the falling snow in *The Chimney Sweeper*. But the fire rises and the snow falls on roughly the same plane across these two pages. Blake's drawing for *London* (pl. 46 {18}) has an ominous shadow slanted in this same direction (the version colored for Robinson duplicates the plane in a second shadow at the lower left of the page).[14] *Holy Thursday* (pl. 33) in *Experience* depicts a supine, dead child, head at the left; in the background, the contour of the dark mountain is the threatening lower-right to upper-left diagonal. Its slope reverses that of the mountain behind the poet and cherub in the frontispiece to *Experience* (pl. 28), hence is its moral opposite.[15] Finally, the drawing for *Infant Sorrow* in *Experience* (pl. 48) reverses the orientation of the figures in the companion drawing of *Innocence*, which accompanies *A Cradle Song* (pl. 17). The child in the later poem is now awake and protesting; he appears naked and kicking at the left of the drawing, his mother bending toward him and reaching left. In the first illustration (which is also an end drawing), the thrust was to the right, and the mood was one of calmness (also of anticipated or symbolic death). In the stormy, left-oriented picture, however, the pall-like backdrop has been partly drawn aside (to the left), whereas in the calm drawing facing right the pall covers the entire back of the scene. Virtually every detail of the second drawing is the mirrored reverse of counterparts in the first, and the key would seem to lie in the thrust of each illustration. It is true that the poems *Infant Sorrow* and *Infant Joy* are closer to being paired opposites, but as drawings *Infant Sorrow* and *A Cradle Song* make a pair.

The poems depicting Blake's "Two Contrary States" are often mirror images of each other. Not every poem of one State has an exact counterpart in the other, but the total effect of *Innocence* and *Experience* is one of balanced opposites, each fulfilling and completing the other. The same principle generally applies to the

[14] In copy B, a heavy shadow on the "pall" falls in the "Experience" diagonal. It is less dark in Z of the same pl. 17.

D.V.E.: For a different view of this "shadow," see the discussion below, pp. 420-421 and n.

[15] The second mountain in pl. 33, with a lower left to upper right diagonal (ordinarily "Innocence"), is a broken line of cliffs, hence no longer a line of safety.

designs that symbolize or illustrate each poem. Marginal vines and branches that more or less balance each other and join between stanzas or at the top of the page suggest calm, symmetry. Their "circle" is complete and thrusts neither way. A boy plays with his hoop of self-contained happiness in the right margin of the first page of *The Ecchoing Green* (pl. 6), and on the second page, grapevines trail evenly up each margin of the two stanzas, the children plucking the grapes of joy. Grapevines appear in the margins of four other of Blake's *Songs* (pls. 6, 27, 38, 53), but this is the only design in which the fruit is actually being picked and gives pleasure. The playing children of the end drawing for *Nurse's Song* almost complete a happy circle by joining hands (pl. 24), the Little Boy found by God his father (pl. 14) is nearly circled about by the arching branches and curving roots of great trees (God's head circled by a great halo), and of course the joined hands of the poet and the cherub of the second frontispiece (pl. 28) close their circle. There is a crucial difference between the circle about to be completed by human gesture (*Nurse's Song*, pl. 24) and the circle completed. That difference will be further discussed below.

More needs to be said first, however, of the threatening diagonals extending from lower right to upper left: *The Little Boy lost* (pl. 13) shows the child moving left, arms out, with trees above him bending up and left, and the famous Tyger (pl. 42) marches left, the dead tree at his right reaching up and left, but in only a tentative manner. The lower-right to upper-left diagonal can also become the clockwise motion, as already mentioned, in *The Sick Rose* (pl. 39). In Robinson's copy the color for this flower is no longer the rich carmine last seen to bloom in *Infant Joy* (pl. 25) but that shade gone awry in the way red roses often turn violet as they age. The thorny stem rises straight up the left margin, and bends over at the very point where the "invisible worm," a camouflaged caterpillar, attacks a leaf. Two small, strange figures, one prone and one kneeling, perch on two of the lowered branches above the text. The main stem descending the right margin, the flower itself lies dead center at the bottom of the page. The spirit of the rose's joy reaches imploringly from the heart of the blossom, threatened and apparently bound by the worm which Blake elsewhere equates with priestcraft.[16] Contrary to the Rose, the blossom

[16] The threat of priestcraft appears literally both in drawing and text for

of *Infant Joy* (pl. 25) is triumphant at the top of its page, and two stems, in countermotion, surround the text. The Rose's sickness is seen in the single, clockwise movement of the thorny stem. No other drawing in Blake's *Songs* so surrounds and defeats its subject with so perverse, single, and complete a motion. The direction in the headpiece to *The Angel* (pl. 41), which depicts a reclining maiden rejecting the love of her benevolent guardian, is also clockwise, but at least the text of the poem is not strangled by the whole design.

The opposite circular motion has already been shown in the counterclockwise thrust of the second frontispiece (pl. 28). The end drawing for *The Little Black Boy* (pl. 10) is another example of this movement. Finally, of course, motion in either direction is stilled, and the circle itself remains, completed in the joined hands of the Poet and Covering Cherub of the second frontispiece.[17] At first glance, a full circle seems to be implied in the drawing for *The Little Vagabond* (pl. 45). The figure of God the Father kneeling arches over a nude youth crouched in His embrace. The outer contour of the pair is a great "O," but within the configuration also appears the more meaningful "S" curve. It begins with God's head, follows His shoulder and arm to the penitent's head, his curving back, and thigh. In another sense, each figure is itself an "S" curve: that of God a normal "S," that of the penitent an "S" reversed, just as the *Divine Image* was a reversed "S." As we have already seen, the Christ figure at the lower right of *The Divine Image* (pl. 18) becomes a compositional equivalent, at the lower right of *Infant Joy* (pl. 25), to the normal "S" curve stem growing there. That stem, when the bud lifts and enlarges into a blossom, will relax and lower itself into a reverse "S." Christ (divinity) "becomes" Infant Joy (the Divine Image,

---

The Garden of Love (pl. 44), and symbolically in the writhing worms of the right margin of the poem. The kneeling figures in the drawing face right, and the third (a priest) gestures down to the grave in a movement that carries the eye clockwise to the bottom of the page. There the line "And binding with briars my joys and desires" rests above looping thorns. Appropriately, the eye movement is confused and lost in this bramble patch.

[17] A mother's and child's joined hands form a circle in the drawing for *The Fly*, but it is more truly an ellipse skewed to the ominous lower right. John E. Grant reads the mother's aid as sinister, since the boy appears old enough to walk unaided; see "Interpreting Blake's 'The Fly,'" in Frye, *Essays*, 51.

man created as the reversed, that is the Mirrored Image, of God). In *The Little Vagabond* drawing, therefore, the "S" of God's figure embraces the reversed "S" of the Vagabond. The figures *together* become the normal and final "S" curve which is also the initial shape of God. The outer contour of the pair, once again, is a great "O," but the real line movement within is that of the great "S."

The endless counterthrusts of the "S" curve must have fascinated Blake. Elaborate "S" capitals in the lettering of the three title pages for *Songs* make this apparent. So do the designs of that letter in titles of individual poems. The large graceful leaf device which *is* the Divine Image is a reversed "S" curve. And we must not ignore the twining trunks of trees, and vines, in many margins of the *Songs*. The most obvious appear in the title page for *Innocence* (pl. 3), the frontispiece for *Innocence* (pl. 2), the first *Introduction* (pl. 4), *The Ecchoing Green* (pl. 7), *The Lamb* (pl. 8), *The Little Girl Found* (pl. 36), and *The School Boy* (pl. 53). The "S" curve is the unending quest to repeat the Divine Image, but in forming itself it sometimes fails to reverse into the second sweep, and merely turns inward to make a self-sustained "O." The fact that the Divine Image resolves thrust into counterthrust is part of Blake's dramatization of the "Two Contrary States," and perhaps also their resolution. We have seen how that shape evolves from the simpler compositional lines of the diagonals. Innocence is the line of the Piper's instrument in the first frontispiece (pl. 2), lower left to upper right. Experience is the line of the flames in the general title page (pl. 1), or of the falling snow in *The Chimney Sweeper* (pl. 37), upper left to lower right. The diagonals may then begin a clockwise or counterclockwise movement which, provided it does not entirely close in upon itself, always has the chance to reverse itself and fulfill the second curve of the Divine Image "S." Thus the incomplete ring of figures in *Nurse's Song* (pl. 24) does not need to close to a circle as the children play; they can still become an "S" figure, although in fact they appear to be planning a spiral. The lead youngster seems headed to pass beneath a loop or scarf held between the last two children of the line, who alone are stationary. Perhaps a kind of "London Bridge" game is being played here, but before the "bridge" falls down, the spiral line that would result reminds us of the many spiraling tendrils and vines of Blake's margins and interlinear spaces in the *Songs*. These are spirals which reach out, like springs, rather than turning inward, ever closer to the center. They are curves that have the potential of the "S" shape, and indeed in some cases are both spiral and "S": they are both of these in the twin vines embracing the trunk of the tree that appears on the title page of *Innocence* (pl. 3). These vines, as Keynes remarks (pl. 3, commentary), represent "Christianity embracing the tree of sinful life." Damon's view (note 3, above) differs slightly. At any rate, the curved vines are divinity itself, a normal "S"; not the Divine Image "S" (a reversal, or mirror image). They are Christ embracing sinful life in the sense of Christ being a man and experiencing the punishment for sin which man cannot bear alone. The fact that *Songs of Experience* had to be written along with *Songs of Innocence* is implicit in the compositional design of the *Innocence* title page itself, though we read that design better for having examined the movement or flow of design in all of the *Songs*.

10

The Presence of Cupid and Psyche

IRENE H. CHAYES

How do source studies contribute to an understanding of Blake's "visionary forms"? What is the relation of traditional iconography to the imagery in both his poetry and his designs? In his case, it is especially true that the work is to be trusted more than the man, and in spite of his strictures on "the classics" his work itself shows that Blake was sufficiently a product of his age to draw on the traditional Greek and Roman myths as well as on more esoteric material for the complex purposes of his two parallel arts. Behind the eccentric proper names and the composite episodes of the epics we can recognize from time to time the familiar figures of Demeter and Persephone, Zeus and Prometheus, Apollo, Poseidon, or Hephaestus. Among the designs, there may be the surprise effect of a fall of Lucifer that is also the fall of Phaëthon, as on plate 5 of *The Marriage of Heaven and Hell*, or, on the last plate of *Europe*: *A Prophecy*, a revision of Aeneas' flight from Troy, in which the dead Creusa seems to be substituted for the aged Anchises. It is true that these are usually only fleeting echoes or allusions with a limited function, and the very familiarity of the originals undoubtedly left little for Blake to do by way of adaptation or variation that would have been an adequate challenge to his imagination. There was one classical myth, however, whose special history and associations set it apart from those that had become hackneyed through overuse by the time Blake began work.

This was the myth of Cupid and Psyche, which is best known as an interpolated story, or parable, or fable, in *The Metamorphoses* (IV, 28-VI, 24), popularly called *The Golden Ass*, by Apuleius of Madaura. Apuleius, in turn, had received his material from a tradition of myth and ritual which may have originated in the Orphic Mysteries and which has survived mainly in the iconography of a variety of minor antique works of art—funerary reliefs, statuary, frescoes, mosaics, engraved gems. In a third tradition, the writers on mythology in later ages, from Fulgentius in the sixth century, to Boccaccio, to the speculative mythographers of the eighteenth and early nineteenth centuries, preserved a continuity of their own in discussions of Cupid and Psyche, both together and separately, as independent mythic figures. By the time of the Romantics, when there was a new interest in Cupid and Psyche among major and minor writers alike,[1] all three traditions were available and in varying combinations affected the way in which the myth was understood, even when Apuleius' literary version continued to be the main source. Through his training in art and his professional work as an engraver, as well as through his more conventional literary interests, Blake was in a position to regard the two figures and the myth from more than one standpoint and in more than one context of meaning. The evidence is that he did precisely that, and from what he saw chose motifs for both his poetry and his designs which furnished him with considerably more than a means of appealing to what his audience already knew or of acknowledging that "the classics" sometimes had anticipated his own characters and situations. Although the results remain purely Blake's own, to trace the separate motifs back to their probable origins and forward in new variations and combinations is to learn much that is valuable about the workings of his imagination, both verbal and visual, and about the relation of his two arts to each other.

The remainder of this section will be concerned with Blake's most direct uses of Apuleius' fable. His more complex adaptations

[1] Thomas Taylor's prose translation of Apuleius' fable (1795) was followed by adaptations in verse by Mary Tighe (1795) and Hudson Gurney (1799); Mary Shelley began a translation of her own in 1817 but left it unfinished. Erasmus Darwin and Thomas Moore as well as Keats and Coleridge wrote poems with specific allusions to the myth; references to Cupid and Psyche both together and separately recur among Coleridge's published and unpublished prose. On sources of the myth in literature and art that were available to the Romantics, see E. H. Haight, *Apuleius and His Influence*, reprinted New York, 1963, chs. 6 and 7, and Ian Jack, *Keats and the Mirror of Art*, Oxford, 1967, ch. 12.

Work on this essay was assisted in part by grants from the American Council of Learned Societies and the American Philosophical Society. For information and courtesies, I am indebted also to the Prints Division of the New York Public Library, the Department of Prints and Drawings of the British Museum, and P. & D. Colnaghi & Co., Ltd., of London.

of the iconography of Cupid and Psyche from both Apuleius and other sources will be the subject of the later sections.[2]

At the beginning of the episode of Vala's regeneration in *Four Zoas* IX, Luvah speaks from a golden cloud and Vala responds to his "creating voice." In a passing note, S. Foster Damon was reminded of Apuleius' fable: "Possibly Blake intended to suggest the unfallen Psyche and the invisible Cupid."[3] His allusion was to the idyllic period after the wedding, when Psyche is content to receive her mysterious husband in the dark. In recent years, Damon's insight has been elaborated upon by Kathleen Raine, who has also found evidence of Apuleius' influence in other Blake poems, notably *The Sick Rose* and the manuscript lyric "I saw a chapel all of gold."[4] Miss Raine, however, assumes that Blake would have read Apuleius with the Neoplatonic lenses of Thomas Taylor, who translated *The Fable of Cupid and Psyche* separately, with an allegorizing commentary, in 1795.[5] Hence she overlooks the poems in which motifs from the fable serve dramatic or ironic meanings and the shock of recognition seems to be part of the calculated effect. In *The Angel*, for example, the "maiden Queen" is a Psyche who does *not* fall, because she spurns her supernatural visitor from the beginning; the accompanying design shows a naked, winged figure who quite clearly is Cupid. In *The Crystal*

[2] Since the aspects of Blake's designs that will be considered belong to the composition or the primary outline rather than to modulations of shading or color, they are not affected by differences among the original colored copies of *Songs of Innocence and of Experience*. For convenience, therefore, discussions of the *Songs*, both text and designs, are based on copy Z, available in the Blake Trust facsimile of 1955 and in the Orion Press facsimile of 1967. Designs in other illuminated works have been consulted in original copies or Blake Trust facsimiles.

[3] Damon, *Philosophy*, 393. Blake's reference to Apuleius in *VLJ* (E546/ K607) is relatively late (1810) and concerns the whole work, not the interpolated chapters on Cupid and Psyche.

[4] "Blake's Debt to Antiquity," *Sewanee Review*, LXXI (1963), 365-382; revised and expanded as "Blake's Cupid and Psyche" in *Blake and Tradition*, ch. 7. (Miss Raine's book did not become available until after this essay was in draft, and there is some duplication of comparative illustrations. For others, not included here, the reader is referred to her selection.)

[5] The commentary is now available in *Thomas Taylor the Platonist: Selected Writings*, ed. Kathleen Raine and G. M. Harper, Bollingen Series LXXXVIII, Princeton, 1969, 429-434.

Cabinet, from a later time, the male speaker undergoes a fall like Psyche's when he tries to exceed the limits set on his enjoyment of the miniature world within the Cabinet; in striving to seize "the inmost Form," he breaks the Crystal Cabinet (as an image, a variant of Psyche's magic palace) and finds himself exiled and weeping "upon the Wild." Even *The Sick Rose* is ambiguous in its relation to the chapters in *The Golden Ass.* The uncommon use of the second person, the curious tone, with its hint of *Schadenfreude,* and the reference to the nocturnal visits of the corrupting "invisible worm" recall not the voice of the narrator but the slanders of the jealous sisters, who tell Psyche that her unseen husband is actually a monstrous, poisonous snake and who eventually destroy themselves in their successive efforts to replace her in Cupid's favor.

As it happens, the poem with the clearest parallels to Apuleius' fable is *The Book of Thel,* which Miss Raine considers in another context entirely. Thel's quest, during which she interviews a succession of personified natural objects—the Lily of the Valley, the Cloud, the Worm, the Clod of Clay—follows the same folklore pattern as Psyche's series of penitential tasks, which she is able to perform only because of the kindness of the similarly assorted magic helpers that come to her aid: the Ant, the Reed, the Eagle, and the Tower. (The Eagle of "Thel's Motto" may have had his origin in Jupiter's royal bird, which does "know what is in the pit," since he helps Psyche by filling her jar with water from the Styx.) The climactic task is a descent to the Underworld, whose dangers Psyche is able to evade on both her way down and her journey back; Thel, too, visits the land of the dead and returns unscathed. The concluding parallels are ironic: both Psyche and Thel are left in their respective paradises; but whereas Psyche is reunited with Cupid and deified as well, permitted at last to take her place among the gods on Olympus, Thel can only return alone to the world she left in discontent, the unchanging earthly paradise of the Vales of Har.[6]

In the Renaissance, there were three notable series of frescoes illustrating scenes from Apuleius' *Cupid and Psyche:* by Raphael

---

[6] If, as some commentators have proposed, Blake borrowed the setting of *The Book of Thel* from the Garden of Adonis in *The Faerie Queene* (III, vi), he may have been reminded of Apuleius' fable by the glimpse of the reunited Cupid and Psyche in stanzas 49-51.

at the Villa Farnesina in Rome, Perino del Vaga at Castel Sant' Angelo, also in Rome, and Giulio Romano at the Palazzo del Tè, Mantua. There was also a series of thirty-two drawings by the Flemish artist Michiel van Coxie, a pupil of Raphael, which were sometimes attributed to Raphael himself. Although the original drawings were lost, they were known through engravings, of which George Cumberland owned a set, evidently acquired early.[7] It would have been possible for Blake, through his personal association with Cumberland, to have seen van Coxie's illustrations, and two in particular bear an illuminating relation to his own work. The scene with the earlier relevance is no. 13 {119}, engraved by Agostino Veneziano, which for the moment brings together *The Book of Thel* and a very different poem, *Europe: A Prophecy*.

In the last section of *Thel*, the lament from the grave-plot concludes with a protest against the failure of sexual consummation: "Why a tender curb upon the youthful burning boy! / Why a little curtain of flesh on the bed of our desire?" In the design on plate 4 of *Europe* {47}, Orc, Blake's personification of revolutionary energy, lies asleep, face down, with a flame playing about his head. Above him, kneeling on a cloud, a nude woman who is probably Enitharmon leans forward in a sweeping gesture and lifts a cloth to reveal him. The next to last line of the text, "Then Enitharmon down descended into his red light," seems closest to the design in reference, but it is not adequate to the actual scene, which might be a pictorial answer to the verse lament. Both clusters of images have such a definite character, in spite of their differences in medium and context, that they give every evidence of having had the same source, which appears to have been Agostino's engraving of the discovery of Cupid, Psyche's violation of the taboo of darkness that was the condition of her marriage.

Psyche leans forward on the bed with her left knee bent (it is

---

[7] See George Cumberland, *An Essay on the Utility of Collecting the Best Works of the Ancient Engravers of the Italian School*, London, 1827, 184-198. Three of the engravings, nos. 4, 7, and 13, are by Agostino Veneziano (de' Musi); the others are by the so-called Master of the Die. Cumberland attributed the latter to Marcantonio Raimondi and all the original designs to Baldassare Peruzzi (*Essay*, 170-171).

Among the plates in Cumberland's *Thoughts On Outline*, London, 1796, are five scenes of Cupid and Psyche, loosely related to Apuleius' narrative, which were "invented" by Cumberland himself and engraved by Blake. (See {117}, {118}, and nn. 8 and 22, below.)

Enitharmon's right knee that is similarly bent), and with her left hand she holds the lamp near the face of the sleeping Cupid. In the fable, a drop of hot oil from the lamp falls on Cupid's wing and scorches the "god of all fire," as Apuleius calls him ("ipsum ignis totius deum"). In both Thel's lament and *Europe* 4, Blake transfers the light-giving flame from the lamp wholly to the "youthful burning boy" who is being discovered; fire, of course, is an attribute of Orc also. The heavy curtain shrouding the bed becomes the symbol of virginity in the verse passage and also, perhaps, the symbol of the radical disparity between mortal and immortal, "a little curtain of flesh." In the design, the curtain has merged with the concealing darkness, becoming literally a mantle of night and sleep, which Enitharmon is lifting to waken Orc, as Psyche figuratively lifted it from Cupid with her light. And why "the bed of our desire"? In the engraving, the bed is the most prominent object in the central scene; in the fable, when Psyche discovers Cupid's beauty she flings herself upon him, enflamed with passion.

Blake might well have composed the closing lines of Thel's lament from the grave-plot with both Apuleius' narrative episode and the van Coxie-Agostino illustration (which has its own verse inscription) fresh in his mind. The design on plate 4 of *Europe* is more remote from Apuleius and seems to be related to the illustration in conjunction with Thel's lament.[8] Neither original source, the fable or the engraving, is responsible alone for either form of imagery, verbal or pictorial. The full three-cornered (or, for *Europe* 4, perhaps four-cornered) relationship is needed in each instance for an understanding of Blake's meaning; and in

[8] A further, intermediate source for both Blake and Cumberland may possibly have been an early drawing by Henry Fuseli illustrating the discovery scene. (See Frederick Antal, *Fuseli Studies*, London, 1956, pl. 23b.) Enitharmon's face and hair in *E4* {47} resemble those of Fuseli's Psyche, and the position of Fuseli's figures—the sleeping Cupid in the foreground and Psyche leaning toward him from behind, half-turned toward the viewer—reappears in the two versions of the discovery scene in Cumberland's *Thoughts*, pls. 12 {117} and 16. A faint pencil sketch by Blake in the MS of *FZ* II seems to be still another variant of the same scene, with another orientation of the figures, which is closest to Cumberland's pl. 16; see Bentley, *Vala*, 28 (facsimile). To complete the circle, the source that has been proposed for Fuseli's drawing—one of the frescoes by Perino del Vaga (Antal, p. 49 and pl. 23a)—evidently was based on van Coxie's original composition, as in {119}.

each instance, although the meaning that ultimately emerges—
concerning desire frustrated in *Thel*, energy roused in *Europe*—is
his own, its total effect depends upon the interaction of the original associations with the new contexts and with the new combinations and variations of the borrowed motifs.

Although in no other example to be cited in this essay will the
relationship be so classically clear, Blake's poetry and designs
will continue to interact with each other and with other traditional material to produce further new meanings in his own
terms. There will be occasion to refer again to the van Coxie illustrations (Blake too may have believed that they were actually
by Raphael, as he once believed in the authenticity of Ossian and
Thomas Rowley), and there will be further echoes of Apuleius'
fable itself. More immediately, the two other available sources
of Cupid and Psyche motifs become applicable. If Apuleius' literary version offered a finished and complex plot structure and
a set of narrative episodes compelling in themselves, the work
of the ancient artists and craftsmen and the commentaries and
interpretations of the mythographers suggested other possibilities
of treatment and other emphases, along with different images
and different patterns of relationship or process. It was from such
suggestions that Blake adapted the motifs that will be examined
in sections II and III.

· II ·

The earliest appearance of Blake's iconography of Cupid and
Psyche was in the poem reputedly his earliest, the song in *Poetical
Sketches* beginning "How sweet I roam'd from field to field." The
"I" who speaks tells of unexpectedly meeting and being enter-
tained, captured, and then held prisoner by someone called only
"the prince of love":

> With sweet May dews my wings were wet,
>   And Phoebus fir'd my vocal rage;
> He caught me in his silken net,
>   And shut me in his golden cage.
> He loves to sit and hear me sing,
>   Then, laughing, sports and plays with me;
> Then stretches out my golden wing,
>   And mocks my loss of liberty.

The epithet "prince of love"—the same that Blake was to use for Luvah in *The Four Zoas*—suggests that the captor is Cupid, and at first there may seem to be something odd about his role here. By a traditional conceit, which can be traced back to the Greek Bucolic poets, it was Cupid who was prone to capture in a net or imprisonment in a cage,[9] apparently because of his resemblance to a bird. The wings which in Blake's poem are wet "with sweet May dews" are obviously not the feathered bird wings conventionally emblematic of Cupid, and the identity of the speaker clarifies the use of the net and the cage by Cupid himself. The "golden wing" of the last stanza, together with earlier references to human features and feminine adornment ("He shew'd me lilies for my hair, / And blushing roses for my brow"), supplies the best clue: Cupid's prisoner is Psyche, who in classical art was usually portrayed as a young woman with butterfly wings—the personification of the human soul, which an even older tradition symbolized by a butterfly (ψυχή). There is no winged Psyche in Apuleius' fable, nor an encounter in which she is put in a cage by Cupid, although her sojourn in the palace is a kind of imprisonment. In the illustrated compendia of classical antiquities that were available in the eighteenth century, however, Blake would have found ready models of very similar situations, identified with Cupid and Psyche by name or emblem. One general collection that was widely used in England was Joseph Spence's *Polymetis* (1747); an earlier and even more ambitious encyclopedic work, the Abbé de Montfaucon's *Antiquité Expliquée*, had been translated in 1721-1722 in five folio volumes, followed by a five-volume supplement. It is not unlikely that Blake the engraver, even as early as the years of his apprenticeship, would have had occasion to consult Spence or Montfaucon in the course of his work, and the articles as well as the plates "explaining" antiquity may have had effects which in subtle ways would continue to influence his own imaginative productions long afterwards.

In Montfaucon's first volume, Cupid and Psyche both together

---

[9] For the net, see Spenser, *The Shepheardes Calender*, "March" (including the woodcut). Among artists in Blake's time, the cage probably would have been best known by its association with the theme of *The Selling of Cupids*, derived from a recently discovered Roman wall painting. On the influence of this painting, see Rosenblum, *Transformations*, 3-9 and pls. 1-5. See also nn. 13, 28, and 34, below.

and separately are the subject of several full-page plates, each of which is made up of a number of small engravings from a variety of sources. No. 3 in plate 61 (fig. 7), for example, one of three

Fig. 7. The wedding of Cupid and Psyche. Montfaucon, *Antiquity Explained*, vol. i, pl. 61, no. 3

depicting the wedding of Cupid and Psyche, is from a cameo signed by Tryphon, which in Blake's time belonged to the Duke of Marlborough and was so well known that James Gillray could use it as the basis of a caricature intended for popular circulation.[10] Psyche can be recognized by her butterfly wings (Cupid, as always, has the feathered wings of a bird), and in most of the other illustrations in Montfaucon's plate 61 {121} she wears the same identifying emblem. In several, however, there is no personifying human figure but instead the insect itself, a butterfly or a moth, which is poised over a lyre (no. 15), has just emerged from a corpse (no. 4), is being plucked from a woman's bosom by a bodiless hand (no. 10), or hovers near a skeleton (no. 5).

That in "How sweet I roam'd" the Psychelike singer is captured

[10] See M. D. George, *Hogarth to Cruikshank: Social Change in Graphic Satire*, New York, 1967, 110, 111.

The Marlborough Gem has a place in two works with which Blake was associated as an engraver: as the frontispiece to Jacob Bryant, *A New System, Or, An Analysis of Ancient Mythology*, London (vol. i), 1774, and as the subject of a verse description in "The Economy of Vegetation," part i of Erasmus Darwin's *The Botanic Garden*, 3rd edn., London, 1795, 165 and n.

and held prisoner by a Cupid with a hint of cruelty in his behavior has a quality which might be recognized as already typically
Blakean; but it is also perfectly in accord with the tradition represented by the illustrations to Montfaucon and Spence. In Greek
epigrams, Psyche was often represented as suffering at the hands
of Love, or Cupid, and this became one of the allegorical themes
used on engraved gems of the Hellenistic period.[11] The most
striking scenes in Montfaucon's plate 61 are those in which either
a butterfly or a butterfly-winged Psyche is being threatened or
physically tortured by one or more Cupids. In no. 11, Psyche is
kneeling, with her hands behind her back; in no. 13 (not illustrated here), she is being bound to a small tree by one Cupid
while another approaches her with a rod, as though to beat her.
Montfaucon (via his English translator) says of the former that
it is "a certain Mark of the Slavery a Soul is brought to, that
suffers it self to be subdued by its Passions."[12] Although there is
no overt physical torture in "How sweet I roam'd," the prince
of love's gesture of stretching out his captive's golden wing[13] is
different mainly in degree from no. 6, in which Cupid, with
hammer raised, is about to nail a butterfly to a tree; no. 9, Cupid
holding a torch close to the wings of a butterfly on the ground;

[11] Cf., for example, the burning motif in no. 9 of {121} and fig. 8 with
the following by Meleager: "If thou scorch so often the soul that flutters
round thee, O Love, she will flee away from thee; she too, O cruel, has
wings" (*Select Epigrams from the Greek Anthology*, tr. J. W. Mackaill, Mt.
Vernon, N.Y., 1943, 26). When Apuleius' Psyche burns Cupid's wing, she is
in effect retaliating against him in behalf of her precursors; cf. sec. III, below.

[12] *Antiquity Explained, And Represented in Sculptures*, tr. David Hum-
phreys, London, 1721-1722, I, 118.

It should be noted that twentieth-century scholarship has returned Cupid
and Psyche to the context of Orphism and has found even more complex
allegorical meanings in the iconography of Cupid alone, especially as he
was depicted in Renaissance art. See, variously, Jane Harrison, *Prolegomena
to the Study of Greek Religion*, reprinted New York, 1955, 532; Erwin
Panofsky, *Studies in Iconology: Humanistic Themes in the Art of the Renaissance*, reprinted New York, 1962, ch. 4, "Blind Cupid"; Edgar Wind, *Pagan
Mysteries in the Renaissance*, rev. edn., Harmondsworth, Eng., 1967, ch. 10,
"Amor as a God of Death."

[13] Since the reference to the "golden cage" (see n. 9) precedes the "golden
wing" by only three lines, it may be noted that in Joseph-Marie Vien's painting *La Marchande d'Amours* (Rosenblum, *Transformations*, pl. 1) the ped-
dler is lifting one of her Cupids in such a way that his wings are distinctly
stretched.

or no. 12 (not illustrated here), two Cupids tearing the wings from a butterfly they hold between them. In no. 5, the human form of Cupid has been dispensed with and as a bird he attacks the butterfly directly. Spence's *Polymetis* shows another threat of burning (fig. 8) and an assault by Cupid which has flung Psyche to her knees (fig. 9).

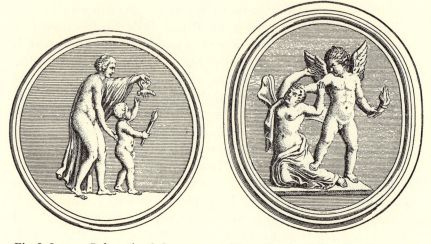

Fig. 8. Spence, *Polymetis*, pl. 6, no. 4   Fig. 9. Spence, *Polymetis*, pl. 6, no. 6

The familiar view of "How sweet I roam'd" is that, in addition to being a slight though charming lyric, it is "a protest against marriage."[14] Read against a background of the traditional iconography of Cupid and Psyche, the poem becomes something much more subtle and nearer to what Blake would do in his maturity. Already implied here is the kind of relationship between male and female which was to continue and develop in the poetry and the designs of a much later time. In particular, analogues of the speaker's imprisonment and of her captor's mocking gesture were to recur in considerably more complex situations. The butterfly and bird imagery which was also associated with Cupid and Psyche in art is only lightly suggested in "How sweet I roam'd," but later it was to undergo a development of its own among Blake's various winged or flying creatures, male and female, human and non-human.

[14] Damon, *Dictionary*, 331.

· III ·

Blake the graphic artist might have been expected to be independently attracted to the ancient butterfly symbol for the soul, and there are designs in which he uses it directly, with much the same meaning as the similar insignia on Greek and Roman sarcophagi or burial monuments. Among his engravings illustrating Young's *Night Thoughts*, for example, there is one, in Night Four, in which a naturalistically drawn butterfly with open wings is placed just beyond the upper border of the text, while at the opposite corner, below, a figure of Christ leans toward an awakening nude man.[15] Similarly, a butterfly (or moth) rises from between the feet of the newly awakened figure in the engraving of *Albion rose* {91}. In both scenes, there is another image as well, a jointed, wormlike creature which is half-coiled on the ground near the left foot of the figure in *Albion rose* and in the *Night Thoughts* illustration lies in profile—resembling a tiny human corpse—exactly on the line that borders the text; the butterfly is just above it. This is, of course, the larva, the first form in the process of insect metamorphosis that culminates in the emergence of the butterfly. Its presence in Blake's designs reflects still a third conception of the mythic Psyche, which he would have known not only through reproductions of ancient art but also through notes and commentaries, especially those by the mythographers of his own time.

Jacob Bryant, for example, could say of Psyche (to whom, as to Eros, he gave an Egyptian origin): "The most pleasing emblem among the Egyptians was exhibited under the character of Psyche, Ψυχη. This was originally no other than the Aurelia, or butterfly: but in aftertimes was represented as a lovely female child with the beautiful wings of that insect. The Aurelia, after its first stage as an Eruca, or worm, lies for a season in a manner dead; and is enclosed in a sort of coffin. In this state of darkness it remains all winter: but at the return of spring it bursts its bonds, and comes out with new life, and in the most beautiful attire. The Egyptians thought this a very proper picture of the soul of man, and of the

---

[15] *The Complaint and the Consolation, Or, Night Thoughts*, London, 1797, 90; cited as *NT* IV, 90 (no. 148 eng.). The butterfly image, which is lacking in the water color, is similar to that in fig. 11.

immortality, to which it aspired."[16] As a source of analogy for their various concepts of evolutionary change from a lower to a higher state, or for a Dantesque ascent by way of descent, this process had a particular appeal for the Romantics, especially for Coleridge, who more than once in his later prose specifically uses the name of Psyche for the triumphant end-product of the metamorphosis.[17] Blake is nearest to his younger contemporaries in this respect in *Four Zoas* IX and Enion's speech anticipating her reunion with Tharmas:

> . . . Soon renewd a Golden Moth
> I shall cast off my death clothes & Embrace Tharmas again
> For Lo the winter melted away upon the distant hills
> And all the black mould sings. (132:21-24:E386/K373)

Earlier, however, especially in the lyrics of the mid-1790's, Blake assimilates the metamorphosis of the butterfly to other processes and patterns, and pictorially as well as verbally he sows confusion by the variety of names and images he uses for the first and last stages in the process, the "worm" and the "fly."[18] In his verse, the word "worm" may refer to the earthworm, usually a symbol of humble mortality; the caterpillar, which has sinister and repressive connotations; the larva, which may also be a caterpillar; or the chrysalis, the pupa in its case (fig. 10), which finally becomes the winged butterfly. In *The Book of Thel*, the "weak worm" on its "dewy bed" at first seems an earthworm; yet as "an infant wrapped in the Lillys leaf" (E5/K129) and as (in some copies) it is shown in the design, with the suggestion of human

---

[16] *A New System*, II, 385-386. See also Montfaucon, I, 118, and Joseph Spence, *Polymetis*, London, 1747, 71. Figs. 10, 11, 12 are from Bryant's pl. x, opposite II, 386; since it is signed by Blake's master, Basire, it may have been engraved by Blake himself.

[17] See, e.g., *The Notebooks of Samuel Taylor Coleridge*, ed. Kathleen Coburn, Bollingen Series L, New York, 1957-, II, 2556 f74ᵛ (on "transmutation" by the performance of duty); Coleridge, *Aids to Reflection*, Burlington, Vt., 1829, 162 (on sufferings as "pains of growth"). Almost as though he were looking at Blake's *Albion rose*, Wordsworth in *Prelude* XI wishes for man to "start out of his earthy, worm-like state, / And spread abroad the wings of Liberty" (ll. 251-253).

[18] An interesting complement to the discussion here and in sec. V below is Edward J. Rose, "Blake's Human Insect: Symbol, Theory, and Design," *Texas Studies in Language and Literature*, X (1968), 215-232.

Fig. 10. Chrysalis. Bryant, *Mythology*, Fig. 11. Aurelia. Bryant, *Mythology*,
vol. II, pl. 10   vol. II, pl. 10

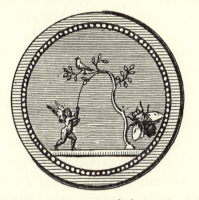

Fig. 12. Musca. Bryant, *Mythology*, vol. II, pl. 10

features, it is a chrysalis. In the frontispiece to *The Gates of Paradise* (1793) there is another baby-faced chrysalis, reposing on a leaf, while a caterpillar clings to another leaf overhead; an earthworm appears on plate 16. The design for *The Sick Rose* {3} goes further and includes in the same scene a caterpillar, a serpentlike worm which is entering the rose, and a tiny female figure who at the same time thrusts her way out of the blossom with upraised arms, like a newly hatched butterfly rising on its first flight.

A similar ambiguity, with more important consequences, governs Blake's use of the image of the "fly." Judged by the text alone, the Song of Experience entitled *The Fly* seems to be about a housefly, which would represent extreme transience of life and hence would be even more remote from the butterfly of

227

resurrection and immortality than the earthworm is from the chrysalis. Yet in the margin beside the last stanza is etched the silhouette of a butterfly, which might be the one from *Albion rose* much reduced.[19] In a poem whose essence is verbal ambiguity and logical paradox, one effect of the juxtaposition is that the butterfly not only lends some of its associations of resurrection and immortality to the housefly but also attracts to itself some of the latter's fragility and vulnerability.[20] Either winged insect, therefore, might be the one killed by the "thoughtless hand." If it is a butterfly, the irony is intensified, as it is in one of the water color drawings for *Night Thoughts*. In *NT* v, 26 (no. 181: "From a Friend's Grave, how soon we disengage?"), a butterfly perching on a gravestone is about to be trapped by a boy who approaches it with his hat raised, like a net. Since by Blake's own symbolism the butterfly might be the newly risen soul from the grave below, the boy's thoughtlessness seems about to lead to a double killing, on two different levels.

Although the circumstances are different, the *Night Thoughts* scene is a pictorial analogue of the capture of the butterfly-winged singer in "How sweet I roam'd," and only one of several, mostly variations on the motif of catching a butterfly in a hat, which were recurring in both Blake's verse and designs before he undertook the Young illustrations. The hat as a substitute for a net seems to have made its first appearance in plate 7 of *Gates of Paradise* (fig. 13), which shows a young man, his hat raised in his right hand, charging forward in pursuit of a tiny, flying, but wingless figure, while another lies on the grass as though dead. Like the original "prince of love," the pursuer here is male, while his victims (according to the legend added in the 1818 re-

---

[19] A similar image—a butterfly, or moth, resting on a woman's thigh—appears in one of Blake's engravings after Fuseli, *Falsa Ad Coelum Mittunt Insomnia Manes* (ca. 1790). The presence of a Cupid who is aiming his arrow at the butterfly, while an elephant-headed demon points to the lettered inscription, imports the traditional torture motif into a situation that recalls Fuseli's famous *Nightmare*. Although the effect of the conjunction is typical of Fuseli, Blake's own method in the design for *The Fly*, as that is interpreted below in sec. III, is not essentially different.

[20] Cf. fig. 12, in which the housefly ("Musca") in company with a Cupid and a bird seems to be a butterfly substitute.

Fig. 13. *The Gates of Paradise*, pl. 7

issue) are female: "What are these? Alas! the Female Martyr."[21] In the design for *The Fly* the hunting motif is further modified and the sex relation of the aggressor and the victim is reversed. Visible in the background is a young girl who holds a racquet in her right hand, poised to hit a shuttlecock which is falling through the air toward her. Since she is facing toward the rear, her pose is almost an exact inversion of that of the youth with the hat in *Gates of Paradise*; moreover, as we can see, the shuttlecock is a flying object with feathered wings, like a bird—or like Cupid.

On the etched plate, both the upraised racquet and the falling shuttlecock are placed just below the stanza in which the philosophizing "I" foresees that one day he, too, may be struck down in his "play": "some blind hand / Shall brush my wing." In the full context of the poem, therefore, the girl's gesture with the racquet is a blow directed vicariously against the male speaker, ironically confirming his own expectations. But in a larger context, the gesture has a more important meaning: it is the girl's symbolic retaliation, during her own kind of play, against those males who in the pursuit of their purposes have variously captured,

[21] In both the Introduction to *Europe* and the MS poem *The Fairy* (E466/K178), hats are similarly used for the capture of fairies, and explicit comparisons are made to butterfly-catching. Both captors and both prisoners, however, are male.

struck down, or slain either butterflies or butterflylike females—
the prince of love and the youth of *Gates of Paradise* as well as
the unthinking killer of the "fly" itself. For this, too, there was
a precedent in the tradition of Cupid and Psyche. Although the
illustrations to Spence and Montfaucon happen to show only the
allegorical sufferings of Psyche at the hands of Cupid, another of
the standard themes on the engraved gems which might have
been known to Blake was the complementary tormenting of Cupid
by Psyche. (The example reproduced here {118} is an imitation,
a design by George Cumberland which Blake himself engraved
in 1794 for Cumberland's *Thoughts On Outline*.)[22] Apuleius
tipped the balance in the opposite direction and made Psyche the
sole aggressor, who, when she prepares to violate the taboo, equips
herself with a dagger as well as with a lamp (see {119}). Assault
and retaliation, the exchange of symbolic blow and counterblow
in a struggle for mastery, are an essential part of Blake's own myth
of male-female conflict, the typical form that the relation of "the
sexes" takes in the depths of the life of Generation. Male and
female contend for power and possession in *The Crystal Cabinet*,
which begins with the Maiden as pursuer and the dancing male
speaker as her captive, a reversal of earlier roles until he becomes
possessive in turn. In *The Mental Traveller*, where the myth is
most fully realized, the archetypal man and woman alternate in a
rising and falling pattern of conflict, disparity, and frustration
which coincides with a highly complex, cyclical pattern of human
and cosmic ages.[23] *The Fly* is a step toward both, linking them
with "How sweet I roam'd" of long before by way of the motif
of butterfly- and bird-hunting. Logically and chronologically,
however, the evolution of Blake's sexual myth is not complete
without two other poems, which have not yet been mentioned.
Like *The Fly* they belong to *Songs of Innocence and of Experience*, and their relation to the iconography of Cupid and Psyche
also involves their relation to each other.

[22] Was Cumberland somehow influenced by "How sweet I roam'd"? Since
Cupid is the prisoner and Psyche the captor, the wing is Cupid's, and its
feathered tip is being curled back, not stretched, the situation in this scene
is very nearly an inversion of that at the end of Blake's lyric. With the details
of Cupid's wing, the tree trunk, and the perching butterflies, cf. fig. 7, no.
6 of {121}, and fig. 14.

[23] On *The Mental Traveller*, see my "Plato's *Statesman* Myth in Shelley
and Blake," *Comparative Literature*, XIII (1961), 361-368.

· IV ·

As the first stanza indicates, the poem *Infant Joy* takes its start from an allegorical personification ("I happy am / Joy is my name"), not unlike that by which Apuleius' Psyche bears Cupid a daughter, Voluptas, or Pleasure.[24] (In Milton's *Comus*, lines 1004-1011, where Psyche gives birth to twins, one of the offspring is in fact named Joy.) "Arise, you little glancing wings, and sing your infant joy" will be Oothoon's song in *Visions of the Daughters of Albion* (E50/K195) celebrating "lovely copulation," and the "little glancing wings" can be seen in the design accompanying *The Blossom* {13}, a poem to which *Infant Joy* is close enough in situation to be a sequel. The naked, winged cherubs fluttering and sporting about the plantlike phallic shape are recognizable as Blake's versions of the *putti* or *amorini* of classical and Renaissance painting, which survived in the eighteenth century mainly in rococo decoration. In other words, they are figures of Cupid, the mischievous infant Cupid without Psyche, and the erotic meaning of their playful flights was thoroughly conventional when Blake turned it to his own use, in this design and elsewhere.

The Blossom is a song about copulation and conception, expressed by both the garden conceit of the text[25] and the somewhat more explicit imagery of the design, which also includes a winged woman, holding one of the *putti* to her breast. In *Infant Joy*, birth has already occurred, and the mother and child are tentatively establishing a relationship with each other. In terms of the personification, this means that through the question and answer about his name, sexual joy, the willingly captured *putto*, is being redefined as the different, "sweet" and "pretty" joy of the nursery. The woman in her turn acknowledges a separate identity for her Joy (in contrast to the passive and oblivious Blossom, who alone is "happy") and learns to respond by song and blessing: "Thou

---

[24] See *The Faerie Queene* III, vi, 50.

[25] The flight of the Sparrow, "swift as arrow," carries a double allusion, to Cupid's conventional weapons and to one of the emblems of his mother, Venus. Cf. "Come hither my sparrows / My little arrows" (*The Fairy*, E466/K178). In Apuleius' fable, Psyche's falling in love with Cupid is symbolized by her pricking her finger with one of his arrows; see the small right-hand scene in {119}. The size disparity in {13} between the winged woman and the cherub has a parallel in van Coxie's designs, where Cupid is consistently portrayed as a child, while Psyche is a full-sized woman.

dost smile. / I sing the while / Sweet joy befall thee." In the verse text, there are only voices, and by the second stanza the implied point of view has become the mother's. The design {2}, on the other hand, shows both the mother and child as they cannot see themselves, and places them in a scene which reveals more than the limited perspective of Innocence allows them to know.

Together with a third figure, they compose a group inside the cup of an enormous, stylized blossom, probably an anemone, whose petals have been partly cut away around them. The young mother and the baby resemble similar pairs in other *Songs of Innocence* (e.g., *Spring*). The other figure, however, who occupies a prominent position in the scene, standing at almost the exact center of the blossom and facing the mother and child from the right, has no counterpart elsewhere in the sequence, and in the text there has been no indication of the presence of a third person. Both "fairy" and "angel" are imprecise terms from Blake's writings which do not apply to the image actually shown in the design.[26] The short, spotted butterfly wings nevertheless do supply the clue: this is a standard figure of the winged Psyche, such as Blake could have seen early and easily enough by going no further than the illustrations to Spence or Montfaucon, or a similar collection (see figs. 14 and 15). The wings, the hair, the suggested "Greek" line of the profile, are all so faithful to traditional representations that the figure was surely intended to be recognized and to contribute her associations to the total meaning of the poem.[27]

[26] Original responsibility for the vagueness concerning this figure probably rests with J. H. Wicksteed, who found no incongruity in turning the butterfly wings into a symbol of resurrection and their wearer into the angel of an Annunciation. (See *Blake's Innocence and Experience*, New York, 1928, 123.) That other viewers have seen a "fairy" suggests that some popular representations of fairies have been imitated at third or fourth hand from older portrayals of the winged Psyche. Raine (I, 108) calls the figure a "butterfly-winged spirit of vegetation"; by way of the anemone, she relates the infant to Spenser's Garden of Adonis—about which see n. 6, above.

[27] The wings are simplified from Bryant's Aurelia (fig. 11); cf. also {118} and {88}. (These should be distinguished from the more fanciful kinds of wings, including butterflies', which Blake the illustrator sometimes bestowed on various of his pictorial figures, especially when he was improvising on someone else's text. Such images, and others like them, pose a special problem for students of Blake's iconography.) For the profile, see, e.g., {119} and {118}. Like the mother's, the hair of the winged figure is drawn back in a low braid or loop, a step toward the famous "Psyche knot," which appears

232

Fig. 14. Spence, *Polymetis*, pl. 6, no. 3   Fig. 15. Spence, *Polymetis*, pl. 6, no. 5

Equally neglected by commentators, although it too leaps to the eye, is the position of the Psyche-figure's arms, which she holds before her, bent at the elbow and slightly raised, as though waiting for something to be put into her hands. In the scene as it is composed, she can only be waiting to receive Joy from the arms of the mother, and again, the significance of such a transfer is not to be found in the limited domestic situation the text implies. In other Songs of Innocence—*The Ecchoing Green* and *A Cradle Song* are two examples—the designs may hint of future events which are never suspected by the Innocent speakers in the texts. In the anemone plant, too, there is the suggestion of a temporal progression, from the drooping, phallic bud, to the womblike blossom opening to give birth, to the symbolic scene the blossom houses. Since he properly belongs to Blake's eternity, Infant Joy is an analogue of Cupid, Eros, the love god, in his unequal union with a mortal, who is represented in two different "ages," the mother and the maidenly winged figure, within the flower of Generation. "Eternity is in love with the productions

---

elsewhere in the *Songs*—e.g., *Holy Thursday (Exp.)*, *The Little Girl Lost*, *Nurses Song (Exp.)*—and an incidental confirmation of the sex of this personage. The long-sleeved, high-waisted gown is not classical, but among female figures it will reappear on the girl in *The Fly* and on the younger of the two women in *To Tirzah* (reproduced in E30/K220).

of time." Time may also fall in love with eternity, as Apuleius' Psyche fell in love with Cupid when she discovered his beauty, and the half-extended arms of the winged figure mimic an embrace which one day will, or may, replace the mother's. Even with her hair unbound and without butterfly wings, the girl in *The Fly* is a variant of the same figure, and she in turn gives way to the younger of the two women in the design for *To Tirzah*. The mother, too, reappears in different and more mature guise in both of these *Songs of Experience*, which carry the male infant forward into childhood and youth—even, in *To Tirzah*, to death.

At the time Blake composed and first etched *Songs of Innocence*, an embrace was perhaps all he intended to suggest by the incomplete gesture in *Infant Joy*. Nevertheless, the later development of arm and hand imagery in both his poetry and his art (see the essay by Janet Warner, above) lends an ambiguity to the gesture. There is, for instance, an implicit criticism of the winged figure's poised and forward-thrusting hands in one of the portrayals of Oothoon in *Visions of the Daughters of Albion*. On the page containing the "Argument" {21}, she is shown kneeling with her hands crossed on her breast, leaning forward to receive the kiss of a small male figure, who with outstretched arms springs up toward her from a flower (vaguely rendered, but probably the marigold of the text).[28] With her Greek profile and her hairdress— a high Psyche knot, plus light tresses like those in the Cumberland outline {118}—Oothoon might herself be the Psyche of classical art, and the manuscript lyric (E461/K179) often quoted in connection with this design,

> He who binds to himself a joy
> Does the winged life destroy
> But he who kisses the joy as it flies
> Lives in eternity's sun rise

could serve also as a motto to the first part of Apuleius' fable. Although she acts by the spontaneity of desire, her enslavement

[28] D. V. Erdman has called attention to the contrast between Oothoon's gesture in this design and that of the female Cupid-seller in the painting by Vien (Rosenblum, *Transformations*, pl. 1). (See "Blake's Vision of Slavery," *JWCI*, xv [1952], pls. 51a, 51b, and p. 250. See also n. 13, above.) Contrast also the small figures on the title page of *The Book of Thel*, enacting an erotic flight and pursuit as they emerge from flowers which, significantly, are anemones. (For a botanical identification, see Raine, I, 105.)

in *Visions* makes Oothoon a conspicuous "female martyr" as well.

In *The Crystal Cabinet*, the captive at first follows Oothoon's example and is content to kiss without touching: "I bent to Kiss the lovely Maid / And found a Threefold Kiss returnd." But he destroys his miniature paradise when he forgets his restraint and tries to "sieze the inmost Form / With ardor fierce & hands of flame." "Hands of flame" might also be a descriptive phrase for the hands of the winged Psyche of *Infant Joy*, with their stiffly spread fingers terminating in sharp points—points which visually rhyme with the pointed leaves of the anemone plant and the flame-like petals of the blossom. Is her "ardor," too, a potential threat, which would make her also a figure of Apuleius' Psyche? In the Song of Innocence, whatever threat there may be is only potential, and the descended Joy is "bound" only in the sense that he has allowed himself to become a source of pleasure and an object of knowledge to the woman whose first, maternal embrace he has readily accepted.

Oppressive "binding" and another pair of pictorial "hands of flame" both occur in the poem which is the formal counterpart of *Infant Joy* in *Songs of Experience*. Using the first person and the past tense, the speaker in the text of *Infant Sorrow* tells of a birth that has been sorrowful for the child and the parents alike. The boy who appears in the design, however {17}, is scarcely a newborn infant; rather, he might be a less mature version of Oothoon's athletic joy, or a wingless Cupid who has been trapped in a domestic setting. Again, Blake seems to have been borrowing from the engravings of van Coxie's illustrations to Apuleius, for here, as in *Europe* 4, the composition broadly recalls the discovery scene {119}. The large bed in the background is heavily draped, like the nuptial bed of Cupid and Psyche; the child is at the left, on a small wicker bed; and the mother (standing on the same side of the child as the mother's successor in *Infant Joy*) reaches toward him from the right, her body arching in a long curve, like the curious Psyche with her lamp, or like Enitharmon waking Orc. The mother this time is modestly capped and kerchiefed, and her carefully outlined hands are neither withheld nor "ardent" but relaxed and open, extended in invitation and compassion to the struggling child.[29] But he has turned away and is

[29] Cf., in the color print *Pity*, the hands of the Valkyrielike rider who leans down to take the "new-born naked babe" from the exhausted mother.

raising his own arms as though in an appeal to someone or something situated above him and to the right rear, outside the picture. On his upturned hands, the fingers are tense, slightly curled inward, and pointed, like small tongues of flame.

If Infant Joy is the energy of eternity in voluntary erotic descent, like Cupid visiting his mortal bride, Infant Sorrow is the same energy after a reluctant fall, protesting and aware of his helplessness, an Orclike "fiend hid in a cloud." In the second stanza of the text, the child comes to terms with his bondage and decides to accept the comfort that is available: "Bound and weary I thought best / To sulk upon my mother's breast." The design shows the truth behind the words of resignation, and a more appropriate inscription might be the closing lines of Thel's lament from the grave-plot. On a literal bed of desire, obstructed by a bank of all too palpable curtains, this new avatar of the "youthful burning boy" is trying to escape the tender curb of maternal pity in his yearning for something—release, deliverance, return—that is beyond his reach. (The link with the van Coxie-Agostino scene —ironic, as it appears—may be the departure of Cupid after he has been seen by Psyche and burned by her lamp. In the left background of the engraving, he is shown flying out the window, while Psyche vainly tries to hold him back by seizing his leg.) The presence of the waiting Psyche in a similar though not identical pose in *Infant Joy* only compounds the frustration; for even though there may be such a figure in the future of the Cupid-Orc of *Infant Sorrow*, and even though she may offer the means by which he ultimately can return to eternity, the temporal pattern requires her to follow the mother, and in rejecting one embrace he is rejecting both, reaching upward and away from the level on which the two kinds of female love must be given.

As verse songs, *Infant Joy* and *Infant Sorrow* are almost model "contraries"; the designs, however, are complementary in a complex and ironic way, which sets the Psyche of one and the Cupid of the other at hopeless cross-purposes to each other. It is at this point that the two figures enter Blake's evolving sexual myth and contribute their frustrated gestures to the pattern of variously

---

Reoriented from vertical to horizontal, the relation of the figures in this composition is much like that in the design for *Infant Joy*.

reaching arms and grasping hands which extends from "How sweet I roam'd" and the stretched golden wing, through the scenes of butterfly-catching, *The Fly*, and *The Crystal Cabinet*, to the culmination of both the myth and the gestic pattern in *The Mental Traveller*. On the whole, male hands are likely to be aggressive by nature and to destroy only unintentionally, like the "blind" and "thoughtless" hands in *The Fly*. (The racquet, however, is an extension of the girl's hand, and in the blow about to be struck her hand will not be "blind.") Aggressive female hands, when they find an object, tend to be destructive in a far more deadly fashion. In *The Mental Traveller* the transfer that was implicitly promised in the design for *Infant Joy* is finally accomplished when the male Babe is "given" at birth to the Woman Old, and the eager gesture of the Psyche figure is finally completed in action, although not in the action that originally appeared to be indicated, when the Woman Old uses her hands in a variety of tortures of her victim. As the climactic torture, "Her fingers number every Nerve / Just as a Miser counts his gold / She lives upon his shrieks & cries / And she grows young as he grows old." In a later cycle of the poem, when the Babe has grown old in turn, he renews himself by embracing a Maiden, who seems as passive as the Babe: "And to allay his freezing Age / The Poor Man takes her in his arms." With the intensification of both the conflict and the cross-purposes of male and female, ardor has become cruelty, and yearning, physical destitution. The nearly reciprocal gestures of *Infant Joy* and *Infant Sorrow* have been thrust even further apart and schematized, as probing female hands and freezing male arms, and in the Land of Men and Women there is no way they can be brought together.

· V ·

The three themes from the tradition of Cupid and Psyche which in their Blakean guise have been the subject of the preceding sections—the descent of the love god into unequal union with a mortal woman, the allegorical conflict between the two (as Love and the soul), the metamorphosis of the butterfly soul—reappear in new modifications and combinations and with new emphases in Blake's later and longer works. Among the *Night Thoughts* drawings, this time not an illustration of the text but a decoration

237

on the contents page of Night VII {88}, is a significant variation of the design for *Infant Joy*. Within an almost identical anemone blossom, a single female figure in an odd stance—half-sitting and half-kneeling at the right, balanced on her toes—combines something of both the mother and the Psyche figure, with perhaps a reminiscence of Oothoon kneeling to kiss the joy as it flies. Although she lacks butterfly wings, the two sides of her white collar are blown back from her shoulders in the suggestion of small feathered wings—bird wings, in fact, like Cupid's. A butterfly appears in its own form further to the left. The emblem from the engraving for Night IV, 90 (no. 148 eng.) has been transferred to a new setting, for just below the mature insect is its first state, the larva, or "worm," held in both hands by the woman.

In the new symbolic scene, the emphasis has shifted from descent to apotheosis, and the Vegetative-Generative life has become the vehicle of a new gestation, spiritual rather than material, over which the woman presides as a guardian. Like the bud in the earlier design, the exhausted little figure on the stalk, who apparently is male, is a token of the original sexual conception, now well in the past. In relation especially to the imagery discussed in section IV above, there are two iconographic clues to the changed female role here: the Cupidlike bird wings, which may indicate that the woman herself ultimately belongs to eternity, like the winged woman of *The Blossom*; and the position of her hands as she holds the "worm"—with palms up and index fingers extended, a protective gesture of the kind that was promised in the hands of the mother in *Infant Sorrow*.

In *The Four Zoas*, all three familiar themes recur. When Apuleius' fable is evoked in Night IX by the regeneration of Vala (E380-385/K366-372), it does not again contribute the pattern of Psyche's penitential tasks, although the echoes of *The Book of Thel* recall Blake's earlier borrowings. Instead, the honeymoon episode is revised to avoid Psyche's fall entirely. Like Cupid, Luvah is invisible, except in Vala's dream, but he visits her in daylight, and Vala does not yield to the temptation of either curiosity or lust. Elsewhere (Nights I, IX), the butterfly metamorphosis is condensed as a process of death and resurrection, sleep and renewal, and the two key stages are divided between females and males, respectively:

In Eden Females sleep the winter in soft silken veils
Woven by their own hands to hide them in the darksom grave
But Males immortal live renewd by female deaths[,] in soft
Delight they die & they revive in spring with music & songs
(5:1-4:E298/K266)

The distinction is preserved in an apparently contradictory passage. "Man is a Worm," says one of the Eternals in Night IX; "wearied with joy he seeks the caves of sleep / Among the Flowers of Beulah in his Selfish cold repose / . . . Folding the pure wings of his mind" (133:11-14:E386/K374). "Folding the pure wings of his mind" would mean preparing to return to the first stage after having reached the last; hence, the males are being warned against trying to undergo in their own persons the sleep of the chrysalis that precedes the awakening. The Eternals' remedy is to introduce another biological pattern of rest and revival, which will belong to the male alone and is in keeping with the broader planting-and-harvest theme of the last Night: "then inclosd around / In walls of Gold we cast him like a Seed into the Earth" (133:15-18). Otherwise, in both narrative and metaphor the conflict of male and female is brought to an ideal (though impermanent) resolution in this poem, not by the decisive victory of one over the other but by the willing sacrifice of the female and the grateful acceptance of the male: "Immortal thou[,] Regenerate She . . . Thus shall the male & female live the life of Eternity" (122:12-15).

One of the "female deaths" by which the males "live renewd" appears to be illustrated on the title page of *Jerusalem* {5}, where a female figure lies in an extravagant pose of death or sleep, her drooping butterfly wings—no longer the modest Aurelia type—elaborately marked with the sun, moon, and stars; nearby, other winged creatures mourn her. In the overall narrative of *Jerusalem*, Albion's rejected Emanation undergoes an ordeal of exile which makes her somewhat an analogue of Apuleius' Psyche,[30] and eventually she too is restored, by Albion's spontaneous change of heart. In the rhetorical texture, the insect metamorphosis lingers

---

[30] Psyche's palace is reflected again in the "Pillars of ivory & gold," "Pavements of precious stones," and "Walls of pearl" Albion associates with Jerusalem (24:18-20:E168/K647). Cf. Vala's "bright house" (E382/K369).

mainly in the passage in which Hyle becomes a "winding Worm" beneath Gwendolen's "veil" (82:45-50:E238/K726). Since Hyle is also called "an infant Love" (line 37) and a "weeping Infant" (48), and "The desarts tremble at his wrath: they shrink themselves in fear" (51), there seem to be echoes of *Infant Joy*, *The Crystal Cabinet*, and *The Mental Traveller* as well, with a significance that reflects back to the discussion in section IV. The most striking "presence" of Cupid and Psyche in *Jerusalem*, however, is in one of the designs, which does not directly illustrate the text it accompanies but which does bring together motifs from earlier works, both poetry and designs, that *Jerusalem* as a whole might be presumed to have left behind. Since it serves as a coda to the aspects of Blake's sexual myth that have already been considered, this design suitably brings the present survey to a close.

At the bottom of plate 25 {6}, Albion is shown on his knees, held prisoner by two women, while a third spreads her arms above the whole group. Albion's pose is an intensification of the victim's in the water color *The Stoning of Achan*. With her outstretched arms and floating hair, the figure overhead resembles the baleful, hovering spirit on the last plate of *Visions of the Daughters of Albion*. The mesmerizing gaze of the woman beside Albion at the left is from the design for *To Tirzah*, and she herself is half-sitting and half-kneeling, balanced on her toes,[30a] like the guardian of the worm in the *Night Thoughts* design {88}. Once again, there is a play on gesture. As though mocking the delicacy of Oothoon, the woman at the left does not touch Albion with her hands; yet Albion, whose own arms are locked behind his back, is "bound" by her gaze.[31] In contrast, the arms of the woman op-

[30a] Except for a shift in orientation from left to right, the position of her legs is virtually identical with that of Eve in Michelangelo's *The Fall*. (The *Night Thoughts* figure, although it is the earlier, is less close to what must have been Blake's source, probably seen in an engraving.) Such a crouching pose had erotic connotations in antiquity.

[31] Contrast the mesmerizing woman in *To Tirzah*, who has placed her right hand on the right side of the prostrate man's chest. Her gesture reverses, or is reversed by, that of the Christ at *NT* IV, 90 (see n. 15), whose left hand rests above the heart of the awakening man; the line marked in Young's text is "That touch, with charm celestial heals the soul."

In the relation of females to male, the compositions of both *To Tirzah*

posite are raised and her hands are actively engaged; with her left hand, she is drawing a long cord out of Albion's navel and rolling it into a ball, while with the right she appears to be drawing the cord out further. Her antecedents are literary rather than pictorial: the Woman Old, numbering the male Babe's "every Nerve," or Enion, whom Tharmas reproves for examining "every little fibre of my soul / Spreading them out before the Sun like Stalks of flax to dry."[32] From the downturned hands of the third woman, curious lines stream toward the rocks on which her two allies are placed; these may be the "Fibres of Life" which Rahab and Tirzah cut from the Atomist rocks and use to "weave a male" on their golden looms (67:1-14:E217-218/K704). "Such are the Feminine & Masculine when separated from Man."

And what of Cupid and Psyche? Van Coxie's illustrations to Apuleius again become relevant, possibly because in 1816 or soon thereafter the part of Cumberland's private collection of engravings in which they were included was acquired by the Royal Academy,[33] where Blake as a visitor might have renewed his acquaintance with the whole sequence. No. 21, engraved by the Master of the Die {120}, illustrates one of the episodes after Psyche's fall, her punishment by "Tristezza" and "Angoscia" (in the language of the verse inscription) in the presence of Venus. The bowed head and shoulders and the forward-pulled hair of Psyche reappear in the woman who is mesmerizing Albion; her

---

and J 25 parody the Deposition scene illustrating NT IX, 115 (no. 533), in which the dead Christ is surrounded and supported by the three Marys (or the two Marys and John?) within a sunlike perfect circle of mourning.

[32] FZ I, 4:28-32:E298/K265. (At J 22:20-24, Jerusalem repeats Tharmas' protest as her own, reproving Albion.) "Anatomy" (l. 30) as the product of manual probing is evidently a pun, and in the light of the hand imagery discussed above in sec. IV, it does not appear an accident that the object of the anatomizing is "infant joy." When Tharmas calls Enion "a flower expanding" and "fruit breaking from its bud / In dreadful dolor & pain" (4:40-42), he (or Blake) might actually be looking at the design for Infant Joy.

[33] See Cumberland, Essay, 12. Cumberland's collection, which was divided between the Royal Academy and the British Museum, has not fared well since. The B.M. portion is now dispersed without identification among the general holdings of the Print Room; the remainder, amounting to more than three hundred engravings, was acquired from the R.A. by a private gallery in 1967.

right profile and braced left arm are the contribution of another engraving, no. 7, in which Psyche is seen in very much the same pose, drying her hair. In no. 21 Venus sits at the right, watching the punishment; her legs and lower torso have been borrowed for the woman eviscerating Albion. The arm used in the evisceration, however, is not from this engraving but from no. 13, the discovery scene {119}. Psyche's original gesture of curiosity with her lamp has been modified to become a gesture of "anatomizing" domination.[34]

In the context of chapter 1, which plate 25 concludes, what is happening to Albion in the design is at once retributive punishment for his own sin and one aspect of that sin itself, the "crucifying cruelties of Demonstration" (*J* 24:55), by which Luvah has been slain and which now is given a symbolic female agency. At the same time, the allusiveness of the portrayals of his captors adds a further meaning to Albion's torture. In recalling the hovering spirit of *Visions*, who perhaps is an adumbration of Vala, the figure overhead also recalls her predecessor's implied threat of vengeance for the enslavement of Oothoon. The Venus and Psyche of Apuleius and van Coxie, Cupid's mother and bride, tend to merge with Blake's figures of Rahab and Tirzah here and with each other, like the similar mother and bride images in *The Crystal Cabinet* and *The Mental Traveller*. Since the Tirzah figure is almost identical with van Coxie's Psyche who is being whipped, so that the former victim has acquired a victim of her own, Albion's torture becomes also, in part, a vicarious penance for the sufferings of Blake's long line of mistreated females, variously assimilable to the Psyches of tradition, including Jerusalem herself, the stricken butterfly on the title page (whose celestial symbols are like Albion's), Oothoon, the Female Martyr of *Gates of Paradise* (fig. 13), and ultimately, once more, the original captured singer of Blake's first poem. Having slain Luvah, Blake's "prince of love," Albion for the moment is a surrogate in the role Luvah

---

[34] Worth noting, despite their wide separation in time, is the similarity in conception between *J* 25 and a remarkable drawing (ca. 1775) on the Cupid-selling theme by the ubiquitous Fuseli (Rosenblum, *Transformations*, pl. 4). A shrunken and cringing Cupid, recognizable only by his wings, is trapped between two women who are concluding the transaction; both are arrested in active gestures, and their cruel expressions parallel the cruel actions of Blake's figures.

might have played. This is all the more appropriate because Albion's curse (23:36-40) has perpetuated in his own terms the old pattern of seesaw conflict, of pain inflicted and pain received, injury and vengeance, which is lamented from Beulah in the short passage of text on plate 25 and which first appeared in Blake's poetry and designs as a struggle between male and female.[35]

[35] Although it bears no direct relation to the traditional iconography of Cupid and Psyche, the design on *J* 99 {103} has a place in this essay, for it finally completes, on a different level and with different personages, the embrace that was frustrated in *Infant Sorrow*. Pity and forgiveness bring together the Universal Man and his Emanation, as they bring together man and God and Albion and his "children." Against a background of upward-sweeping flames which have replaced the oppressive curtains, Jerusalem's pose combines elements from both figures of *Infant Sorrow*: the upraised arms of the child, and the compassionate gesture the child rejected. The upraised arms now express reception rather than yearning, and the gesture is offered to the heavens, toward which Jerusalem is rising in the embrace of a repentant, Jehovahlike Albion whose own arms are lowered. Pity and forgiveness may also come from below.

11

Blake and Urizen

JOHN SUTHERLAND

A POET'S VISIONS, Blake tells us, come during timeless moments—
moments "less than the pulsation of an artery" in duration, each
of which, nonetheless, is "equal in its period & value to Six Thousand Years."[1] Blake's visions, as elaborated in his prophetic books,
probably came during such peak moments of "four-fold" vision;
however, the visions themselves do not concern otherworldly
events. Instead, they concern themselves with cyclic patterns of
struggle, universalized in terms of underlying archetypal forces,
which repeat themselves through all the human worlds of time
and space. Such struggles are reconciled only in eternity—about
which the visions tell us relatively little.

In Blake's subjective experience, the contests of Luvah and
Urizen, of Los and the Spectre of Urthona, were repeated within
his own psyche during the course of youth, maturity, and age.
Simultaneously, similar contests raged within the nation (within
the psyche of the fallen giant, Albion); between nations—insofar
as England, under Pitt, seemed to be dominated by Urizen, while
England's great antagonist, revolutionary France, seemed to be
dominated by Luvah; and throughout ages of time and space—as
recorded in history and myth, and as perceived (imagined) in
vision.

Thus no attempts to identify individual events in the allegories
of the prophetic books should be taken as exclusive. Nonetheless,
a basic hypothesis of the present essay is that Blake's primary attention was directed inward, and that both direct and symbolic
references to outward events may be best understood when they
can be related to the fairly systematic theory of psychology which
(together with fragments of his own psychic history) Blake gradually elaborated throughout his work. A closely related hypothesis
is that Blake had deeply ambivalent feelings about that aspect
of human mental activity which he allegorized as Urizen.

[1] M 28:62-63 (E126/K516).

Some sort of *reason*, of course, was necessary to Blake in his system-building. In *Jerusalem*, plates 10 and 11, Blake/Los drives his Spectre, the "Holy Reasoning Power" which is also the "Abstract objecting power," to great and painful labors, as he attempts to "Create a System." There seems little doubt that Blake's primary ability was his creative, visionary imagination—as symbolized by Urthona/Los. However, the clear, hard lines with which he insisted on delineating his visions, and the precision with which he worked out complex relationships in his writings, point to reason—symbolized by Urizen—as a strongly developed secondary ability.

Few writers, in all literary history, have left evidence of having matured and individuated as fully as did Blake. All accounts of his old age contribute to a picture of psychological security and serenity, of calm creativity, of inward joy, and of rational clarity. Needless to say, this final state was achieved only after many years of inward and outward conflict, of "mental" warfare—much of which is mirrored in his art.

Most critics and biographers agree that one of the major crises of Blake's life took place during the years 1803 and 1804. In these years he went through a series of climactic experiences: he broke free of his dependent relationship with Hayley in the spring of 1803; he was accused by the soldier, Schofield, of having uttered "seditious expressions" during the summer of 1803; he returned to London in the fall of 1803; he stood trial for sedition and was acquitted in January 1804. At that time, he reports in a letter to Hayley, he "was again enlightened with the light I enjoyed in my youth, and which has for exactly twenty years been closed to me as by a door and by window shutters." A key aspect of this experience seems to have been his sudden conviction that he had at last "reduced that spectrous Fiend to his station, whose annoyance has been the ruin of my labors for the last passed twenty years of my life. He is the enemy of conjugal love and is the Jupiter of the Greeks, an iron hearted tyrant, the ruiner of ancient Greece . . ." (E702-703/K851-852).

Various explanations of the significance of this peak experience have been suggested. Arguing from the second part of Blake's description of the "spectrous Fiend," George Mills Harper has suggested that Blake at this point decisively turned away from Greek philosophy and mythology, and in particular from Platonism, in favor of Hebrew mythology and a philosophy of Christian forgiveness.[2] Arguing from the first part of the same description, Bernard Blackstone has suggested that, twenty years before, "for the first time, Blake felt the full strength of the bonds of marriage, and of the malice of that spectrous fiend jealousy—whom he afterwards identified thoroughly with Urizen or Jupiter, the god of the Greeks."[3] David Erdman has pointed out, in an essay published in 1949, that Blake's "lost" twenty years preceding 1804 correspond exactly to the period in which Blake set up as an engraver and devoted most of his energies to a struggle for commercial success.[4] And in *Blake: Prophet Against Empire* Erdman remarks (387-388 [416-417]) that "after the renewal of the war in 1803 Blake never quite emerged from an ambivalent view of the American and French Revolutions as having been either too warlike or not revolutionary enough." He concludes that "it is evidently historical change rather than theology that led Blake to shift his emphasis from Energy to Forgiveness, from warlike men to the solitary seditious monk [the "Grey Monk" of *J* 52], and to revile the heralds of peace-through-revolution as having been false prophets."

Each of these suggestions has much to be said for it; indeed, Blake's crisis of 1804 seems to have been of the sort caused by multiple, converging forces. And doubtless the relief of his acquittal was an important predisposing factor. However, another possible cause deserves notice. Typically, the death of a father forces a son on to another stage of psychological adjustment—or, hopefully, development. Blake's father, James Blake, died in the early summer of 1784. It seems possible that Blake, after his father's death, may have moved a perceptible step further away from the visionary openness of his youth. The "shades of the prison-house" may have begun to close about him as part of a sequence which Wordsworth was to find irreversible—and which Blake only decisively reversed twenty years later.

Blake, by 1784 in his mid-twenties, was by all evidences immensely energetic, perceptive, and idealistic; however, there is no evidence that he was ready to think kindly of father figures of any

[2] *The Neoplatonism of William Blake*, Chapel Hill, 1961, 34-35.

[3] *English Blake*, Cambridge, Eng., 1949, 120-121.

[4] "William Blake's Exactness in Dates," *Philological Quarterly*, XXVIII (1949), 465-470.

description. Indeed, for the succeeding twenty years the chief antagonists in Blake's psychological dramas can be generalized as repressive father figures of one sort or another. These antagonists include "old Nobodaddy aloft" who so much enjoyed capital punishment and repressive warfare; the "Priests in black gowns" who prohibited free expression of love and sexuality; "God & his Priest & King" who made up a "heaven" out of the "misery" of the little chimney sweepers;[5] "the starry king" of *A Song of Liberty*;[6] William Hayley, whose benevolent, blind patronage so tried Blake's spirit during the years at Felpham; and most climactically and dangerously, the King himself—as represented by the King's soldiers and the King's courts which so directly threatened Blake in the sedition trial of January 1804. These antagonists, of course, are all represented by the archetypal "primeval priest," Urizen, who was first introduced by name in 1793, and whose character and antecedents were developed at length the next year, in *The Book of Urizen*.

By 1804, Blake was getting too old to be automatically antagonized by father figures. For other reasons, too, it seems likely that he was more than ready to move on to another stage on his mental travels. In 1793 he had prepared a series of plates entitled *For Children: The Gates of Paradise*. These include four visionary, humanized portraits of the four elements (water, earth, air, fire) arranged to suggest that these represent symbolically the basic constituents to be found, in varying proportions, in every human psyche. In the same year, in *The Marriage of Heaven and Hell*, he represented the four functions of the psyche symbolically as dragons, a viper, an eagle, and lions ("A Memorable Fancy," pl. 15). About 1797, in the first part of *The Four Zoas*, Blake put more explicitly his belief that "Four Mighty Ones are in every Man: a Perfect Unity / Cannot Exist, but from the Universal Brotherhood of Eden / The Universal Man. . . ."[7] To proclaim this was to acknowledge the desirability of coming to terms with each of the "Mighty Ones" in his own personality.

Blake seems always to have been more or less at ease in the

---

[5] "Let the Brothels of Paris be opened . . ." (E490/K185); *The Garden of Love* (E26/K215); *The Chimney Sweeper* (E22-23/K212).

[6] *MHH* 25. Damon (*Dictionary*, 422) suggests that this is the first appearance of Urizen in Blake's work.

[7] *FZ* 1 3 (E297/K264).

worlds of Tharmas, Luvah, and Urthona. Tharmas (the physical senses) and Urthona (imagination/intuition) seem dominant in the mental worlds presented in the *Songs of Innocence*. Luvah (passion) and Urizen (moralistic judgment) seem to be dominant, and in conflict, in the worlds of the *Songs of Experience* and *The Marriage of Heaven and Hell*. As a partisan devil in the *Marriage*, Blake seems to be associated with the forces of both Orc (fallen Luvah), and Los (fallen Urthona). However, at this stage in his thinking, Blake may not have distinguished clearly between Orc and Los. He may have assumed that visionary imagination and rebellious emotional energy go naturally together—as indeed they must have in his own personality.

The well-known frontispiece to *Europe* (1794) (also printed separately, and often called "The Ancient of Days"), provides a significant image of one aspect of Blake's vision of Urizen at a relatively early stage in his career (see {8}). One is immediately surprised by the degree to which the figure seems to be dignified— even glorified. However, negative aspects of the image suggest that it may have been intended (at least in part) as covert comment on Proverbs 8:27, and on Milton's account, in *Paradise Lost* VII, 225-227, of God's using "the golden compasses . . . / . . . to circumscribe / This Universe and all created things. . . ." (One is reminded of Blake's more forthright address to the Divine Circumscriber: "If you have formed a Circle to go into / Go into it yourself & see how you would do" E508.) Nonetheless, the degree to which the form of the picture as a whole involves the glorification of a Urizenic figure suggests that, as early as 1794, Blake accepted (at least theoretically) the need to comprehend a rational father/creator figure within his system.

The whole thrust of Blake's thought seems to have been toward some sort of realistic comprehension of the disparate elements of mental experience, as well as toward the achievement of some sort of enlightenment. Indeed, he uses the word "enlightenment" to describe the peak experience he enjoyed following his visit to the Truchsessian Gallery. At the same time, he gives thanks for being restored to the "light of Art" (E703). Enlightenment is properly the business of the god of light, Urizen/Apollo—as is Blake's ideal of precision and clarity in the visual arts. ("Dark" Urthona's Dionysian visions need considerable refinement before they can emerge as works of art.)

To call Urizen a god of light is not precisely to call him a sun-god. In terms of the basic symbolism of the Zoas, none of the four can literally *be* the god of any external force—since each represents primarily an aspect of the human psyche. As Los at one point tells Enitharmon (although she is in no mood to accept the information): "in the Brain of Man we live, & in his circling Nerves. / . . . this bright world of all our joy is in the Human Brain" (*FZ* I 11:E302/K272). The external sun is, as it appears to us, created by the human imagination—by Urthona/Los. It appears as a ball of fire, or as a golden guinea, or as a chorus of angels. Simultaneously, the sun may be perceived as the globe of blood passed as a vortex when human awareness shifts from eternity to the external, temporal world: "The red globule is the unwearied sun by Los created" (*M* 29:E126/K517).

Nonetheless, Urizen in his eternal aspect is more properly associated with the sun than any of the other Zoas. Urizen's place in eternity is the south—the place of the sun. His seizure of the north from Urthona is (in Blake's early version of the myth) a part of the cause of the fall of man. At one time Blake amused himself, and teased Crabb Robinson, by telling how the spiritual sun appeared to him on Primrose Hill and made clear that he (the sun) was not Apollo—that the sky was Apollo (and also Satan). In saying this Blake was asserting, essentially, that Apollo was fallen Urizen—Urizen after he had usurped Urthona's place in the north. Plate 4 of *Gates of Paradise* (entitled "Air" and later inscribed "On Cloudy Doubts & Reasoning Cares") was first produced about the same time as the frontispiece to *Europe*. This plate (which is very nearly the opposite, in every symbolic implication, from the splendid, but seemingly more conventional, "Ancient of Days") shows a neurotic sky-god who may reasonably be identified with Urizen/Apollo.

The image of the sun, in Blake's work, is associated in different places with at least three of the Zoas; however, the sun does not serve as an allegorical equivalent for any one of them. For example, in a poem in a letter to Butts, dated 22 November 1802, Blake reports that Los appeared to him "in the sun." "Twas outward a sun," Blake explains. "inward Los in his might."[8] Luvah, too, had his turn with the sun. In *The Four Zoas*, acting out a

---

[8] E693/K808. Digby (pp. 69-70) argues from this example that the spiritual sun "is" Los.

part of the process of the fall of man, "Luvah siez'd the Horses of Light, & rose into the Chariot of Day." However, he (as his fallen variant, Orc) later confesses to Urizen that "I stole thy light & it became fire / Consuming. Thou Knowest me now O Urizen Prince of Light / And I know thee. . . ."[9] In *Milton* 21 (E114) "Luvah's Bulls each morning drag the sulphur sun out of the deep." (Foster Damon remarks that "the 'sulphur sun' . . . is the material sun, as contrasted with the spiritual sun.")[10] In *The Four Zoas*, Urizen after his usurpation of the north is surrounded by cold and dark; he is shrouded in "the Direful Web of Religion"; all light is intercepted by "the tree of Mystery"; nonetheless, he still is conventionally addressed as "Prince of Light," and he still worships in "the temple of the Sun." As soon as he abandons his efforts to repress man's natural functions, he rises like the sun: "Then glorious bright Exulting in his joy / He sounding rose into the heavens in naked majesty."[11]

Before 1804, Blake seems to have entertained hopes that the quasi-Dionysian forces of Orc and Los could help all human society break through to freedom—to Jerusalem. After 1804, his attention seems more immediately directed to the problems of individual enlightenment. Much—probably most—of the work Blake produced during the 1790's expresses sympathy with repressed creative energy, and with the victims of repression; it expresses hope for some sort of breakthrough—both in terms of personal "improvement of sensual enjoyment" in a freer expression of sexuality and in the heightened perceptions of visionary experience—and in terms of some sort of revolutionary success in the achievement of a more just society. The solitary individual is envisioned as repressed by the limitations of his own senses: "For man has closed himself up, till he sees all things thro' narrow chinks of his cavern" (*MHH* 14). Individuals in society are envisioned as repressed, exploited, and tortured by the iron laws of church and state.

After 1804, Blake seems more concerned with communicating a method he has discovered by which men may win free from individual, internal tyranny—a method by which an individual may free himself from the domination of one distorted aspect of

[9] *FZ* I 10 (E301/K271); viia 80 (E349/K324).
[10] *Dictionary*, 389.
[11] Night viii 103 (E361/K345).

his own psyche (either from Urizen, or from the Spectre of his dominant Zoa—in Blake's case, from the Spectre of Urthona). Although Blake never relinquished his dream of building "Jerusalem, / In Englands green and pleasant Land" (*M* 1), he seems to have become far less hopeful of any immediate transformation of the outward social and political scene. His adjustment to "historical change"[12] seems to have involved, simultaneously, an increased sensitivity to the faults of revolutionary France (Luvah), and an increased desire to come to terms with imperialist England (Urizen, or Albion in the grip of his own Spectre).

Examination of differences between Nights vIIa and vIIb of *The Four Zoas* may clarify some of the changes which took place in Blake's thinking during the period immediately before the climactic events of 1804. Night vIIb, almost certainly the earlier version, presents a dream in which Urizen is still very much an external enemy. The primary allegorical referents of the action are probably to be found in the battles of the war with France before the Peace of Amiens,[13] although Blake, as usual, ranges widely in search of significant parallels. The focus of the narrative seems primarily extraverted. Urizen is not recognized explicitly as the selfhood; instead, his attributes are seen in the actions of Pitt and the English establishment, who make war on France, and in the actions of the Romans and the Jews, who crucified Jesus.

In Night vIIa, the later version, the focus is on Los and Enitharmon. The chief external references of the allegory seem to be to the personal lives of Blake and his wife; however, the allegory seems predominantly to look inward, into the mental experiences of Blake/Los. In the chief turning point of the action, Blake/Los recognizes his Spectre as part of himself, and is convinced that by uniting with his Spectre he will be turning decisively toward reintegration and enlightenment. The story is told in a form parallel to Milton's account of the temptation in Eden. The "spectre of Urthona" is cast as Satan. He tempts Eve (Catherine Blake/Enitharmon), telling her that he is "now a Spectre wandering / The deeps of Los the Slave of that Creation I created . . ."

[12] vIII 102-103 (E360-361/K344-345), IX 121 (E376/K362).

[13] *Prophet*, 299ff. [325-326]. For details of current puzzlings over the dating of parts of *FZ*, see G. E. Bentley, Jr.'s edition (Oxford, 1963) and Erdman's critique, "The Binding (Et Cetera) of *Vala*," *The Library*, xix (1964[1968]), 112-129.

(VIIA 84:E352). The Spectre seems in part to be Enitharmon's nightmare vision of the psyche. It describes itself to her as "insane brutish / . . . ravening devouring lust," and tells Enitharmon that it "cannot crave for anything but thee. . . ." It offers to "bring down soft Vala" to seduce and gratify the body it inhabits (that of Los/Blake); in this way it (the Spectre) will in a sense have Enitharmon to itself.

Thus we have a vision of the Spectre, incarnate in Los and thus the slave of *time*, appealing to *space* for mercy (for more complete incarnation). Enitharmon envisions Blake/Los's physical desire for her as "brutish . . . lust," and is tempted by this vision to fall— that is, to accept a religion of moralistic judgment. The Spectre persuades Enitharmon that the "tree of Mystery" (p. 85)—which is "Urizens tree" (p. 87), the tree of conventional religion—"Is given us for a shelter from the tempests of Void and Solid" (p. 84). The circumstances of this temptation suggest that Catherine was emotionally very disturbed. Her "shadow in the deeps beneath" labors to bring forth "a wonder horrible." Her condition seems to have disturbed Blake, opening him, too, to the temptations of the Spectre: "While Enitharmon shrieked / And trembled thro the worlds above Los wept his fierce soul was terrifid. . . ." "But then the Spectre enterd Los's bosom Every sigh & groan / Of Enitharmon bore Urthonas Spectre on its wings . . ." (p. 86). The precise moment at which the Spectre enters "Los's bosom" is represented by the birth of an idlike "howling Orc" to Enitharmon's shadow. She is given charge of the babe by its father, the Spectre, and at this moment she falls, and Los's fall is foreshadowed: "Then took the tree of Mystery root in the World of Los."

The Spectre at last rises from the unconscious "deeps of Los" to full consciousness. Blake/Los accepts with "irresistable conviction" (p. 86) the notion that he must come to terms with this Spectre if he is to achieve enlightenment, *and* if he is to be reconciled to his wife. The Spectre's crowning argument is: "Thou never canst embrace sweet Enitharmon terrible Demon. Till / Thou art united with thy Spectre Consummating by pains & labours / That mortal body & by Self annihilation back returning / To Life Eternal . . ." (p. 85).

Los embraces both Enitharmon and the Spectre, and in this moment comes close to the threefold bliss of Beulah. "Clouds would have folded round in Extacy & Love uniting /But Enitharmon trembling fled & hid beneath Urizen's tree . . ." (p. 87). Los stood on "the limit of Translucence," but then turned back because of Enitharmon, who, Evelike, offered him some of the "ruddy fruit" she had gathered "in the Deeps." The fruits here offered seem to be on the physical level Enitharmon/Catherine Blake's breasts, which she presents in very erotic, tempting fashion in the sketch on page 86 {90}. Thereafter Blake/Los apparently achieves the sexual consummation which had for some time been withheld; however, it is in good part spoiled for him by the sense of guilt and degradation which Enitharmon now seems to connect with sexuality.

Enitharmon/Eve/Catherine Blake's nightmare is characterized both by the association of guilt and sin with the body and by a dark sense of the vulnerability of the body to cruel patterns taken by the life-force. She tells Los that she has learned "In the Deeps" "That Life lives upon Death & by devouring appetite / All things subsist on one another. . . ." She expresses a deeply felt need for the scapegoat-savior of the conventional Urizenic mystery religion: "I knew / That without a ransom I could not be savd from Eternal death" (p. 87). Los, like Adam, accepts the fruit from his wife's hands, and eats (this, presumably, suggests the moment of sexual consummation). Immediately infected with "despair," Blake/Los's only comfort during the period immediately after this fateful moment is the sense that "Urthona's spectre in part mingling with him" is "a medium" between himself and Enitharmon/Catherine Blake. Thus they lament together like Milton's Adam and Eve after the fall.

Doubtless Blake was amused to parody the fall of man, tempted by Satanic falsehoods, with an account of the fall of Los (and himself), tempted by the doctrines of conventional Urizenic religion. In each case, only the woman is completely deceived; both Adam and Blake/Los go along, at least in part, because of compassion for their wives. However, Blake seriously implies that one cause of the fall of man is the acceptance—directly or indirectly—of Urizenic religion. The irony of this particular "happy fall" is that Blake/Los finds that compassionate love between himself and his wife grows out of a sharing of spectrous depressions and fears.

After this, Blake/Los persuades Enitharmon to join him in his artistic labors. Together they draw "From out the ranks of Urizens war" various archetypal forms. Finally, they draw "Urizen['s]

Shadow away / From out the ranks of war separating him in sunder / Leaving his Spectrous form which could not be drawn away . . ." (p. 90). Thus Blake/Los makes the significant discovery that it is possible to separate the "Shadow" of Urizen from the fearful, war-making "Spectre." The "Shadow" is appropriately named: it must indeed have been insubstantial, since it was separated both from the giant form of Urizen in eternity, and from the perverse strength of the ego-ridden Spectre. Perhaps, more than anything else, the Shadow represents *pity*—a quality which Urizen had exhibited freely since the first weaving of the "net of religion" (*U* 25).

Blake may have come to feel, perhaps after the renewal of hostilities in 1804, that his attitude toward his giant forms—and chiefly toward Urizen—had become distorted by the emotionally overwhelming, oppressive atmosphere of the seemingly interminable hot and cold war with France. Night viia as a whole represents an effort to play down the allegory of politics and war in favor of an allegory based on psychology and metaphysics. And the chief event of the book—at its very end—is Los's discovery that he loves the "Shadow" of his old enemy: "Startled was Los he found his Enemy Urizen now / In his hands, he wonderd that he felt love & not hate / His whole soul loved him he beheld him an infant / Lovely breathd from Enitharmon he trembled within himself."[14] Appropriately, the Urizenic "Shadow" babe is born of Enitharmon, since it is the fruit of her embracing of Urizenic religion. Thus Blake/Los is taught by his love for a woman to accept an aspect of the human potential to which he had previously been cold.

The chief event of Night viii of *The Four Zoas* is the crucifixion of the "Lamb of God." To set the stage for this, the Spectre of Urizen again "in self-deceit his warlike preparations fabricated" (p. 101:E359/K343). As Erdman has suggested, the immediate reference here, and in the battle imagery which follows, is very likely the renewal of war following the failure of the Peace of Amiens (*Prophet*, 369[397]).

[14] *FZ* viia 90 (E357/K332). Janet Warner suggests: In this not *Pity* "like a naked, New-borne Babe, / Striding the blast . . ."? See the color print (Darrell Figgis, *The Paintings of William Blake*, London, 1925, pl. 74) where the babe is born of a woman who—significantly—resembles Eve in *Satan Exulting Over Eve* {108}.

Blake/Los's attitude toward the war seems to differ from what it had been before the beginnings of his reconciliation with his Spectre, and with Urizen. Now he feels the war primarily as an outrageous disturbance of the creative spirit—as an attack on the human creative potential which he in turn must counter directly: "The battle howls the terrors fird rage in the work of death / Enormous works Los Contemplated inspired by the holy spirit / Los builds the Walls of Golgonooza against the stirring battle. . . ." As Erdman has emphasized (p. 371 [p. 399]), Blake *for the first time directly faces the facts of modern war.*" War itself—not one side or the other in the war—takes "a form / Which he [Urizen] intended not a Shadowy hermaphrodite black & opake / The Soldiers named it Satan . . ." (VIII 101:E359). War itself is the enemy.

Satan thus is recognized as a state—not an archetypal individual—not Urizen (although the Spectre of Urizen was still in the state of Satan). Now the Spectre of Luvah (France) could also be seen as Satanic: "When Luvah in Orc became a Serpent he descended into / That state calld Satan. . . ." Now both Urizen and Luvah could be saved, even though "The State namd Satan can never be redeemd in all Eternity" (p. 115:E366/K351).

According to Blake, the crucifixion takes place when the human/divine spirit sacrifices itself freely and lovingly for all who are in the Satanic state, in order that "the Spiritual body may be reveald." This sacrifice for those in the state of Satan (in particular, for Luvah and Urizen) is freely offered and performed by Jesus. It is not a single historical event—the sacrifice of a scapegoat to assuage a sense of guilt—but rather takes place "time after time" wherever and whenever the spirit of love and forgiveness triumphs in men's lives.[15]

The crucifixion leads to the Last Judgment (in Night IX) as the sorrow of Blake/Los for the apparent death of Jesus leads him to an act of despair which seems to symbolize his need to entirely reorganize the world in which he has lived his mental life: "Los his vegetable hands / outstretched his right hand branching out in fibrous Strength / Siezd the Sun. His left hand like dark roots covered the Moon / And tore them down cracking the heavens

[15] VIII 115, 104, 115, 104 (E366, 363, 366). See the interpretation in John Middleton Murry, *William Blake*, London, 1933; reprinted New York, 1964, ch. XI.

across . . ." (IX 117). This act seems also to be symbolic of the destruction of the shell of the ego—which from inside looks like the whole world—and which must be broken if the psyche is to get a glimpse into eternity. Thus the symbolic destruction which follows may apply as much to Blake's own previous world view as to the conventional Urizenic world view (the world view of the confident establishment patriot/warmonger) which he had opposed in what now seemed to him too narrow and partisan a fashion.

The "Eternal Man" who is awakened by this destruction is, first of all, the "Eternal Man" within Blake. On another level, he is the "Eternal Man" who comprehends both England and France, and who may awake (Blake hopes) to millennium. The Eternal Man laments the "war within his members." He lifts his head from a "Horrible rock far in the south" where Urizen first started all the trouble by giving "the horses of Light into the hands of Luvah."

Urizen is the first figure the Eternal Man calls upon when he addresses himself to the task of self-reconstruction. He addresses Urizen formally as "Prince of Light," equivocally (ironically) as "schoolmaster of souls," and disparagingly (yet accurately) as "great opposer of change" (p. 120). Urizen is made to repent his bloody and disruptive efforts to control "dark futurity" by his incessant labors "with the sword & with the spear / And with the Chisel & the mallet. . . ." With nervous forebodings, like a retiring policeman, Urizen relaxes his efforts to control all man's mental functions. He cries: "let dark Urthona give / All Strength to Los & Enitharmon & let Los self cured / Rend down this fabric . . . / Rage Orc Rage Tharmas Urizen no longer curbs your rage" (p. 121).

Urizen's forebodings prove to be unjustified. After some initial difficulties, the result of his abdication is the reintegration of "the human form divine" (p. 139:E392). Luvah and Vala are reunited, and return to the "place of seed." Blake is no longer dominated by Los—and it appears that Los has been all along "the Spectre Los / . . . the Spectre of Prophecy" (p. 138), essentially the Spectre of Urthona of Night VIIa, and thus Urizenic in spite of his having entertained such violent surface antagonisms against Urizen.

Insofar as Blake is reintegrated as the "Eternal Man," he is born again in a new world of innocence. This world is dominated

256

by Tharmas (the body and its senses) and Urthona (the divine/human imagination). The internal world Blake now observes is in part very innocent: "For Tharmas brought his flocks upon the hills & in the Vales / Around the Eternal Mans bright tent the little Children play / Among the wooly flocks . . ." (p. 138). Urthona introduces fiercer images reminiscent of the world of Experience, but they are perceived in the spirit of innocence and found harmless: "The hammer of Urthona sounds / In the deep caves beneath his limbs renewd his Lions roar / Around the Furnaces & in Evening sport upon the plains / They raise their faces from the Earth conversing with the Man / How is it we have walkd thro fires & are not consumd?"

Luvah, no longer a partisan in the battles for heart and head, no longer the thief of the horses of instruction, is put to his proper task as grand expediter of sexuality, and of all generation: "Luvah was put for dung on the ground by the Sons of Tharmas & Urthona" (p. 137).

Blake/Urthona, reintegrated, enlightened by the sun of Urizen, goes hopefully forth "to form the golden armour of science / For intellectual War." It seems likely that this "armour" is constructed of Urizen's gold, rather than Urthona's iron, because the repressive "primeval priest" has been recognized as the poet's own selfhood and reclaimed as a god of light. Possibly Blake hopes to put on his selfhood (like a Jungian *persona*) as armor with which to face the intellectual wars of a better world, once the war with France is over. And, of course, "science" (in the broad, old-fashioned sense of the word) is Urizen's special concern in Eternity. Thus, in the last line of the poem, the great change in Blake's perception of Urizen is celebrated: "The dark Religions are departed & sweet Science reigns" (p. 139). (As a prophecy of the beneficent effects of the Peace of Amiens, this vision proved dismally inaccurate. As a description of the outcome of Blake's own mental wars, it has much to recommend it.)

Nonetheless, Blake was not satisfied with the account of the reintegration of the "Eternal Man" as he worked it out in *The Four Zoas*. The failure of political events to fulfill the prophetic part of his allegory doubtless helps to explain his attitude. Moreover, he had experienced new, mind-changing visions which demanded expression in their own terms. I suggest that the title page of each of his two greatest prophetic works, *Milton* and

Jerusalem, bears the date 1804 because in that climactic year he conceived and planned each of these works—and in a rush of energetic enthusiasm began work on the first plates of each.

In *Milton,* Blake calls back the poet Milton, specifically to come to terms with his (Milton's) Spectre, Satan. At the time of the writing of *The Marriage of Heaven and Hell,* Blake seems to have sympathized with (although he may not completely have identified with) "the voice of the Devil." This "devil" asserts, of course, that Milton betrayed his own poetic vision in his structuring of *Paradise Lost,* and that in his characterizations of God and Satan he reversed true values. In spite of this, the Satan with whom Milton is to be reconciled, according to Blake's vision of ca. 1804, is closer to the God of *Paradise Lost* and to fallen Urizen (he is associated with "Holiness / Oppos'd to Mercy . . ." [*M* 39]), than to either the Satan of *Paradise Lost* or the creative devils of *The Marriage of Heaven and Hell.* This Satan is "the Spectre; the Reasoning Power in Man" (*M* 14), the conventional god of this world.

Thus Milton's purportedly climactic announcement: "I in my selfhood am that Satan: I am that Evil One!" (*M* 14:30), seems, from another point of view, close to an anticlimactic assertion of reconciliation with his own God (the spectrous God of *Paradise Lost*). The insight involved seems more appropriate to the state of mind of Blake at that time, than to a state of mind which might be imagined as Milton's. (Although it represents, of course, a part of Blake's current diagnosis of the cause of Milton's difficulties.) Since the insight is also a part of the mechanism which brings Milton back to incarnation in the body of Blake, it is—at least in a roundabout way—attributed by Blake to himself.

Blake's newly stabilized opinion that the ultimate enemy, Satan, is the selfhood might seem, from a psychoanalytic point of view, to represent a desirable expansion of consciousness—an assimilation of the superego by the ego. In a sense this is true; however, Blake was no psychoanalyst, and from his point of view the Spectre, Satan, still had the same negative characteristics which had first, more easily, been perceived when the Spectre was projected and identified with an external, repressive enemy. To Blake, the chief value of the new insight seems to have been that it made it emotionally possible to love and forgive Satanic types, as he recognized that that which made them Satanic also identified them with his own selfhood. He could, for example, without changing his basic principles recognize that the various repressive father figures with which he had been so long at odds were—in archetypal essence—identical with his own selfhood. And the emotions of love and forgiveness associated with this perception made it possible for him to "annihilate" his own spectrous selfhood, and thus win through to timeless moments of illumination and imaginative vision.

Milton provides an essentially introverted view of the change in Blake's outlook. A more extraverted view of the same change is provided in the first plates of *Jerusalem*. Blake sees around him, as before, a desolate scene of oppression and exploitation. However, he now focuses on the blindness of the giant Albion, "the perturbed Man," whose insecure, angry psyche is made up of the generality of the population of England. Albion insists on his own lack of unity—"Saying. We are not One: We are Many. . . ." He clings stubbornly to his nightmares in "the Sleep of Ulro." Blake speaks out his own message directly: "Awake! awake O sleeper of the land of shadows, wake! expand! / I am in you and you in me, mutual in love divine: / Fibres of love from man to man thro Albions pleasant land." However, the "perturbed man," in his blindness and fear, "turns down the valleys dark." He fears in particular "Love! which binds / Man the enemy of Man in deceitful friendships!" He denies the very existence of that fulfillment of freedom and happiness which Blake names "Jerusalem" (*J* 4).

Ruled entirely by his Spectre, the giant Albion believes only in pragmatic science, property rights, an arbitrary moral code, and—as final arbiter of all things—physical violence and war:

> By demonstration, man alone can live, and not by faith.
> My mountains are my own, and I will keep them to
>   myself:
> The Malvern and the Cheviot, the Wolds Plinlimmon &
>   Snowdon
> Are mine. here will I build my Laws of Moral Virtue!
> Humanity shall be no more: but war & princedom &
>   victory!   (*J* 4)

The new system which Blake was developing made it possible for him to be fairer to Urizen. The system also made possible a more accurate allegorical exploration of his own psychic state. Blake was never in any danger of being dominated by Urizen;

nor was he ever in danger of being dominated by Urizen's conventional antagonist, Luvah/Orc. However, he was at times very much in danger of being dominated by Los, the Spectre of Urthona (or—in alternative phrasing of the allegory—he was in danger, as Los, of being dominated by his own Spectre). Finally, he had at one time made the serious mistake of confusing his own Spectre with the giant form of the Zoa, Urizen. (In Jungian terms, he had confused his own *Shadow* with a personification of the basic psychic function of *thinking*.)

Perhaps the necessity for a shift in symbolism first became apparent when Blake came to allegorize some of the reactionary changes within revolutionary France, as well as changes in his own attitudes toward the governments of both France and England. As noted in the discussion of *The Four Zoas*, he developed the doctrine of *states* in order to represent Luvah as falling into the state of Satan. For consistency (as well as for important personal reasons) fallen Urizen came to be described as being in the state of Satan, rather than as being himself Satan. While the concept of a state of Satan is used in *Jerusalem*, the system of spectres represents the same idea more simply, and is used more generally.

Urizen is still associated with Albion in this new scheme. Since Albion's dominant Zoa, in the eighteenth century, was Urizen, Albion, when in the grip of his Spectre, *was* still fallen Urizen. However, Urizen was perceived to be an individual, not a state. Thus both Albion and Urizen could be redeemed—reintegrated into the unity of the Eternal Man.

However, redemption can be at best only an intermittent process in this fallen world. As long as an individual like Blake remained active in Ulro, his Spectre was very necessary to him. Man needs a strong sense of selfhood to survive. Los drove his Spectre hard, he tells us, to produce *Jerusalem*. Nonetheless, in order to experience the vision necessary to plan *Jerusalem*, Blake/Los—with the help of the compassionate love and continual forgiveness of sins symbolized by Jesus—had to annihilate his Spectre in order to become for timeless instants Blake/Urthona.

To comprehend all this, as Blake did, demands a relatively complex intellectual system. Blake was also well aware of the comic inconsistency of "Striving with systems to deliver Individuals from Systems" (*J* 11). But in a fallen world in which even Los was forced to endure the company of his own Spectre, "systems" provided one of the best possible means for communicating with the spectrous intelligences of the many "redeemed" individuals who might collectively, if only they could be enlightened, bring about the reintegration of the giant Albion. Urizen, as a personification of the thinking function, must be concerned with systems of all kinds. As primeval priest, he favors the obscurities of systems which enslave; in Eternity, presumably, Urizen is concerned only with making clear the details of those systems which may enlighten.

In a satiric stanza, Blake once remarked ironically "That God is colouring, Newton does show / And the devil is a black outline all of us know . . ." (E507/K554). The ambivalence of this comment may convey something of the attitude I am attempting to describe. Urizen, to Blake, always remained in one way or another "the bound or outward circumference of Energy" (*MHH* 4)—"a Black outline." However, Urizen becomes Satan when, as "primeval Priest" he attempts moralistically to restrain, to judge, and to punish. In these lines Blake retains the verbal ironies of *The Marriage of Heaven and Hell* yet reverses their application by associating a Urizenic god with the fashionable "colouring" which he deplored, and by associating an energetic Orclike devil with his favored "Black outline."

During the 1790's, and up to 1804, Urizen's Satanic form loomed large over the head of rebellious Blake. Yet by 1809, Blake—in arguing for the kind of art he had always practiced— could argue freely (in effect) for Satan, and for Urizen:

> The great and golden rule of art, as well as of life, is this: That the more distinct, sharp, and wiry the bounding line, the more perfect the work of art; and the less keen and sharp, the greater is the evidence of weak imitation, plagiarism, and bungling. . . . The want of this determinate and bounding form evidences the want of idea in the artist's mind. . . . How do we distinguish the oak from the beech, the horse from the ox, but by the bounding outline? How do we distinguish one face or countenance from another, but by the bounding line and its infinite inflexions and movement? . . . What is it that distinguishes honesty from knavery, but the hard and wiry line of rectitude and certainty in the actions and intentions. Leave out this line and you leave out life itself; all is chaos again, and the line of the almighty must be drawn out upon it before man or beast can exist. (*DC* xv:E540/K585)

261

(Note the final reference, here, to the "line of the almighty"—which may be the line of Urthona. Nonetheless, the jumbling together of references to precision of imagination and to "morality" and "rectitude" suggests something of the growing alliance between Urizen and Los—reason and intuition—in the mind of Blake.)

Lines from the conclusion of *Jerusalem* may remind us how Apollonian Urizen became—how much a god of those visual arts with which Blake was most involved. When Albion awakes and calls his Zoas to the great consummation, Urizen is called first, and appears in trappings of honor: "Fourfold the Vision for bright beaming Urizen / Layd his hand on the South & took a breathing Bow of carved Gold / Luvah his hand stretch'd to the East & bore a Silver Bow bright shining / Tharmas Westward a Bow of Brass pure flaming richly wrought / Urthona Northward in thick storms a Bow of Iron terrible thundering" (*J* 97).

We are again reminded that Urthona may be the source of all vision—but like Los laboring at his forge, he is concerned with iron, not gold, and with dark and terrible secrets. Urizen is much more civilized; his work is essential to all artistic communication. (For example, way back in the *Songs of Experience*, it must have been Urizen who showed us *The Tyger*. Los, of course, forged the fierce lineaments of the animal in the smithy of his imagination; however, it took poor, fearful Urizen, with all his neurotic questionings about things he feared to face—"What the hammer? What the chain, / In what furnace was thy brain?"—to work it out as poem and picture.)

In the conclusion of *Jerusalem*, after the "Druid Spectre" has been annihilated by the "Arrows of Intellect," two types of human genius, both of which, in fact, draw upon intuition as well as reason—or reason as well as intuition—can at last stand freely together: "Bacon & Newton & Locke, & Milton & Shakespeare & Chaucer." The emphasis in this listing is clearly on the alliance of reason and imagination—not on the alliance of emotion and imagination which a reader of only the early poems might have expected. The marvelous worlds of Eternity are, in this vision of a millennium, the construct of "the wonders divine / Of Human Imagination . . ." (*J* 98). These wonders at last are perceived and delineated, without constriction or judgment, by Urizen.

12

Orc as a Fiery Paradigm
of Poetic Torsion

GEORGE QUASHA

Theory: A Myth of the Functioning Artist

For the darkness of Asia was startled
At the thick-flaming, thought-creating fires of Orc.
—*The Song of Los* 6:6

When I make sculpture all the speeds, projections, gyrations, light changes are involved in my vision, as such things I know in movement associate with all the possibilities possible in other relationships. Possibly steel is so beautiful because of all the movement associated with it, its strength and function. Yet it is also brutal, the rapist, the murderer, and death-dealing giants are also its offspring. . . . I have carved marble and wood but the major number of my works have been steel, which is my most fluent medium and which I control from start to completed work without interruption. There is gratification in being both conceiver and executor without intrusion. . . .   —David Smith[1]

THE birth or rising of Orc, seen in archetypal perspective as the first phase of a cycle, has come to seem an inevitable component of Blake's meaning. Yet "the Orc cycle" may be a more characteristic creation of Northrop Frye's cartography than of Blake's poetic system, which strove for escape from circular closure in space and time. A careful reading of *America*, either from a strictly historical perspective, as employed by David Erdman, or from the perspective established by intrinsic structural analysis, seriously raises the question of the relevance of any cyclic symmetry to the poem engraved in 1793.[2] Frye himself is careful to leave Orc in his first

[1] "Notes for David Smith Makes a Sculpture," *Art News* (Jan. 1969), 48.
[2] See Erdman, *Prophet*, esp. 6-7 and 53-60 [56-63]; also Erdman's note above in "*America*: New Expanses," and Simmons, above, on Fuzon.

263

appearance some breathing space: ". . . Orc is the power of human desire to achieve a better world which produces revolution and foreshadows the apocalypse; the 'Preludium' to *America* represents him as having arrived at puberty determined to set the world on fire as a promising youngster should do. To the reactionaries, of course, he is a demonic and hellish power, rising up to destroy everything that is sacred and worth conserving" (*Symmetry*, 206). Careful, further, to indicate the auspicious aspect of the cyclic view: ". . . Orc, then, is not only Blake's Prometheus but his Adonis, the dying and reviving god of his mythology. Orc represents the return of the dawn and the spring and all the human analogies of their return: the continuous arrival of new life, the renewed sexual and reproductive power which that brings, and the periodic overthrow of social tyranny. . . . Orc dies as the buried seed dies, and rises as it grows; winter nights become long and gloomy, but at the depth of winter the light slowly returns" (p. 208). The "cyclic" inseparability of Orc and Urizen, however, records Blake's "pessimism" about actual political revolutions, though opposing principles do maintain their separate identities and potentialities: "If the dragon is itself old Orc, then surely is not Orc simply a dragon who has the power to shed his skin from time to time?" (p. 210). Frye, finally, notes the probability that Blake came to emphasize Orc's identity with his opposite only *gradually*.

If we are to consider the full poetic implications of this evolution of the archetypal perspective, we must define not only Orc's function in the early prophecies but also the principle inherent in his particular action there. Clearly we must identify Orc with political revolution, mainly in its productive role, but to discover the principle involved we must explore its more complex psychological and aesthetic operations as well.

Blake's mode of visionary thought, as Frye demonstrates extensively, involves each poetic meaning in the furthest possible ranges of a dynamic metaphoric system. His mental habit of seeing every Particular as containing the cosmos—ontogeny recapitulating phylogeny—relates him to the earliest mythopoeic thinkers. Recognition of the creative act (*poiein*) as a metaphor for its own process—a Zagreus-Dionysus myth—is characteristic of the ancient oral-traditional prophetic poet, who sees his art—the very powers of tradition, order, truth, and vision—as a craft and as literal performance.[3] Art delights in art (to paraphrase Blake's "Life delights in life") and is self-begetting. It is the duty and burden of such a poet to realize continually the human capacity for skillful self-renewal in the here and now, to *make* history. The future, as a perception within the generative poetic act, is continuous with past and present. So Blake resembled the primordial poets he honored, while to an unexampled degree he converted phenomenological awareness into creative principle. Verbal invention came to imply perpetual revolution within the expanding vortex of human consciousness. And the violent birthlike experience of apocalypse he embodied in a language structure which from our vantage point resembles organic evolution: a cumulative, temporally linear, unpredictably irregular progression toward more complex forms.

Early in his work Blake embraced an affirmative principle of growth:

> . . . the ratio of all we have already known is not the same that it shall be when we know more. . . .
> The desire of Man being Infinite the possession is Infinite & himself Infinite. . . .
> As the true method of knowledge is experiment the true faculty of knowing must be the faculty which experiences. This faculty I treat of. (E2/K97-98)

Over the years his description of Intellectual and Imaginative expansion varied, emphasizing Poetic Genius and Prophetic Character and deemphasizing "experiment," but the fundamental notion endured: that the prophetic poem is the vehicle of visionary travail, the Chariot of Genius. If art is the process of evolving spirit, the working artist is the agent of remodeled man, at his best conceiving or inventing unexampled forms, expanding the medium:

> I know my Execution is not like Any Body Else. I do not intend it should be so; none but Blockheads copy one another. My Conception & Invention are on all hands allowd to be Superior. My Execution will be found so too.
> (*PA*: E571/K601)

[3] See Albert B. Lord's study of oral-traditional poetry, *The Singer of Tales*, New York, 1965, from which my assumptions about traditional poetry derive.

In no respect does Blake seem more contemporary than in this conception of man (metaphorically the working artist) as the willing inhabitant of a universe of open possibilities: "Every thing possible to be believ'd is an image of Truth" (*MHH* 8). There is practically no end to parallels with Blake in our contemporary world of artists, and even the manner of expression of a sculptor like David Smith seems Blakean: "Everything imagined is reality / The mind cannot conceive unreal things."[4] In one stream of the "modern"—the structurally "open" and experimental—form does not obey paradigm but takes the particular impress of the creative act, which shapes "barren" nature (*MHH* 10:68) into human identity. "Invention depends Altogether," insisted Blake, as do many artists and poets of our time, "upon the Execution or Organization; as that is right or wrong so is the Invention perfect or imperfect" (Annotations to Reynolds: E626/K446). And in this definition, perfection means accurate *function*, the flawless transmutation of medium into shape; it is "relative" in Einstein's sense of particularity in a universe without geometric paradigm, but "absolute" in the aesthetic sense of irreducible formal identity. For creative man, as for his analogue the body politic, erection of a standard of authority outside the imagination is an absurdity, an enslavement by perverse religion or commercialism, a failure to realize the potentials of indeterminate direction. Falsely closed form is a Narcissistic parody of creation.

Orc in *America*, I intend to argue, is a specific manifestation of a principle of renewal through "thought-creating fires," the basis for enduring social and political revolution: primal (and primordial) Energy released as *formative power*, the creative force

---

[4] *David Smith by David Smith*, ed. Cleve Gray, New York, 1968, 67; see also 132-135. Celebration of the open artistic mind in an open universe of possibilities relates Blake's world to that of such contemporary poets as Charles Olson and Robert Duncan and such a composer as John Cage— the latter notably in his application of *I Ching* chance and indeterminacy principles to musical procedures. Some "new" directions in modern thought similarly are quite Blakean, often consciously so, as in Thomas J. J. Altizer's important application: *The New Apocalypse: The Radical Christian Vision of William Blake*, East Lansing, Mich., 1967. Blake's faith in the formative power of human identity has striking parallels in Lancelot Law Whyte's *Accent on Form: An Anticipation of the Science of Tomorrow*, London, 1955, and R. Buckminster Fuller's *No More Secondhand God and Other Writings*, Carbondale, Ind., 1963.

of the universe alembicated by human vision-in-action, metaphorically the generative action of a dying-reviving god. To be sure, Orc, the active creative principle, must ultimately be "married" to the principle of poetic prophecy or message, its "contrary" in a fallen, self-divided world. The early Los, as he emerges in *The Book of Urizen,* exemplifies the worst tendencies of passive intellect subserving misguided prophecy and false authority; having "shrunk from his task" (5:1:E76), he is trapped in Urizen's circle of dead forms until he finds courage to heat up his smithy with Energy's transforming fires. In this symbolic drama of the poet's struggle toward material message, the later "Orc cycle" enacts a failure of generative power to unite with stable and relevant social vision. Culture gives way to inertia; evolutionary progression grinds to a halt from the pull of historical gravity.

A partial realization of the Orc principle is Fuzon, an inferior poet, so to speak, who leaves Urizen's Egypt but lacks the genius to forge a new orb (in *The Book of Ahania*). He confuses or fuses mere novelty, and consolidates rather than transcends the Urizenic limits. His Robespierrean perversion of generative action to destructive ends (see Erdman, *Prophet,* 289-290 [315-316]) illustrates for Blake the tragic failure of imagination, on every level, to discover appropriately functional order. The result is empty rhetoric, Narcissistic self-deception ("I am God, said he, eldest of things!"); fire in tyrannical hands—Orc as pyromaniac—dramatizes the reversibility of any principle in the absence of vision: Orc failing into cycle is the medium without the message.

Yet a message not continually rediscovered through an evolving medium is a still greater risk, and the Orc cycle is paralleled in Blake's cultural ecology in the failure of the main English poets, starting with Dryden, to carry on where Chaucer, Shakespeare, and Milton left off. Settled in a socially unrealistic and poetically limiting passivity, the Neoclassicists saw nothing new under the sun, and their technique knew, from Blake's point of view,

> Enough of Artifice but Nothing Of Art. Ideas cannot be Given but in their minutely Appropriate Words nor Can a Design be made without its minutely Appropriate Execution. . . . Unappropriate Execution is the Most nauseous of all affectation & foppery.   (*PA:* E565/K596)

Johnson's disdain for the streaks of the tulip, the poetic unit of discrete evolution, meant settling for the tautology of mere literature, "Pope's Metaphysical Jargon of Rhyming," abstraction rather than "Knowledge . . . by Perception at once" (E565, 653). To the inertia of poetic closure Blake posed the prosodic counterprinciple, symbolized by Orc, of forced progression through the fertile penetration of *any* closed system.

On the level of the medium itself, *poiein* is the Orc-Poet's breaking *into* the mind of the reader who "sees all things thro' narrow chinks of his cavern": "this I shall do, by printing in the infernal method, by corrosives, which in Hell are salutary and medicinal, melting apparent surfaces away, and displaying the infinite which was hid" (*MHH* 14:E38-39/K154). As by a Cubist painting, a Surrealist movie, or Brechtean-Artaudean theater, the reader-viewer is not permitted to be a serene spectator of the cultural artifact; he must enter directly the infernal, transforming process which "rouzes the faculties to act" by alienating him from the comforts of conventional literary form. As Orc shatters the stony law and scatters "religion" to enable the inhabitants to rush together with renewed force, Blake would confuse the faculties—Rimbaud's "dérèglement de tous les sens"—to enable the imagination, through a fortunate fall of the senses, to hatch from its shell of Innocence: once revived by its fiery entrance into perilous passage, the expanded inner eye gazes, from a perspective of the infinite, at the world outside the poem.

This translation of Zagreus-Adonis into aesthetic function metaphorically extends both the surface-piercing heat of the "infernal method" and its equivalent in verbal action, which I suggest calling *poetic torsion*. Torque, a turning or twisting force, is what produces a rotary effect or torsion. Its prosodic and syntactic dynamics characterize the poetry of "process," as distinguished by Frye from the poetry of "artifact."[5] If the latter is Aristotelian, aesthetic, and structurally conventional, the poetry of process is Longinian, psychological, and often unconventional or nonparadigmatic. Linguistically, the poem conceived as conventional artifact refines the model of "intensive" syntax, in normalized grammar (rational or closed discourse); the poem conceived as psychological or visionary process develops out of the

[5] See "Towards Defining an Age of Sensibility," *Fables of Identity*, New York, 1963, 130-137.

associational or "extensive" syntax of the spoken language (expressive or open discourse).[6]

If we define poetic structure as the concrete embodiment of the principles which generate it, we can say that an ideal reader re-enacts those principles by following the temporal sequence of the text and of any variant accompaniment such as Blake's illuminations. Within their symbolic drama, the plots of Blake's narrative poems direct the reader-viewer along the curve of visionary experience, generally that of an opening circle or series of epicycles leading, ideally, to human action in the literal world. An expanding vortex of "centerfleeing" force in the poem must be alembicated by a "centerseeking" force in the reader's mind. In other terms, the movement from artistic fission—a splitting or rending action—to perceptual fusion or reconstitution repeats the process of human redemption, the movement from fall or self-division to reunion, wholeness, incarnation. Poetry saves man by energizing the spiritual process that revives the bonds of communication, and Blake's Orclike attempt to arouse young men of the new age seems, from today's perspective, to herald the action-poetry of "howl," the oral art-form of anticultural defiance, or the poem as rapist and death-dealing giant.

An Allegory: Opening the Mind

The plot or mythos of *Visions of the Daughters of Albion* essentially resembles that of *America* (Preludium and Prophecy) as an imitation of the action of universal propagation, human progression and, by implication, evolution. The general paradigm of penetration-fertilization-birth specifically modulates in *America* to a pattern of sexual, political, and poetic redemption which may be followed on several dramatic levels: a potent young man rescues

[6] The perception that "process" and "organic" poetry are orally structured relates Blake and much modern poetry to ancient oral verse (see Lord, n. 3, above). Blake's vision of future "harmony" is an aural perception "Within the unfathomd caverns of my ear" (*J* 3:E144/K621). Cf. Walter J. Ong's application of Auerbach's belief in a Hebraic-Christian "well-spring of mankind's genuine historical awareness"—a heritage "rooted in an oral-aural notion of knowledge, not in the more visual Hellenic . . . ," a verbal world of "ineluctable interiority, related to this irreducible and elusive and interior economy of the sound-world" ("A Dialectic of Aural and Objective Correlatives," *Essays in Criticism*, VIII [1958], 166-181). Cf. also Marshall McLuhan's *Verbi-Voco-Visual Explorations*, New York, 1967.

his mother from a cruel and illegitimate father (an "Oedipus complex" myth); a national hero saves a fallen continent from a fierce dragon (an epic myth, comparable to *Beowulf* or the story of St. George); youth defiantly steals the source of power from the aged (a Promethean myth); the Male Will to change triumphs over the Female Will to stasis (a yin-yang analogue of organic and poetic process). In bare outline the allegorical action is:

rape—forced break in a closed system; human touch; friction or the traction of contraries in contact;

outcry—human sound, initially lamentation; verbal "seed" of fertile human identity in "barren" natural ecology; torsion; a system of forces, released in waves;

prophetic form—the increment of formative power or the birth of new form itself; poetry; revolution; eventually, apocalypse.

It is my working hypothesis that Blake intends us to read the dramatic action of *Visions* as foreshadowing and, in a sense, producing that of *America*, and I see the Preludium, written after both poems, as a mythical regression to a time "earlier" than either drama that structurally bridges the two.

In the narrative of *Visions*, Oothoon's apparently willing but precarious passage from Innocence toward Experience is redirected by Bromion's rape to produce her rapid and powerful self-actualization, which supplies the controlling dynamics of the poem. Consider her new perception of the distortions of appearance: ". . . Theotormon is a sick mans dream / And Oothoon is the crafty slave of selfish holiness. . . . the youth shut up from / The lustful joy shall forget to generate & create an amorous image. . . . Are not these . . . / The self enjoyings of self denial? . . . Can that be Love, that drinks another as a sponge drinks water? . . . Such is self-love that envies all!" (6-7:E48-49). It is hardly accidental that brutal "interference" has engendered this poetic expression of Blake's own revolutionary psychology, since the price of true vision in the fallen (modern) world is a harsh exaction. And by the redeeming logic of the fortunate fall, Oothoon by facing that rending with clarity and courage rises a step higher in the spiritual evolution of mankind.

The poetic rite of Oothoon's passage repeats the Orc paradigm:

rape—forced division of her virgin world ("in twain") despite her good intentions in leaving Leutha's vales;

outcry—her call, first, to Theotormon's eagles and, second,
to Theotormon himself, lamenting his refusal to accept her;

prophetic form—her new identity and long final speech, symbolic of the birth of poetry, the language of Blake's own
thought.

Dramatically, her function is that of revolutionary Orc and of the
Prophetic Character generally, to voice a Declaration of Independence from the manacles of slave morality and church oppression and to state the grounds of positive morality, "for every thing
that lives is holy!" (her concluding words: 8:10; cf. *A* 8:13). Poetry
here is the Adamic naming of newly perceived realities, deepening
from psychological to political perspectives.

Structurally the allegory presents the seed of prophetic Orc,
as fertilized in the body of America: "the child / Of Bromion's
rage, that Oothoon shall bring forth in nine moons time" (2:1-2)
—implicitly the poetic body of *Visions*. The later poem will
"bear" the mature Orc visibly, struggling from the womb-earth
in the second Preludium page, then liberated, in the upper left
corner of the first Prophecy page—as if phallically entering the
body of *America*. Oothoon's morning song celebrates this approaching realization: "Red as the rosy morning, lustful as the
first born beam" (*VDA* 7:27).

In a modulating poetic sequence, Oothoon metaphorically becomes the shadowy daughter of Urthona ("American plains":
A 2:10), much as Orc transfuses into Fuzon, or as visual figures
metamorphose from plate to plate—e.g., the leaping female at the
top right of the *America* title page {25} transforming into a leaping
male at the top left of *America* 3 {29} (the *spirit* of Oothoon inher-
ing in Orc?). And a still more important bridge between the poems
establishes the dramatic necessity for a second rape of the American body, this time by her own child. In *Visions* Oothoon's psychological liberation is ultimately unsuccessful, never progressing
beyond mere words, the same dull round of lamentation over and
over ("every morning":8:11). And her role as Echo to a Narcissus-
Theotormon, reaching us as the echoing voices of enslaved Daughters, is twice removed from effective prophecy. What is this femi-

271

nine self-enclosure in complaint but a more insidious form of the self-enjoyings of self-denial? And how can this cry for "little glancing wings" (of poetry?) do other than petrify, finally, into an "iron tongue" (*A* 1:9)? Blake's meaning—like Ezra Pound's in his insistence on "ideas into action"—is that a poetry which deplores the evils of a time, without offering a positive vision of action, is but a disguised version of the basic evil of intellectual passivity, a self-satisfied withdrawal to literary cloisters. True poetic lament, like Enion's (*FZ* II 35:E318) which voices Blake's own anguish over art's failure to transmute evil, figures only as a moment within evolving prophecy, which transcends pathos.

If self-pitying Oothoon cannot bring "Expansion to the eye of pity" (*VDA* 8:3), she does sing poetry's tortuous struggle to break the closed circuit of self. In its torque of genesis her language expresses the tragic joy of Orc, and of poetry that sometimes has to function within the isolated self as both male and female. Yet Blake's kind of poetry is not parthenogenic, any more than the upward curve of the Orclike twining in D'Arcy Thompson's description below is a pure phenomenon of willpower. Both vine and poem must climb through uncertain torsions, their traction resulting from actual confrontations of contraries. Unlike Wordsworth, Blake did not suffer a direction-reversing disillusionment over political revolution. Appalled by its failures, he reenacted it himself, in mental rather than corporeal warfare. Orc may dwindle allegorically into cycle, but the Orc principle fires the smithy of the major prophecies.

Verbal Torsion

In "twining" plants, which constitute the greater number of "climbers," the essential phenomenon is a tendency of the growing shoot to revolve around its vertical axis. . . . This tendency to revolution—circumvolution, as Darwin calls it, revolving nutation, as Sachs puts it—is very closely comparable to the process by which an antelope's horn (such as the koodoo's) acquires its spiral twist, and is due, in like manner, to inequalities in rate of growth of the growing stem: with this difference between the two, that in the antelope's horn the zone of active growth is confined to the base of the horn, while in the climbing stem the same phenomenon is at work throughout the whole length of the growing structure. The growth is in the main due to "turgescence," that is to the extension, or elongation, of ready-formed cells through the imbibition of water; it is a phenomenon due to osmotic pressure. . . . The essential fact . . . is that in twining plants we have a marked tendency to inequalities in longitudinal growth on different aspects of the stem. . . . There is very generally to be seen an actual *torsion* of the twining stem—a twist, that is to say, about its own axis. . . . When a stem twines around a smooth cylindrical stick the torsion does not take place, save "only in that degree which follows as a mechanical necessity from the spiral winding": but . . . stems which had climbed around a rough stick were all more or less, and generally much, twisted. . . . The mechanical explanation would appear to be very simple. . . . In the case of the roughened support, there is a temporary adhesion or "clinging" between it and the growing stem which twines around it; and a system of forces is thus set up, producing a "couple." . . . The twist is the direct result of this couple, and it disappears when the support is so smooth that no such force comes to be exerted. . . . The effect of torsion will be to intensify any such peculiarities of sectional outline which [the twining stem] may possess, though not initiate [them] in any originally cylindrical structure. . . .

—D'Arcy Wentworth Thompson, *On Growth and Form*[7]

> By no means an orderly Dantescan rising
> but as the winds veer
>   . . . as the winds veer and the raft is driven
>   and the voices . . .
>   as the winds veer in periplum . . .
>
> —Ezra Pound, *Canto LXXIV*

Vinelike torsion—pictured literally in the vine of *America* 2—is manifested in the dramatic structure by, for example, a persona's reaction to brutal waves of outside force, the "interference" of selfhood by Experience. Oothoon, deflowered and newly pregnant, registers the penetration-action of Bromion ambivalently as both her suffering and her sexual excitation: "But she can howl incessant writhing her soft snowy limbs" (2:12); "can" implies

---

[7] Cambridge, Eng., 1959, II, 887-892, "A Further Note on Torsion."

the capacity she is discovering for both kinds of experience. Similarly in *America* a counterpoint of anguished writhings in response to antipathetic or antithetical forces produces the couple and twist Thompson describes. Fertile and progressive engagement of contrary forces is seen as the involvement of a dramatic character in definitive action brought about by a sort of Darwinian "resistence"—though the notion is opposed by Thompson's specific morphology. In this sense prophecy becomes what Yeats, thinking of poetic drama, called "Character isolated by a deed."

Structurally the couple is a temporal point in language, a node of verbal energy which by its recurrence defines the poetic plot, an irregular pattern of vectors in a self-fulfilling but inconclusive poetic process.[8] In *Visions* and the Preludium of *America* the recurrent couple is the action of rape which centers in image-words of tearing and rending. Both Argument and Preludium initiate the pattern in an overturelike prefiguring which provides the prophetic poem that follows with the ordering effect of strong poetic closure, without resort to such conventional dramatic resolution as Fortinbras' ceremonial entrance or the terminal couplet of a Shakespearean sonnet. Oothoon's initial monologue, spoken from a point of vantage above or beyond her chained lament at the end of the poem, provides a *generative* verbal order by establishing the plot of *rending*:[9] "But the terrible thunders tore / My virgin mantle in twain." This mythic overview of primordial rape, recurring in the Preludium, gives an evolving poetic meaning both to dramatic inconclusiveness (Oothoon's failure to actualize her liberation) and to structural open-endedness (her endless daily cycle of

[8] Recurrence appears to be the basic feature of poetic, as of musical, structure, and the high incidence of repeated key words and motifs in Blake ought to be definable in linguistic terms. Such "nodes" may be related to the "summative" words which linguists have found to be the center of phonic patterns in certain sonnets and other short forms: see J. Lynch, "The Tonality of Lyric Poetry: An Experiment in Method," *Word*, 9 (1963); Dell Hymes, "Phonological Aspects of Style: Some English Sonnets," *Style in Language*, Cambridge, Mass., 1960, 109-131. Claude Lévi-Strauss offers a broader definition of recurrence: "La répétition a une fonction propre, qui est de rendre manifeste la structure du mythe" (*Anthropologie structurale*, Paris, 1958, 254).

[9] The generative verb for "rending" in Argument and Preludium may be the summative word of n. 8, above, suggesting that the long sections of the poem are in fact musically expanded versions of these overtures, or that the latter are condensations. The revolutionary child is father of prophetic man.

lamenting). The effect of the poem's thus seeming to spill out of its aesthetic frame is to suggest opposing possibilities: unity and unlimited gnomonic extension of a pattern. While the perverse body-and-mind-opening rape by Bromion results in aimlessly circular open-endedness, its repetition by Orc corrects and redirects it toward the gate-opening of the affirmatively unresolved termination of *America*. (Compare the end of *Europe*: "Till morning ope'd the Eastern gate.")

The *rending* plot of these poems is borne along on a terminology of torsion of which the Minute Particular or discrete terminological unit is any dialectical verb (the "action word" of grammar) such as "rend." Because of semantic ambiguity, such a verb generates both extensions of itself and of its opposite, which in turn regenerate the original word. The result is a "logological" system, to use Kenneth Burke's vocabulary, wherein each verbal operation stands for the whole poetic machinery in which it functions.[10] A particle serves as catalyst of a changing Gestalt, which in turn redefines the particle. Thus the *term* (a torsion word) is the ontogenetic embryo of the *grammar* (the "logic" of torsion language) which is the phylogenetic pattern embodying its own operative principles. That pattern is the process symbolized by Orc.

Thus "rend" generates, first, images of itself, analogues or synonyms ("tore my virgin mantle in twain") emblematic of the whole class of divisions of being (Fallen Man, separation of continents, split of mind and body, etc.), sexual and aural "piercing," physical and verbal "writhing" and "wrenching," and so on. Second, it generates different levels of opposing principles or antonyms: reunion or reconstitution of the liberated body politic, sexual union of revived youth, "rushing of th' inhabitants together," etc. Generation of contraries on a verbal level is tantamount to an "identity of opposites" in poetic process based on metaphoric thought. From this perspective the Orc cycle is one extreme of poesis, modeled on the theological doctrine of circumincession, that each member of the Trinity inheres in the others—Orc and Urizen being reciprocal, because interdependent, human possibil-

---

[10] My method here derives from Kenneth Burke's notions of poetry as "symbolic action" and the "dancing of an attitude" in *The Philosophy of Literary Form*, New York, 1957, and in *The Rhetoric of Religion: Studies in Logology*, Boston, 1961.

ities. In Blakean metaphoric process the Orc *cycle* is a failed marriage of contraries, a loss of identity due to a double misunderstanding of the creative process, the false assumptions being that marriage means a passive union of opposites rather than active engagement and that a dialectical system (of thought, language, life) seeks a binding synthesis. Properly it seeks a purer extension of its dynamics in newer and newer visionary orders; metaphor, like the Trinity, is the work of the creator, and all created things bear the essential stamp of his mind: the rending is the marriage and true marriage is perpetual visionary rending.

By "expanding" the poetic dialogue of *Visions of the Daughters of Albion* into a full-scale prophetic opera in *America,* Blake demonstrates creative powers of Genius in the phono-aesthetic resources of language. (Here I assume familiarity with David Erdman's close analysis of the verbal-visual progression in *"America: New Expanses."*) The rape-outcry-prophecy paradigm develops as the course of evolving human communication, beginning with Orc's conversion of cosmic silence into primal verbal presence, in the shadowy daughter's newborn words, and continuing through Washington's courageous speech, Orc's Declaration of Independence, the verbal apocalypse of plate 8, and the pure musicality of the rest of the poem. Aesthetically the highest stage of this evolution of communication is the poem itself, its verbal-visual-musical modality.

Structurally the Preludium appears to *produce* the Prophecy, the primal rape generating the antithetical torsion of mental warfare, the symbolic drama of apocalypse. As if to test the medium of poetry itself—its presumption, for example, that "Mental things alone are real"—Blake presents an instance where mental struggle must turn into human action or lose a portion of the infinite. Orc, though chained, spiritually accumulates the revolutionary energy to save the continent: ". . . Rivets my tenfold chains while still on high my spirit soars" (*A* 1:12: see the illustration of *MHH* 4). And his suffering contains the plot of the paradigm he must later enact (emphasis added):

> . . . & sometimes a whale I *lash*
> The raging fathomless *abyss,* anon a *serpent folding*
> *Around* the pillars of Urthona, and *round* thy dark limbs,
> On the Canadian wilds I *fold,* feeble my *spirit folds.*

276

For chaind beneath I *rend* these *caverns*; when thou
   bringest food
I *howl* my joy!

"Fold" is the dialectical verb here, which generates both the "awful" circularity of the shadowy female and the vinelike torque
of the serpent whose winding is indeterminate—and creative—
and whose movement *around* pillars and limbs is also a movement
up, eventually to "burst the stony roof" (8:9) and pierce the
"Invulnerable tho' naked" womb. Similarly, elsewhere, "infold"
can suggest both Los's false creation—"Human Illusion . . . in-
volvd" (*The Book of Los*, last line: E94/K260)—and his true
creation, the "infinite infolding" of *Jerusalem*. Positive rotary
action opens into progression, by virtue of waves of centrifugal
creative force:

The hairy shoulders rend the links, free are the wrists of fire;
Round the terrific loins he siez'd the panting struggling womb;

and of penetrative power: "It joy'd"; and of reactive torque:
"then burst the virgin cry."

Self-Interference as Self-Generation

For nothing can be sole or whole
That has not been rent.
         —Yeats, *Crazy Jane Talks*
             with the Bishop

Poetry Fetter'd, Fetters the Human Race!
                —*J* 3

By using the Orc paradigm of opening a body (inward and
then outward) as its mode of operation, prophetic poetry becomes
a self-extending system with a built-in procreative mechanism, a
verbal torque of self-interfering process. Thus in "A Prophecy"
soul-piercing "sullen fires," reported in ear-rending sounds, produce Orc fires and revolutionary diction, and so on. Blake evidently was thinking of evolution on the level of organic morphology and embryology,[11] and his Orc initiates the chief cosmic event

[11] Carmen S. Kreiter, "Evolution and William Blake," *Studies in Romanticism*, IV (1965), 110-118, suggests that Blake had knowledge of early theories
of evolution, embryology, and the biogenetic law; however, Kreiter's analysis
does not go beyond linking the diction of *The Book of Urizen* to contempo-

in biological terms: "the Zenith grew" (4:4). The human organic system, no less than freed slaves (pl. 6), breaks out of apparent limits, and the image of *bursting* stands for birth out of the womb of closed systems (2:2, 6; 6:5, 8:9, etc., leading to 15:19: "The doors of marriage are open"). Spiritual evolution is phylogenic progression, the entropic cycle breaking into epicycle and moving on the track of actual time. Apocalyptic expansion of Man's body is "human blood shooting its veins all round the orbed heaven" (4:5), a massive torsion that modulates into the open circuit of nerves and vines:

> They feel the nerves of youth renew, and desires of
> ancient times,
> Over their pale limbs as a vine when the tender grape
> appears (15:25-26)

This visionary rebirth foreshadows the drama in *Jerusalem* of Man's hatching the egg of his limited world: "There is a Void, outside of Existence, which if enterd into / Englobes itself & becomes a Womb" (*J* 1:1-2:E143/K620).

Higher human form, a sort of Superman "Wonder" (5:7), is engendered by the power of heat, which penetrates the body, as opposed to light, which reveals the play of appearances:

> Intense! naked! a Human fire fierce glowing, as the wedge
> Of iron heated in the furnace; his terrible limbs were fire . . .
> . . . heat but not light went thro' the murky atmosphere
> (*A* 4:8-11)

Orc as phallic wedge in the smithy of human re-creation links with Los as artist of "infernal method." At every stage of development from generative principle to prophetic principle, true creation is born of some sort of marriage of the two. Orc-Los, the poet-prophet, as a man-transmuting alchemist uses the traditional and clearly sexual Rod of Fire[12] to effect a transcendent form:

---

rary science, except to offer the curious argument that Orc represents a "devolution" from the "higher" state of innocence symbolized by the worm.

[12] See Gaston Bachelard's *The Psychoanalysis of Fire*, Boston, 1964, a key (along with Bachelard's other works, mostly untranslated) to a phenomenological analysis of poetry—and apparently an important influence on the method of Northrop Frye (who supplies an Introduction). Bachelard discusses the sexual meanings of alchemy—the phallic Rod of Fire and the smithy which was often shaped as a sexual organ (51ff.).

man's "feet become like brass, / His knees and thighs like silver, & his breast and head like gold" (8:16-17). The journey toward *Jerusalem*, locomoted by torsion, is a marriage of heaven and hell, a vinelike spiritual "ascent," blossoming in sunlight, and a magical "descent" through the condensed heat of smithy, body, and imagination.

The body-piercing and surface-rending heat, extending the metaphor of infernal *poiein*, suggests that Blake as primal poet sees his function as releasing the energies and "desires of ancient times" pent up beneath closed surfaces. Closer to eighteenth-century pseudoscience than to the poetics of contemporaries who accepted the "bondage" of a prosody of restraint, his Visionary Forms of tactile release suggest a hidden metaphor of ritual friction. For the pseudoscientist (such as Blake's "Inflammable Gass") "Everything that rubs, that burns, or that electrifies is immediately considered capable of explaining the act of generation."[13] A treatise by Charles Rabiqueau of 1753, *The Spectacle of Elementary Fire or A Course in Experimental Electricity*, for example, develops "an electrical theory of the sexes" based on a theory of friction. Torque itself—of demonic winding serpent, coupling vine, or twisting fire—relates to the electrifying friction of con-

[13] This and other relevant passages quoted by Bachelard, 26ff.; cf.: "The equation of fire and life forms the basis of the system of Paracelsus . . . [and] Boerhaave. It is the hidden fire that must be utilized for the curing of sickness and for procreation. Nicolas de Locques [1665] bases all the value he attributes to fire on its inwardness. Fire is 'internal or external; the external fire is mechanical, corrupting and destroying, the internal is spermatic, generative, ripening' " (73). David Erdman calls my attention to Kathleen Raine's discovery (I, 25-26) of "a direct link" between Blake's chimney sweepers "and Orc, who is Blake's Eros," in Blake's use of a passage in Swedenborg about the spirits "from the Earth Jupiter" who are called "Sweepers of Chimnies, because they appear in like Garments . . . with sooty Faces" and are in a region that corresponds to "the seminal Vessels." What is somewhat cryptically presented in the passage quoted but is spelled out fully in Swedenborg is that the Sweepers, who have "a burning Desire to be admitted into Heaven" and who, at the call of an Angel, cast off their raiment "with inconceivable Quickness from the Vehemence of [their] Desire," illustrate exactly in their quickness and vehemence the correspondent quickness of seminal ejaculation, a demonstration of the swiftest way to enter Heaven "and become Angels." Blake, of course, ironically reverses the transformation in his own Memorable Fancy (*MHH* 24) of the Angel who becomes a Devil.

See n. 17 to the essay by W.J.T. Mitchell, above.

traries. Frazer cites friction-caused ritual fires, with sexual significance, and Bachelard (pp. 31-32) cites a fire ritual "which unites the Sun festival and the harvest festival . . . above all a celebration of the *seeding* of the fire. In order that it may have all its force, this seeding must be seized in its first intensity, when it comes fresh from the rubbing tool." As ritual, the progression from Orc to Los moves from fire-seeding Minor Prophecies to harvesting Major Prophecies—as the wheat-yielding illumination of "A Prophecy" visually suggests.[14] In the terms I have been using, poetic self-interference is the ritual self-seeding and -firing which leads to the self-reaping of prophecy (message) and myth (structure).

The marriage of Orc and Los or process and message, dramatized in plate 8 of *America*, justifies a poetry of "terrific form" (7:7), analogue of "fearful symmetry." The dialogue of Orc and Albion's Angel, a traction of verbal contraries, intensifies the dialectics of *Visions of the Daughters of Albion* to apocalyptic breaking point. The progression is electrically generated from verbal pronouncement (Orc's speeches, *A* 6 and 8), to increasingly violent reactive verbal torsions (the Angel's augmenting hysteria in 7 and 9), then on to waves of expanding force (the Angel of Boston's "rending off his robe," pls. 11 and 12, involuntarily seeding the flame that "folded roaring fierce"), and finally beyond discourse to pure verbal action (flames magnetizing citizens, etc., pl. 14). Plate 6, Orc's Declaration, is the agent of primary force, but plate 8 is the fertilized seed, the strongest node in a moving field of forces. The latter defines revolutionary identity: the *cognito* or self-naming ("I am Orc"), the serpentine torsion ("wreath'd round the accursed tree"—kernel of the "wreaths" of renewal in 15:21), the fiery acceleration of history toward collapse into apocalypse ("The times are ended"), and, by implication, the rending of all temporal and mind-forged chains as rehearsed in the Preludium. In the spiritual birth process the open discourse of Orc contrasts symmetrically with the closed shriek of Albion's Angel, held within the envelope of musical refrains in plate 9. The visibly stony womb of plate 8 encloses Orc's apocalypse, with Urizen sitting over it like a hen on an egg, until two plates later

---

[14] See the essay by E. J. Rose at the end of this volume.

it "gives birth" to fiery Orc, as though verbal seeds had burst into visionary flames.

This link between plates 8 and 10 suggests further that pregnant *America* contains the kernel of *Europe*. As the womb that "Heaves in enormous circles" (9:10) crosses the Atlantic in widening force-waves, poetic systems interpose in a larger self-interfering system. *America* 10 {38} may, as Erdman suggests, illustrate the concluding lines of *Europe*; or rather, the serpent-hair of Orc pictured in *America* 10 emerges verbally in *Europe* 15 as the "snaky thunders" on the *reared* head of Los. And *America* climaxes in renewed vines and opened gates of perception that reopen into *Europe* as "Five windows" lighting "the cavern'd Man" (viz., the reader) and as "the eternal vine" (*E* 3:1-2). *America* 8 is, I suggest, the main generative torque for both poems and the vector determining their open endings—structurally the ontogenesis of their phylogenesis.

The Minute Particular of this long-range linking is Orc's fertilizing action within plate 8. The stony law he stamps "to dust" becomes ejaculated seed that "scatter[s] religion abroad / To the four winds as a *torn book*"—the Holy Bible itself rent and impregnated within this Bible of Hell. Taking the Book into its smithy, *America* disseminates seeding sparks to "make the desarts blossom" and reincarnate God in the living body of religion (Man as Jesus, Poet as Creator). Man returns to inner sources as the "deeps shrink to their fountains," waking Albion to "infinite infolding." Again Orc-seeding leads us to Major Prophecy; the image of fires that "inwrap [cf. Milton's "instruct"] the earthly globe, but man is not consumed," will grow into the vision of Night IX of *The Four Zoas*:

> How is it that we have walkd thro fires & yet are not consumd
> How is it that all things are changd even as in ancient
>   times . . .
> The Expanding Eyes of Man behold the depths of wondrous
>   worlds   (138:39-40, 25:E391/K379)

Poetic alchemy reverses, as if by magnetic repolarization, "life by magic power condens'd; infernal forms art-bound" (*A*b:14:-E57/K204), and the poet becomes Prometheus unbound.

As an allegory of poetics, Orc embodies the principle of expansion by prosodic and structural unfettering, the opening inward by syntactic, rhythmic, and other formal means directly to energies of creative process. The self-interfering poem and book become a self-regulating economy, like the bird learning its limits by soaring on its own wings. "Allegory" is a term hardly adequate to this perception. Herbert Weisinger argues in his essay on "The Mythic Origins of the Creative Process" that the archetypal dying-reviving-god pattern of myth and ritual, viewed in the light of evidence from both literature and science, becomes "the symbolic representation of the creative process, that is to say, the mind's figuring forth of itself . . . the mode of operation of the mind . . . as essentially dramatic and dialectical, of proceeding by what amounts to leaps, falls and higher leaps. . . ."[15] Orc initiates a process which, in authentic prophecy, must determine poetic structure by enacting "the primal law of the inner life of man" that

> . . . *ontogeny recapitulates phylogeny,* . . . as it would appear that that is the law of history and nature itself. As I try to visualize the movement of the mind during the creative process, I see an *unfolding from within, a reaching beyond, another unfolding,* and another stretch; an ever *shifting center radiating out* to ever *widening circumferences, not circular, but irregular,* with deep bays of regression, flat beaches of futility, and sudden promontories of achievement. In any event, I do not see the movement as a circle, of a beginning returning in on itself, but rather an *uneven ascending spiral.* I suppose that from the point of view of God as he looks down on the process it is a circle (as I suppose it is too from the point of view of Satan as he looks up at it) but from the point of view of man standing midway and looking head-on, the circle is a spiral, and what hope he has comes from the difference in location and angle of vision. . . . The creative process is therefore by its nature profoundly *revolutionary,* a *built-in device which immediately upsets any state of equilibrium or stasis* it encounters. By its *interposition* it transforms rest into motion, altering and recasting, until the *friction* of *resistance* and effort slows it down into form or

[15] *The Agony and the Triumph: Papers on the Use and Abuse of Myth,* East Lansing, Mich., 1964, 250.

formula, a new state of rest whose balance it again upsets, so that now each new mirror in the corridor reflects one subtly altered image after another. . . .

(Weisinger, 252-253; emphasis added)

Together with the vine morphologue from Thompson, this account gives us a vocabulary for self-correcting verbal action and structure in Blake which lead us beyond the poem, where the poet would have us go, and then back into its evolving economy, equipped then with expanded critical tools. We may learn thereby the full meaning of the "going forth & returning" of *Jerusalem* 99.

A Note on the Bard's Rending of His Harp

The stern Bard's curious action at the end of the Preludium seems to have a structural meaning in the light of the present analysis:

> . . . asham'd of his *own song*; enrag'd he swung [rotary action]
> His harp aloft sounding [rent music], then *dash'd its shining frame* [rending] against
> A ruin'd pillar in *glittring fragments* [seed-sparks]; silent he turn'd away [negative torque],
> And wander'd down the vales of Kent in sick & drear lamentings.
>
> (*A* 2:18-21:E51/K196; emphasis added)

I suggest that his shame results from recognizing the shadowy daughter as a real part of his own mind and sensing that the poet of Experience can become his own lamenting song and close himself within it, like Oothoon. As Swedenborg had failed to do, the poem must embody Orc by opposing even his own creation, "tearing" the book by canceling plates (a potentially sinful division of the visionary body), re-ordering the system, providing new contraries for new igneous power, and so on. Visually, the paradoxical fires rage across the pages of *America* or burst from its center (pl. 10 {38}) as if threatening to consume the book itself. Yet the visionary book is unconsumed; "A Prophecy" is unimpeded by the broken harp. Indeed this act of self-denial or self-interference assures the birth of authentic prophecy through friction and resistance. Blake is not only describing mental warfare, he is undergoing it—as his cancellation of this troublesome plate indicates. Will this additional destruction of a frame lead to expansion of art? The poet cannot possibly know in advance; so his own creative act is always running the risk of destroying art. Even as he breaks the frame, however, he sees it as "shining"; his hope is that its "glittring fragments" will become seeding sparks to fertilize the silence of barren nature. The Bard joins common man in his lamentings, for true prophecy can only take root in the actual soil of literal history; the vine of prophecy must produce "Divine Revelation in the Litteral Expression" (*M* 42:14).[16]

[16] The vine as organic life evolving into prophecy and as the torque which generates vision has a visual equivalent in *America* 2 {27}, where it twines upward (paralleling Orc's birth struggle below) and couples with the text to become the actual words of poetry.

13

Metamorphoses of a Favorite Cat

IRENE TAYLER

WHEN Walpole's cat, Selima, met her appointed fate, Thomas Gray commemorated the occasion in an *Ode on the Death of a Favourite Cat: Drowned in a Tub of Gold Fishes*. And half a century later, Blake responded to the occasion again—distinctively, in his own manner, as the "visionary" illustrator of Gray's poems. The whimsical Cat Ode is also, of course, a cautionary tale addressed to the ladies. Its humor and point derive from the proverbial similarities between the two species: their self-love and their self-indulgence. The cat, enamored of her reflection in the water, spies a pair of goldfish and plunges after them, to her death; just as the ladies may be similarly beguiled, through wantonness and complacency, to seek what glitters and fall to dishonor. It will be obvious that Gray's tone and double purpose present special problems to the illustrator.

The little allegory amuses as it instructs, teasing fun out of the beast fable and the moralizing elegy. Where Blake found in Gray's elegiac banter not only humor but also intimations of the kind of "vision" that transcends "allegory," Dr. Johnson simply found himself critical of the way the fable is related to the moral, complaining that some lines are applicable only to the cat, others only to the ladies. Gray apparently had a good deal of fun in confusing distinctions, making the fable and the moral compete for the reader's attention by allowing the ladies to serve as a vehicle for the cat even as the cat serves as a vehicle for talk about the ladies. The cat, exposed to temptation, appears as that "hapless nymph"; her "feet"—not paws—are beguiled, and she falls a "Presumptuous maid"; as she stretches for the prize, the poet asks parallel but separate rhetorical questions, one each for moral and fable:

> What female heart can gold despise?
> What cat's averse to fish?[1]

---

[1] Quotations from *Ode on the Death of a Favourite Cat* are taken from the 1790 Murray edition used by Blake.

285

And the last stanza makes the moral amusingly explicit:

> From hence, ye beauties, undeciev'd
> Know, one false step is ne'er retriev'd,
> And be with caution bold.
> Not all that tempts your wand'ring eyes,
> And heedless hearts, is lawful prize,
> Nor all that glisters, gold.

Logically considered, the last line remains, in Dr. Johnson's uncompromising words, "a pointed sentence of no relation to the purpose"; for, as Johnson resolutely maintained, "if what glistered had been 'gold,' the cat would not have gone into the water; and, if she had, would not the less have drowned." Indeed the sententious close will do for neither the fable nor the moral. Dr. Johnson is, as usual, right in asserting that cats do not dive for gold; and we may go on to observe that only very literal-minded, or very immoral, ladies take the plunge entirely for gold. Those "wand'ring eyes" and "heedless hearts," that "one false step" that is "ne'er retriev'd"—all these unmistakably represent the usual cautions against sexual indiscretion; but they open the truism, "nor all that glisters, gold," once again to the kind of objections Dr. Johnson directed against the fable. Addressed to the ladies, rather than the cat, the truism in the context of the whole poem would have to mean something like: "Indeed, what glisters may turn out to be of no more worth than a fish! (—and prone to be as elusive too)." As we pursue these distinctions the delicate parallel between feline and feminine becomes obliterated, and the poem begins to fragment into fable and wholly detachable moral.

From his illustrations we may infer that Blake was struck not only by the sexual connotations of Gray's moral but also by the shifting relationship between fable and moral. Blake in fact appears to have perceived the richest meanings of the poem in just those wavering distinctions that Johnson found logically reprehensible. The art of illustration was for Blake an encounter—in Eternity, he might have said—of one visionary experience with another, the confrontation of two images of the truth. "Visions" of "eternal principles or characters of human life appear to poets in all ages," observed Blake in speaking of Chaucer; and in *The Marriage of Heaven and Hell* he asserted that "Every thing possible to be believ'd is an image of truth." That it was an image only, constantly in need of development and revision, seems to have been Blake's experience with his own vision as it exfoliates in his poems and prophecies. Such revision of vision was, in a sense, what he conceived himself to be doing for Milton in his own poem of that name, and in an important sense it is what he did on each occasion that he illustrated the work of another poet. The distinction appears again in Blake's notion of "Fable or Allegory": "The Hebrew Bible & the Gospel of Jesus are not Allegory, but Eternal Vision or Imagination of All that Exists. Note here that Fable or Allegory is seldom without some Vision" (E544/K604). If this Platonizing seems excessively solemn when placed next to the Cat Ode, perhaps we need to remind ourselves that for Blake, no less than for Freud, levity has its own weight and seriousness, a fact that does not so much undercut the humor as complicate and enrich it. Accordingly, Blake's illustrations are delightfully comic and yet play quite seriously with the interrelationships of human, animal, and imaginary worlds in Gray's modest allegory. For here, amid these shifting interrelationships, lay the "vision" within the "fable."

In 1797, fifty years after the untimely death of the fabled Selima, Blake stood at a kind of turning point in his career. Most of his short prophecies were completed, and in his struggles with *Vala* he found himself moving toward the longer visions of *Milton* and *Jerusalem*—vastly important works in the canon but destined, as he was himself aware, for a small public. On the other hand, he seems to have had substantial hopes of reaching a wider public through his illustrations. "Poetical painting," as it was called, seemed to be in vogue. There was the success of Boydell's "Shakespeare Gallery," and Blake's friend Fuseli was currently laboring over his "Milton Gallery." Blake himself had dreamt of financial success with his massive set of illustrations to Young's *Night Thoughts*; although this ambitious edition failed commercially, Blake may have felt that the fault lay with the money crisis of 1797 rather than with the artist or the venture itself. (In fact Blake did succeed in reaching a wider public through his illustrations: even today he is more highly appreciated in many circles for his designs to Milton, *Job*, and Dante than for his own prophetic books.) It was at this point in his career, at this point in his development as creative illustrator of other men, that Blake turned to Thomas Gray.

287

Blake's six illustrations to the Cat Ode (see {64-69}) form part of a series of 116 that the artist designed for the wife of his friend John Flaxman; sold after Flaxman's death, the entire series dropped from sight until 1919 when, newly rediscovered, the unique copy elicited from Professor Grierson the observation that he knew of "no collection which illustrates so fully the range of Blake's power."[2] For Blake's use the margins were trimmed away from pages of Murray's 1720 edition of Gray's poems and then each sheet was carefully pasted against a very slightly smaller rectangle cut out near the center of a large sheet of folio drawing paper. Each page, when Blake had finished his work of illustration, thus presented a rectangular box of printed text surrounded by a water color drawing. The number of illustrations to a poem is therefore directly related to the number of pages it occupied in the printed volume.

The six illustrations to Gray's *Favourite Cat* depict the cat and the paired fish of the fable in progressively shifting shapes, extensions of the little allegory itself and of hints in Gray's language. The first two designs are in effect general, or introductory. The first appears on the title page, setting the tone and preparing for the action of Gray's beast fable. Blake entitles the picture by quoting from Gray's third stanza: " 'Midst the tide / Two angel forms were seen to glide"; as we learn in the next line, these angelic goldfish are the "Genii of the Stream." What Blake actually chooses to show, however, is a leering, beckoning exchange between forms neither human nor animal but rather a kind of mocking, demonic perversion of both. Across the top of the box reserved for the text (in this case for the title) reclines Selima, a sort of comic gargoyle with a furry, catlike body but slyly human face, pointed ears located down the side of the head where human ears belong, arms furry but human in shape, and lower legs that end in wispy claws neither human nor quite feline; she sports both corset and shawl, and gestures with coy wickedness, intensified by the glint in her red eyes, toward the two goldfish swimming beneath. The goldfish also combine human forms with attributes of the subhuman: scaly torsos and finlike wings make them resemble menacing goblins; their wide-flung arms seem almost to invite Selima to join them while at the same time they are swimming

---

[2] *The Times* (London), 4 November 1919, p. 15.

rapidly away. In this ribald, mischievous exchange Blake manages to parody specifically the animals of the mock elegy and the ladies toward whom the moral is directed.

Even a black-and-white reproduction conveys some sense of the enormous visual energy of this design; it is one of Blake's best, most vigorous and appealing. But the colors are an even greater source of power—they are at once brilliant and dense, beautiful and a little terrible. These colors—dark bluish-green for the water, harsh red-orange for the fish—intensify the sense of perversity, of an entire world violent and misshapen in its metamorphoses. The whole is a splendid comic creation, and it demands our laughter; but it is by no means the laughter of self-approving joy. The gargoyle violence, the coy thrust of the gestures, prepare us for what will prove to be Blake's overall view of the action of the poem, and for his visionary interpretation of it.

The second introductory illustration surrounds Blake's list of picture titles, and the title of this particular design is "Demurest of the tabby kind," a line from Gray's first stanza. Here Selima—for the only time in Blake's series do we see a wholly catlike cat—again reclines on the inserted box, though this time in a position roughly the reverse of that in the preceding design; and below her in the water swim two wholly fishlike fish. All three figures are relatively small and huddled close against the text-box, leaving the rest of the page an undecorated expanse of yellowish air and blue water, perhaps to suggest a special connection here between figures and text. The curiosity of the illustration is that astride each animal figure sits a human one—a naked "nymph" with an elaborate hairdo rides the cat, leaning demurely and rather self-consciously on her arm and looking out at the reader. Two less distinctly drawn, more conventional nymph-figures ride the fish. This design illustrates not so much Gray's gently ironic judgment of Selima's character—her "demureness"—as it does the sense in which she is "of the tabby kind." For what we see is a comic literalizing of the poetic technique of layered meanings, a visual parody of the allegorical method in which the "real subject" is made to "ride" astride the ostensible one, the two combining as they do in this poem to point the moral for the ladies. As the cat-lady receives fuller treatment by Gray, so Blake also draws her as a recognizable character; the fish-figures remain less distinctly individual in poem and picture alike.

Each of these first two designs, then, seems largely self-contained, each a general comment on the poem—the first on the theme of hunter and prey implicit in the cat and fish story, the second on the literary method of allegory that would have us read a fable and find a moral. The third, fourth, and fifth form one movement to which the sixth and final illustration stands as conclusion: the titles for all these are lines quoted from the poem, but all depend more broadly on the whole poem than the technique of quoted single lines would imply. Finally they depend upon the "vision" in the "fable."

This is of course a handling of the poem quite foreign to Gray and to his contemporary illustrator, Walpole's friend Richard Bentley, who joined Gray in regarding the whole affair with amused detachment.[3] A glance shows Bentley's details to be at once more realistic and more elaborately "arty" (see {70}). His cat is thorough cat; his bowl even reflects the windowpanes that light our view. But that little domestic scene is overwhelmed by the elaborate inventiveness, and indeed the sheer mass, of its decorative surroundings. The scene is framed—the word "framed" is insufficient—by a decorative entablature supported by caryatids of a river god stopping his ears to Selima's cries (so phrased in the accompanying "Explanation of the Prints") and Destiny cutting the nine threads of her life; and the whole structure is further embellished by a mandarin-cat seated in a pagoda, fishing in a Chinese vase, another cat drawing up a massive net from another Chinese vase, various elegant flowers and draperies, and a number of jubilant mice. At the foot of the entire structure, and displayed with conscious pomp, are the signatures of Gray and his illustrator; the poet's initials inscribed on a lyre, the artist's on a pallet.

Bentley, like Blake, worked up small hints from the language of the poem, making from the mention of Chinese vase a complete Oriental setting with costumed cat, and of the "wat'ry God" and "malignant Fate" robust imitations of Greek architectural statuary. The picture itself is a paradigm of Bentley's technique: the household cat surrounded in mock solemnity by the rich culture of fashionable eighteenth-century England, its deference to classical tradition, its vogue of chinoiserie, its decorous but pervasive accolade to the artist as gentleman-maker.

[3] Richard Bentley, *Designs by Richard Bentley, for Six Poems by Mr. Thomas Gray*, London, 1753.

But if the two illustrators worked from some of the same hints, it was to wholly different effect. Bentley, perfectly catching Gray's stylish irony, returns the poem all the more forcefully to the public world of its social and literary context; we are safely located in time and space. You will notice that just as the cat's bowl faithfully reflects the light that illuminates our view of it, so too the framing figures are faithfully shaded for us, emphasizing our role as observers of a fixed scene; it is our familiar world, however fancifully played upon, and we are reassured in our sense of the reliability of reality. Flights of fancy take off from the ground, but like the thrown stone they return there too.

Not so with Blake. Gone is the picture frame, gone even the social frame of the parlor, and we are alone among those shifting shapes whose continual metamorphoses suggest that whatever reality is, it is no matter of stable physical structure. In this world of more than Ovidian mutability it is the imaginative form that asserts itself visually, not the physical form. And he who watches these mutual metamorphoses of eye and object within the six designs must ask what stretch his own eyes have made in response to the "objects" that are these designs. Blake says of some of his artist friends: "I found them blind: I taught them how to see." We know that with Blake how we see determines what we see. And what we see in Gray's poem is not only the lamented Selima of Arlington Street.

We recall that Blake usually associated allegory with fable, finding both "totally distinct and inferior" to "Vision or Imagination." And we recall that Blake's distinction is based on his contention that what he calls "vision" or "imagination" must be "a Representation of what Eternally Exists, Really & Unchangeably," whereas allegory is topical, that is, applicable only to a given time or set of ethical principles. In literature it is the difference, say, between the Bible (which Blake called "Vision itself") and Dryden's *Absalom and Achitophel*. The meaning and suggestiveness of the Bible expand as man's knowledge and understanding expand, whereas Dryden's poem contracts a biblical episode to fit a passing set of facts, which explains why without fairly thorough footnotes much of Dryden's poem escapes a modern reader, and partially explains what Blake meant by asserting that allegory "is Form'd by the daughters of Memory" (E544/K604).

To find "vision" in Gray's fable, Blake would have us look for what "eternally exists" in the story—in what ways Gray's allegorizing of Walpole's cat suggests pervasive truths of human experience. And to discover with Blake what "eternally exists" we must attend not to Bentley's chinoise cat about to drown in eighteenth-century mock splendor, not even to the cat of Arlington Street that in 1747 expired in Gray's playful elegy, but rather to the cat who is woman, the feline feminine who becomes the object of Gray's moral and who forms the subject of Blake's "vision."

The final four illustrations complete a sequence that follows the action of Gray's fable—but with important shifts in emphasis. The first of the four, which surrounds the first page of the poetic text, shows, in the words Blake uses to abridge the first two stanzas,

> The pensive Selima
> Her ears of jet and emerald eyes
> She saw and purr'd applause.

In this, the first stage of the action, we view Selima, a dainty lady with a rather catty face, cat-ears, and a tail protruding from her long skirt, absorbed in admiration of her reflection. The mirror image, which reveals only the face and torso, is just sufficiently distinct so that we can remark the startling fact that it reflects none of the catlike attributes, only those of the pretty young lady. What we see in part is another illustration of Gray's literary technique: the lady-like cat of the fable appears on the verge, the lady of the moral is mirrored in the water. But the reflection also prefigures Selima in what Blake sees as her essential, or perfected form, as we will see her in the final design. Here, as in all but the final illustration, there is no suggestion, as there emphatically is in Bentley, of a world outside the water and the air immediately above it. Air and water, most often barely separated by their pale coloring, are divided only by the horizontal halving of the page. Gray had described the scene from somewhere across the parlor:

> 'Twas on a lofty vase's side,
> Where China's gayest art had dy'd
> The azure flowers, that blow;
> Demurest of the tabby kind,
> The pensive Selima reclin'd,
> Gaz'd on the lake below.

Whereas Bentley had complied with Gray's sense of physical and ironic distance, in Blake's illustration we are invited to join a world of cat and fish: the flowers seem to be growing in an actual lake, no longer the purely metaphorical "lake" of the poem, and nestled among them, tenderly embracing in an echo of Selima's loving self-admiration, are the goldfish, the "Genii of the Stream," depicted as "humanized" male and female figures, each with softly yellow, finlike wings folded against his side. What is imaginative or figurative in Gray tends toward the literal in Blake, and the goldfish bowl has become the world.

The following illustration shows the second stage of the action: Selima, with the head, shoulders, and forepaws of a cat—but draped from the waist down with clothes that reveal beneath them human feet, ready in Gray's phrasing to be "beguil'd." Hovering close, and drawn with an elaborate seriousness that echoes Gray's mock-epic tone, sits Fate, scissors in hand, preparing to slit the thick-spun thread of Selima's life. In the water below we see the Genii, their forms still much as they were in the preceding illustration but displaying in flight more of their finny wings, which are now more orange in color. Whereas the preceding illustration seemed relatively static, this design, more violent even in its coloring, begins the cycle of action between hunter and prey hinted at in the first of the two introductory illustrations.

The climax follows in the next design, which Blake significantly conceives to be a clockwise circle of movement: at top center sits Fate (or Fortune, who traditionally dominates circular motion),[4] her arms extended over Selima, whom she has just shoved into the water; Selima, here depicted entirely as a human girl, falls headlong down the right. Across and up from the bottom rise the Genii, their position almost the same as in the preceding picture but their figures completely transformed. Their metamorphosis may be

---

[4] Blake seems to have confused the functions of Fate and Fortune, but at least he has respectable precedent for inaccuracy in *Lycidas*, where Milton appears to have confused the Fates with the Furies:

> Comes the blind Fury with the abhorred shears,
> And slits the thin-spun life.

Moreover, if we take Gray's "Malignant Fate" to refer with classical precision to Atropos (the text does not so insist, it seems to me), then Bentley also errs, for his "Explanation of the Prints" calls her "Destiny."

traced to a cue in Gray, but it is a slight one and by no means suggests the elaborate extension Blake made of it; three stanzas earlier Gray had described the glittering scales of the fish as "scaly armour," and now Blake again literalizes the figurative talk of eighteenth-century poetry, showing the Genii as human male and female costumed for war, brandishing long fish spears. The male—now harsh gold-green—grimaces fiercely at the viewer, while the female looks back over her shoulder, apparently regarding Selima's fall with feminine alarm. The cycle of action is complete also in its reversals: the fish, dressed for attack, have become the fishers, as they take on the fully human forms they do not possess for Gray; the warriors of a fallen world of humans, they wear the lineaments of destruction. In this climactic metamorphosis the hunter becomes the hunted, and the countering aggressiveness of the prey stands revealed.

This reversal of roles is not noted directly by Gray, though his poem does ape the theme of the fall from greatness. The ode begins with the "favourite," Selima, atop a "lofty" vase, purring applause at the sight of her own "fair round face." But then she spies a new object of desire and, in stretching to capture it, falls, losing her friends with her footing and affording the occasion for the moral to the "beauties." The fall from greatness may of course be taken to represent one half of the wheel of fortune, and this is apparently what Blake invites us to see in the illustration. In the poem "Fate" passively "sits by" in a parenthetical line, whereas Blake lends his goddess a wider, far more active role: she figures largely in two out of the six illustrations, and here she occupies the top center position, thus taking Selima's place on the wheel after having actively pushed Selima to her death. The circular pattern is completed by the fish, who fling themselves actively upward —human-shaped, armored for battle—as Selima falls. Although Blake, in his own role of creative illustrator, seems to have taken us far from the poem as it is written by Gray, we have to realize that Blake is not misunderstanding Gray; rather he is attempting to draw out the "visionary" implications, that which "eternally exists," in the little beast fable, whether it exists as a result of Gray's intentions or in spite of them.

In the sixth and final illustration we are shown Selima as a young woman "emerging" from the water, her hands folded in prayer. Again Blake may seem to have misunderstood Gray. In

Blake's title to the picture—"*Nine* times emerging from the flood / She mew'd to every wat'ry god"—Blake miscounts Gray's "*eight* times emerging," and in this way arrives at the number beyond which cats proverbially do not emerge from water. Whereas Gray's "eight times" allows for the ninth and fatal submersion, Blake's "nine times" dismisses the feline point, making explicit in the ninth submersion the death only anticipated by Gray, then raising the "spiritual body"[5] for a tenth—and new—life. And in the distance one can just make out the form of a shore with trees, the first sign in Blake of a world outside the deadly circle of this drama. Blake, then, carries his conclusion beyond that of Gray's poem; at the level of fable what we see emerging could be read as the feminine soul of the cat. But at the level of vision the cat has died within the woman to release her into her fully "human form." Put another way, the literal death of the cat becomes for Blake the figurative death of the fable—the fable dies with the cat, leaving the "moral level" to survive alone both in text and in illustration. The cat is gone from Gray's final stanza; and Blake's title and design both suggest that the cat, become woman, may survive with a tenth and new life—her own, this time, as she is freed from the destructive cycle of hunter and prey and emerges from that watery world of generation and death which is for Blake always a symbol of the fallen universe, the sea of time and space, this present dispensation in which we all live somewhat less than fully human lives. Beneath her in the picture, and swimming off to the right, her former prey, her adversaries, are now seen to be two flatly realistic fish who depart glassy-eyed and oblivious.

Fable and moral have finally split, then: no one rides the fish, and there is no cat beneath the girl. Instead, one realistically portrayed figure remains from each "level"—an extraordinary denouement for an allegory. Also gone are the parallel shifts in the relationship of cat to fish; the oscillation between them has ceased. They are completely separate at last, and as one would expect with a supplicating girl and two fish in water, they pay no attention to each other.

It seems to have been more than anything else the allegory—the relationship of fable to moral—that attracted Blake to the poem, and that makes his illustrations to it provocative and inter-

[5] Blake uses this Biblical phrase in his plate *To Tirzah* (reproduced in E30/K220), whose theme is closely related to his theme in these designs.

esting. Remember that for Blake "Fable or Allegory is seldom without some Vision," that is to say, some awareness of those pervasive shapes that human experience assumes again and again, however different the reasons and circumstances in each case. In taking Walpole's drowned cat and giving her human dimensions Gray released a "fable" with wider suggestions than perhaps he realized or intended. Part of what Blake found there, buried in such words as "armour," "bold," and "prize," was a story about woman as predator, whose relationship with her prey is a cyclical and mutually dangerous one. "As the eye, so the object," Blake constantly maintained, and where the eye is man's, every object should be fully human. But in these illustrations we see the eye and object of Gray's story—the cat and fish, woman and the object of her desire—shifting to fit one another in grotesque and sub-human ways.

Blake regarded as disastrous the view of sex that sees lovers as antagonists and the sexually experienced woman as "fallen," a prey, by revealing metaphor, to the man who made love to her. A society that demanded coyness of the woman, or that regarded the beloved as a possession rather than a partner, was for Blake the type and result of humanity's real fall. Thus the degraded half-human parodies of the title page demonstrate how each party in the relationship of hunter to prey draws the other into a scheme of malicious coyness. And thus the parallel shifts of cat and fish throughout define their interdependency. When Selima is the object of her own self-love, the fish are their own lovers too. As she prepares her attack they become fleeing and vulnerable "angels," their long webbed wings betraying nonetheless a telling relationship to that master of hypocrisy, Satan. In Selima's fall, when she exchanges in herself the preying cat for the vulnerable woman, the fish become human attackers, seeming to find strength in her weakness. The final illustration brings us full circle, and out: the hunter-prey exchange on which Selima had engaged was invoked, it suggests, by her faulty view both of herself and of her object. Man's view of the universe is self-regarding, according to Blake: see yourself as a predator and you will be likely to find yourself preyed on as well. "As the eye, so the object" means, in other terms, "as ye sow, so shall ye reap." By dividing off the "levels" of the allegory in this final illustration, Blake seems to be allowing the fable to swim away with the fish, leaving a clearer-eyed young woman free of her entrapment.

In visionary terms this has been the story not of the lamented Selima who died in Arlington Street, but rather of a coy, terrible, and piteous Selima who grows—like the tree of Mystery—in the human brain, whenever it mistakes love for war or the fruits of love for possessions. The Selima of Blake's reading is a partially misguided woman struggling to find her humanity. Her cat-ness is interesting to us only negatively, that is, insofar as she must rid herself of it, "cast" her "Spectre Into the Lake,"[6] and assume in spiritual self-fulfillment the human form that Gray gave Walpole's Selima by way of moralizing allegory. Whereas Dr. Johnson had found in Gray's wavering distinctions between feline and feminine the source of poetic illogic, Blake discerned there the vision that transcends fable.

We appear to have come a long way from the poem printed on the page, and yet the two areas of Blake's visionary interpretation are surely central to Gray's poem: these are the analogies of temperament between cat and lady, and the analogies between their aggressiveness in the hunt and their downfall. Thus, for example, the metaphor "scaly armour," which alludes to the war-games of cat and fish, expands for Blake to become one of the central images in the poem, paralleling as it does his own constant use of scales to symbolize forces of domination and evil. And the water in which Selima struggles is the fallen world, depicted as a sea of time and space by Blake and the Neoplatonists before him. As for Gray's confusions of identity, they must have seemed to Blake the proof of Gray's poetic genius: in Blake's reading the poem is precisely about the problem of identity, the movement toward humanity, the mutations of form along the way. In this view we are right as readers to feel the language appropriate to cats and to ladies—and incidentally to warriors—competing for our attention, as this very competition illuminates the meaning of the poem. We are left to hope that Selima will be ready for dry land and a truly human life, no longer a subject of "Fate" because no longer a believer in her wheel, on which all human relationships are necessarily those of up and down, oppressor and oppressed.

[6] The phrase appears in *Jerusalem*, in mirror-writing on a scroll beside a figure self-enclosed "in his Spectre's power." Reproduced in E182/K669.

For Blake, however, the story of Selima assumed an even wider perspective, offering an even more private, though corollary, way to understand the visionary meaning of the tale. Blake saw the fish in designs 3, 4, and 5 not only as the objects of Selima's lust, but also as embodiments and examples of a mutual love that she lacks and desires to experience. We first see Selima narcissistically admiring her own reflection (her face and bonnet are suggestively heart-shaped), in contrast to the "angels" who lie below in mutual embrace. Her plunge would then be in envy of such a love, her death the death of "selfhood," her redemption her new capacity for selflessness. The progress is not explicitly explained in these designs, and so remains decidedly private—as it is also decidedly foreign to any intention of Gray's. But readers familiar with Blake's other work can trace the connections throughout. A loose but suggestive parallel to design 3, in which Selima admires her own image as the fish embrace below, may be found in the 1808 illustration to *Paradise Lost* entitled *Satan Watching the Endearments of Adam and Eve*.[7] There Satan, at the top of the design, regards and embraces a serpent (the extension of himself) in interesting analogy to the self-contemplating Selima. Below Satan, Adam and Eve, like the fish of the Gray design, lie clasped in mutual embrace, encircled by a flowery bower. Milton's lines tell us that Satan envies their bliss, "Imparadis'd in one anothers arms," as he can feel only "fierce desire . . . still unfulfill'd," a phrase that echoes throughout Blake's pronouncements on the fallen human condition.[8]

Clearly the vision Blake had of Milton's Adam and Eve under the envious watch of the self-loving Satan is not in all respects parallel to his vision of Selima and the fish; the connection lies in the sterility of the self-loving figures and their envy of the flower-encircled mutual lovers below. The psychology of envy operates in Satan and Selima alike, making predators of both. But there the similarities between their two stories end; the next step in Selima's progress is not to be understood from the story of Satan

[7] Reproduced in John Milton, *Poems in English with Illustrations by William Blake*, London, 1926.

[8] Note that this is a composition on which Blake exercised some thought, as it is an alteration of the 1806 version, in which the serpent lies at Adam's feet.

but rather from an understanding of the visionary meaning Blake saw in the fish.

Gray had called the fish "The Genii of the Stream" by way of polite eighteenth-century periphrasis. But Blake had observed in *The Marriage of Heaven and Hell* that "The ancient Poets animated all sensible objects with Gods or Geniuses, calling them by the names and adorning them with the properties of woods, rivers, mountains, lakes, cities, nations, and whatever their enlarged & numerous senses could percieve." Blake himself exercised this poetic prerogative constantly, and treated Gray's use of it with respect. Almost twenty years later, again illustrating Milton, Blake's mind returned to the figures he had used in response to Gray's phrase. In the *Il Penseroso* design entitled "The Spirit of Plato unfolds his Worlds to Milton . . ." Blake pictures Milton in his chair beneath "the Circles of Plato's Heavens" and surrounded by "The Spirits of Fire, Air, Water & Earth." The Spirits of Water are a pair of spread-armed fish-humans (see detail, {71}) closely similar in both form and gesture to those of Blake's design to the title page of Gray's Cat Ode {64}. These later figures lack the gargoyle faces of the Gray title page (they resemble in this the figures of design 4 {67}), but they perform much the same function as those fish-turned-fishermen, for in the Milton design Blake shows them catching in fishnets a plunging human similar to the plunging Selima of design 5. Even the coloring is similar to that of the Gray designs, combining the bright gold-orange finny wings of the fish in the Gray title page with the pallor of the falling human form in design 5. These fish-humans are "Spirits of Water" in Blake's visionary sense, where water means what it did in plate 10 of *Gates of Paradise*: there only the hand of a drowning man remains stretched above a sea of water, and the caption reads "Help! Help!" to which Blake later added the fuller caption, "In Time's Ocean falling drown'd."[9] The spirits of this water are indeed captors, their nets those among which Blake's prophetic figures are so often seen to struggle; but it is revealing that after almost twenty years Blake should again return, in a picturing of watery entrapment, to the rather comic little fish of these Gray designs. That he did is, I think, an indication of their original meaning and importance to him.

[9] Reproduced in E262/K771; for fuller caption, see E266/K771.

Finally, even casual readers of Blake can recognize the falling Selima of design 5 as similar to the countless lost figures who plummet downward in Blake's pictures;[10] they clasp their heads in fear, as distinct from those who dive or float fearlessly, connoting a state of spiritual freedom in which no direction is really down. And Selima's final rise, in prayer, is again a familiar one in Blake designs: an analogy may be found close at hand in the last of the 116 Gray illustrations, which shows one spirit conducting another heavenward, the conducted spirit in an attitude of wonder.

This is, then, a prophetic sequence in which all the stages are familiar to those well acquainted with Blake's designs, however far afield such a reading lies from Gray's intent. Yet this quite private Blakean reading is not in all ways foreign to some interpretations of recent criticism. William Empson rightly observes that in Gray's poem both nymph and cat are the main subject, but adds that "the clash is not only between *nymph* and *cat* but between two metaphorical nymphs; between snatching at a pleasure, real but dangerous . . . and mistaking a false love for a true one . . . —believing that happiness to be permanent which will, in fact, be fleeting."[11]

The distinction is a valuable one, and something like it may surely be found in the poem. Gray's final stanza offers three compact and separable warnings: what you ladies seek, he says, may be too dangerous ("one false step is ne'er retrieved"), immoral ("not all . . . is lawful prize"), or deceptive ("Nor all that glisters gold"). The central tie in the poem between lady and cat, moral and fable, lies in a punning split of the word "goldfish"—"gold" applies to the desires of ladies, "fish" to cats. Yet the word "gold," used alone only twice in the poem, is there used in two different ways. In the line "What female heart can gold despise" it is used literally to mean money, implying in the ladies an equation of sexual and financial acquisitiveness that reduces love to lust and Gray's satire to unwonted savagery. But in the final line, so trying to critics from Johnson to Gosse,[12] the word "gold" is used figura-

[10] See, for example, Blake's painting of *The Last Judgment* in its various versions; one of these is reproduced in E550f. Compare also *God the son casting the rebel angels into hell*, reproduced in Milton, *Poems in English*.

[11] *Seven Types of Ambiguity*, New York, 1961, 122.

[12] Edmund Gosse in *Gray* (English Men of Letters; London, 1882, 81), dismisses the final line as "a specious little error."

tively to mean "of true worth." Thus Gray's turn on this pivotal word allows the literal distinction between real gold and fool's gold to enter by metaphor the moral realm of the poem and suggest that of his three warnings (against danger, immorality, and deception) the last is actually the inclusive one, implying not an audience of ladies to be deterred only by threats of danger or the wagging of a tutorial finger, but of ladies who seek true value (read also "love") and need only to be taught to distinguish it from false. We are thus returned to the second of Empson's "two metaphorical nymphs" and to that gentler satire that readers have always found in Gray's poem.

Blake's idiosyncratic reading has important and interesting alliances, then, with Empson's, for Blake, too, saw something like two distinguishable nymphs, but he saw them as two states of the individual. One is the fallen woman who "seeketh only Self to please" with a love whose method is "to bind another to Its delight,"[13] who snatches her prey with lustful possessiveness, and who dies the death of the cat, drowned in the sea of time and space. The other is the struggling daughter of Albion within her, who dies to "rise from Generation free"[14] in the final design, human-formed at last in her repudiation of "self-love that envies all" (E49/K194). The first is the woman who is cat, "snatching at a pleasure real but dangerous," in Empson's words; the second is that milder lady who seeks "true gold," whom Empson elsewhere calls "the more spiritual nymph" and Blake "the Human Form Divine."

That the same plunge should bring death to one and life to the other is to be understood from Blake's early views about sex. Love in the fallen world is never uncomplicated by jealousy, possessiveness, and cruelty; these are the motives of the cat, and they drown her.[15] But "fierce desire" is in itself a mark of life; the effort to gratify desire (rather than repress it) is a movement toward salva-

---

[13] The phrases are from *The Clod & the Pebble* (E19/K211).

[14] The phrase is from the text of *To Tirzah*.

[15] There is a provocative and altogether curious alliance between the Cat Ode designs and Blake's later designs to Milton's *L'Allegro* and *Il Penseroso*. I have already alluded to the reappearance of Gray's fish as "The Spirits of Water" (in {71}), but his cat may be found as well. The first *L'Allegro* design, entitled "Mirth," personifies "wanton wiles" as a young lady with fine catty whiskers—she is the dainty Selima of design 3, even to her heart-shaped face and bonnet (see detail {72}).

tion as it is both a partial repudiation of selfhood and the expression of an energy. These are the motives of the woman, and they drown her catness to save her humanity. In pictorial terms, plunging is a movement toward life, away from self-restriction; but self-contemplation is self-enclosure, and deadens the soul.

Gray's tone and double purpose do indeed present special problems to the illustrator, enormous ones if like Blake he aspires to be critic and interpreter as well. As we saw, Bentley brilliantly caught the tone, but ignored the double purpose. Blake carried the tone rather beyond its limits, yet he did not, I believe, intend to violate it. Rather he intended to expand the comic proportions of the poem until they reached those of a miniature divine comedy, concluding with a visionary glance toward paradise. The double purpose he thus extended even more forcefully. Ignoring the cautionary purport of Gray's moral, Blake felt he recognized in its elusive suggestiveness a visionary truth about love in the fallen world. Within the confines of that world it is grotesque and destructive and deserves satiric treatment. Interestingly, the same *Il Penseroso* design that yielded "Spirits of Water" analogous to those of the Gray designs also yields a tiny study of that love here satirized. At the top of the Milton design sit "The Three Destinies," each positioned over one of the "Circles of Plato's Heavens." According to Blake, "these Heavens are Venus, Jupiter & Mars." The Heaven of Venus—placed, perhaps significantly, beneath the cutting Destiny—depicts the love goddess presiding with voluptuous grace over two sets of tiny figures, a male and female bound back to back with serpents or thorny vines (they are unclear in reproduction, but in any case a version of those "iron threads of love & jealousy & despair" mentioned in *Jerusalem*, pl. 45 [31]), and on the other side two paler figures, a shunned and weeping female and a male departing from her, his left arm pushing her away behind him. The scene is of course again a vision of the love that binds and grieves.[16]

But where human love exhibits a desire to break the confines of the fallen world, to transcend selfhood and seek "true gold" like the gold of that burning bow with its arrows of desire celebrated at the outset of Blake's *Milton*—in short, where it is re-

[16] Compare to the plate of *VDA* which shows Oothoon and Bromion bound back to back on the shore of the sea of time and space, while near them sits the self-enclosed Theotormon, shunning Oothoon's offers of love.

demptive love—then it is a subject no longer proper for satire, but rather for jubilant prophecy.

Gray had divided his poem into a fable and a moral for the eighteenth-century ladies; looking far beyond Gray's moral, Blake sought to reveal in the story of Walpole's cat both a satiric view of the fallen world and a prophetic glance toward eternity. For those readers of Gray who are unfamiliar with Blake's work and his distinctive philosophy, these illustrations offer witty if rather loosely pertinent embellishment to the poem. But the student of Blake can find there, complete in only six designs, a singularly clear paradigm of Blake's method in his larger works, particularly revealing because it takes as its starting point not Blake's own prophetic mythology, but a modest poem which we all feel we can understand, and demonstrates before our eyes how Blake's literalizing art presses metaphor into metamorphosis, and makes of allegory a form at once visionary and intensely dramatic.[17]

[17] D.V.E. and J.E.G.: We look forward with great interest to Irene Tayler's forthcoming volume of and on *Blake's Illustrations to the Poems of Thomas Gray* (Princeton, 1971) reproducing and discussing all 116 of the designs.

14

Envisioning the First
Night Thoughts

JOHN E. GRANT

THE most important of Blake's unpublished works is the series of
537 water colors for Young's *Night Thoughts* that he painted
from about 1795 to 1797. Together with the 43 engravings selected from the first 156 drawings and published in 1797, and
the 15 or more copies of these engravings which were hand-colored
according to two or more basic schemes, the *Night Thoughts* pictures represent more than a quarter of Blake's productions as
an artist. Except for the descriptions of some 120 of the drawings
made by Shields in 1880 and essays by Comyns Carr in 1875,
Keynes in 1927, and Margoliouth in 1954, little of importance
about the designs themselves has been published before 1968.[1]

The problems involved in presenting both descriptions and
interpretations for the designs even of a single Night are formidable, and it seems advisable to begin with a plain verbal description of all the designs.[2] I shall complicate yet simplify this by

[1] See Frederick James Shields (B&N no. 1234B), J. Comyns Carr (B&N
nos. 993A and 993B), Geoffrey Keynes (B&N nos. 315 and 1462), and H. M.
Margoliouth (B&N nos. 1579A and 1579B); also Hagstrum, esp. pp. 121-123;
also W. E. Moss, "The Coloured Copies of Blake's 'Night Thoughts,'" *Blake
Newsletter*, II (1968), 19-23—written about 1942; G. E. Bentley, Jr., "A Census of Coloured Copies of Young's *Night Thoughts* (1797)," *Blake Newsletter*, II (1968), 41-45 (Bentley mentions the suggestive theory of Martin
Butlin, who is at work on a catalogue raisonné of Blake's painting, that the
colored copies were done in two batches, one in 1797, the other about 1805);
and Morton D. Paley, "Blake's Illustrations to Young's *Night Thoughts*," in
Rosenfeld, *Essays for Damon*.

[2] I write as one of a team preparing an edition, with commentary, of all
the *Night Thoughts* designs—the publication date not yet predictable. On
Night the First, the subject of the present essay, E. J. Rose and M. J. Tolley,
my principal collaborators, have completed a draft commentary with the
assistance of extensive notes and photographs I made in 1963. This essay
draws on their commentary and benefits from their criticism, but it is an
independent attempt to discuss the structure and meaning of Blake's designs.
I wish also to express my gratitude to our other associates in the project,

indicating certain thematic groupings in the sequence. I shall then discuss many of the designs at length, with particular reference to two formal and substantial questions, which may be headed "Young and Universals" and "Identity and Organization." But first a prefatory word about the relationship between the two "authors" of this work, Young and Blake.

Blake's attitude toward other authors is so forthright, especially in his marginalia, that it often seems simple as well—until we try to sum it up. His attitude toward Young is scarcely revealed in his few verbal references, but the evidence of his illustrative-illuminative collaboration is that it was similar to his attitude toward Thomas Gray, whose poems inspired his second-longest series of illustrations. That is, Blake was always critical, almost always hopeful, and occasionally grateful to his distinguished predecessor for telling important truths. He would never have undertaken this enormous project without feeling considerable sympathy for Young.

In his Preface Young states that "the occasion of this Poem was real, not fictitious," and that "the narrative is short and the morality arising from it makes the bulk of the Poem." Blake tended to accept the "morality" of Young's declaredly spontaneous reflections as an expression of the author's own imagination. But he was also inclined to ignore, or even subvert, the "morality" when it comes across as codified prescriptions for human behavior, rather than as what really interested him, the archetypes of human action and relationships, or "Universals." Thus on the title page for Night the First {74} of *The Complaint or Night-Thoughts on Life, Death, and Immortality* Blake has drawn no figure immediately recognizable as Edward Young, either as man or as author. Instead there is a scene in which a woman and children are about to be gathered into the hand of Death while another woman is in process of being translated, "new worlds to inherit." On the textless verso of the title page, however, where Blake is free to make his comment unlimited by Young's words, there is a remarkable scene {75} in which the scroll of a sleeping poet is transported down to be copied by a little old man. Together these designs

D. V. Erdman and Irene Tayler, for their suggestions, and to Judith Rhodes for her assistance. Perhaps I should make clear that work is well advanced on commentaries for most of the other Nights.

present a two-page pictorial table of contents in which the first episode of universal human ethics is contrasted with the more particularized and personalized comment on Young's capacities and habits as a poet.

Interpreting these pictures would be easier, though less interesting, if one could confidently recognize and relate identical characters every time they appear. It is sometimes difficult to be sure who is being depicted, however, even in the cases of Christ, Young, and Death, the three most important characters. The appearance of similar characters elsewhere in Blake's work is often a clue to the identity of a problematic figure or gesture. But the exact connections among these are sometimes more problematical than those among the characters in a single picture. One must also exercise discipline even in relating *Night Thoughts* designs that are far removed from one another, lest he fall into a web of subordinate relationships and lose track of the main thing, which is always the particular picture before him. The serious interpreter is committed to a preliminary consideration of such minutiae as hair style and color, eye color, clothing, and posture, among other factors, if he wants to be tolerably confident that he is responding to Blake's meaning rather than fabricating explanations that account for a few striking details of imagery. It has been implied by some commentators that the *Night Thoughts* designs are simpler and more obvious in meaning than the designs for Job or Dante, which were done when Blake was old. Other commentators have indicated that Blake merely used Young's text for jumping-off points for his own visions. Both schools can find supporting evidence, but neither provides an adequate theory for understanding the whole series.

The best immediate guides to Blake's meaning in most of the designs are to be found in Young's poem, where the most relevant lines are usually marked by Blake with a cross in the margin, though this device was not employed until well on in Night the First. Often the reader will understand the pictures best if he disregards the historical order of composition of poem and pictures and treats whole passages of the text as if they were rather plodding and frequently erroneous verse expositions of the pictures such as might have been produced by Crabb Robinson— who had talked with Blake and sometimes understood him. Used in this way, Young's poem will be found more "reliable" than the brief "Explanation of the Engravings" included in most copies of the published book, though the poem is always subject to "correction." Granted that Blake was more imaginative than Young, and that he was able to discover implications in Young's imagery that the elderly clergyman would never have recognized, one of the primary satisfactions to be gained from these designs is to see how Blake exploits the latent, often biblical, energy in Young's verses. Blake almost always found something in the approximately twenty lines of text on the typical page which he could illustrate or at least use as a point of departure. In most cases I shall take little explicit notice of Young's text, but this is simply to reduce the amount of data to be mentioned. The interpreter who disregards such information does so at his peril.

Any serious viewer of the designs will notice that there are thematic and imagistic connections between designs at various places throughout the series, as well as a preponderance of pictures dealing with the titular subject of each particular Night. That there is some overall organization of the designs is indicated by the fact that the two frontispieces (for the two volumes in which the designs were originally bound) are pictures of the resurrecting Christ. First (no. 1) he is the liberator who pushes aside heavy clouds as he mounts up from his cast-off grave clothes, which remain below to be venerated by tame angels; then (no. 265) he is the awakener, who returns to enlighten tormented sleepers in Death's realm of endless night. But these unmistakable connections of theme and character are no more decisive than the slightly less apparent connections of form and typology between the first and last (no. 537) designs. In this relationship the initial vision of Christ is complemented by the concluding picture of Samson, his prototype who liberated Israel by pulling down the columns of the Philistine temple or theater of Dagon, and, in so doing, assumed a position very like that of his successor when he unfolded the obscuring clouds. The fact that the pictures of these two great exemplars bracket the second and penultimate pictures (nos. 2 and 536), which contain the first and last portraits of Young, implies much about the relative importance in the series of Universals and the author of the *Night Thoughts*. As we shall see, however, Blake does begin the designs for Night the First with a strenuous attempt to delineate the character and capacities of Young.

Less evident than these large structural connections is an infra-structure of picture groups, consisting of two or more designs each, which form distinct and meaningful units within each of the Nights. The criteria for identifying a group must be quite flexible and there is usually more than one major theme or image in a group, which makes each group subdivisible. In general one should look for sequences of designs that are of similar length and are made up of interlocking concerns, often quite sharply distinguished from the design at the end of the previous group. In Night the First each of the units begins with a major incursion into the scene of a superhuman character from another realm of existence. This occurs in designs 6, 8, 13, 18, 24, 29, and 34 and marks the division of the Night into units of two, five, five, six, five, five, and two designs. This symmetry is complicated by the fact that the incursive figure in no. 13 is not a grand character from above like Death in nos. 8, 18, and 29 but a butterfly-winged boy who has broken up through the surface of the Earth-egg. And the small woman who flies in at the left in no. 34 might hardly be noticed by the casual viewer. Moreover Death makes an entrance in no. 31 which is even more impressive than his appearance in no. 29. Many other such objections can and should be raised, but the dimensions of this hypothesis cannot be truly understood until one has achieved a thorough familiarity with the particulars of each design. A synopsis of the designs for the Preface and Night the First follows, accompanied by my outline of the infrastructure.

Descriptions of the Designs

The following descriptions are factual rather than interpretive, except that the characters are usually designated by the names indicated in the relevant lines of Young's poem. This may seem like a harmless attempt to sophisticate the presentation, but errors at this primary level would, of course, seriously distort the subsequent interpretation.[3]

[3] The number assigned to each design is the one penciled (not by Blake) at the bottom center of the framing inlay paper. Only colors with a distinct or unusual function are mentioned, and pentimenti are disregarded. The eleven engraved versions of designs for Night the First are treated as variants and are designated only by the arabic number and the abbreviation eng., which indicates that the design was engraved and included in the 1797 illustrated edition, B&N no. 422. Engravings for the first two Nights are repro-

Prefatory Designs

The first five designs—the general frontispiece, the recto and verso of the general title page, and the recto and verso of Young's general Preface—serve to introduce the entire series. They will be discussed only as they relate to Night the First, but they contain prefigurations of many of the important images of the whole series. All are described here to let the reader see how Blake sets forth what he thinks Young is about. Four themes are announced:

A (no. 1) Resurrection: Christ
B (2-3) Young
C (4) Woman and Children
D (5) A Poet Inspired

No. 1 (eng. used as title page for Night the Fourth). Used as the frontispiece for the first of the two volumes in which the designs were bound after being inlaid in larger sheets of paper. The naked Christ in Resurrection mounts through clouds and parts them with his hands. At either side below, winged angels kneel and contemplate the rejected shroud. (Hagstrum pl. 64.)

No. 2. Title page. Young as a young curly-headed man sits up, bare-chested, in bed and reads from a large book by the light of a shell- or leaf-shaped lamp. At the left and behind, a young nude man leans back while standing cross-legged and resting his right hand on the handle of a shovel as he looks out. Below him, an old white-bearded man lies in a grave. At the right above Young's head, a pile of dark clouds is being climbed by a nude young man.

No. 3. Verso of title page. At the left and below the text a dark patch of sky with six huge stars is surrounded by white clouds. Mounting the clouds with a stick in his left hand is a nude young man who has yellow curly hair. As in the previous design, the reader assumes the wayfarer must be Young himself.

No. 4. Preface. In a patch of blue sky at the right a young woman in a white dress with wonderfully long yellow hair holds in her arms twin infants with yellow curly hair who raise their arms as she looks down at them.

No. 5. End of Preface. Below and at the left a powerful Poet with long wavy yellow hair and blue eyes and wearing a blue robe looks up into the light descending from a yellow luminary which appears as a crescent otherwise obscured by a dark circular object. He leans

duced, rather faintly, in Butterworth, B&N no. 423. Water colors reproduced in other books are indicated when they are not included in the present volume.

on his right elbow and holds a poised white plume in his hand, ready to write on a huge scroll which rests in his lap and bends around his knees and under him to form the base of a scroll-shaped couch that is raised at the left end, on which he leans {73}.

Designs for Night the First

Blake's designs for the first Night are symmetrically divided into five major groups. A central section of six designs is preceded and followed by groups of five. These are bracketed by two minor groups, introductory and concluding pairs. Among designs which cohere as a group, careful study will reveal decisive thematic and imagistic connections. At the same time, individual designs are often related to designs in other groups and in other Nights.

Group I (nos. 6 and 7) The Complaint and the Devolution

No. 6 (and 6 eng.). The huge figure of Death as a bearded old man looms over a woman and five children as he bends down and sweeps them away with his right hand. The woman holds a distaff on her right leg and draws a thread from it with her left hand. Two children play at the harp. Two others stand at the woman's knee, a girl reading and a boy presenting a scroll to her. The fifth, in scribal position in front, plies his pen on a sheet. Death's open left hand rests on his knee, providing a platform for a nude young woman, seen from the rear, who rises as a clothed semitransparent spirit to be greeted by two angels. The ends of Death's bow and arrow are visible beside his right foot {74}.

No. 7. Above the (empty) text-box, a writer with a laurel crown has fallen asleep, pen in hand, over his enormous scroll, which is being carried down by two male spirits to the lower area beneath the box, where it is read by a small, bearded old man in white—he is Death much reduced in stature—who is seated in a scribal position beneath a barren tree with a pen poised to write on a sheet of paper {75}.

Group II (nos. 8-12) Night Thoughts: Transcendence Frustrated
        A (no. 8) Thinking
        B (9-10) Night, Thought
        C (11-12) Quest, Limit

No. 8 (8 eng.). Young as a young man completely muffled in his robe, except for his head and right toes, leans on his right elbow and probably holds in his right hand a large object, which is hidden by his robe, perpendicularly a little above the ground. He is lying sleepless with a vine at his head while a woolly dog and a flock of sheep are being visited by winged "Sleep," who bears a wand and is silhouetted against the starry night sky as he bends to the flock. In another break in the clouds above the text a smaller man in white sleeps peacefully on his side {76}.

No. 9. The gigantic, dark, long-haired, muffled figure of "Night," seen against a dark cloud background, holds a scepter and spreads her robes over half a planet, the bottom of which is lost in white clouds {77}.

No. 10. "Thought" as a small young woman in yellow rises at the right above the grasp of the seated and muffled figure of "Darkness" and supplicates a great white-winged female, "Silence," who appears above the text with her finger raised to her lips. Behind her a dead branch projects from under her robes down toward a green skull which lies face up in water at the bottom left near the covered feet of Darkness {78}.

No. 11. A figure of the "Mind" as a naked masculine pilgrim, with a stick in his left hand and shading his eyes with his right, strides up toward three children at the left; they are: a girl reading, a boy flying a kite, which is shown above the text, and another boy who holds a cricket bat and points to the right. Behind the pilgrim is a stone sarcophagus with a vaguely delineated statue of a woman on it, foliage hanging over it, a headstone leaning against it, and a dead branch on the ground near it {79}.[4]

No. 12. Above the text, a supplicating woman in a blue dress, "Fears," prays distractedly, while a kneeling woman in a yellow dress, "Hopes," peers down the side of the text at a huge man below. He is seen by the viewer head on with long hair hiding his face and bare outspread arms, lying prone on a black cloud {80}.

Group III (nos. 13-17) The Circle of Destiny and Edward Young
    A (no. 13) Male Aspiration
    B (14-15) Young's Distractions
    C (16-17) Female Aspiration, Masculine Error

No. 13. Below the text, a boy with spotted violet butterfly wings mounts in a flameburst, with outspread arms and trailing his left leg in a crack, to the surface of a planet. Above, a boy sleeps silhouetted against an oak leaf {81}.

No. 14 (14 eng.). Below sleeps the gray-clad loosely draped Poet, pen in hand, with his head resting on his book. Above the cloud over his head and around the text are six dream episodes enacted by six nude males and a draped female: he ventures beneath barren trees, cavorts

---

[4] There is another water color version in the Huntington Library. It is on vellum and reversed, with a different text and variant details. Evidently derived from no. 11, probably by Blake, it has a status comparable to that of an engraving. See C. H. Collins Baker, B&N no. 541, pl. 31.

among clouds, dances with the yellow-clad woman, holds onto a dead branch, falls headlong, and swims on water at the lower left {82}.

No. 15. A young man in a white gown kneels and prays at the foot of a newly dug grave, which is beneath a tree that projects a leafed branch over the text and above the head of the mourner.

No. 16. Below the text, a great broken blue eggshell releases a long-haired naked female spirit, who ascends at the right. Above the text a yellow cocoon is silhouetted against an oak leaf while the stem of another oak leaf curls around the right corner of the text and the leaf itself is at the right edge of the text {83}.

No. 17. Below is a chain-encircled dark sphere, within which an aged human-torsoed green caterpillar, "Reason," with a long beard and bald head, looks at himself in a mirror held in his left hand. His sphere partly surrounds the text and hangs by a chain from a huge starred blue sphere, the bottom of which appears across the top of the picture. At the left a draped female spirit looks at the scene below with her hands raised in dismay {84}.

Group IV (nos. 18-23) The Poet Awakened to Visions of the
Empire of Death
A (nos. 18 + 20) Death
B (19 + 21) Mortality
C (22 + 23) Bondage

No. 18 (18 eng.). The huge, long-bearded figure of Death with a bell in his left hand advances at the right and awakens the Poet, who had been sleeping bare-chested under a blue coverlet and now looks up with alarm. Behind him, on a table under the text, are an hour-glass, a plume and inkwell, a lighted lamp, and an open book {85}.

No. 19. Below the text, "domestic Comfort," a woman in a long pink dress and open-toed yellow sandals, bends over to mourn "Bliss," a boy in a white gown who is laid out on her legs. On two stalks of yellow wheat, which issue from beneath her and curve through the text, are three small female "Moments," holding sickles in their right hands. An ear of wheat hangs at the left and another naked small female with a sickle rises up at the right behind the woman.

No. 20 (20 eng.). Bearded "Death" in white holds the sun in his left hand above the text and prepares to smite it with an arrow held in his right hand. His feet rest on the white draped intertwined bodies of two crowned kings, who represent "Empire." In the water color version the king at the left has been decapitated {86}.

No. 21. "Thought," a nude youthful male murderer, looks up while holding a bluish dagger in his right hand. On the rocks below lies the outstretched nude body of a male victim. At the left above stand at least six female departed "Joys," who wear white dresses and huddle together while the central one throws up her arms in distress.

No. 22. At the right, "Oppression," a crowned dark-haired woman who wears a yellow scaly breastplate and a long skirt, holds a chain in her left hand at her knee and a scepter in her right, which rests on the text-box. Behind her right arm are a bishop's flat orange hat and a yellow miter as well as a crozier. A chain dangles down at the left from the head of the scepter. Below in a cavern two male miners, dressed in yellow and blue, who are representatives of "mankind," kneel and wield picks, while a third, dressed in light brown, carries off a yellow basket on his back. (Hagstrum, pl. 66a, also in Margoliouth, B&N nos. 1579A and B.)

No. 23. Below the text, two enslaved oarsmen in skirts, but with naked torsos, are chained to oars with which they propel a rowboat through water. Above at the left are dark clouds, against which are seen a flight of five birds. (In Keynes, B&N no. 315.)

> Group v (nos. 24-28) The Empire of Disease
> > A (no. 24) Sin
> > B (25-26) Quests
> > C (27-28) Losses

No. 24 (24 eng.). At the right, a lithe female figure in a long gray and yellow dress that loops above the text, dives down and with her left hand empties the contents of a vial into the ear of a shepherd who reclines while leaning on his left elbow. He wears a deep blue skirt, and carries a crook over his right shoulder, under which part of his mantle is displayed. With her right hand the woman discharges the contents of another vial toward a sheep which lies above and behind his lap. "Disease" is contained in the vials, but the woman herself is identifiable as Sin. Against a background of two hills are at least two other sheep, which sleep beside a short-haired dog.

No. 25. Below the text, against a background of two hills, a naked man with a short beard strides off to the left, a stick in his left hand. Behind him the lion of "Fate" paces with mouth open. Above the text a looping spotted snake of "Passion" reaches down toward the man with open mouth.

No. 26. At the lower right, an old man with a beard is seen from behind. He wears a long brownish gown and holds a stick in his right hand as he reaches up with his left hand toward a spotted yellow butterfly. He has passed by five blue, bell-shaped flowers and four roses, which grow beneath a thin tree that gently bends over the text and has a few tiny pale leaves at the right.

No. 27 (27 eng.). Below the text, a man with loose yellow-green knickers and bare chest lies back with his arms stretched out against two rocks, which are backed by a third and shaded by foliage. Around him is wrapped a spotted snake of "Misfortune" with its mouth open. Kneeling at his side is a woman with blowing hair and wearing a long pink dress, absorbed in holding back a small boy wearing only trousers who is trying to catch a variegated bird. In the engraved version eight flying birds are added at the left and the text is draped at the sides by a double leafy vine that grows from the top. A singing bird is seated in the vine.

No. 28. Below the text, "Earth," a large girl wearing a white dress, rests her elbows on a hillock with her legs stretched out to the right. She raises her hands in despair as she looks down at two naked "joys," who are stretched out beside pieces of drapery, one supine, the other, wearing a turban, prone. At the left, a small joy wearing a long white dress departs in sorrow. At the right above, a bird flies away into the clouded sky. (In Keynes, B&N no. 315.)

Group VI (nos. 29-33) Death's Power and the Ages of Man
    A (nos. 29-30) Death and Philander
    B (31) Death and the Family
    C (32-33) Senility

No. 29. Below the text, in a dark spot amidst bright clouds, bearded "Death" points with his left hand at the white draped, stretched-out, round-faced figure of "Philander," whose head rests on green, bladelike leaves and whose feet are blended into the area at the right. With his right hand Death beckons in a huge curled brown worm which is poised at the right. Above the text is an hourglass in which the sand has run down.

No. 30. Below and at the right, naked Philander sits with his right leg stretched out on a long rock of "Adamant" under the text and holds up in his right hand the mop of a yellow distaff which rests on his right thigh. He looks open-mouthed at the reader as he handles a thread falling from the bunch with his deeply shaded left hand near the end of the rock at the lower right. Above, four small women in red, yellow, blue, and green dresses come out of a cloud and enter the bunch of fibers. Below, at the left, the sun is setting behind a dark blue hill.

No. 31 (31 eng.). At the left, bearded "Death" swoops down with a feathered arrow poised in his right hand to strike a reclining woman in white who leans on her right elbow. Her right breast is bared but part of the white coverlet is draped over her head. Kneeling before her, embracing and kissing her, is a naked small boy who is also in the line of the stroke. The background is a dark purple canopy, the lighter edge of which extends around the text.

No. 32. At the bottom lies a long-bearded old jester wearing a dunce's cap with a bell at its tip and a pale shirt beneath a matching yellow robe. His face is rested disconsolately in his left hand, and in his right hand limply stretched along his thigh he holds a pinwheel stick. On either side of the text behind him grow up curling branches of a grapevine with leaves and a bunch of green grapes above his head.

No. 33. At the left, in front of a hill, stands a bearded middle-aged man in a blue robe, supported by crutches and counting two coins in his left hand. He carries a money bag on his right wrist. On the hillside at the right are roots, around which are growing vines with unnaturally sinister triangular leaves.

Group VII (nos. 34-35) What Moved Young

No. 34 (34 eng.). Below the text, Young, as a young man dressed in a long white gown and wrapped in briar vines with tiny leaves, his left ankle chained with a manacle, is stretched out on grass reading from a book. At the left, a small woman plunging downward has caught her long yellow dress in a branch of the briars. Beneath her the open-mouthed "Nightingale" is singing in a fork of the vine near the Poet's head. Above the Poet are four stars in a dark sky. In a clouded area at the right are three women in long dark dresses; one sitting on the Poet's rump, one departing on his legs, and one rising up and away. A fourth uncolored one can be seen entering a white cloud at the upper right. Flying above the text is a tiny brown "Lark" {87}.

No. 35 (35 eng.). At the left, the Poet, in a long white gown and holding a curved yellow lyre in his upstretched right hand, aspires to fly, but is held down by a manacle and chain on his right ankle. Below and to the right are coils of the briar thicket from which he has escaped, now showing more distinct tiny leaves, but barren at the right.

Personae of Young in the Designs of the First Night

The contrasting designs on the title page and the textless verso, nos. 6 and 7, the second of which was not engraved, signify the division of attention in Night the First between the public "Complaint" that Young knew he was making and the personal "Night Thoughts" in which, through a kind of free association, Young reveals more than he realized to Blake, the artistic analyst of imagination. This distinction between the public poem in which the preacher speaks with public validity and the private poem which betrays the weaknesses of Edward Young is not rigorously maintained throughout the series, but it need not be since the viewer has been given such unmistakable notice of the discrimination at the outset. For the sake of brevity my discussion will concentrate on authorial figures, but in many designs the vision is not peculiarly applicable to Young in any of his roles. It would be a mistake to suppose that the inside or personal story was all that really interested Blake. His idealist premises do, however, necessitate a continuous assessment of the author even when he is uttering conventional generalities—even ones Blake himself agreed with. Folly remains folly, whether it is spoken with the voice of one or of many. The same is true of wisdom.

The first major section of five designs, which I have entitled "Night Thoughts: Transcendence Frustrated" (Group II), recapitulates motifs appearing in the prefatory designs. I shall not pause to document this assertion in detail, but the connection between the wakeful reclining Young in no. 2 and the figure of Young in no. 8 is patent. In the latter design he appears, not clearly as a poet nor even quite as a shepherd, but as an insomniac, the main figure below the text. He is contrasted with the small figure above the text, who is evidently one of those mentioned in the poem "who wake no more," but is nevertheless to be understood as sleeping rather than finally dead. This is because "Mercy chang'd Death into Sleep" (*To Tirzah*) in the Resurrection of the Spiritual Body depicted in no. 1 and also no. 264. This simultaneous image of Young and his contrasted double occurs throughout the series at crucial times, after having been adumbrated in nos. 2 and 7. In no. 9 the humanized image of "Night" is a closer analysis of the dark area in no. 8. She in turn is modulated into the figure of "Darkness" in no. 10, where the winged figure of "Sleep" in no. 8 has become modulated into winged Silence, though she occupies the position of the sleeper above the text. Her pupil, Young's "tender Thought," whom she is converting into *"Reason,"* is a modulation of the sleeper in no. 8, though she occupies the position of the wings of Sleep. The fatal consequences of this miseducation for Young himself are shown at the bottom left, by the feet of Darkness. The skull sunk in the water beneath the barren branch of Silence is a degeneration of the wakeful Young beside his vine in no. 8 and was prefigured by the old man in the grave in no. 2.

In no. 11 the relationship of male and female is reversed, with

Young projected as the active, questing pilgrim with his staff who leaves behind the barren branch as he climbs in pursuit of childhood—but who also passes by the tomb in which the remains of his emanation are buried, doubtless as a consequence of her conversion into "Reason" in no. 10. In no. 12 he has mounted higher than the kite of no. 11 and higher even than the dark cloud in the background of Night in no. 9, but in so doing he reaches a dead end of active transcendence and there despairs from a sense of unfulfillment at having become the possessor of that mere vacuum, "a dread Eternity." The position he takes is at once sovereign and defeated, being that of divine malefactors, such as the ancient sky-god who smites with disease in *The House of Death* {93} or Albion's Urizenic Angel in *America* 8 {36} or, on the other hand, defeated benefactors, such as the long-haired angel in the frontispiece to *America* {24}. The emanation of this Albion in no. 12 is split into the distraught women called by Young his Fears and Hopes and by Blake, Vala and Jerusalem. The yellow-clad Hopes is derived from no. 10 and the blue-clad Fears will occur again in no. 17. In understanding this climactic design the reader must concentrate on the implications of Young's crucial line 64, "A dread Eternity! How surely *mine!*" Young's insistence on developing his Reason at the expense of his emanative faculties recapitulates the archetypal error of Urizen: his very success traps him into assuming the form of an unholy spirit brooding over a vacuum. This fatal commitment is the essence of Blake's case against Young, but Blake must have thought it a glorious error too, such as could only have been committed by a poet who had the power as well as aspirations to reach such heights.

Young's error recapitulates those of other great men of the Age of Reason, such as Bacon and Newton and Locke, or Alexander Pope, and even John Milton. Thus Blake would hardly wish to dwell on Young's own personal shortcomings for the rest of the *Night Thoughts*, since they were symptomatic of his age and of a whole anti-imaginative attitude toward life which Blake believed was responsible for the misery in the world. Consequently, in the following section Blake's reader looks at a sequence of human endeavors which Young himself is now able to see in their true perspective for the first time. As usual, cosmic scenes are interspersed with mundane ones because Truth cannot be understood when looked at exclusively from one or the other perspective.

The reader of Blake encounters many treadmill stories in which promising new beginnings fade away into ancient errors and perennial frustrations. Blake called this progress the "Circle of Destiny" and Northrop Frye has given it the useful name of "the Orc cycle." Nos. 13 and 17 together provide a thorough summary of the cycle from Orc to Urizen. In no. 13, below the text a winged boy, a combination of figures in *Gates of Paradise* 3 and 6, rises like the dawn from a sphere which is at once the earth and a round egg. The sleeping boy and the oak leaf above are a compound of images in the frontispiece to *Gates of Paradise, Holy Thursday* in *Songs of Experience*, and *America* 11 {39}. The contrast between the sleeping figure above and the waking one below also parallels no. 8 and, like it, is derived from no. 7, though the vision here is more impersonal. It is part of Blake's subversive symbolism that regeneration should come from below but, as has been observed, the bottom is a great way down, and it is difficult for even a radical analysis to get to the root of the difficulty. Blake does so pictorially in no. 17 by presenting a vision of what it is that prevents the boy in no. 13 (a more cosmic version of the boy in *America* 2 {27}) from getting his other foot loose. The starry sphere at the top of no. 17 is a macrocosmic blow-up of the diurnal sphere of no. 13, and it is penetrated by the connecting link of the chain which fades off and implicitly links with the quasi-umbilical line beneath the boy's left foot in no. 13. In no. 17 it is unmistakable that Blake intends Young's text to be recognized as part of the anti-progressive link-up. The author himself confesses to his complicity in lines 157-161:

> How, like a Worm, was I wrapt round and round
> In Silken thoughts, which reptile *Fancy* spun,
> Till darkened *Reason* lay quite clouded o'er
> With soft conceit of endless Comfort *here*,
> Nor yet put forth her Wings to reach the skies!

But even now he does not see that *Reason*, not *Fancy*, is at the bottom of his difficulty. The problem displayed is universal; schematically we can see he is an old mole who has lost or buried his initiative and accepted the motherhood of the worm in *Gates of Paradise* 16, and cannot see anything but himself through the narrow links in his chain. Though he is more degenerate and his surroundings seem less prepossessing, he is Har or Adam Struldbrug.

One also recalls the great Ancient of Days frontispiece to *Europe* {8} and Blake's Reprobate impudence *To God*, viz. "If you have form'd a Circle to go into / Go into it yourself & see how you would do" (E508/K557). The symbolism of a human caterpillar derives from the frontispiece to *Gates*. Though here it is connected to an old man, the beginning and end of this creature are pretty much the same. The mirror, on the other hand, is the traditional *speculum vanitatis*, but Blake's overall vision of this home of reaction has a more specific derivation.

Most of the crucial details in the picture can be found in Book III of *Paradise Lost*, either literally or by parodistic inversion. According to Milton's cosmology, the universe with Earth at its center is hung from Heaven by Means of the Great Chain of Being. This rationalization of traditional symbolism Blake must have thought appalling, since by analogy such cosmology tends to legitimate any other system of bondage that depends on chains to hold it together. But in III, 418ff. Milton describes a Limbo of Vanity or Paradise of Fools, a kind of darkened anti-Earth, on which Satan (later to be a great worm) first lands on his journey up out of Hell. He then travels on from this as yet unpopulated place and arrives at the Sun where, in disguise, he talks with the unfallen angel Uriel, who is stationed in the source of light. In Night the Seventh, Young remembered Uriel, and Blake drew a splendid picture of that angel in his illuminated sphere (no. 339), but Young's conception of the sublime could not easily contain a conception as rough and satirical as Milton's limbo of Vanity. In no. 17 Blake exchanges Milton's Heaven for the firmament, depicts a chain of bondage rather than one of dependency, expropriates the dark sphere of Vanity, and combines the great worm with a parody of the great angel to construct Urizen, "darkened Reason." The gray-haired female soul in blue at the left is also operationally identical with the disguised Satan in Milton, while her specific lineage in these designs is from the distraught fearful blue-clad emanation in no. 12; she is the opposite of the liberated emanation in no. 16 and represents a lower state of ineffectuality than the hopeful yellow-clad emanation who looks down in no. 12. Plate 4 of *Thel* is practically captioned by the first line: "Then Thel astonish'd view'd the Worm upon its dewy bed" and is the pictorial prototype of this design. Here the dominant emotion of the errant emanation seems to be pity, and it is dubious whether this

319

emotion can in any way be helpful in the necessary task of rending this dungeon that is held together by a chain of self-indulgences.

The great caterpillar is locked into his snug darkness by his own fashionable and vain night thoughts. As such he represents a "consolidation of error" still more appalling than that depicted in no. 12 at the end of the first main movement within the designs. This benighted enclave is more contemptible too when seen, as even the timorous emanation sees it, divested of the contingencies and amenities that make folly seem tolerable, or even dignified, in the created universe of time and space. In his verses Young himself came close to envisioning his own problem, but true recognition was obscured by his proliferation of images, which are fancifully conceived rather than organically imagined. It has sometimes been implied that in deriving his images from the *Night Thoughts* Blake's motivation was not more serious than that of a man who plays a game with another man's equipment. To Blake, however, it must have seemed that his art had to include psychological, sociological, and religious dimensions and that what he had to show was how these matters could be articulated without being understood by their sententious, verbose, clergyman-author. When that old fool looked into the mirror, there was no reflection and thus he couldn't recognize what he had become. The following words in Young's text on this page provided themes and images for Blake's synoptic design: Time, Death, Flight, threescore years, push, Eternity, Human Thought, smother, souls immortal, Dust, soul immortal, spending, Fires, wasting, strength, strenuous Idleness, Tumult, raptur'd, alarm'd, this scene, threaten, or indulge, Censure, myself, Heart, encrusted, World, self-fetter'd, groveling Soul, like a Worm, wrapt round and round, silken thought, reptile *Fancy*, spun, darkened *Reason*, lay, clouded o'er. In short, every-. thing Young said was used against him. And, to repeat, something like this is what Young was actually trying to say himself, both consciously and implicitly. Young's self-criticism sprang not from false modesty but an uneasy awareness that he was not what he should be. The error which underlay all the shortcomings to which he confessed, however, continued to elude Young. He could not make the imaginative connection which is the teleology of his words. What Blake did was to put all these elements together in a simple intelligible whole in order to show what the drift of these verses implies. No wonder the emanation is dismayed at the revelation.

This way of accounting for Blake's accomplishment is too mechanistic, but it indicates how much assistance Young unwittingly provided. Blake was not primarily concerned either to analyze or discredit Young, whose limitations are significant only as they exemplify universal human failings. If one imaginatively stands apart from immersion in the processes of a society or an age, as Blake certainly did from what had survived of the Age of Reason, he quickly sees how appalling are the images that the society or age is content to project of itself. In such a perspective what these groups complacently profess as their virtues are frequently less attractive than the secret vices alleged by their enemies. The same mechanisms are at work in individual vanity, as Blake reminds us by the use of the traditional mirror: the vermin-man presumably thinks his humanoid bust is splendid, whereas, if he were able to see himself as others do, he would discover that it is his huge caterpillar tail that is at least wonderful in size, whereas his human characteristics are not at all attractive. By connecting this design as a formal sequel to no. 13 Blake wished to present a comprehensive account of the way of the world in history. There can perhaps be other views of the matter than Blake's, but it is doubtful whether they take so much into account.

It is evident that no. 17 contains satire directed against "Reason," but both the lineage and meaning of the symbolism and the concern of the observing soul make it apparent that the dis-humanized caterpillar represents cosmic error and corruption. When the prophet Ezekiel took up his lamentation against the King of Tyre he discovered that his malefactions were larger and more disturbing than the foul deeds commonly perpetrated by kings, and thus demanded mythical expression. In this perspective the King appeared to be nothing less than the Cherub who prohibits man from exercising his birthright of feeding from the Tree of Life. Blake was to give the Covering Cherub his ultimate verbal definition in the text of *Jerusalem* 89. While this caterpillar-man is not as pernicious as a king, his extraordinary self-absorption is the psychological precondition for sublime malefactions. Symbolically it is only a short step from this worm chained in vanity to the uncontrollable dragon that the angel struggles vainly to subdue in the great painting *Michael and Satan* (Blunt, pl. 39a). In the final plates of *Jerusalem* Los and Albion and evidently Blake himself must work out their spiritual relationship with this monster. After having sunk into such an abysmal state during his sleep of reason, an awakening from this oblivion in no. 18, the first design of the next movement, was inevitable.

Designs 14, 15, and, to a lesser extent, 16 confirm the diagnosis of Young's case and show how closely regeneration is related to degeneration but also why they are not inextricably bound together. No. 14 combines the optimistic vision of the general title page, no. 2, with the pessimistic vision of the verso of the title page of Night the First, no. 7. Here Young sleeps by a book he is writing, whereas in no. 2 he was awake reading a book and in no. 7 he slept over a scroll he was writing. As before, the small figures enact the hopes and fears of his mental quest. The optimistic progress up the right side above his head in no. 2 is continued over the top of the text in company with a dancing girl in yellow, who is derived from the girls in nos. 10 and 12. Then the little dream man falls headlong down at the left, like the scroll-porters in no. 7, into water in which it is at least possible to swim. Between the swimmer in no. 14 and the drowned skull of no. 10 Blake's symbolism includes the drowning man of *Gates of Paradise* 10, who is just conscious enough to cry "Help! Help!" The dream explorer of the dead woods in no. 14 is a timorous successor of the bold pilgrim of no. 11 but foreshadows Los, who, as a clad adventurer, will explore the Caverns of the Grave by entering a gothic doorway in the first page of *Jerusalem*.

In no. 15 a rather epicene person, decently clad, is praying humbly at the foot of a grave such as the more energetic nude figure had dug in no. 2. That this simple act of piety is nevertheless exceptionable is subtly suggested by the exaggeratedly horizontal branch of the "Cypress" tree that strives to spread its "gloom" over his head, thus delineating a sinister square quasi-lintel over the text—see *Gates of Paradise* 15, etc. These leaves are similar to those that shaded the tomb of the emanation in no. 11. In general the error dealt with in this design is that Young was notorious as the very type of the graveyard poet, and such obsessions with death, however respectable, must be recognized as necrophilia. We have already seen in no. 2 the old man in the grave, whom an independent-minded person would not need nor wish to venerate, especially after having had a closer look at him as Death in no. 6, and again as Urizen the scribe in no. 7. If it seems excessively ingenious to derive so much significance from so simple a design as this, it is because we have not yet learned to understand Blake's designs in their pictorial context the way we would, as a matter of course, expect to approach his poetry.

A corroboration of the view presented here is contained in the whole design for *The Garden of Love* in *Songs of Experience*. There a priest leads a boy, who looks extremely like the devotee in no. 15, as well as a girl, in prayer at the foot of a grave. Being a clergyman himself, Young couldn't see what is wrong with this kind of behavior, but by employing a kind of X-ray vision in the Song, Blake had already shown his reader the invisible worms who have inherited the Garden of Love. In no. 15 Blake presents what seems to be the first example of a wholly natural vision in the *Night Thoughts*. The lack of a "spiritual cause" in this picture makes it seem at first anecdotal and then enigmatic until one recalls the proleptic explanation in the Song. And to confirm the effective presence of the unseen worm in no. 15, Blake will shortly display the ultimate religious caterpillar in no. 17, the antichrist who feeds on "the rejected corse of Death." It is significant that the mourner is by himself in no. 15 because his only future, for better or for worse, is downward and alone. Further confirmation of this interpretation of the design is contained in the fourth illustration for Gray's *Elegy*, no. 107 of the designs for Gray's poems, which combines motifs from the *Night Thoughts* designs with ones from *The Garden of Love*. Such analogies make it perfectly clear that the criticism of morbidity is not directed against Young alone, but this author characteristically is at pains to associate himself with mourners who wish they were dead. To mope in this way is really the opposite of the kind of reverence Blake felt for his dead brother Robert because, for Blake, Robert was still a vitalizing presence in his life, whereas the dead in Young's life tended to be haunting spirits who encouraged the poet to interminable effusions.

There is a declension from the butterfly boy and the human boy on an oak leaf in no. 13 to the "dishumanized" chrysalis on an oak leaf above the text in no. 16. But the yellow color of the cocoon connects it with the yellow-clad girls of nos. 10, 12, and 14. The fact that the extra oak leaf beside the text is now unoccupied indicates that the male has fallen away while his yellow emanation is reduced to a condition of subhuman latency. This state objectifies the hermaphroditic plight of the mourner in the previous design, in which the female principle becomes introjected or suspended when the male principle is absorbed with death. But a kind of homeostasis operates in human affairs: the dark emanation is shown effecting an escape from this world, which is changed in symbolism from an insect egg, as in no. 13, to a blue bird's egg or "mundane shell," a traditional symbol for the potentially vital world which Blake had already used in *Gates of Paradise* 6. Young's lines show that he knew this oviparous symbolism as well as any clergyman should who had read the opening of *Paradise Lost*. At any rate, this emanation will be only dimly perceived until she appears again at the end of the Night.

Whereas the analysis in nos. 14 and 15 is mundane, that in nos. 13 and 16 is universal and prepares the way for a cosmic analysis in no. 17. Specifically, no. 16 reminds the reader that woman had been almost left out of the account in no. 14, was totally absent from the picture in no. 13, and was hidden far within in no. 15. The symmetry of design and mutually parodistic imagery of nos. 13 and 16 are essential for an understanding of how it is with men and women. A thorough interpretation of no. 16 would require that the design be located within Blake's vision of the relationships of the sexes. Since there is no adequate published summary of this tangled subject, I shall not attempt to deal with it here. But I believe Blake would have been happy if the spectator recalled no. 16 when he saw Jerusalem on the penultimate page of his last epic. (See {103}.)

The last three major sections have much less particular applicability to Young as a Poet or even as a man. The obvious exception to this rule is no. 18, where the man as delinquent poet is rudely awakened from his slumbers by the intervention of Death the Bellman. This occurs at the start of the only section which has as many as six designs.

Each of the major concluding sections begins with the onset of a supernatural being: in IV (no. 18), Death the awakener to alert the sleeping Poet; in V (no. 24), Disease as Sin the soporific to perpetuate the slumbers of a sleeping shepherd; in VI (no. 29), Death the concluder to do away with the dead Philander. Each of the sections ends with a scene of bondage in which some element of

324

hope can still be discerned. At the end of IV (no. 23) the galley-slaves are set against the five birds, which recall to the reader the following apothegm etched on the walls of Hell:

> How do you know but ev'ry Bird that cuts the airy way,
> Is an immense world of delight, clos'd by your senses five?
>
> (E35/K150)

At the end of V (no. 28) the dead joys and the mourning Earth are set against the escaping female spirit and the departing bird of paradise. Most of these images are repeated from the illuminated books: the gesture of "Earth" recalls that of the emanation in no. 17, but the figure particularly recalls that of the heroine in *Thel* 4, while the dead male joy is in the same position as the spirit of a cloud in the same plate and the dead girl joy is repeated from *Gates of Paradise* 7; the departing spirit is identical with the Lily depicted in *Thel* 2. And the bird is practically identical with the one on the title page of *Songs of Innocence and of Experience* {9} which is able to weather the wrath falling on Adam and Eve—the prototypes of the two dead joys. For the student of Blake, these affinities are assurances that discernible implications of hope actually occur in the pessimistic no. 28. In VI (no. 33) crippled miserly Prudence has least to hope for, in spite of the fact that his objective circumstances seem less bereft than those in nos. 23 and 28, at least as the world judges. But if he is halt, he is still ambulatory, and on the road in spite of himself. And his hair is still that of a man not in extreme old age. Like the gaffers on crutches depicted in *London* {18} and in *Jerusalem* 84 {100} he might still be redeemed by a child.[5] Even those ominous leaves on the roots at the right can be overcome by the man who will press on, for very similar ones that grow on the trunk of the tree at the right in the frontispiece to *Songs of Experience* {15} do not deter the image of the youthful bard or the mental traveler who there confronts the

---

[5] This projection of a future may seem too speculative to be critically legitimate or too sentimental to be imaginatively satisfying. But Blake's conscious task as a prophet-artist was to delineate all the paradigms of human life, that the reader-viewer learn to see the "result" of going on in any particular life-style (cf. E607/K392). In the more pessimistic perspective offered by *Gates* 14 and 15 we can say also of the man in no. 33 that he may well not be rescued at Death's Door by an innocent child but instead decline to the haunted nether world of Hecate and the worm. Indeed, this fortune is assured unless he lifts up his eyes from his money.

reader. This regenerate man accepts the perils of an activist creative life because he can depend on the good guidance of the winged child.

I have emphasized the consoling implications in these terminal designs because their disturbing ones are clear enough. In the succeeding five hundred designs, Blake will find occasion for a thorough exploration of the lower depths of despair which are only prefigured in Night the First. Still these visions from nos. 17 to 33, which are related to the horrific ones in *The Marriage of Heaven and Hell*, ought to have been adequate to stimulate Young to do his duty as a Poet—if terrors *could* be the cause of inspiration, as eighteenth-century theorists often declared them to be. For Blake negations are never sufficient to arouse the imaginative faculties to act. Another kind of intermediacy is necessary to persuade Young to be a Poet rather than a vicarious reader.

The Poet per se, as distinguished from the nonliterary identities of Mr. Young, is not unequivocally present in nos. 19 through 33, and when he does appear again in no. 34 {87} (group VII) it is not in an active, creative role but in the passive role of a reader in bondage. In this design his plight represents an intensification of his predicament as previously delineated. In no. 2 he is reading a book, but he is also alert and in his own bed. In no. 7 he has the prophetic scroll, but he is wrapped up in it and asleep, unable to perfect the word. Instead, two conforming spirits are delivering the word (not without evidence of strain) to that epitome of conformity, Death—who has his own literary aspirations, or at least seeks to extract laws from poetic tales that he can impose on everyone. In no. 8 the protagonist is not visibly literary at all, though this Mr. Young evidently conceals something the size of a book beneath his gown. In no. 14 Young is still asleep, now over a book he was trying to write, and dreaming of masculine adventures like those indicated in no. 2. In no. 18 he is awakened and at least has a lighted lamp, very like that in no. 2 (particularly in the engraved version, no. 18 eng.), between his open book and ready pen and ink. Now in no. 34 the written book absorbs him more than ever. A review of the lineage of the other motifs in this design would confirm one's impression that in no. 34 there occurs a convergence of major images from practically all the other designs of Night the First except, perhaps, for nos. 11 and 25, which show the most positive action.

The involvement of the image of Young with doubles—mentioned and unmentioned in the *Night Thoughts*—has been frequently remarked. In no. 34 the two sides of Young as Poet are symbolized by the two birds alluded to in the text, the Nightingale and the Lark. Here the reading Poet is almost equidistant between the Nightingale, which he claims as the exemplar of his song, and Midnight, the hour which characterizes his song. But Young admits that, rather than trying to write, he usually recites the inimitable verses of the masters, notably Milton, Homer, and Pope, who are mentioned by name on the last page. In the symbolism of this picture, the great poets are identifiable with the open-mouthed Lark of day singing far above the scene of nocturnal bondage where the singer of *Night Thoughts* is incarcerated.

Thus the arrival of a yellow-clad emanation, a redemptive figure who has been out of the pictures since no. 16 (though she can also be recognized in the white-clad departing joy of no. 28), is highly dramatic. In her yellow dress she may hope to undo the damage caused by the incursion of yellow-clad Sin in no. 24; so far her efforts to bring the spiritual sunrise down to Dr. Young have not availed because the Poet is attuned not to the Lark but to the darkling Nightingale, who cannot see the dawn coming. Already this Muse's dress has snagged on the briars of Grief and Woe, and there is another briar branch behind the bird which is in a position to interdict her way to the Poet. The descent of Young's emanation is bound to remind the reader of the descent of Ololon in *Milton*, who leaves the realms where the great poet's "real self" is sleeping to join his temporal self questing below. This later episode is described in the greatest nature poetry Blake ever wrote, much of it particularly apposite to this design:

Thou hearest the Nightingale begin the Song of Spring;
The Lark sitting upon his earthy bed: just as the morn
Appears; listens silent; then springing from the waving Corn-
    field! loud
He leads the Choir of Day! trill, trill, trill, trill,
Mounting upon the wings of light into the Great Expanse:
Reechoing against the lovely blue & shining heavenly Shell:
His little throat labours with inspiration; . . .
All Nature listens silent to him & the awful Sun

Stands still upon the Mountain looking on this little Bird. . .
Then loud from their green covert all the Birds begin their
    Song . . .
The Nightingale again essays his song, & thro the day,
And thro the night warbles luxuriant; every Bird of Song
Attending his loud harmony with admiration & love.
This is a Vision of the lamentation of Beulah over Ololon!
                              (*M* 31:28-34; 36-37; 39; 41-45)

The similarity of Blake's basic imagery to Young's can hardly
have been accidental, but here, as so often elsewhere, one observes
Blake's technique of echoing and "correcting" at the same time.
Blake's point is that Young became trapped by the cult of the
Nightingale and (like Coleridge in *Dejection: An Ode*) took to
reading more as an escape from his creative depression than for its
own sake. *As distraction*, books are no more admirable than the
jester's pinwheel or the miser's tally. At this juncture, a rescue by
the emanation must have been attempted even if Young neglected
to write about it.

In the more decisive awakening in *Milton*, it is expressly stated
that the ultimate "Lark met the Female Ololon descending" and
Blake adds that the immortal "Lark is a mighty Angel" (36:10,
12). Later Blake depicted the angelic form of the Lark (described
E663) as he appears at the beginning of Milton's glad day, but
Young has still to wear out his night in response to the complaints
of Philomel which, though heartfelt and beautiful, celebrate only
the futile things already done and undone. Such plangent songs
can scarcely move.

The hours are the human forms of the four stars, which provide
whatever light the man has to read by, and also constitute the four
links in the chain of darkness. The three who are clad in blue and
dark blue recall the dark lady witnesses of nos. 12 and 17 and even
the brunette figure of Oppression in no. 22. But the figure of the
midnight hour who sits looking at the Poet has yellow hair in the
water color version, and thus becomes associated with the sinister
ladies in yellow of the earlier designs. By contrast, although the
descending emanation is dressed in yellow, the briars could well
divest her of this assumed garment of Sin, which is slit by an accident rather than by fascinating design, and her barely visible
hair seems to be gray, not yellow, the color of those who, in nos.
16 and 17, have learned wisdom through sorrow.

No. 34 does not reveal how successful the rescue was, though it does make clear the long odds against its success. In no. 35 we see the Poet with lyre in hand liberated from the briars but still tethered by the chain of darkness, in spite of the fact that the night has now turned to day. It should be observed that the chain has been lengthened but is now attached to his *right* ankle; this is an important indication as to what has happened, for Young is now bound on the side of his lyre, the poetic instrument which is not in evidence in any of the previous designs except in no. 6, where it is shared by two of the children about to fall prey to Death. One might, indeed, suspect that it was his lyre rather than a book that Young was hiding in no. 8, but it is not necessary to be certain as to the identity of the secreted instrument in order to understand the issues raised in no. 35.

It cannot have escaped Blake's attention that the deference to Pope expressed by Young in the closing lines is fulsome, and Blake would have thought such a declaration of inferiority degrading or at least debilitating for any poet who aspired to creativity. Moreover, Young's thought that Pope could have written better the poem he himself was aspiring to write must have seemed proof enough to Blake that Young had something deeply wrong with him, since Blake believed, with most of the later Romantics, that Pope's accomplishment was inauthentic and that his influence had been disastrous for poetry. Young's own lines imply something like this, but what Young attributed to inadvertence on Pope's part Blake was sure derived from a corrupted essence and anti-imaginative preoccupations.

By the time he came to write the Preface to *Milton* Blake was also very critical of Homer as a "silly slave of the sword," one who, with Virgil, had misled even John Milton. In his later tractate *On Homer's Poetry* Blake explains his antipathy in more detail (E94 and 267). But in 1796 all Blake had to see was the tribute to Pope to confirm the suspicions he must always have had about Young. Such subservience to a vicious tradition would have seemed to Blake a kind of effeminacy, and it is doubtless no coincidence that the poet in the final design for Night the First does not appear as masculine as he did in the previous design. Indeed, it is noteworthy that Shields took the figure to be female, and that both he and the writer of the "Explanation of the Engravings" took the figure to represent the Poet's *soul*, rather than the author himself. And it is even possible that the curious suggestion of a beard on the chin of the descending emanation in the engraved version of no. 34 (not the water color) relates to this. Earlier cases of possible bisexuality are the figure kneeling at the grave in no. 15, whom I identified with Young, and the figures of Philander in nos. 29 and 30. Since both Young and Philander are behaving in a feminine manner, the former playing the part of "wretched Thought" and the latter plying the distaff, effeminate characterizations are hardly inappropriate. In this connection it is important to recall two things: first, that Blake spoke of false and uncreative intellectual unions as being "hermaphroditic"; second, that although he was entirely prepared to recognize the tradition of the hairy poet, he did not feel easy in the tradition of the pretty poet. Inspiration by the Muse is essential for Poetry, but premature introjection of the Muse produces enervating uxoriousness.

An image of the Poet delineated in his ideal perfection adequate to serve as the standard throughout the series can hardly be the man who reads in bed at night depicted in no. 2. Rather he must be the powerful masculine figure who is depicted in no. 5, poised to write on a scroll as big as himself while he receives inspiration from on high. It is striking that his inspiration is transmitted without human mediacy by huge beams of yellow light descending from a partially obscured yellow luminary, a crescent of which is revealed. Because of its shape and because of the role many Romantic poets including Blake assigned to the moon as a source of poetic creativity, it is natural at first to assume that the luminary must be the moon, the moon shaded by the earth, that is. However, because this crescent is so perfectly horizontal, so "dry," as the moon never is elsewhere in the series, and especially because of the huge volume of light emitted, it is probable that what is portrayed is an eclipse of the sun.[6] Either it is a total eclipse that is now ending or it is a partial eclipse, neither of which can completely interdict the clear light of eternity being poured on the

[6] The persuasiveness of this view of the symbol is weakened when one recalls J 100 {104}, where the woman influences a perfectly dry crescent moon (in which a figure perhaps is lying) that emits great rays of light down to a scroll-shaped end of the Druid Serpent Temple. Yet one must resist piecemeal explanations; the complexity of Blake's cosmic symbolism is exemplified in J 70, which probably depicts a sun in eclipse in the black-and-white copies but an unobscured luminary in the colored copy. In the case of no. 5, the functional meaning of the luminary is much the same whether moon or eclipsed sun.

true visionary. The meaning is essentially the same if one should insist that the luminary is the moon, but to assume this to be the case deprives the opening Nights of a fine anomaly. In spite of the fact that this poem is known as *Night Thoughts* and that Blake often depicts and refers to the moon, no distinct example of this luminary occurs in these designs until Narcissa makes her super-lunary appearance on the title page for Night the Third (no. 78).[7] Young does appear writing, in the company of the Muse and under the influence of a wet waning moon, shortly after, in no. 80.

A more important piece of symbolism, in this context, is the huge pale yellow scroll in which the Poet is wrapped; it is hardly distinguishable from the couch on which he reclines and it curves out of his lap so as to become almost part of him. When this scroll is compared with that of the sleeping Young in no. 7, it becomes clear why, as Young admits himself at the end of Night the First, he is only occasionally inspired. For the scroll of the would-be poet comes out from behind his head and binds down his legs be-fore it is brought down for scrutiny, and perhaps improvement, to little old Urizen seated under a blasted tree. It cannot be doubted that Blake is saying in the fifth design that poetry comes out of the guts of the living, whereas in the seventh his point is that what comes out of the head of the sleeping is likely to be turned into law.

The only other scroll in Night the First occurs in no. 6. It is very much smaller than the two enormous ones in the designs adjacent to it. One can hardly explain its significance without considering in some detail the family group that is about to be swept away by the hand of death. Probably one needs more help from Blake's other work to understand this design than is the case with any other in the first Night. The association of Vala with the distaff is quite consistent in the later prophecies and this woman's apparent expression or irritation or annoyance at the gift she re-ceives (at least in the water color—this is less evident in the en-graving) indicates that she is a sinister figure, one who prefigures Sin in no. 24. Indeed she is as different as possible from the chil-

---

[7] Narcissa has blue eyes, as does the inspired Poet in no. 5, whereas it is not until Night the Fourth (no. 138) that a figure identifiable as Young achieves this clear-eyed color. This fact and the curious one that the only other character with blue eyes in Night the First is Philander in no. 30 will someday have to be accounted for.

dren around her, who are engaged in activities which in themselves are undoubtedly creative. They are in fact closely related to the three daughters of Job who stand with their parents in the final design for the Book of Job.[8] From right to left they hold, respectively, a lyre, a scroll, and an open book, the same implements as are employed by the standing children in no. 6. But the Job design shows a scene of blessedness after the night of experience has passed, whereas in the title page for Night the First, not only is the hand of white Death about to exterminate the woman and children, but there is also an ominously dark patch of sky at the left, behind Death's bow and arrow, which must be night coming on. It is also noteworthy that there are four standing children, but only three implements, and that they are all turned inward toward this "mother of my mortal part," rather than outward, like the liberated girls in the Job pictures.

In the water color version, a girl holds the harp, and the figure who stands behind her and plays it is at least as effeminate as the chained lyrist in no. 35. Blake must have thought this symbolic comment was too obscure. In the engraved version the youth is certainly depicted as a boy. It is possible to think that the boy and girl are making beautiful music together, but in the context of the entire design and of Night the First as a whole, it seems probable that the girl is the boy's emanation and that such teamwork, in which two do the work of one, can only be to the detriment of the Music. In the greatest human joy Blake ever depicted, the communal singing at the end of Job, everybody plays his own instrument. Similarly the scribe, who could be designing with a pen or a graver and would thus represent Painting, is also of rather ambiguous sex but probably a boy in both versions. But this scribal posture is not the proper one for creativity, which was shown in its perfection in no. 5. Rather, his hunched-up position at the feet of Vala is best suited for taking notes, and is therefore assumed by Urizen when he composes his prohibitions under the Tree of Death in no. 7. Further perspective on the suspect scribal position is given by the fourth illustration for Gray's *Ode to Adversity*, the thirty-seventh of the Gray designs. There the harsh figure of Adversity holds a scribal figure in her lap. Gray thinks this is good tutelage, but Blake shows by the compasses she holds

[8] The picture is well reproduced and discussed in *Blake's Job: Blake's Illustrations of the Book of Job*, ed. S. Foster Damon, Providence, 1966.

that she is fit only to teach law and order to "Virtue," not the truth that makes us free.

The third child, uniquely naked, who presents a scroll at the right knee of Vala and disturbs her with his message of Poetry, is not compromised as the others are. He can best be understood as a combination of several Blakean figures, some of which were drawn much later. His leg position is characteristically Blakean and is usually associated with positive characters, such as several of the children in the second page of *The Ecchoing Green*. It is also the position of Christ's legs in the draft pencil drawing for the general title page (no. 1 verso), except that Christ rests on his right leg while this boy rests on his left. This is possibly related to the fact that he is bearing bad news, like the first messenger to reach Job in the fourth design of that series. The fact that the messenger in the Job design is more importunate does not invalidate the basic relationship between the two designs. But the precedent for the gift of a scroll is the opposite of announcing the wrath of God. In the second version of the Genesis title page, the central deed is the handing of a scroll from Christ to Adam, which I have elsewhere argued must be the Everlasting Gospel. This, of course, is the counterpart of the Stony Decalogue given to Moses on Sinai, which is the story Blake usually seemed to accept. Later (in no. 333) Moses will be depicted as himself breaking this covenant of negation and, in effect, leaving it to Orc to "stamp the stony law to dust" (*MHH* 27, *A* 8). Actually, Blake implies, Moses himself also received a liberal covenant from that God "Who in mysterious Sinai's awful cave / To Man the wond'rous art of writing gave" (*J* 3). Even more to the point, he painted a picture of Moses, the shepherd, with his flock in the presence of the burning bush, holding a scroll in his right hand. The text must be identical with the Everlasting Covenant which was given to Adam in the beginning and would never be rescinded by its original donor.[9]

[9] The Genesis title page and the picture of Moses face each other as pls. 1 and 2 in Damon's *Dictionary*. Reviewing this book in *Philological Quarterly*, XLV (1966), 533-535, I pointed out that the former picture is the second, not first, version of the title page, done on 1825 paper, and that the nude figure who rushes across the top of the design with outspread wings must be identified as the Holy Spirit in the person of Orc. These corrections have not found their way into the second issue of the volume (1967). Though the Genesis manuscript has not been as egregiously neglected in proportion to its magnitude as the *Night Thoughts* series, Blake studies also need a more

Certain confirmation that Experience is entering into this family group can be found by comparison of various motifs occurring in *Songs of Innocence and of Experience,* but the true mother-centered community of love depicted in the title page of *Songs of Innocence* {11} offers the clearest standard for showing what is

precise interpretation of these pictures than can be found either in Damon or in Nanavutty, B&N no. 1649. Even the great Dante series gives no such clear vision of what, in the end, Blake believed it must have been like in the beginning.

I can at least assist this work by pointing out that my own brief remarks were also too simplified to be perfectly accurate as a description of Blake's symbolism. It is in the *first* version of the Genesis title page, not the second, as I implied, that God the Father holds a (straight) bow at his left side as he divides the waters about the firmament from those beneath it with his right hand and his feet. In the second version this bow has been replaced by Newtonian compasses while the bow is given to Orc, the Holy Spirit. But in his hand it is no longer the bow of wrath wielded by Christ in *Night Thoughts* no. 325 or in the seventh design for *Paradise Lost,* nor yet the bow-book of disease deployed by the blind old man from his chariot of clouds in *The House of Death* (see {93}). Instead it is "a Bow of Mercy and Loving-kindness" (*J* 97:13), as big as the rainbow of promise, and discovered so late that it breaks the sketched frame of the picture. The strings of this bow constitute the bow of an ark suitable to carry the whole human covenant over these supernal waters. (For further observations on the Genesis title page see the next essay in this volume, n. 22.)

The occurrence of scroll and compass in this design, together with the frequent contrast between scrolls and books, requires some comment here. As a maker of books, Blake was a lover of them too, but he knew they could become absorbing to the point of distraction, or the instruments of tyranny if one believed the letter rather than the spirit. In this they are not very different from compasses, which were handled with impunity by Christ in the Carpenter's Shop (repr. Keynes, B&N no. 543, item 108)—and by Christ in *Night Thoughts* no. 62 (II, 29)—but which misled Newton into devotion to an abstraction. All these things find their proper place, however, on the several levels of *Jacob's Ladder:* see Blunt, pl. 44. At the lowest turning of the vortex a Newton with compass and scales looks at the great scroll being returned by a female spirit to the source of light. And descending below them, just behind the gifts of spiritual food, are a male and a female angel, the first carrying a scroll and showing it to the other, who carries a book that as yet is sealed. When she has learned her everlasting lesson these seals will become, not a device for binding down the Word, but instruments for gathering the scattered leaves in a single meaningful volume. Such binding confers intelligibility, the form of Revelation, to materials which, however energized, tend to atrophy when they are only looked at here and there. A case in hand is Blake's designs for *Night Thoughts.*

wanting here. In this design a seated mother with bound hair holds in her lap a book which is being studied—from their own points of view, no doubt—by a girl and boy, both of whom are draped. In no. 6, on the contrary, the girl is still content to study a book at her mother's knee, but the boy has received a higher message (doubtless from the angel seated on the "N" of SONGS in the title page of *Innocence*) which Vala is unable to understand. Had she not been too proud to bridge this generation gap, she would have responded as does the less prudent woman, depicted in the left section of the upper picture of the title page of *America* {25}, who is accepting the tutelage of a small boy. Nothing is legible on the scroll of no. 6, of course, but insofar as the message is prophetic, its burden must be everlastingly the same: "If you go on So, the result is So" (E607/K392). This is the message of Life to the agent of Death, but it is not easy to communicate with Death the giant, who has his eyes shut and is about to assert his tyrannical prerogatives. His lethal right hand, however, cannot negate the Immortality being achieved with Death's own cooperation in the upper part of the design. There is a sense, too, in which all four unwinged males in this picture represent aspects of the author, but only Young when young has a message. The two other forward youths are growing into Young when old, who is anagogically blind Mr. Death himself.

15

Text and Design in
Illustrations of the Book of Job

BEN F. NELMS

A GENERAL impression of Blake criticism is that his *Illustrations of the Book of Job* represent virtually a rewriting of the book by Blake in his own terms and that the interrelations of text and design are less important than they usually are in his books.[1] Blake's series is indeed much more than a mere sequence of illustrations of the original; yet it is not a complete rewriting. It is rather, as Northrop Frye has pointed out, a profound commentary characterized by an attitude of critical acceptance.[2] Blake's exegetical methods are, characteristically, bold; the visual symbolism of his central designs is amplified (in the engraved version) by border designs and by a careful selection and arrangement of texts.

The Book of Job clearly invites the kind of commentary Blake provides, for the bitter defiance of Job's speeches, the divine denunciation of the friends, the ambiguity of Elihu's imagery, and the unresolved enigma of the message from the whirlwind all represent challenges to the orthodox reading of the Bible. "But in the Book of Job," Blake wrote in *The Marriage of Heaven and Hell*, "Milton's Messiah is call'd Satan" (E34/K150). What he did

---

[1] Cf. Joseph H. Wicksteed, *Blake's Vision of the Book of Job*, London, 1924, 43-47; Keynes, *Bible*, 12; S. Foster Damon, *Blake's "Job,"* Providence, 1966, 3 and *passim*. I have also consulted the Morgan Library edition of 1935 (B&N no. 301), which includes the water color designs and pencil drawings.

[2] In *Fearful Symmetry* (427) Frye wrote that Blake's work, "though a profound commentary on that poem, is clearly not a series of illustrations to it, but an independent art-form." In his recent essay, "Blake's Reading of the Book of Job" (Rosenfeld, *Essays for Damon*, 221-234), he says, "Everyone realizes that Blake re-created the Book of Job in his engravings and was not simply illustrating it. At the same time he appears to be following the book with some fidelity, and his attitude toward it . . . seems to be on the whole an attitude of critical acceptance." My essay was completed before I had an opportunity to see Frye's, but I have been able to insert a few references to it.

not add was that Job's God in the first two chapters and Milton's Messiah are also closely related. When he quotes in the first *Job* plate, "It is Spiritually Discerned" (1 Cor. 2:14),[3] he means, among other things, that the work is being read in its infernal or diabolical sense.[4]

Blake's allusions to Job in other works show that it came to represent for him the pilgrimage of the human soul—its descent into hell, the necessity of death and rebirth. Harold Bloom points to a verbal echo of Job in *The Four Zoas*.[5]

What is the price of Experience? do men buy it for a song
Or wisdom for a dance in the street? No, it is bought with the price
Of all that a man hath, his house, his wife, his children.
Wisdom is sold in the desolate market where none come to buy,
And in the wither'd field where the farmer plows for bread in vain.

Job had cried out:

But where shall wisdom be found? and where is the place
of understanding?
Man knoweth not the price thereof; neither is it found in
the land of the living.   (Job 28:12-13)

Since wisdom is not found in "the land of living," it must be sought in the grave. *Gates of Paradise*, quoting Job 17:14, makes precisely this point: "I have said to the Worm: Thou art my mother & my sister."

[3] As is usually true, this brief text implies and is clarified by a longer passage from which it is quoted. "But the natural man receiveth not the things of the Spirit of God: for they are foolishness unto him; neither can he know *them*, because they are spiritually discerned" (1 Cor. 2:14).

[4] E43/K158. Some possibilities for an ironic-diabolical reading of the Bible have been pointed out by Martha England. She refers to the ironic applicability of the Pharisees' accusation, "This man receiveth sinners still," and continues, "This reading of Luke 15:2 has become orthodox. But Wesley went beyond 'orthodoxy' in his daring use of such ironies. Quite recently I have seen him criticized for an interpretation of Matthew 25:27 in his journal. . . . The words of the Elect which authorized the crucifixion were, 'His blood be on us / and on our children.' Wesley said it was the greatest prayer a man could speak. This interpretation is not yet 'orthodox,' and it is proof of Wesley's 'divine audacity,' but it is only proper to point out that in this reading he was merely paraphrasing his favorite poet, the holy Mr. Herbert' ("Blake and the Hymns of Charles Wesley," *BNYPL*, LXX [1966], 111-112).

[5] Bloom, *Apocalypse*, 238.

There are many ways of entering into Blake's *Book of Job*, but a central theme is illustrated at the center of the book, plate 11 {110}. Above the caption, "With Dreams upon my bed thou scarest me & affrightest me with Visions" (Job 7:13-14), this design shows Job on his couch pushing away the God in his own image who hovers menacingly over him. With his right hand this God points to the tables of stone revealed in lightning above, and with his left to the black flames below in which the three tormentors are revealed. Two of the scaly tormentors pull Job downward at the feet and loins, and a third brings chains for his head. Job's God is shown with cloven hoof and a serpent twined around him.

The Scripture quoted above the design, read diabolically, has a threefold irony: "Satan himself is transformed into an Angel of Light & his Ministers into Ministers of Righteousness" (2 Cor. 11:14-15). First, the simplest irony is that from Job's point of view just the opposite has happened. His God, whom he has supposed to be the only angel of light, is revealed as Satan, the supreme Accuser, a terrible but accurate vision of a God who sends fire from heaven. While he points to the tables of stone—the proscriptive law—with one hand, he points to the fiery gulf below with the other. Since, from Blake's point of view, Satan has been masquerading as God in Job's mind all along, this is not really a scene of metamorphosis but of recognition, and like all true recognition scenes it involves potentially more of self-revelation than anything else. This ambiguity of the roles of God and Satan is implicit in the Bible account (as many commentators have discovered to their chagrin), for in Job 1:12 Jehovah grants Satan permission to persecute Job, "Behold, all that he hath is in thy power"; but in Job 2:3 Jehovah refers to Satan as the inciter and himself as the agent of destruction, "thou movedst me against him, to destroy him [literally, to swallow him] without cause." To the Blakean reader, there is no radical exegetical problem here, for the difference between permission and execution, between commissioner and commissioned, is negligible.

In the second place, the transformation of Satan into an angel of light, referred to in the text in plate 11, inevitably suggests a prior transformation: the traditional and Miltonic legend of the fall of Lucifer, the daystar.[6] Since light imagery dominates the

---

[6] Though I do not at this point refer to Lucifer as the first Eye of God, I do think that his relation to Jesus, the seventh Eye, is related to my point.

latter half of the *Book of Job*, particularly the light of stars, it might be well to follow the ironic implications of this cyclic identity for a moment; traditionally, Lucifer, an angel of light, was transformed into Satan; now, in some prophetic sense, Satan is said to be transformed into an angel of light.

For the most part the first ten plates are dominated by the "fire fallen from heaven," that is, heat without light, or, in a stricter sense, destructive lightning and flames. The text at the top of this page, which is interlaced with tongues of flame, continues this imagery, as do the jagged lightning and black flames of the design. "My bones are pierced in me in the night season & my sinews take no rest." "My skin is black upon me & my bones are burned with heat" (Job 30:17, 30). The main theme of the next ten pages will be the Redeemer who will "fallen, fallen light renew" (E18/K210). In a sense, Christ is the renewal of the fallen light of Lucifer. Two New Testament passages are relevant here. The first is 2 Peter 1:19.

> And we have the word of prophecy made more sure; whereunto ye do well that ye take heed, as unto a lamp shining in a dark place, until the day dawn, and the day-star arise in your hearts. . . .

The other is Revelation 22:16.

> I Jesus have sent mine angel to testify unto you these things for the churches. I am the root and the offspring of David, the bright, the morning star.

Christ, the fulfillment of prophecy, can be seen as a second and more benevolent day-star, a day-star in our hearts.[7]

---

[7] My only purpose in citing these Scriptures is to establish the relationship between Lucifer and Christ; however, I think there is at least one other layer of subtlety there through which I have not penetrated. The connecting link may be the second quatrain of the Epilogue to the *Gates of Paradise*:

> Tho thou art Worshipd by the Names Divine
> Of Jesus & Jehovah: thou art still
> The Son of Morn in weary Nights decline
> The lost Travellers Dream under the Hill.
> (E266/K771)

The gist of this quatrain in relation to the two New Testament passages I have quoted is perhaps best expressed as "Better fallen light than no light at all," or "Thank God for a starry floor."

Structurally, therefore, an allusion to Lucifer in plate 11 is very appropriate, coming as it does midway between the darkness of his fallen state and the potential light of his risen counterpart. In connection with this aspect of Satan, the text at the very bottom of the page should be read in its original context.

> Let no man beguile you in any wise: for it [i.e., the day of the Lord] will not be except the falling away come first, and the man of sin be revealed, the son of perdition, *he that opposeth and exalteth himself against all that is called God or* that *is worshipped*; so that he sitteth in the temple of God, setting himself forth as God.
>
> (2 Thess. 2:3-4; Blake's quotation italicized)

The revelation of the man of sin is, of course, the subject of this design; but it should be remembered that the phrase that Blake quoted might just as well have been applied by the Pharisees, the Elect of their day, to Jesus. And, ironically, they would have been right, for Jesus did exalt himself above all that *they* called God or worshiped.

This suggests the third edge of irony, that is, the fact that this Satan-God really is an angel (or Messenger) of light and a minister of righteousness, for only after this recognition scene in which his nature is fully comprehended, this dark night of the soul, can Job's ascent begin. The starry light and benevolent visions of the next few plates must be preceded by the recognition and purgation of Error. This Satan-God is actually Job's twofold error, the repression and compensatory self-righteousness of religious legalism. Thematically and visually, therefore, plate 11 is the turning point of the drama.[8] Job is seen prostrate here for the last time. In fact, the only other time he is prostrate is in plate 6 where he is being smitten with boils, and even there his shoulders are slightly raised and his head is thrown backward as if in some contortion of skyward appeal. Significantly, I think, Job is never shown standing until plate 18 where he offers prayers for the three

[8] Frye calls plate 13 the turning point; but as Damon has pointed out, plates 11 and 13 are contraries (Rosenfeld, 230, 232; Damon, *Philosophy*, 32). It would perhaps be more accurate, therefore, to speak of the one as the end of the beginning and the other as the beginning of the end. I have selected plate 11 because it is the middle plate in the series of twenty-one and, more significantly, in it alone is Job prostrated by his adversities.

friends, but from plate 11 on his posture is much more relaxed and his expression more serene. Two of the marginal texts of plate 11 also mark this as a climactic event.

> Why do you persecute me as God & are not satisfied with my flesh. Oh that my words were printed in a Book that they were graven with an iron pen & lead in the rock for ever For I know that my Redeemer liveth & that he shall stand in the latter days upon the Earth & after my skin destroy thou This body yet in my flesh shall I see God whom I shall see for Myself and mine eyes shall behold & not Another tho consumed be my wrought Image (Job 19:22-27)

The references to printing and engraving are an appropriate Blakean signature, particularly as they stand in such close juxtaposition to the first mention of redemption and life after death in the engravings. The verbal ambiguities in this passage, as Blake quoted it,[9] are highly provocative. The implicit connection between Blake, the printer-engraver, and the Redeemer who "shall stand in the latter days upon the Earth" is not as uncalled for as it might seem at first, for Job's words have always been peculiarly vulnerable to the misinterpretations of the Elect, from Eliphaz and company to the early Christian overemphasis on the patience of Job, to the present. Modern textual scholarship has even shown substantial distortions resulting from the bias of the Masoretes, the scholars who established the standard Hebrew text. Minor changes in orthography and omissions, we are told, "enabled the Masoretes to turn Job's defiant and bitter protest against divine injustice into an affirmation of complete trust and submission."[10] The translators of the King James Version did not counteract this tendency; so, in the case of this book at least, Blake's diabolical

---

[9] The King James Version reads "Why do ye persecute me as God, and are not satisfied with my flesh? Oh that my words were now written! oh that they were printed in a book! That they were graven with an iron pen and lead in the rock for ever! For I know that my redeemer liveth, and that he shall stand at the latter day upon the earth: And though after my skin worms destroy this body, yet in my flesh shall I see God: Whom I shall see for myself, and mine eyes shall behold, and not another; though my reins be consumed within me."

[10] *The Anchor Bible*: "Job," trans. Marvin H. Pope, New York, 1965, xli. This statement made in reference to a specific passage is applicable to treatment of passages throughout the book of Job.

reading with its textual alterations was probably closer to the original intention than most of the translations.

In a more literal sense, however, the Redeemer stands upon the earth in the latter days of plate 17, where the anticipatory "yet in my flesh shall I see God" is answered in the triumphant "I have heard thee with the hearing of the Ear but now my Eye seeth thee" (Job 42:5).[11] In the margin of plate 11 a line from the flames divides the last line of this text between "for Myself" and "and mine eyes" and underlines *destroy* in the next to the last line. This division calls attention to a syntactic ambiguity in the King James Version which must not have escaped Blake. In the clause "Yet in my flesh shall I see God" the prepositional phrase "in my flesh" can refer to either the speaker or God, and thus can be taken to mean "Yet I shall see God in myself or in my own flesh." A bit more farfetched, but syntactically possible, is the idea that *mine eyes* is the object, not the subject, of *shall behold*. Thus the *whom* clause would be taken to mean "I shall see God for myself and shall behold mine eyes and not Another." Of course, this analysis of the syntax is not necessary to show that for Blake the God whom Job sees is not Other—the visual similarity and marginal texts in plate 17 {116} do this—but it is the kind of verbal foreshadowing which one comes to expect of Blake, and it contributes to the richness of plate 11.

A more certain and more relevant implication, however, concerns what is being destroyed in this purgatorial experience and what is being retained. In a phrase which Blake did change substantially from the highly speculative King James rendering, Job says, "after my skin destroy thou This body yet in my flesh shall I see God." The only way to make sense of this is for *This body* to be something different from *skin*, which will be destroyed before it (which in fact is being destroyed now by the boils—"my skin is black upon me"), and from the *flesh* in which he will see God. Further, I take it to be the same as the *wrought Image*, a phrase that is also a product of Blake's own translation—and

---

[11] A slight change in wording here allows Blake to make a point not in keeping with the letter of the original. The original is "I have heard *of* Thee. . . ." By omitting the *of* Blake can distinguish between the Voice in the Whirlwind and the Man-God, Jesus—a perfectly valid distinction considering Job in the context of the whole Bible.

capitalization. (In the marginal design of plate 11 {110} the words *wrought Image* are printed vertically up the right side of the page in the flames. Thus, in a nice visual touch, this *wrought Image* is literally being consumed up the side of the page by marginal flames.) It would be consistent with the meaning of the whole book and with the central position of this design to hold that *This body*, this *wrought Image*, is Job's own mistaken self-image which he must recognize concretely as he recognizes the true nature of his Satan-God and which must be purged away before the regeneration or redemption of the next six plates can take place. The *wrought Image* invites comparison with the words "graven with an iron pen & lead in the rock for ever." Both seem to imply the need for embodying error in concrete, visible form. Thus Blake's engraving of Job's terrifying dream, like Job's own paintings in his palace of art in plate 20, implicitly shares in the redemptive act, fulfilling Job's prayer at the same time that it records it and giving permanence to the concrete visualization of Job's purgative experience.

The title caption of plate 11 is one of three textual references to dreams in Blake's *Job*. It looks back to the dream of Eliphaz in plate 9 {109}, with which it shares the aspect of terror if not the tone of Gothic superstition. The entire section on which Blake based plate 9 is quoted below, with Blake's quotations underlined:

> Now a thing was secretly brought to me, and mine ear received a little thereof. In thoughts from the visions of the night, when deep sleep falleth on men, Fear came upon me, and trembling, which made all my bones to shake. *Then a spirit passed before my face; the hair of my flesh stood up*: It stood still, but I could not discern the form thereof: an image was before mine eyes, there was silence, and I heard a voice. . . . (Job 4:12-16)

The secrecy, the partially heard voice, and the indiscernible form are all hallmarks of a false or misinterpreted vision. So, probably, is the ominous, empty black cloud above the head of the sleeping Eliphaz.[12] It would seem that the vision of Eliphaz was intended

[12] Marion Milner is probably right in her interpretation of this cloud, though for some reason she identifies the sleeping figure as Job. "Here the

as a warning for him which he did not have the imaginative perception to discern.

If the dream of Job in plate 11 shares in the terror of the dream of Eliphaz, it shares also in the instructive grace of the dream Elihu refers to in plate 12: "In a Dream in a Vision of the Night in deep Slumberings upon the bed Then he openeth the ears of Men & sealeth their instruction" (Job 33:15-16). This needs, however, to be put in the context of Blake's interpretation of the character and message of Elihu.

Visually and verbally, Elihu dominates plate 12 {111}. Until the final plate, he is one of the few standing human figures in the book.[13] He advances on his left foot, which—if we follow the symbolism as urged by Wicksteed (p. 151)—illustrates the text, "I also am formed out of the clay" (Job 33:6). With his right hand he silences the three friends, and with his left he points toward the starry heavens. As an "Interpreter One among a Thousand," he has an affinity with Blake himself.[14] Although most critics emphasize Blake's departure from the Bible account with Elihu,[15] it is easy to see what must have been attractive to him in the biblical Elihu. He comes in wrath (Job 32:2), not in pity as the three friends originally did; he is young, and they are very old (Job 32:6, quoted in caption of plate 12). He claims divine inspiration at the same time that he boldly speaks his own opinion.

---

most striking thing to me, in the purely feeling aspect of the picture, was the great, dark, empty space above Job's dreaming head—a pregnant emptiness" ("Psycho-Analysis and Art," in *Psycho-Analysis and Contemporary Thought*, ed. John D. Sutherland, London, 1958, 97).

[13] The only other which invites comparison is the son (?) in plate 2. The eldest son trying to keep the roof from caving in in plate 3, the running messengers in plate 4, and the hunched and crippled beggar in plate 5 are all standing, but in distorted positions. The accusers enter standing in plate 7 but never make it to their feet again. Job finally stands in plate 18. The friends bringing gifts stand in plate 19 in contrast with Job, who was sitting and waiting for the crippled beggar to come to him in plate 5. Everybody stands in the last plate. The only spiritual figures who stand are Satan in plate 6, the God of Eliphaz in plate 9, the Sons of God in plate 14 {114}, and the Father in plate 17 {116}.

[14] Blake was called Interpreter by his followers, and he must certainly have thought of himself in this role.

[15] E.g., Wicksteed, *Blake's Vision*, 64-65.

But there is a spirit in man: and the inspiration of the Almighty giveth them understanding.

Therefore I said, Hearken to me; I also will shew mine opinion.

For I am full of matter; the spirit within me constraineth me.[16]   (Job 32:8, 10, 18)

To find Elihu's speech altogether in agreement with Blake's conception, all that one must do is to read it diabolically, that is, in opposition to the conventional reading. For *God*, read something like Divine Imagination or Humanity Divine. For *the wicked*, read corporeal man or human abstract, depending on the context. Read *righteousness* in the Reprobate sense, not as the Elect's "Thou shalt not." Though at first this may seem a radical interpretation, it soon makes more sense than the orthodox one; and it has the added advantage of better explaining what the Elihu speeches are doing in Job anyway, for read in the usual sense they merely repeat the arguments of the three friends and yet sound much too brash and imaginative to be an interpolation of the Elect. Several passages, besides the ones Blake uses in the margins, which are usually explained by orthodox commentators on Job as textual inadequacies, support this view without a substantial rereading. For instance, in Job 36:5 Elihu says: "Behold, God is mighty, and despiseth not any: he is mighty in strength and wisdom." Though this is usually emended to say that God does not despise the innocent or pure, it literally translates, "Lo, God is mighty and does not despise, mighty in strength of heart"— a much more Christian concept of God.[17] Similarly, Job 34:11, "For the work of a man shall he render unto him, and cause every man to find according to his ways," is closer to the Christian "Seek and ye shall find." God's providence (his "bright cloud") is described in Job 37:13 as coming "for correction, or for his land, or for mercy." The modern rendering again may be closer to Blake's diabolical understanding: "Whether for discipline, or for grace, / Or for mercy, he makes it find its mark."[18] All of the other speakers have reasoned from power, "the multitude of oppres-

[16] The modern translation of the last phrase, "My belly is full of wind," would not seem inappropriate to Blake, I imagine. *Anchor Bible*, 211.

[17] *Anchor Bible*, 232.   [18] *Anchor Bible*, 240.

sions," "the arm of the Mighty," but Elihu dares ask, "Where is God my maker, who giveth songs in the night?" (Job 35:10, 11). At any rate, Blake's reading is not as perverse as one may have been led to believe: it seems to be suggested even in the King James Version.

Elihu must be contrasted with Eliphaz. Even their names clash, Elihu ("God is he") suggesting a considerably more relevant message to Job than Eliphaz ("God is fine gold"). Job (in plate 10) is interested in coming forth like gold himself (Job 23:10). Ironically, after his purging he does, but his gold is then that of God, the divine humanity. The message of Eliphaz frightens as his dream does, but does not instruct. The pictorial details contrast: Eliphaz kneels and points with his left hand into his own perverted vision. He faces toward the left, the side of the setting sun. Elihu faces the side of the rising sun. The figure of Elihu also recalls that of the young man in plate 2, presumably Job's son; but he too faces the setting sun and looks not to his own vision or the starry heavens, but to Job's book, "the letter that killeth." He precedes the triumph of Satan (plate 6) as Elihu precedes the triumph of Christ (plate 17) {116}. The figure of Christ might indeed be said to incorporate the humanity of Elihu and the divinity of the God of Eliphaz, unbinding the arms of the latter and controlling the angry external directions of the former.[19]

Job had asked, in plate 10, "And dost thou open thine eyes upon such a one & bringest me into judgment with thee?" Elihu in his central text answers the question: "For his eyes are upon the ways of Man & he observeth all his goings" (Job 34:22). All the texts at the top of plate 12 {111} are taken from Job 33, and refer back to the previous plate, where Job's self-righteous pride and repressed sensuality are revealed to him. The nature of the Redeemer or Ransom is further clarified. God speaks to man time and again, Elihu says, but man doesn't hear. He instructs man in a dream or in a vision in order to rescue him from pride and the pit. If someone will but act as Interpreter, God's grace has provided a ransom.

The crucial imagery of both the text and the plate, however, is not of the pit but of the stars, not of darkness but of light. All that has preceded has been God's work with man "to bring back

---

[19] This reading attempts to give some unity to the meaning of the standing figures. It may be pressed too far, but the pictures do suggest analogies.

his Soul from the pit to be *enlightened with the light of the living*"
(Job 33:29-30; quoted in margin of plate 12; italics mine). The
two passages which follow (Job 35:5-7) are of peculiar significance.
First, Elihu says, "Look upon the heavens & behold the clouds
which are higher than thou." But Elihu appears beneath not a
cloudy but a starry sky; and this passage, instead of soaring off
into the heights, is printed on Job's belly in the lower margin
of the plate. In fact, the twelve bright, prepossessing stars of the design are nowhere mentioned in the marginal texts or in Elihu's
speeches in the Bible account. But the meaning of this twofold
irony is surely clear. Though the clouds themselves may be higher
than we, their meaning lies within us; and though they may appear outwardly to corporeal sight as clouds, they may enlighten
those who see with the light of the living. The last part of Elihu's
speech, as he sees the storm approaching, is in fact filled with
references to light, particularly to some strange undecipherable
phenomena translated in the King James Version as *bright clouds*.
(See especially Job 37:11, 15, 21. Verse 11 is quoted on plate 15.)
One of these furnishes the key to our interpretation: "And now
men see not the bright light which is in the clouds: but the wind
passeth, and cleanseth them" (Job 37:21). The next plate brings
the cleansing whirlwind and the voice of God, "who maketh the
Clouds his Chariot" (Psalms 104:3). The stars and the ascending
female figures in the design of the upper margin of plate 12 {111}
are encased in clouds on which the texts themselves are engraved.
These cloudy inscriptions serve as instructions for the discern-
ment of the inner spiritual vision.

The second part of Elihu's last text is printed under the head
of Job in the lower margin. The Job figure is reclining, presumably experiencing a vision of the night. Of this text, Wicksteed
says (p. 65):

> Elihu says that it is impossible God should have any motive
> other than pure justice because he is removed from the possi-
> bility of either benefit or injury at Job's hands. "If thou sin-
> nest what doest thou against him, or if thou art righteous
> what givest thou unto him?" Blake in quoting these words in
> the margin of the twelfth design, certainly understood them,
> not as showing that God must have a disinterested desire to
> punish sin, but as showing that God takes no interest in either

sin or righteousness, which were for Blake radically false conceptions.

Though Wicksteed is partially right, he has missed the main thrust of these verses. It is not so much that God is not touched by man's wickedness, but that *man is*! Both man the sinner and man the sinned against. And to this extent good and evil are still meaningful concepts in Blake's system. Moral codes based on abstract duty to a sky-god, "higher than thou," affect neither God nor man, and this has been Job's morality. But Blake must have expected us to understand verse 8 also, with his redefinitions of wickedness and righteousness: "Thy wickedness may hurt a man as thou art; and thy righteousness may profit the son of man." A recent comment on this is, "Man's good or evil affects only man, and cannot benefit or harm God. So also man's wisdom or folly affects only himself, Prov. 9:12."[20] But to Blake whatever affects one's fellow man or one's self—that is ultimately what affects God. When verses 6 and 7 are read in context, Blake's rereading of them does not seem so radical. The question at this point is not so much whether sin and righteousness matter, but to whom they matter and by whose standards they will be defined.

Like Frye, I see Elihu as a heroic and thematically significant figure; but whereas Frye assigns him a role similar to that of Newton in *Europe*, I identify him as a prophet or Interpreter, almost a persona for Blake himself. Blake's selection and placement of inscriptions in the margins indicate his resistance to the view that Elihu is merely another one of the accusers. His appearance in plate 12, occurring between the contrary visions of the abyss in plate 11 and the cleansing whirlwind in plate 13, suggests that his role is to interpret the one and prepare for the other.

One aspect of the picture itself requires further comment. Frye describes Elihu as "pointing to twelve stars, representing the cycle of the zodiac."[21] In neither the engraved nor the water color versions does he actually point *to* the stars; rather he appears to point *beyond* them or *through* them. In the engraved designs he appears to point to the marginal material in the extreme upper left-hand corner, including the texts (Job 33:14, 15) which refer to God's speaking to man in dreams or visions. The texts are in-

20 *Anchor Bible*, 228.
21 Rosenfeld, *Essays for Damon*, 227; cf. Damon, *Philosophy*, 34.

scribed on clouds, beneath which is a constellation of three stars (perhaps Orion, referred to later). The two columns of figures ascending in the right and left margins originate with the sleeping Job in the lower margin but rise to form a human canopy, extending out of the upper margin, apparently into infinity. They seem to be the human or visionary counterpart of the tentlike structure formed by the bare lines in the margin of plate 1. One sees here a wholesome exuberance as contrasted with the austere prudence of the illustration, marginal design, and texts of plate 1. The twelve stars which appear so bright in the illustration recur in the upper margin, scattered and relatively insignificant beneath the human canopy and cloudy inscriptions. It seems to me that Elihu's stars are more closely related to the "bright clouds" of his speech and hence to the possibility of vision than to the mechanical or rationalistic view of the universe. If so, Elihu's vision, though limited, is not false. It rises above a "starry floor"; it gives way to the fuller enlightenment of the succeeding plates and foreshadows the infinite and human vision of the morning stars of plate 14 {114}.

Elihu's high heavens and bright clouds have prepared for the Voice out of the Whirlwind, whose question echoes Elihu's earlier assertions (Job 34:37; 35:16): "Who is this that *darkeneth* counsel by words without knowledge?" (Job 38:2; italics mine). But after the cleansing of the whirlwind the darkness gives way to the brilliance of plate 14: Elihu's stars, now indubitably humanized, prevail.

In Orion and the Pleiades, which dominate the upper margin of plate 14, the Bible furnished Blake constellations replete with splendid classical lore. Orion's exploits cover the span of the created world. As Neptune's son, he was a giant who could walk on the floor of the ocean without getting his head wet. Though he is said to have sprung from the urine of the gods, he is elevated to the skies after a life of daring exploits—his futile attempts to win Merope, his blind journey to the sun where his sight is restored, and his eventual death at the hand of Diana, who loves him and gives him his place among the stars.[22] The Pleiades, the

[22] J.E.G.: Nelms does not emphasize his departure from earlier interpretations of plate 12—according to which Elihu is benighted because he seems to repeat the arguments of the three erring friends and points to the stars to justify his contentions. But, as Nelms notes, Elihu does not actually point

seven dovelike daughters of Atlas, are changed into a constellation to escape the amorous pursuit of Orion. Blake places the three stars of Orion in the upper right-hand corner and the seven Pleiades in the upper left-hand corner, rendering visible both Merope, who sometimes is said to fade away in shame because of her union with the mortal Sisyphus, and Electra, who is said not

---

at any of the stars. Even if he did, he would not necessarily be guilty of error; Blake criticism must abandon the dogma that stars are invariably sinister symbols of "materialism" or "reason." Insofar as their courses through the heavens are seen as unchanging and inexorable, they are culpable objects of superstition, but insofar as they light the darkness of night, they are windows to bright Eternity. And they are potentially human, as the angelic morning stars are revealed to be in plate 14 {114}.

If one were to try to measure the spiritual status of Elihu by his posture he might be badly misled by the figure of Satan who stands in a similar position, though with his right leg forward, at the lower left of that remarkable and too-little-known picture *The Fall of Man* (Keynes, *Bible*, no. 12). Apart from the possibility that Satan is here shown engaged in what is, in some respects, a commendable instigation, the fact that figures are shown cascading down *both* sides of the picture makes the contrast with *Job* 12 maximal, for there the border figures pour upwards on both sides, though the old man is yet asleep. And there can be no doubt at all that the resurrection of these figures is a positive redemption, since the center of action is at the lower left, above the feet of the old man, where two angels gesture upwards with their right arms while one passes a scroll to a rising woman. This gesture is closely related to the intervention of Jesus to raise man, which is depicted on the Genesis title page, where he passes to Adam a scroll which I have identified elsewhere as the Everlasting Gospel. See my review of Damon's *Dictionary, Philological Quarterly*, xlv, 534, and essay 14, n. 9, in this volume. It is notable, however, that the figure being raised in the Job design is a woman, for the woman was not yet attended to in the action shown in *The Divine Image*. She may be identified as Eve or Britannia, but in Blake's lyric symbolism she is called "Earth," as in the *Introduction* to the *Songs of Experience*, where she is shown as not yet risen from the starry floor in spite of the call of the Bard. But in the *Job* design the regeneration of the protagonist must begin with his emanative portion, who is depicted in the main picture at the nadir of despair as Job himself had been in the previous design.

Another evidence that Elihu is on a truly prophetic mission can be seen in *NT* no. 363, where a similar young man is routing a congregation of purveyors of traditional ignorance. His gesture is not as commanding as that of Elihu, in that he raises his hand to his bared breast rather than holding it out to silence the accusers, but his other hand is straight up as an invocation of supernal authority. Indeed, the contrast of this solitary with the crowd is in all respects sufficient evidence of the authenticity of his witness.

to have been able to bear the sight of the fall of Troy. This peculiar combination of three and seven stars is anticipated in the upper margin of plate 12, Elihu's starry world, on the left- and right-hand sides above the ascending emanations of the sleeping Job, and recurs under the right and left arms of God in his Ancient of Days posture of plate 15 {115}. The bonds of the Pleiades and the bands of Orion in the constellation remind one of T. S. Eliot's *Burnt Norton*, in which

> . . . the boarhound and the boar
> Pursue their pattern as before
> But reconciled among the stars.
> (II, 13-15)

The chaos of Leviathan in the Sea of Time and Space of the bottom margin of plate 14 contrasts with the order of these constellations, but the order is not achieved at the expense of motion and humanity, but rather the all too human pursuits are raised and reconciled in the stars, as in the myth and in Blake's design.

The Genesis myth of creation, substantially repeated in Job 38 and 39 and depicted in the side margins of plate 14, is analogous in its achievement of order without abstraction. At the top of the left panel is light, the creation of the first day; at the top of the right, the sun, moon and stars, creation of the fourth day. Below these are the firmament, the second day, and sea creatures and fowls, the fifth day. At the bottom are sea and land, the third day, and creeping things and cattle, the sixth day. Again Blake is fortunate in the symmetrical arrangement he inherits from the Bible account, which enables him to picture creation arising from the depths of chaos through sublunary earth to the heavenly lights.

The main design of the page with its mandala structure pictures man, who as creator of the worlds within is himself faced with the task of establishing light and order out of dark and chaotic depths. The sense of the design, as Marion Milner has effectively demonstrated, is that the depths cannot be ignored. The four parts represent man's four faculties. The lowest portion, the cavelike darkness beneath the heavy cloud, where the five mortals sit looking upward, is the area of the five senses. In the right middle section (to the left of the Deity), the winged moon goddess whose chariot is pulled by two serpents represents the passions. Corresponding to her on the other side is the sun god,

whose chariot is drawn by four horses. This would be the area
of reason. The top portion of the design is the area of inspiration
or imagination. It is filled with a myriad of stars and a triumphant,
apparently infinite, interlocking chain of the Sons of God. The
caption of the design is "When the morning Stars sang together
& all the Sons of God shouted for joy." The divine potential of
Lucifer is beginning to be realized. The false pride of Eliphaz and
the Elect gives way to the true pride of Elihu and the Reprobate.
As the Christian dispensation was heralded by the light of a star,
the triumph of light and the divine humanity in Christ is marked
in plate 17 {116} by another reference to stars: "When I behold
the Heavens the work of thy hands the Moon & Stars which thou
hast ordained. then I say. What is Man that thou art mindful of
him? & the Son of Man that thou visitest him" (Psalms 8:3, 4).
This passage echoes one in Job which Blake remarkably does not
use in this series of engravings:

> What is man, that thou shouldest magnify him? and that
> thou shouldest set thine heart upon him?
> And that thou shouldest visit him every morning, and try
> him every moment?   (Job 7:17-18)

This trial and Lucifer's fallen light are both recalled in the uppermost caption on plate 17: "He bringeth down to the Grave &
bringeth up" (1 Sam. 2:6). Christ is the embodiment of the "light
of the living" who have been saved from the pit. Henceforth,
Elihu's stars may fade in the light of what Blake elsewhere refers
to as "the more bright sun" {1}, represented in this picture by
the nimbus of God.

Before leaving the starry heavens, however, I should comment
briefly on the relation of plates 14 {114} and 15 {115}. In the
latter, Orion and the Pleiades are in the physical universe below
the clouds but safely above the grotesque turmoil of Behemoth
and Leviathan and outside their rigidly bounded circle. Certainly
14 and 15 are meant to be complementary and are thought of
as a part of the self-recognition necessary before the rejection of
Satan (plate 16) and the triumph of Christ (plate 17). Probably
they represent man's inner world and man's outer world, human
nature and Nature. These are not two different worlds, however,
but the same seen from different perspectives—looking up and
looking down. The first, except for the lower part, the senses, is

unbounded, apparently infinite, and is embraced, redeemed, and supported by the divine imagination. The second is strictly bounded, and the attitude of the deity toward it is almost Urizenic. Two of the marginal texts of plate 15 are from the "bright cloud" section of Elihu's speech, suggesting again the necessary perspective developed there—the cleansed, imaginative vision of the natural world. "Can any understand the spreadings of the Clouds / the noise of his Tabernacle?" (Job 36:29). The answer is yes. Anyone can who views them fearlessly and in their concrete forms. The three quotations from the Voice in the whirlwind show that Nature and the natural man must be formed, not ignored. "Behold now Behemoth which I made *with thee*" (Job 40:15; italics mine). The interpenetration of subject and object in perception is the basis of knowledge, and an awareness of this is the beginning of art and the humanizing of environment. Thus Behemoth is "the chief of the ways of God" (Job 40:19). Leviathan likewise can be hooked, but as he is a creature of the sea, not of the land like Behemoth, the task is more difficult. He is also more dangerous and reigns as "King over all the Children of Pride" (Job 41:34), for the proud cannot admit his chaotic existence in themselves or in Nature and so instead of controlling him are controlled by him.

Damon's view of this picture as "the unredeemed portion of the psyche" and Marion Milner's identification of Leviathan and the serpents of the moon goddess as the repressed depth or female portion of Job's rational, masculine mind seem to me to point in the right direction, but to stop short.[23] In this picture they are not dominant or out of control—as the circle, their concrete, visible forms, the presence of the recording angels, and the selection of marginal texts show. They are still chaotic, irrational, and very much alive, but not as violently sinister in fact as

---

[23] Damon, *Philosophy*, 40; Milner, "Psycho-Analysis and Art," 87-88. To Miss Milner the circle denotes an inner world, and the theme is the "two levels of the mind—the surface or conscious mind and the depth or unconscious mind." "Also Blake seems to be saying that this awakening comes through the acceptance of, equally with the male, what he seems to look upon as the female phase of mental functioning; also that the full experience of this female phase means a willingness to accept a temporary submergence below the surface consciousness." Orion is depicted in his human form in *NT* no. 502 (Night IX, 84), as well as the last design for *Il Penseroso* {106}.

Leviathan is in plate 14: they are recognized, acknowledged, and forgiven, we may say, but not abolished.

The analysis of text and design in plate 11 has taken me into the details and interrelations of a good many other plates and the reverberations go on almost indefinitely, but what is needed now is a view of the total structure of the series in both its visual and verbal effects.[24] The structure is obviously cyclic and dialectical simultaneously, for the first and last designs are contraries. In the first, Job and his wife are sitting with books outspread before them and their musical instruments hung on the tree above them. The sons are kneeling, holding their shepherd's crooks, one wearing a lyre. In the background are the setting sun on the left

[24] Wicksteed (*Blake's Vision*, 74-75) regards plate 11 as the nadir in a four-act drama. "The work then divides itself symmetrically thus: i-vi, Job loses the things of the earth; vii-xi, Job loses the things of heaven; xi-xv, Job, by the help of Elihu, recovers the things of earth in a new vision; xvi-xxi, Job discovers the things of heaven in the eternal vision."

Damon (*Dictionary*, 217) bases his interpretation of the structure on the design of the title page, which "shows the path of Experience which Job must tread, symbolized as the seven Eyes of God, seven angels descending and reascending clock-wise. They are the path of Job's sun, which sinks into the underworld but rises again at the end. The turning point is Shaddai, the State of Accusation, who looks backward. Once he is passed, the Eyes ascend again, ending with Jesus, who turns his face inward, toward the spiritual life."

At first Damon's scheme seems less arbitrary than Wicksteed's and truer to the details of the book; but on closer analysis this does not seem so obvious. For one thing, he applies the Eyes to the plates in a peculiar way, a pair of designs being assigned to each Eye for the first fourteen plates, then one plate to each Eye in reverse order and with reversed significance. This scheme is not particularly relevant either to the title page, where the seven Eyes form a cycle, not seven descending and seven ascending, or to the twenty-one plates, of which only three or four are particularly appropriate to the Eye that Damon assigns them. Plate 3 is relevant to Molech, who was worshiped by the sacrifice of children, especially if one accepts Damon's thesis that the sons are not actually killed but are destroyed only in Job's mind; and plate 9 is very suitable for Pahad (Horror) if the horror of Eliphaz is intended. These are two insights that I should regret giving up. More disappointing in Damon's scheme, however, is that Shaddai, whom he describes as the turning point in the design of the title page, is not associated with plates 10, 11, and 12, the turning point in the sequence—all of which are relevant to Shaddai's role as Accuser. Nor does he assign more benevolent roles to the three ascending Eyes, which are not only in the ascent on the title page but also on the right-hand side from the perspective of a Last Judgment scene.

and a sinister hill, waning moon, and single evening star on the right. A Gothic church reaches up to the sun, and tents of ease (or barns of plenty) are spread out under the moon. The sheep in the foreground are flanked by two rams, and the dog in the center is no more watchful than the sheep he should be guarding. In the last design, Job and his family are all standing playing on the musical instruments. Job is playing the harp with his right hand and worshiping God with his left. His and his wife's musical instruments enhance their sexual roles. The three daughters now face outward. The scroll held by the middle one replaces the books in the first design. The one on the right holds a lyre, and the one on the left a book—an illuminated book, no doubt, as painting is the only one of the three sister arts not otherwise represented. The shepherd's crooks have now disappeared, but one lies on the ground in the lower margin. The rising sun is now on the right, and the waxing moon and two morning stars are on the left. Even the sheep look less drowsy now, and there is a ram on Job's side of the page and a ewe on his wife's side—surely a good sign! The dog looks a bit more like a dog and more alert. His bright eye is open, and he appears relaxed, but not sluggish. In the margin the ram and the bullock have reversed positions.

Among the texts, the prayer of the first design, obviously a rote repetition from a book (Our Father which art in Heaven . . .), has been replaced by the song of Moses and the Lamb (Rev. 15:3). The emphasis on the heavenly presence of God has given way to an emphasis on his works and ways, verbal echoes of the references to moon and stars in plate 17 and Behemoth in plate 15: "Great & Marvellous are thy works / Lord God Almighty"; "Just & True are thy Ways / O thou King of Saints." The texts on the altar are parallel, both rejections of legalism. They recall the lines from the Prologue to *Gates of Paradise*:

> Jehovahs Finger Wrote the Law
> Then Wept! then rose in Zeal & Awe
> And the Dead Corpse from Sinais heat
> Buried beneath his Mercy Seat
> (E256/K761)

The habitual routine piety of Job's beginning, "Thus did Job continually" (Job 1:5), gives way to the rich blessing of his end, "So

the Lord Blessed the latter end of Job more than the beginning"
(Job 42:12).

Within this framework the progress of the designs can be compared to the cycle of the seven Eyes of God, suggested in the design of the title page. The middle of the cycle is Shaddai, the
Accuser, looking backward in accusation, but going forward in
redemption. This portion of the cycle begins in plate 10 with the
false accusation of the friends and Job's false self-justification,
continues in plate 11 through Job's self-accusation and recognition, and leads up to the true accusation of Elihu in plate 12.[25]

Lucifer, false Pride, is readily apparent in the first two plates
in Job's confidence in his material prosperity and moral perfection, with his family yet about him and his God securely enthroned
in heaven. But the fire falls from heaven (as Lucifer fell) in plate
3, and false pride is undermined. Ironically, all that Job had has
been in Satan's power all along, but he has been unaware of it.
The sons are destroyed amidst relics of Job's prosperity and their
revelry. A counterpoint to this is the heroic pride of the eldest son
with his child, his mistress, and his Herculean resistance to Satan
and the false God of his father.

Plate 4 ushers in Molech, the Executioner, with his fire and
lightning. The young men are slain with the sword. Satan with
bat wings and a sword is seen "going to and fro in the earth."
Destruction touches Job for the first time and his dead joys are
symbolized by the tiny prostrate figures on the upper corners of
the design. Molech's ravages continue, upsetting the stasis of
heaven in plate 5 and inflicting Job with boils in plate 6.

The presence of Elohim, the Judge, is less apparent in plates 7
and 8 but is implicit in the appearance of the three friends who
have prejudged Job's case. All the judgments rendered in these
plates are false; and this false system of Justice is symbolized by
the barren forest of Error in plate 9 {109}. Perhaps the falsest
judgment of all is Job's curse on the night he was born—the bitter
self-judgment in plate 8. In a way, the only true judgment in the
set is the ironic sense of the microscopic text at the bottom of
plate 7: "Ye have heard of the Patience of Job and have seen the
end of the Lord" (James 5:11). The end of the Lord, in the sense

---

[25] The sleeping figure of Job in the lower margin confirms the redemptive
movement. Wicksteed's interpretation (151-158) is impeccable, but too long
for summary here.

of the rejection of the false god and the fulfillment of divine humanity, is the most significant judgment pronounced in the book.

Proceeding forward from Shaddai, the Accuser, the Eyes must be interpreted more benevolently than usual, for they are in the ascent. Pahad, or Terror, must, therefore, be Awe, a proper fear of God or proper respect for divine humanity. This would be entirely appropriate to the whirlwind in plate 13 and the storm which lays low the forest of Error. Awe would again be the proper response to both plates 14 and 15 {114 and 115}, wherein the awesome heights and depths of man's creative faculties are realized.

Jehovah, the Lawgiver, might be ushered in by the angels writing on the tablets in the upper corners of plate 15, but plates 16, 17, and 18 depict the law of love, not the law of sin and death, the spirit that giveth life, not the letter that killeth. Jehovah, therefore, is presented in his more benevolent aspect of Mercy as opposed to the Justice of Elohim.[26] The first step of both Mercy and lawgiving is to cast out wickedness in high places. Thus the Jehovah cycle begins with the rejection of error—Satan and the now fully formed bodies of Job and his wife. Here is the consummation of *This body* and the *wrought Image* of plate 11.

Moreover, in the texts of the four margins of plate 16 the four earliest and more sinister Eyes of God are referred to as being in some way cast out. In the right margin (the left side of the Judgment scene) Lucifer as the Prince of this world is cast out, and just below, Satan is said to fall like lightning from heaven. In the upper margin Destruction (Molech) has no covering to save it from the wrath of God. The judgment of the wicked (Elohim) is fulfilled, as noted in the bottom margin. In the left margin (the right side of the Judgment scene) the Accuser is cast down, but the Almighty (Shaddai in his more visionary aspect) is preserved in the text: "Canst thou find out the Almighty to perfection?" Not only are the texts appropriate to the design, but their positions on the page are a part of the design and a relevant part of their meaning.

In plate 17 {116} Jehovah as Mercy sends Christ. "Know that after Christ's death, he became Jehovah" (E35/K150), and Job assumes the posture of Christ or Mercy in plate 18. In other words, the law of love is given in the former and obeyed in the latter; the

---

[26] Damon, *Dictionary*, 205-206.

identity of Jehovah and Jesus is stated in the one, and the identity of Jesus and Man is demonstrated visually and thematically in the other. Thus, he becomes as we are that we may become as he is.

The last three plates belong to Jesus, or God in Man, and so only human figures appear. Job is now God Incarnate. The acceptance of the gifts in plate 19 is accompanied by the fruiting of the fig tree and the grain. The margins are elaborately decorated with palms of victory, and the lily and rose. Job appears again in the cruciform position in plate 20 encompassing his daughters and repeating the position of God in the whirlwind in the painting behind him. His arms embrace the three daughters who correspond to the three arts, which are further represented on the page by the musical instruments, the paintings in the main picture, and the poetry quoted in the upper margin. The reference to their beauty in the marginal texts associates them with Job's new awareness of femininity: "There were not found Women fair as the Daughters of Job in all the Land & their Father gave them Inheritance among their Brethren" (Job 42:15). Their names as given in the biblical account mean "dove" (the bird sacred to Venus), "cassia" (a variety of perfume), and "antimony" (a kind of makeup thought to enhance seductiveness).[27] The marginal decorations are again luxurious with foliage and ripened grapes. Two embracing figures on each corner of the design recall the dead joys in a similar position in plate 4. The marginal texts, however, recall the suffering as do the paintings on the left and right behind Job and his daughters in plate 20.

> He bringeth Low & Lifteth Up (1 Sam. 2:7)

> If I ascend up into Heaven thou art there
> If I make my bed in Hell behold Thou art there
> (Psalms 139:8)

Thus, both in details of design and in the structure of the whole, there is an interdependence of quoted text and design, the one enriching and clarifying the other. Likewise, the contexts of the quoted Scriptures are implied in the quotations and can interpret and be interpreted by the designs with which they are associated. Not only has Blake produced a new account of Paradise lost and regained, but he has also produced a triumphant vindication and example of his new form of art.

[27] *Anchor Bible*, 392.

16

Epic Irony in
Milton

BRIAN WILKIE

IN CALLING Blake an epic poet we need no longer feel that we are being whimsical or using sleight of hand with the term *epic*. Blake revealed his own intentions clearly enough in his well-known letter of 1803: "I have in these three years composed an immense number of verses on One Grand Theme Similar to Homers Iliad or Miltons Paradise Lost the Persons & Machinery intirely new to the Inhabitants of Earth (some of the Persons Excepted),"[1] and since Northrop Frye's noble commentary in *Fearful Symmetry* (313-325) it has been clear that Blake himself understood the epic dynamics much as other poets had done.

Yet there is more to be said about Blake's epic strategy. Despite the poignant fact of his obscurity in his own lifetime, we need to see his attempts at epic as part of the whole Romantic attempt to refurbish epic as a vehicle for both propaganda and imaginative expression. Furthermore, we need to see Blake's epics in a wider context than that of his British epic ancestry, mainly Spenser and Milton. This second point is especially important, for although it is obvious that Blake enters the epic arena in order both to enlist Milton's aid as a brother prophet and to confute or convert him, it is less obvious that he does much the same thing with the whole general tradition of literary epic. In his long poems, and particularly in *Milton* and *Jerusalem*, the dazzling and sardonic ironies that Blake is master of are directed not merely at such perennial targets as eighteenth-century deism, Newtonian science, and man's seemingly infinite capacity to destroy his own happiness and mental health but also at a number of other targets toward which the epic tradition helps him to direct and steady his aim.

Nor should one feel uneasy in marrying the terms *epic* and *irony*. Some readers feel that epic is so solemn, noble, and sincere a form as to be above the calculating double-edgedness of irony,

[1] To Butts, 25 April 1803 (E697/K823).

but in fact all the great epic poets have been ironists to at least some extent. They tend to say things they do not mean literally and to encourage double-takes, as Milton does when, in Book IX of one of the most imitative and allusive poems in the world, he speaks scornfully of imitation. What Milton, like most epic poets, really means is that he *is* using epic gimmickry, though somewhat subversively: in the service of a new and higher truth. In many ways Blake does the same thing.

Like several of his fellow Romantics, however, Blake sometimes goes farther than this kind of gradualism and attempts to stand the whole epic tradition on its head while still drawing on it, as Byron does in *Don Juan* when in casting for the role of epic hero he selects a lover, and a casually easygoing one at that, over the heads of military adventurers of past and present. Even this kind of epic inversion depends on fairly strict verbal and mechanical echoes of the definitive epics which readers have come to accept unselfconsciously, as Byron's repeated appeals to epic precedent again make clear.

I wish to concentrate on the poem *Milton*, the shortest of Blake's three "major prophecies." I do so partly because it *is* relatively short and can therefore be treated in a brief essay. But there are other, less mechanical reasons too. For *Milton*, besides being an epic, is also a kind of dramatized essay on epic. One of the poem's central subjects is the way in which the impulse of inspired epic is propagated. Part of the epic poet's inspiration (here, Blake's own) comes directly from his unmediated, inspired vision, but part of it too must come from the pages, the living memory, of earlier poets and prophets, whom Blake likes to link, together with himself, in a mighty scheme, as he does in some epistolary verses to Flaxman in 1800: "Now my lot in the Heavens is this, Milton lov'd me in childhood & shew'd me his face. / Ezra came with Isaiah the Prophet, but Shakespeare in riper years gave me his hand" (E680/K799). It is thus not enough for Milton to become reincarnate in William Blake (as happens in plate 15 when Milton falls on the tarsus of Blake's left foot); it is also necessary that Los, the timeless and eternal representative of poetic inspiration, should be incarnated in both poets (the new trinity being completed in plate 22).

Milton is also a useful index to Blake's epic practice because it is the most "human" of the long poems, the most personal and most directly concerned with events that can be located on familiar earth (in Blake's garden at Felpham, for example) at the same time that it includes the "scenes in heaven" and the cosmic allegorical figures that dominate *Jerusalem* and *The Four Zoas*. Better than either of these *Milton* exhibits the dynamics of the relationship between literally human beings and the figures of Blake's mythology. In short, it illustrates the epic use of "machinery," the interplay between earth and heaven—a matter I shall return to presently.

It has been suggested that *Milton* (only two books long, though originally projected as having the standard epic twelve) be regarded as what Milton called "brief epic" (*Symmetry*, 313). This label is useful, but only in a limited way. Except for Milton's own contribution, which earns the title by authorial fiat, the "brief epic" hardly exists as a tradition demanding allegiance—unless we wish to cite Milton's own idiosyncratic precedent, the Book of Job, or advert to Aristotle's purely hypothetical prescription that future epics be as long as a series of tragedies presented on the same day.[2] To the extent, though, that Blake was focusing specifically on John Milton, the point about "brief epic" has its own ironic implications, because of the subject matter and title of *Paradise Regained*. For Blake's *Milton* is another poem about paradise regained, but with an ironic twist imparted to the prefix *re*. In Blake's poem John Milton is moved by a bard's song (an epic reminiscence in itself) to renounce the security of his place in the Church Triumphant, to reconsider such Miltonic values as chastity, to find within himself the Satan who had been conquered in Milton's "brief epic." Blake's *Milton* is a vicarious palinode which might well have been subtitled *Paradise Re-Regained*.

We need not reexamine here the intricate relationship, implied in the subject matter and titles of both poets' works, between Blake's epics and Milton's. Blake's critics have gone over the matter pretty thoroughly, and most of the important parallels with Milton's poems are obvious even to a casual reader of Blake—for example, the ironic parallel between the decision of Blake's Milton to forsake Eternity in order to redeem his errors and his Emanation and, in *Paradise Lost*, the Son's decision to become human

---

[2] *Poetics*, 24, 1459b.

and redeem a humanity that has fallen through the "vegetable" agency of the Tree. But, behind Milton, Blake is aware of the whole epic tradition, as of a backdrop in front of which his own epic action is to be played. The relationship between action and backdrop is essentially one of ironic contrast, as is so often true of the method which makes epic poets try to destroy earlier epic edifices in order to build something new from the rubble. In *Milton* Blake indicts the entire rationalist and "moral" tradition of the ancient classical world, with the epic poets, the "silly Greek & Latin slaves of the Sword" (pl. 1), bearing the brunt of his indignation.[3] Blake is not simply letting off steam in such passages or ingenuously expressing Romantic modernism or egocentrism; he is using a standard epic strategy of the kind that all epic poets use at times. That his antagonism to the ancient classics is a rhetorical cloak put on for a special occasion becomes clear if we compare these angry passages with the usual tenor, at least prior to 1805 or so, of his comments on the Greek and Roman ancients.[4]

[3] Blake champions the Bible in preference to "The Stolen and Perverted Writings of Homer & Ovid: of Plato & Cicero, which all Men ought to contemn"; he exhorts the young men of his age to ignore "Greek or Roman Models" and follow their own Imaginations (pl. 1); he has Milton complain that "The Nations still / Follow after the detestable Gods of Priam; in pomp / Of warlike selfhood, contradicting and blaspheming" (14:14-16); he makes Rintrah and Palamabron, in their fear of Milton's approach, anathematize "Laws from Plato & his Greeks to renew the Trojan Gods, / In Albion" (22:53-54).

[4] Although he could at times refer contemptuously to antiquity, as he did in a letter to Hayley (28 May 1804: K845) when he called the adulation of Washington and Buonaparte "Grecian, or rather Trojan, worship," his typical attitude toward the ancients before and while he composed *Milton* seems to have been friendly enough. He placed Aesop, Homer, and Plato among "The wisest of the Ancients" and answered his own rhetorical question "What is it sets Homer Virgil & Milton in so high a rank of Art?" by explaining that like the Bible they "are addressed to the Imagination which is Spiritual Sensation & but mediately to the Understanding or Reason" (E676-677/K794: to Trusler, 23 August 1799). In a letter to Cumberland of 2 July 1800 he hailed "the immense flood of Grecian light & glory which is coming on Europe" (E678/K797). He tried to decribe his "Grand Theme" itself by likening it to "Homers Iliad or Miltons Paradise Lost" (E697/ K823: to Butts, 25 April 1803), and his famous definition of poetry as "Allegory address'd to the Intellectual powers" is by Blake's own admission similar to the Platonic definition (K825: to Butts, 6 July 1803). Peter F.

362

In *Milton* his anti-epic invective serves the same half-artificial purpose it had served for Milton in *Paradise Lost* when he rejected contemptuously fabled knights in battles feigned along with the whole older tradition of derring-do. Both Blake and Milton, like all standard epic poets, are locating their poems in the line of an epic ancestry and at the same time informing their readers, through the poets' restiveness about that ancestry, of their attempt to go beyond the older epic values.[5]

When he wrote his letter to Butts mentioning his "long Poem . . . on One Grand Theme Similar to Homers Iliad or Miltons Paradise Lost," Blake was apparently referring to *Milton*,[6] and when he went on to say that the "Machinery" was "intirely new to the Inhabitants of Earth," he was not only pressing his claim to the status of inspired epic poet but also singling out a term which is central both in the epic tradition and in Blake's own peculiarly ironic epic strategy. "Machinery," the name given by epic theorists to those divine agents that intervene in human affairs, is traditionally used in the epic to give direction and meaning to the heroism of human actors and at the same time to define the limits of human power in the universe. This relationship between man and God is crucial to *Milton* as it is to almost all of Blake's work, and in the poem he uses machinery both in a fairly traditional way and in a very subversive one. Blake believes that, as Frye puts it (*Symmetry*, 31) "God is the perfection of man," but "man is not wholly God." To the extent that Blake wishes to explore the horror and pain of life in a fallen, vegetated world— the fact, in other words, that man is not wholly God—he insists on this duality of planes of action. Thus, for example, the winepress of Los, operated by the sons and daughters of Luvah, is in Eternity

---

Fisher, in his perceptive analysis of Blake's attitude toward classical civilization and art, states that Blake "did not deny that under the 'apparent surfaces' of classical myth and Greek philosophy was hidden genuine vision obscured and distorted by the limited ends it had been made to serve" and that he "had a way of recording his disagreements and absorbing his agreements without comment" ("Blake's Attacks on the Classical Tradition," *Philological Quarterly*, XL [1961], 1, 17).

[5] I have urged this view of the dynamics of epic in *Romantic Poets and Epic Tradition*, Madison, 1965, 3-16.

[6] The point is problematical, but see Erdman, in E727.

the passion of full and truly human love, but in our fallen world it is a terrible parody of Eternity: "This Wine-press is call'd War on Earth . . ." (27:8). Similarly, Milton's Shadow is vegetated when he embarks on his epic ordeal-journey to "Eternal Death," but simultaneously his "real and immortal Self" remains under the cherishing protection of the Seven Angels of the Presence (15:1-16).

On the other hand, it is also through his machinery and certain of his comments on its implications that Blake insists on God's humanity, on God as being the fulfilled potential of man. This is where his machinery becomes subversive. Los is no god of the *Aeneid* or the *Iliad*; he does not take sides with or direct human actors to whom he is superior, but rather fuses himself with the presently human William Blake and the historically human John Milton. At the very beginning of the poem proper, Blake, with an acrid glance both at Genesis and at *Paradise Lost,* locates "Paradise" in "the Portals of my Brain," planted there not by a Nobodaddy but by "The Eternal Great Humanity Divine" (2:7-8). "Seek not thy heavenly father then beyond the skies," Blake in his own voice urges "mortal man" (20:31-32), and in the context of the epic tradition the exhortation is a denial of the limitations of human power which that tradition had always tried to make poignantly, and from Blake's point of view defeatistly, emphatic. His rebellion against the dualism of epic machinery is grounded in the same aversion Blake felt toward religious and philosophical dualism.

Perhaps the most pungent of Blake's major epic ironies emerges in his treatment of a subject central to the epic: the role of woman and her relationship to heroism. In epic, woman is generally an ignoble alternative to stern heroic duty. Hector must leave Andromache, however sadly; Ulysses must leave Calypso, outwit Circe, and take precautions against the sirens' songs; Aeneas must renounce Dido's love; Tasso's Rinaldo and Spenser's enamored knight must not be allowed to bid farewell to arms with Armida and Acrasia. In his treatment of this subject Blake finds the general epic tradition even more useful to him than *Paradise Lost* is in particular, for despite the fit of uxoriousness that contributes to Adam's fall Milton generally treats human sexual love sympathetically, in his major epic at least.

In different ways and depending on his kaleidoscopically shifting point of view, Blake both rejects this antifeminine tradition of epic and endorses it in his inimitably ironic way. The ordinary simple and literal distrust of sex as a distraction from martial heroism he rejects stridently enough. The climactic instance of this reversal is the casting off of virginity by Milton's Emanation, Ololon, near the end of the poem (42:3-6). The same reversal of epic precedent is illustrated, perhaps even more clearly, in Blake's implied judgment on the casting out by Satan of his emanation Leutha, an act which clearly parallels, in its suicidal self-destructiveness, the driving away of Ahania in Night III of *The Four Zoas*.[7] Leutha, repentant, describes Satan's Urizenic motives:

> . . . in selfish holiness demanding purity
> Being most impure, self-condemn'd to eternal tears, he drove
> Me from his inmost Brain & the doors clos'd with thunders sound . . .
> . . . Alas what shall be done [the Sick-one] to restore?
> Who calls the Individual Law, Holy: and despises the Saviour.
> Glorying to involve Albions Body in fires of eternal War—
> (*M* 12:46-49; 13:4-6)

But, like Blake's other poems, *Milton* contains its own symbolic type of antifeminism: in his distinctive way Blake could portray the female threat to heroism (Blake's own version of heroism) as direfully as any of the great epic poets. Leutha's repentant confession, from which I have just quoted, exhibits this side of Blake's attitude too. Leutha has seduced Satan as in *Paradise Lost* Sin does, but Blake has his own way of defining the siren's wiles:

> Ah me! the wretched Leutha!
> . . . entering the doors of Satans brain night after night
> Like sweet perfumes I stupified the masculine perceptions
> And kept only the feminine awake. Hence rose his soft
> Delusory love to Palamabron: admiration join'd with envy
> Cupidity unconquerable! (12:3-8)

[7] *FZ* III 43-44 (E322-323/K294-295:110-145).

The Divine Voice later reproaches the "Daughter of Babylon" for her insubordination:

> When I first Married you, I gave you all my whole Soul . . .
> Then thou wast lovely, mild & gentle. Now thou art terrible
> In jealousy & unlovely in my sight, because thou hast cruelly
> Cut off my loves in fury till I have no love left for thee.
> Thy love depends on him thou lovest & on his dear loves
> Depend thy pleasures which thou hast cut off by jealousy. . . .
>
> (33:2-9)

Blake puts the point most succinctly in one pungent, understatedly didactic couplet:

> The nature of a Female Space is this: it shrinks the Organs
> Of Life till they become Finite & Itself seems Infinite.
>
> (10:6-7)

Blake's irony on the subject of woman is even more complex, however. For his endorsement of this somewhat ironic version of epic antifeminism is itself based on a rationale exactly opposed to that which operates in the standard epics, though like earlier epic poets Blake sees love and war as parts of the same problem of human values. The irony, in other words, is put through an extra inversion. The siren figures in Blake do not tempt men to lay down their arms in order to rest in voluptuary bliss. On the contrary, the sinister females in Blake's mythology, the representatives of the "female will" in the worst sense, make the cruelty of bloodshed the very price of sexual blandishments. They are, simply, blood-swilling whores who represent the final distillation of the attitude Dryden summed up in the words "Only the brave deserve the fair." The hermaphroditic voices which, while he is struggling with Urizen, tempt Milton to become King of Canaan boast that "bright Tirzah triumphs: putting on all beauty / And all perfection, in her cruel sports among the Victims"; they demand that Jerusalem be brought "with songs on the Grecian Lyre" and offered up to "Holiness." The Images of the Lamb of God

> . . . are born for War! for Sacrifice to Tirzah!
> To Natural Religion! to Tirzah the Daughter of Rahab
>   the Holy!

366

She ties the knot of nervous fibres, into a white brain!
She ties the knot of bloody veins, into a red hot heart!

(19:44-56)

One of the most appalling passages in all of Blake's poetry is the description of the "Human grapes" in the winepress of war, and here the connection with sex is explicit enough:

> In chains of iron & in dungeons circled with ceaseless fires.
> In pits & dens & shades of death: in shapes of torment
> & woe.
> The plates & screws & wracks & saws & cords & fires &
> cisterns
> The cruel joys of Luvahs Daughters lacerating with knives
> And whips their Victims & the deadly sport of Luvahs
> Sons.
> They dance around the dying, & they drink the howl &
> groan,
> They catch the shrieks in cups of gold, they hand them
> to one another:
> These are the sports of love, & these the sweet delights of
> amorous play
> Tears of the grape, the death sweat of the cluster the
> last sigh
> Of the mild youth who listens to the lureing songs of
> Luvah. (27:32-41)

Blake's ambivalent view of sex and of the female will is thus a paradox, but one that is simply resolved. From the viewpoint of the person in the earthly state of vegetation and generation, woman's love is a noble and healthy alternative to war; by the standards of the fiery imaginative realm of Eden, sex symbolizes at best (as in Beulah) a mild and pleasant relaxation from the active ardors of Eternity, at worst a sinister betrayal of the full imaginative life. This life of total imaginative energy is for Blake true heroism, and he, like other epic poets in the service of another heroism, makes it a severely masculine principle.

The reexamination of woman's role in relation to heroism is a preoccupation Blake shares with other Romantic authors of epic: the Byron of *Don Juan*, the Southey of *Joan of Arc*, the Shelley who in *The Revolt of Islam* gives the heroine Cythna a heroic role separate from but equal to Laon's. But the question of woman is only part of a still larger preoccupation which Blake shares with other Romantics. Like them, Blake wants to redefine heroism in terms of mental and spiritual experience and to substitute this new heroism for war and empire-building. And, again like most other Romantics, Blake finds the precedent of Milton useful to this strategy, since Milton had claimed to renounce "Wars, hitherto the only Argument / Heroic deem'd" in favor of "the better fortitude / Of Patience and Heroic Martyrdom" (*Paradise Lost* IX, 28-32). Milton had not gone far enough, however, and therefore, for example, Blake can attribute to Rintrah and Palamabron a fear that Milton's religion, along with its eighteenth-century heritage, will make war "With cruel Virtue . . . upon the Lambs Redeemed; / To perpetuate War & Glory . . ." (22:44-45). The siren voices tempt the struggling poet to be bound in "the bands of War" (20:5). It is this corrupt tendency in himself and in his work, coupled with his genuine but not sufficiently clear-sighted disgust with martial heroism, that makes Milton volunteer for "Eternal Death," for, as he goes on to say, "The Nations still / Follow after the detestable Gods of Priam; in pomp / Of warlike selfhood, contradicting and blaspheming" (14:14-16). And along with Milton, Blake indicts the entire epic tradition: "the silly Greek & Latin slaves of the Sword" (pl. 1), "the Trojan Gods" (22:53).

Yet Blake also reserves for this subject an irony almost as rich as that which informs his treatment of the feminine theme; like Shelley in *The Revolt of Islam*,[8] Blake repudiates war but preserves the metaphor of warfare. He vows, "I will not cease from Mental Fight, / Nor shall my Sword sleep in my hand" (pl. 1). The life of Eden is essentially a kind of warfare:

> As the breath of the Almighty, such are the words of man
>   to man
> In the great Wars of Eternity, in fury of Poetic Inspiration,
> To build the Universe stupendous: Mental forms
>   Creating. . . .

[8] *Romantic Poets and Epic Tradition,* 139-140.

But literal earthly war is sadly different:

> ... the Gods of the Kingdoms of the Earth: in contrarious
> And cruel opposition: Element against Element, opposed
>   in War
> Not Mental, as the Wars of Eternity, but a Corporeal
>   Strife. . . .
>
>   (30:18-20; 31:23-25)

Ololon, gazing into the "Heavens of Ulro," puts the matter most poignantly and at the same time makes the ironic parallel with standard epic values nearly explicit:

> How are the Wars of man which in Great Eternity
> Appear around, in the External Spheres of Visionary Life
> Here renderd Deadly within the Life & Interior Vision ...
> Those Visions of Human Life & Shadows of Wisdom &
>   Knowledge
> Are here frozen to unexpansive deadly destroying terrors.
> And War & Hunting: the Two Fountains of the River
>   of Life
> Are become Fountains of bitter Death. . . .
>
>   (34:49-35:3)

For Blake to call the occupations of Eternity "War & Hunting" is more than an affirmation of the energy of Eden; it is also both a sardonic redefinition and a kind of redemption of the most important single source of epic imagery—hunting—and its standard subject matter—war.

One of the key facts about the epic and Blake's relationship to it is that epic, like the Bible, has a strong historical bias, a tendency to celebrate the unique effect of certain moments in time which are important precisely because they will never occur again. Such for Virgil is the moment when Troy fell, for Camoëns the first rounding of the Cape, for Milton the moment when the Tree of Knowledge was despoiled. Such for the Old Testament writers were the moments when Abraham left Chaldea and when the Covenant was contracted at Sinai. For the New Testament writers such were the times when John the Baptist began his ancillary ministry and when Jesus was born; the authors of Matthew and Luke are as careful to locate these events in particular periods and reigns as the authors of Genesis are to establish the exact ages of the patriarchs.

Myth, on the other hand, concerns itself with what happens perennially, in a sense outside of historical time entirely—the enduring phenomena of nature such as the change of the seasons and the predictable rhythms of the human psyche such as the dynamics of puberty and of the other climacterics. And it is impossible to deny that Blake is a mythic poet in exactly this sense; that is one reason why he prefers to avoid linear continuity and chronology in his poems and to fuse or create overlaps in his characters (Los and Milton and Palamabron and Blake; Urizen and Satan and Jehovah and Newton). It is also one reason why Blake has such startling insight into and power over his readers.

It is quite true, of course, that both the biblical and the epic writers draw freely on the mysterious reservoir of mythic insight. The opening chapter of Genesis depends on Babylonian creation myths, and when Moses draws water from the stone in the desert the incident is somehow mythically and psychologically akin to such far-flung analogues as Wordsworth's Arab who hastens to do the opposite, to preserve the stone and shell in the face of the threat of watery engulfment.[9] Aeneas' descent into the underworld with the help of the talismanic golden bough is obviously mythic enough in its implications, and Milton compares the Garden of Eden to Proserpina's fair field of Enna. But in the last analysis these authors and works are fairly militantly antimythic (in the sense of *myth* I have just outlined). The authors of Genesis insist that their pagan sources are merely grotesque parodies of the unique truth (God is not in nature but rather made it, bit by bit and day by day); Moses' striking of the rock was a particular enough event so that some mysterious delinquency in the act earned him the punishment of not reaching Canaan; Aeneas' visit to the underworld results in a vision of imperial Rome at the time of Augustus; Milton's Eden was real while Enna is a timeless fable. If they had anticipated later systems of measurement, Matthew and Luke would doubtless have insisted that Jesus was born on a Thursday, at 11:14 P.M., weighing seven pounds three ounces. In short, for all these authors time and history have a shape, utterly unique and preciously particular.

[9] Cf. Part 2, "The Stone and the Shell," in W. H. Auden, *The Enchafèd Flood*, New York, 1950.

The biblical and epic obsession with time and history is important in interpreting Blake's many poetic statements on the subject. The metaphysical problem of time is important in itself to him, but it is also important because it is a central concern in the epic tradition he is exploiting, however ironically. The irony in his treatment of time, however, lacks the cutting edge of his other epic ironies; in this area he is ironic in the "New Critical" sense which sees irony as an attempt to balance or reconcile ambiguities, without necessarily serving a satiric purpose. For the most part Blake subscribes to the historical rather than the mythic view. A number of times in *Milton* he claims that the six-thousand-year trial which the world has had to endure is approaching its climax (e.g., 21:51-52; 22:15-18; 23:55), and he insists that the Christian cycle of history is to be the last one, ending in a unique apocalypse. The despair implied in an endless series of cycles is foreign to his vision: "Time is the mercy of Eternity; without Times swiftness / Which is the swiftest of all things: all were eternal torment" (24:72-73). The most eloquent and moving expression of the precious particularity of time (and of space and circumstance) is put into the mouth of Los:

> . . . not one Moment
> Of Time is lost, nor one Event of Space unpermanent.
> But all remain: every fabric of Six Thousand Years
> Remains permanent: tho' on the Earth where Satan
> Fell, and was cut off all things vanish & are seen no more
> They vanish not from me & mine, we guard them
>   first & last.
> The generations of men run on in the tide of Time
> But leave their destind lineaments permanent for
>   ever & ever.   (22:18-25)

Blake is generally more ambiguous, however, in his treatment of time and timelessness, and even in the passage I have just quoted it is significant that the words of Los are delivered just after his mythic fusion with William Blake, an event which illustrates a collapsing of time as much as time's culmination. The description in plate 28 of the building by Los's sons of vehicles for every unit of time ("Moments & Minutes & Hours / And Days & Months & Years & Ages & Periods; wondrous buildings") ends with a daring apothegm which is equally compatible with both the mythic and historic visions:

> Every Time less than a pulsation of the artery
> Is equal in its period & value to Six Thousand Years.
> For in this Period the Poets Work is Done: and all the
>   Great
> Events of Time start forth & are concievd in such a Period
> Within a Moment: a Pulsation of the Artery.
>
> (28:44-29:3)

Universality and particularity blend here in a way which makes the categories of myth and history inadequate at least. And indeed Blake seems to be trying in *Milton* to achieve some kind of synthesis or reconciliation of these two kinds of vision. This is, to draw an analogy, what happens in the Christian liturgy for Holy Week, which in circumstantial detail celebrates on Good Friday and again on Easter Sunday important and unique events in time but on the intervening Saturday celebrates the typology (water, fire, light) of a redemption which is personal, perennial, timeless, and universal. In poetry such syntheses had best been achieved before Blake by Dante and Spenser, two other poets who tried to combine a sense of epic etiology with allegory addressed to the intellectual powers and thus produced, as Blake did too, a fascinating species of hybrid genre. Which is a reminder that, although the epic tradition can help us understand much about Blake's long poems, it will not take us all the way. Blake can be finally grasped only in terms of himself and of his unique vision.

17

The Formal Art of
The Four Zoas

HELEN T. MC NEIL

The Four Zoas, Blake's most experimental poem, shares the thematic ambitions of *Milton* and *Jerusalem*. Like them, it is of epic length and significance, with a mythic scope and superhuman protagonists. Formally, however, *The Four Zoas* goes beyond the innovations of both its companion epics: it dispenses with exposition or explanation and concentrates on an intense exchange of action and reaction, statement and counterstatement. This concentration creates an epic of situations, in which action has been reduced to a series of violent, absolute confrontations taking place in a cosmic limbo.

Since *The Four Zoas* lacks exposition, character reveals itself by behavior within a given encounter. During these encounters, the ferocity shared by the Zoas is more striking than their differences: each is a potential tyrant. Constantly descending and fragmenting into Emanations and Spectres, the Zoas act according to the requirements of the present situation, not according to a concept of stable personality. This creates an emphasis on action rather than on agent. Urizen the destroyer, the sufferer, the unrequited lover, the radiant guest at an apocalyptic feast are all the same "living creature,"[1] acting in apparently contradictory ways according to the roles that analytic intellect may play between the beginning and the end of fragmented human consciousness.

In *Milton* and *Jerusalem*, the giant Albion, the Zoas, the Vortex and other characters and powers are introduced in the context of antecedent cultural images which the reader is likely to recognize. But the reader of *The Four Zoas* searches in vain for *Milton's* explanations of Blakean terminology and the guiding—if ironically limited—perspective of a narrator. Nor will he find those references to the Bible and Britain which connect the narrative

---

[1] Blake's four Zoas are the "living creatures" of *Ezekiel* 1:5-24 and Revelation 4:6-8.

of *Jerusalem* with external history, theology, or myth. The Zoas themselves sporadically posit pasts or structure the present, but their accounts, flawed as they are by the passions of the moment, are not consistent. In Night the Fourth, Tharmas forces Los to create a physical world and the familiar Orc cycle of a creation-fall leading toward an eventual apocalypse begins to emerge, but even so, cosmology in *The Four Zoas* remains conspicuous by its absence. Later on in the poem, the presence of two versions of Night the Seventh indicates that Blake was uncertain about the kind of role that a historical cycle should play in a work characterized by the encounters of supernatural beings. More than any other of Blake's poems about universal disaster and ultimate recovery, *The Four Zoas* operates without a context, even a Blakean one.

The absoluteness of *The Four Zoas* has the effect of forcing the reader immediately into the poem's chaotic world. Blake could have made explicit the parallels between facultative psychology and his own, but he opted to draw the Zoas without apology or explanation. Thus the internecine warfare of the "living creatures" offers the reader an embodiment of certain battles of the mind, but the one does not explicitly represent the other: *The Four Zoas* is not *psychomachia*. Instead, it develops operational definitions which absorb our previous notions about the psyche. The Zoas offer an independent image which can be recognized as accurate but never fully grasped in terms not its own. The inarticulateness induced by this lack of reference makes the reader hesitate to apply his own version of the mind's form to the poem. Without a mimetic link between poem and world, it is difficult to translate Vala into "Nature" or Tharmas into "Desire" and feel confident that the equivalences are meaningful.

Milton and *Jerusalem* gradually lead the reader to an acceptance of Blakean world view and terminology: *The Four Zoas* aggressively presents that world view as a *fait accompli*. Ideally, then, it attempts to accomplish by shock techniques what the other long poems attempt by measured development: the moment of psychic renovation when the reader accepts the reality of the Blakean myth as final. At this point, the visionary drama and the real would become one, and its actors would be no longer fictive tools but the true forms of imagination. The reader, subject to the ravages of mental powers like those in *The Four Zoas*, is shown by example that he, as a type of the fallen Albion, can aspire to the relative unity of the poem's conclusion.

The Four Zoas emerged from its parent manuscript, *Vala*,[2] as the result of a series of formal dislocations. To the extent that it can be considered a separate poem, *Vala* began with what is now Night the Second of *The Four Zoas*. The opening of Night the Second offers a brief, but clear, exposition of the relation between Albion the Eternal Man and his "Sons" or constituent qualities, the Zoas. "Rising upon his Couch of Death" (23:1), Albion bequeaths his scepter to Urizen, who begins to build the Mundane Shell (as in *The Book of Urizen*), limiting the universe for the first time. This straightforward opening seems not to have satisfied Blake, and he added the dislocations of Night the First.

Immediately after the penciled title "The Four Zoas," which precedes the present Night the First, Blake provides a half-title, an epigraph, an invocation, an appeal to authority, and definitions of subject and hero. Some of these are subsequently ignored, others prove to be ironic or trivial, and still others turn out to be central to an understanding of the poem. Much of Blake's independence from conventional structure lies in the simple fact that he does not inform the reader which are which.

First the poem defines an ostensible (but immediately discarded) subject in the half-title, "The torments of Love & Jealousy in / The Death and Judgement / of Albion the Ancient Man." Albion's torments and judgment would seem to provide the poem's material, but references to Albion or to his heroic epithets, the Ancient Man, the Eternal Man, and the Slumbering Man, are so scattered that Albion is at most a referential frame for the action, and not a character, as he is in *Jerusalem*. Next follows the motto "Rest before Labour," which is the opposite of what the Zoas do. Above the title "VALA / Night the First" Blake places an epigraph from Ephesians 6:12 in the original Greek; in the King James Version it reads:

> For we wrestle not against flesh and blood, but against principalities, against powers, against the rulers of the darkness of this world, against spiritual wickedness in high places.

[2] In *Blake's Vala*, Oxford, 1956, H. M. Margoliouth begins *Vala* with the present Night the Second of *The Four Zoas*. The edition gives an interesting impression of a more conventionally structured text beneath the revised poem, but it rests on the assumption, difficult to prove, that a certain intermediate draft of the poem can be identified and taken to be a single entity.

The epigraph accurately describes *The Four Zoas*' assignment of battling spiritual wickedness in high places, but it misleads the reader into thinking that Blake's "rulers of darkness" are the same as the Bible's.

The poem proper begins with a reference to "The Song of the Aged Mother," Eno.[3] These lines place her song in the past; their diction is deliberately majestic:

> The Song of the Aged Mother which shook the heavens
>   with wrath
> Hearing the march of long resounding heroic Verse
> Marshalld in order for the day of Intellectual Battle
> (3:1-3:E297/K264)

The Aged Mother has heard Blake's heroic verse, ready for intellectual battle. Is *The Four Zoas* to be an attack on intellectual error, with the Earth Mother Eno the embodiment of the anti-Blakean forces? We hear no more, however, of Eno's wrath or of the historical Blake.

Lines 4 through 8 of Night the First offer a skeletal version of the poem's cosmic scheme and the status of the characters. The passage mixes standard exposition and irony:

> Four Mighty Ones are in every Man;
>   a Perfect Unity   John XVII c. 21 & 22 & 23 v
> Cannot Exist. but from the Universal
>   Brotherhood of Eden   John I c. 14 v
> The Universal Man. To Whom be
>   Glory Evermore Amen   και· εσκηνωσεν εν· ημιν
>
> What are the Natures of those Living Creatures the Heavenly
>   Father only
> Knoweth no Individual Knoweth nor Can know in all Eternity

The marginal references to John 1 and John 17 attach Blake's epic myth to the Bible. Albion is implicitly identified with the Christ who is sent into the world "that they all may be one" (John 17:21). The resurrection of the dead Albion would provide a

---

[3] In the manuscript, many erasures indicate some uncertainty about which female character should bear the weight of response. Eno and Vala were both written and erased; Enitharmon replaced Eno, and finally the whole first line was rewritten without naming the Aged Mother, the mother of our mortal part.

second resemblance to the New Testament, but it is not announced until Night the Eighth.[4] The first indication of less than complete fidelity to the views of the Bible appears in perfunctory flatness of Blake's brief prayer: "To Whom be Glory Evermore Amen." The prayer applies equally to Blake's fallen immortal, "The Universal Man," and to the Christian God. Only later in *The Four Zoas*, as the action proceeds, do the invidious consequences of Christian belief emerge. Immediately after saying that no individual, but "the Heavenly Father Only," can know the natures of the Zoas, Blake proceeds to demonstrate his own extensive knowledge of Tharmas and, in time, of all the other Zoas as well.

In the next stanza of Night the First, Los-Urthona, the most conventionally creative of the Zoas, is introduced as the poem's apparent hero. The fall and resurrection motif, first attached to Albion, is transferred to Urthona. It is he of whom the Blakean muses are urged to sing:

> Los was the fourth immortal starry one, & in the Earth
> Of a bright Universe Empery attended day & night
> Days & nights of revolving joy, Urthona was his name,
> In Eden; in the Auricular Nerves of Human life
> Which is the Earth of Eden, he his Emanations
> propagated
> Fairies of Albion afterwards Gods of the Heathen,
> Daughter of Beulah Sing
> His fall into Division & his Resurrection to Unity
> His fall into the Generation of Decay & Death & his
> Regeneration by the Resurrection from the dead
>
> Begin with Tharmas Parent power. darkning in the West

In spite of the introduction of Urthona, when the action of *The Four Zoas* does begin, neither Albion nor Urthona but Tharmas is the agent, "darkning in the West." This passage also contains

---

[4] The Bible is not overtly acknowledged again as an authority until p. 111 of Blake's manuscript. As the apocalyptic harlot Rahab "triumphs over all" (111:19), "John saw these things Reveald in Heaven" (111:4). Familiar biblical terms like "the Lamb of God" recur in the text, but the wise reader withholds approval until it becomes clear in Night the Eighth that it is only in the fallen, corporeal world that Luvah takes on the form of the Lamb of God.

The Four Zoas' version of an epic invocation, "Daughter of Beulah Sing / His Fall . . . ," but it is not addressed to the classical muses, daughters of Memory. In a slap at the Lockean conception of the poetic mind as a storage bin for past sensory impressions, Blake calls on the daughters of Beulah, daughters of Inspiration, to aid his song.

Blake's introduction of the status of the Zoas is almost parenthetical. Urthona propagated his Emanations "in the Auricular Nerves of Human Life." He is thus connected with the sense of hearing and exists within the human form.[5] Human life, in turn, is "the Earth of Eden," the place where we stand or fall. If the terms of this passage were maintained by consistently psychological or "interior" imagery, *The Four Zoas* could be read with some justice as the account of the battle of contraries within every man. It is this, but Los is also "immortal," "starry," ruling "the Earth / Of a bright Universe"; Tharmas darkens "in the West" and sits "weeping in his clouds" (4:27); and soon after, the females of "Eden," which had seemed to be identified with "human life," have a limitless universe of time and space to play with when they begin to weave their constricting veils. The mind and the universe are interchangeable metaphors for the place where the Zoas battle. Their strife and its faltering resolution can be said to internalize a myth of creation, fall, and apocalypse, providing a *Götterdämmerung* with its psychological commentary built in—or, alternately, the Zoas externalize basic disputes of the spirit. Since for Blake the fully realized man and the imagination were one, he would take any final placement of a myth inside or outside man as a severe limitation on the validity of its conclusions.

The reader, subjected to Blake's abrupt shifts in focus, may have difficulty assessing the relative importance of a given passage, but Blake gives his references casually, as if the reader were expected to know already who the Zoas are and whether a particular incident is ironic, trivial, or important. Many of the poem's oblique references are explained in *Milton* and *Jerusalem*, so that *The Four Zoas* seems to be dependent on the two other works for context. Since, however, the present version of *The Four Zoas*

[5] In his Commentary on 3:9-4:3(E865) Harold Bloom associates the "Earth of Eden" with the "Auricular Nerves," but since the relative clause reads "Human life / Which is the Earth of Eden," using a singular verb, "Earth of Eden" must refer back to all of human life.

is a deliberate one and the matter of the poem is Blake's central myth, rather than an ancillary tale, the poem's confident lack of reference must be taken seriously. All of Blake's longer poems argue explicitly and by their example against the bondage of imagination to preexisting historical, religious, or philosophic conceptions of the human, but only *The Four Zoas* is written as if the battle against alien forms had already been won. *The Four Zoas'* independence of form amounts to the creation of an internally consistent but externally unexplained world. A creation of this sort, even if Blake did not carry it beyond manuscript stage, has tremendous formal implications. It bluntly abandons the associative obligations of major poetry, and by so doing threatens the mimetic mode itself. Such a threat, if carried through, could return major poetry to a pre-Homeric primitivism, or, more hopefully, it could give a literary form to any phenomenology which, like Blake's, sees the perceiver and the perceived as one.

By the fifteenth line of *The Four Zoas*, Blake's mutual contradictions leave only the sense that the work is to be of great moment. Blake withholds further explanations or equivalences and begins the epic's first scene: the reader is plunged *in medias res* without a guide. Before us is Tharmas, "parent power," bewailing the loss of his Emanation, "sweet Jerusalem" (4:8). He says alternately that he has hidden Jerusalem and that Enion has taken her away. As he, weakened by this loss, begs Enion for pity, he expresses pity for his even weaker Emanation, Enitharmon. Enion's whining reply objectifies Tharmas' fears: she blames their apparently already degraded state on a cowardice which she cannot or will not explain:

> Enion said—Thy fear has made me tremble thy terrors
> have surrounded me
> All Love is lost Terror succeeds & Hatred instead of Love
> And stern demands of Right & Duty instead of Liberty
>
> (4:16-18)

What has terrified Tharmas? What has he done to cause Enion to blame him—rightly or wrongly—for her loss of liberty? Was she, and is she, so utterly dependent on him as she says? Why does she speak so fatalistically? These questions are never answered; the situation is taken to be self-explanatory.

Enion wants to end her existence, to turn into a shadow and

hide in Tharmas as Jerusalem has done, but at the same time she attacks him. With irrevocable caprice she says that she "cannot return." Her utterance of these fatal words weakens Tharmas to a point where he can no longer hope to return himself or Enion to their original united state. Enion's anatomizing destroys the spontaneity on which Tharmas' identity depends:

> I have lookd into the secret soul of him I lovd
> And in the Dark recesses found Sin & cannot return
>
> Trembling & pale sat Tharmas weeping in his clouds
>
> Why wilt thou Examine every little fibre of my soul
> Spreading them out before the Sun like Stalks of flax
>   to dry
> The infant joy is beautiful but its anatomy
> Horrible Ghast & Deadly nought shalt thou find in it
> But Death Despair & Everlasting brooding Melancholy
> $$(4:25-32:E298/K265)$$

This passage raises more questions: What is the fatal flaw that Enion claims to have found? If Tharmas and Enion represent psychological powers, should they not be acting more consistently? If they are gods, why are they so vulnerable to mere speech? If demigods, how can they be, as Tharmas says, "a victim to the living" (4:7)? The Zoas cannot be human, since creatures called Emanations can spring from them and since they can move through "clouds" and fade into "a Shadow in Oblivion" (4:21). They seem rather to be fluid, nonhuman powers, constantly subject to change and redefinition.

Tharmas and Enion's exchange of lament and accusation throws the reader into a complex, embittered, and precipitous situation. It is as if another *Paradise Lost* were to begin with Eve's (or here, Enion's) laments and machinations immediately after an undescribed fall. Her destructive persuasion of Adam would then be the first action of an epic whose end and cause were unknown. Even so, in *Paradise Lost* Adam and Eve are familiar to the Christian reader, who would immediately recognize their plight and its history. Eve is given motives and Adam hesitations and scruples which are clearly recognizable as human. The roles and hierarchical standing of God, the Angels, Satan, and Adam and Eve have all been made clear to the reader. In *The Four Zoas*, by

contrast, neither the recognition of frame nor the recognition
of psychology is available. The point of the epic can only be derived from the scenes of which it is composed, and these follow a
hectic, disruptive pattern of their own.

There are four levels of characters in *The Four Zoas*. When first
extracted from the text they may seem to form a hierarchy, with
the Eternals at the top, Albion "the Eternal Man" next, the Zoas
in the middle, and, finally, man at the bottom. Much of this apparent order is illusory. Albion is no more than a frame for the
poem's action. The Eternals, described only in passing, function
like the sylphs in Pope's *The Rape of the Lock*: they are machines,
introduced to provide a parody of causality in a world that seems
quite capable of functioning without it. At best the proposed
causality of the Eternals is perfunctory. More often it serves an
ironic function, as in the following passage from Night the Sixth.
Urizen is in the midst of one of his last ominous journeys:

> Endless had been his travel but the Divine hand him led
> For infinite the distance & obscurd by Combustions dire. . . .
>
> (72:2-3:E342/K316)

Urizen staggers away from the latest and most deathly of his successive creations. The Divine hand is mentioned only once, at
Urizen's moment of greatest despair, when it has become clear
that the laws of bondage in books of "brass & iron & gold" (71:40)
will be, and must be, written; Urizen's frantic creations have been
proved to be cruel hoaxes for him as well as for man. In this situation Urizen's character has created his fate, and the Divine hand
is an externalization of his impulse to continue to create, whatever the price. By tempting the reader with a chance to cast the
blame for these creations on a vague divinity, Blake exposes our
craven desire to pity the weeping executioner. Even if the Divine
hand were considered a separate power, it would make a sardonic
commentary on Christian determinism, since it would have led
Urizen on a spiraling descent which created, among other horrors,
the ironclad world which Blake designates as our own.

Among the Zoas, next in the hierarchy, Urizen does not attain
the preeminent position he enjoys in other of Blake's poems. He
creates his cumbrous worlds, but the poem focuses equally on the
other Zoas, whom he does not consistently control. There is little
theodicy in *The Four Zoas*, little questioning of the harsh ways

of a God whom we have inflicted on ourselves. Nor can the tangle of the middle Nights be blamed on a Kafkaesque bureaucrat-god, whose commands, ambivalent to begin with, never reach those for whom they were intended. Each of the Zoas creates his own imperatives and then suffers from them absolutely, as if the tyranny were external. Each, however, must remain responsible for the destruction he wreaks, whatever his actual or declared hierarchical level.

The creation of man, the loathsome "Human polypus of Death" (56:16:E331/K304), marks the greatest debasement of the Zoas, and the annihilation of man is one of the conditions for the apocalypse of Night the Ninth. On this basis, man might be considered less valuable than the cosmic figures of the poem, but the Zoas are superior to him only in vigor and immediacy: morally and emotionally they often represent man's worst qualities. In fact, many of the sketches in *The Four Zoas* manuscript depict the Zoas and their female Emanations as subhuman serpent, bird, and sphinx-like forms with ravaged human faces.[6] The poem's extended concentration on the stark, atavistic, and unrestrained encounters of these debased but perversely energetic powers finally lessens our respect for them. Also, since the whole action of *The Four Zoas* is aimed at showing a human audience its potential restoration to an original unified splendor, man can well be regarded as the highest level of the poem.

Will and action are not separated in the powers who populate *The Four Zoas*, although such a separation might be expected in a human character or a mythic character adhering to the patterns of the human (Keats's gods, for example). To the Zoas, impulse

[6] See, for example, the drawings on pp. 7, 13, 26 {89}, 70, and 100 reproduced in Bentley, *Vala*.

D.V.E.: The drawings on page 26 (folio 13ᵛ) are ingeniously interpreted in alchemical terms by Piloo Nanavutty in "*Materia Prima* in a Page of Blake's *Vala*," in Rosenfeld, *Essays for Damon*, 293-302. The interpretation hinges, however, on our being able to see, issuing from the dragon woman at the bottom of the page, "a child whose head is held firmly in the mouth of the dove that had proceeded from the womb first" (p. 297). Such a vision must derive from poor photography; a fresh examination of the original manuscript disclosed no child, no dove; for this volume we ordered an infrared photograph {89}, which leaves no lines in the drawing fainter than what the naked eye can see. To be very specific: all the lines drawn between the two shorter mermaid tails of the dragon are outlines of the scales on her long central tail.

and act are simultaneous. No Zoa, Emanation, or Spectre nurses unacted desires since, in the nonphysical world depicted for most of the poem, the articulation of a desire means that the desire is being acted upon. Each situation carries with it a peculiar zest for destruction or, less often, for union, giving it a tension like that of dramatic *peripeteia*, but without the opportunity for resolution offered by the drama. For most of the poem, the end is invisible, and when the apocalypse does draw near, it is as much because of exhaustion as because of actual reformation. The Zoas themselves seem terrified by the apparently endless absolutism of action afforded them. Not only the vast changes wrought by Urizen, Los, and Orc demonstrate this fearful thrust toward destruction of self and others: each lovers' quarrel has the capacity to annihilate either or both partners. Tharmas is fragmented by Enion, who in turn is driven into Non-Entity, and Los and Enitharmon spitefully debase each other. The greater the degree to which a Zoa or Emanation permits fear to weaken his impulses, the greater the crippling effect of his fearful act.

In his restructuring of the psyche Blake has not chosen a higher inner world of Platonic essences over a lower, shadowy outer world. The Zoas are mythic, but they are not Platonically ideal. Their actions are not different in kind from actions in the everyday world. In Blake's version of the mind's form, the Zoas function roughly as characters but have no division between outer and inner, no clear line between affecting and affected, and no linear past that faithfully marks off the present. To put it another way, in *The Four Zoas* the real becomes the plausible, whatever is accepted as believable at any point in the poem. By removing an external reality, ironizing any ideal or heavenly reality, and moving swiftly among several levels of action within the local reality of *The Four Zoas*, Blake compels the reader to accept his floating world as accurate without reservations. Since the reality of *The Four Zoas* is the plausibility of a given scene, its authenticity as an acting out of some aspect of the human condition, the poem becomes, in this special sense of the word, more "real" as it proceeds. Repetition and variation replace linear narrative: several versions of the same event or slightly different versions of the same type of event can coexist without damaging the truth of any given version. To the degree that Blake succeeds, the reader should be increasingly willing to follow the Zoas without nostalgia for more direct forms of mimesis. One test of acclimatization to *The Four Zoas* is the shock of Night the Eighth, after the education of the first seven Nights has made external history and Christian terminology seem delusive and irrelevant. Now the pain and bafflement which one felt at the initial invasion of the Zoas are felt at their temporary submission to an historical scheme in which Jesus plays a partially redeeming role. The outer reality which presumably had been our standard before the poem now seems no more than a retreat from the actual, violent world of Blake's "powers."

Albion's fragmentation into the warring Zoas has preceded the beginning of the poem, so that *The Four Zoas* depicts a post-lapsarian age. The Zoas' fall from unity marks the beginning of their long descent. It is only the first of the poem's many ironies that Albion's destruction was necessary to create the visible middle world of the Zoas. As in the Preludium to *Europe*, the world available to poetic description must have already suffered a pernicious division into warring powers. By the time primeval unity separates enough to yield form and outline it is, according to Blake, beginning to die. The action of *The Four Zoas* intersects *Jerusalem* during the confused separation of the Zoas from the dying Albion, approximately plates 17-41. Thus its placement resembles the intersection of plate 4 of *The Book of Urizen* by *The Book of Los*. Both *The Book of Los* and *The Four Zoas* stand as independent poems, but each serves as an expansion of concerns that the poem it intersects could not deal with without losing its characteristic form. While *Jerusalem* provides the full Blakean myth and *Milton*, the most personal of the epics, examines the role of individual genius, *The Four Zoas* expands and offers alternate retellings[7] of

---

[7] In *The Four Zoas*, the creations of Los are ordered by Tharmas, not by Urizen (as in *The Book of Urizen* and *Jerusalem*), but once these creations begin, Blake absorbs most of chapter IV (b) of *The Book of Urizen* into the later text verbatim. Ahania's costly awakening to emotion in Night the Second and Night the Third *passim* enriches the stark narrative of *The Book of Ahania*, chapter v, which is itself a continuation of *The Book of Urizen*. The apocalypse of Night the Ninth parallels the conclusion of *Jerusalem* with some diminution in grandeur and scope: in this case, *Jerusalem* seems the more authoritative version. The division of *The Four Zoas* into nine Nights indicates the formal influence of Young's *Night Thoughts*, also written in nine Nights, of which the last is both the longest and apocalyptic (see also Grant's essay, above). Blake wrote the second half of the text of *The Four Zoas* on proof plates of his engravings for *Night Thoughts*.

the trying middle state between the fall that begins time and the apocalypse that will end it.

Many of the actions in Nights one through seven are placed one after the other, even though they do not necessarily develop or progress inevitably. The first six Nights describe the falls of Tharmas, Luvah, Los-Urthona, and Urizen, several impermanent and interchangeable reorderings, and the recognition of the conditions of renewal by the fallen. The poem begins a slow move upwards in Night the Fourth, when Los narrows the range of error and the human body is created, but the poem has begun to change as early as the close of Night the Second with Enion's lament, the first real moment of recognition in the poem. By the end of Night the Sixth even Urizen has realized that if the terms of thought are changed, the results of thought, or of any mental act, can be changed as well. In Night the Seventh (version a) conversation begins to replace invective and lament; the Zoas listen to each other. Gradually the term "human" is redeemed, and slumbering Albion, the potentially whole man, revives. The forces of evil crystallize as Rahab and Tirzah in Night the Eighth, and Urizen loses his remaining power to Orc, who prepares human history for the apocalypse of Night the Ninth.

A précis like the above may cover the historical events of *The Four Zoas*, but it distorts the actual weight given to the events it covers. It also implies a more conventional notion of time than may in fact exist in the poem. *The Four Zoas* begins a moment after the fragmentation of Albion but, to the degree that the Zoas are his separated mental powers, the clashes of the poem may occur during a single instant of his thought. The Zoas themselves posit radically different pasts according to the emotions of the present. Indeed, time recalled from the perspective of a distinct present, and temporal movement toward a future which constantly realizes itself in the present can hardly be said to exist in *The Four Zoas*. The past seems to be invented at will to satisfy the needs of rhetoric; there is no linear time-line with regular demarcations until Night the Eighth. Sometimes, as in dream narrative, certain events seem to get "stuck," seem to keep happening. These are not quite repetitions (Urizen's creations, for example, worsen as he grows weaker), but each time the event occurs it is redolent of the failure of the last time. The most striking examples of these folds in time are the successive false creations, but in the mutual denunciations of Zoa and Emanation, each bitter accusation and lament seems to have already been anticipated in slightly different form. Far from granting the speaker freedom from the trammels of the past, the realization of emotion in a scene is a tool of the past. Once something has happened, once it has been uttered, it becomes real and can happen again.

The violence of action in *The Four Zoas* would seem to make it a very verbal poem. In fact, when Blake describes the actions of the Zoas, he tends to use participial constructions. Actions described with these participial forms are forced into a kind of continual present. The reader is overwhelmed by a spate of actions all in the process of occurring, but he is rarely relieved by their completion. This spreading out of action does not completely freeze what is happening, but it does make it seem as if the reader were watching the Zoas' acts from a different time perspective, a warped type of slow motion. The Zoas' acts are of a continuing nature without the continuation affording the richness of an interlocking plot. This spreading out of the present or of the immediate past is most surprising when it appears in a passage of violent action. In Night the Third, Urizen has banished his bride Ahania into Non-Entity as punishment for her discomfiting concern with the future. Suddenly a terrible cry rings out as Tharmas, unbalanced by this shift in power, begins to fall to the level of the human:

> Loud strong a universal groan of death louder
> Than all the *wracking* elements deafend & rended worse
> Than Urizen & all his hosts in curst despair down *rushing*
> But from the Dolorous Groan one like a shadow of smoke
>   appeard
> And human bones *rattling* together in the smoke &
>   *stamping*
> The nether Abyss & *gnasshing* in fierce despair. *panting*
>   in sobs
> Thick short incessant *bursting sobbing*. deep *despairing*
>   *stamping struggling*
> *Struggling* to utter the voice of Man *struggling* to take
>   the features of Man. *Struggling*
> To take the limbs of Man at length *emerging* from the
>   smoke. . . .
>
>   (44:11-19:E323/K295-296; italics mine)

386

The participial construction conveys the claustrophobic terror of Tharmas' fall.

This phenomenon should not, however, be called an actual solidification of time, because Blake uses that figure to signify the descent of the Zoas into corporeality. In Night the First, as Enion dissolves, losing "all her spectrous life" (9:8:E300/K270),

> Then Eno a daughter of Beulah took a Moment of Time
> And drew it out to Seven thousand years with much care
>   & affliction
> And many tears & in Every year made windows into Eden
>   (9:9-11)

To protect themselves from terrors they have invented themselves, the daughters of Beulah have given up limitlessness and created the restricted world of "Moony spaces" (9:19) in which Los and Enitharmon, the children of Experience, will be nurtured.

Eno turns next to an atom of space:

> She also took an atom of space & opend its center
> Into infinitude & ornamented it with wondrous art
> Astonishd sat her Sisters of Beulah to see her soft
>   affections   (9:12-14)

For Tharmas, an atom of space was minuscule, a fit simile for weakness: "I am like an atom / A Nothing" (4:42-43); but Eno fits a whole world into this negligible space. A space which is measurable by the standards of distance and proportion found on earth is possible only in a shrunken universe. What Harold Bloom calls "the relieving world of temporal appearances"[8] is achieved only at the price of freedom of movement. The daughters of Beulah think they have protected themselves by giving a physical dimension to space, but their protection soon turns to imprisonment. Slowly but surely their perceptions are clouded and pastoral sport becomes destruction.

The absolutism of action in *The Four Zoas* bars repentance or retraction. Once Tharmas begins to address Enion as a creature separate from himself, both he and she are doomed. If Tharmas, the sensual power, were perfect, he would not feel the need to objectify a natural love and then desire it. For sensuality itself to *feel*, rather than *be*, desire, it must have lost both scope and

[8] Bloom, *Apocalypse*, 214.

power. A division like that of Enion from Tharmas may provide the immediate ease of sexual companionship, but this pleasure by two separate parties is temporary, since the divisive process continues relentlessly once it has begun.

Once Enion, in her drift away from Tharmas, has shown the capacity for a given accusation, the substance of that accusation is accepted automatically by her victim. After she has uttered the word "sin," no return to innocence is possible. Every estrangement can be proved to be well founded. The destructive thought *is* the destructive act. An evil or deluded *human* action can sometimes be undone, but the dissolution of a mode of thought and the confused clashes of its fragments are final. Enion's cowardice is conceptual; she plants "sin" in Tharmas as a facile rationalization of the widening distance she perceives between herself and him. The term is painfully inadequate, and the sinful past she posits seems to have been fabricated to fit her conclusion, but Tharmas accepts both. After this opening attack he is easily "anatomized" and relegated to the chaotic sea. From being the parent power of the emotive self, Tharmas sinks to the level of any melancholy Petrarchan lover, shuttling between the impotence of hope and the impotence of self-pity.

Action, then, is not a consequence of thought in *The Four Zoas*, but rather the way a thought is expressed. The wish, the casual speculation, and the false surmise are all manifested with the power of a divine edict. Words are as irrevocable as incidents: however mistaken or inadequate a phrase is, once it has entered the world of the Zoas it must be coped with as fully as any more honest act. Enion sins, both in the conventional sense and in the Blakean sense of committing an act which further fragments the universe, when she attacks Tharmas. The initial formulation of the object (be it a beloved or an aspect of mind) as an external also takes a visionary revenge on its maker by making him or her merely another set of externals. In Night the Third, for example, Urizen banishes Ahania to Non-Entity, only to find himself drawn there soon after. Los and Enitharmon each become whatever one has accused the other of being. The merger of agent and the object acted on becomes more pronounced as *The Four Zoas* continues. One of its most explicit expressions is found at the close of Night the Fourth, when Los shrinks from his task of false creation. His weakened imagination has exhausted itself:

In terrors Los shrunk from his task. his great hammer
Fell from his hand his fires hid their strong limbs in
  smoke
For with noises ruinous hurtlings & clashings & groans
The immortal endur'd. tho bound in a deadly sleep
Pale terror siezd the Eyes of Los as he beat round
The hurtling Demon. terrifd at the shapes
Enslavd humanity put on he became what he beheld
He became what he was doing he was himself transformd
(55:16-22:E331/K304-305)

Once he has conceived of man, Los takes on man's shape.

Even when a result appears to be the direct consequence of an act, it is difficult to apply normal causality to *The Four Zoas*. For example, the very act of anatomizing another seems to drain the newly exposed fibers of all life and make them evil at the same time. Yet, as with Enion and Tharmas, the accusation does not cause the sin; it seems rather to articulate it, to uncover its hitherto only potential strength. A mental act cannot "cause" the creation of a consequence separate from itself. A gesture of anger may dissolve a gesture of love, or a sensation of fear may leave behind it a spectral fragment. But the fragment, whether it be the spectre of Tharmas, the hatred replacing Los and Enitharmon's infant love, or the human polypus as created by Urizen, was always present *in potentia* inside the parent emotion. The spectre of Tharmas is a piece of him, drawn forth less by the summary action of Enion than by his own state of weakness. Had he retained his full primal strength, her willful attack would not have affected him.

If action and causality are distorted in *The Four Zoas*, can the poem be said to have a history? The variety of true, untrue, and ironic histories proposed by the Zoas makes even the reader armed with a knowledge of *Milton* and *Jerusalem* fear that no one story will ever triumph over any other. Since *The Four Zoas* is an epic of situations with only the most perfunctory exposition, the reader is tempted to believe that the "true" account, the one he should believe, is simply situational truth, the truth as it is presented at any given point. This truth can be far from honesty, as the destructive fantasies of the Zoas indicate. Eventually a fairly reliable history of the Zoas' fall and recovery can be patched together, but not before the reader has been tricked into believing a dozen

false ones. The reader seeking a lucid epic like the *Aeneid* is un-
pleasantly reminded of a Proverb of Hell: "Every thing possible
to be believ'd is an image of truth."

After the reader has followed the Zoas through their maze of
false choices and dead ends, he begins to realize that there will not
be any reward of a moral at the end of the poem. The energetic
is not the good in *The Four Zoas*, but neither do the meek inherit
the earth. One may also question whether so intensely dialectic a
poem as *The Four Zoas* can ever arrive at the unity of an apocalyptic conclusion. At the end of the poem the "terrible wine
presses of Luvah" crush the "Human Grapes" into a pure wine,
but the Zoas do not merge into a single form (136:1,21:E389/
K376,377). Vala, the emanation of Luvah, enjoys her higher innocence cordoned off in "lower paradise" (128:30) and Tharmas,
or his shadow, still pursues a reluctant Enion: "In infant sorrow &
joy alternate Enion & Tharmas playd" (131:17). The Zoas remain
distinct, even though they now share many qualities. *The Four
Zoas* closes in the present tense, as the "fresh Earth" (139:3) of
the last three Nights survives and the renewed Zoas look forward
to continued intellectual warfare:

> . . . Urthona rises from the ruinous walls
> In all his ancient strength to form the golden armour of
>   science
> For intellectual War The war of swords departed now
> The dark Religions are departed & sweet Science reigns
> (139:7-10:E292/K379)

In other words, although the "war of swords" has been won, the
dialectic encounters of the Zoas will go on forever.

The war of ideologies has also been won in *The Four Zoas*.
Instead of propounding a new mythology to replace worn-out but
still dangerous creeds, Blake acts as if his mythology has long since
been accepted. He then proceeds to offer the reader a new, loose,
antimimetic form in which his mythic actions are played out. By
confidently presenting the fragmented world of *The Four Zoas*
as self-evident, Blake also implicitly argues that the high rant and
bone-crushing agony of most of the poem are not merely the
idiosyncrasies of a private horrific vision. They are, he indicates,
the actual and inescapable conditions of the riot of mental powers
in every fallen man.

18

Narrative Structure
and the Antithetical Vision of
Jerusalem

HENRY LESNICK

ALTHOUGH *Jerusalem* continually reiterates and offers variations
on a few elements of action and imagery, the narrative may be
seen to be somewhat progressive. Numerous critics have commented on the poem's narrative structure. They have discussed
the correspondences between specific thematic and narrative elements and individual chapters and have also recognized that the
simultaneous occurrence of antithetical elements is one of the
primary characteristics of the poem's structure.[1] What has not
been adequately treated by these critics is the way in which specific plates which introduce and conclude each of the four chapters
help to define the material included in each chapter, and what has
not been fully recognized is the extent to which the structural
antithesis reflects the truly paradoxical nature of Blake's vision.

The poem begins with the fall an accomplished fact: "Awake!
awake O sleeper of the land of shadows . . ." (*J* 4:6). It then pro-

---

[1] Frye (*Symmetry*, 357) believes that the four chapters present an account
of the fall, man's struggle in the fallen world, redemption, and apocalypse.
Karl Kiralis, "The Theme and Structure of *Jerusalem*," in *The Divine
Vision*, ed. Vivian De Sola Pinto, London, 1957, 141-162, argues that, following an introductory chapter, the narrative is organized around the concept
of the three ages of man, the three regions immense of childhood, manhood,
and old age which correspond to Judaism, Deism, and Christianity, religions
of those addressed in the prefaces of the last three chapters. S. Foster Damon
adopts this view in his *Dictionary*, 210. E. J. Rose, "The Structure of Blake's
Jerusalem," *Bucknell Review*, XI (1963), 35-54, challenges Kiralis' basic
thesis, maintaining that the progression begins with old age rather than ends
with it, and that each part is dominated by a Zoa. Frye (p. 357) explains
the structural antithesis as the presentation of "a phase of imaginative vision
simultaneously with the body of error which it clarifies." Bloom (*Apocalypse*,
404) states, "Each of *Jerusalem*'s four chapters founds its structure upon a
gradually sharpening antithesis between two contrary forces."

ceeds to examine various phases of fallen existence until plate 89. At the same time, throughout the first eighty-eight plates, Los is engaged at his furnaces in his redemptive labors, and visions which hold promise of man's redemption are disclosed: Golgonooza is revealed; Los builds the moon of Ulro; the Divine Vision forms the limits Satan and Adam, and of the latter forms woman that himself in process of time may be born man to redeem; Allegory becomes Divine Analogy. These elements occurring throughout the poem have redemptive implications, but it is not until the Covering Cherub is revealed (pl. 89), Los views the nations amalgamating in his furnaces (pl. 92), and Bacon, Newton, and Locke give the apocalyptic Signal of the Morning by worshiping Babylon (pl. 93) that redemption is finally achieved. The major division in the narrative occurs between the first eighty-eight plates, in which the primary focus is on the fallen condition, and the last twelve, which describe the restoration of man. To the extent that the poem does offer a narrative progression, discrete segments of which correspond to individual chapters, the progression is one which presents the successive stages of the fall.[2] This is clearly the case in the first three chapters. The fourth chapter brings this progression to its culmination in the revelation of the Covering Cherub and to its ultimate resolution in the restoration of fallen man. The various stages of the progression are punctuated by the plates which begin and end each chapter.

Each chapter presents a phase of fallen experience, the limits of which are defined by the half-plate designs which head and conclude the chapters and by the addresses which precede them. The only exceptions to this pattern are the address "To the Public" and the design which heads chapter 1; both of these serve as introductions to the material of the entire poem as well as to that of the first chapter. The full-plate designs which occur after each chapter are transitional, reflecting in part the material of the chapters which precede them and anticipating the material of the chapters which follow them; the only exception is, of course, plate 100.

After stating the overall concern of the poem, the passage through eternal death and awakening to eternal life, which is depicted in the design of plate 4, the first chapter proceeds to describe the disintegration of Albion. His children flee, Jerusalem is drawn eastward

[2] This view of the narrative progression is implicit in many of the recent studies which treat the poem's structure.

(*J* 5:46-47,14:31-32), he sinks down in pallid languor on the edge of Beulah and casts the veil of moral virtue into the deep to catch the souls of the dead (*J* 23:20-26), the sun flees from his forehead (*J* 24:10). The degradation of Albion is summarily presented in the design of plate 25 (see {6}), where Albion is shown under the dominion of the female. Albion is on his knees, surrounded by three female figures; one of them supports his head in her lap, a second grasps his umbilical cord, a third towers above him surrounding all the figures of the design with the fibers of corporeal existence which hang from her outstretched arms.[3] Albion's disintegration appears to be incomplete at this point, for although the sun has fled from his forehead (a small, mournful-looking sun-face is shown above his right knee), twelve stars are displayed on his body and limbs; the starry heavens have not yet fled his mighty limbs.[4]

Plate 26 shows Hand at the left of the plate and Jerusalem at the right with her hands raised in a gesture of fear or repulsion. Their names are incised beneath the two figures. Jerusalem's raised hands suggest her resistance to being drawn eastward in maternal anguish by the starry wheels (cf. *J* 5:46-47, 14:31-32), which are identified with the twelve sons (*J* 18:5-8). Hand represents the aggregate of the twelve sons (*J* 8:43), who also, in the aggregate, become one great Satan (*J* 90:40-43). A characteristic of Blake's symbology is the identification of symbols which have the same symbolic function. It is because of this that Hand displays stigmata in most copies of plate 26. The stigmata establish the identity between Hand and the vegetated Christ, who is in turn identified with the Evil-One, Satan (*J* 90:35). There is a dimension of Hand which is Satan, and it is this dimension which is expressed in the design of plate 26. The design alludes not only to the drawing eastward of Jerusalem described in chapter I but also to Jerusalem's fall eastward, which is presented immediately following the appearance of Satan in the address of chapter II; or, more precisely, it depicts Jerusalem's recognition of the significance of Hand-Satan's influence.

The addresses, particularly the last three, to the Jews, the Deists, and the Christians, reflect the progression of the successive stages

[3] Joseph Wicksteed, *William Blake's Jerusalem*, London, 1954, 155-156, identifies these women as Vala or Gwendolen, Rahab, and Tirzah.
[4] Cf. *J* 27.

of the fallen condition treated in each chapter. The address to the Jews precedes chapter II because their culture occupies a position in history analogous to the position of this chapter in Blake's vision of history. As the Jewish culture is an early postlapsarian one which preserves the memory of Edenic existence, continues the process of the fall, and at the same time produces the spiritual verse (*J* 48:6-12) instrumental to man's salvation, so this chapter recalls the lost innocence ("Every ornament of perfection and every labour of love, / In all the Garden of Eden, & in the golden mountains / Was become an envied horror . . ." [*J* 28:1-3]), continues the process of the fall, and describes the events which will yield the restoration of man.[5]

The lyric included in the address is particularly appropriate because its treatment of the whole of history is similar to those of the Old Testament and of this second chapter. It begins with a vision of past innocence, then describes the labors of fallen man and the realities of fallen existence, and concludes with the realization that Jerusalem will be restored. Each of the subsequent addresses includes a lyric, and it can be shown that each lyric reflects a significant aspect of the chapter it precedes.

The second chapter explores the limits of Beulah, the married land. And although humanity knows not of sexes, Beulah does afford a sanctuary from Ulro. The spiritual topography of Beulah extends to the edge of Eden at the upper level and to Ulro at the lower. These limits are explored in the first and last designs of the chapter.

The design of plate 28, which introduces the chapter, presents a male and female embracing and, in an early proof, perhaps copulating; they sit on a lily and are partially enveloped in a fibrous mantle; the Morgan proof {95} displays a caterpillar on the petal immediately below the figures.[6] Beulah is at once both a sweet place, a "pleasant lovely shadowy Universe / Where no dispute can come; created for those who Sleep" (*J* 48:19-20), and a place

[5] Blake's vision of fallen man always includes elements which provide for man's restoration. Yet Golgonooza and Los's labors at the furnaces are aspects of our condition which exist continually; unlike the building of the moon of Ulro or the establishment of the Limits, they are not events which occur at specific times in the linear sequence of fallen history.

[6] For an account of the alterations made in this design see David V. Erdman, "Suppressed and Altered Passages in Blake's *Jerusalem*," *Studies in Bibliography*, XVII (1964), 18-20.

where the male enters the female "And becomes One with her mingling condensing in Self-love / The Rocky Law of Condemnation & double Generation, & Death" (*J* 44[30]:36-37). Elements of this second aspect of Beulah might appear to be implicit in the design, but the sexual character of the design is not necessarily expressive of the maleficent aspect of Beulah; the redemptive quality of Beulah is also associated with its sexuality: "Thou shalt no more be termed Forsaken; neither shall thy land any more be termed Desolate: but thou shalt be called Hepzibah (my delight is in her), and thy land Beulah: for the Lord delighteth in thee, and thy land shall be married. For as a young man marrieth a virgin, so shall thy sons marry thee: and as the bridegroom rejoiceth over the bride, so shall thy God rejoice over thee" (Isaiah 62:4-5). Thus it could be maintained that the design defines the lower limits of Beulah, but because the sexuality of Beulah is also benign, the design might be emblematic of the sanctuary Beulah affords. The obliteration of the ominous caterpillar in the final form of the plate, and the predominance of a warm, orange-yellow wash in the Mellon copy tend to corroborate this second interpretation of the design.

As Luvah tears forth from Albion's loins, animating the dragon temples, the souls of the dead break forth from Beulah's hills and vales (*J* 47:4-10); the soft slumberous repose of Beulah yields the dreams of Ulro in which men rage like wild beasts in the forests of affliction and repent of their human kindness (*J* 42:61-62). The single vision of Newton's sleep is latent in Beulah's night. The concluding design of chapter II describes the element of human consciousness, Ulro, which is always latent in Beulah and which manifests itself as the dominant element in the condition of man as the process of the fall continues, as man falls from the upper limits of Beulah to and beyond the lower limits.

The design of plate 50 (fig. 16) shows Hand sitting on Albion's cliffs with three awful and terrible heads, each of which bears a crown, and three brains in contradictory council brooding incessantly; the three forms are named "Bacon & Newton & Locke"; Hand's brothers issue from a hideous orifice in his chest (*J* 70:1-15). Hand sits upon an island which represents England. He and his brothers are surrounded by a swirling funnellike cloud, the vortex of the dead (*J* 48:54).

The significance of other elements of the design is less obvious.

Come, O thou Lamb of God and take away the remembrance of Sin.
To Sin & to hide the Sin in sweet deceit. is lovely.'!
To Sin in the open face of day is cruel & pitiless.' But
To record the Sin for a reproach: to let the Sun go down
In a remembrance of the Sin: is a Woe & a Horror.'
A brooder of an Evil Day. and. a Sun rising in blood
Come then O Lamb of God and take away the remembrance of Sin
End of Chap. 2.

Fig. 16. *Jerusalem*, pl. 50, detail

A small full moon (washed in gray in the Mellon copy) is at the left of the plate; a larger crescent moon is at the right, along with two suns, the smaller of which is rising and the larger of which may be rising or setting. It is possible, as E. J. Rose suggests, that the two suns are both rising and represent the sun of This World and the Eternal Sun respectively.[7] I think it is more likely that the astronomical imagery represents the confusion of the material world of Ulro, for the illuminated side of the crescent moon is not toward either of the suns, and consequently cannot receive its light from them. The two suns may illustrate the consequence of the doctrine of vengeance for sin:

> . . . to let the Sun go down
> In a remembrance of the Sin: is a Woe & a Horror!
> A brooder of an Evil Day, and a Sun rising in blood
> (*J* 50:27-29)

[7] "Blake's Hand: Symbol and Design in *Jerusalem*," *Texas Studies in Language and Literature*, VI (1964), 150.

The smaller sun, as seen in the Mellon copy, displays a red tail.[8]

One other element of the design which warrants some consideration is the bird's head and beak at the extreme left of the plate. Lightning issues from the beak or from some point next to it. The white ring around the eye suggests that the bird is a cormorant. The cormorant is best known for its voracity, which probably accounts for Milton's comparison of Satan to the cormorant in *Paradise Lost* (IV, 195). This element and the suns at the right are emblematic of the ethic of Ulro, the ethic of Satan the accuser, who demands vengeance for sin.

The exploration of Ulro and its limits continues in the plates immediately following and throughout the third chapter. Plate 51 depicts a less abstract aspect of Ulro existence, Vala's court of despair. In addition to Vala, who sits upon a Druidic stone throne with her crowned head bowed, the design presents Hyle with his head between his knees, and Skofield standing stoop-shouldered in chains. Hyle (whose name in Greek means "matter") represents the degraded form of natural man; he becomes the winding worm of plate 82. Skofield was the soldier who in 1803 accused Blake of seditious utterance. In *Jerusalem* he is the ninth of Albion's sons, in whom the last three become one—in whom, in turn, the other eight are involved, "To separate a Law of Sin, to punish thee in thy members" (*J* 7:50). However, he appears on plate 51 as another victim of the condition caused by the accuser rather than an active agent of the accuser; he is, here, another "hapless soldier."

The address "To the Deists" (pl. 52) is unique in that it is the only one which does not offer a vision of the restoration of man.[9] This absence is appropriate because Deism represents the nadir of man's spiritual existence, a system of beliefs concomitant to, or perhaps even responsible for, our deepest night of Ulro.

The design which introduces the third chapter is the counterpart of the one which concludes the second. After describing Hand as he appears on plate 50, the text of plate 70 proceeds to

---

[8] Wicksteed, 203, suggests that this smaller sun with its tail is a meteor, but the design has more relevance to the text if we regard it as a sun rising in blood. Donald K. Moore suggests that the bloody orb may be causing an eclipse of the orb above it, possibly not the moon but the earth.

[9] Compare plates 3: "Heaven, Earth & Hell . . . shall live in Harmony"; 27: every land "Mutual shall build Jerusalem:/Both heart in heart & hand in hand"; and 77: "Our souls exult & Londons towers,/Receive the Lamb of God. . . ."

describe his feminine counterpart, Rahab, as she appears on plate 53 (see {96}):

> . . . Rahab
> Sat deep within him hid: his Feminine Power unreveal'd
> Brooding Abstract Philosophy. to destroy Imagination,
>   the Divine-
> -Humanity A Three-fold Wonder: feminine: Most beautiful:
>   Three-fold   (J 70:17-20)

The design depicts Rahab sitting facing us on a crown-shaped throne which occupies the center of a sunflower. She holds her head in her hands and wears three crowns piled one on top of the other, which represent her threefoldness and correspond to the three crowns of three-headed Hand. Above her shoulders are seen the twelve stars, Albion's sons. A small globe is seen above her left shoulder and a small moon above her right.

The arrangement of the earth and the moon helps to define the condition which this design represents and also indicates that Blake had more than a casual understanding of astronomical phenomena. The side of the moon which is furthest from the earth and toward the left of the plate is illuminated. There is a sun somewhere at the left implicit in the illuminated moon. Given that the sun is at the left, the inclination of the earth indicates that the season in the northern hemisphere is winter. Furthermore, the positions of the earth and the moon with respect to the sun are those which yield a solar eclipse. The appropriateness of this imagery to the part of the poem which explores Ulro is clear.

These two designs on plates 50 and 53 taken together represent the dichotomy of the dragon forms. They are the Female hid within the male, "Mystery Babylon the Great: the Abomination of Desolation / Religion hid in War: a Dragon red, & hidden Harlot" (J 75:19-20). The design which concludes the third chapter, the seven-headed dragon of plate 75, Rahab-Babylon, is a composite expression of the two-dimensional "Female hid within the Male."

Thus Rahab is revealed (J 75:18); the body of error is given a form that it might be cast out forever. The concretion of this spiritual nadir is itself an aspect of the Signal of the Morning. The remaining plates of the poem which precede the restoration explore various manifestations of the consolidation of error, and (often simultaneously) present images and elements of action which adumbrate the vision of the life of immortality with which the poem ends.

Plate 76 {98} depicts the vegetated Christ, the hermaphroditic blasphemy, the Evil-One; Jesus assumes the Satanic body of holiness, his maternal humanity, that it might be put off (*J* 90:34-38). Los has previously announced that by his maternal birth Jesus redeems man (*J* 42:32-34). Generation, the image of regeneration, is the means of the deliverance of form out of confusion; it is the medium of redemption. Yet in these lines from plate 90 it is clearly Satanic. Jesus, in his generative existence, becomes—is—that Evil-One. The Lamb of God is only fully realized in Generation, and his total realization is as Satan. The epiphany of Anti-Christ is coincident to and logically identical with the epiphany of Christ. They are the same event. Thomas J. J. Altizer offers a somewhat cryptic statement of Hegel's in an attempt to explain the dialectic which is at the heart of much of Blake's work: "Every opposite creates itself as its own other and can only be united with that other by negating itself."[10]

The transformation of the Transcendent into the Immanent, or more accurately, their union, is achieved only as the alien other, Satan, the God of This World and of traditional theology, is united with its dialectical opposite, by which it has been created, and the product of that union experiences the anguish of regeneration, the terrors of self-annihilation. As Jesus becomes Satan in order to be truly Jesus, so the Transcendent, Satan, passes into the Immanent, Jesus. Thus the rationale behind Los's imperative, "Come Lord Jesus take on thee the Satanic Body of Holiness" (*J* 90:38), becomes clear. Man must become God that God may become Man.

As Jesus becomes Satan, the Eternal Sun breaks. Albion stands Christlike with his arms outstretched, looking up and to his right at the crucified Christ.[11] Christ's head is encircled in sunlight, and a less pronounced sunlight is seen at the extreme left of the plate.

[10] *The New Apocalypse: The Radical Christian Vision of William Blake,* East Lansing, Mich., 1967, 179.

[11] The action depicted in this design might be construed as a kind of devil-worship. But it must be understood that in viewing the Satanic body of holiness that has been put off, Albion is also viewing the archetype of Self-Annihilation.

It could be argued that the sun at the left simply suggests the final setting of the Christ-sun seen above Albion's head, that the design illustrates a passage presented in chapter II:

> Then the Divine Vision like a silent Sun appeard above
> Albions dark rocks: setting behind the Gardens of Kensington
> On Tyburns River, in clouds of blood. . . .
>
> (*J* 43[29]:1-3)

It is more likely that the sun at the left is the Eternal Sun, which rises in the west as a direct consequence of crucifixion—particularly in light of the fact that the design immediately precedes the fourth chapter, in which we learn that crucifixion, the putting off of maternal humanity, is a necessary requisite of regeneration.

Plate 78 {99}, the first of chapter IV, presents a large sun, about one quarter of which is shown at the extreme left of the plate. A seated figure facing it is at the right. He has a muscular, male body, a powerful neck, and the head of a bird. He incongruously displays both a cock's comb and a predatory beak.[12]

The design is basically ironic. The cock's comb might suggest that the design depicts the dawn, that the figure is announcing the rising of the sun. In fact, the sun at the left is setting, and the setting of this sun marks the beginning of the deepest night of Ulro. Plate 84, in the Mellon copy, displays a sun in approximately the same position. The text of that plate reveals that "Night falls thick . . ." (line 20), as London is led through the streets of Babylon.[13] The beak of the figure is clearly not a cock's beak, but is rather the "rav'ning beak" of ignorance which is a concomitant of Hand's absorbing his brethren and condensing his emanations (*J* 8:43-9:13). It is emblematic of the spectres of Albion's sons "Raging against their Human natures, ravning to gormandize / The Human majesty . . ." (*J* 19:23-24), "ravning to devour / The Sleeping Humanity . . ." (*J* 78:2-3). The figure seated at the right of the design is Hand, who by synecdoche represents all of the spectrous sons.[14]

---

[12] Wicksteed, 226, believes that the figure is Los and that the cock's comb indicates that the sun is a rising one.

[13] The sun of plate 97, which also appears at the left and is rising, is not a natural sun.

[14] In this respect Hand's function is like that of Reuben, with whom he is identified; see *J* 30 [34]:36.

400

Hand and his brethren, in the fourth chapter, "took their Mother Vala, & they crown'd her with gold: / They namd her Rahab, & gave her power over the Earth" (*J* 78:15-16). The Daughters unite into one "With Rahab as she turned the iron Spindle of destruction" (*J* 84:30). "Jerusalem took the Cup which foamd in Vala's [Rahab's] hand" (*J* 88:56). Rahab and Tirzah crucify the terrible hermaphroditic form which is revealed as the Covering Cherub, the Anti-Christ, a human dragon (*J* 89:1-11). Rahab, elevated by the sons, is identified with the Anti-Christ; Bacon, Newton, Locke worship "The God of This World, & the Goddess Nature / Mystery Babylon the Great, the Druid Dragon & hidden Harlot" (*J* 93:23-24).[15] These events constitute the "night" of chapter iv. Hand is instrumental in precipitating this night, and therefore it is appropriate that he be presented in this design in which the fall of the night is depicted.

The significance of the cock's comb is a function of the value of this particular night. The night marks the nadir of fallen existence, the culmination of the night of death. The worship of Babylon-Rahab is "the Signal of the Morning which was told us in the Beginning" (*J* 93:26). Insofar as Hand gives Rahab dominion over the earth, creates Babylon, he has given a body to falsehood that it might be cast out forever. With the fall of Hand's night, the night of death "is far spent, the day is at hand" (Romans 13:12), and it is this day which is adumbrated by the otherwise malevolent Hand.

That the sun of plate 78 is setting is also corroborated by the dark brown which, in the Mellon copy, covers the sun, the clouds which surround the seated figure, and sea presented between him and the sun. Conversely, the sun of plate 19 is washed in orange and bright yellow, and the dominant tint of the design is pink. Albion is shown lying outstretched, "his Giant beauty on the ground in pain & tears" (*J* 18:46), "His Giant beauty and perfection fallen into dust" (*J* 19:8). He is "self-exiled from the face of light & shine of morning" (*J* 19:13), and it is this condition which is depicted in the design (see fig. 17). His head is at the extreme left of the plate, turned away from the rising natural sun seen at the right.

Perhaps the most significant clarification of Blake's use of solar

15 Cf. plate 52.

Fig. 17. *Jerusalem*, pl. 19, detail

imagery and directional symbolism in general is provided by plates 95 and 97 of *Jerusalem*, and plate 39 of *Milton*. Plates 95 and 97 are very similar. Plate 95 {101} describes the awakening of Albion: "The Breath Divine went forth upon the morning hills, Albion mov'd / Upon the Rock, he opened his eyelids in pain . . ." (lines 2-3). He rises with his right hand raised and his right foot forward, toward our right. His left hand rests on a rock. He looks to his right. He has risen from his outstretched position in plate 94, where he is shown, as he was in plate 19, with his head at the left of the plate and his feet at the right. Plate 97 {102} shows Albion in a position similar to the one he assumes in plate 95, although there are a few crucial differences between the two.[16] Albion's right foot is still forward, but it is now toward the left of the plate; his left foot is stretched behind him toward the right. He faces inward, and stretches his left hand into infinitude to take his bow fourfold (lines 5-6). The "Bow" which Albion lifts in his left hand is the sun of Eternal Day, as clearly evidenced in the design. Albion's fourfold bow is an emblem of mental war, a central image of the

---

[16] Wicksteed, 245, maintains that the figure of this design is Los, but the text (lines 6-7) seems to suggest that he is Albion. Wicksteed himself had earlier identified the figure as Albion in *Blake's Vision of the Book of Job*, London, 1910, 136. His later judgment seems to have been prompted by a desire to see an exact symmetry in the relationship between this design and the frontispiece.

regenerated spiritual condition, and thus is appropriately identified with the regenerated spiritual sun.

The resurrection of Albion depicted on plates 95 and 97 is described in the text at the end of *Milton*. The text explains the two
designs and the differences in Albion's attitudes almost completely:

> Then Albion rose up in the Night of Beulah on his Couch
> Of dread repose seen by the visionary eye; his face is toward
> The east, toward Jerusalems Gates: groaning he sat above
> His rocks. London & Bath & Legions & Edinburgh
> Are the four pillars of his Throne; his left foot near London
> Covers the shades of Tyburn: his instep from Windsor
> To Primrose Hill stretching to Highgate & Holloway
> London is between his knees: its basements fourfold
> His right foot stretches to the sea on Dover cliffs, his heel
> On Canterburys ruins; his right hand covers lofty Wales
> His left Scotland; his bosom girt with gold involves
> York, Edinburgh, Durham & Carlisle & on the front
> Bath, Oxford, Cambridge, Norwich; his right elbow
> Leans on the Rocks of Erins Land, Ireland ancient nation. . . .
> He movd his right foot to Cornwall, his left to the Rocks of
> Bognor
> He strove to rise to walk into the Deep, but strength failing
> Forbad & down with dreadful groans he sunk upon his Couch
> In moony Beulah. Los his strong Guard walks round beneath
> the Moon
>   (M 39:32-52)

The events described in these lines are identical with those depicted in the designs, with one very notable exception. The awakening of Albion in *Milton* is incomplete; he is unable to rise and
walk, and therefore he sinks back upon his couch. He does not
achieve reunion with his Emanation; the Zoas are not reunited
in him; he does not throw himself into the furnace of affliction,
experience the "little Death" which culminates the resurrection of
man.

As Albion struggles to rise in plate 95 {101}, his right foot is in
front of him, toward our right, and his left foot is stretched behind
him. It is this posture which is apparently described in lines 32-40
of the *Milton* passage: "His right foot stretches to the sea on Dover
cliffs, his heel / On Canterburys ruins" (just west of Dover); "his

left foot near London / Covers the shades of Tyburn"; "London is between his knees"; "his face is toward / The east." His left hand still covers Scotland in *J* 95, but, because his struggle "to rise to walk into the Deep" is successful in *Jerusalem*, his right hand is raised, his elbow no longer leans on Erin's land, his right hand no longer covers lofty Wales.

Albion alters his supine sitting position in line 49;[17] the position of his feet is reversed. His right foot, previously on the eastern coast, is now moved to Cornwall on the western coast. His left foot is now east of the right, on the Rocks of Bognor, on the south-central coast, about a mile from Felpham. Albion no longer faces east, but is now striving to rise to walk into the Atlantic Deep. Plate 97 depicts this reversal. Albion's right foot is still forward, but is now at the left of the plate, and his left foot is toward the right. Plate 97, unlike the *Milton* passage, presents Albion standing. His awakening is complete, as indicated by the presence of the Sun of Eternal Day, which he lifts in his left hand from the abyss of the Atlantic Deep at the left of the plate.

Thus there can be no doubt that the right of these plates is east, the left is west, and that the sun rising at the left of plate 97 is not a natural sun. The natural sun sets in the west and the Eternal Sun rises in the west in accordance with the same rationale which makes Los's gate and Death's Door logically identical.[18]

The lyric included in the address to the Christians ends with a vision of the restoration of England which is presented in the present tense. However, the text which immediately precedes and follows the address presents the revelation of Rahab-Babylon and the elevation of Rahab by the sons of Albion. Similarily, as the daughters unite into one with Rahab, they take the Falsehood which grows until it becomes the Space and Allegory named Divine Analogy (*J* 84:29-85:7). The antithesis seen in these plates is basically the same as that seen in earlier chapters, the only difference being that the dichotomy of This World delineated in the first part of

---

[17] The complexity of this geographical imagery is heightened by the fact that Albion is at once both stretched across England east to west, i.e., placed *on* England, and *is* England, stretching north to south: his bosom involves York, Edinburgh, Durham, and Carlisle. Were his bosom *on* the northern part of England, his limbs could not be disposed as they are.

[18] For a discussion of this identity see my "Perspective in Blake's *Jerusalem*," *BNYPL*, LXXIII (1969), 49-55.

the poem is conceived in terms of the processes through which the reintegration of fallen man and the destruction of Jerusalem may be achieved, whereas the last chapter treats the antithesis in terms of the absolute extension or products of the processes. Quite simply, the maleficent forces of This World yield in the latter quarter of the poem to images which symbolize the consolidation of error; forces, images, and events which held promise of redemption yield to images which either immediately anticipate redemption or are themselves manifestations of the restored condition of man. The first three chapters describe the successive stages of fallen existence and elements of imaginative vision which will ultimately lead man out of that existence. The fourth chapter carries the process of the fall to its conclusion, revealing various forms of consolidated error and images of Eternity.

Even when, in the concluding plates, the focus of the poem shifts to the restored condition of man, images of the fallen world remain an integral part of the eternal reality. The reintegration of man with his emanation is depicted in the design of plate 99 {103}, which concludes the last chapter. The black-and-white copies present a naked female at the left with upraised, outstretched arms receiving and being embraced by an aged, bearded figure at the right. Flames surround both figures. A rather large, white nimbus is seen behind the head of the male. Two significant differences in the Mellon copy are that the nimbus is blue, and that within the nimbus, encircling the head of the male, is a gray, jagged-edged halo similar in texture to the oak-leaf caps worn by the figures of the title page and reminiscent of the crown of thorns. Blue is associated in *Jerusalem* with vegetative death. Luvah is stained "with poisonous blue, they inwove him in cruel roots / To die a death of Six thousand years bound round with vegetation" (*J* 65:9-10); the extent to which Albion has fallen is indicated by the appearance of blue death in his feet (*J* 33[37]:10).

The meaning of this design is intimately connected with the events described in the text and designs of plates 94-98, the awakening of Albion and his union with Jerusalem-England. The plate most relevant to this one is 96, where an aged, bearded male at the left is seen embracing a naked female at the right. These figures appear to be the ones presented on plate 99. The major difference between the two designs is that the positions of the figures in one are reversed in the other. Wicksteed (p. 244) identifies the male of plate 96 as Albion and suggests that the design "represents the ancient race of Man in the act of rising from Earth (with bared Right foot to symbolize his spiritual ascent), while the Feminine figure of his consort in Eternity (a pure unadorned spirit of Emanation) rises from her Left foot off the Earth into which we were all born." If the male of this design is seen to be Albion, it is necessary to realize that he is not wholly identifiable with the rising Albion of plate 95 {101}, who is beardless;[19] but rather, he is a manifestation of the Satanic aspect of Albion, of the Covering Cherub-self which marches eastward against Jesus from Sinai and Edom into the wilderness of Judah (J 96:9-13). The union of the two figures is, on plate 96, an imperfect one, for the female faces the reader while the male is presented in profile; her hip is toward his body. Altizer (p. 206) says of plate 96, "We may surmise that this illustration is a vision of the universal process of Crucifixion if only because Satan and Jerusalem are engaged in mutual negation of that Selfhood which isolates each from the other. Satan becomes spirit and Jerusalem becomes flesh." According to Altizer, the "Divine Image" dies in Jesus to abolish the solitary God; "Crucifixion embodies the movement of Satan from flesh to spirit, and of Jerusalem from spirit to flesh, from right to left, which is the movement of incarnation." This approach to the relationship of the two plates is basically sound, but Altizer fails to provide the correct analysis of these designs because he regards right and left as absolute categories. As evidenced by the inscription at the top of plate 3, the reader's right corresponds to the spiritual left. The movement of incarnation is from right to left, yet when seen in the vegetable glass, i.e., from our perspective, it is from left to right.[20]

Thus the change in the positions of the figures in plates 96 and 99 does not represent the movement of Jerusalem from spirit to flesh, and of Satan-Albion from flesh to spirit. The Emanation dividing from her male counterpart, assuming a corporeal form, represents a stage of the fall.[21] The disorganized, degraded Jerusalem already has a separate, corporeal identity prior to the con-

[19] Also see plates 25{6}, 33[37]{97}, 76{98}.

[20] See the design of plate 31[35], which presents the movement of incarnation, Jesus' move from left to right, forming woman of contraction's limit that "Himself may in process of time be born" (J 42:34).

[21] See J 17:49-56, 67:2-14, 86:50-62, 90:1-13.

406

clusion of the poem. She is "Shrunk to a narrow doleful form . . ."
(*J* 79:63), a worm wandering in affliction, encompassed by the
frozen net of vegetative existence (*J* 80:1-4). This condition is expressed by the position of Jerusalem in plate 96. The Urizenic
male of plate 96 is that alien other, the selfhood, the solitary God
which must be put off eternally. He is the God afar off (*J* 4:8),
whose annihilation is achieved only as he becomes the vegetated
Christ. It is in plate 99, not plate 96, that he is presented in his
corporeal form. The darkened nimbus and the jagged-edged halo
which encircle his head in the Mellon copy are emblematic of
the vegetative condition into which he must pass. As the Spectre
of Albion, "the Selfhood / Satan: Worshipd as God by the Mighty
Ones of the Earth" (*J* 29 [33]:17-18), becomes flesh (Jesus), the
fallen Jerusalem is restored,[22] and the union of man, who is God,[23]
with his Emanation is consummated. This union is expressed in the
design of plate 99. The bodies of the two figures are now almost
completely contiguous. This plate, in its final form, indicates that
the Edenic condition is achieved through the medium of This
World.

Although there is a time after which "Time was Finished . . ."
(*J* 94:18), and Albion awakes from the dream of history to behold
the visions of his deadly sleep of six thousand years dazzling around
Jesus' skirts like a serpent (*J* 96:11-12), there is considerable evidence to indicate that the eternal inheres in time. Eternity may be
held in an hour (*Auguries of Innocence*); Jesus "Opens Eternity
in Time & space; triumphant in Mercy" (*J* 75:22). Blake's great
task is also

> To open the Eternal Worlds, to open the immortal Eyes
> Of Man inwards into the Worlds of Thought: into
>   Eternity. . . .
>
> (J 5:17-18)

The interval separating the historical and the eternal is spacial
rather than temporal:

> The Vegetative Universe, opens like a flower from the Earths
>   center:

[22] The restored Jerusalem cannot become flesh because, as the feminine
becomes a veil and net of veins, of red blood, she ceases to be man's emanation (*J* 90:1-5).

[23] Blake wrote in his copy of Berkeley's *Siris*, "Man is All Imagination
God is Man & exists in us & we in him" (E654/K775).

In which is Eternity. It expands in Stars to the Mundane Shell
And there it meets Eternity again, both within and without. . . .

(J 13:34-36)

Cambel and her Sisters sit within the Mundane Shell forming

According to their will the outside surface of the Earth
An outside shadowy Surface superadded to the real Surface;
Which is unchangeable for ever & ever Amen. . . .

(J 83:46-48)

The poem defines two planes of existence, two categories of
reality, which are usually thought to be mutually exclusive, or
at least of unequal ontic status. The coincidence of the eternal and
historical realities as they are normally conceived yields a genuine
paradox, for the existence of an unchangeable, infinitely extended
reality, that is, Eternity, precludes the existence of any other.
Blake may appear to overcome this ontological dilemma merely by
defining it out of existence, by stating that the World of Mortality
is but a shadow of the Eternal World of Imagination (<i>J</i> 71:19). Yet
an obvious concession to the reality of fallen history and consequently to the paradoxical nature of the poem's ontological order
may be seen in the observation of those in Great Eternity who
contemplate death:

   . . . What seems to Be: Is: To those to whom
   It seems to Be, & is productive of the most dreadful
   Consequences to those to whom it seems to Be: even of
   Torments, Despair, Eternal Death. . . .

(J 32[36]:51-54)

Compare this passage with its direct contrary, which occurs immediately after the revelation of the Covering Cherub and the
amalgamation of Briton, Saxon, Roman, Norman in Los's furnaces: "Will you suffer this Satan this Body of Doubt that Seems
but Is Not / To occupy the very threshold of Eternal Life"
(<i>J</i> 93:20-21). The ontologies of This World and Eternity are logically irreconcilable—at least as they are presented in these passages.

This paradox is reflected in the temporal structure of the narrative. The perspective of the narrator is grounded in both This
World and Eternity. The narration of the poem begins in a sim-

408

ple progressive present tense: "This theme calls me in sleep night after night, & ev'ry morn / Awakes me at sun-rise, then I see the Saviour over me" (*J* 4:3-4), and ends in what may be called the prophetic past: "And I heard the Name of their Emanations they are named Jerusalem" (*J* 99:5). Blake sees the Savior hovering over him at sunrise "Spreading his beams of love, & dictating the words of this mild song" (*J* 4:5). It could be argued that the past tense defines the time during which the Savior dictates, the period at sunrise in which events—past and future—are disclosed to Blake. The present, although predicated on a prophetic knowledge of past and future, is not grounded in an extratemporal reality, that is, it is not itself prophetic, but is merely that period subsequent to the sunrise disclosures, the day and night during which Blake sits trembling, writing (*J* 5:16-24). This explanation would provide a temporal fix on the statement occurring at the beginning of chapter II and repeated at the end of chapter III, "But now the Starry Heavens are fled from the mighty limbs of Albion" (*J* 27, 75:27). The immediate reality is one in which man is fragmented and fallen. However, this explanation does not adequately account for the descriptions of vision occasionally presented in the present tense: "I see the Past, Present & Future existing all at once" (*J* 15:6); "I see Albion sitting upon his Rock in the First Winter" (*J* 15:30).

It could also be argued that the prophetic past has implicit in it a prophetic present subsequent to the time when "Time was Finished," grounded in an extratemporal perspective like that afforded man after he awakes from his deadly sleep of six thousand years. However, this explanation fails to account for the fact that the reality of fallen history is presented in the present tense, that now the starry heavens are fled.

The apprehension of past, present, and future all at once projects Blake into and beyond history all at once. Although Eternity is extratemporal, it is manifest in time. And although it is manifest in time, it cannot logically admit of a temporal dimension; it cannot be that infinitely extended reality which precludes the existence of any other reality. The world of appearances is merely a shadow of the Eternal World; yet what seems to be, is. The Moment of Eternity is history: man, conversing in visionary forms dramatic, is "Creating Space, Creating Time according to the wonders Divine / Of Human Imagination . . ." (*J* 98:31-32). It is clear that the relationship between This World and Eternity is not simply a linear or sequential one. The poem creates an ontic hierarchy. It presents two antithetical categories of existence, the historical and the eternal, and asserts that the condition of man, fallen or restored, is ultimately grounded in both.

Thus we see, concomitant to the restoration of man, that all human forms are identified,

> . . . living going forth & returning wearied
> Into the Planetary lives of Years Months Days & Hours
>   reposing
> And then Awakening into his Bosom in the Life of Im-
>   mortality
>
> (J 99:2-4)

Even as man realizes existence in the eternal world, as he achieves the eternal reality, the historical remains an integral part of his condition.

These lines have been subject to various interpretations. Harold Bloom maintains that they describe the eternal alteration of contrary states, the living and going forth of Eden, and the returning wearied and reposing of Beulah.[24] However, in light of the coincidence of the eternal and historical worlds found elsewhere in the poem, and the design of plate 100 {104}, which illustrates these lines, it is necessary to recognize that the state to which man returns wearied is not an extramundane one. Blake's Eternity is not simply of the post-temporal, pie-in-the-sky-when-we-die variety.

The final plate depicts the restored condition of man. A male at the extreme left of the plate, Los's Spectre, carries the Eternal Sun on his left shoulder. Los stands in the middle holding the tools he used throughout the poem in his redemptive labors, the tongs and hammer. Enitharmon stands at the right of the plate holding a spindle-shaped device in her left hand and in her right the threads or fibers of Generation, which are draped over an ark-moon—and are painted blood-red in the Mellon copy.[25] The set-

---

[24] *Apocalypse*, 481.

[25] Enitharmon's action here is somewhat ambiguous. The object in her left hand could be a spindle on which she gathers the fibers held in her right, which serves as a distaff. It is also possible, and perhaps more likely, that the object in her left hand is a small, spindle-shaped shuttle of the type used to hold the thread one manipulates in knotting and netting. Enitharmon might then just be unwinding the thread from the shuttle, draping it over

ting of this design is also representative of existence in This World. Depicted immediately behind the figures and extending across the plate is the Druid Temple of Avebury.[26] It is set on a green hill (in the Mellon copy) and covered with vegetation. As the fallen serpent is emblematic of the restrictive and corrupting aspects of fallen nature (*J* 43:76-80), so the serpent temple is an "image of infinite / Shut up in finite revolutions . . ." (*E* 10:21-22).

Although Blake maintains in *A Vision of the Last Judgment* (E555/K617) that error or creation will be burned up and outward creation is as dirt upon his feet, the restoration of man at the conclusion of *Jerusalem* is not accompanied by the destruction of the World of Generation, but rather by its reconstruction. The all-wondrous serpent is not destroyed, but is humanized in the forgiveness of sins (*J* 98:44-45). The aspect of This World which was meant for the destruction of Jerusalem has been annihilated, but Generation still remains as the medium through which Eternity is realized. The cry of triumph over moral law is heard "from the Great City of Golgonooza in the Shadowy Generation" (*J* 98:55).

The moment of Eternity is reconstructed history. But perhaps more important, it is also the act of reconstruction, the transformation of the reality of This World by Imaginative Vision. It is the period between the pulsations of an artery when the artist's work is done, and it is at the same time that work. The terrible eternal labor of the golden builders of Golgonooza is itself Eternity. Imaginative acts performed by men in This World, in shadowy Generation, are the substance of Eternity: "The Eternal Body of Man is The IMAGINATION. that is God himself The Divine Body"

---

the ark-moon of Generation. The difficulty in maintaining this view of Enitharmon's action is that only a single thread hangs between the shuttle and her right hand, and many threads hang from her right hand. However, this same problem is encountered in plate 45 [31], where Vala is seen inweaving Jerusalem in her dark threads. Vala holds a device similar in appearance to this one in her right hand. A single thread issues from it to her left hand, from which three threads extend to the net in which Jerusalem is caught. The action on plate 45 is clearly from the spindle-shaped object to the net. Enitharmon's action is also similar to Vala's action in the design of plate 25. The ark-moon symbolizes the corporeal form of man; see *J* 32[36]:1-4 and the designs of plates 24 and 39 [44].

26 Ruthven Todd, *Tracks in the Snow*, New York, 1947, 48.

(*The Laocoön*: E271/K776); "God only Acts & Is, in existing beings or Men" (*MHH* 16). It is clear why Blake, defending Paine, writes, "Is it a greater miracle to feed five thousand men with five loaves than to overthrow all the armies of Europe with a small pamphlet. look over the events of your own life & if you do not find that you have both done such miracles & lived by such you do not see as I do" (Annotations to Watson's *Apology*: E606/K391). Like the golden builders, like those in Great Eternity, Paine and Blake also converse in visionary forms dramatic and repose in the planetary life of years, months, days, and hours.

19

Blake's Cities:
Romantic Forms of Urban Renewal

KENNETH R. JOHNSTON

THE EPITHET which Frank Kermode bestowed upon Baudelaire, "the great poet of the modern city," can be applied with equal justice to Blake, English Romanticism's most urban poet and the modern city's first myth-maker.[1] The aptness of the tribute to the author of *London* and *Jerusalem* is evident, but its pertinence to the entire range of his work has not been fully appreciated. Scholars (especially Northrop Frye) have emphasized the importance in Blake's poetry of the dialectical myth of a heavenly city and a fallen city, adapted principally from the Jerusalem and Babylon of Revelation, where both share—one as bride, the other as whore—the human aspect that is central to his mythopoeia.[2] Yet a study of the cumulative development of Blake's urban imagery, emphasizing the connection between mythic cities and historical cities, will clear away some more of the reputed obscurity of his work and may also allow us to see ourselves more clearly, *sub specie urbis*.[3]

Although Blake might have acknowledged the sociological accuracy of Baudelaire's famous comparison of the poet's role in the city to the prostitute's, it would have shocked him because of the degradation of human imaginings which it implied and accepted. Unlike Baudelaire, who views the *fourmillante cité* with a pessimistic realism, Blake plumbs its depths of consciousness and lays bare in an intellectualized and abstract symbolism the forms of life it creates for good as well as evil. He brings urban myth and urban reality together in his illuminations as well as his texts. Though he pictures human and vegetative forms predominantly, the occasions on which he presents visual representations of cities are sig-

---

[1] Frank Kermode, *Romantic Image*, London, 1957, 5.

[2] Frye, *Symmetry*, ch. 11, "The City of God." For indication of the influence of the myth of the heavenly city on Frye's own criticism see his *Study of English Romanticism*, New York, 1968, 18-19.

[3] See "Note on Other Romantic Visions of the City," below, p. 441.

nificant, while smaller architectural details function throughout his work as passing allusions to the extensive urban schemes developed in his texts. Pyramids or domed structures represent tendencies toward repression and imaginative failure, especially if topped by a cross. The same is true, with important exceptions, of his Druidic structures. The ideal city of unrepressed imagination, on the other hand, is represented by Gothic buildings with delicate, open arches.

Blake's awareness of the positive potential of urban imagery did not spring full-blown from his first consciousness of his surroundings. On the contrary. His earliest work, *Poetical Sketches* (1783), reflects the antiurbanism which had become conventional among his near-contemporaries, the tired poets of Sensibility, in their reaction against the satiric urbanity of the great Neoclassic writers. In some of the experimental prose-poems with which he filled out his first volume, Blake explicitly rejects the city as a source of poetic inspiration, in favor of the country:

> Clamour brawls along the streets, and destruction hovers in the city's smoak; but on these plains, and in these silent woods, true joys descend. (*Contemplation*:E433/K37)

Manuscript fragments from this period underline his early antipathy toward the city. They depict cities as symbols of vice and folly, conceived on models like Sodom and Gomorrah. Such cities exist only to be denounced, not satirized, as residences of evil—personified in the abstractions of the Augustan moral vision:

> . . . Pride, inspird by [Ambition], Prophetic Saw the Kingdoms of the World & all their Glory. . . . Cains city. built with Murder. Then Babel mighty Reard him to the Skies. Babel with thousand tongues . . . Then Nineva & Babylon & Costly tyre. And evn Jerusalem was Shewn. the holy City. Then Athens Learning & the Pride of Greece. and further from the Rising Sun. was Rome . . . the mistress of the world, Emblem of Pride ("then She bore Pale desire . . .":E437/K41)

During the next fifteen years, Blake's estimate of the value of the city relative to the country reversed itself almost completely —sign and symbol of his affirmation of the inherently creative power of imagination which announced his "case against Locke." In Blake's version of the great Romantic dialectic between Nature and Imagination, it is not fair to say that his attitude toward nature per se ever became entirely negative, but he rejected ideas of human community based on "natural" premises as utterly as he scorned similarly grounded theories of perception and systems of theology. Stages along the way of this development are marked by the forms of cities which become increasingly marvelous affirmations of the power and transcendent value of Imagination. From "Cain's city built with Murder" Blake moves to a realistic yet symbolic analysis of *London* in the *Songs of Experience* (published 1794, but composed ca. 1789-1792), and then into his despairing visions of the cities of fallen man, in the minor prophecies (1793-1795). *The Four Zoas* (ca. 1796-1807?) is the great battleground of Blake's imaginative development, and its urban imagery reflects the direction he takes in *Milton* and *Jerusalem*: from it emerges not only Golgonooza, the urban form of Jerusalem in the fallen world, but also Babylon, its mirror image and the real metropolis of history, part Vanity Fair, part factory town, in which the fall is eternally recapitulated.

Even in his earliest work, however, there is evidence that Blake's attitude toward the city is more than conventional. He does not reject cities out of hand, but attacks them as places where self-love flourishes, perverting the ways of man to man just where, paradoxically, man's "neighborhood" is closest:

Go see the City friends Joind Hand in Hand. Go See. the Natural tie of flesh & blood. Go See more strong the ties of marriage love. thou Scarce Shall find but Self love Stands Between   ("then She bore Pale desire . . .":E439/K43)

Although this is prose, the rhythms and concerns anticipate the simple compelling insistence of *London*, which in text and picture brings to a level of major artistic achievement Blake's earliest attitude toward the city, summed up in this fragment as an attack on Pride: "Guile & fraud . . . live in the Smoke of Cities . . . alas in Cities wheres the man whose face is not a mask unto his heart" (E438-439).

By the early 1790's, when he had completed *London*, Blake's vision was developed to the point where he could see through the masks, "And mark in every face I meet / Marks of weakness, marks of woe." As David Erdman has shown, Blake's *London* is the Lon-

415

don of 1794, as well as that cynical, self-tyrannizing state which we call "experience." Yet a close study of the text, the picture engraved above it, and early manuscript versions show that the poem is not an expression of simple despair but a profound analysis of human misery in cities, an example of what Raymond Williams has identified as Blake's ability to make "a genuine connection" between social alienation and personal alienation.[4]

Sometime before he began drafts of *London*, Blake put down in his *Notebook* eight lines of simple response to the grievances of city life, parts of which he salvaged for the poem.

> Why should I care for the men of thames
> Or the cheating waves of the charterd streams
> Or shrink at the little blasts of fear
> That the hireling blows into my ear
>
> Tho born on the cheating banks of Thames
> Tho his waters bathed my infant limbs
> The Ohio shall wash his stains from me
> I was born a slave but I go to be free
>
> (E464/K166)

This preliminary view of the economic and emotional ills of London, though elliptical, displays a shrewd realism much advanced from the deductive abstractions of *Poetical Sketches*. Nevertheless, the speaker's response is the perennial human reaction to urban ills: escape. In the terminology of Blake's mature myth, the speaker's response is that of Unorganized Innocence; his imagination does not respond to challenge because it has not come through the contrary of Experience. America was frequently for Blake a symbol of individual liberty; in this fragment it functions also as a natural paradise.[5] The Ohio River (in 1790 the frontier of the Western Territory) represents both political and economic freedom, yet the symbolic force of its name derives from Blake's assumption that its water is not literally polluted like the Thames's. The ironies that time has forced upon this symbolism are obvious enough, but instructive; residents of present-day Ohio

[4] Raymond Williams, "Prelude to Alienation," *Dissent* (Summer 1964), 304.

[5] Nancy Bogen, "Blake on 'The Ohio,'" *Notes & Queries*, xv (1968), 19-20, finds that Blake may have been influenced in his view of the Ohio region by the glowing description in Gilbert Imlay's *Topographical Description of the Western Territory of North America*, 1792.

cities (and a hundred others) are in much the same predicament as Blake's speaker, but escape is not so easy. The economic exploitation which turns pure water into "the cheating waves of . . . charterd streams" will very likely turn Ohio's Lake Erie into a swamp before it is taken to task by imaginative anger. The entire process, in Peter Fisher's description of Blake's view of it, is this: "withdrawal from vision is a cyclical repetition of the fall."[6] In the relationship between Nature and Imagination as it exists between country and city in most modern industrial countries, this means that the attempt to escape imaginative challenge by fleeing to nature ends by bringing nature down around our ears in ruin.

When he came to draft *London* itself, Blake made word choices which specifically prevent a simple escapist response to the dreadful city of Experience. In his manuscript *Notebook* he described London with pejorative adjectives: "dirty street," "dirty Thames," "dismal streets." But in the engraved poem he substituted adjectives that are at once more neutral and more symbolically weighted ("charter'd street," "charter'd Thames," "midnight streets"), thereby indicating that London's evils are not the fault of the city per se, but faults which Englishmen have brought upon themselves. The most telling of these changes is from "german forg'd links" to the famous "mind-forg'd manacles," which he hears echoing in the cries of both Innocence and Experience:

> In every cry of every Man,
> In every Infants cry of fear,
> In every voice: in every ban,
> The mind-forg'd manacles I hear.

The chimney sweeper, the conscripted soldier, and the prostitute in the poem are undeniably victims, but Blake's changes point to his conviction that repression is not simply the result of "bans" handed down from above. German George III issues the bans, Blake knows, but even he cannot forge the manacles with which we shackle our spirits into obeying them; man's "marks of weakness" are partially the cause of his "marks of woe."

The design across the top of *London* {18} is an excellent example of the way in which Blake's designs at their best enrich the verbal statement of the poems. Because it does not relate directly

---

[6] Peter Fisher, *The Valley of Vision*, Toronto, 1961, 53.

to anything in the text, the design at first confuses, but its effect does jar the reader's perceptions out of the verbal and into the visual mode. On first viewing, the aged cripple and the child who seems to be leading him appear as two victims of the evils of contemporary London, but on closer inspection—of independent visual elements counterpointing independent verbal elements—we recognize a dramatization of the statement of the first stanza: the child and the ancient "mark" (see) in each other's face "woe" and "weakness," respectively. Or, more simply (since the old man may be blind), they *are* the marks—evidences—themselves. Furthermore, there is a profound irony in the situation if, as seems likely, the child is supposed to be leading the old man. Viewed against the text this is a mockery, since every stanza after the first contains a detail about the victimization of children in London. But what seems a mockery to common sense may be a profoundly sustained ironic contrast to the author of *The Marriage of Heaven and Hell*. If we generalize the child as Innocence and the aged cripple as Experience, we can interpret the design in the larger context of the *Songs Of Innocence and Of Experience, Shewing the Two Contrary States of the Human Soul*. Does the design parallel the text by showing the inadequacies of Innocence and Experience as *separated* modes of consciousness, or is it to be read counter to the text, as a hopeful sign of human progress, a glimpse of the day when the wisdom of Experience moves forward in the city guided by the fresh simplicity of Innocent desires?[7]

Although it would be hard to answer this question affirmatively in the face of such a bitter statement as the text of *London*, Blake's capacity for such ironic reversals between text and design should not be underestimated. This can be seen with special clarity if we look ahead some twenty-five years in his career, from *London* to plate 84 of *Jerusalem* {100}, which displays almost exactly the same design. Here the design is a more direct illustration of the text. It depicts part of the song the daughters of Albion sing to Los from their captivity in Babylon:

[7] Cf. John Grant, "The Colors of Prophecy," *The Nation*, CC (25 January 1965), 92; E. D. Hirsch, *Innocence and Experience: An Introduction to Blake*, New Haven, 1964, 265. Both Grant and Hirsch see the design as optimistically contrary to the text. Hirsch sees both the old man and the child as emblems of weakness and woe: "Like the poem, the design telescopes cause and effect."

> I see London blind & age-bent begging thro the Streets
> Of Babylon, led by a child. his tears run down his beard
>
> (84:11-12)[8]

With reference to *London*, these lines might seem to suggest that its design carries only negative connotations, but the suggestion is unreliable, because Albion's daughters are not capable of telling the whole truth, and their song functions ironically in its context. They are singing partially to entice and partially to encourage Los, but, as he recognizes, they are confused and misleading about their own situation. Nevertheless, Blake in the space of four lines puts in their mouths a lament which focuses the urban dimension of their confusion on London, bringing an enormous scope of time and space to bear upon his own street corner:[9]

> The voice of Wandering Reuben ecchoes from street to street
> In all the Cities of the Nations Paris Madrid Amsterdam
>
> The Corner of Broad Street weeps; Poland Street languishes
> To Great Queen Street & Lincolns Inn, all is distress & woe
>
> (*J* 84:13-16)

All of these images are suggested to a certain extent by the design, as is the daughters' earlier claim that they "builded Jerusalem as a City & a Temple" (84:3). The Gothic cathedral and Romanesque temple in the left background of the design are additions to Blake's conception of the scene in *London*, and they are crucial to the ironic counterpoint of text and design.

Although London is reported by Albion's daughters to be walking through the streets of Babylon, the architecture depicted is identified in the text as Jerusalem. It is of course possible that the daughters duplicate Jerusalem's architecture as they "build Baby-

[8] Although the design obviously illustrates these lines, it is characteristic of Blake's mature artistic technique that one design may pick up echoes of two or three passages of text, suggesting alternate meanings. Thus, the design also catches associations from lines near the end of plate 83:

> So Los spoke, to the Daughters of Beulah while his Emanation
> Like a faint rainbow waved before him in the awful gloom
> Of London City on the Thames from Surrey Hills to Highgate
>
> (*J* 83:66-68)

[9] For a discussion of the way in which Blake raised common sights in his neighborhood to epic proportions in his prophecies, see Erdman, *Prophet*, 266-267 [288-291].

lon on Euphrates" (84:8), but the text suggests something more on the order of an emergency military camp (84:9-10). Rather, I think Blake means us to see the buildings as Jerusalem, or to remind us of Jerusalem, so that the design presents an eternal instant in which past, present, and future appear simultaneously. Furthermore, no matter what attitude one takes toward the *arcana* of left/ right orientations in Blake's illuminations, it is apparent that the two figures have rounded a corner ("the Corner of Broad Street"?) not available in the *London* version of the design, that they are moving to (the reader's) left into the light instead of to the right into darkness, and that they have passed by a door (reminiscent of "Death's Door"; *Gates of Paradise* 15) which they were just approaching in *London*.[10]

[10] This parallel and several other details of the design are discussed by John E. Grant in a note from work in progress which he has kindly offered as an appendix to my interpretation:

J.E.G.: A sounder principle than Wicksteed's hypothesis of right as the spiritual direction and left as the material—which depends on variables of ethics (e.g., when "left" is or is not sinister) and of perspective (whether the viewer's or the actor's or the stage's left and right are in question)—is that whenever a little child leads an old man he does not mislead him, if we mark their progress to the end. Karl Kiralis, in " 'London' in the Light of *Jerusalem*," *Blake Studies*, I (1968), 5-15, is trapped by the Wicksteed formula into declaring that the old man, in *London*, is being misled by the boy "to the (stage) left" into the darkness, whereas he is on the right track in *J* 84 because he is going to the (stage) right, toward the "rising sun, which shows quite clearly on [but only on] the colored copy." Yet in *London* the old man is not blown into "Death's Door" as in *A* 12 and *Gates of Paradise* 15; he is led past the door by the enlightened child. Kiralis errs in indicating that the pair are going into darkness in copy Z (Blake Trust facsimile); in Z and in AA and B (Micro Methods films) it is clear that the pair are illuminated from on high, as though by a searchlight. If we then consider *J* 84, we see that they have not quite passed the Door of Death but have reached a corner where a better vista is evident and there will be no more darkness at all.

Consider in *London* the marginal scene of the boy warming himself by a fire. In copies Z and AA he is identified with the boy guide by identical green clothing (in B the guide is in white). He keeps the fire of life burning in the midst of an eternal winter, in readiness to perform a redemptive act— returning a favor experienced by the Little Boy found (pl. 14) which the deplorable times cannot render impossible. London lost is a truth only of midnight streets: real but not final.

Those who find poetical-pictorial counterpoint difficult and are looking for something to make the picture as despairing as the poem may take com-

In short, the major orientation points of the design have been reversed, but even without *London* as a gloss, the tone and action of the design of plate 84 would seem to warrant a less dire commentary than that provided by Albion's daughters. It would be too mechanical an interpretation to say that the design is optimistic because Gothic architecture usually carries optimistic connotations in Blake's work, but the sun (added in the Mellon copy) which bathes both buildings in brilliant color would support such a reading. Also, the child's right hand points directly into the archway of the Gothic cathedral, probably indicating it as his goal rather than the Romanesque temple. If the design were viewed simply as an ideograph, this could be taken to indicate that salvation (Jerusalem) is near at hand despite the proximity of enslavement (Babylon). However, it would be forcing line 3 to say that "City" and "Temple" refer to the spires and the dome, respectively, and that the former illustrates the true Jerusalem and the latter its Babylonian inversion. It is much more likely that Blake simply means to evoke the traditional double image of Jerusalem as Holy City and Holy Temple.[11]

Nevertheless, it is clearly Blake's intention in the large sweep of his myth to assert that the city is a place of infinite possibility,

---

fort in the sinister worm across the bottom. But in the last copy Blake placed an extraordinary plumed tail on the worm which covers a dark spot visible in earlier copies. The redeeming characteristic must have been there all the time; if Blake hadn't seen this potential embellishment long before, he'd have moved out of the city into the suburbs and stayed there.

Blake was no idolater of the young; he could look unblinkingly at the disturbed motivation beneath the alienated condition politely called *Infant Sorrow*. But that prudent elders were incompetent to lead he was so firmly persuaded that critics have complained of the tactlessness of the *Voice of the Ancient Bard*. This was Blake's message; he who wants to hear a prophet say "Come, let us reason together" will have to find another author.

Edward Young also aspired to speak out loud and clear on this issue, and Blake devotes an important sequence of *Night Thoughts* pictures (nos. 359-363) to the theme. A youth, in no. 362, follows a string that he is winding into a ball through a dark forest—prefiguring the still younger wayfarer in *J* 77. This little boy, because he found himself by following the clue, changed his robe from white (as in *J* 77 and copy B of *London*) to blue and was thus able to lead London from a state of Aged Ignorance into the light of Eternity's sunrise that is shining now through the eastern gates of Paradise.

[11] William R. Hughes, ed., *Jerusalem: A Simplified Version*, New York, 1964, 216.

and that we build a Jerusalem or a Babylon depending on how we choose to exercise our imaginations. Though the two buildings here are represented too schematically to permit exact identification, it would be hard not to see the domed temple as St. Paul's, since other dominant features of London and its environs are cited repeatedly in the text of plates 83 and 84 as proof that Los is present in London, supporting by his presence his impassioned plea to Albion: "Found ye London! enormous City!" (83:23). Los promises to manage the spiritual part of this massive urban renewal project by assimilating London to Golgonooza (83:43), the so-called "City of Art." Because,

> The land is markd for desolation & unless we plant
> The seeds of Cities & of Villages in the Human bosom
> Albion must be a rock of blood. . . .   (83:54-56)

His promise counters the song of Albion's daughters that London is Babylon, and completes the circle of ironic counterpoint between this design and its texts (which Blake first conceived in *London*), because they sing to weaken his resolve.

A large part of Los's resolution, in each of Blake's three epics, is to build Golgonooza—that is, to establish a form or vessel for the life of Imagination upon the contracted limits of fallen human nature. The appearance of Golgonooza about 1797, in Night the Fifth of *The Four Zoas*, is an important milestone in the development of Blake's urban vision after *London*.[12] Before it, with but one noteworthy exception (in the abandoned *French Revolution*)[13] Blake's cities partake of the despairing appearance of the

---

[12] E737-739. Cf. Bentley, *Vala*, 159-162. Since Night v cannot be dated with certainty, it is impossible to say exactly when Blake first thought of Golgonooza. Probably it entered his MS late in the first concerted stages of composition. However, the description of the building of Jerusalem in Night IX may be earlier, which would place the conception of Golgonooza in the early 1800's rather than the late 1790's. Although there are of course images of cities in Blake's earlier work, David Erdman has pointed out to me that there is no description of city-*building* before *The Four Zoas*.

[13] *The French Revolution* (1791) marks a break between the mode of Blake's early and late urban imagery; the former is largely historical, the latter predominantly mythic. In the first (and only) book of this projected historical epic, we hear one of Blake's most striking voices in the speech of the Abbé de Sieyès; mixing myth and social reality, he speaks for "the voice of meek cities," proclaiming the triumph of a civilized urban economy

"proto-*zoas*" in the minor prophecies, and of their failure to "graduate" to vision.[14] Once he conceived Golgonooza, however, he took a giant step forward in his search for a concrete expression of the redemptive side of prophecy.[15]

The cities in *The Four Zoas* are the massive creations of Blake's giant Zoas, symbols of the fundamental modes of consciousness which, divided from their prelapsarian unity, have successively tyrannized man's history. Since Blake rejected any philosophic notion of pure being, holding instead that action becomes the man, the cities the Zoas build are literally the form of their being; they are "city-states," simultaneously geo-political units and the states of mind which create them. (The conception is a natural extension from *London*.) Given the dialectical cast of all Blake's thinking and his indebtedness to biblical models, it is not surprising that these cities work dialectically, each calling forth its contrary. We can follow the action of all three of his epics by distinguishing, for example, between the grotesquely subdivided "developments" of Urizen (Moral Rationalism) and the self-renewing cities planned by Los. The fullest significance of Blake's cities is much better gauged by analyzing their function in the movement of the poem than by attempting to make sense of them by tracing the etymologies of their odd names. Like the Zoas themselves, their cities are giant human forms with enormous potential for good and evil. Also like his Zoas, Blake's cities are not vicious (when they are) according to conventional moral categories, but through a lack of respect for the integrity of all modes of being, which inevitably results in psychic tyranny or repression. What the truncated cities in *The Four Zoas* lack is "human scale," and human scale is what, in typically literal descriptions, Blake gives to Los's vision.

---

with full employment over the forests of error and repression. In his vision, peasants are not "driven back by the . . . pestilent fogs [of war, disease, deprivation, ignorance, and sloth] round the cities of men," but enter in as true *citoyens* (pp. 11-12). The Abbé's optimism parallels Los's, but unlike the Paris of 1789, Golgonooza is on no map but the chart of human consciousness that Blake first laid out fully in *The Four Zoas*.

[14] H. M. Margoliouth, *William Blake*, New York, 1951, 91.

[15] To view Golgonooza solely as a city is of course to limit its symbolic richness. For fuller discussion of its varied possibilities, see, among others, John Middleton Murry, *William Blake*, London, 1933, 196-210, and Bloom, *Apocalypse*, 377-382.

The larger movements of *The Four Zoas, sub specie urbis*, are as follows. There are basically two cities in the poem, actually two versions of Golgonooza, which, for convenience, we may identify by the names they ultimately assume, Jerusalem and Babylon. They are very different from each other, yet their activities are closely paralleled because Babylon is a deadly parody of Jerusalem that certain aspects of consciousness (particularly the Urizenic) attempt to foist off on others as human necessity. After the dissolution of the unity of the Zoas at the beginning of the poem, the action progresses to the destruction of Jerusalem at the end of Night the First. Nights II and III witness the rise of Urizen's cathedral city or fortress which, taken in its largest dimensions, is the "Mundane Shell" of fallen nature, or the universe at the present time. In Night v and again in Night VIIa there are accounts of the building of Golgonooza, and in Night VIIb and Night VIII the two cities' preparations for war are contrasted.

At each of these stages the destruction of cities, or the construction of cities along misguided plans, is presented as the destruction of humanity. The gleeful song of the demons at the wedding of Los and his Emanation, Enitharmon, in Night I (a marriage of convenience if there ever was one) celebrates the fact:

> And This the Song! sung at The Feast of Los & Enithar-
> mon . . .
> With wine of cruelty. Let us plat a scourge O Sister City
> Children are nourishd for the Slaughter; once the Child
> was fed
> With Milk; but wherefore now are Children fed with
> blood . . .
>
> Call to thy dark armd hosts, for all the sons of Men
> muster together
> To desolate their cities! Man shall be no more! Awake
> O Hosts
> The bow string sang upon the hills! Luvah & Vala ride
> Triumphant in the bloody sky. & the Human form is no
> more   (pp. 14-15:E304/K274-275)

Urizen's attempt to restore order to this chaos in Night II brings Jerusalem "down in a dire ruin over all the Earth," "Petrifying all the Human Imagination into rock & sand" (p. 25:E310). H. M.

Margoliouth's comment (p. 111) on Urizen's action, "Rationalism and planning are evils used to fight the evils of chaotic emotion," plus his witty summation, that "after softheadedness comes
hardheartedness," are truths too painfully relevant to most official
responses to urban crises to need elaboration. The mass reaction
to Urizen's action is also familiar. It is acquiescence, the willingness to be tyrannized which Blake touched on in *London*, which
is echoed at all times in demands for "law and order" in the face
of apparent chaos. As Urizen struggles,

> . . . many stood silent & busied in their families
> And many said We see no Visions in the darksom air
> Measure the course of that sulphur orb that lights
>   the darksom day
> Set stations on this breeding Earth & let us buy & sell
> (p. 28:E312/K283)

These are the conditions of life without imagination: nature reduced to scientific measurement, sexual relationships degraded to
breeding contracts, and business as usual. Soon enough, Urizen as
"Architect divine" constructs a geometric city that is the fitting
concrete form of such a life:

> . . . such the period of many worlds
> Others triangular right angled course maintain. others obtuse
> Acute Scalene, in simple paths. but others move
> In intricate ways biquadrate. Trapeziums Rhombs Rhomboids
> Paralellograms. triple & quadruple. polygonic
> In their amazing hard subdued course in the vast deep
> (p. 33:E315-316/K287)

Blake's sense of absurd humor is evident here, but he does not neglect to give Urizen credit for the beauty of his construction,
despite its mechanical rationalism: "infinitely beautiful the wondrous work arose / In sorrow & care." The tone of this faint praise
is more wistful than ironic, because Urizen's rational skills are
necessary to man's full redemption, though destructive when set
to work in isolation.

At the beginning of Night III, Ahania, Urizen's emanation of
creative repose, puts her finger on his city's flaw: "Golden & beautiful but O how unlike those sweet fields of bliss / Where liberty
was justice & eternal science was mercy" (E320). Her memory of a

social order where liberty and justice were identical is pastoral, as befits her character, but the ultimate contrast in Blake's mythology to Urizen's dreadfully ordered city is, even more than Golgonooza, the literally humanized city described in the major set piece in chapter 1 of *Jerusalem*:

> What are those golden builders doing? . . .
>
> . . . near mournful
>
> Ever weeping Paddington? . . .
>
> Lo!
>
> The stones are pity, and the bricks, well wrought affections:
> Enameld with love & kindness, & the tiles engraven gold
> Labour of merciful hands: the beams & rafters are
> forgiveness:
> The mortar & cement of the work, tears of honesty. . . .
>
> (*J* 12:25ff.)

Los, architect of this capital, knows the intimate connection between urban renewal and human renewal, whereas Urizen's construction in *The Four Zoas* has all the marks of a city, but it is substance without spirit. At the end of Ahania's speech Blake inserted in pencil two lines which make the contrast between these urban entities explicit: "Whether this is Jerusalem or Babylon we know not All is confusion All is tumult & we alone escaped" (E751). The addition was presumably made at a time when he had fully realized his urban mythology, for the struggle between these two opposite but equal orders is a central organizing principle in both *Milton* and *Jerusalem*. Indeed, Ahania's confusion is much like that of the daughters of Albion examined above, and Blake's use of it is similarly ironic, for within five pages of her "escape" Ahania is cast down into "Non Entity" by Urizen.

There are two different versions of the founding of Golgonooza in *The Four Zoas*, which reveal Blake's difficulty and dissatisfaction with the poem as a whole. Reduced to its simplest form, the dissatisfaction has to do with Vala's role in the reestablishment of Jerusalem, which is to say, the place of Nature, or "life," in the process of Imaginative vision, or "art."

If we narrow the range of Golgonooza's possible meanings between its position as the last downward stage of the fall and the first stage up toward regeneration, then the city that Los builds in Night v is clearly at the nadir of possibility. The difference does not seem great, but to a poet who took literally Christ's teaching that the Kingdom of Heaven is within, the slightest difference in point of view can make all the difference in the world. This Golgonooza, built "in dark prophetic fear" of "brass & silver & gold fourfold," is vaguely reminiscent of Urizen's cathedral city, and Los's cruelly jealous treatment of Orc (revolutionary energy) confirms the inauspicious parallel.

By contrast, the Golgonooza built in Night viia—presumably the later of the two versions of this Night—is evidence of the poem's first move toward unity: Los's reunion with Enitharmon and his pity for his "brother" Orc. (The reunion is parodied in the opposite camp by Urizen's crucifixion of Luvah, "Prince of Love" and Zoa of the emotions.) The reconciliation between Los and Enitharmon, seen as the union of Time and Space, makes possible a new vision of Golgonooza: "new heavens & a new Earth [open] beneath & within" (E354/K329).

Blake brings together his two urban symbols (Urizen's cathedral city and Los's Golgonooza) in a fully developed parallelism about halfway through Night viii, but the texts of the poem, to say nothing of its dense symbolic logic, make it difficult to see exactly what is happening. However, the recent editions by David Erdman and G. E. Bentley, Jr. reveal that many of Blake's struggles to project a unified vision in his first epic took place in passages dealing with cities.

In the earlier version of Night the Seventh (viib), Blake described still another city, constructed by Urizen and Vala—as Moral Rationalism and Nature, the villain and villainess of the poem and, to Blake's mind, of the century. This unnamed city springs up not as a sign of love (like the second Golgonooza) but as a device of jealousy. If the Golgonooza in viia is a large step up from the Golgonooza of Night v, then this city is, by a nice contrast, a substantial step down from Urizen's splendid cathedral city in Night ii. That city was at least orderly, but in this one order is achieved by falsehood, reflected in a religion based on mystery, an economy based on slavery, and a politics based on militarism—in short, the British Empire as Blake saw it.

First Trades & Commerce ships & armed vessels he builded laborious
To swim the deep & on the Land children are sold to trades

Of dire necessity still laboring day & night till all
Their life extinct they took the spectre form in dark despair
And slaves in myriads in ship loads burden the hoarse
 sounding deep
Rattling with clanking chains the Universal Empire groans
          (p. 95:E392/K333)

A confrontation between these two cities is hinted at in the earlier version of Night the Seventh, but Blake apparently felt he had to make the positive potential of Golgonooza more striking. This appears to have been a large part of his reason for drafting a second version of Night VII, in which he drops out Urizen's city altogether. He even recapitulates Golgonooza's construction at the beginning of Night VIII—actually the fifth description in the poem of a city under construction—and only then does he proceed to describe the two urban orders, fully developed, standing over against each other on his symbolic landscape, "the Limit of Translucence"—i.e., the last ditch, where the issues of human survival are to be decided. In the middle of Night VIII the looms of Los and Enitharmon are busy creating Jerusalem's veil—the covering of her form in Nature—while "the firm of Satan, Og, & Sihon"[16] are just as industriously *un*creating.

     . . . Satan Og & Sihon
Build Mills of resistless wheels to *un*wind the soft threads
 & reveal
Naked of their clothing the poor spectres before the
 accusing heavens
While Rahab & Tirzah far different mantles prepare
 webs of torture
Mantles of despair girdles of bitter compunction shoes
 of indolence
Veils of ignorance covering from head to feet with a cold
 web   (p. 113:E362/K346; emphasis mine)

The activities are identical, but the mill wheels run in opposite directions. One city's product is redemptive form, while the other strips form away, placing man in the light of a judgment he cannot bear, preparing to hurl him into the depths of Ulro, or formless "Non Entity." All that makes the two cities different is the

---

[16] The witticism is Erdman's (*Prophet*, 436n. [472n.]), probably not intended by Blake.

428

subtle error—correct from a Urizenic or strictly rational view-point—of accepting human perceptual limitation as fixed forever.

Night VIII has two inconsistent actions at its end, neither of which can properly be called a conclusion or an adequate preparation for the apocalyptic regeneration which occurs in Night IX, even though one of them is qualifiedly optimistic. My interest, however, is not to try to resolve what is only the largest of many inconsistencies in *The Four Zoas*, but to observe that Blake describes the final regeneration, when Urizen shakes off his "aged mantles," as an urban renewal:

That we his Children evermore may live in Jerusalem
Which now descendeth out of heaven a City yet a Woman
Mother of myriads redeemd & born in her spiritual palaces
By a New Spiritual birth Regenerated from Death
(p. 122:E376/K362-363)

The pattern of urban imagery which Blake evolved in *The Four Zoas* is refined and extended in *Milton* and *Jerusalem*. His cities continue to represent the significant form of creative and destructive modes of consciousness, but his descriptions of the conflict between them, which in *The Four Zoas* reflect his conflicting conceptions of the poem as a whole, are now accomplished with more precision and purpose, juxtaposed at more regular intervals in the text, and transformed into important structural landmarks. In the best tradition of Romantic creativity, Blake transmutes an imaginative difficulty into a source of greater inspiration. Urban renewal, "continually building & continually decaying" (*J* 53:19), becomes a central metaphor for the theme of eternal intellectual warfare which is a defining principle of *Milton* and, especially, of *Jerusalem*.

In *Milton*, the famous prefatory lyric announces Blake's primary epic subject, to build Jerusalem "in England's green & pleasant Land." This reminds the reader that the literary topics broached in *Milton* are not "secondary" epic subjects (a distinction Blake would not allow), but directly related to social prophecy. In the poem proper, the two city-states which emerged from the workshop of *The Four Zoas* confront each other near each of *Milton's* three roughly equidistant climaxes, which mark past, present, and future time (plates 13, 29, 43). The confrontations are even more finely drawn than in *The Four Zoas*, because Blake's emphasis in *Milton* is on the thin line between inspiration and failure of nerve.

By far the most significant extension of Blake's urban vision in *Milton* occurs in the second of these movements (plates 14-29, the "present"). In a hierarchy of three elaborately conceived cities— Golgonooza, Bowlahoola, and Allamanda—Blake ranks alternatives to the finitude of the senses which Satan's agents have imposed upon man's past history, culminating in Locke's philosophy and Newton's science. These three are described in a large digression (plates 21-29) from the main narrative, which begins at the startling moment when Blake himself enters the action, as a character identified with Milton, Los, and Jesus, following his dream-vision of how close man stands to eternity: "in brain and heart and loins / Gates open behind Satans Seat to the City of Golgonooza / Which is the spiritual fourfold London, in the loins of Albion" (20:38-40). The other characters' confusion about which city is which (carried over from the poem's first large movement, where Golgonooza, "the Limit of Contraction," is juxtaposed to Satan's realm, "the Limit of Opacity") is, if anything, compounded by the apparition of Blake. Rintrah and Palamabron mistake him for the murderer of prophets like Wesley and Whitefield, and fear for the life of what little imaginative power is left in them: "The Witnesses lie dead in the Street of the Great City . . . How long shall *we* lay dead . . ." (22:59, 23:11; emphasis mine). Los cannot convince them that Blake is not an agent of Babylon until he descends with them to his terrible winepress ("call'd War on Earth, it is the Printing Press / Of Los") and shows them that the apocalypse Blake announces will begin precisely at the point where their prophetic powers are most abused:

> The Wine-press on the Rhine groans aloud, but all its
> central beams
> Act more terrific in the central Cities of the Nations
> Where Human Thought is crushd beneath the iron hand
> of Power.
> There Los puts all into the Press, the Opressor & the
> Opressed
> Together, ripe for the Harvest & Vintage & ready for
> the Loom.   (*M* 25:3-7)

But, even with Blake acknowledged as its human herald, the revolution is not yet, and much of the rest of the digression is taken up with a discussion of "prerevolutionary" Golgonooza,

Bowlahoola, and Allamanda as staging grounds for the apocalypse. The latter two are cities of Law and Commerce, respectively, and their names suggest, to Blake's fanciful sense of etymology, anthropomorphic parallels to their civic function: "bowels" and "alimentary."[17] Their function in the poem, however, is to serve as foils to Golgonooza, "namd Art & Manufacture by mortal men" (24:50). Los warns Rintrah and Palamabron not to invest their energies in them, because such cities, however efficient and necessary, fail to respond to the exercise of imagination (24:51-56). Thus, as is appropriate in a "secondary" or "art" epic, Blake rules out at once all revolutionary programs not based on Art, just as he protested in his annotations to Reynolds that Art cannot be other than revolutionary: "The Arts & Sciences are the Destruction of Tyrannies or Bad Governments" (E625). In Golgonooza, literally the artifice of Jerusalem, man shores up his defenses against chaos by creating out of the one unfallen art, Architecture—the urban art par excellence—temporal equivalents for the fallen arts (for Painting, Surgery; for Music, Law; and for Poetry, Religion), "that Man may live upon Earth till the time of his awaking" (27:61).

Blake's attitude toward Golgonooza is not totally enthusiastic, because as a fallen creation its splendor is sometimes more akin to Urizen's tightly closed cathedral city than to Jerusalem's open traceries. This ambiguity of Golgonooza is probably embedded in its name, with its antithetical suggestions of "New Golgotha" and "Golconda."[18] In the hint of Golgotha we see that Blake has recast, as a city, the lowest point in the Christian story of the regeneration of Nature. In the place of a cross, he sets a crossroads of possibilities; Golgonooza is the "City of [present] Time," and in its zones the timeless visionary instant opens upon perspectives of eternity:

For in this Period the Poets Work is Done: and all the Great
Events of Time start forth & are conceivd in such a Period
Within a Moment: a Pulsation of the Artery.   (*M* 29:1-3)

Or if, as Harold Bloom has suggested, the name Golgonooza is Blake's rough attempt to coin from Hebrew a word meaning

---

[17] Damon, *Dictionary*, 17, 57; Erdman, *Prophet*, 402n. [432n.].

[18] Speculations on the meaning or derivation of these and other of Blake's names are almost as numerous as the names themselves. For these, I am indebted to Erdman, *Prophet*, 356 [384].

"hidden hub,"[19] then we may conceive Blake's apocalypse as originating in the central city—defined as that point around which any man's exercise of imagination instantly shapes his universe out of chaos into form:

> The Sky is an immortal Tent built by the Sons of Los
> And every Space that a Man views around his dwelling-
> place:
> Standing on his own roof, or in his garden on a mount
> Of twenty-five cubits in height, such space is his Universe
> (M 29:4-7)

"In the same way," as Kevin Lynch says of "imageability" in urban design, "we must learn to see the hidden forms in the vast sprawl of our cities."[20] For in the city, as in *Milton*, ideal dimensions ("Spiritual fourfold") are reflected, inverted, in nightmare alternatives, and around the visionary instant rumble the mills and looms of Satan and Rahab, in the wastes of Entuthon Benython, eastward of Golgonooza (29:53-63).

The connection between mythic Golgonooza and real London is strikingly dramatized in the last of *Milton*'s three major progressions (the "future"), when Blake *in propria persona* awakens on his own garden mount at Felpham to see Los hovering over London: "Los listens to the Cry of the Poor Man: his Cloud / Over London in volume terrific, low bended in anger" (42:34-35). In this vision, and in his decision to remove from the false idyll of the Felpham seashore to return to his labors in the city,[21] we see Blake acting in his own myth, yet acting realistically. He sees London as a city beset by real social evil, not the Golgonooza of "mighty Spires & Domes of ivory & Gold" he saw in his dream, yet he returns, for this London, as Northrop Frye has said, "is the symbol par excellence of the material with which the visionary deals, the redeemable conscious life of the fallen world, a mixture of imagination and nature, like the Biblical Jerusalem a great dream of a heavenly city expanding out of a dirty and iniquitous earthly one."[22]

[19] Bloom, "Commentary," in E846.
[20] Kevin Lynch, *The Image of the City*, Cambridge, Mass., 1960, 12.
[21] See Erdman, *Prophet*, 356 [384].
[22] Frye, *Symmetry*, 379.

In *Jerusalem*, London functions under slightly different auspices. Blake continues his technique of marking the major divisions of the epic with urban set pieces,[23] but the most significant *extension* of his city imagery in *Jerusalem* is to make London the factor by which the urban dimension of his myth is raised, so to speak, to the twenty-eighth power. In the myth, the regeneration of Albion in Golgonooza cannot be accomplished by Los alone— no more than England could be renewed in London solely by an obscure poet-painter-prophet. So Blake turns to England's ancient sources of "inspiration," the original twenty-eight cathedral cities of England, Scotland, and Wales, and shows them acting in concert with London. This expansion of his urban vision actually begins in Book II of *Milton*, when the redemption of English poetry (by Blake through Milton) is shown to lead to the redemption of all England, since Albion's body is delineated by references to cities, counties, streets, and geographical markers all over the land, and "London & Bath & Legions[24] & Edinburgh / Are the four

---

[23] The only technical variation from *Milton* is that he places these set pieces at the beginning rather than the end of each movement. In the opening invocation, he asks his Muse's aid "While I write of the building of Golgonooza" (*J* 5:24); plates 10 through 16 describe its construction—which is introduced as an explanation for much of the intervening action ("*Therefore* Los stands in London building Golgonooza"; 10:18, emphasis mine). See also chapter II 29[33]:12-16 and chapter III 53:15-24. Although chapter IV opens with the newly constructed City of Art desperately besieged, the reader is assured of Jerusalem's ultimate triumph by the heroic call to action with which Blake concluded his address "To the Christians" on the chapter's prefatory plate (*J* 77): "And now the time returns again: / Our souls exult & Londons towers / Receive the Lamb of God to dwell / In Englands green & pleasant bowers." The urban structure of *Jerusalem* is of course only one of its many dimensions. But I would add to the various insights of Damon, Frye, Bloom, Erdman, Kiralis, Rose, and others the observation that, as Blake adapted the epic tradition, he recognized that major divisions in the action tend to begin with grand set pieces, and his vision demanded that in his epics these should concern the creation or destruction of giant city-states. Moreover, though he could have found no precedent in the tradition for beginning each book with the *same* action, he obviously felt that the urban dimension of his myth was important enough to use it in this structurally repetitive way.

[24] "A city mentioned by Geoffrey of Monmouth (III, x; v, v; IX, xii); Holinshed identified it with Caerlheon." It got its name when invading Roman legions set up winter quarters there. (Damon, *Dictionary*, 237.) Blake's substitution of Canterbury for it in *Jerusalem* has the obvious advantage of familiarity, whatever other reasons may be adduced.

pillars of his Throne" (*M* 39:35-36). As usual, Blake appropriates Christian tradition to his own uses in very literal fashion: the need for religion to be redeemed into its eternal form, imaginative vision, was to him a real need if not a strong hope. Further, he knew from experience that the form of a city affects the forms of individual lives; so too he recognized that true urban renewal extends beyond individual cities to entire regions and nations,

bringing all together in coherent though varied unity. Thus the twenty-eight cities in *Jerusalem* converge, seven each, into four "regions" (London, Canterbury, York, and Edinburgh), and these four converge in one: London-Golgonooza-Jerusalem. Though they are not grouped together with much geographical consistency, their relationships form a network of focal points which literally bind the land together—as S. Foster Damon's helpful diagram in *A Blake Dictionary* makes clear.[25] Thus political

Fig. 18. *Jerusalem*, pl. 57, details

history and geography are "mythicized" in *Jerusalem* as literary history was in *Milton*.

These new combinations in the pattern of Blake's city imagery are augmented in the visual designs by his bringing together on the same plates his giant human and architectural forms in breath-

[25] *Dictionary*, 70. Damon hazards some ingenious speculations about Blake's association of each city with contemporary personages, on the understanding that "The Communion of Saints, seen close to, consists of Individuals; so consequently do the Cathedral Cities. . . . For Blake . . . they are spiritual forces operative in his day" (p. 71).

takingly literal accommodations of mythic form to the form of physical and historical reality. A prime example, which we have already seen, is his reworking of the design of *London* for plate 84 {100}: he added the towers and temple which take up half the illustration, and the new context enlarges the symbolic stature of the child and the ancient. Also, on plate 46 [32] {7}, the cross-topped dome in the lower left corner and the Gothic spires in the lower right are the cities, respectively, of Vala and Jerusalem, who are depicted at a dramatic moment of decision in the foreground. On plate 57 (fig. 18) the orb of the fallen universe, spun from the fingers of the daughters of Albion, is shown to be polarized between a Romanesque London (and York) and Gothic Jerusalem. On plate 92 (fig. 19) Jerusalem trembles amid the dissolving forms of her former tyrants (Amalek, Egypt, etc.), with the stark trilithons "Where Druids reard their Rocky Circles to make permanent Remembrance of Sin" (92:24-5) looming around her in the

Fig. 19. *Jerusalem*, pl. 92, detail

background. This design pattern culminates, appropriately, on plate 100 {104}.

The picture is the focus of Albion's vision following his resurrection. It represents no single moment in the text, but recapitulates much of the form and action of the entire poem. In particular, it recalls the activity of Los and Enitharmon which begins with renewed vigor on plate 85, ending with the awakening of England and Albion on plates 94 and 95.[26]

The "urban" form of the design is the curving line of trilithons, which closely resembles William Stuckeley's serpentine reconstruction of the ruins at Avebury (1743). The structure is different from similar edifices in Blake's work because it is coherent and complete. Elsewhere, the trilithons stand separately, at odd angles to each other, some fallen or indistinguishable from massive unhewn rocks nearby, never in a complete circle (*M* 4 and 6; *J* 69, 70, 92, 94). In a very general way, these earlier structures can be seen as preparations for plate 100, which represents their fulfillment. Also, in the Mellon copy of the plate {104} the trilithons rise from richly foliated, green and gold surroundings rather than the bleak or darkly forbidding waste landscapes in which Blake usually placed them. They recall the serpent temples of fallen priestcraft, yet Wicksteed's passing suggestion that the structure is Golgonooza can be justified in several ways.[27]

First, we must remember how the twenty-eight cathedral cities in *Jerusalem* become foci of regeneration following *their* redemption from "Druidic" error (i.e., the ancient abuses against humanity which they perpetuated in Christian form), and how these

[26] The identity of the three figures in *J* 100 is still a subject of some disagreement. Erdman (*Prophet*, 449 [486]) identifies them as, left to right, Los, Urthona, and Jerusalem (or Enitharmon). Digby (p. 86, fig. 77) proposes Los, Urthona, and Enitharmon; or, the Spectre of Urthona, Los, and Enitharmon. See also Henry Lesnick's essay in the present collection. Since several of these interpretations, as well as my own, agree that Blake is representing the temporal and eternal perspectives of reality simultaneously on plate 100, it is possible that all these identifications are correct, depending on which perspective one takes. Thus, in temporal perspective we have Los's Spectre, Los, and Enitharmon, with a suggestion that the Spectre is now working for Los rather than against him. In eternal perspective, we have Los, Urthona, and Enitharmon, and Los's "exit" is unqualifiedly triumphant.

[27] Joseph Wicksteed, *Jerusalem: A Commentary*, London, 1953, 251. Cf. Ruthven Todd, *Tracks in the Snow*, London, 1946, 47-52.

redemptive forms of England's ancient imagination coalesce in Golgonooza. Second, and more important, the form of the design itself presents strong evidence that the curving line of trilithons is "the great City of Golgonooza in the shadowy Generation" (98:55). Many commentators on Blake have remarked the importance of circular symbols in both his poetry and engraving. Like most Blakean symbols, the circle has a fallen and an eternal significance. After the fall, the circle is the indefinite—not infinite—cycle of recurrence.[28] But there is a circle inside this circle, "wheels within wheels" moving counter to it: the flywheel of imagination whose "hidden hub," following Bloom's suggestion, is Golgonooza. There are numerous circular forms on plate 100: the trilithons in the center, the two smaller circles in the lower corners, the sun on Los's shoulder, the crescent moon under Enitharmon's right arm, and the face of Los's hammer and the hinge of his tongs (held by Urthona, Los's eternal form).

If, as seems likely, the trilithons are to be seen as a continuation, in architectural form, of the veil of natural generation which Enitharmon is pulling from her spindle, then the "plot" of the design suggests that natural substance (associated with the moon and the imagery of the fallen garden it evokes in Blake) is here given form and literally turned-in-to the bright sun of imagination by the prophet-smith. For the tongs, placed squarely in the center forefront of the design, can also be seen as a stiff caliper-compass (indeed, Urthona holds them lightly between thumb and first and second fingers, as one would hold a compass) whose points approximately delimit the inside circumference of the circle in the background. This suggests a visual representation of that part of Blake's myth which tells of the reunion of Urizen and Los, or Reason and Imagination, which he no less than Wordsworth or Shelley longed for in the intellectual life of his times. The compass associated with Urizen, creator of horizons and limits, is taken over at the end by Urthona-Los as the tongs with which he turns the matter of his prophecy. Clearly the design represents a process, not a stasis: the continuous resolution of the endless revolutions of the fall. Like the plots of many of his poems, Blake's imagery of urban renewal projects a cycle of never-ending activity.

The larger movement of the design is also circular: falling down from Enitharmon's hand, through the convolutions of fallen his-

28 Frye, *Symmetry*, 384.

tory redeemed by Los and now presided over by Urthona, and up onto the shoulder of Los—who is, as it were, about to spring off the page of Blake's prophecy into the realm of its realization, now bearing on his shoulder like a prize the light of inspiration which has guided him from the beginning (plate 1). The black and red vertical lines along the right margin of the plate and the bright gold lines along the left margin impart a sense of falling motion to the moon and rising motion to the sun, indicating that they "fit" the circles below them—allowing for a diminution in perspective from foreground to background, from top to bottom, and (especially) from eternal to temporal dimension. Civilization, represented by architectural form, is wound up from Nature, where it has fallen, into the coherent and perfect form of Golgonooza by Los's tools, and then released upward with him into the eternity of Imagination. (It would be convenient to this interpretation to say that the line of trilithons winds around upon itself to form the central circle, but it is hard to tell if the circle is separate or connected to the curving line. Still, Blake has clearly created this ambiguity on purpose, by his placement of Urthona and Enitharmon.) Finally, the face of Los's hammer is of the same circumference as the two smaller circles. The compass-tongs give form to Nature, but the smith's mighty hammer first makes it malleable. Together, the two implements and their respective circles remind us of Los's work of creating forms to retard the course of the fall, depicted as early as *The Book of Urizen*. In particular, they recall the small designs on plate 32[36] and plate 73, where he is shown violently beating a brilliant orb on an anvil, though the texts indicate he is working for preliminary stages of regeneration: "Building the Moon of Ulro" (32[36]:4), and "Dissipating the rocky forms of Death" (73:43). In short, the interplay of forms on plate 100 suggests a visual representation of the dialectic of destruction and creation which is the essence of Blake's imagination. On the basis of this "circular" evidence, Golgonooza can be seen here as the mediating form of the eternal form (Sun) of Imagination; in Golgonooza, eternity begins, and in Golgonooza all merely natural cycles end.[29]

[29] It is almost possible, with some sympathetic allowances for distorted perspective, to see the sun and moon as having the same circumference as the large center circle. Granted this, one could then argue that the temple on the hill is a "mold" in which the incomplete form of Nature—represented

Like several other designs in *Jerusalem*, plate 100 represents a conflation of spheres of time—not of past, present, and future (like plate 84), but of Time and Eternity. It is a moment—"a Pulsation of the Artery"—in which the Zoa of Imagination, in his eternal as well as spectral and emanative forms, pauses at last from the perpetual labor which has echoed throughout the poem, particularly following the turning point in its action:

Here on the banks of the Thames, Los builded Golgonooza,
Outside of the Gates of the Human Heart, beneath Beulah
In the midst of the rocks of the Altars of Albion. In fears
He builded it, in rage & in fury. It is the Spiritual Fourfold
London: continually building & continually decaying
    desolate!
In eternal labours. . . .   (*J* 53:15-20)

In this instant, it becomes possible to identify the architecture of the plate not only as Golgonooza, but more simply and obviously: as Jerusalem in her urban aspect, the eternal form for which Golgonooza has been the preparation, "builded . . . as a City & a Temple" (84:3), the ancient temples of inspiration redeemed into the eternal urban form of Blake's Apocalypse, "Eternity . . . in love with the productions of time."

In these two additions to the development of his urban imagery —the plot line of the twenty-eight cities and (especially) the giant forms dominating the foreground of his urban designs—Blake represents symbolically the "action" of consciousness upon phenomena: in the act of perceiving it defines and creates its universe ("every Space that a Man views . . . is his Universe": *M* 29:5-7). In the more mundane sphere of urban affairs, one can speculate that this action approximates the impact of a city upon its sur-

---

by the half-circle moon—is brought to fulfillment: the sun of Imagination. The smaller circles could then be taken as the fallen or temporal forms of this eternal process. However, such a close mechanical look at the design may be more annoying than illuminating, for reasons of taste, approaching what might be called the "ideographic fallacy" in the study of Blake's mixed media. (The label is particularly suited to many arguments about his left/ right orientations.) Nevertheless, though the reader of poetry—as distinct from the viewer of paintings—may resent having to interpret an ideograph as his last act in the poem, Blake's art disallows an easy distinction between the two.

roundings: one piece of practical knowledge we learn from Blake's city planning is that the city focuses the country. Such a speculation leads us back to Blake's often misunderstood idea of the Imagination's relation to Nature: just as Imagination focuses—gives form to—Nature, so Blake's cities are creative centering points for his land. To say that Jerusalem-London "focuses" Albion-England is to say in symbols what Blake means literally, that the form of life in the metropolis is the form of a nation's imagination. (Cf. Ruskin: "All good architecture is the expression of national life and character.") The relation between city and country is ideally dialectical; we can see its two terms embedded in the little lyric at the beginning of chapter IV (a coda to its more famous sister-piece in *Milton*): "Our souls exult & Londons *towers*, / Receive the Lamb of God to dwell / In Englands green & pleasant *bowers*" (E231; emphasis mine). It is important that the dialectical tension not be lost. The terms are not equal, but even though Imagination is always dominant, it (or its city) does not tyrannize or usurp Nature's green pleasures. Rather, it makes them possible, letting them appear in a new vision. Imagination gives a form to Nature and holds it from death and dissolution—not vice versa, as Wordsworth came close to asserting, much to Blake's disgust.[30]

Jerusalem is, admittedly, of all poems in the language the least suited to "application" to everyday life, but there is a sense— Blake's sense of the living reality of his myth[31]—which demands it. I have little doubt but that during the composition of his masterpiece he occasionally had in his mind's eye a vision of England renewed through her cities. His prescience was remarkable, to see in "the increasing accumulation of men in cities, where the uniformity of their occupation produces a craving for extraordinary incident" (Wordsworth, Preface to *Lyrical Ballads*), the deadening effect of eighteenth-century empiricism extended onto the lives of men in nineteenth-century industrial forms. Still more remarkable is his daring to project a vision of renewal in and through the city,

[30] "I see in Wordsworth the Natural Man rising up against the Spiritual Man Continually & then he is No Poet but a Heathen Philosopher at Enmity against all true Poetry or Inspiration" (Annotations to Wordsworth's *Poems*, 1815:E654/K782).

[31] Edward J. Rose, " 'Mental Forms Creating': 'Fourfold Vision' and the Poet as Prophet in Blake's Designs and Verse," *Journal of Aesthetics and Art Criticism*, XXIII (1964), 173-183.

rather than out and away from it, a vision which, though tragically unfulfilled, still feeds the eye of the best spirits among us. Like Blake, perceptive modern city planners go beyond city plans to plans for regions; Blake went further, to plans for nations, or worlds. Granted, somewhere in these progressive enlargements of focus, "plan" becomes an inadequate word, and must be replaced by "vision," but that is as Blake would have it. From man to city to nation to world, even to the revolution of history and conscious-ness: thus Blake's urban symbolism fits into the story of the fall and regeneration which provides the basic plot for most of his major work.

A Note on Other Romantic Visions of the City

Blake was not alone among his contemporaries in viewing the city as a giant mythic entity. The inordinate and continuing emphasis on Romantic poetry as subjective "nature poetry" sometimes obscures an urban tradition in Romantic poetry which extends from Blake to the present day. Wordsworth's distaste for London is well known, but we tend to forget the mythopoeic stature of the images in which he expressed it—or attempted to reconcile himself to it. The "mighty heart" image in the Westminster Bridge sonnet derives from the same impulse as Blake's more elaborate anthropomorphic images. Also, in *Prelude* VII, Wordsworth expresses the depth of his early enchantment with the very idea of London by allusions to Babylon, Persepolis, and reports "by pilgrim friars of golden cities" (lines 77-86). (Cf. Charles Williams, *The Image of the City and other Essays*, ed. Anne Ridler, London, 1958.) Byron's imagery is similarly biblical-mythological when he describes Juan's approach to London: it is "mighty Babylon" (*Don Juan* XI, xxiii, 2), and is associated with Stonehenge and the Druids (XI, xxv, 1-3)—a comparison strikingly akin to Blake's. Urban forms are not among Shelley's several characteristic imagistic "signatures," but he invokes them as images of spiritual power in many important contexts (cf. *Mont Blanc*, lines 104-108). The subtitle of his first ver-sion of *The Revolt of Islam* is "The Revolution of the Golden City: A Vision of the Nineteenth Century." Among the Romantic essayists, it is interestingly DeQuincey, that unhappy convert to the Lake School, who most clearly adopts the mythic mode to describe London, "this mighty orb," in the chapter of his autobiography entitled "The Nation of London." Lamb, by contrast, constructs his image of the city out of memory—a mode in some respects antithetical to the mythic.

Granting their common indebtedness to traditional and biblical archetypes, what almost all these Romantic versions of London share is a sense of mystery, an awe compounded of fear and wonder at a social phenomenon that was manifestly *there*, but at the same time very difficult to imagine. From the vantage of hindsight, one sees relatively much more tension and fruitful ambiguity in the Romantic mythic view of the city than in the Victorian. The latter tends to be more realistic as well as pessimistic, though often with mythic undertones (as in Dickens). Ruskin is the clear link between Blake and more recent manifestations of this Romantic tradition. At many points, his imagination partakes of the literalness of Blake's; his arguments for moral architecture are not less difficult, or more easily misapprehended, than some of Blake's urban symbolism. The dialectic Ruskin sets up between Gothic and Renaissance Venice parallels Blake's very closely, though Ruskin's myth is more historical than psychological. The dialectic continues between Dublin and Byzantium in Yeats, and in the tension Stephen Daedalus and his creator felt between Dublin and the European capitals of art.

In American literature, the tradition extends from Emerson and Whitman ("In a dream I saw a city invincible") through the more popular optimism of Sandburg's *Chicago* to Hart Crane's *The Bridge*, Williams' *Paterson*, and beyond. (Cf. David Weimer, *The City as Metaphor*, New York, 1966.) Michael H. Cowan, in *City of the West: Emerson, America, and Urban Metaphor*, New Haven, 1966, goes far toward correcting the easy assumption that American Romantic literature is largely negative in its attitude toward the city. Still, as Cowan and others point out, Americans have until very recently thought more about the distinction between city and country, or man and nature, than about the distinction between a city of perverted spirit and one of fulfillment. Cf. Leo Marx, *The Machine in the Garden*, New York, 1964.

Reflecting the explosive growth of Western cities since the Industrial Revolution, "urban literature" of all kinds has increased to the point that it constitutes almost a new genre, with its own tropes and conventions, as subtle as the traditional antipastoral. (Cf. Paul Ginestier, *The Poet and the Machine*, tr. Martin B. Friedman, Chapel Hill, N.C., 1961.) One of the most important of these connections is dialectical pattern and imagery which allow the writer or critic to spin out theses and anti-theses almost endlessly. The present essay is no exception. Another recent example is Maynard Mack's study of Pope, *The Garden and the City*, Toronto, 1969.

20

"Forms Eternal Exist For-ever":
The Covenant of the Harvest in
Blake's Prophetic Poems

EDWARD J. ROSE

THE PURPOSE of this essay is to discuss the way in which Blake employs the seasonal cycle as a symbolic structure, how he directs his mythopoeic drama toward a final harvest associated typically with the autumn season but untypically with an eternal spring, and how he sees this harvest as a process by which "every particular Form" becomes the "Form" of the "Divine Vision." All three of Blake's major poems, *The Four Zoas*, *Milton*, and *Jerusalem*, conclude with a visionary harvest. As Frye points out, when discussing the end of *The Four Zoas*, "An imaginative spring is approaching, and the seeds begin to push upward into eternal daylight. . . . The last spring has now gone through the last summer and is waiting for the harvest of the last autumn, a season which can no longer be called a 'fall.' "[1] Shakespeare, in his well-known sonnet "That time of year," draws the analogies often associated with the autumnal season. The analogies are directed toward the human condition. Autumn is a time of day (evening) and a "region" of man (age).

In general Blake critics have accepted the relation between the four seasons and the four Zoas in man's day: Luvah-Orc is spring, morn, and youth; Urizen is summer, noon, and manhood; Tharmas is autumn, evening, and age; Urthona is winter, night, death. But man's vegetable day is really night in Blake's work. Thus the action in Blake's long poems takes place in the night-world of the Spectre of Urthona whom Los puts off. In the night-world or temporal winter, Los is the only living or fully awake being. Vegetable man has three regions, "Childhood, Manhood & Age" (*J* 14; 98). This is the life of generation, "holy Generation [Image] of regeneration" (*J* 7). But the "Human Majesty" has "Four Re-

---

[1] Frye, *Symmetry*, 307.

gions" (*J* 18) and that fourth region is not death but eternity.[2] While in generation spring, summer, and fall end in winter, as morn, noon, and evening end in night and childhood, manhood, and old age end in death—a fourfold seasonal recurrence—in regeneration they end in the fourfold reintegration of man in God. Thus the first of Blake's long poems concludes with an everlasting autumnal harvest. Furthermore, it is a "Human Harvest" and not a vegetable one. Several illustrations for Young's *Night Thoughts* explicitly portray this kind of harvest, for example, the water color drawings for the Night I title page (no. 6 {74}) and Night II, 16 (no. 49), both of which were engraved. In generation man is cast *like* a "Seed into the Earth" (*FZ* IX:E386/K374), but in regeneration he is matured from another seed, the "seed of Contemplative Thought" (*VLJ* 68:E545/K605) through which the "Imaginative Image returns." Although men and all things in the vegetative world change and pass, man's eternal form and the eternal forms of all things in his imagination exist forever.

Autumn-age is traditionally the time of the vintage years, the twilight time in which man, having reaped life, now anticipates the winter-sleep of death-night. For Blake this is the time, however, when man is "To go forth to the Great Harvest & Vintage of the Nations" (*M* 43). The ultimate autumn of the visionary or of imagination is contrasted with the fall of fallen man in the vegetable cycle. Having reached the "perfect summer life"[3] at last, a summer that never decays and a noon that never declines, regenerated man does not go gently into the death-night of winter, for he has drawn time to its period (*J* 92). The morn in which the

[2] The three regions or seasons without the fourth are "Three Immense Wheels" (*J* 18:E161/K640). Like the twelve signs of the zodiac wheeling around the heavens (like the knights of Arthur's round table and the tribes of Israel), the Twelve Sons of Albion wheel in the "orbed Void" of fallen space building a "Kingdom among the Dead" (*J* 18). They enslave the children of Jerusalem after the manner of the kings of Babylon and the pharaohs of Egypt who commanded the children of Israel in bondage to build temples and tombs. See also *J* 13:E156/K634 and *J* 89-91:E245-49/ K734-739. Blake associates these monuments to cruelty with the temple in Jerusalem, the serpent temples of Britain, and the temples of Mexico. As modern research has demonstrated in amplifying the discoveries of the eighteenth century, they are not only to be associated with human sacrifice and the mythology of agricultural civilizations but also functioned (as in the case of Stonehenge) as calendars.

[3] This phrase is taken from the "Conclusion" to Thoreau's *Walden*.

twenty-eighth lark (Los's messenger in *Milton*) mounts is the day on which nightingales sing at noon.[4] Throughout *Fearful Symmetry*, Frye calls this an apocalypse. In *The Four Zoas* and *Milton*, Blake describes it as a harvest and by so doing is able to identify temporal sequences with a nontemporal event. There are no swallows twittering in Blake's autumn sky, preparing to go where spring and summer have gone.

Blake's identification of temporal sequences with nontemporal events affects his use of zodiacal imagery, which is employed after the manner of Revelation, where the signs of the zodiac dramatize history and history dramatizes the signs of the zodiac. History and the zodiac are then employed analogically to make a statement about the nontemporal. Blake's association of Boötes with Arthur and Arthur with Albion is a case in point (*DC* v: E533/K577; *J* 54). In the *Night Thoughts* drawings, for example, he develops specifically the imagery of Revelation. The title page for *Night* III, no. 78, which was engraved, portrays the woman crowned with stars. The verso page, no. 79, extends his point. The woman is Virgo, the last sign of summer, who ushers in the autumn of the year. Traditionally she is portrayed holding a spike of grain signifying the harvest to come. As such Virgo can be associated with the virgin female will and with Vala but not with Jerusalem, who is liberty, liberty from the turning and seasonal vegetative world. In *A Vision of the Last Judgment* (*VLJ* 80-81: E548-549/K609-610), Blake distinguishes between Jerusalem and the woman crowned with stars, between the bride of *risen* man and redeemed *nature*. As the *sixth* sign of the zodiac, which echoes Blake's number symbolism, her demonic form appears (as in Revelation) in the figure of the Whore of Babylon, associated by Blake with Rahab (see the title page for Young's Night VIII, no. 345), who rides the Beast whose number is 666.

In the last of the twelve *L'Allegro* and *Il Penseroso* designs (the number of months in the year), we see the aged Milton in whom we may behold the autumn of life (Milton died in November) (see {106}); however, the sky above him is not an autumn sky. Instead we see the five constellations—Aries, Taurus, Orion, Gemini, and Cancer—that are visible in the northern hemisphere as a

---

[4] Cf. Shelley's *Epipsychidion*, line 444. The apocalypse in *Prometheus Unbound* also begins at "noon." Cf. the "grosser Mittag" that concludes Nietzsche's *Also Sprach Zarathustra*.

group only in the winter and spring skies. The four zodiac signs are those of spring and summer from the equinox to the solstice or noon of the year. For Blake that time of year (Blake was born in November) in which we await the onset of winter is not the drizzly November of the soul which Melville's Ishmael experiences. Instead, it is associated with birth, with the spring and summer that follows winter. Age and autumn and twilight are the beginning of life, the year, and the day, not the end of life or the year or the day. The visionary sees beyond the cycle of the vegetable world by using the vegetable world analogically. Generation is an image of regeneration. Blake manipulates the seasonal cycle in much the same way that he manipulates the cycle of the worm and the fly.[5] Man may be a worm of seventy winters in the vegetable world, but when he leaves the cocoon of vegetable existence, which he can do only in imagination, he becomes a human form. He cannot do it simply by dying as a worm. "This World Is a World of imagination & Vision."[6] To die without imagination is just the same as to live without imagination. "The Traveller" who "hasteth in the Evening" toward "Death's Door" acknowledges with Job that the worm is his mother and his sister (*Gates of Paradise*, emblems 14-16). He lives by the word of "The Accuser who is The God of This World," who is "The Son of Morn in weary Night's decline," and who had deluded man into *reasoning* that he can find his lost dream "under the Hill," that is, in the grave (*Gates of Paradise*, epilogue); "to the Eyes of the Man of Imagination, Nature is Imagination itself. As a man is, So he Sees. As the Eye is formed, such are its Powers. You certainly Mistake, when you say that the Visions of Fancy are not to be found in This World. To Me This World is all One continued Vision of Fancy or Imagination. . . ."[7]

Nature without imagination is cyclical after the pattern of the reasoning process, but since "to the Eyes of the Man of Imagination, Nature is Imagination itself," the cyclical processes of nature

[5] See my essay "Blake's Human Insect: Symbol, Theory, and Design," *Texas Studies in Literature and Language*, x (1968), 215-232. See below, n. 19.

[6] Letter to Dr. Trusler, 23 August 1799: E670/K793-794.

[7] *Ibid.* See my essays "The Symbolism of the Opened Center and Poetic Theory in Blake's *Jerusalem*," *Studies in English Literature*, v (1965), 587-606 and "The Structure of Blake's *Jerusalem*," *Bucknell Review*, xi, 3 (May 1963), 35-54.

become ever-renewing creations, as they are to Los (*J* 16).[8] This world's day is really the dark night of the soul in which man's existence is a bad dream. The "Great Code of Art"[9] begins, in fact, by specifying it was evening and then morning, one day. The structure of each of Blake's long poems is based upon the imaginative vision of the fallen night-world as one long winter-death.

Blake writes in *A Vision of the Last Judgment* that "The Nature of my Work is Visionary or Imaginative it is an Endeavour to Restore what the Ancients calld the Golden Age" (*VLJ* 72: E545/K605). In *The Four Zoas* the cosmic nervous breakdown in fourfold man precipitates the "fall" of man in the natural body. The *fall* of the vegetated Tharmas produces a vegetated spring (Luvah) and a vegetated summer (Urizen). The result is the wintery life of fallen man—his vegetative history in Urthona's dark earth. This is the pattern of the first four Nights. The next four Nights examine the psychology of this history. The entire action of the poem records the events of the night-winter world, which dramatize fallen man's spiritual condition. The visionary harvest of the last Night produces a visionary day-year which reaps the seeds sown in time in a perennial autumn that is a spring-morn and the summer-noon. The night-winter that intervenes between the evening-autumn of vegetable existence and the visionary morn-spring which begins the eternal day—the restored golden age—is the whole of temporal experience. By analogy the four seasons are contained in a harvest without end, just as the four seasons are parodied in the four intervals of each day contained in turn by an "eternal winter" or a night seemingly without end. With imagination man can see that the metaphorical relation between the year and the day explains the relation between temporal and eternal existence. With imagination man sees that day is night and that "Chronos or Time as a very Aged Man" is fable. Because "the Real Vision of Time is in Eternal Youth," autumn is really spring. Man wakes up to find that that in which he was seemingly awake was a dream. That time of year which is age is youth, since it is the beginning of the day-life of eternal man. The time of year and time of day he has known—the four seasons and the four intervals of the day—exist only in the winter-night of his ratiocinative sleep-

[8] Cf., for example, *J* 13:E156/K634.
[9] *The Laocoön*: E271/K777.

death. Without imagination a tree is "only a Green thing that stands in the way" and is subject like man to decay and death. It cannot be spoken to and cannot speak in return. That is, it has no form or imagination.

In eternity all things are "Vocal" (*FZ* vi:E341/K315). The most significant characteristic of the final pages of each of Blake's three long poems is the restoration of the dialogue of creation, stressed at great length at the conclusions of *The Four Zoas* and *Jerusalem*. The Eternal Man casts Luvah, Vala, and their children into "The World of shadows, thro' the air, till winter is over & gone."

> But the Human Wine stood wondering in all their delightful
>   Expanses
> The elements subside the heavens rolld on with vocal
>   harmony
> Then Los who is Urthona rose in all his regenerate power
> The Sea that rolld & foamd with darkness & the shadows of
>   death
> Vomited out & gave up all the floods lift up their hands
> Singing & shouting to the Man they bow their hoary heads
> And murmuring in their channels flow & circle round his feet
>   (*FZ* ix:E390/K378)

This chorus is sung against the background of the winter-night-death that is about to be "over & gone."

>   Nature in darkness groans
>   And Men are bound to sullen contemplations in the night
>   Restless they turn on beds of sorrow. in their inmost brain
>   Feeling the crushing Wheels they rise they write the
>   bitter words
>   Of Stern Philosophy & knead the bread of knowledge
>   with tears & groans
>
>   Such are the works of Dark Urthona Tharmas sifted the
>   corn
>   Urthona made the Bread of Ages & he placed it
>   In golden & in silver baskets in heavens of precious stone
>   And then took his repose in Winter in the night of Time
>   (E391/K379)

By dramatizing this night-winter of "Dumb despair,"[10] Los or the imaginative artist gives it vision and speech. The sun that he carries into Albion on plate 1 of *Jerusalem* must eventually leave its "blackness" and find a "fresher morning," as at the end of *The Four Zoas*, when "Man walks forth from midst of the fires." The renewed youth of risen man does not belong to the deathbed life of the vegetative seasonal cycle but to a new vision, where

> The Sun arises from his dewy bed & the fresh airs
> Play in his smiling beams giving the seeds of life to grow
> And the fresh Earth beams forth ten thousand thousand
>   springs of life   (E392/K379)

The harvest which Blake describes takes place in an unfallen autumn, a fall that is always visible "to the Eyes of the Man of Imagination," where "Nature is Imagination itself." Such a vision reaps countless "springs of life" continually. In such a harvest the "Eternal Image & Individuality" of imaginative form which "never dies" is continually recreated "by its seed; the seed of Contemplative Thought." It is these seeds in *The Four Zoas* that beam "forth ten thousand thousand springs of life" in the "Human Harvest."[11] What we see at the conclusion of Blake's three long poems is the restoration of the golden age of ancient times, that autumnal ripeness from which man fell into his winter-night sleep but to which he reawakens.

In order to make his harvest symbolism work, in order to capitalize on the imagery of the seasonal cycle of the fallen or vegetative world, Blake cannot simply point to a new spring. As an artist he must describe the fulfillment of that spring by harvesting the eternal forms that fructify in the "perfect summer life" and that will create an eternal autumn free of the "Universe of Death & Decay" (*FZ* IV:E325/K298). The vegetated Tharmas is renewed in the imagination by the power of Los. This is the answer to the questions raised by the vocal Lions at the end of *The Four Zoas*, when they ask:

10 Albion's melancholy is given voice by Los's wondrous art in Blake's art; nevertheless, language is specified in *J* 36[40]:58-60 (E181/K668).

11 *M* 42 (E142/K353); see *FZ* IX 125:17-21 (E379/K366:335-339) for how the human harvest begins and for the seed-grave symbolism. Cf. Damon, *Dictionary*, 176. See also *J* 77 (E229/K716-717) for the "Divine Harvest."

How is it we have walked thro fires & yet are not consumd
How is it that all things are changd even as in ancient
 times   (*FZ* ɪx:E391/K379)

At the human harvest the Lions along with all things and beings
converse with the Eternal Man:

> The stars consumd like a lamp blown out & in their stead
> behold
> The Expanding Eyes of Man behold the depth of
> wondrous worlds
>
> One Earth one sea beneath nor Erring Globes wander
> but Stars
> Of fire rise up nightly from the Ocean & one Sun
> Each morning like a New born Man issues with songs
> & Joy
> Calling the Plowman to his Labour & the Shepherd to
> his rest

The days and nights, like the seasons, of the Eternal World of
vision are instantaneously one, their passage no longer sequential
as in the "night of Time."

> He [the one Sun who is "like a New born Man"] walks
> upon the Eternal Mountains raising his heavenly voice
> Conversing with the Animal forms of wisdom night & day
> That risen from the Sea of fire renewd walk oer the Earth
>
> For Tharmas brought his flocks upon the hills & in the
> Vales
> Around the Eternal Mans bright tent the little Children
> play
> Among the wooly flocks The hammer of Urthona sounds
> In the deep caves beneath his limbs renewd, his Lions
> roar
> Around the Furnaces & in Evening sport upon the plains
> They raise their faces from the Earth conversing with the
> Man

This is autumn under the aegis of the "Spirit of Prophecy" rather
than the "Spectre of Prophecy," for Urthona is now in "all his

ancient strength" and Tharmas again a little boy.[12] The vegetated, devouring tongue of the darkened parent power that talked away the golden age ("Lost! Lost! Lost!" *FZ* I 4:6:E297/K264) speaks a prophecy of newborn innocence (*FZ* IX 132:36-39:E386/K373; IX 134:5-29:E387/K374-375). All the Zoas converse with one another at the Golden Feast, for all have contributed to and taken part in the harvest of the human form from the winter-night of time which takes place in a restored golden age, an autumn of countless springs. If "Ripeness is all," then we must understand Blake's harvest to be a dramatization of the creative process that produces that ripeness. Art is "conversing" with images of wonder in imagination. The harvest symbolism relates directly to the reader's or spectator's attitude toward the vision he has just witnessed. Each of Blake's long poems is a harvest, not only for him but for the reader-spectator. "If the Spectator could Enter into these Images in his Imagination approaching them on the Fiery Chariot of his Contemplative Thought if he could Enter into Noahs Rainbow or into his bosom or could make a Friend & Companion of one of these Images of wonder which always intreats him to leave mortal things as he must know then would he arise from his Grave then would he meet the Lord in the Air & then he would be happy" (*VLJ* 82). This passage recalls 1 Thessalonians 4:17 and explains in part why Blake says, "The Nature of my Work is Visionary or Imaginative it is an Endeavour to Restore what the Ancients calld the Golden Age." Art must give eternal form to the acts of time.

The resurrection of man of which Paul speaks in 1 Corinthians was forever meaningful to Blake. The illustration for *To Tirzah* quotes in part 1 Corinthians 15:44: "It is Raised a Spiritual Body." Paul's epistle is often the source for Blake's orientation to the resurrection, especially 15:35ff. and 15:43-44. Paul also invokes the harvest symbolism of Matthew 13:39-43. In addition, his epistle is related to Blake's distinction between the spiritual and natural bodies. Los, the archetype of the artist-prophet with whom Blake identifies, preserves the intercourse between time and eternity (see Matt. 13:12-32). It is he who prepares man's intellectual life by planting the seeds of eternity in time. Hence, man's natural body is related to the spiritual body as a grain or a seed is related

---

[12] See *FZ* IX 130:7 (E383/K370:510-511).

to the harvest (1 Cor. 15:37-38), which is why it is possible "To see a World in a Grain of Sand." With the advent of the millennium, the bodies of believers are instantaneously changed (1 Cor. 15:42-44), because their vision of the world has become creative. This is a kind of mental travel distinct from corporeal wandering. It can be expressed only in terms of the ripening of Los's vision in the human imagination. As such Blake's works are educational (perhaps didactic) because they are visionary and assert a critical theory, biblical in image and origin. Man must understand through visionary art not only what God speaks but how he speaks. To participate in the harvest of time, man must become a reaper of images of wonder, otherwise he shall be cast as spectre-spectator into the lake (Rev. 20:4-5;14-15; see also J 37[41], the inscription on the scroll in the design). Therefore, dying to the world and to time is related not only to the millennium, but also to any individual experience which permits man to "leave mortal things." This kind of conversion is a matter of vision or perception and is related to how we see, affecting, in turn, what we do see. The fiery chariot of contemplative thought which is Ezekiel's is the spirit of prophecy, not a theological *deus ex machina*. It carries us past mortal things by annihilating the natural body (which Blake calls an "Obstruction") and by renewing the spiritual body. It is the vehicular form of the process that reveals reality by changing the "image of the earthy" we have borne into the "image of the heavenly" (1 Cor. 15:49).

The seeming pleas for conversion in the prose passages in *Jerusalem* must be understood rightly not as ordinary attempts to preach and convert but rather as the effort to converse in "Visionary forms dramatic." The Covenant between God and Man is a continuing dialogue: "God's act of creation is speech; but the same is true of each lived moment. The world is given to the human beings who perceive it, and the life of man is itself a giving and receiving. The events that occur to human beings are the great and small, untranslatable but unmistakable signs of their being addressed; what they do and fail to do can be an answer or a failure to answer. Thus the whole history of the world, the hidden, real world history, is a dialogue between God and his creature; a dialogue in which man is a true, legitimate partner, who is entitled and empowered to speak his own independent word out of his own being."[13] The harvest symbolism in *Milton*, much abbreviated from *The Four Zoas*, is made subordinate in *Jerusalem* to the symbolism of the Covenant, for the "whole history of the world," as Buber writes, is seen there as a dialogue between God and Man. Noah's harvest of the pairs of creation in Genesis and the Covenant there signified by the bow are in *Jerusalem* the humanizing of all the events by which man was addressed. Once man grasps the meaning of the bow (Gen. 9:8-13), he can reply to God with "ardor" and rejoice in the "Fourfold Annihilation" of the winter-night of time that has flooded his world.

In his *Vision of the Last Judgment*, Blake describes this covenant in aesthetic terms. "If the Spectator . . . could Enter into Noahs Rainbow or into his bosom," this is what he would see: "The Persons who ascend to Meet the Lord coming in the Clouds with power & great Glory. are representations of those States described in the Bible under the Names of the Fathers before & after the Flood Noah is seen in the Midst of these Canopied by a Rainbow on his right hand Shem & on his Left Japhet these three Persons represent Poetry Painting & Music the three Powers in Man of conversing with Paradise which the flood did not Sweep away" (*VLJ* 81:E548/K609).[14] In *Milton*, we are told that "in Eternity the Four Arts: Poetry, Painting, Music, / And Architecture which is Science: are the Four Faces of Man" (*M* 27). But we are also told that this is "Not so in Time & Space." In time and space, "Three are shut out, and only / Science remains. . . ." It is Los who maintains the ability of Man to converse with Paradise. Both in *Milton* and in *Jerusalem*, he harvests the events of time and space by laying "his words in order above the mortal brain" and building the "structure of the Language" (*M* 27:8-10; *M* 30:18-20; *J* 36[40]).

The making "Permanent" of "every little act, / Word, work, & wish, that has existed" (*J* 13:E156/K634) in the visionary "bright Sculptures of / Los's Halls" from which "every Age renews its powers" (*J* 16) depends upon Los's "wondrous Art." Los or imagination holds converse with God and that converse is the "real world history" in "Visionary forms dramatic." The covenant of

---

[13] Martin Buber, *Israel and the World: Essays in a Time of Crisis*, New York, 1963, 16. Cf. Blake on prophecy in the marginalia to Watson's *Apology* 14 (E606-607/K392) and Matt. 13:43: "Who hath ears to hear, let him hear."

[14] Cf. Damon, *Dictionary*, 300-301; 139; pl. I.

which the bow is token is related in *A Vision of the Last Judgment* to the alteration of the seasonal cycle after the flood, because "beneath the feet of Seth two figures represent the two Seasons of Spring & Autumn while beneath the feet of Noah Four Seasons represent the Changed State made by the flood" (*VLJ* 83). Before the flood, there is only spring and autumn, sowing and reaping, birth and maturation, a perennial dialogue which harvests countless beginnings. In order to restore that condition to man, imagination must keep the covenant by comprehending, like Elijah, "all the Prophetic Characters" from its "fiery Chariot" (*VLJ* 83). It is only in this way that Jerusalem can be built "In Englands green & pleasant Land."

When discussing Zen, Suzuki writes that by "expressing ourselves we realize that the experience grows deeper and clearer. A dumb experience is no experience at all."[15] The concluding plates of *Jerusalem* underscore how important Los's building of the structure of the language is to the reintegration of man. He not only acts against Albion's despair by vocalizing his nightmare so man can see what he has become, but also establishes the "rough basement" for a creative discourse in which all things "Humanize."[16] The events of Genesis concerning the flood and God's punishment and mercy belong to the winter of time, like the four seasons; by analogy these events prophesy that when man can speak as God speaks, he will be a legitimate partner in the dialogue of creation and will speak his part and "give" as well as be spoken to and "receive."

The time that the Ancients called the golden age is restored in *Jerusalem* because man is once again a creator, not simply a creature. When he speaks the Universal Father speaks "in him" (*J* 97). It is then that Albion stretches his hand into "Infinitude" in order to take God's bow, which is in fact "his Bow." And once he can do this for himself, he can do it for all "living creatures." The cloud over London in which Los "low bended in anger" (*M* 42) unfolds, for man has taken hold of the token of the covenant and the "Night of Death is past."

[15] "Existentialism, Pragmatism and Zen," *Zen Buddhism: Selected Writings of D. T. Suzuki*, ed. W. Barrett, New York, 1956, 172.

[16] Cf. *J* 36[40]; *J* 63:18-22; *J* 71:15-19; *J* 98. See my essay, "Visionary Forms Dramatic: Grammatical and Iconographical Movement in Blake's Verse and Designs," *Criticism*, VIII (1966), 111-125.

Blake's analogy—Los's "Divine Analogy"—is at work again. Man's vision, like his nerves of sensation, is now distributed all over his body spiritual. He feels-sees completely. Like God, he is all vision. The flood of sensations that rolled and crashed against the shores of his rocky, opaque life now flows from him as the water of life. The dim chaos brightens beneath, above, and around where once was shadowed forth a punishing God (*J* 49). Man now sees the Divine Analogy from the point of view of the Universal Father. And each man is lifted by the spirit of the Zoas after the manner of Ezekiel's vision.

Plate 99 of *Jerusalem* uses time metaphorically to describe the nature of the creative conversation defined on plate 98, hence the movement back and forth:

> All Human Forms identified even Tree, Metal, Earth
> & Stone. all
> Human Forms identified, living going forth & returning
> wearied
> Into the Planetary lives of Years Months Days & Hours
> reposing
> And then Awaking into his Bosom in the Life of Immor-
> tality.
> And I heard the Name of their Emanations they are
> named Jerusalem   (*J* 99:E256/K747)

The relation of the image of time to the form of eternity or of generation (the "Image" of regeneration) to regeneration describes the "whole history of the world, the hidden, real world history," which "is a dialogue between God and his creature." No longer created *in* time, man now creates time as a vehicle of speech —a vehicular form—through which he describes his relation to eternity, for in eternity the "mutual interchange" with another is like the movement of time toward eternity (*J* 88; cf. *J* 71:16-19). The "Night of Time" began when man's emanations refused form in each other's bosom, causing things to "roll apart in fear" and causing the gates into Jerusalem to be walled up. But Jerusalem is built or identified by a mutual giving and receiving of the emanations of all things by all things. The seeming cyclical description of life in plate 99 is actually a description of the dialogic relationship between the emanations of all living things humanized and God, based upon a temporal metaphor. The "mutual interchange" of plate 88 is the "Mutual Covenant Divine" of plate 98—the word of God—which is variable and which is *like* the relation of time to eternity.[17]

Forgiveness of sins is on the moral level the act of entering another's bosom, and the act of entering another's bosom, which can be accomplished only through imagination,[18] is on the visionary level the act of "Awaking into his Bosom in the Life of Immortality." When this happens all men are one man (as each man is all men). When this happens the human form is recognized as the divine (as the divine is seen in all life). To awake "into" God's bosom is to raise the temporal to the eternal and the human to the divine. To converse in "Visionary forms dramatic" is to speak God's vehicular word, to "Enter into Noahs Rainbow or into his bosom," to "make a Friend & Companion" of the divine image in one's imagination, to "Humanize" all life and thus to make it divine. The name of the emanations of "All Human Forms identified" is Jerusalem, because it is those emanations that "unite" man with man, the only way in which Jerusalem can exist. The human forms of plate 99 are the "Human Fourfold Forms" that "mingle" in "thunders of Intellect," that is, Human Forms

[17] It is not the purpose of this essay to convince critics who have insisted upon a cyclical reading of the last two plates of *Jerusalem* that Blake is no prophet of eternal recurrence, but I should like to point out briefly that as a fundamentally Christian poet he conceives of time as a pilgrimage toward eternity. Time is in fact, as he says, the mercy of eternity (M 24:71: E120/K510; cf. J 88:49:E245/K734). In the vegetable world, man conceives of time after the manner of the philosopher and sees only the cycle of the days and the seasons—sees eternity and God only as something *other*, a heaven and a Father afar. A man of imagination lives *in* Los, who keeps time with the beat of his hammer (see J 73:29ff:E266/K713). Los labors *in* the moment that *is* eternity and from which "all the Great / Events of Time start forth & are concievd" (see M 28:62-63; 29:1-3; cf. M 24:68-70 and VLJ 79, 91: E546, 553/K607, 614). Los "walks up & down continually" in the six thousand years (see, for example, J 74-75) which are contained in the moment in which all things are changed. The harvest-covenant of human forms at the end of *Jerusalem* uses the planetary lives of the wheeling universe analogically, in order to demonstrate that time is the vehicle in which the bard sees the past, the present, and the future, but is not limited by its horizons. There are many moments and many words, but they are contained in one moment and one word which are revealed continually. Time, like *Jerusalem*, is a "Song."

[18] See especially J 71:15-19, J 88:3-15. Cf., also, VLJ 82-84: E550/K611.

that speak the "Words of the Mutual Covenant Divine" which makes all things "Humanize," "even Tree Metal Earth & Stone" as well as "every Colour, Lion, Tyger, Horse, Elephant, Eagle Dove, Fly, Worm, / And the all wondrous Serpent. . . ." The human harvest at the end of *Jerusalem* is a visionary act, a work of art describing the creative process that built *Jerusalem* in "Englands green & pleasant Land." Earlier in the poem Blake speaks of Jerusalem as the emanative force that creates unity out of mutual forgiveness and individual liberty (*J* 54). The identification of Jerusalem with liberty, mutual forgiveness, the Divine Vision, and "Form" is very important. "Visionary forms dramatic" are forms that are particular and that are peculiar so far as the light they shed is concerned. When all the particular and peculiar characteristics of man are freely expressed the human harvest becomes divine.

The "ubi sunt" speech of the living creatures on plate 98 of *Jerusalem* contrasts the human condition in time with the human condition in "Great Eternity." The snows of the "winter of human life," yesteryear as it were, are melted by the "more bright Sun of Imagination" which the youthful Milton sees in his dream in the last of the *L'Allegro* designs; this design should be contrasted with the dark and constellation-filled sky of the last of the *Il Penseroso* designs that arches over the mossy cell in which the aged and blind Milton awaits death, somewhat like Albion on plate 21 of *Jerusalem*, where the Cosmic Man wishes "that Death & Annihilation were the same!" In *Milton*, Blake has Milton return not to die a vegetative death again but to enter the state of eternal annihilation in which the selfhood is put off. (As I pointed out earlier in the essay, the twelve designs for *L'Allegro* and *Il Penseroso* can be read against the metaphor of twelve visionary months in the year-life of Milton. The twelfth "December" design {106} portraying the aged Milton under the sky of the winter solstice should be contrasted with the sixth "June" design of the summer solstice {1} in which the youthful Milton sees the real sun—the "more bright Sun of Imagination." Once Milton annihilates the selfhood, he overcomes death.)[19]

[19] In the *L'Allegro* and *Il Penseroso* designs, Milton is seen as piper (the poet of youth and spring) and as bard (the poet of age and autumn). When he sees the "more bright Sun of Imagination," he is *alseep* and *dreams* ambitiously of following in the dancing steps of Shakespeare and Jonson

The "ubi sunt" theme appears in two distinct ways in *Jerusalem*: on plate 20 Jerusalem laments the golden age and on plate 98 the "Living Creatures" hark back to the nightmare of history. Jerusalem's speech on plate 20 foreshadows plate 99 by recalling the golden age in terms that anticipate the movement of the human forms identified on the last plate of *Jerusalem*:

> Wherefore hast thou shut me into the winter of human life
> And clos'd up the sweet regions of youth and virgin
>   innocence:
> Where we live, forgetting error, not pondering on evil:
> Among my lambs & brooks of water, among my warbling
>   birds:
> Where we delight in innocence before the face of the
>   Lamb:
> Going in and out before him in his love and sweet
>   affection   (*J* 20:E163/K642)

The "Going in and out before him in his love and sweet affection" is parallel to the "going forth & returning . . . reposing / And then Awaking into his Bosom in the Life of Immortality." Plate 21 (lines 42-49) describes the fact of the Covenant of Priam, which is recalled on plate 98. It is the covenant of cruelty and the covenant of the dying and reviving "Vegetated Christ" (cf. *J* 90:28-38) which "must be put off Eternally / Lest the Sexual Generation swallow up Regeneration." By entering into images in his imagination (Los), Milton in *Milton* and Albion in *Jerusalem* become (with Blake) one with Los, who is of the likeness and similitude of Jesus. Speaking in "Visionary forms dramatic" man

---

(see Grant's prefatory note, above, p. xi), but when he retreats into his mossy cell, he has assumed the mantle of the exiled prophet who *awake* but *blind* chastises in solemn voice the heedless spirits of the Restoration. In designs 6 and 12, we see two Miltons, both of whom Blake admired but also believed to be incomplete (if not contradictory). Milton finally overcomes death not by dying as a blind old man in possession of Sophoclean wisdom learned too late but by becoming one with Los (as in *Milton*), a final stage of development that would have been impossible had Milton not progressed beyond the stage of a pastoral dreamer. For a fuller discussion of the illustration for Milton's companion poems, see my essay, "Blake's Illustrations for *Paradise Lost*, *L'Allegro*, and *Il Penseroso*: A Thematic Reading," *Hartford Studies in Literature*, II, 1 (1970), 40-67.

converses with man in God and humanizes all life. Whereas "every thing that lives is holy" to the visionary in time, everything in "Great Eternity" is human. It is human because man has "put on Intellect" and given forms to events, thus shaping eternity with the stuff of time. The human harvest in *Jerusalem* is the imagination's ethical and aesthetic victory—an act of vision—over generation, the winter life of the times of trouble. By using generation as an image of regeneration, the prophetic and visionary poet has made the temporal cycles of the year and the day image forth or emanate the peculiar light of every particular form which is in one body the form of the Divine Vision.[20] The human form divine holds converse with every particular form he has identified in the labor and the harvest of his six thousand day-years and now reposes in God like the creator he is:

> And they conversed together in Visionary forms dramatic which bright
> Redounded from their Tongues in thunderous majesty, in Visions
> In new Expanses, creating exemplars of Memory and of Intellect
> Creating Space, Creating Time according to the wonders Divine
> Of Human Imagination, thoughout all the Three Regions immense
> Of Childhood, Manhood & Old Age[;] & the all tremendous unfathomable Non Ens
> Of Death was seen in regenerations terrific or complacent varying
> According to the subject of discourse & every Word & every Character
> Was Human. . . .   (*J* 98)

Jerusalem concludes with the "Words of the Mutual Covenant Divine," a literal expression of the converse in "Great Eternity" that harvests "every little act, / Word, work & wish" (*J* 13). These become, in the Divine Analogy of six thousand years, the converse

20 Cf. *The Laocoön*: E271/K776 and the Annotations to *The Works of Sir Joshua Reynolds* 60: E637/K459: "One Central Form composed of all other Forms" is to Blake "The Imagination," "The Eternal Body of Man."

between man and man in the human *form* divine. The mutual covenant divine is a harvest of "ten thousand thousand springs of life." Such is the nature of imagination, whose "Forms Eternal" are the "Human Existence itself."[21]

[21] See Damon, *Dictionary*, 340: "When Eno, who has prophetic insight, draws out a moment of time 'into a Rainbow of jewels and gold,' she is perceiving in time a pre-vision of eternity (*J* 48:35). After Erin has expounded the Forgiveness of Sins and invoked Jesus, her 'lovely Bow enclos'd the Wheels of Albion's Sons' with the hope of his coming (*J* 50:22).

"Noah's rainbow is the hope and promise of immortality, as it symbolizes the spiritual body. See NOAH.

"On *Jerusalem* 14, the vision of Jerusalem is overarched by a rainbow, for she is the hope of a perfect society.

"A rainbow sweeps across the title page of *Visions of the Daughters of Albion*. It is the only sign of hope in the whole book. It signifies that in spite of the storm, the sun is shining; and that there is hope for the solution of Oothoon's problems, though perhaps only in the spiritual body."

For Noah and for man in the flood of time, the significance of the bow is also such a sign. It is by no means unusual for a poet or painter to identify the rainbow with the archer's bow, especially since it arches over the world. When Eno "draws out a moment of time" (the moment in each day that Satan cannot find) "into a Rainbow of jewels and gold," Blake suggests the action of drawing the bow to be that of the painter in mental war. The "Arrows of Intellect" that the fourfold bowstring "breathes with ardor" are the armaments that he employs in the intellectual battles that are waged in the "Mental Fight" of visionary art. Visionary arrows penetrate the opacity of man and "Open the hidden Heart in Wars of mutual Benevolence, Wars of Love" (*J* 97; cf. lines 12-17 and *J* 88:2-15, where Blake speaks of the male, the female, and children). The vision of Jerusalem is overarched by a rainbow on *Jerusalem* 14 (fig. 20), as Damon notes, because she *is* the only "perfect society"; the bow symbolizes the power of a creative vision that goes beyond the mortal and the finite (the flood of time) into infinitude (Eden or Eternity) which while Albion sleeps is only a "pale reflection" from his tomb. The rainbow is also the *palette* of the painter-poet-prophet whose "Visionary forms dramatic" redound from a prophetic tongue, "creating exemplars of Memory and of Intellect, / Creating Space, Creating Time according to the wonders Divine / Of Human Imagination. . . ." Erin's hopeful exposition of the Forgiveness of Sins at the end of chapter II is matched at the end of chapter IV by a final realization of the covenant of the Forgiveness of Sins. As I have pointed out in other essays (see note 7), the symmetrical parallels between the closing plates of chapters II and IV in *Jerusalem* are very important features of the structure of the poem. It is important to observe that in chapter II (*J* 48), when Eno draws out the moment of time "into a Rainbow," it appears only as "a mild Reflection from / Albions dread Tomb" where "the *Human Harvest* waves abundant in the beams of Eden"

Fig. 20. *Jerusalem*, pl. 14, detail

And as we have borne the image of the earthy, we shall also bear the image of the heavenly. . . .

Behold, I show you a mystery: We shall not all sleep, but we shall all be changed,

In a moment, in the twinkling of an eye, at the last trump; for the trumpet shall sound, and the dead shall be raised incorruptible, and we shall be changed. . . .

Therefore, my beloved brethren, be ye steadfast, unmov-

(my italics). At the end of *Jerusalem*, the rainbow is no longer "a mild Reflection," for once the "Hand of Man" has grasped God's token, he has "Clothed himself" with it. Albion has risen from his tomb and the human and the divine have been identified in a spiritual body clothed in bows and arrows fourfold, which have hitherto only been a hope or promise symbolized by the bow set in the cloud by God as a token of his covenant with Noah, his seed, and every living creature. Cf. *J* 77; also *VLJ* 85 (E552/K613) for the rainbow that surrounds the Beams of Glory that surround Jesus and the throne.

able, always abounding in the work of the Lord, forasmuch
as ye know that your labor is not in vain in the Lord.

(1 Cor. 15:49; 51-52; 58)[22]

Blake did all his work in Paul's moment and saw all things
changed. His harvest of eternal forms by which he transformed
the world of corporeal command into visionary and dramatic
mental signification was his sign that he had kept the covenant.

[22] Cf. *M* 28:44-62; *M* 29:1-3, and *M* 35:42-45 for this moment of which
Paul speaks. For the moment as grain, see *J* 35:1-3 and *J* 39:1-3. Cf. also
Buber's "each lived moment."

Then said he unto his disciples, The harvest truly *is* plenteous, but the labourers *are* few;

Pray ye therefore the Lord of the harvest, that he will send forth labourers into his harvest.

Matthew 9:37-38

action, suggested by visibilia, 87; political, 98; dynamic, 100-01; revolutionary, 115; fertilizing, 281; relation to time, 385-89; seasonal, 447-48

Adam, 186; and Eve, 100-01, 101n, 207-08

Aeneas, in burning Troy, 133n, 134n, 214

Agostino Veneziano, {119}, 218

Ah! Sun-Flower, 115, 122n

Ahania, 425-26

Ahania, 161, 168; title page, 149n

Albion, 178-79, 186, 259, 377, 384, 393, 401, 402-04, 406, 436, 457; function of, 375; visual contrast with Urizen, 77-78; daughters of, 418-19, 422

Albion and the Letter That Killeth, 194

Albion rose, {91}, 176, 178, 178n, 179, 185, 225, 228; contrasted with *Europe* frontispiece, 77-78

All Religions Are One: *plate 4* (fig. 6, p. 180), 179-80; *plate 7*, 179; *plate 10*, 82

Allamanda, 430-31

allegorical anonymity, 68

Allegro, L', and *Il Penseroso* illustrations: *no. 1* (Mirth), {72}, 301n; *no. 3* (Great Sun), xiv; *no. 6* ("more bright Sun"), {1}, xi-xiv, 457, 457n; *no. 9* {71}, 299, 301n; *no. 11* (Milton's Dream), xiv, *no. 12* (peaceful Hermitage), {106}, xi, xiii, 353n, 445-46, 457, 457n

Altizer, Thomas J. J., 399, 406

America, 161n, 168, 194; global movement, 41n; picture-gallery form, 87; composition and background, 94; machinery as improvement on Barlow, 95; visualized sound, 95-98; opening tableaux, 99-100; Preludium, 100-01; depiction of central drama, 101-10; progressive movement, 100-01, 103-05; king forms, 106-08; comparison with *Europe*, 115-16, 131, 133; general paradigm, 269-70 *frontispiece*, {24}, 95-96, 99-100, 176, 193, 317; *title page*, {25}, 95, 95n, 96, 99-100, 102, 189, 235, 271; *plate 1* (Preludium), {26}, 100, 102, 121, 124n, 190; *plate 2* (Preludium), {27}, 101, 109, 271, 276-77, 318; *plate 3* (Prophecy), {29}, 102, 106, 108n, 109, 134, 271; *plate 4*, {31}, 106-07,

107n, 186n, 190; *plate 5*, {33}, 107-08, 190; *plate 6*, {34}, 176, 191, 192; *plate 7*, {35}, 110, 176; *plate 8*, {36}, 79-80 (compared to plate 10), 109, 176, 180, 181-82, 186, 188, 281, 317; *plate 9*, {37}, 176, 190-91; *plate 10*, {38}, 79-80, 109, 181, 187, 281, 283; *plate 11*, {39}, 131n, 318; *plate 12*, {40}, 192, 420n; *plate 13*, {41}, 109, 110, 184, 194; *plate 14*, {42}, 125; *plate 15*, {43}, 102, 104; *plate 16* (finis), {44}, 98, 103, 104-05, 131n, 136n, 176, 193; *canceled plates: a* {28}, 106n; *b* {30}, 106, 106n; *c* {32}, 106n, 108-09

"Ancient of Days, The," See *Europe*, *frontispiece*

Angel, The, 211, 216

Angel of the Revelation, The, 47n

antifeminism, in *Milton*, 364-69

Antiquity Explained (Montfaucon), {121}, fig. 7, p. 222

antithetical structure, 391ff; categories, 408

antiurbanism, 414

Apocalypse, 40, 95, 102

Apuleius, 214

archetypes, visual, 175-76

architecture, Gothic versus Romanesque, 414, 419, 421, 435

Arlington Court painting, 176, 189, 193

Armageddon, 102, 106, 109, 119, 130, 139-43

arms, 243n. *See also* outstretched arms

art forms: combinations of, 57; Blake's reluctance to separate, 58. *See also* composite art

Atlantic deeps and mountains, 109-10

Alantis myth, 41n, 95

Aurelia (Bryant's *Mythology*), fig. 11, p. 227

autumn, 444, 446

Babylon, 401, 419, 421, 424, 426

Bachelard, Gaston, 278n

Baker, Collins, 174n

bard: on divan, 208, 208n; rending harp, 283-84

Barlow, Joel, 95, 98

Bastille, 38

bat-winged creature, 92, 184

Beer, John, 30n, 31n, 134n, 136-37n, 138n

Behemoth, 352, 353

bent kneeling figure, 193
Bentley, Gerald E., Jr., 135n,
148n, 190, 304n, 427
Bentley, Richard, illustration of Gray's
Ode, {70}, 290, 292-93
Berger, Pierre, 30n
Beulah, 252, 394-95; daughters of, 387
Bible: relation to Blake's designs, 88-89;
to thought and images in *Europe*,
126n, 129, 135-36; to epic, 369-70;
mythic elements, 370; ironic treatment
of, 377; Blake's illustrations of, 132n.
*See paintings by title; see also
separate books*
Binyon, Laurence, 174
birds, 110, 110n, 176, 194, 325, 397
bird-headed figure, 400
Blackstone, Bernard, 246
Blake, James, 246
Blake, Robert, face in *Island* MS, 28n
Blake, William: face in *Island* MS,
28n; creative use of sources, 32; 1803-04
crisis, 245-46; attitude toward father
figures, 246-47; early ambivalence
toward Urizen, 248; emphasis on
individual after 1804, 250; Blake/Los,
Enitharmon, and Spectre, 251-54;
reconciliation with Urizen, 254-55;
new attitude toward war, 255; need
to reorganize mental life, 255-56;
recognition of selfhood, 258-59;
attitude toward Gray's ode, 286-87,
297-303; toward Young, 305-07;
alleged antagonism to classics, 362-63
Bloom, Harold, 30n, 31n, 53n, 93n,
121n, 142n, 337, 387, 391n, 410, 423n,
431, 437
Blossom, The, {13}, 185, 201-02, 231, 238
Blunt, Sir Anthony, 58n, 77, 175n,
183n
body as political metaphor, 44
"Body of Hector, The," 183n
Bogen, Nancy, 416n
Bowlahoola, 430-31
boy, sleeping, 318
Breach in a City, A, {23}, 99, 99n
Bronowski, Jacob, 30n
Browne, Sir William, 13-14
Bryant, Jacob, 222n, 225, 226n, 227
(figs. 10, 11, 12), 232n
Burke, Edmund, 84
burning motif, 223n
Butlin, Martin, 304n
butterfly symbol, 225-30
Byron, Lord, 360, 367, 441

Carr, Comyns, 304
Cat Ode, Blake's illustration of, 288-95
caterpillar, 226-27, 394-95; human,
319-20
chain, 318, 329
Chatterton, Thomas, 11, 12n
chiasmus, 168n
children, 124, 190-91, 332-33. *See also*
secret child
Chimney Sweeper, The (*Experience*
pl. 37), 207-08, 212; (*Innocence*
pl. 12), 205
chimney sweepers, 279n
Christ: designs, 178-79, 186; relation to
Lucifer, 339n; vegetated, 399-400.
See also Jesus
Christ Taking Leave of His Mother, 178
Christ's Troubled Dream, 183
chrysalis (fig. 10, p. 227), 226-27, 323
Churchill, Charles, 14
cinematic elements of Blake's art, 93,
93n, 94
circle, 78, 209-10, 437-38; of Destiny,
318-24
city: visual representation of, 413-14;
Blake's early antiurbanism,
414-15; his vision of in *London*,
415, 417-18; in *The French
Revolution*, 422n, in *The Four
Zoas*, 423-29; in *Milton*, 431-32; in
Jerusalem, 419-22, 433-41; Golgonooza,
422, 424, 426-29, 431-32; other
Romantic visions of, 441-42
classical tradition: Blake's attitude,
362n
clockwise movement, 100, 103, 104, 202,
206, 210, 211, 293
Clod & the Pebble, The, 207, 208
cloud imagery, 38, 50, 52-54, 110,
347, 349
Coleridge, Samuel T., 215n, 226
Collins, William, parodied in *Island*, 20
color: use of, 74-76, 289; symbolism, 64n
compasses, 116-17, 437-38
composite art: nature and historical
background, 57-61; function in Blake,
61-62; in *Marriage of Heaven and
Hell*, 63-66; Blake's departure from
tradition, 66-69; his art forms as
critiques of their own media, 69-72;
dialectic as key to symbolism,
73-80; complexity of, 92-94. *See also*
sister arts
Comus (Milton), 231
Conjugal Union of Cupid and Psyche
(Cumberland), {118}, 218, 232
Connolly, Thomas, 58n

Contemplation, 414
contraction-expansion, 77-78
contraries, 63-65, 354-55, 378
conversion, as visionary process, 452
1 Corinthians, 451, 452; 2 Corinthians, 338
corpse, 176, 190-91
counterclockwise motion, 100, 202, 206, 211
couple (language structure), explained, 274
courtly love, 151
Covenant, symbolism of, 453
Covering Cherub, 194
Cradle Song, A, 205, 209, 233
Crane, Hart, 442
creative fingers, 176, 186
creation, accounts of, 117-19
crucifixion, 155-56, 255, 399-400, 406-07
Crucifixion: Christ Taking Leave, The, 178
cruciform gesture, 177-78
Crystal Cabinet, The, 168, 217, 230, 242, 277
Cumberland, George, 218, 219n, 230, 241, 241n; inscriptions in *Europe*, 117n, 123, 128n, 130, 131, 133n; in *Marriage of Heaven and Hell*, 183n; *Conjugal Union of Cupid and Psyche* (engr. Blake), {118}, 230; *Psyche Disobeys* (engr. Blake), {117}, 219n
Cupid, Discovery of (Van Coxie; engr. Agostino), {119}, 218-20, 235, 236, 241-42
Cupid and Psyche (Apuleius), 216-17, 218n, 238
Cupid and Psyche, wedding of (Montfaucon), fig. 7, p. 222
Cupid and Psyche myth: elements in *Thel*, 217-20; in *Europe*, 128n, 218-20; in "How sweet I roam'd," 220-24; in other works, 216-17; butterfly-soul designs, 225-30; sexual themes, 231-37; apotheoses, 238ff; merging with figures of Albion and Rahab-Tirzah, 242-43
curves, 196-97, 201-03

Damon, S. Foster, 30n, 35n, 52n, 59n; 113, 116, 123, 124, 128n, 134, 135, 137, 193, 194, 202, 204, 213, 216, 224n, 247n, 250, 333n, 336n, 340n, 353, 354n, 391n, 431n, 433n, 434, 434n, 449n, 460n
Daniel, 140
Dante: *Divine Comedy* illustrations, *no. 3* (Angry God), 180; *no. 10*

(Circle of Lovers), {107}, 104; *no. 14* (Plutus), 191; *no. 37* (Boiling Pitch-Pool), 108
Darwin, Erasmus, 215n, 222n
David Delivered Out of Many Waters, 184, 194
Death, figure of, 324
decoration versus illustration, 199
DeQuincey, Thomas, 441
design, Blake's studies of, 58n
Deuteronomy, 135
diagonals: constructive, 200-01; threatening, 197-98, 207-09, 210
Digby, George Wingfield, 58n, 134n, 176n, 191, 194, 436n
directional symbolism. *See* left-right symbolism
Discovery of Cupid (Van Coxie; engr. Agostino), {119}, 218-20, 235, 236, 241-42
Divine Analogy, 455; hand, 381; image, 212
Divine Image, The, {14}, 199, 201-02, 203, 211, 350n
divinity, indicated by outstretched arms, 177
domed structures, 414
Douglas, Dennis, 118n
Dream, A, 204
drowning, 322
Druidic architecture, 414, 435-36

eagle, 217
earthworm, 226
Ecchoing Green, The, 185, 198-99, 210, 212, 233, 333
egalitarianism, 37, 43
egg, 111, 324
Egypt, 131-32, 132n, 161n
elements, four, 169-70
Elihu, 344-45, 347-49
Eliphaz, 346
Elohim, 356, 357
Elohim Creating Adam, {94}, 156n, 184, 189, 191, 194
emblem tradition, 60
embryo (of change), 110
Emerson, Ralph W., 442
Empson, William, 300
England, Martha, 337n
Enion, 226, 379, 387, 388
Enitharmon, 118, 122, 122n, 124n, 126n, 141-42, 149, 158, 218-19, 251-53, 410, 410n, 437; creation of, 156; children of, 128n, 143n; night of, 125-30
Eno, 376, 387
Enscoe, Gerald E., 113-14

Ephesians 6:12, 375-76

epic: Romanticism and the tradition, 359-60; "brief epic," 361; machinery, 95, 363-64, 381; love, war, and heroism, 364-69; relation to history, 369-72; relation to cities, 433n; *French Revolution* not epic but prophecy, 31, 35; *Four Zoas*, epic of situations, 373

epic irony, 359-60, 367-68; in *Milton* (of genre, 361; by contrast with tradition, 362; by subversive machinery, 364; in treatment of woman, 364-69; in use of time, 371-72); in *Four Zoas*, 381

Erdman, David V., 30n, 34n, 116n, 124n, 126n, 140, 142n, 143, 144, 194n, 246, 254, 255, 263, 394n, 415-16, 419n, 427, 428n, 431n, 432n, 436n
  notes and comments, 13n, 27, 27n, 99n, 100n, 123n, 126-27n, 161n, 182n, 183n, 191, 234n, 382n

Eternal Man, 256

eternal recurrence, 456n

Eternals, the, 381

eternity in time, 407ff

Europe, 41n, 168; cycle of history in, 112-13; mood in forms, 115; creation design, 117-19; Preludium, 117-22; Prophecy: Oothoon, 123-25; Enitharmon's night, 125-30; depiction of miseries, 130-34; account of Fall, 135-39; toward Armageddon, 139-43; morning, 143-45
  Cumberland inscriptions, 117n, 123, 128n, 130, 131, 133n
  frontispiece ("Ancient of Days"), {8}, 78, 116-17, 150, 248, 319; *title page*, 194; *plate 1* (Preludium), {45}, 121, 123, 208n; *plate 3* (Prophecy), {46}, 123-25, 126-27n (punctuation problem), 190, 208n; *plate 4*, {47}, 115, 128, 218-20, 235; *plate 5*, {48}; *plate 6*, 128, 130-31, 176, 190, 191; *plate 7*, 131; *plate 8*, {49}, 132-33 and n; *plate 9*, 131-32, 189, 190; *plate 10*, 135-38; *plate 11*, 128; *plate 12*, {50}, 116, 191; *plate 13*, 133-34; *plate 15*, 133n, 134, 134n, 214, 281

Eve Tempted by the Serpent, 192

evolution, spiritual, 277-78

Exodus: allusions or imagery in *Europe*, 129, 129n, 131, 135n, 136, 140

expansion: negative aspects, 79; apocalyptic, 278; and contraction, 77-78

Eyes of God, 354n, 356

Ezekiel, imagery in *Europe*, 135

Ezekiel's Vision, 181n

Faerie Queene, The (Spenser), 217n

Fairy, The, 229n

fall, account of, 135-39; as embracing subjectivity, 156; Urizenic version of, 161n; parodied, 253; and resurrection motif, 377; of the Zoas, 384, 385, 386

Fall of Man, The, 350n

falling figures, 176, 190, 300

Farrer, Austin, 32-33n

fate, 293, 293n

father figures, Blake's attitude toward, 246-47

female will, xii, 366-67

Fielding, Henry, 23

finite and infinite, in *Urizen*, 159-65

fire, 98, 140, 339

fish, 288-95

Fisher, Peter F., 363n, 417

flame-flowers, 70-71

flowers, 176, 194, 232, 235

Fly, The, 211n, 226-30, 233n, 234, 237

flying figure, 175, 189-90

foetus posture, 123, 193-94

Foote, Samuel: his theater and company, 3-8; Blake's knowledge of his theatricals, 3, 8-15, 27

forgiveness of sins, as imaginative art, 456

form, independence of, in *Four Zoas*, 379

Four Zoas, The, 161n, 168, 226, 238-39, 247, 281, 337; picture-gallery form, 87; Cupid and Psyche myth in, 216, 219; Nights VIIa and VIIb compared, 251-54; apparent obscurity, 373-74; formal dislocation, 375; introduction of Zoas, 377-78; deliberate independence of form, 379; perplexity of first scene, 379-81; nature of the oZas, 381-83; drawings in, 382; reality in, 383-84; relation to other poems, 384, 384n; action and time, 385-89; cities in, 423-29; seasonal action, 447-48
  page 2, 101n; *page 3*, 189; *page 26*, {89}, 382n; *page 70*, 107n; *page 71*, 107n; *page 86*, {90}, 253; *page 139*, 189

French Revolution, The: Book of Revelation as source, 31; verbal pictures, 34; scenic structure, 35; not epic but prophecy, 35n; scenes analyzed: (1), 37-38; (2), 38; (3), 39; (4), 39-48; (5), 48; (6), 49-50; (7),

50-51; summary and diagram of movement, 51-52 (and fig. 1); figurative language, 52-54 (imagery), 54-56 (similes); levels of action (fig. 1); picture-gallery form, 87; urban imagery, 422

friction, 279

Friedman, Albert, 16, 22n

Frye, Northrop, vii, 30n, 41n, 82n, 94, 112 (Orc cycle), 136, 138, 143n, 175, 193, 194, 263-64 (on Orc), 336, 336n (on *Job*), 340n, 348, 359, 391n (on *Jerusalem*), 413, 432, 437n, 443, 445

Fuseli, Henry, 124n, 219n, 228n

Fuzon, 160, 267

Garden of Love, The, 210n, 323

garment, as metaphor for color, 76

Garrick, David, 4, 6, 8, 22

Gates of Paradise, The, 247, 355; *frontispiece,* 319; *plate 3,* 318; *plate 4,* 176, 193, 249; *plate 5,* 190; *plate 6,* 190, 318, 324; *plate 7* (fig. 13, p. 229), 189, 228-29, 242, 325; *plate 10,* 299, 322; *plate 11,* 181, *plate 14,* 325n; *plate 15,* 176, 192, 322, 325n, 420, 420n; (pls. 14-16, 446); *plate 16,* 16, 107n, 176, 192, 193, 318; *epilogue,* 107, 184, 194, 339n

generative verbal order, 274

Genesis, imagery in *Europe,* 137-38; illustrated title page, 333, 333n, 350n

gesture, types of, 174-76, 243n

girl in yellow (*Night Thoughts*), 322, 323

Gleckner, Robert E., 181

God: and man in *Milton,* 363; Job's, depicted by Blake, 338

God the son casting the rebel angels into hell, 300n

Golden Ass, The (Apuleius), 214

Goldenberg, Shelley, 110n

Golgonooza, 67, 422, 424, 426-29 (*Four Zoas*), 431-32 (*Milton*), 436, 437-39 (*Jerusalem*)

Good and Evil Angels, The, 182n, 184, 187

Gothic architecture, 414, 419, 421, 435

grain of sand, 111-12, 452

Grant, John E., viii, 194, 418n, 420n *notes and comments:* 63n-64n, 95n, 96n, 98n, 99n, 100n, 101n, 102n, 105, 107n, 108n, 109n, 116n, 128n, 131n, 133n, 182n, 349-50n, 420n

grave, 322

Grave, The (Robert Blair, illus. by Blake): *title page,* 108n; *plate 3* (Death's Door), 76, 192; *plate 13,* 191-92

Gray, Thomas: *Ode to Adversity,* 332; *Elegy* (Blake's illustration no. 107), 323; *Ode on the Death of a Favourite Cat:* Dr. Johnson and the moral, 285-86; Blake's illustrations for, {64-69}, (circumstances of composition, 287-88; discussion of designs, 288-95; Blake's treatment of the allegory, 295-303); illustration by Richard Bentley, {70}

gray-haired female (*Night Thoughts*), 319

Great Balloon Ascension, 16

Great Red Dragon and the Woman Clothed with the Sun, The, {63}, 187-88

Grey Monk, The, 112-13

grieving figure, 193

growth, principle of, 265

guilt and sexuality, 253

Gurney, Hudson, 215n

Hagstrum, Jean, 58n, 174n, 176n, 179-80, 304n; notes and comment, 168n

Halliburton, David, 30n, 35n, 52n

Hand, 393, 395, 400, 401

Handel, George Frederic, 25, 26, 26n, 27; and pastoral tradition, 8, 18, 18n; and foundlings, 23

hands, 79, 176, 234; upturned, 185-86; downturned, 186-87; human, on dragon, 107n

Harper, George Mills, 245

Harris, James (*Daphnis and Amaryllis*), 19, 19n

harvest: as dramatization of creative process, 451-52; human, 444 (in *Night Thoughts* illustrations), 449-51, 457 (as visionary art), 459 (victory of imagination)

hat, functioning as net, 228-29

Hayley, William, 4n, 27, 247

Haymarket (Little Theater), 5-7

head-clutching figure, 106-08, 190

hell, as Bastille, 38

heroism: in *Milton,* 363-65; Blake's conception of, 368

Hirsch, E. D., 418n

Hirst, Désirée, 178n

history, 19, 145, 374; in epic, 369-70; contrasted with myth, 370

Holy Thursday: (*Experience*), 131n, 190, 206, 209, 233n, 318; (*Innocence*), 23, 205-06

Homer, 85, 329
Horace, 60
hours, human forms of stars, 328
House of Death, The, {93}, 182n, 183, 186, 317, 334n
hovering figure, 182-84, 242
"How sweet I roam'd," 220-24, 230
huddled forms, 176
Hughes, William R., 421n
human form, 67, 68, 88, 175, 188n, 456, 459, 460; fused with animal form, 288-95
hunched figure, 193-94
hunting motif, 221
Hyle, 193, 397

"I saw a chapel all of gold," 216
iconic poetry, 85-86
identity, problem of, 297
ideographic fallacy, 439n
illustrated book conventions, 83
illustration, Blake's concept of, 58
imagination: in Blake's illustrations of Gray, 291-92; role in keeping Covenant, 454; in relation to nature, 440
Inchbald, Elizabeth, 12, 16
Infant Joy, {2}, 201, 203, 211, 231-32, 234-38, 241n
Infant Sorrow, {17}, 209, 235-38, 243n
intellectual vision, 92-93
Introduction. See Songs of Innocence and of Experience
irony, 376-77; between text and design, 418. *See also* epic irony
Isaiah, 137, 144, 395
Island in the Moon, An, 3-29; similarity to Foote's theatricals, 8-15

Jacob's Ladder, 137, 138, 334n
Jehovah, 357
Jerusalem, a city, 67, 89, 419-21, 424, 426, 455; yet a woman, 379, 393, 406-07, 445, 456
Jerusalem, 3, 259, 453; picture-gallery form, 87; antithetical structure, 391-92; narrative progression, 391ff; ch. I, 393; addresses and lyrics, 393-94; ch. II, 394-97; ch. III, 397-98; ch. IV, 399-404; final plates, 404-08; paradoxical structure, 408-10
  frontispiece (pl. 1), 76, 322, 438, 449; *title page* (pl. 2, {5}), 239, 258; *plate 4,* 101n, 191-92; *plate 6,* 92, 184; *plate 14* (fig. 20, p. 461), 460n; *plate 19* (fig. 17, p. 402), 401-02; *plate 20,* 458; *plate 21,* 457-58; *plate 25,* {6},
240, 242, 393; *plate 26,* 189, 393; *plate 28,* {95}, 394, 394n; *plate 31,* 184; *plate 32,* 438; *plate 33,* {97}, 184; *plate 37,* 194; *plate 39,* 70 (formal strategy); *plate 41,* 193; *plate 46,* {7}, 189, 190, 435; *plate 50* (fig. 16, p. 396), 395, 398; *plate 51,* 193, 397; *plate 52,* 397; *plate 53,* {96}, 398; *plate 54,* xii; *plate 57* (fig. 18, p. 430), 435; *plate 58,* 109n; *plate 69,* 436; *plate 70,* 330n, 436; *plate 73,* 438; *plate 75,* 398; *plate 76,* {98}, 176, 178, 179, 186, 194, 399; *plate 77,* 421n; *plate 78,* {99}, 400-01; *plate 82,* 397; *plate 84,* {100}, 192, 325, 418-19, 421, 435; *plate 85,* 436; *plate 92* (fig. 19, p. 435), 107n, 435-36; *plate 93,* 189; *plate 94,* 402, 436; *plate 95,* {101}, 402-04, 406, 436; *plate 96,* 405-07; *plate 97,* {102}, 76, 402, 404; *plate 98,* viii (quoted); *plate 99,* {103}, 189, 243n, 283, 324, 405-07, 455-56, 456n, 458; *plate 100,* {104}, 322, 330n, 410, 436, 436n, 437-39, 456n
Jesus, 119, 121, 125, 129, 399. *See also* Christ
Job, Book of, 118, 129; Satan and God, 338, 340; verbal and syntactical ambiguities, 341, 342; Elihu's speech, 345-49
Job, Illustrations of, 53n, 168; picture-gallery form, 87; Job and his God, mirror images, 194; Job's posture, 340-41; Blake's illustrations as commentary, 336; Elihu's speech, 345-49; plates 3-18 discussed, 356-57; structure of the series, 354-58
  plate 1, xi, 354-55; *plate 2,* 346; *plate 3,* 134, 356; *plate 4,* 356, 358; *plate 5,* 356; *plate 6,* 178, 193, 340, 346, 356; *plate 7,* 356; *plate 8,* 176, 356; *plate 9,* {109}, 343, 356; *plate 10,* 189, 356; *plate 11,* {110}, 184, 338, 340-41, 342-44, 348, 356-57; *plate 12,* {111}, 344-51, 356; *plate 13,* 184, 348, 356; *plate 14,* {114}, (the drawing, {113}), 118n, 180, 185, 186, 189, 344n, 349, 350n, 351-54, 357; *plate 15,* {115}, 351-53, 355, 357; *plate 16,* 352, 357; *plate 17,* {116}, 189, 342, 344n, 352, 355, 357; *plate 18,* 340, 357; *plate 19,* 358; *plate 20,* 176, 184, 186, 358; *plate 21* (final design), xi, 332, 355
John, gospel of, 122, 126n, 376-77

Johnson, Samuel, 20, 285-86
Jonson, Ben, xii
Joshua, 135n
Joyce, James, 442

Keats, John, 37n, 85, 215n
Kemper, Claudette, 73n
Keynes, Sir Geoffrey, 58n, 59n, 126n,
    176n, 213, 304, 336n
King of England, three forms of, 106-08
Kiralis, Karl, 72n, 391n, 420n
knee-raised figure, 179-82
Kreiter, Carmen S., 277n

Lamb, Charles, 441
Lamb, The, 198, 199, 206, 208, 212
language, 172; pictorial, 174-75
lark, 327, 328
Last Judgment, The. See Vision of
    the Last Judgment
left-right symbolism, 73n, 133n, 162-63,
    197-200, 200n, 402, 403, 404,
    406, 420, 420n
Lesnick, Henry, 160n
lettering, 66, 102, 196-97, 212
Leutha, 365
levels of action and meaning, 34, 51, 228
Leviathan, 352, 353
Levine, George, 58n
light (in Job), 339, 340, 346-47, 352
linearity in Blake's art, 73-74
literary pictorialism, departure
    from, 67
Little Black Boy, The, 78, 206, 211
Little Boy Found, The, 210, 420n
Little Boy Lost, The, 183n, 193, 210
Little Girl Found, The, 192, 212
Little Girl Lost, The, 206, 233n
Little Theater (Haymarket), 5-7
Little Vagabond, The, 211
London, 430, 432-33
London, {18}, 192, 209, 325, 415,
    417-18, 420n, 425, 435
Los, 144-45, 150, 155, 249, 256, 267,
    378, 426, 437, 451, 453-55, 456n;
    pictorial matching with Urizen,
    152-53; and Enitharmon, 251-53;
    Spectre of, 92, 410
Los-Urthona, 377
Los, The Book of, 168
Los, The Song of, 168
love and war, relation of, 364-68
Lucifer, 339, 340, 352, 356-57
Luvah, 250, 395

machinery, epic, 95, 363-64, 381
Malkin, Benjamin Heath, 24n

Man Who Built the Pyramids,
    The, 166
Margoliouth, H. M., 304, 375n, 423n, 425
Mark, gospel of, 126n
Marlborough gem, 222, 222n
Marriage of Heaven and Hell, The,
    161n, 167, 168, 247, 258; the spiders
    in, 13n; thematic relation to
    The French Revolution, 31n, 38
    title page, {3}, 63-66, 63n-64n;
    movement on, fig. 2, p. 65; plate 3,
    65, 189; plate 4, 182n, 184; plate 5,
    98n, 214; plate 11, {19}, 182,
    182n, 183, 183n, 184, 186; plate
    14, 176, 183; plate 16, 101n;
    plate 21, 191; plate 24, 181;
    relation to title page, 63n-64n
Master of the Die, 218, {120}
Matthew, 181, 451
Mental Traveller, The, 168, 230,
    237, 242
Merchant, W. Moelwyn, 26, 27n
Michael and Satan, 322
Michelangelo, 98n, 182n, 191, 240;
    detail of Sistine Chapel ceiling,
    {112}, 191
Milner, Marion, 343n, 351, 353
Milton, John, 85, 360; link with Handel,
    18, 18n; derivative satires, 19-20;
    Blake's criticism of, 31n, 368; in
    designs for L'Allegro and Il
    Penseroso, xiii, 457, 457n
Milton, 186, 194, 258-59, 453; as essay
    on epic and index to Blake's practice,
    360-61; "brief epic," 361; relation
    to tradition, 362-63; machinery,
    363-64; love, war, and heroism,
    364-69; historical and mythic elements,
    369; treatment of time, 371-72
    title page, 257-58; plates 4 and 6,
    436; plate 15, 181; plate 29, {92},
    186; plate 38, 109n; plate 39,
    402; plate 42, 124n, 184
mind, as "place" of The Four Zoas, 378
Miner, Paul, 135
mirror, 319
mirror imagery, 31, 149, 150, 176,
    194-95, 209-10, 292, 319
Mitchell, John E., 82, 84, 148n
Molech, 356-57
Montfaucon, Abbé de (Antiquity
    Explained), 221-22; illustrations
    from, fig. 7 and {121}
moon, 330-31, 396, 398, 410, 428n
Moore, Thomas, 215n
"more bright Sun" design, {1}, xi-xiv
Moss, W. E., 304n

Mother Cole, 14-15
motion, 32, 37, 41n, 48, 100-01, 103-05
mundane shell, 78, 111-12, 324
Murry, John Middleton, 255n, 423n
Musca (Bryant's *Mythology*), 227
 (fig. 12), 228
music, 95, 332
My Pretty Rose Tree, 193
myth, 370

nameless shadowy female, 115, 117,
 119, 121, 123
Nanavutty, Piloo, 334n, 382n
Narcissa, 331, 331n
Narcissus motif, 147, 150, 151, 298
narrative order, 69-70, 391-92; tenses,
 408-09
natural religion, 157-59
nature, 158
Newton, Isaac, 130, 134n, 141-42, 142n
Newton, 166, 187
night (of Enitharmon), 125-30
Night, 204, 206
Night Thoughts (Edward Young),
 Blake's illustrations: attitude toward
 Young's poem, 305-07; problems of
 interpretation, 306-07; thematic and
 imagistic structures, 307-08;
 description and discussion of designs
 (*nos. 1-5*, 305, 309-10, 316; *nos. 6-7*,
 310, 316, 331, 332, 335; *nos. 8-12*,
 310-11, 316-17, 322; *nos. 13-17*,
 311-12, 318-24; *nos. 18-23*, 312-13,
 324-25; *nos. 24-28*, 313-14, 324-25;
 nos. 29-33, 314-15; *nos. 34-35*,
 315, 326-35)
 other references: *NT no. 2*, 189;
 no. 5, {73}, 123n, 208n, 330-31;
 no. 6, {74}, 444; *nos. 7-10*, {75-78};
 no. 11, {79}; 110n; *no. 12*, {80};
 no. 13, {81}, 131n, 190; *no. 14*,
 {82}; *nos. 16-17*, {83-84}; *no. 18*,
 {85}, 107n; *no. 19*, 190, 193; *no. 20*,
 {86}, 108n; *no. 26*, 192; *no. 27*,
 185, 185n; *no. 28*, 193; *no. 34*, {87};
 no. 38, 108n; *no. 49*, 444; *no. 62*,
 334n; *no. 78*, 331, 445; *no. 79*, 445;
 no. 138, 331n; *no. 148*, 225, 238;
 no. 149, 123; *no. 163*, 136n; *no. 181*,
 228; *no. 190*, 105; *no. 244*, 110;
 no. 264, 316; *no. 272*, {88}, 238, 240;
 no. 313, 123; *no. 325*, 334n; *no.
 339*, 319; *no. 345*, 445; *nos. 359-363*,
 421n; *no. 363*, 350n; *no. 403*, 189;
 no. 413, 189; *no. 435*, 189;
 no. 502, 353n
nightingale, 327, 328

Noah, 460n
Notebook, page 96 of, 116
Number of the Beast is 666, The,
 106n
Nurmi, Martin K., 117n
Nurses Song (Experience), 233n
Nurses Song (Innocence), 210, 212
nymph figures, 289

oak leaf, 318, 323
old man, 98, 98n, 179, 180-81, 319, 325;
 bent, 176, 192. *See also* Urizen
On Anothers Sorrow, 204
On the Morning of Christ's Nativity
 (Milton), 118, 119-20
Oothoon, 183, 231, 234, 270-71;
 possibly the figure in *Europe* pl. 3,
 123-34
opacity, beneficial aspect, 78
open possibilities, universe of, 266
opera, 6; analogy to Blake's form, 94;
 ballad opera, 16
Orc, 109, 115, 125, 158, 181, 182, 187,
 218-19; identity with Urizen, 79-80,
 80n; in *America*, 98n, 99, 99n,
 101-02, 161n; sleeping, in *Europe*,
 127-28; not quite to be identified
 with Christ, 143-44, 145n; Blake's
 Prometheus and Adonis, 264;
 principle of renewal and formative
 power, 266-67; Fuzon a partial
 realization of, 267; as symbol of
 poetic process, 275; link with Los,
 278-79; dialogue with Albion's
 Angel, 280; fertilizing action,
 281
Orc cycle, 79, 80n, 112-14, 263-64
 (questioned), 276-77, 318, 374
Orc paradigm, 270-71, 277
ordering devices, in *The French
 Revolution*, 33
orientation symbolism, 163. *See also*
 left-right symbolism
Orion, 349, 352, 353n, 445
Orpheus and Eurydice, xii, xiii
Our End is Come, 94, 107n, 133
ouroboros, 136n
outstretched arms (visual archetype):
 four basic poses (standing 177-79;
 knee-raised, 179-82; hovering,
 182-84; prostrate, 184-85); others,
 189; variations in hand positions
 (upturned, 185-86; downturned,
 186-87). *See also* arms, hands,
 standing figure

Pahad, 357
Palamabron, 128-29
Paley, Morton D., 304n
palms. See hands
Paradise Lost (Milton): pictorial idealism, 91; Urizen as parody of, 167; as source and background, 19, 31, 39, 40, 117-18, 248, 319; Blake's illustrations of, 100n, 186, 334n
Paradise Regained (Milton), ironic relation to Milton, 361
parody, visual, 289
pastoral: parodies of, 18-20; serious use in Island, 21; vision in French Revolution, 40, 41, 41n
Penseroso, Il. See L'Allegro
Perino del Vaga, 218
personification, 88
Pestilence—the Death of the First Born, 132n
2 Peter, 339
Phaëton myth, 98n
pictorial conventions, 73; language, vii, 174-75; pictorialism, 84
picture-gallery form, 86-87
Pilon, Frederick, 16
piper, 65n, 105, 105n, 161n, 212
Pity, 235n, 254n
planetary lives, 410, 412
Pleiades, 350, 352
poet, figure of, 326, 329-30
poetic genius, 179, 181, 186
poetic torsion, explained, 268-69
Poetical Sketches, 88, 414
poetry of "process," 268
poiein, 268
Poison Tree, The, 189
pole star, 138-39
Polymetis (Spence), 224 (figs. 8 and 9), 233 (figs. 14 and 15)
Pope, Alexander, 329
Pound, Ezra, 273
praying figure, 322
Praz, Mario, 82n
progressive cartoons, 100-01, 103-05
prone figure, 189
prophecy, relation to epic, 31, 35, 360
Prophecy of the Crucifixion, The, 178
prophetic bard, 123n
prostrate figure, 184-85, 340
Proverbs, Book of, 117, 348
Psalms, 129, 352
Pysche Disobeys (Cumberland; engr. Blake), {117}, 219n
Psyche, Punishment of (Van Coxie), {120}, 218, 241-42
puppets, 6, 12n
pyramids, 166, 414

Queen Katherine's Dream, 26, 27n

Rabiqueau, Charles, 279
Rahab, 398, 401, 445
rainbow, 46on
Raine, Kathleen, 48n, 216, 216n, 232n, 234n, 279n
Raphael, 217
reader as spectator, 85; involved, 374; perplexed, 380-81
reason, 155; Blake's ambivalence toward, 245; satire against, 319, 321
recurrence: structural device, 35, 274n; eternal, 456n
refrain lines, 97
religion, rational (natural), 159
rending plot, 274-75
Revelation, Book of, 89, 187-88; and The French Revolution, 31-56; and Europe, 127, 136, 140, 144; and Blake's Job, 339, 355; its zodiacal imagery, 445
revolution, 112-14. See also Orc cycle
Reynolds, Sir Joshua, 84n
right-left symbolism. See left-right symbolism
Rintrah, 128-29
Romanesque architecture, 419, 421, 435
Romano, Giulio, 218
romanticism and epic tradition, 359-60
Rose, E. J., 72n, 73n, 114, 185n, 226n, 319n, 396, 44on
Rosenblum, Robert, 67n
Ruskin, John, 442

"S" curves, 202-03, 211-13
1 Samuel, 352
Sandburg, Carl, 442
Satan, 258, 296, 298, 340, 399; form of, 178, 184; as a state, 255; fallen Urizen, 260; Job's God as, 338, 340
Satan Calling Up His Legions, 178, 189
Satan Exulting Over Eve, {108}, 184
Satan Watching the Endearments of Adam and Eve, 298
Satan's and Raphael's Entries into Paradise, {105}, 187
School Boy, The, 212
Schorer, Mark, 31n, 82n
scroll, symbolic, 208n, 331-33, 334n, 350n
seasonal cycle, as symbolic structure, 443
seasons: usual association with Zoas, 443
seated male nude, 191-92
secret child, 119-22, 124
sedition trial, 245
self-love, 296, 298
serpent, 136-37; serpent temples, 436

sexuality: attitudes toward, 253; Blake's
attitude, 296, 301-02, 365-67
(in *Milton*)
Shaddai, 356, 357
Shakespeare, William, xii
Sharp, Cecil J., 22n
Shelley, Mary, 215n
Shelley, Percy B., 367-68, 441
Shepheardes Calender, The (Spenser),
221n
Shepherd, The, 206, 208
Shields, Frederick James, 304
Shuter, Edward, 6, 21
Sick Rose, The, {4}, 199, 202n,
206, 216, 227
Siddons, Sarah, 26, 27
silence, in *America*, 97, 98, 99
similes, 54-56, 109
Simmons, Robert E., notes and
comments, 108n, 161n
single visualizable picture, 94, 111
sister-arts tradition: Blake's language
related to practices of iconic poetry,
85-86, of picture-gallery form,
86-87, and of personification, 88; his
forms and "ideal" reality, 90-91.
See also composite art
Skofield, 397
Sloss, D. J., and J.P.R. Wallis, 142n
Small Book of Designs, The, 59n
Smart, Christopher, 5
Smith, David, 263, 266
Song of Liberty, A, 103n, 182n
Song of Los, The, 168
Song of Solomon, 121, 129
songs, Blake's, in *An Island*, 17-26
Songs of Innocence and of Experience,
elements of design: diagonals
(threatening, 197-98, 207-09, 210;
constructive, 200-01); verticals, 198-99;
curves (in letters, 197, 198; vegetal
designs, 201-03; "S" curves,
202-03, 211-12); marginal decorations,
203-06; clockwise motion, 206; the
circle, 209-10

  general title page (pl. 1), {9},
196-97, 207, 208, 212; *Innocence*
frontispiece (pl. 2), {10}, 200-01,
212; *Innocence* title page (pl. 3), {11},
197-98, 207, 212-13, 334; *Introduction*
(*Inn.*) (pl. 4), {12}, 199, 200, 206,
212; *Experience* frontispiece (pl. 28),
{15}, xiii, 200-01, 206, 209-10, 325;
Experience title page (pl. 29), {16},
176, 206, 207, 208; *Introduction*
(*Exp.*) (pl. 30), {12}, 123n, 192,

206-08, 208n, 350n. *See also*
poem titles
Songs of Innocence, 78, 168, 185
sound, 95-98
Southey, Robert, 367
Spence, Joseph (*Polymetis*), 221, 224
(figs. 8 and 9), 233 (figs. 14 and 15)
spiders in *The Marriage of Heaven and
Hell*, 13, 13n
Spring, 203-04, 206, 208, 232
Squintum, 9, 14, 15
standing figure, 103, 103n, 177-79,
340-41, 344, 344n, 346, 346n
stars, 138-39, 346-47, 349, 352
states, 301; of man, 175
Stoning of Achan, The, 240
striding figure, 189
structure: of *America*, 87, 95-98, 100-05;
of *Europe*, 119; of *The Four Zoas*,
375, 379; of *The French Revolution*,
35, 51-52; of *Jerusalem*, 391-93,
408-10; of *Job*, 354-58; of *Night
Thoughts* I, 307-08; of *Urizen*,
163-65
subjective view of reality, 154-56
sun, of Imagination, xi-xii, xiv; of
revolution, 39, 50; association with
Los, 144, with Urizen, 249-50;
temporal or eternal, 396, 399-401,
404, 438n
supine figure, 189
Swedenborg, Emmanuel, 279n
Swinburne, Algernon Charles, 30
symmetry: of scenes in *The French
Revolution*, 36; defined, 146-47; kinds
of in *Urizen*, 147-62; in structure of
Urizen, 162-65; implications of in
Urizen, 165-67; in various works,
167-71; alternative to, 171-73; in
designs of *Night Thoughts* 13 and
16, 324; in the *Job* series, 354
syntax, 268-69, 386, 408-09

tactile release, 279
Taste (Foote), 6
Taylor, Thomas, 215n, 216
Tea at the Haymarket. See Foote,
Samuel
"terrific form," poetry of, 280
text and design, relation of, 62, 418,
419n. *See also* composite art
Tharmas, 377, 378, 379-80, 386, 388;
Spectre of, 193
Thel, Book of, 217-20, 226, 234n, 238;
title page, 176, 189; *plate 2*, 325;
plate 4, 319, 325
"then She bore Pale desire," 414, 415

Theotormon, 193
There is No Natural Religion, 179, 184, 190; *plate 1*, 192; *plate 7* (fig. 5, p. 180), 185
1 Thessalonians, 451
2 Thessalonians, 340
Thompson, D'Arcy Wentworth, 272-73
Tighe, Mary, 215n
time, views and uses of, 49n, 55, 371-73, 385-89, 409-10, 445, 447, 455, 456n
Tiriel, 132, 133
To Tirzah, 233n, 234, 240
To Winter, 98n
Todd, Ruthven, 411n, 436n
Tolley, Michael: comment, 105n
torsion, poetic, explained, 268-69; verbal, 273, 280
transcendence frustrated, 316-17
translucence, negative aspects, 79
Troy, escape from, 133n, 134n, 214; moment of fall, 183n, 389
Tyger, The, 166, 168
tyranny, art in service of, xii

ubi sunt theme, 457-58
Ulro, 396, 397
unity, devices for (in *The French Revolution*), 33
universe, as the "place" of *The Four Zoas*, 378
urban imagery, 413-14
"Urizen on the Stone of Night" (*America* 8), 79-80
Urizen, 109, 127, 181, 182, 373, 381, 425; visual contrast with Albion, 78; matching with Orc, 79-90, with Los, 152-53, 156; as old man, 98; in *Europe* frontispiece, 116-17; on first and last plates of *Urizen*, 148; subjective view of reality, 154; as creator, 158
  ambiguity in Blake's early design of, 248; association with sun, 249-50; as god of conventional religion, 252; Blake reconciled with, 254-55; as Prince of Light, 256; distinguished from Satan, 260-61
Urizen, Book of, 193, 194; bibliographical note, 147n-48n; types of symmetry (subject-object, 147-52; reason-senses, 152-57; nature-religion, 157-59; finite-infinite, 159-65); structure analyzed, 163-65; implications of symmetry, 165-67 (fig. 3, p. 164); four elements in, 169-71 (fig. 4, p. 170); language of, 172

plate 1, {51}, 148, 162; *plate 3*, 162, 189; *plate 5*, 180-81; *plate 6*, {57}, 156, 162, 176, 185, 190; *plate 7*, {59}, 152-53, 191; *plate 8*, {60}, 152-53; *plate 10*, 156, 162; *plate 13*, {53}, 149; *plate 14*, 162; *plate 15*, {56}, 150; *plate 16*, {61}, 153, 156; *plate 17*, {55}, 150, 162, 167; *plate 18*, {54}, 150, 162; *plate 20*, 162; *plate 22*, {62}, 153, 156, 176; *plate 23*, {58}, 162, 166; *plate 27*, 162; *plate 28*, {52}, 148, 162, 186
uroboros, 136n
Urthona, 126n, 249, 378, 437; daughter of, 121n; Spectre of, 251-52, 256, 260
ut pictura poesis, viii, 60-61, 85-89

Vala, 331, 411n, 445
Van Coxie, Michiel, 218, 220, 231n, 235 236, 241-42, and {119, 120}
vegetal designs, 201-03
veil, as metaphor for color, 76
Venus stance, 176, 192
verbal pictures, 34; torsion, 273, 280
vertical element of design, 199
Vien, Joseph-Marie, 223n, 234n
vine of prophecy, 284
Virgo associated with Vala, 445
vision: relation to clouds in *The French Revolution*, 53; intellectual, 92-93; character of Blake's thought, 264-65
Visions of the Daughters of Albion, "quoted" in *America*, 110; *America* as expansion of, 276; general paradigm, 270-71
  title page, {20}, 128n, 182n, 183, 189, 460n; *Argument*, {21}, 176, 189, 234; *plate 1*, 128n; *plate 3*, 184; *plate 4*, {22}, 193; *plate 6*, 101n, 124n; *plate 7*, 190; *plate 8* (finis), 183, 183n, 240; *tailpiece*, 302n
Vision of the Last Judgment, 34n, 53n, 190, 300n, 445, 447, 451, 453, 454

war, Blake's changed attitude, 254-55; ironic use as metaphor, 368-69
Warner, Janet A., 131n, 149n; notes and comments, 96n, 101n, 254n
Weisinger, Herbert, 282-83
Whitefield, George, 14-15
Whitman, Walt, 442
"Why should I care for the men of thames," 416-17
Wicksteed, Joseph H., 190, 200n, 202, 202n, 205n, 232n, 336n, 344, 354n, 356n, 393n, 397n, 400n, 402n, 405-06, 420n, 436n

Williams, Raymond, 416
wings, 221-24
woman, treatment in *Milton*, 364-69
Wordsworth, William, 226n, 440, 441
worm, 226, 319; worm-serpent-dragon, 176, 194

Yeats, William B., 442

Young, Edward, Blake's attitude toward, 305-07; personae of, in Blake's designs, 315-24

Zoas, 378; hierarchy and tyranny, 373, 381-82; as aspects of man, 382-83; as city-states, 423; seasonal aspects, 443
zodiacal imagery, 444n, 445-46

Index prepared by *Donald K. Moore*

Plates

{1} For Milton's *L'Allegro*, water color no. 6

{2} *Infant Joy, Songs of Innocence*

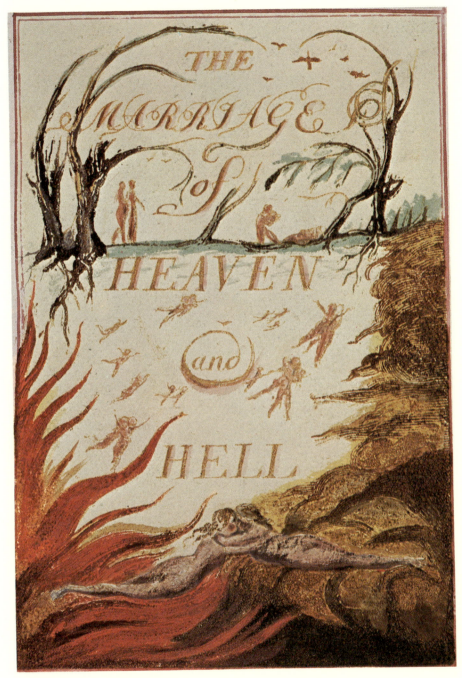

{3} *The Marriage of Heaven and Hell,* title page

The SICK ROSE

O Rose thou art sick.
The invisible worm.
That flies in the night
In the howling storm:

Has found out thy bed
Of crimson joy:
And his dark secret love
Does thy life destroy.

{4} *The Sick Rose, Songs of Experience*

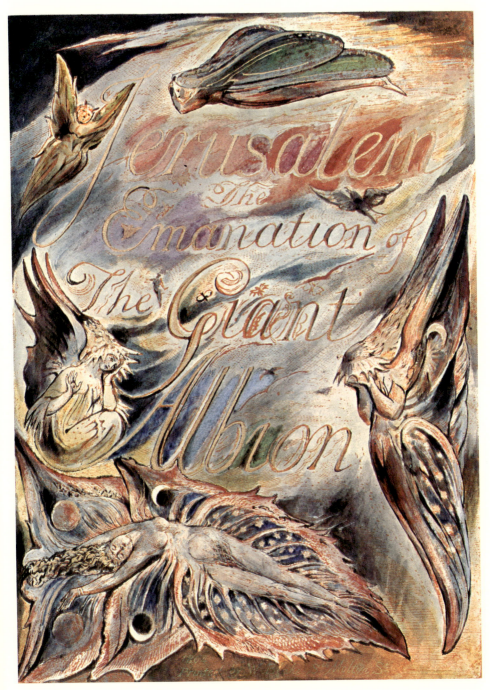

{5} *Jerusalem*, title page

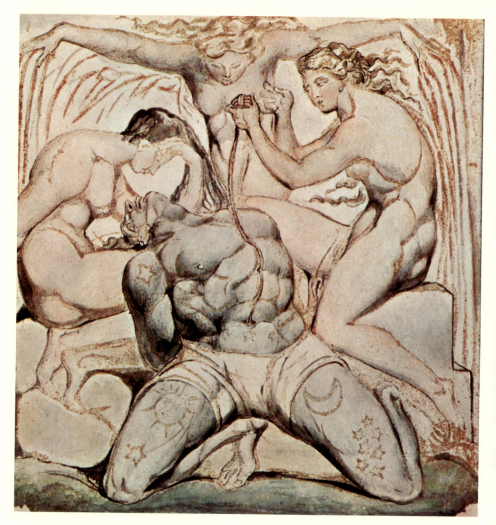

{6} *Jerusalem*, pl. 25, colored proof, detail

{7} *Jerusalem*, pl. 46[32], colored proof, detail

{8} *The Ancient of Days*, color print, variant of *Europe* frontispiece

{10} *Songs of Innocence*, frontispiece

{9} *Songs of Innocence and of Experience*, general title page

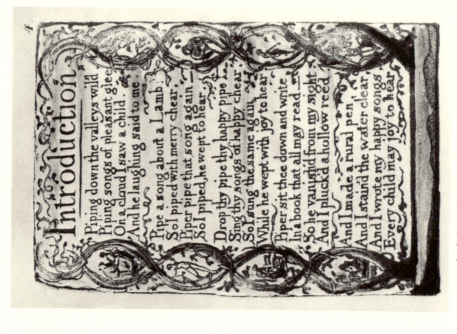

Introduction.

Piping down the valleys wild
Piping songs of pleasant glee
On a cloud I saw a child.
And he laughing said to me.

Pipe a song about a Lamb:
So I piped with merry chear,
Piper pipe that song again—
So I piped, he wept to hear.

Drop thy pipe thy happy pipe
Sing thy songs of happy chear,
So I sung the same again
While he wept with joy to hear.

Piper sit thee down and write
In a book that all may read—
So he vanish'd from my sight
And I pluck'd a hollow reed.

And I made a rural pen,
And I stain'd the water clear,
And I wrote my happy songs
Every child may joy to hear

{12} *Introduction, Songs of Innocence*

The Author & Printer W Blake

{11} *Songs of Innocence, title page*

{14} *The Divine Image, Songs of Innocence*

{13} *The Blossom, Songs of Innocence*

{15} *Songs of Experience*, frontispiece

{16} *Songs of Experience*, title page

{18} *London, Songs of Experience*

{17} *Infant Sorrow, Songs of Experience*

The Eye sees more than the Heart knows.

Printed by Will:^m Blake : 1793.

{20} *Visions of the Daughters of Albion*, title page

1 The ancient Poets animated all sensible objects
with Gods or Geniuses, calling them by the names and
adorning them with the properties of woods, rivers,
mountains, lakes, cities, nations, and whatever their
enlarged & numerous senses could perceive.

And particularly they studied the genius of each
city & country; placing it under its mental deity;

Till a system was formed, which some took advantage of & enslav'd the vulgar by attempting to
realize or abstract the mental deities from their
objects; thus began Priesthood.

Choosing forms of worship from poetic tales.

And at length they pronounced that the Gods
had orderd such things.

Thus men forgot that All deities reside
in the human breast.

{19} *The Marriage of Heaven and Hell*, pl. 11

The Argument

I loved Theotormon
And I was not ashamed
I trembled in my virgin fears
And I hid in Leutha's vale;

I plucked Leutha's flower,
And I rose up from the vale;
But the terrible thunders tare
My virgin mantle in twain.

{21} *Visions of the Daughters of Albion, Argument*

Where shadows dwell the wretched
Drunken with woe forgotten, and shut up from cold despair.

Tell me where dwell the thoughts forgotten till thou call them forth.
Tell me where dwell the joys of old! & where the ancient loves;
And when will they renew again & the night of oblivion past?
That I might traverse times & spaces far remote and bring
Comforts into a present sorrow and a night of pain.
Where goest thou O thought! to what remote land is thy flight?
If thou returnest to the present moment of affliction
Wilt thou bring comforts on thy wings, and dews and honey and balm;
Or poison from the desert wilds, from the eyes of the envier.

Then Bromion said: and shook the cavern with his lamentation

Thou knowest that the ancient trees seen by thine eyes have fruit;
But knowest thou that trees and fruits flourish upon the earth
To gratify senses unknown? trees beasts and birds unknown;
Unknown, not unperceiv'd, spread in the infinite microscope,
In places yet unvisited by the voyager, and in worlds
Over another kind of seas, and in atmospheres unknown:
Ah! are there other wars, beside the wars of sword and fire!
And are there other sorrows, beside the sorrows of poverty!
And are there other joys, beside the joys of riches and ease?
And is there not one law for both the lion and the ox?
And is there not eternal fire, and eternal chains!
To bind the phantoms of existence from eternal life?

Then Oothoon waited silent all the day, and all the night.

{22} *Visions of the Daughters of Albion, pl. 4*

{23} *A Breach in a City the Morning after the Battle*, water color, earliest version

{24} *America,* frontispiece

{25} *America,* title page

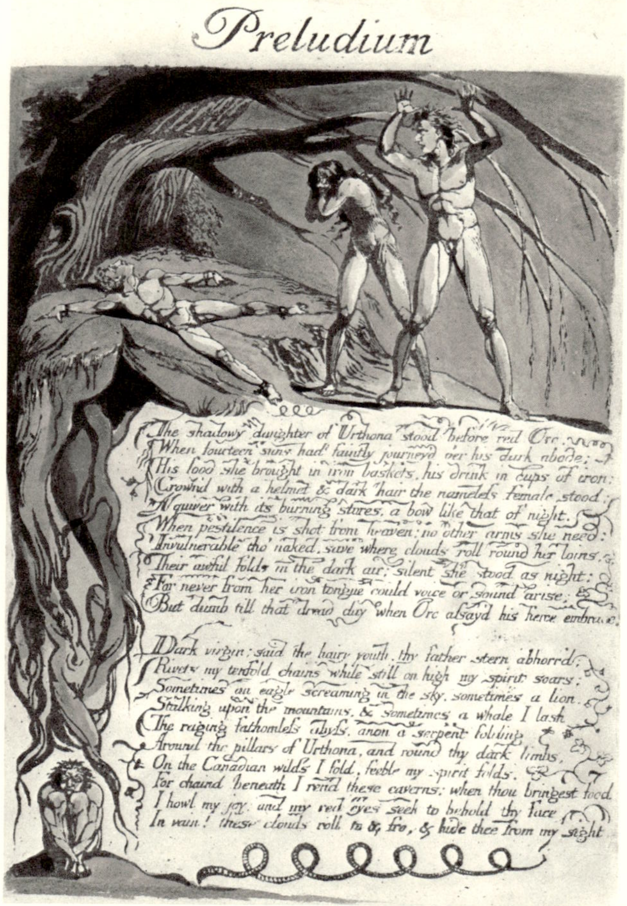

{26} *America*, Preludium, pl. 1

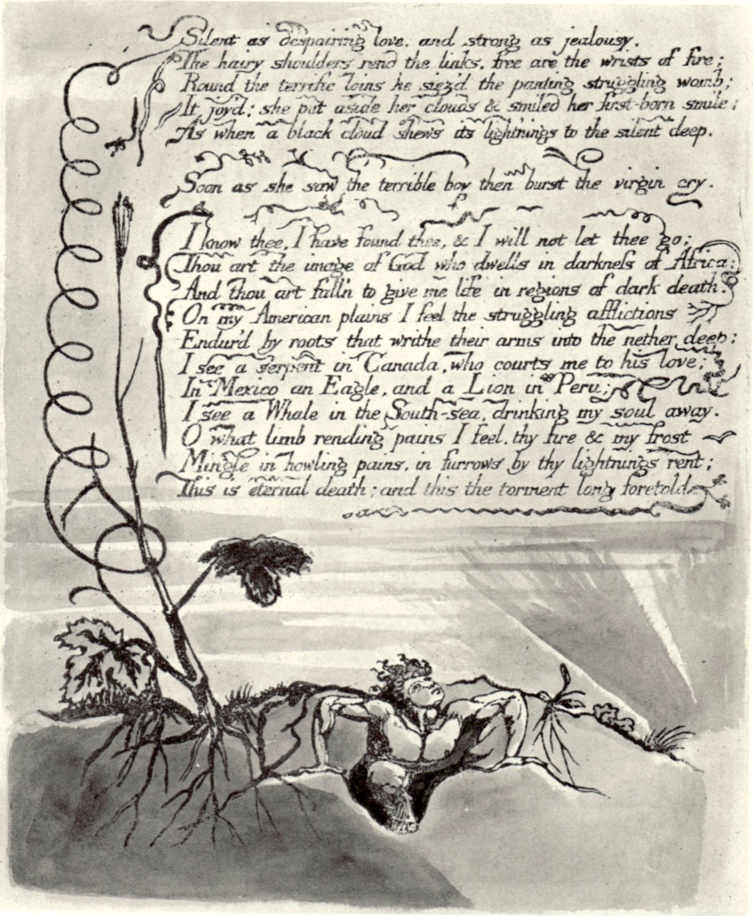

{27} *America*, Preludium, pl. 2

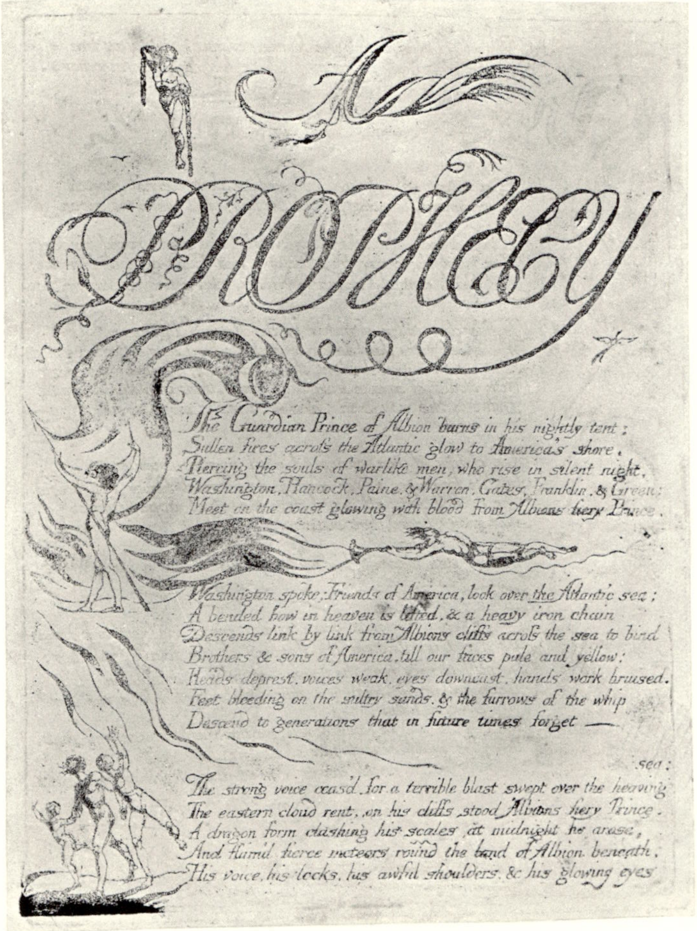

{28} *America*, pl. a (canceled)

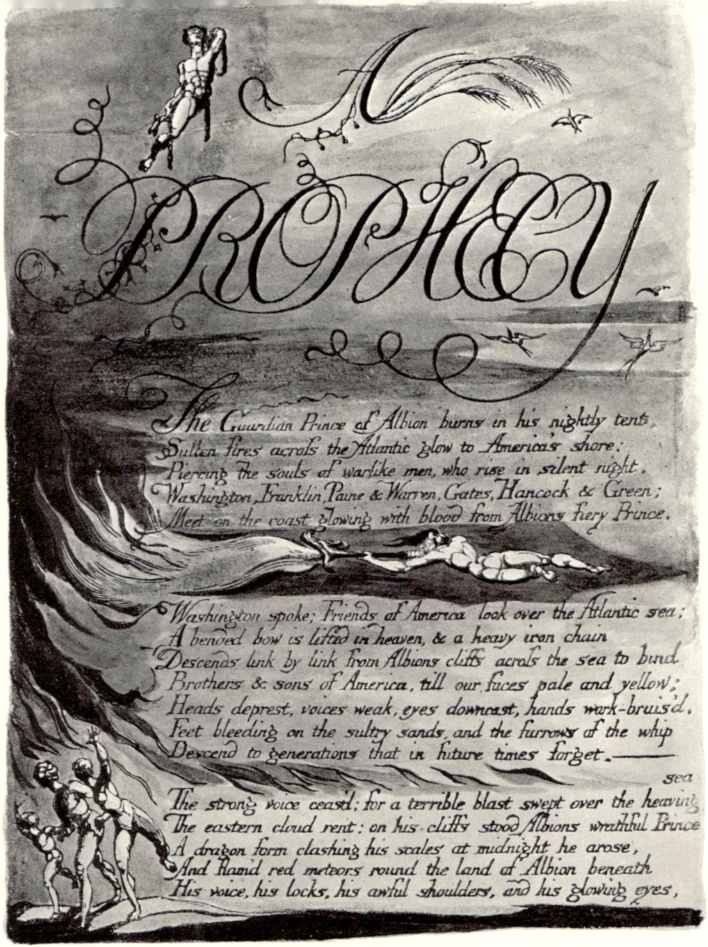

{29} *America*, pl. 3

Appear to the Americans upon the cloudy night.

Solemn heave the Atlantic waves between the gloomy nations
Swelling, belching from its deeps red clouds & raging fires!
Albion is sick! America faints! enrag'd the Zenith grew.
As human blood shooting its veins all round the orbed heaven
Red rose the clouds from the Atlantic in vast wheels of blood
And in the red clouds rose a Wonder o'er the Atlantic sea;
Intense! naked! a Human fire fierce glowing, as the wedge
Of iron heated in the furnace; his terrible limbs were fire
With myriads of cloudy terrors banners dark & towers
Surrounded; heat but not light went thro' the murky atmo-
sphere

The King of England looking westward trembles at the vision

{31} *America, pl. 4*

Reveal the dragon thro' the heavens, coursing swift as fire
To the close hall of counsel, where his Angel form renews.

In a sweet vale shelter'd with cedars, that eternal stretch
Their unmovd branches, stood the hall; built when the moon
shot forth,
In that dread night when Urizen call'd the stars round his feet;
Then burst the center from its orb, and found a place beneath;
And Earth conglob'd, in narrow room, roll'd round its sulphur Sun.

To this deep valley situated by the flowing Thames;
Where George the third holds council. & his Lords & Commons meet:
Shut out from mortal sight the Angel came; the vale was dark
With clouds of smoke from the Atlantic, that in volumes roll'd
Between the mountains, dismal visions mope around the
house.

On chairs of iron, canopied with mystic ornaments
Of life by magic power condens'd; infernal forms art-bound
The council sat; all rose before the aged apparition;
His snowy beard that streams like lambent flames down his
wide breast
Wetting with tears, & his white garments cast a wintry light.

Then as arm'd clouds arise terrific round the northern drum;
The world is silent at the flapping of the folding banners;
So still terrors rent the house: as when the solemn globe
Launch'd to the unknown shore, while Sotha held the north-
ern helm,
Till to that void it came & fell; so the dark house was rent.
The valley moved beneath; its shining pillars split in twain,
And its roots crack across with shrieks on shrieks on th' angelic seats.

{30} *America, pl. b* (canceled)

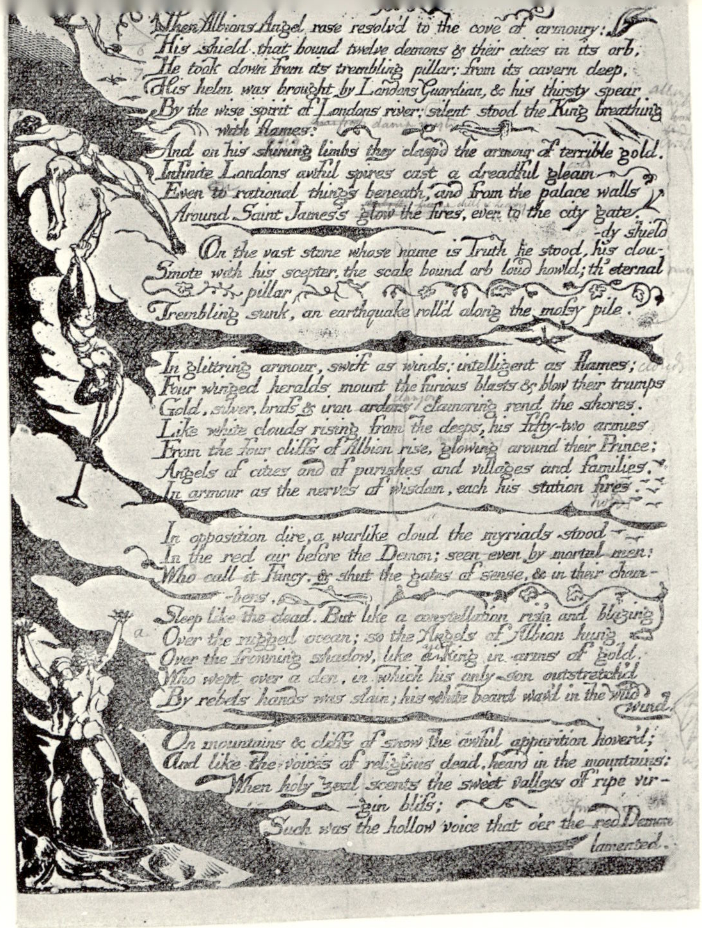

{32} *America*, pl. c (canceled)

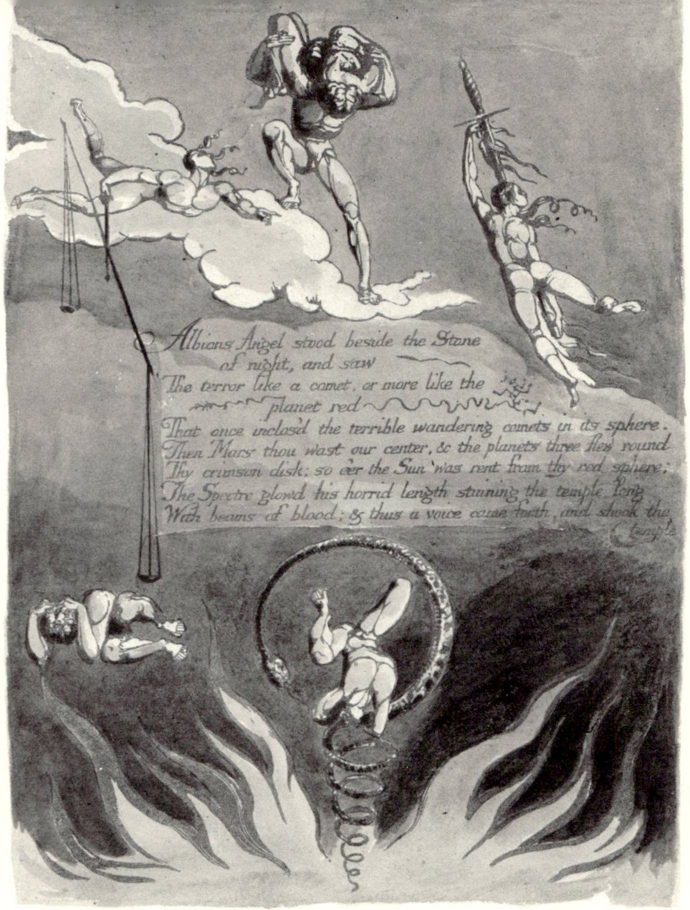

{33} *America*, pl. 5

In thunders ends the voice. Then Albions Angel wrathful burnt
Beside the Stone of Night; and like the Eternal Lions howl
In famine & war, reply'd. Art thou not Orc, who serpent-form'd
Stands at the gate of Enitharmon to devour her children;
Blasphemous Demon, Antichrist, hater of Dignities;
Lover of wild rebellion, and transgresser of Gods Law;
Why dost thou come to Angels eyes in this terrific form?

The morning comes, the night decays, the watchmen leave their stations;
The grave is burst, the spices shed, the linen wrapped up;
The bones of death, the cov'ring clay, the sinews shrunk & dry'd.
Reviving shake, inspiring move, breathing! awakening!
Spring like redeemed captives when their bonds & bars are burst;
Let the slave grinding at the mill, run out into the field:
Let him look up into the heavens & laugh in the bright air;
Let the inchained soul shut up in darkness and in sighing,
Whose face has never seen a smile in thirty weary years;
Rise and look out, his chains are loose, his dungeon doors are open.
And let his wife and children return from the opressors scourge;
They look behind at every step & believe it is a dream.
Singing. The Sun has left his blackness, & has found a fresher morning
And the fair Moon rejoices in the clear & cloudless night;
For Empire is no more, and now the Lion & Wolf shall cease.

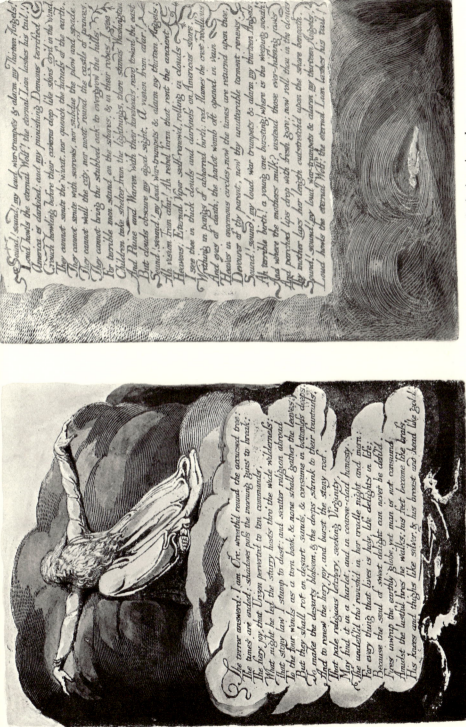

{36} *America*, pl. 8

{37} *America*, pl. 9

Fiery the Angels rose, & as they rose deep thunder roll'd
Around their shores: indignant burning with the fires of Orc
And Bostons Angel cried aloud as they flew thro' the dark night.

He cried: Why trembles honesty and like a murderer,
Why seeks he refuge from the frowns of his immortal station
Must the generous tremble & leave his joy, to the idle: to
the pestilence!
That mock him? who commanded this? what God? what Angel!
To keep the gen'rous from experience till the ungenerous
Are unrestraind performers of the energies of nature;
Till pity is become a trade, and generosity a science,
That men get rich by, & the sandy desert is giv'n to the strong
What God is he, writes laws of peace, & clothes him in a tempest
What pitying Angel lusts for tears, and fans himself with sighs
What crawling villain preaches abstinence & wraps himself
In fat of lambs? no more I follow, no more obedience pay.

{10} *America pl 11*

Thus wept the Angel voice, & as he wept the terrible blasts
Of trumpets, blew a loud alarm across the Atlantic deep.
No trumpets answer; no reply of clarions or of fifes,
Silent the Colonies remain and refuse the loud alarm.

On those vast shady hills between America & Albions shore;
Now barred out by the Atlantic sea: call'd Atlantean hills:
Because from their bright summits you may pass to the Golden world
An ancient palace, archetype of mighty Emperies,
Rears its immortal pinnacles, built in the forest of God
By Ariston the king of beauty for his stolen bride.

Here on their magic seats the thirteen Angels sat perturb'd
For clouds from the Atlantic hover o'er the solemn roof.

{38} *America, pl. 10*

{41} *America*, pl. 13

{40} *America*, pl. 12

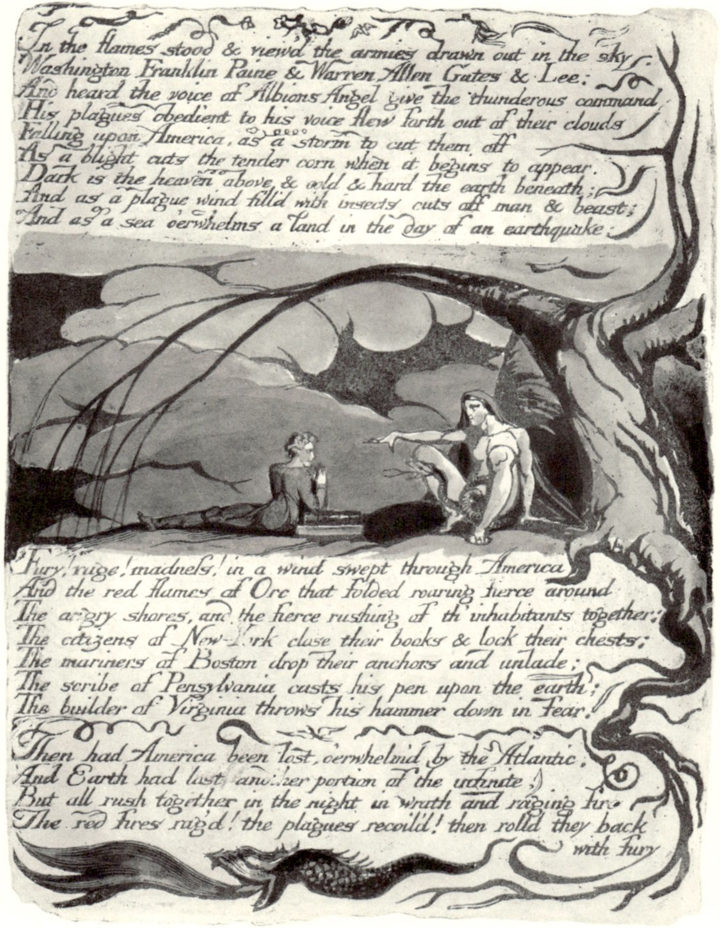

{42} *America*, pl. 14

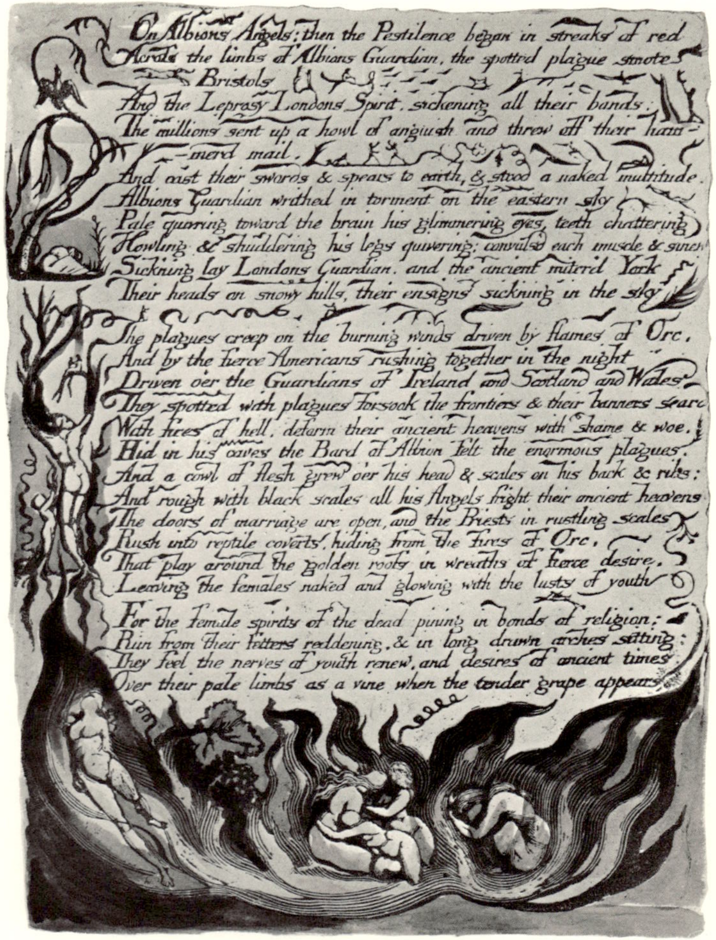

{43} *America*, pl. 15

Over the hills, the vales, the cities, rage the red flames fierce;
The Heavens melted from north to south; and Urizen who sat
Above all heavens in thunders' wrap'd, emerg'd his leprous head,
From out his holy shrine, his tears in deluge piteous
Falling into the deep sublime! flag'd with grey-brow'd snows
And thunderous visages, his jealous wings wav'd over the deep;
Weeping in dismal howling woe he dark descended howling
Around the smitten bands, clothed in tears & trembling shuddring cold.
His stored snows he poured forth, and his icy magazines
He open'd on the deep, and on the Atlantic sea white shivring.
Leprous his limbs, all over white, and hoary was his visage.
Weeping in dismal howlings before the stern Americans
Hiding the Demon red with clouds & cold mists from the earth:
Till Angels & weak men twelve years should govern oer the strong;
And then their end should come, when France recievd the Demons light.

Still shudderings shook the heav'nly thrones! France Spain & Italy,
In terror view'd the bands of Albion, and the ancient Guardians
Fainting upon the elements, smitten with their own plagues
They slow advance to shut the five gates of their law-built heaven
Filled with blasting fancies and with mildews of despair
With fierce disease and lust, unable to stem the fires of Orc:
But the five gates were consum'd, & their bolts and hinges melted
And the fierce flames burnt round the heavens, & round the abodes of
men

{44} *America*, pl. 16

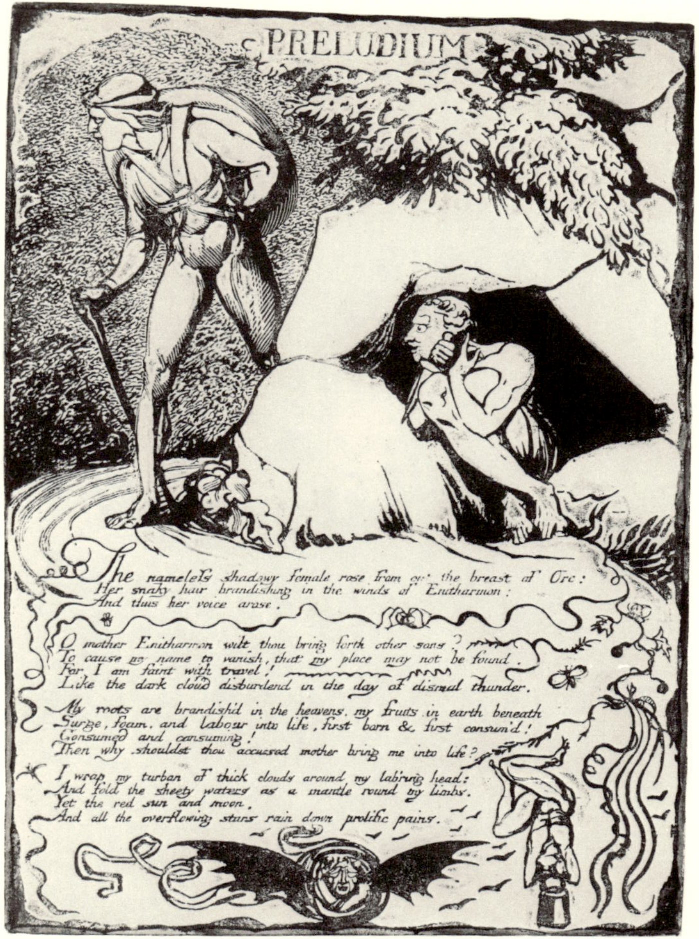

{45} *Europe*, Preludium, pl. 1

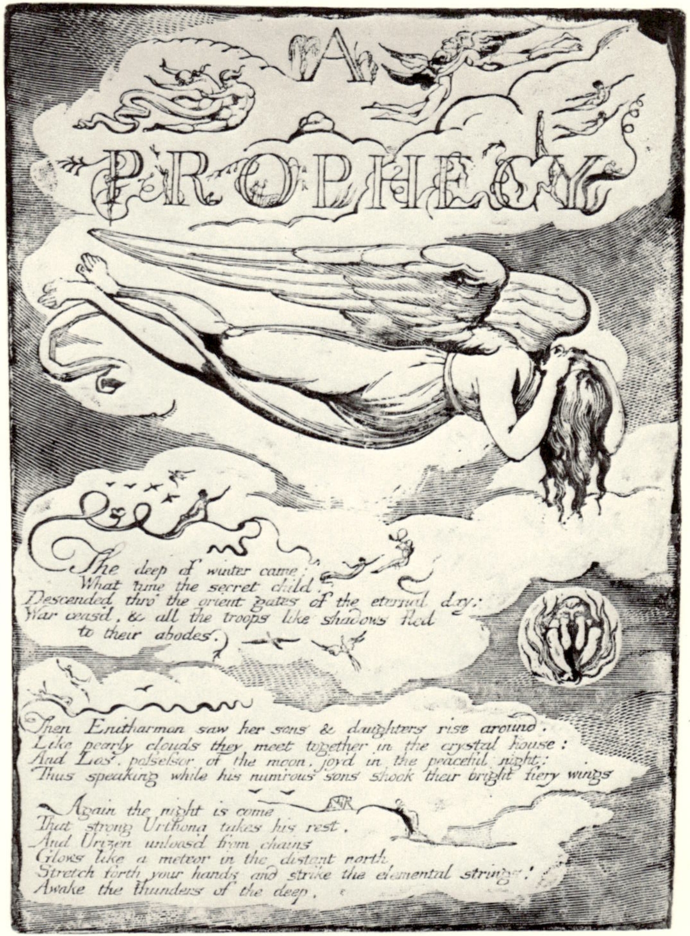

{46} *Europe*, pl. 3

The shrill winds wake!
Till all the sons of Urizen look out and envy Los:
Sieze all the spirits of life, and bind
Their warbling joys to our loud strings
Bind all the nourishing sweets of earth
To give us bliss, that we may drink the sparkling wine of Los
And let us laugh at war,
Despising toil and care,
Because the days and nights of joy, in lucky hours renew.

Arise O Orc from thy deep den,
First born of Enitharmon rise!
And we will crown thy head with garlands of the ruddy vine;
For now thou art bound;
And I may see thee in the hour of bliss, my eldest born.

The horrent Demon rose, surrounded with red stars of fire,
Whirling about in furious circles round the immortal fiend.

Then Enitharmon down descended into his red light,
And thus her woes rose to her children, the distant heavens reply.

{47} *Europe, pl. 4*

{48} *Europe, pl. 5*

{49} *Europe*, pl. 8, color print

{50} *Europe*, pl. 12

{52} *Book of Urizen,* pl. 28

{51} *Book of Urizen,* pl. 1

{54} *Book of Urizen, pl.* 18

{53} *Book of Urizen, pl.* 13

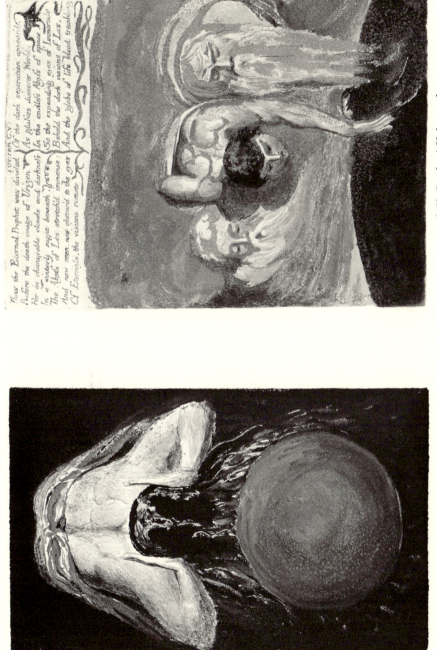

Thus the Eternal Prophet was divided
Before the death image of Urizen
For in changeable clouds and darkness
In a winterly night beneath.
The Abyss of Los stretchd immense:
And now seen, now obscurd to the eyes
Of Eternals, the visions remote

JUrizen CV:
Of the dark separation appeard
As glasses discover Worlds
In the endless Abyss of space
So the expanding eyes of Immortals
Beheld the dark visions of Los
And the globe of life blood trembling

{56} *Book of Urizen,* pl. 15

{55} *Book of Urizen,* pl. 17

{58} *Book of Urizen*, pl. 23

{57} *Book of Urizen*, pl. 6

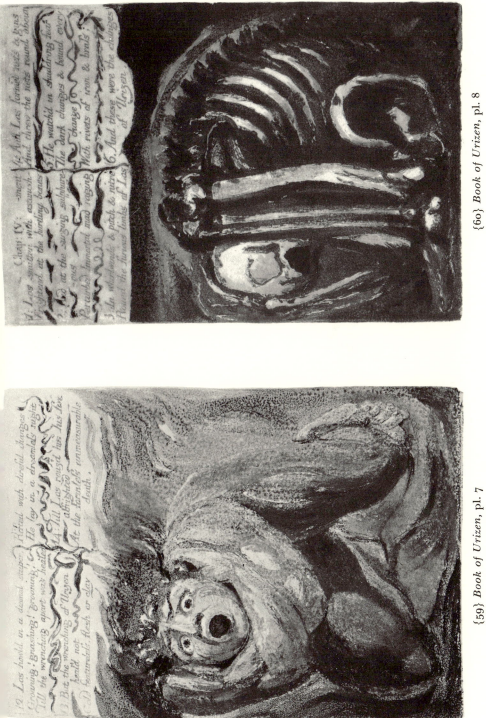

{59} *Book of Urizen*, pl. 7   {60} *Book of Urizen*, pl. 8

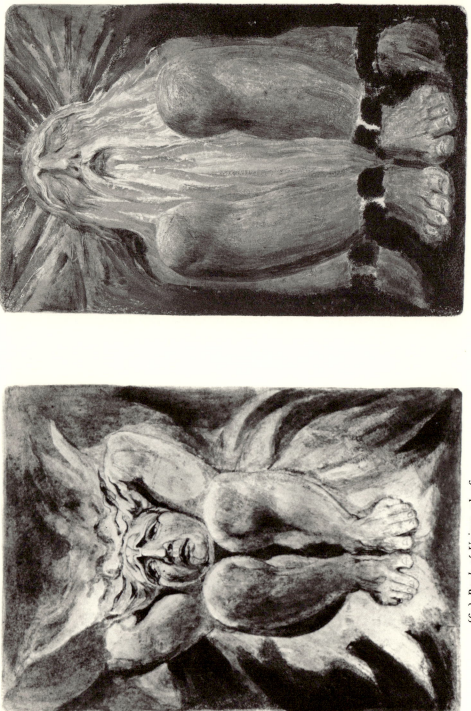

{62} *Book of Urizen*, pl. 22

{61} *Book of Urizen*, pl. 16

{63} *The Great Red Dragon and the Woman Clothed with the Sun,*
water color, for Revelation 12:4

{65} For Gray's *Ode*, no. 2

{64} For Gray's *Ode on the Death of a Favourite Cat*, water color no. 1

{67} For Gray's *Ode*, no. 4

{66} For Gray's *Ode*, no. 3

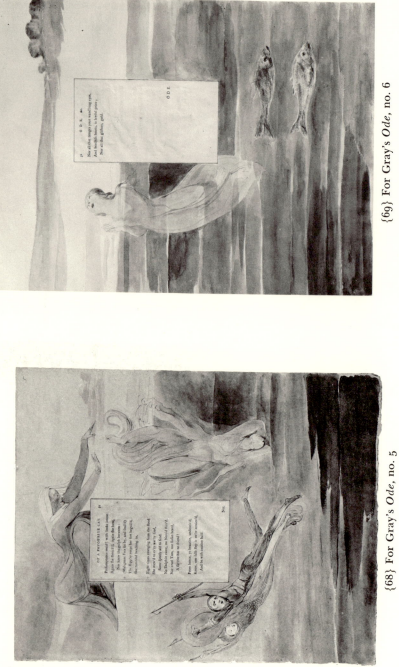

{69} For Gray's *Ode*, no. 6

{68} For Gray's *Ode*, no. 5

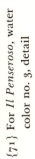

{71} For *Il Penseroso,* water color no. 3, detail

{72} For *L'Allegro,* no. 1, engraving, detail

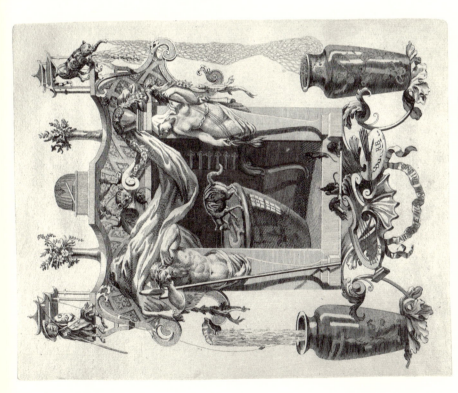

{70} Richard Bentley, for Gray's Ode. From *Designs . . . for Six Poems by Mr. Thomas Gray*

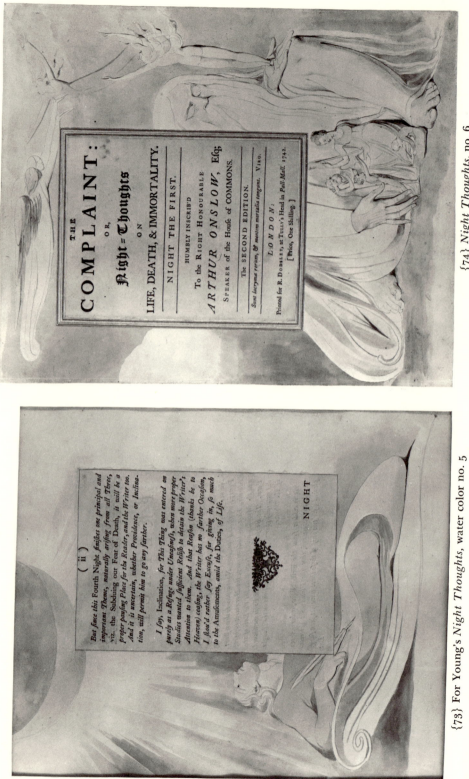

{74} *Night Thoughts, no. 6*

{73} For Young's *Night Thoughts*, water color no. 5

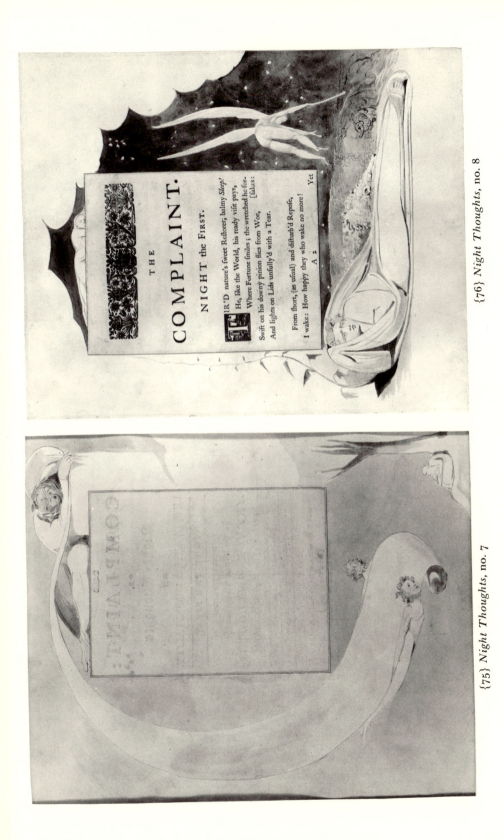

{76} *Night Thoughts*, no. 8

{75} *Night Thoughts*, no. 7

(5)

An aweful pause! prophetic of her End.
And let her prophecy be soon fulfill'd;
Fate! drop the Curtain; I can lose no more.

Silence, and Darkness! solemn Sisters! Twins
From antient Night, who nurse the tender Thought
To Reason, and on reason build Resolve,
(That column of true Majesty in man)   30
Assist me: I will thank you in the Grave;
The grave, your Kingdom: There this Frame shall fall
A victim sacred to your dreary shrine:
But what are Ye? Thou, who didst put to flight
Primeval Silence, when the Morning Stars
Exulting, shouted o'er the rising Ball;
O thou! whose Word from solid Darkness struck
That spark, the Sun; strike Wisdom from my soul;
My soul which flies to thee, her Truth, her Treasure; 40
As misers to their Gold, while others rest.

Thro'

{78} Night Thoughts, no. 10

(4)

Yet that were vain, if Dreams infest the Grave.
I wake, emerging from a sea of Dreams
Tumultuous; where my wreck'd, desponding Thought
From wave to wave of fancy'd Misery,
At random drove, her helm of Reason lost;
Tho' now restor'd, 'tis only Change of pain,
A bitter change; severer for severe:
The Day too short for my Distress! and Night
Even in the Zenith of her dark Domain,
Is Sun-shine, to the colour of my Fate.   11

Night, sable Goddess! from her Ebon throne,
In rayless Majesty, now stretches forth
Her leaden Scepter o'er a slumbering world: 20
Silence, how dead? and Darkness how profound?
Nor Eye, nor list'ning Ear an object finds;
Creation sleeps. 'Tis, as the general Pulse
Of life stood still, and Nature made a Pause;

An

{77} Night Thoughts, no. 9

(6)

Thro' this Opaque of *Nature*, and of *Soul*,
This double Night, tranfmit one pitying ray,
To lighten, and to chear: O lead my Mind,
(A Mind that fain would wander from its Woe,)
Lead it thro' various fcenes of *Life and Death*,
And from each fcene, the nobleft Truths infpire;
Nor lefs infpire my *Conduct*, than my *Song*;
Teach my beft Reafon, Reafon; my beft Will
Teach Rectitude; and fix my firm Refolve   50
Wifdom to wed, and pay her long Arrear.
Nor let the vial of thy Vengeance pour'd
On this devoted head, be pour'd in vain.

The Bell ftrikes *One*. We take no note of Time,
But from its Lofs. To give it then a Tongue,
Is wife in man. As if an Angel fpoke,
I feel the folemn Sound. If heard aright,

I1

{79} *Night Thoughts*, no. 11

(7)

It is the *Knell* of my departed Hours;
Where are they? with the years beyond the Flood:
It is the *Signal* that demands Difpatch;
How Much is to be done? my Hopes and Fears
Start up alarm'd, and o'er life's narrow Verge
Look down——on what? a fathomlefs Abyfs;
A dread Eternity! how furely mine!
And can Eternity belong to me,
Poor Penfioner on the bounties of an Hour?

How poor? how rich? how abject? how auguft?
How complicate? how wonderful is Man?
How pafling wonder He, who made him fuch?
Who center'd in our make fuch ftrange Extremes? 70
From different Natures, marvelloufly mixt,
Connection exquifite of diftant Worlds!
Diftinguifht *Link* in Being's endlefs Chain!
Midway from *Nothing* to the *Deity*!

A Beam

{80} *Night Thoughts*, no. 12

(9)

O'er Fairy Fields; or mourn'd along the gloom
Of pathless Woods; or down the craggy Steep
Hurl'd headlong, swam with pain the mantled Pool;
Or scal'd the Cliff; or danc'd on hollow Winds,
With antic Shapes, wild Natives of the Brain?
Her ceaseless Flight, tho' devious, speaks her Nature
Of subtler Essence than the trodden Clod;
Active, aerial, tow'ring, unconfin'd,
Unfetter'd with her gross Companion's fall: 100
Ev'n silent Night proclaims my Soul immortal:
Ev'n silent Night proclaims eternal Day:
For human weal, Heaven husbands all events,
Dull Sleep instructs, nor sport vain Dreams in vain.

Why then *their* Loss deplore, that are not lost?
Why wanders wretched Thought their tombs around,
In infidel distress? are *Angels* there?
Slumbers, rak'd up in dust, Etherial fire?

   B   They

{82} *Night Thoughts, no.* 14

(8)

A Beam etherial sully'd, and absorpt!
Tho' sully'd, and dishonour'd, still Divine!
Dim Miniature of Greatness absolute!
An Heir of Glory! a frail Child of Dust!
Helpless Immortal! Insect *infinite!*
A Worm! a God! I tremble at myself,   80
And in myself am lost! At home a Stranger,
Thought wanders up and down, surpriz'd, aghast,
And wond'ring at her *own:* How Reason reels?
O what a Miracle to man is man,
Triumphantly distrest? what Joy, what Dread?
Alternately transported, and alarm'd!
What can preserve my Life? or what destroy?
An Angel's arm can't snatch me from the Grave;
Legions of Angels can't confine me There.
'Tis past Conjecture; all things rise in Proof: 90
While o'er my limbs *Sleep's* soft dominion spread,
What, tho' my soul phantastic Measures trod,

       O'er

{81} *Night Thoughts, no.* 13

(11)

And make us Embryos of Existence free.
From *real* life, but little more remote
Is *He*, not yet a candidate for Light,
The *future* Embryo, slumbering in his Sire.
Embryos we must be, till we burst the Shell,
Yon ambient, azure shell, and spring to Life,
The life of Gods : O Transport ! and of Man.

Yet man, fool man ! here burys all his Thoughts ;
Inters celestial Hopes without one Sigh :
Prisoner of Earth, and pent beneath the Moon,
Here pinions all his Wishes ; wing'd by Heaven
To fly at infinite ; and reach it there,
Where *Seraphs* gather Immortality,
On life's fair Tree, fast by the throne of God :
What golden Joys ambrosial clust'ring glow,
In *His* full beam, and ripen for the Just,
Where momentary Ages are no more?

Where

130

140

B 2

(12)

Where Time, and Pain, and Chance and Death expire?
And is it in the Flight of threescore years,
To push Eternity from human Thought,
And smother souls immortal in the Dust?
A soul immortal, spending all her Fires,
Wasting her strength in strenuous Idleness,
Thrown into Tumult, raptur'd, or alarm'd,
At ought this scene can threaten, or indulge,
Resembles *Ocean* into Tempest wrought,
To waft a Feather, or to drown a Fly.

Where falls this Censure? It o'erwhelms myself.
How was my Heart encrusted by the World?
O how self-fetter'd was my groveling Soul?
How, like a Worm, was I wrapt round and round
In silken thought, which reptile *Fancy* spun,
Till darken'd *Reason* lay quite clouded o'er

With

150

2

(15)

Of sweet domestic Comfort, and cuts down
The fairest bloom of sublunary Bliss.

Bliss! sublunary Bliss! proud words! and vain!
Implicit Treason to divine Decree!
A bold invasion of the rights of Heaven!
I clasp'd the Phantoms, and I found them Air. 200
O had I weigh'd it e'er my fond Embrace!
What darts of Agony had mis'd my heart?
Death! Great Proprietor of all! 'Tis thine
To tread our Empire, and to quench the Stars;
The Sun himself by thy permission shines,
And, one day, thou shalt pluck him from his sphere.
Amid such mighty Plunder, why exhaust
Thy *partial* Quiver on a-Mark so mean?
Why, thy *peculiar* rancor wreck'd on me? 210
Infatiate Archer! could not One suffice?
Thy shaft flew thrice, and thrice my Peace was slain;
                                                    And
I

{86} *Night Thoughts*, no. 20

(13)

With soft conceit of endless Comfort *here*,
Nor yet put forth her Wings to reach the skies?

Night-visions may befriend, (as sung above)
Our waking Dreams are fatal: How I dreamt
Of things Impossible? (could Sleep do more?)
Of Joys perpetual in perpetual Change?
Of stable Pleasures on the rolling Wave?
Eternal Sun-shine in the Storms of life?
How richly were my noon-tide Trances hung
With gorgeous Tapestries of pictur'd joys?
Joy behind joy, in endless Perspective! 170
Till at Death's Toll, whose restless Iron tongue
Calls daily for his Millions at a meal,
Starting I woke, and found myself undone?
Where now my Frenzy's pompous Furniture?
The *cobweb'd* Cottage with its ragged wall
Of mould'ring mud, is *Royalty* to me!
The *Spider's* most attenuated Thread

{85} *Night Thoughts*, no. 18

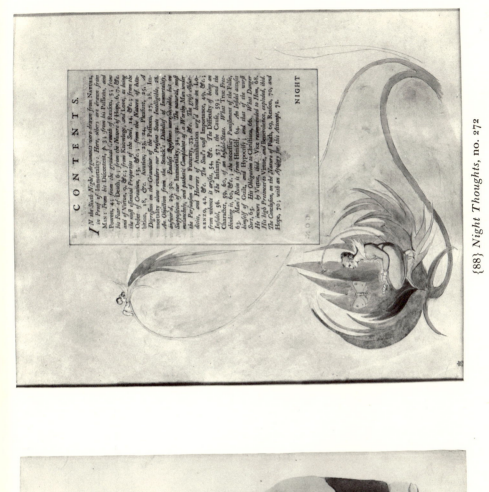

{88} *Night Thoughts*, no. 272

{87} *Night Thoughts*, no. 34

Vala incircle round the furnaces where Luvah was clos'd
In joy she heard his howlings & forgot he was her Luvah
With whom she walkd in bliss, in times of innocence & youth

Hear ye the voice of Luvah from the furnaces of Urizen

If I indeed am Valas King & ye O Sons of Men
The workmanship of Luvahs hands: in times of Everlasting
When I calld forth the Earth-worm from the cold & dark obscure
I nurturd her I fed her with my rains & dews, she grew
A scaled Serpent, yet I fed her tho' she hated me
Day after day she fed upon the mountains in Luvahs sight 50
I brought her thro' the Wilderness, a dry & thirsty land
And I commanded springs to rise for her in the black desart
Till she became a Dragon winged bright & poisonous
I opend all the floodgates of the heavens to quench her thirst

And

{89} *The Four Zoas*, p. 26 (infra-red photograph)

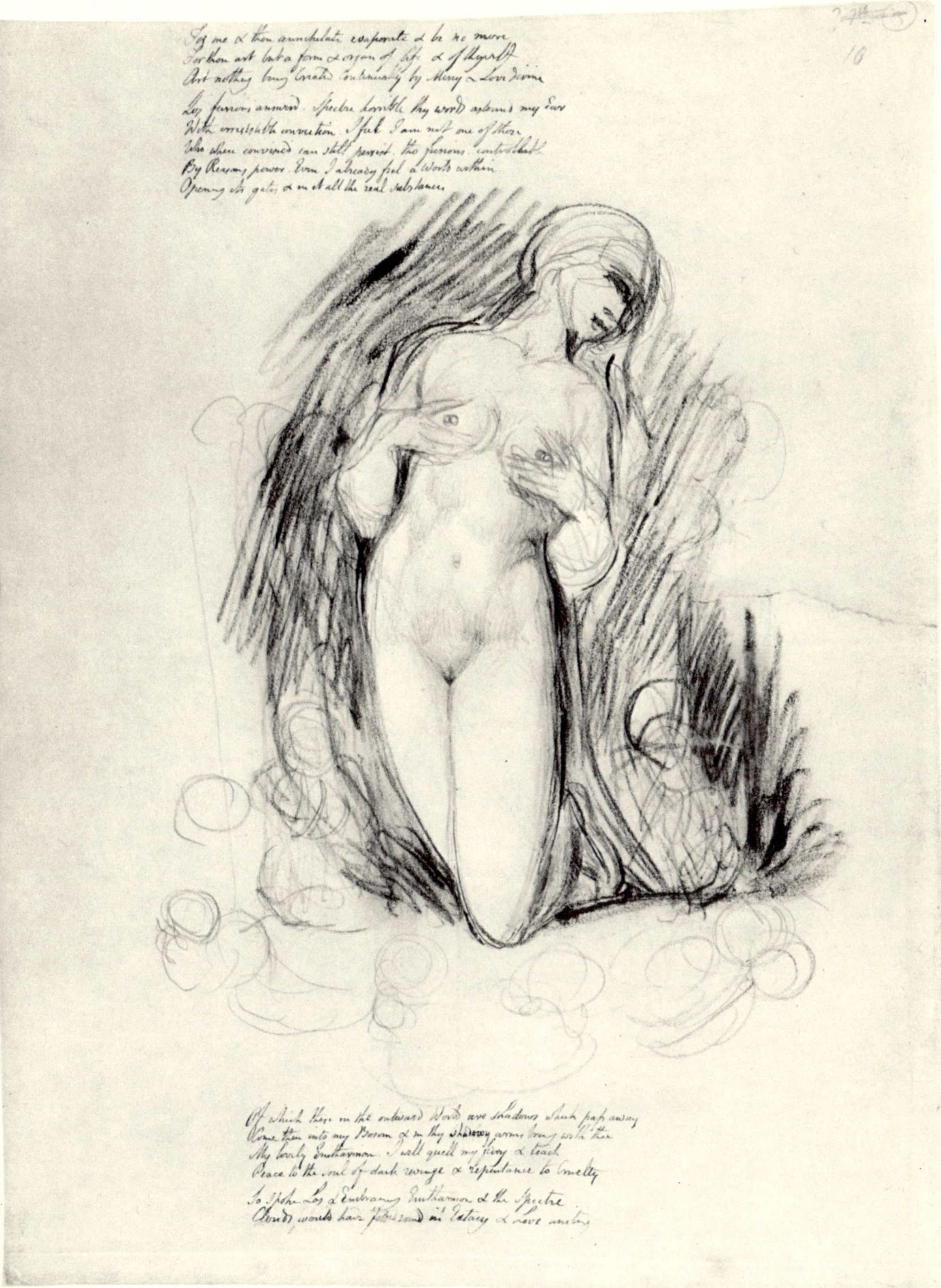

{90} *The Four Zoas*, p. 86 (infra-red photograph)

{92} *Milton*, pl. 29

{91} *Albion rose*, engraving

{93} *The House of Death*, color print

{94} *Elohim Creating Adam*, color print

{95} *Jerusalem*, pl. 28, proof copy, detail

{96} *Jerusalem*, pl. 53, detail

And One stood forth from the Divine Family & said

I feel my Spectre rising upon me! Albion. arouze thyself!
Why dost thou thunder with frozen Spectrous wrath against us?
The Spectre is, in Giant Man; insane, and most deformd.
Thou wilt certainly provoke my Spectre against thine in fury!
He has a Sepulcher hewn out of a Rock ready for thee:
And a Death of Eight thousand years forgd by thyself, upon
The point of his Spear! if thou persistest to forbid with Laws
Our Emanations, and to attack our secret supreme delights

So Los spoke: But when he saw blue death in Albions feet
Again he joind the Divine Body, following merciful:
While Albion fled more indignant; revengeful covering

{97} *Jerusalem*, pl. 33[37]

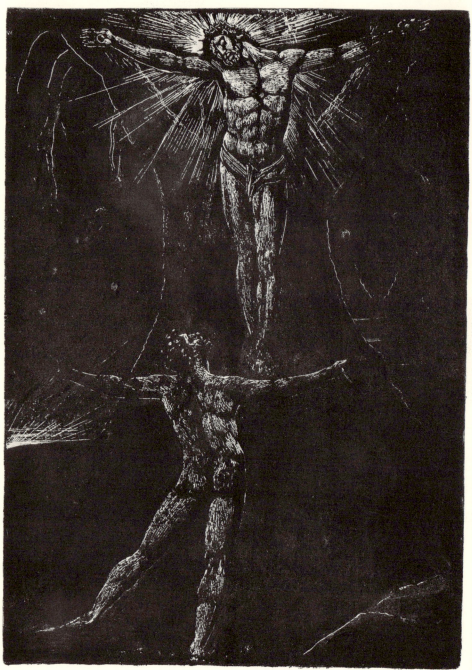

{98} *Jerusalem*, pl. 76

{99} *Jerusalem*, pl. 78, detail

{100} *Jerusalem*, pl. 84, detail

{101} *Jerusalem*, pl. 95, detail

{102} *Jerusalem*, pl. 97, detail

All Human Forms identified even Tree Metal Earth & Stone, all
Human Forms identified living going forth & returning wearied
Into the Planetary lives of Years Months Days & Hours reposing
And then Awaking into his Bosom in the Life of Immortality.
And I heard the Name of their Emanations they are named Jerusalem

The End of The Song
of Jerusalem

{103} *Jerusalem*, pl. 99

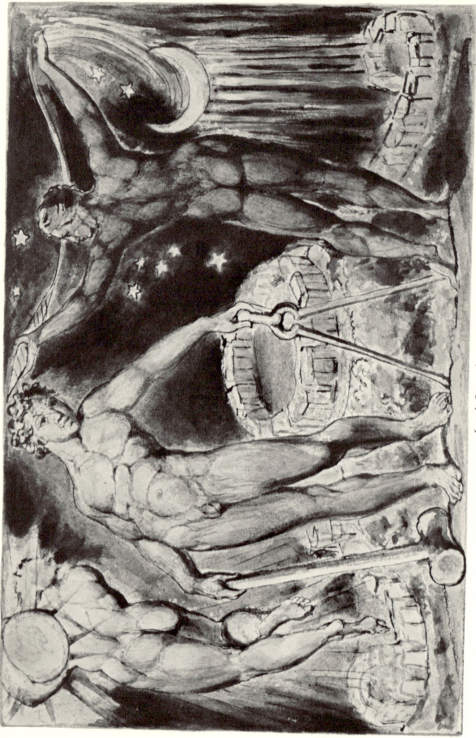

{104} *Jerusalem*, pl. 100

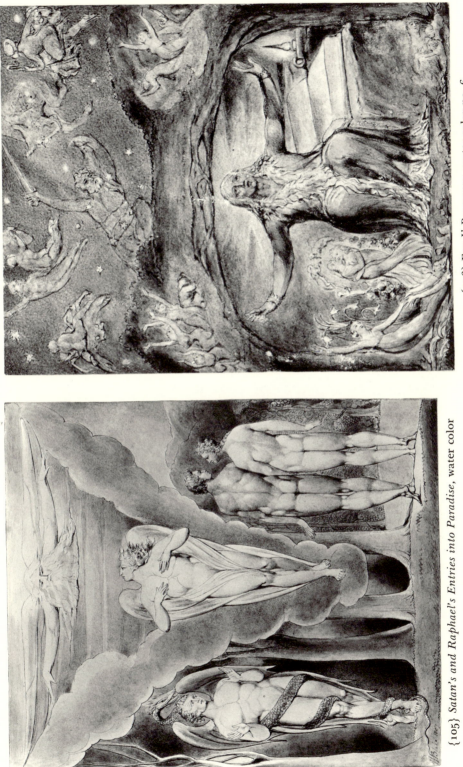

{106} For *Il Penseroso*, water color no. 6

{105} *Satan's and Raphael's Entries into Paradise*, water color

{107} For Dante's *Inferno*, no. 10, engraving

{108} *Satan Exulting Over Eve,* color print

Shall mortal Man be more Just than God? Shall a Man be more Pure than his Maker? Behold he putteth no trust in his Saints & his Angels he chargeth with folly

Then a Spirit passed before my face the hair of my flesh stood up

WBlake invenit & sculpsit

{109} *Illustrations for the Book of Job, pl. 9*

My bones are pierced in me in the
night season & my sinews
take no rest

My skin is black upon me
& my bones are burned
with heat

The triumphing of the wicked
is short, the joy of the hypocrite is
but for a moment
Satan himself is transformed into an Angel of Light & his Ministers into Ministers of Righteousness

With Dreams upon my bed thou scarest me & affrightest me
with Visions

Why do you persecute me as God & are not satisfied with my flesh. Oh that my words
were printed in a Book that they were graven with an iron pen & lead in the rock for ever
For I know that my Redeemer liveth & that he shall stand in the latter days upon
the Earth & after my skin destroy thou This body yet in my flesh shall I see God
whom I shall see for Myself and mine eyes shall behold & not Another tho consumed be my wrought Image
Who opposeth & exalteth himself above all that is called God or is Worshipped

W Blake invent & sculp

{110} *Job*, pl. 11

For God speaketh once yea twice & Man perceiveth it not

In a Dream in a Vision of the Night in deep Slumberings upon the bed

Then he openeth the ears of Men & sealeth their instruction

That he may withdraw Man from his purpose & hide Pride from Man

If there be with him an Interpreter One among a Thousand

& saith Deliver him from going down to the Pit

then he is gracious unto him

I have found a Ransom

For his eyes are upon
the ways of Man & he observeth
all his goings

I am Young & ye are very Old wherefore I was afraid

Lo all these things worketh God oftentimes with Man to bring
back his Soul from the pit to be enlightened
with the light of the living

Look upon the heavens & behold the clouds
which are higher
than thou

If thou sinnest what
doest thou against him, or if thou be
righteous what givest thou unto him

W Blake invenit & sculpt

{111} *Job*, pl. 12

{112} Michelangelo, Sistine Chapel ceiling, detail

{113} *Job*, water color drawing for pl. 14

When the morning Stars sang together. & all the
Sons of God shouted for joy

W Blake Invenit & Sc

{114} *Job*, pl. 14

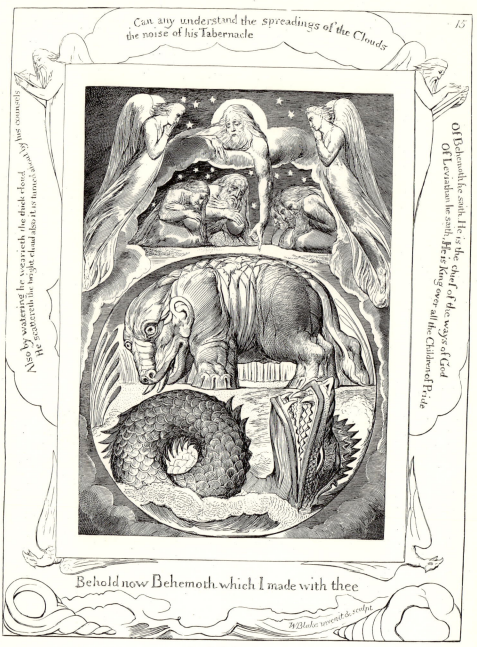

Can any understand the spreadings of the Clouds
the noise of his Tabernacle

15

Also by watering he wearieth the thick cloud
He scattereth the bright cloud also it is turned about by his counsels

Of Behemoth he saith He is the chief of the ways of God
Of Leviathan he saith He is King over all the Children of Pride

Behold now Behemoth which I made with thee

WBlake invenit & sculpt

{115} *Job*, pl. 15

He bringeth down to the Grave & bringeth up

We know that when he shall appear we shall be like him for we shall see him as He is

When I behold the Heavens the work of thy hands the Moon & Stars which thou hast ordained. then I say. What is Man that thou art mindful of him? & the Son of Man that thou visitest him

I have heard thee with the hearing of the Ear but now my Eye seeth thee

He that hath seen me

If ye had known me ye would have known my Father also and from henceforth ye know him & have seen him

Believe me that I am in the Father & the Father in me

Hethat loveth me shall be loved of my Father & I will love him & will manifest myself unto him

He that loveth me not keepeth not my sayings

I & my Father are One

hath seen my Father also

At that day ye shall know that I am in my Father & you in me & I in you

If ye loved me ye would rejoice because I said I go unto the Father

And the Father shall give you another Comforter that he may abide with you for ever

Even the Spirit of Truth whom the world cannot receive

W Blake inv & sculp

{116} *Job*, pl. 17

{118} Cumberland, *Conjugal Union of Cupid and Psyche,* engraved by Blake (*Thoughts on Outline,* pl. 15)

{117} Cumberland, *Psyche Disobeys,* engraved by Blake (*Thoughts on Outline,* pl. 12)

Vedila qui colferro, e'l lume ardente
    sopra il bel fanciullin di citherea,
il qual trouando in luogo di serpente,
    pentita lascia quel, che far uolea,

piagasi un dito con un stral pungente,
    e à mirar torna il figlio dela dea,
che poi che'l cocente oglio lo risuiglia,
    fugge uolando et ella a un pie s appiglia

{119} Van Coxie, *Discovery of Cupid*, engraved by Agostino Veneziano

In questo per trouar l'alato amante
    Va la fanciulla à l'amorosa stanza,
& per le chiome à Citerea dauante
    Sin dala porta è tratta da l'Vsanza

La dea sgrida la misera tremante
    poi batter falla senza dimoranza,
Da la Tristezza, e da l'Angoscia dira,
    & grattasi l orecchia per molt ira,

{120} Van Coxie, *Punishment of Psyche*, engraved by the Master of the Die

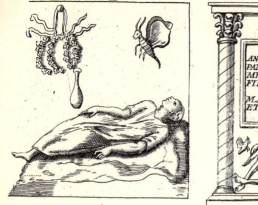

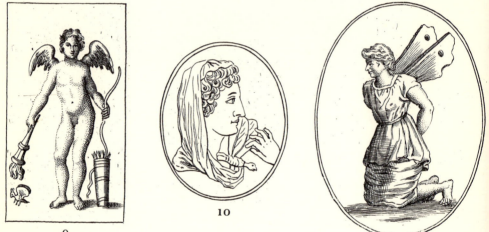

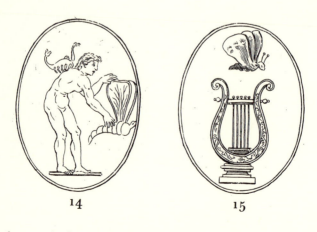

{121} Montfaucon, *Antiquity Explained*, vol. 1, pl. 61, nos. 4, 5, 6; 9, 10, 11; 14, 15